Generis
PUBLISHING

National and International Legal and Constitutional Order

Convergent and Divergent Studies and Essays

Marius Andreescu

Title: **National and International Legal and Constitutional Order**

Convergent and Divergent Studies and Essays

ISBN: 979-8-89248-683-5

Author: Marius Andreescu

Cover image: www.pixabay.com

Publisher: Generis Publishing
Online orders: www.generis-publishing.com
Contact email: info@generis-publishing.com

NATIONAL AND INTERNATIONAL LEGAL AND CONSTITUTIONAL ORDER. CONVERGENT AND DIVERGENT

STUDIES AND ESSAYS

Dr. Marius Andreescu

Scientific researcher

Andrei Rădulescu

Legal Research Institute of the Romanian Academy

2024

CONTENTS

FOREWORD

Man is essentially a social being, he is a product of society and a producer of society. In the social framework, man enters into a multitude of social relations with his fellows. Some of these social relations become legal reporters if they are subject to their regulation by legal norms.

From a legal perspective, society is a structural system, it implies an order, in relation to which it exists, manifests and evolves and whose content can be legal, political, moral, economic or of another nature. The social order is a reality that has its own coordinates, making possible the difference between society as a higher form of human existential organization, and on the other hand, the simple collectivity.

Unlike any form of human collectivity (the family, more or less organized social groups), society is characterized by a relatively stable order that is imposed, and is primarily legal in nature. It can be said that the law system, as a legal order, is the structuring system of any society that ensures system cohesion, stability, individuality, but also the possibility of its evolution. On the other hand, society is the reality of law, the environment that justifies and legitimizes the normative system. That is why we do not conceive of law as an abstract normative reality, but only as the law of a certain society in relation to which it manifests itself. The legal norm regulates social relations which, in this way, become legal relations. The participants in the legal relations are subjects of law, and the content of these relations are the rights and obligations established or recognized by the laws.

Therefore, although each of the systems, legal and social, has a relative functional and evolutionary autonomy from each other, we retain the essential aspect conferred by the biunivocal correspondence between law and society, or, in other words, the social environment: society involves the legal order, without which the social system could not exist, and conditions, most of the time, determines the specificity and content of the judicial system, giving reality to the law.

On the other hand, law, with all its systemic and functional autonomy, can only be conceived as a social reality, being at the same time the instrument through which the state, the sole creator of law, gives the social the legal order so that the social system can exist, work and evolve. The reality of the law, understood as a social reality, implies a relationship of the adequacy of the law to the social environment, which also expresses a unilateral contradiction, in the sense that the law, the normative system existing at a certain historical moment, can contradict its environment, i.e. society, but society it cannot contradict law as its order and structure, but, moreover, determines its content.

In this context, the meaning of a constitution can be understood as a political and legal settlement of a society, i.e. the main factor shaping the social order through all its components: political, economic, cultural, value and, last but not least, by defining man as an individual and person, but through the abstract form conferred by the subject of law within the diversity of social relations, including those between individual and state, rulers and ruled.

There are inter-conditioning relationships between society, state and law, in the sense that society is the environment in which the state and law manifest themselves, giving it the organization and order necessary for a simple collectivity to become a form of social organization.

Therefore, society and the state appear and evolve together, any concrete way of organizing a society can only be a state one. The expression "organized society state" expresses the correspondence between the state and society. In this broad sense, the state concretizes society, giving it an organization as the sum of three elements: territory, population and sovereignty or power. Organized society thus becomes a state (country), which in turn becomes individualized through the characters and attributes established by the constitution of each country. The state is, in its essence, institutionally expressed as the ultimate form of political authority that creates social order. In other words, the state is the state power which in turn is always political, i.e. oriented and exercised towards the achievement of a general goal, which in a democratic society can only be the public interest.

In any democratic society, the state is defined as the organized power of the people. Power, as a constitutive element, itself expresses the whole being of the state, just as the other two constitutive elements, territory and population, carry within themselves the reality of state-organized society. Regarding the relationship between the state and power and the role of the state as a factor of social organization, the state can be conceived by its own structure and order. It is what is considered in specialized literature to be the restricted (legal) understanding of the state. From this perspective, the state appears as an organized, institutionalized form of political power, the latter having the people as its holder in a democratic society.

We emphasize, all these characteristics have a doctrinal theoretical significance and do not fully reflect the contemporary social and state realities, nor the social status of man.

Hans Kelsen, the main author of the normativist theory of law, emphasized that the state can be considered a coercive legal order, a commanding power and has a will of its own, distinct from that of individuals and situated above them. Thus, the difference in legal status between the rulers and the ruled is explained.

There is an inter-conditional relationship between the state and law. The two realities of social superstructures appeared at once and from the same causes. The state creates law, and law delimits the configuration and limits the actions of the state. This last aspect legitimizes the principle of the supremacy of law in relation to the state, specific to the concept of the rule of law that is the basis of contemporary constitutionalism.

It is a paradoxical situation, in the sense that, although the state is the sole creator of law (there cannot be legal norms that are not, as the case may be, created, recognized or consecrated by the state), nevertheless the legal system imposes its existential authority on the creator state , so that in an institutional organization and functioning of the state, its very legitimacy as a power of command and social organization of power is conferred by law, in particular by the constitutional norms, which essentially regulate fundamental social relations regarding establishment, exercise and maintenance of power.

The state and law have a historical character, materialized in the types of state: slave, feudal, socialist and capitalist. The structure and functions of the state have evolved, but its essence has remained the same: a commanding power and an instrument for organizing human society through law. The being of a nation and its state organization is expressed primarily by its history. The history of a state obviously has a unitary character and cannot be dissociated from the legal phenomenon. Therefore, the proper understanding of the social and political historical realities of a state is also conditioned by understanding the evolution of the legal phenomenon. The state in its historical evolution cannot be conceived only through political or social facts, but also through the legal forms determined by the economic and political elements but which at the same time express these realities.

The unity of a state's history is thus naturally completed by the history of its law. In this sense, Hegel affirmed that reporting to history actually means the consciousness of the existence of the state in its progress towards freedom

The multiple aspects of Romania's integration into the European Union and contemporary globalization produce essential transformations in contemporary state, social and political realities, in the content of man's relationship with the state and society. More specifically, globalization and international integration, the formation of centers of economic, political, military and international legal power are far from generating the best for the social existence of man, but on the contrary they have generated important social and legitimacy crises with the consequence of placing between brackets the dignity and freedom of man as a person, considering this only as an individual included in a social and state mechanism whose goal is domination and alienation and which offers in return the surrogate of an illusory social security.

We, together with the majority of the states of the world, are in a deep crisis of democracy which is manifested by disregarding the existential values that characterize man and society, in particular life, human dignity, the principles of equity, justice, the obligation of the rulers to respect the rights and fundamental human freedoms. All this being the consequence of discriminatory and abusive restrictive measures by the governors under the stated pretext of saving man, society and the state, from various real or imaginary dangers, as happened during the recent health crisis, but this is only an example. Under the pretext of defending fundamental human rights and freedoms, wars were started with hundreds of thousands of victims. According to the classic theory of the rule of law and constitutional democracy, in any circumstance, even in exceptional situations, the state has the obligation, which derives from its very legitimacy, to protect the life, health, freedom, and dignity of every human being, not to destroy them, not to destroy them.

Unfortunately, the rulers of many countries, including Romania, and those who lead the European Union, deliberately do not want to understand that not the measures restricting the exercise of fundamental rights and freedoms, discriminatory and abusive, the disregard of man and his dignity, the serious degradation of some components of the social system such as health, the economy, education, culture and in general public life, can have the effect of solving the multiple contemporary social crises, but a good governance based on positive measures in which every man to be regarded and respected as a worthy and free person, every man never to be regarded as the means but always as the end of the act of government.

Freedom is not and should not be considered only as a fundamental legal right enshrined in constitutions and laws, which in fact are the expression of the power of those who govern. Freedom is much more, it is a divine gift. An essential attribute of human nature and therefore should not be subject to the discretionary and pharisaical will of the rulers of our times.

The message we want to convey to the reader through the interdisciplinary approach to some aspects of man, society and the state can be summed up in the words of Saint Thomas Aquinas: "the individual is for the state, the state for the person and the person for God".

Dr. Marius Andreescu

Scientific researcher at the ''Andrei Rădulscu'' Legal Research Institute of the Romanian Academy

1. NATIONAL AND INTERNATIONAL LEGAL AND CONSTITUTIONAL ORDER. CONVERGENT AND DIVERGENT

Abstract:

The relationship between the national law and the law of the European Union is interpreted differently, there are several doctrinal concepts and different jurisprudence solutions. One school of thought asserts the supremacy of the Constitution, including over European Union law, even if it accepts the priority of application of the latter, in its mandatory rules, over all other rules of domestic law, and another the priority of unconditional application of all the provisions of the law of the European Union compared to all the rules of the internal law, including the constitutional rules.

There are European constitutional jurisdictions that have established that they have the competence to control the constitutionality of European Union law, integrated into the internal legal order, by virtue of the principle of the supremacy of the Fundamental Law

The Romanian Constitution enshrines two principles of a different nature and with specific implications whose effects are convergent but also divergent: the supremacy of the Constitution and the priority of European Union law.

In this study we analyze the interferences between the principle of priority of European Union law and the principle of supremacy of the Constitution with reference to the relevant doctrine and jurisprudence in the matter.

Key words:

National legal and constitutional order / International legal order/ Principle of priority of European Union law / Principle of the supremacy of the Constitution / Obligation of legal norms of the European Union / Conformity national law with European Union la

I. Introduction

One of the most important defining elements of the European Union is the existence of its own system made up of principles, written norms and rules established by jurisprudence. Therefore, it is important to clarify the relations between the European Union law and national law. The solution to this problem is found in a set of rules that are not explicitly provided in the Constituent Treaties but were developed by the Court of Justice through several decisions, some of them controversial. The constitutions of the Member States of the European Union state rules of principle regarding the relationship between European Union law and national law.

In practical terms, the interference between European Union law and national law occurs especially when there are contradictions between the legal norms belonging to the legal systems. Of course, the problem of the relationship between the two categories of legal norms is of interest not only in such a situation, but also in cases where a court can apply a norm of European Union law. One of the most important aspects of this issue is the relationship between the supremacy of the constitution, and, on the other hand, the priority principle of the law of the European Union as well as the competences of the constitutional jurisdiction in the matter of application and interpretation of the rules stated by the legal acts of the European Union.

We believe that this issue can be analyzed on two levels: 1. the relationship between domestic law (other than the constitutional law) and the European Union law; 2. the relationship between the constitutional norms of the Member States, and, on the other hand, the law of the European Union.

One of the most interesting discussions, jurisprudential and doctrinal, involving the constitutional courts of the member states of the European Union, concerns the cooperation mechanisms with the Court of Justice of the European Union. The jurisprudence of the Court of Justice of the European Union, the doctrine, but also the internal legislation refers to the principle of priority or supremacy, primacy, pre-eminence of European Union law over the national law systems.

II. Content

The relationship between the constitutional norms and European Union Law is interpreted differently, there are several doctrinal conceptions. One current of thought affirms the supremacy of the Constitution, including over the European Union law, even if it accepts the priority of applying the latter, in its mandatory norms, over all other norms of domestic law, and another the priority of systematic and unconditional application of all the provisions of the European Union Law in relation to all the norms of the internal law, including the national constitutions. Some traditional European constitutional jurisdictions have reached, at certain moments and historical contexts, the conclusion that it is within their competence to control the constitutionality of the European Union law, integrated into the internal legal order, by virtue of the principle of the supremacy of the fundamental law (for example, the German Constitutional Tribunal).

The Court of Justice reached the development of the principle of priority of the European Union law, considering the rule of public international law, according to which "A party cannot invoke the provisions of his domestic law to justify the non-execution of a Treaty". Another source was represented by the provisions of art. 10 of the Treaty of the European Community, modified by the Treaty of Lisbon. The norm contained in the provisions of art. 10, however, remained unchanged until now and establishes the obligation of the member states to take all the necessary measures to ensure the fulfillment of the obligations resulting from the treaties and acts of the Community institutions. The same provisions impose the negative obligation of the Member States to refrain from taking measures that would endanger the achievement of the Treaty's goals. These are not the only regulations from the European Union Treaties that underpin the principle of priority of the European Union law over the national law.

The principle of priority and obligation of the Law of the European Union was built especially through jurisprudence. In this matter, the historical jurisprudence of the Court of Justice of the European Union is relevant, which marks a certain evolution of the affirmation of this principle in relation to the national law.

A significant moment is represented by the *Costa v. Enel* case[1]. The Italian court submitted two requests for interpretation, one to the Constitutional Court of Italy and the other to the Court of Justice of the European Union. The Constitutional Court considered that the Treaty establishing the European Community can only have a normative value to the extent that it is incorporated into the law national through a law. At the same time, it was admitted that a national law can derogate from the provisions of the Treaty.

The Court of Justice had a different opinion expressed in the pronounced decision: "It follows from these considerations that the legal system born from the Treaty, an independent source of law, cannot, due to its special and original nature, be superseded by the internal legal norms or that would be their legal force, without being deprived of its community law feature and without the very legal foundation of the Community being called into question".

Another moment of the evolution of the jurisprudence of the Court of Justice in this matter is represented by the "International H" cases[2]; "Simmenthal I[3] [35/76, Simmenthal SpA (1976) ECR 1871] and Simmenthal II"[4].

The following considerations from the decision pronounced in the *Simmenthal II* case are relevant for our research topic: "as such, any provision of the national legal order or any practice, legislative, administrative or judicial, which would have the effect of being incompatible with the requirements inherent in the nature of the Community law diminishing the effectiveness of the Community law by refusing the competent judge to apply it, the power to do, at the very moment of this application, all that is necessary to remove the national legal provisions that, possibly, would represent an obstacle to the full effectiveness of community norms. Therefore, the answer to the first question is that the national judge tasked, according to his competence, to apply the provisions of Community law, has the obligation to ensure the full effectiveness of these rules, leaving unapplied, *ex officio*, if necessary, any provision contrary with the national legislation, even later, without requesting or waiting for its prior legislative elimination or by any other constitutional procedure" (para 22 and 24 of the decision).

[1] 6/64 Costa c. Enel (1964) ECR 585
[2] 11/70, Internationale H., (1970) ECR 1125
[3] 35/76, Simmenthal SpA (1976) ECR 1871
[4] 106/77, Simmenthal (1978) ECR 629

Moreover, the Court considered that the national courts have the power to constrain and even sanction the legislative power and the executive power in order to guarantee the full efficiency of the principle of priority of European Union law over national law.

This principle must also be understood from the perspective of the rule of obligation of community acts. The *regulation* has general applicability and is mandatory in all its elements. In contrast, the *directive* is addressed to some or all of the Member States and is mandatory with regard to the result to be achieved, leaving for the national authorities the competence regarding the form and the means they use to achieve the set objectives. The *decision* is binding in all its elements on the addressees it indicates.

The rule of direct application that characterizes some of the legal acts of European Union law is of interest to the understanding and application of the priority principle of the European Union law. The regulations have direct application because they do not require transposition into national law. As the court indicated in its jurisprudence, Member States do not have to adopt national legislation to take over the regulations. Their provisions can be invoked by natural and legal persons directly before the national courts. In contrast, the directive is not directly applicable. It must always be transposed into the legal system of each Member State to which it is addressed. The domestic normative act transposing the directive is the one through which the content of the directive will enter the national legal system.

The principle of priority of the European Union law over the national law must also be understood according to the criterion of the possibility of direct invocation of community acts before national courts. The phrase "direct effect" denotes the attribute of a community normative act to create in the patrimony of natural and legal persons rights that they can invoke directly before the national courts. Without going into details, we emphasize that under certain conditions, regulations, directives and decisions can have a direct effect.

One of the consequences of the principle of priority of the European Union law is the obligation of national courts to interpret domestic law in accordance with the European Union law. In an attempt to ensure the effectiveness and uniformity of the law of the European Union, the Court of Justice of the European Union established several means to stimulate the states to implement the directives correctly and on time and to ensure their implementation. One of these means is the creation of the doctrine of direct vertical effect of directives.

In the hypothesis in which the provisions of an unimplemented or incorrectly implemented directive cannot have a direct vertical effect because they do not meet the condition of being sufficiently clear, precise and unconditional, in order to be able to deduce the right that the litigant wishes to exploit before the courts national, the Court established the obligation, for the national judge, to interpret the national legislation in relation to the content of the directive.

Among the first cases in which this obligation was expressly stated was the *Van Colson* case. The Court held in the considerations of the pronounced decision that the national legislation limits the right to reparation of persons who have been the object of discrimination in the case of exercising the right to work. Such a situation does not comply with the requirements of the effective transposition of Directive 76/207. Therefore, the court in Luxembourg ruled: "It follows that in the activity of applying the national law and in particular the provisions of a national law specially introduced in order to apply Directive 76/207, the national court is required to interpret the national law in the light of the text and the finality of the directive to obtain the result provided for in art. 189 para 3) of the TCE". Consequently, the Court specified: "It is in the competence of the national court to issue laws adopted in order to apply the directive, to the extent that the national law grants it a margin of appreciation, an interpretation and an application in accordance with the requirements of Community law".

The decision of the Court of Justice of the European Union, pronounced in the case of *Seda Kücükdeveci v. Swedex GmbH & Co.*[5], is also edifying. The Court reaffirms the existence of the principle of non-discrimination on grounds of age, as well as the role of the national court in its application. The German regulation which stipulates that periods of work completed before the age of 25 are not taken into account for the calculation of the notice period is contrary to the principle of non-discrimination on grounds of age, as provided by Directive 2000/78. In this situation, the national court must remove, if necessary, any contrary internal regulation, even in the context of a dispute between individuals.

---

[5] Decision C-555/07

From the considerations of this decision, it follows that Directive 200/78 concretizes the principle of equal treatment in the field of employment. The principle of non-discrimination on grounds of age is a general principle of the Union law. Therefore, the national court referred to a dispute in which the principle of non-discrimination on grounds of age, as provided by Directive 2000/78, is brought into question, is obliged to ensure, within the framework of its competences, the legal protection arising for justiciable in Union Law and to guarantee the full right of this principle, removing, if necessary, the application of any provision, possibly contrary, of the national law.

In accordance with these conclusions of the Court of Justice of the European Union, it follows that the Romanian courts, in the situations where they will apply the provisions of a national law implementing a directive, interpret it in accordance with the text and purpose of the directive. From the jurisprudence of the Court, it follows that the national court is obliged, when it has to apply a law implementing a directive, to take into account not only that law, but the whole set of national law rules and to interpret them in accordance with the requirements the respective directive, in order to pronounce a solution in accordance with the purpose pursued by the community act.

Given that the Romanian law is characterized by excessive procedural formalism and especially by significant inconsistencies and contradictions, the realization of this obligation by the national courts will be very difficult.

Moreover, in its jurisprudence the Court of Justice of the European Union considers that this obligation of the national courts is subject to certain limits. The obligation to interpret domestic law taking into account the text and purpose of the directive exists only to the extent that national law grants a margin of appreciation to the court. In this sense, the Court held the following in the Papino case: "The principle of interpretation in the light of the directive cannot serve as a foundation for a *contra legem* interpretation of national law"[6].

We believe that whenever the national law confers on the court a "related competence" that excludes the existence of a margin of appreciation, the aforementioned obligation does not exist for the national judge. By way of example, some of the procedural normative provisions can be included in this category. Also, in criminal matters, the national courts cannot aggravate the

[6] Decision C-105/03

criminal liability of persons in the event that they commit an act criminalized by a directive, if it has not been implemented in domestic law.

Another important issue is the relationship between the constitutional norms, the decisions of the Constitutional Court, and on the other hand the law of the European Union.

Constantly, the constitutional courts of some Member States, especially Germany, Italy and France, considered that the principle of priority of the European Union law does not apply in relation to the regulations included in a constitution, because the fundamental law of a state expresses the identity and national sovereignty. This solution particularly concerned the regulations regarding fundamental human rights and freedoms. Until December 1, 2009, when the Treaty of Lisbon and the Charter of Fundamental Rights of the European Union entered into force, the European Union law did not include a coherent normative system for guaranteeing fundamental human rights. Consequently, the courts of the Member States invoked the internal constitutional regulations in such situations.

Moreover, the practice of the courts of the Member States of the European Union does not offer many examples of conflict between the rules of the European Union law, and on the other hand, the constitutional regulations. This situation is explained by the fact that, following the process of joining the European Union, the Member States adapted their constitutional regulations of principle to the specific requirements of the European Union law and established in one form or another the principle of priority of this legal system against domestic law whenever there is a contradiction between the rules of the two categories of legal norms. Of course, this problem remains open and is far from being solved. We note that in the jurisprudence of the Constitutional Council and the French Council of State in recent years, the concept of "constitutional national identity" has been developed. According to this principle, the national courts will always apply the internal constitutional norms, but also the rules inscribed in the ordinary legislation whenever they have no counterpart in the European Union law.

The Romanian Constitution makes the distinction between the principle of the supremacy of the fundamental law, and on the other hand, the principle of the priority of European Union law over national law. Thus, the provisions of Art 1 Para 5 of the Constitution enshrines the principle of the supremacy of the fundamental law: "In Romania, compliance with the Constitution, its supremacy and the laws is mandatory". This principle cannot be mistaken with that of the priority of the law of the European Union over the contrary regulations of the internal laws enshrined in Art 148 Para 2 from the Constitution.

The jurisprudence of the Constitutional Court of Romania reflects this difference.

By DCC no. 148 of April 16, 2003 regarding the constitutionality of the legislative proposal to revise the Romanian Constitution, our constitutional court clearly distinguishes between the supremacy of the Constitution and the principle of priority of the European Union law, stating: "The consequence of accession starts from the fact that the Member States of the European Union have understood to place the communitarian acquis, the constitutive treaties of the European Union and the regulations derived from them in an intermediate position between the Constitution and the other laws when it comes to binding European normative acts". In the specialized legal literature, with reference to the provisions of Art 148 of the Constitution and in accordance with Decision no. 148 of April 16, 2003, it was stated that "Therefore, it can be stated that in the internal legal order, the legal act by which Romania joins the European Union has a legal force inferior to the Constitution and constitutional laws, but superior to organic and ordinary laws"[7].

In its subsequent jurisprudence, the Constitutional Court seems to have renounced this distinction, basing its decisions only on the principle of the priority of the European Union law[8].

However, by DCC no. 1258 of October 8, 2009[9], which we consider to be of historical importance in subsequent constitutional jurisprudence, the Court finds that an internal law transposing a directive of the European Union into internal law is unconstitutional. Such a solution, in our opinion, enshrines

[7] M. Constantinescu, A. Iorgovan, I. Muraru, E.S. Tănăsescu, The revised Constitution of Romania - comments and explanations, All Beck Publ.-house, Bucharest, 2004, p. 331

[8] DCC no. 308/2006, published in the Official Gazette no. 390/5 May 2006; DCC no. 59:2007, published in the Official Gazette no. 98/8 February 2007; DCC no. 1042/2007, published in the Official Gazette no. 12/8 February 2008 and DCC no. 1172/2007, published in the Official Gazette no. 54/23 January 2008

[9] Published in the Official Gazette no 798/23 November 2009

the principle of supremacy of the Constitution and the obligation to respect it in relation to the principle of priority of the European Union law.

Through the decision with the number above, the constitutional court found that the provisions of Law no. 298/2008 (Official Gazette no. 780 of November 21, 2008) are unconstitutional. From the considerations of the decision, it follows that Law no. 298/2008 was adopted to transpose into national legislation the Directive 2006/24/EC of the European Parliament and of the Council of March 15, 2006, regarding the retention of data generated or processed in connection with the provision of publicly accessible electronic communication services or public communication networks. The Court refers to the legal regime of such community acts, emphasizing that: "(...) it imposes its obligation on the Member States of the European Union in terms of the regulated legal solution, not in terms of the specific methods by which this result, the states benefiting from a wide margin of appreciation in order to adopt them according to the specifics of national legislation and realities". Examining the content of the Law no. 298/2008, the Court found that this normative act is likely to affect the exercise of rights or fundamental freedoms, namely the right to intimate, private and family life, the right to secrecy of correspondence and freedom of expression. The constitutional court considers that the restriction of the exercise of these rights does not correspond to the requirements established by art. 53 of the Romanian Constitution[10].

DCC no. 80 of February 16, 2014[11], on the legislative proposal regarding the revision of the Romanian Constitution is relevant for our research topic. Regarding the interpretation of the provisions of Art 148 regarding integration into the European Union, the Court notes that: the "constitutional provisions do not have a declarative character, but represent mandatory constitutional norms, without which the existence of the rule of law, provided for by Art 1 Para 3 from the Constitution. At the same time, the Basic Law represents the framework and extent in which the legislator and the other authorities can act; thus, the interpretations that can be brought to the legal norm must take into account this constitutional requirement, included in Art 1 Para 4 of the

---

[10] DCC no. 17/21 January 2015, published in the Official Gazette no. 79/30 January 2015 through which our constitutional court established the unconstitutionality of the law on Romania's cyber security

[11] Published in the Official Gazette no 246/7 April 2014

Fundamental Law, according to which in Romania the compliance with the Constitution and its supremacy is mandatory".

Another aspect analyzed in the constitutional jurisprudence refers to the application of the Charter of Fundamental Rights of the European Union within the framework of the constitutional review. Our constitutional court ruled that, in principle, this is applicable within the framework of constitutionality control "to the extent that it ensures, guarantees and develops the constitutional provisions in the matter of fundamental rights, in other words, to the extent that their level of protection is at least at the level of constitutional norms in the field of human rights"[12].

Also in connection with the application of the European Union norms, regarding human rights within the framework of constitutionality control, it was stated that the reporting of the provisions contained in an act having the same legal force as the constitutive treaties of the European Union must be done according to the provisions of Art 148 of the Constitution, and not those stated by Art 20 of the Basic Law, which refers to international treaties on human rights, other than those of the European Union[13]. Our constitutional court ruled that the provisions of Art 41 of the Charter of Fundamental Rights of the European Union, regarding the right to good administration, can be invoked through the prism of Art 148, and not Art 20 of the Constitution[14].

Also, in the constitutional jurisprudence it was established that it is not within the competence of the Constitutional Court to analyze the conformity of a provision of constitutional law with the text of the Treaty on the Functioning of the European Union, through the prism of Art 148 of the Constitution. Such a competence, namely that of determining whether there is a contradiction between the national law and the treaty, belongs exclusively to the court, which also has the possibility to formulate a preliminary question to the Court of Justice of the European Union. It is interesting that the constitutional court considers itself incompetent to verify the conformity of a provision of national law with the text of the constituent treaties of the European Union and for the fact that, if it were to arrogate such competence, a

[12] DCC no. 871/25 June 2010, published in the Official Gazette no. 433/28 June 2010

[13] DCC no. 967/20 November 2012, published in the Official Gazette no. 853/18 December 2012 and DCC no. 206/6 March 2012, published in the Official Gazette no. 254/17 April 2012

[14] DCC no. 12/22 January 2013, published in the Official Gazette no. 114/28 February 2013

possible conflict would be reached of jurisdiction between the Constitutional Court of Romania and the Court of Justice of the European Union, which, at this level, is considered inadmissible[15].

Regarding the cooperation between the Constitutional Court and the Court of Justice of the European Union, our constitutional court stated that it remains at its discretion, in the application of the judgments of the Court of Justice of the European Union or the Court's formulation of questions preliminary in order to establish the content of the European norm. "Such an attitude is related to the cooperation between the national and the European constitutional court, as well as to the judicial dialogue between them, without bringing into discussion aspects related to the establishment of a hierarchy between these courts".

The Court of Justice of the European Union, in its recent jurisprudence, has a different opinion and ruled the supremacy of the legal order of the European Union Law, over the internal legal order and even over the constitutional order.

Thus, through the Judgment delivered on May 18, 2021[16], the Court of Justice of the European Union rules on a series of reforms in Romania regarding the judicial organization, the disciplinary regime of magistrates, as well as the patrimonial liability of the state and the personal liability of judges for judicial errors.

Six requests for a preliminary decision were made before the Romanian constitutional court in the context of the disputes between legal entities or natural persons, on the one hand, and authorities or bodies such as the Judicial Inspection, the Superior Council of the Magistracy and the Prosecutor's Office attached to the High Court of Cassation and Justice, on the other hand. The main disputes are in the context of a far-reaching reform in the field of justice and the fight against corruption in Romania, a reform that has been subject to

[15] DCC no. 1249/7 October 2010, published in the Official Gazette no. 764/16 November 2010 and DCC no. 137/25 February 2010, published in the Official Gazette no. 182/22 March 2010

[16] Decision in connected cases C-83/19, the Association "The Forum of Judges in Romania"/Judicial Inspection, C-127/19, the Association "The Forum of Judges in Romania" and the Association "The Movement to Defend the Status of Prosecutors" and OL/Prosecutor's Office attached to the High Court of Cassation and Justice – General Prosecutor of Romania and C-397/19, AX/Romanian State – Ministry of Public Finances

monitoring at the level of the European Union since 2007, based on the cooperation and verification mechanism established by Decision 2006/928[17] with the occasion of Romania's accession to the Union (hereinafter referred to as "CVM").

In this context, the referring courts raised the issue of the nature and legal effects of the CVM, as well as the scope of the reports drawn up by the Commission pursuant to it. According to these courts, the content, legal nature and temporal extent of the mentioned mechanism should be considered circumscribed by the Accession Treaty, and the requirements formulated in these reports should be binding for Romania. In this regard, however, the respective courts mention a national jurisprudence according to which the Union law would not prevail over the Romanian constitutional order, and Decision 2006/928 could not constitute a reference rule in the framework of a constitutionality review, since this decision was adopted prior to Romania's accession to the Union, and the issue of whether the content, nature and scope of Decision 2006/928/EC falls within the scope of the Accession Treaty has not been the subject of any interpretation by the Court.

Regarding the legal effects of the Decision 2006/928, the Court found that it is binding in all its elements for Romania from the date of its accession to the Union and obliges it to achieve the reference objectives, also mandatory, which appear in the annex to this. The respective objectives, defined as a result of the deficiencies noted by the Commission before Romania's accession to the Union, aim, among other things, to ensure compliance by this member state with the value of the rule of law. Romania is thus obliged to take the appropriate measures in order to achieve the mentioned objectives and to refrain from implementing any measure that risks compromising the achievement of the same objectives.

The Court ruled that the principle of the supremacy of the Union law opposes a national regulation of constitutional rank that deprives a lower court of the right to leave unapplied *ex officio* a national provision that falls within the scope of Decision 2006/928 and which is contrary to the Union law. The Court recalls that, according to established jurisprudence, the effects associated

[17] 2006/928/EC: Commission Decision of 13 December 2006 establishing a mechanism for cooperation and verification of progress in Romania to address specific benchmarks in the areas of judicial reform and the fight against corruption (OJ 2006 L 354, p. 56, Special Edition, 11/vol. 51, p. 55)

with the principle of the supremacy of the Union law are imposed on all organs of a Member State, without the internal provisions relating to the distribution of judicial powers, including constitutional ones, being able to prevent this. Also recalling that national courts are obliged, as far as possible, to give domestic law an interpretation that complies with the requirements of the Union law or to leave unapplied *ex officio* any contrary provision of national legislation that could not be subject to such a compliant interpretation, the Court notes that, in the event of a proven violation of the EU Treaty or Decision 2006/928, the principle of supremacy of the Union law requires the referring court to leave the provisions in question unapplied, regardless of whether they are of legislative or constitutional origin.

Through the Decision of December 21, 2022[18], the Court of Justice of the European Union ruled that the Union law opposes the application of a case law of the constitutional court to the extent that it, in conjunction with the national provisions on prescription, creates a systemic risk of impunity.

The supremacy of the Union law requires that national judges have the power to leave unenforced a decision of a constitutional court that is contrary to this right, without being exposed to the risk of being engaged in disciplinary liability.

In the reasoning of the Decision, the following is essentially noted:

In these cases, the question arises as to whether the application of the jurisprudence resulting from various decisions of the Constitutional Court of Romania (Romania), regarding the rules of criminal procedure applicable in matters of fraud and corruption, is likely to violate the Union law, in particular the provisions of this law that aim to protect the financial interests of the Union, guarantee the independence of judges and the value of the rule of law, as well as the principle of the supremacy of the Union law.

The Court, gathered in the Grand Chamber, confirmed its jurisprudence resulting from a previous decision, according to which the CVM is binding in all its elements for Romania[19]. Thus, the acts adopted before accession by the

---

[18] Decision for the connected cases C-357/19 Euro Box Promotion et al., C379/19 DNA – Oradea Territorial Service, C-547/19 Association "The Forum of Judges", C-811/19 FQ et al., and C-840/19 N

[19] Decision of 18 May 2021, the Association "The Forum of Judges" et al., C-83 C-127/19, C-195/19, C-291/19, C-355/19 and C-397/19 (see also CP no. 82/21)

institutions of the Union are binding for Romania from the date of its accession. This is the situation of Decision 2006/928, which is binding in all its elements for Romania as long as it has not been repealed. The benchmarks that aim to ensure respect for the rule of law are also binding. Romania is thus required to take the appropriate measures to achieve these objectives, taking into account the recommendations formulated in the reports drawn up by the Commission[20].

The Union law opposes the application of a jurisprudence of the Constitutional Court that leads to the annulment of judgments handed down by illegally composed panels of judges, to the extent that this, in conjunction with the national provisions on prescription, creates a systemic risk of impunity for acts that constitute serious crimes of fraud affecting the Union's financial interests or corruption.

It was also noted that in this case, the application of the jurisprudence of the Constitutional Court in question has the consequence that the respective cases of fraud and corruption must be re-judged, if necessary, several times, at first instance and/or on appeal. Given its complexity and length, such a retrial inevitably has the effect of prolonging the duration of the related criminal proceedings.

The Court recalls that, taking into account the specific obligations incumbent on Romania under Decision 2006/928, national regulation and practice in this matter cannot have the consequence of extending the duration of investigations into corruption offenses or weakening the fight against corruption in any other way. On the other hand, taking into account the national statutes of limitation, the retrial of the cases in question could lead to the statute of limitations of the crimes and could prevent the sanctioning, in an effective and dissuasive way, of the persons who occupy the most important positions in the Romanian state and who were convicted of committing acts of serious fraud and/or serious corruption in the exercise of their functions. Therefore, the risk of impunity would become systemic for this category of persons and would call into question the objective of combating high-level corruption.

In the reasoning, the supremacy of the European Union law is invoked and it is noted that the principle of the supremacy of the Union law prevents national courts from being able, at the risk of applying disciplinary sanctions,

[20] Pursuant to the principle of loyal cooperation, enshrined in Article 4(3) TEU

to leave unapplied the decisions of the Constitutional Court contrary to the Union law.

The Court recalls that, in its jurisprudence regarding the EEC Treaty, it established the principle of the supremacy of Community law, understood in the sense that it enshrines the prevalence of this right over the law of the Member States. In this regard, the Court found that the establishment by the EEC Treaty of a legal order of its own, accepted by the Member States on the basis of reciprocity, has as a corollary the impossibility of the mentioned states to prevail against this legal order, a subsequent unilateral measure or to oppose to the right born from the EEC Treaty norms of national law, regardless of their nature, otherwise there is a risk that this right will lose its community character and that the legal foundation of the Community itself will be called into question.

In addition, the executive force of the Community law cannot vary from one Member State to another depending on subsequent domestic laws, otherwise there is a risk that the achievement of the objectives of the EEC Treaty will be jeopardized, nor can it give rise to discrimination on the grounds of citizenship or nationality, prohibited by this treaty. The Court thus considered that, although it was concluded in the form of an international agreement, the EEC Treaty constitutes the constitutional charter of a community of law, and the essential features of the community legal order thus constituted are in particular its supremacy in relation to the law of the Member States and its direct effect of a whole series of provisions applicable to Member States and their nationals.

According to the Court, the effects associated with the principle of the supremacy of Union law are imposed on all organs of a member state, without the internal provisions, including constitutional ones, being able to prevent this. National courts are required to leave unapplied, *ex officio*, any national regulation or practice contrary to a provision of Union law which has direct effect, without having to request or wait for the prior elimination of that national regulation or practice by legislative means or by any another constitutional procedure.

On the other hand, the fact that national judges are not exposed to procedures or disciplinary sanctions for having exercised the option to refer the Court under Art 267 TFEU, which belongs to their exclusive competence, constitutes an inherent guarantee of their independence. Thus, in the hypothesis in which a national common law judge would come to consider, in the light of a Court decision, that the jurisprudence of the national constitutional court is contrary to Union law, the fact that this national judge would leave the said jurisprudence unapplied cannot engage his disciplinary liability.

III. Conclusions

In the opinion of our constitutional court, to consider that the law of the European Union is applied without any differentiation within the national legal order, not distinguishing between the Constitution and the other internal laws, is equivalent to placing the Fundamental Law in a secondary plan compared to the legal order of the European Union. The legitimacy of the Constitution is the will of the people itself, which means that it cannot lose its binding force, even if there are inconsistencies between its provisions and the European ones. Moreover, it was emphasized that Romania's accession to the European Union cannot affect the supremacy of the Constitution over the entire internal legal order.

The Constitutional Court has established that the mandatory acts of the European Union are norms introduced within the framework of constitutionality control[21]. At the same time, the lack of constitutional relevance of the European law norm, interposed in constitutional reference norms within the framework of constitutionality control, was emphasized. In this case, it is inadmissible to refer the Court based on non-compliance with the provisions of Art 148 Para 4 of the Constitution[22]. Through the same decision, the Court established that it is necessary for the legal norm of the European Union law to be circumscribed to a certain level of constitutional relevance, so that its normative content supports the possible violation by the national law of the Constitution – "the only direct norm of reference in within the framework of constitutional control". The constitutional court consecrated, just like the French Constitutional Council, the concept of "national constitutional identity", by which it understands the relevance of the supremacy of the constitution whenever the question of compliance of internal laws with the European Union acts arises[23].

The Constitutional Court of Romania, in a press release, stated the following, with reference to the recent Decisions of the Court of Justice of the European Union issued recently regarding the relationship between the internal constitutional order and, on the other hand, the law of the European Union:

---

[21] DCC no. 668/18 May 2011, published in the Official Gazette no. 487/8 July 2011

[22] DCC no. 157/19 March 2014, published in the Official Gazette no. 296/23 April 2014

[23] DCC no. 64/24 February 2015, published in the Official Gazette no. 286/28 April 2015

according to Art 147 Para 4 of the Constitution, the decisions of the Constitutional Court are and remain generally binding.

Moreover, the CJEU also recognizes, in its Decision of December 21, 2021, the binding feature of the decisions of the Constitutional Court. However, the conclusions of the CJEU Decision according to which the effects of the principle of the supremacy of the EU law are imposed on all organs of a member state, without internal provisions, including those of a constitutional order, being able to prevent this, and according to which national courts are required to leave unapplied, *ex officio*, any regulation or national practice contrary to a provision of the EU law, assumes the revision of the Constitution in force.

In practical terms, the effects of this Decision can be produced only after the revision of the Constitution in force, which, however, cannot be done as a matter of law, but exclusively at the initiative of certain legal subjects, in compliance with the procedure and under the conditions provided for in the Romanian Constitution itself.

We fully agree with the opinion expressed by the Constitutional Court.

Bibliography

Constantinescu, Mihai; Iorgovan, Antonie; Muraru, Ioan, and Elena-Simina Tănăsescu. The revised Constitution of Romania - comments and explanations, Bucharest: All Beck, 2004;

2006/928/EC: Commission Decision of 13 December 2006 establishing a mechanism for cooperation and verification of progress in Romania to address specific benchmarks in the areas of judicial reform and the fight against corruption (OJ 2006 L 354, p. 56, Special Edition, 11/vol. 51, p. 55);

Treaty on the Functioning of the European Union;

Decision of the Constitutional Court of Romania, no. 308/2006, published in the Official Gazette no. 390/5 May 2006;

Decision of the Constitutional Court of Romania, no. 59:2007, published in the Official Gazette no. 98/8 February 2007;

Decision of the Constitutional Court of Romania, no. 1042/2007, published in the Official Gazette no. 12/8 February 2008;

Decision of the Constitutional Court of Romania, no. 1172/2007, published in the Official Gazette no. 54/23 January 2008;

Decision of the Constitutional Court of Romania, no. 17/21 January 2015, published in the Official Gazette no. 79/30 January 2015;

Decision of the Constitutional Court of Romania, no. 871/25 June 2010, published in the Official Gazette no. 433/28 June 2010;

Decision of the Constitutional Court of Romania, no. 967/20 November 2012, published in the Official Gazette no. 853/18 December 2012;

Decision of the Constitutional Court of Romania, no. 206/6 March 2012, published in the Official Gazette no. 254/17 April 2012;

Decizia Curții Constituționale a României, no. 12/22 January 2013, published in the Official Gazette no. 114/28 February 2013;

Decizia Curții Constituționale a Românie, no. 1249/7 October 2010, published in the Official Gazette no. 764/16 November 2010;

Decizia Curții Constituționale a României, no. 137/25 February 2010, published in the Official Gazette no. 182/22 March 2010;

Decision in connected cases C-83/19, the Association "The Forum of Judges in Romania"/Judicial Inspection, C-127/19, the Association "The Forum of Judges in Romania" and the Association "The Movement to Defend the Status of Prosecutors" and OL/Prosecutor's Office attached to the High Court of Cassation and Justice – General Prosecutor of Romania and C-397/19, AX/Romanian State – Ministry of Public Finances;

Decision for the connected cases C-357/19 Euro Box Promotion et al., C379/19 DNA – Oradea Territorial Service, C-547/19 Association "The Forum of Judges", C-811/19 FQ et al., and C-840/19 N;

Decision of 18 May 2021, the Association "The Forum of Judges" et al., C-83 C-127/19, C-195/19, C-291/19, C-355/19 and C-397/19 (see also CP no. 82/21);

Decision of the Constitutional Court of Romania, no. 668/18 May 2011, published in the Official Gazette no. 487/8 July 2011;

Decision of the Constitutional Court of Romania, no. 157/19 March 2014, published in the Official Gazette no. 296/23 April 2014

2. THE PRINCIPLES OF LAW. METAPHYSICAL RATIONALITY AND LEGAL NORMATIVITY

Abstract:

Any scientific intercession that has as objective, the understanding of the significances of the "principle of law" needs to have an interdisciplinary character, the basis for the approach being the philosophy of the law. In this study we fulfill such an analysis with the purpose to underline the multiple theoretical significances due to this concept, but also the relationship between the juridical principles and norms, respectively the normative value of the principle of the law.

Thus, are being materialized extensive references to the philosophical and juridical doctrine in the matter. This study is a pleading to refer to the principles, in the work for the law's creation and applying. Starting with the difference between "given" and 'constructed" we propose the distinction between the "metaphysical principles" outside the law, which by their contents have philosophical significances, and the "constructed principles" elaborated inside the law. We emphasize the obligation of the law maker, but also of the expert to refer to the principles in the work of legislation, interpretation and applying of the law.

Arguments are brought for the updating, in certain limits, the justice – naturalistic concepts in the law.

Key words:

Principles of the law / Essence and phenomenon like aspect of the law / "Given" and "constructed" in the law / Significances of the principles of law / Moral value / Juridic

I. Introduction

In philosophy and, in general, in science, the principle has a theoretical and explanatory value because it is meant to synthesize and express the bases and unity of human existence, of existence in general and of knowledge in their diversity of manifestation. The discovery and affirmation of principles in any science gives certainty to knowledge, both by expressing the first element, which exists by itself, without needing to be deduced or demonstrated, and by achieving system cohesion, without which scientific knowledge and creation cannot exist.

The principle has multiple meanings in philosophy and science, but for our scientific approach, we retain that of: "fundamental element, idea, basic law on which a scientific theory, a political, legal system, a norm of conduct or the totality of laws is based and of the basic notions of a discipline"[24]. The common place of the meanings of the term principle is the *essence*, an important category for philosophy as well as for law.

The principle represents *the given as such*, which can have a double meaning: a) what exists before any knowledge as an a priori factor and basis for science; b) theoretical element and resulting synthesis of phenomenal diversity for reality of any kind. The distinction but also the reality between "given" and "constructed" are important to understand the nature of principles in science and especially in law. In his work "Séance et technique en droit positif", published at the beginning of the 20th century, François Geny[25] analyzes for the first time the relationship between science and legal technique starting from two concepts: the "given" and the "constructed". In Geny's opinion, a thing is "given" when it exists as an object outside the productive activity of man. In this sense, the author distinguishes four categories: real data; historical data; the rational data; the ideal data. From the perspective of our research topic, two of these categories are of interest, namely: the "rational data" which consists of those principles that arise from the consideration that must be shown to man and human relations, and the "ideal data" through which a dynamic element is established, namely moral aspirations and spiritual of a particular civilization.

---

[24] Explanatory dictionary of the Romanian language, Socialist Republic of Romania Press, Bucharest, 1975, p.744

[25]Quoted by Ion Craiovan in the monograph Introduction to the philosophy of law, All Beck Publ.-house, Bucharest, 1998, p.63

A thing is “constructed” when it is made by man, for example a reasoning, a legal norm, etc. The "given" is relative in the sense that it is influenced by the "constructed", by human activity. Regarding the “given”, man's attitude consists in knowing it with the help of science. As far as the “built” is concerned, man is by hypothesis the builder, he can make art or technique in this sense. The sphere of the constructed also extends to the social and political order.

The question arises whether the right is “given”, an object of science, in other words of ascertainment and registration, or is it “constructed”, a technical work? From a historical perspective, law is obviously “given”, an object of science, as old law, contemporary national or international law appears. However, the development of positive law requires “a construction” and in this sense the legal rules are the work of technique.

In the legal literature, this distinction has been retained, according to which science investigates the social climate that requires a certain legal normativity, and the technique aims at the ways in which the legislator transposes into practice, “builds” the legal rules. The relativity of this distinction was also emphasized, considering that the legal technique also implies a creation, a scientific activity[26].

Therefore, the principles represent the “given” as an ideal or basis for science and the “constructed” in the situation where they are elaborated or transposed into a human construction, including through legal norms.

A good systematization of the meanings of the notion of principle is made in a monograph[27]: “a) the founding principle of a field of existence; b) what would be hidden from direct knowledge and requires logical-epistemological processing; c) logical concept that would allow knowledge of the particular phenomenon”.

This systematization, applied to law, means: “a) the discussion regarding the essence of law; b) if and how we would know the essence; c) the operativity

---

[26] Jean Dabin, Théorie générale du Droit, Bruxelles, 1953, p.118-159

[27] Gheorghe C. Mihai, Radu I. Motica, Fundamentals of law. Theory and philosophy of law,All Beck Publ.-house, Bucharest, 1997, p.19

of the placement in the phenomenality of the right, correlated or not with the essence"[28].

The spirit's need to ascend to principles is natural and particularly persistent. Any scientific construction or normative system must refer to principles that guarantee or establish them. This regressive movement towards the unconditional, towards what is absolutely first, is for example the movement that Plato follows in Book VII of the Republic[29], when he posits the existence of "Good" as a first and non-hypothetical principle.

In the same sense, another great thinker[30] speaks of the "first principles" or the eternal principles of the unprovable "Being", the basis of all knowledge and of all existence, beyond which lies only ignorance.

The question then is to know if what seems necessary, in the logical virtue of knowledge, is also necessary in the ontological order of existence. In the "Critique of Pure Reason"[31], Kant will show that such a transition from logic to existence (the ontological argument) is not legitimate. If the unconditioned, as a principle, is necessarily posited by our reason, this cannot and must not lead us to the conclusion that this unconditioned exists outside of it and independently of any reality.

Consequently, the principles, since they aim at existence in all its domains, cannot and must not be immutable, but are the result of becoming. They are a "given", but only as a result of the existential dialectic or as a reflection of becoming in the phenomenal world and of essence.

---

[28] Gheorghe C. Mihai, Radu I. Motica, op.cit., p.20

[29] Plato, Works,5th Volume, Scientific and Enciclopedic Publ.-house, Bucharest, 1982, p.401-402

[30] Aristotle, Metaphysics,Book I, IRI Press, Bucharest, 1996, pp..9-69

[31] Immanuel Kant, Critique of Pure Reason, IRI Press, Bucharest, 1994, p.270-273

II. Content

Law, because it presupposes the particularly complex relationship between essence and phenomena, as well as a dialectic specific to each of the two categories in terms of theoretical, normative and social reality, cannot be outside the principles.

The problem of the status of the principles of law and their explanation has always concerned theorists. The school of natural law argued that the source, the origin, therefore the basis of legal principles is human nature. The historical school of law, under the influence of Kantianism, opens a new perspective in researching the genesis of legal principles, presenting them as products of the popular spirit (Volkgeist) which moves the basis of law from the universe of pure reason to the confluence of historical origins dissipated in a multitude of transient forms. The variants of the positivist school claim that the principles of law are generalizations induced from social experience. When the generalization covers a sufficiently large series of social facts we are in the presence of some principles. There are also authors such as Rudolf Stammler who deny the validity of any legal principle, considering the content of law diversified in space and time, lacking in universality. In the author's view, law would be a cultural category[32].

Referring to the same problem, Mircea Djuvara affirmed: "The whole science of law does not consist in reality, for a serious and methodical research, except to release from the multitude of provisions of the law their essentials, i.e., precisely these ultimate principles of justice from which all derive the other provisions. In this way, the entire legislation becomes very clear and what is called the legal spirit is captured. Only in this way the scientific elaboration of a law is done"[33].

In our opinion, this is the starting point for understanding the principles of law.

---

[32] Rodolf Stammler, Theorie der Recktswissenschaft, University of Chicago Press, Chicago, 1989, pp.24-25

[33] Mircea Djuvara, General theory of law. Rational law, sources and positive law, All Beck Publ.-house, Bucharest, 1999, p.265

In specialized literature, there is no unanimous opinion regarding the definition and meanings of the principles of law[34]. Several common elements can be identified, which we highlight below:

- Legal principles are general ideas, guiding postulates, fundamental prescriptions or foundations of the legal system. They characterize the entire system of law, constituting at the same time specific features of a type of law.
- The general principles of law configure the structure and development of the legal system, ensure unity, homogeneity, balance, coherence and capacity for its development.
- The authors distinguish between fundamental principles of law, which characterize the entire legal system and which reflect what is essential within the respective type of law, and principles valid for certain branches of law or legal institutions.

Thus, in the doctrine, the following general principles of law were identified and analyzed: 1) ensuring the legal basis for the functioning of the state; 2) the principle of freedom and equality; 3) the principle of responsibility; 4) the principle of equity and justice[35]. The same author believes that the general principles of the law have a theoretical and practical importance which consists in: a) the principles of the law draw the guideline for the legal system and guide the legislator's activity; b) these principles are also important for the administration of justice because, "The legal person must ascertain not only the positivity of the law, he must also explain the reason for his social existence, the social support of the law, its connection with social values"; c) the general principles of law can take the place of regulatory norms when the judge, in silence of the law, resolves the case based on the general principles of law[36].

One of the great problems of legal doctrine is the relationship between the principles of law, legal norms and social values. The opinions expressed

---

[34] Ioan Ceterchi, Ion Craiovan, Introduction to the general theory of law, All Publ.-house, Bucharest, 1993, p.30; Gheorghe Boboş, General theory of the state and law, Didactic and Pedagogical Publ.-house, Bucharest, 1983, p.186; Nicolae Popa, General theory of law, Actami Publ.-house, Bucharest, 1999, p.112-114; Ion Craiovan, Elementary treatise on general theory of law, All Beck Publ.-house, Bucharest, 2001, p.209; Gheorghe C. Mihai and Radu I. Motica, General theory of law, Alma Mater Publ.-house, Timisoara, 1999, p.75.

[35] Nicolae Popa, op.cit., pp.120-130

[36] Nicolae Popa, op.cit., p.120-130

are not unified, they differ depending on the legal concept. The school of natural law, the rationalists, the Kantian and Hegelian philosophy of law admit the existence of some principles outside the positive norms and superior to them. The principles of law are based on human reason and configure the value of the entire legal order. Unlike the positivist school of law, Kelsian normativism considers that principles are expressed by the rules of law and consequently there are no principles of law outside the system of legal norms.

Eugeniu Speranția established a correspondence between law and the principles of law: "If law appears as a total of social, mandatory norms, the unity of this totality is due to the consistency of all norms with a minimum number of fundamental principles, themselves presenting a maximum of logical affinity between they"[37].

In relation to this problem, in the Romanian specialized literature the idea was expressed that the principles of law are fundamental prescriptions of all legal norms[38]. In another opinion, it is considered that the principles of law guide the development and application of legal norms, they have the force of higher norms, found in the texts of normative acts, but they can also be deduced from "permanent social values" when they are not expressly stated by the rules of positive law[39].

We consider that the general principles of law are delimited by the positive norms of the law, but there is indisputably a relationship between the two values. For example, equality and freedom or equity and justice are value foundations (values) of social life. They must find their legal expression. In this way, the legal concepts that express these values appear, concepts that become the foundations (principles) of law. Legal norms then derive from these principles. Unlike the norms, the general principles of law have explanatory value because they contain the foundations of the existence and evolution of law[40].

---

[37] Eugeniu Speranția, Fundamental principles of legal philosophy, Cluj, 1936, p.8; Nicolae Popa, op.cit., p.114

[38] Nicolae Popa, op.cit., p.114

[39] Ioan Ceterchi, Ion Craiovan, op.cit., p.30

[40] Nicolae Popa, *op.cit.*, pp.116-117

Together with other authors[41], we believe that the legal norms relate to the principles of law in two senses: the norms contain and describe most of their principles; the functioning of the principles is then achieved by applying in practice the conduct stated by the rules. In relation to principles, legal norms have a narrower teleological explanatory value, the purpose of norms being to preserve social values, not to explain the causal reason for their existence. The principles of law are the expression of the values promoted and defended by law. We could say that the most general principles of law coincide with the social values promoted by law.

For a correct understanding of the issue of values in law and their expression through the principles of law, some brief clarifications are required in the context of our research topic. The different currents and legal schools, from antiquity to the present, have sought to explain and substantiate legal regulations and institutions through some general concepts valued as special values for society. Law is based on value judgments. Indeed, by its nature, law implies an appreciation, a valorization of human conduct according to certain values, representing the finality of the legal order, such as: justice, the common good, freedom, etc.[42].

The values are not strictly and exclusively legal in nature. On the contrary, they have a wider dimension of a moral, political, social, philosophical nature in general. These values must be understood in their historical-social dynamics. Although some of them can be found in all legal systems, such as justice, still the specificity and historical particularities of society leave their mark on them. The values of a society must be derived primarily from the philosophy (social, moral, political, legal) that presides and guides the social forces in that society.

The legislator, in the process of legislation, orienting himself according to these values, expressed especially by the general principles of law, transposes them into legal norms, and on the other hand, once "legislated" these values are defended and promoted in the form specific to the regulation legal. The legal norm becomes both a benchmark for assessing behavior according to the respective social value, and a means of ensuring the realization of the demands of this value and of predicting the future evolution of society.

---

[41] Nicolae Popa, op.cit., pp.116-117, Gheorghe C. Mihai and Radu I. Motica, General theory of law. University course, Alma Mater Publ.-house, Timisoara, 1999, p.78

[42] Paul Roubier, Théorie générale du Droit, L.G.D.J., Paris, 1986, p.267

It should also be added that legal norms materialize legal values relatively, because neither as a whole nor individually they fully indicate a legal value, they do not exhaust its wealth of content.

Regarding the identification of the values promoted by law, the opinions of the authors do not coincide, although they are in close spheres. Thus, Paul Roubier lists *justice*, *legal security* and *social progress* as values[43]. Michel Villey lists four great purposes of law: *justice*, *good conduct*, *serving people* and *serving society*[44]. François Rigaux speaks of two categories, namely: the primordial ones, which he calls formal, *order*, *peace* and *legal security*, and the material ones, *equality* and *justice*[45].

The indisputable value that defines the finality of law, in the view of the most prominent thinkers, since antiquity is justice. The particularly complex concept of *justice* has been approached, explained and defined by numerous thinkers – moralists, philosophers, jurists, sociologists, theologians – who start their definition from the ideas of just, fair, in the sense of giving everyone what is due. The general principle of law, equity and justice is the expression of justice as a social value. Many conceptions of law could be located either in a rationalist line or in a realistic one. Rationalists argue that the principle of justice is innate to man, it belongs to our reason in its eternity. Realists argue that justice is an elaboration of history and general human experience.

Regardless of the theoretical orientation, justice undoubtedly constitutes a complex basis of the legal universe. Giorgio del Vecchio states that justice is compliance with the legal law, the legal law being what includes justice. According to Lalande, justice is the property of everything that is just; Faberquetes considers the law as the unique expression of the principle of justice, and justice as, of course, the unique content of the expression of law. It has also been said that justice is the will to give everyone what is his; it is balance or the proportion of relationships between people, it is social love, or it is the harmonious realization of the essence of the human being[46].

---

[43] Paul Roubier, op.cit., p.268

[44] Qouted by Jean-Louis Bergel in Théorie générale du Droit, Dalloz, Paris, 1989, p.29

[45] Quoted by Ioan Ceterchi and Ion Craiovan in Introduction to the general theory of law, All Publ.-house, Bucharest, 1993, p.27

[46] Gheorghe C. Mihai, Radu I. Motica, Fundamentals of law. Theory and philosophy of law, All Publ.-house, Bucharest, 1997, p.128

Justice as a value and principle of law exists through the legal norms contained in constitutions, laws, etc. This does not mean that objective law, with its expressions, completely and inevitably carries “justice”: not everything that is right in force is just. On the other hand, there are legal norms, such as technical ones, which are indifferent to the idea of justice. As there are circumstances when positive law is more inspired by considerations of utility than justice in order to maintain order and stability in society.

In our opinion, justice, as a social value and at the same time as a general principle of law, is dimensioned in the ideas of fair measure, equity, legality and good faith. In particular, the concepts of fair measure and equity express proportionality.

The principle of justice has this guiding content in a cognitive-actional line: to give everyone what is due to them. A legal system is unitary, homogeneous, balanced and coherent if in all its components it “ensures, protects, enshrines”, so that each natural and legal person is what he is, has what is due to him without harm each other or the social system.

Equity is a dimension of the principle of justice in its consensus with the moral good. This concept rejuvenates formal legal equality, humanizes it, introducing into the legal systems in force the categories of morality from the perspective of which justification is also a doing for good and for freedom. “Considered in this way, equity spreads to the most distant spheres of the system of legal norms, bearing fruit even in strictly technical or formal domains, apparently indifferent to axiological concerns”[47]. Understood by the idea of proportionality, equity concerns the reduction of inequality, where the establishment of perfect equality (also called formal justice) is impossible due to the particularities of the factual situation. In other words, in relation to the generality of the legal rule, equity suggests that we take into account the factual situations, the personal circumstances, the uniqueness of the case, without going to extremes.

The idea of justice evolves under the influence of social-political transformations in society. Thus, in contemporary democratic states, in order to emphasize the achievements of social policy regarding living and working conditions, economic, social and cultural rights, we speak of *social justice*. The achievement of social justice is listed as a requirement of the rule of law in the

---

[47] Gheorghe C. Mihai, Radu I. Motica, *op.cit.*, p.133

document adopted at the Conference for European Security and Cooperation, Copenhagen, 1990.

Another problem of legal doctrine is to establish the relationship between the principles of law and those of morality. Christian Thomasius in his work *Fundamenta juris naturae et gentium ex sensu comuni deducta* (1705)[48], distinguished between the mission of law to protect the external relationships of human individuals through prescriptions that form perfect and punishable obligations and the mission of morality to protect the inner life of individuals only through prescriptions which form imperfect and unsanctionable obligations. This distinction between morality and law has become classic.

Undoubtedly, law cannot be confused with morality, for several reasons analyzed in the specialized literature[49]. However, since ancient times, law and morality have been in a close relationship that cannot be considered accidental. The respective relationship is of an axiological nature. Legal and ethical values have a common origin, namely the conscience of individuals living in the same community. The jusrationalism theory – a modern form of jusnaturalism – tried to argue that there is a fund of principles of universal and eternal justice, because they are inscribed in human reason where they intertwine with the principles of good and truth. Therefore, since law is rational, it is natural, and since it is natural, it is also moral.

Of course, the law eminently regulates the external conduct of the human individual. However, the law is not disinterested in morality, "in that through equity it seeks the good by acting towards the agreement of the outside with the inside, while morality acts towards the agreement of the inside with the outside of the individual, in the same equity"[50].

We consider that indeed morality and law have a common value structure and this can be deduced not only from the fairly frequently encountered statement that "law is a minimum of morality", but also from the finding that there is no moral statement to be denounced as unjust, although

---

[48] Quoted by Ion Dobrinescu in Justice and cultural values, Romanian Academy Press, Bucharest, 1992, p.95

[49] Giorgio del Vecchio, Lessons in legal philosophy, Europa Nova Publ.-house, Bucharest, 1995, pp.192-202; Ion Dobrinescu, op.cit., pp.95-99; Gheorghe Mihai, Radu I. Motica, op.cit., pp.81-86; Ion Ceterchi, Ion Craiovan, op.cit., pp.39-42

[50] Gheorghe C. Mihai, Radu I. Motica, *op.cit.*, p.84

sometimes legal statements are discovered in disagreement with moral principles. The tendency of the law to appeal to values of a moral character is observed in order for them to be introduced in legal regulations. In this sense, Ioan Muraru states that: "Moral rules, although they are usually much more appropriated by natural law and custom, they express the ancestral and permanent desires of mankind. Moral rules, although they are usually not fulfilled, in case of necessary through the coercive force of the state must be legally supported in their realization when they defend the life, freedom and happiness of people. That's why the Romanian Constitution does not lack references to the hypostases of morality. These constitutional references ensure efficiency and validity to morality. Thus, for example, Art 26 and Art 30 protect the 'good morals', Art 53 mentions the 'public moralsd'. Likewise, 'good faith', which is obviously first a moral concept, is enshrined in Art 11 and Art 57"[51]. Therefore, the general principles of law and those of morality have a common value base. Law norms can express values that are originally moral and that are also found in the content of the general principles of law, such as equity or its particular form, proportionality.

The principles of law have the same features and logical-philosophical meanings as principles in general. Their peculiarities are determined by the existence of two systems of dialectical relations specific to law:

a) Principles – categories – norms;
b) Principles – the law, as social reality;

Some more important features of the principles of law can be identified, useful to establish whether proportionality can be considered a principle of law:

A) Any principle of law must be of the essence. It cannot identify with a concrete case or with an individual assessment of legal relations. The principle must represent the stability and balance of legal relations, regardless of the variety of normative regulations or particular aspects specific to legal reality. Consequently, the principle of law must be opposed to randomness and express necessity as its essence.

---

[51] Ioan Muraru, Elena Simina Tănăsescu, Constitutional law and public institutions, 1st Volume Ed. All Beck, Bucharest, 2003, p.8

However, the principle cannot be a pure creation of reason. It has a rational, abstract dimension of maximum generality, but it is not a metaphysical creation. Although of the order of essence, the principles of law cannot be eternal and absolute, but reflect social transformations, express the historical, economic, geographical, political particularities of the system that contains them and, in turn, that underpins them[52]. The principles of law evolve because the realities they reflect and explain are subject to improvement. "In law, every legal relationship is susceptible – equally to improvement. The scientific improvement of legal analysis will never be finished. But, in law, we must immediately give solutions, because practical life does not wait"[53].

Being of the order of essence, the principles of law have a generalizing character, both for the variety of legal relationships and for the rules of law. At the same time expressing the essential and general of legal reality, the principles of law are the basis for all other normative regulations.

There are great principles of law that do not depend on their consecration by legal norms, but the legal norm determines their concrete content, in relation to the historical reference time.

B) The principles of law are enshrined and recognized by constitutions, laws, custom, jurisprudence, international documents or formulated in legal doctrine.

The principles must be accepted internally and be part of the national law of each state. The general principles of law are enshrined in the constitutions. The characteristics of the legal system of a state influence and even determine the consecration and recognition of the principles of law.

The work of enshrining the principles of law in political and legal documents is in full swing.

Thus, in international documents such as the U.N. Charter or the Declaration of the UN General Assembly from 1970, principles that

[52] Mircea Djuvara, Law and sociology, I.S.D., Bucharest, 1936, p.52-56; Nicolae Popa, op.cit., pp.113-114

[53] Mircea Djuvara, General theory of law. Rational law, sources and positive law, All Beck Publ.-house, Bucharest, 1999, p.265

characterize the democratic international legal order are enshrined[54]. The regional legal systems knew and recognized their own principles. The regional legal systems knew and recognized their own principles. For example, the community law system enshrines the following more important principles: the principle of equality, the protection of fundamental human rights, the principle of legal certainty, the principle of subsidiarity, the principle of res judicata and the principle of proportionality[55]. Most democratic constitutions enshrine principles such as: the principle of sovereignty, the principle of legality and supremacy, the constitution, the principle of democracy, the principle of pluralism, the principle of representation, the principle of equality, etc.

Jurisprudence has a significant role in consecrating and applying the principles of law. There are situations in which the principles of law are recognized through jurisprudence, without being formulated in the text of normative acts. Thus, the Italian Civil Code recommends judges to rule in the absence of texts, in light of the general principles of law.

There are legal systems in which not all principles have a normative consecration. We are specifically referring to the great system known as common law, which consists of the existence of three autonomous and parallel normative subsystems: common law (in the narrow sense); equity; and statute-law. Equity represents a set of principles derived from court practice and which are a corrective to common-law rules.

With all the variety of ways of enshrining and recognizing the principles of law, the necessity of at least their recognition is evident in order to be characterized and applied in the legal system. This consecration or recognition is not enough to be doctrinal but must be achieved through norms or jurisprudence. However, a distinction must be made between the consecration or recognition of the principles of law, and on the other hand, their application.

C) The principles of law represent values for the legal system, because they express both the legal ideal and the objective requirements of society, they have a regulatory role for social relations. In the situation where the rule is unclear or does not exist, the settlement of disputes can be done directly based

---

[54] Alexandru Bolintineanu, Adrian Năstase, Bogdan Aurescu, Contemporary International Law, All Beck Publ.-house, Bucharest, 2000, pp.52-71.

[55] Ion Craiovan, *op.cit.*, p.211

on general or special principles of law. Ideally, they represent a coordinating theme for the work of legislation.

D) In the classification of the principles of law, one starts from the consideration that between them there is a hierarchy or a relationship from general to particular[56]. Starting from this finding we can distinguish:

1. General principles of law that form the content of norms of universal application with a maximum level of generality. These are recognized by the doctrine and expressed by normative acts in domestic law or international treaties of particular importance. As a rule, these principles are written in constitutions, thus having a superior legal force over all other laws and over all branches of law. Referring to the theoretical and practical importance of studying the principles of law, Nicolae Popa remarked: "the general principles of law are the fundamental prescriptions that combine the creation of law and its application... In conclusion, the action of the principles of law results in conferring the certainty of law – the guarantee granted to individuals against the unpredictability of coercive norms – and the congruence of the legislative system, i.e., the concordance of laws, their social feature, their plausibility, their opportunity[57].

General principles also play a role in the administration of justice, because those charged with applying the law must know not only the letter of the law, but also its spirit, and the general principles constitute this spirit. Among them we can include: the principle of legality, the principle of enshrining, respecting and guaranteeing human rights, the principle of equality, the principle of justice and equity, etc.

2. Specific principles that express values and that usually have limited action to one or more branches of law. They are written in codes or other laws. The principle of the legality of punishments, the obligation of contracts, the presumption of innocence, the principle of respecting international treaties, etc. can be included in this category. The special principles have their value source in the fundamental principles of law.

For example, proportionality is one of the old and classical principles of law, rediscovered in the modern era. The meaning of this principle, in a general

---

[56] Ioan Ceterchi, Ion Craiovan, op.cit., p.31; Radu I. Motica, Gheorghe C. Mihai, General theory of law, p.77

[57] Nicolae Popa, *op.cit.*, p.117

sense, is that of equivalent relationship, balance between phenomena, situations, persons, etc., but also the idea of fair measure.

Ion Deleanu specifies that: "Originally, the concept of proportionality is outside the law; he evokes the idea of correspondence and balance, even harmony. Appeared as a mathematical principle, the principle of proportionality also developed as a fundamental idea in philosophy and law, receiving different forms and meanings: "reasonable", "rational", "equilibrium", "admissible", "tolerable", etc.[58]. Therefore, proportionality is part of the content of the principle of equity and justice, considered to be a general principle of law. At the same time, through its normative consecration, explicit or implicit, and through jurisprudential application, proportionality has particular meanings in different branches of law: constitutional law, administrative law, community law, criminal law, etc. The definition, understanding and application of this principle, in the meanings shown above, result from the doctrinal analysis and jurisprudential interpretation[59].

[58] Ion Deleanu, Constitutional law and political institutions, Europa Nova Publ.-house, Bucharest, 1996, p.264

[59] Marius Andreescu, The principle of proportionality in constitutional law, Publ.-house C.H. Beck, Bucharest, 2007

III. Conclusions

An argument for which the philosophy of law must be a present reality not only in the theoretical sphere but also for the practical activity of drafting normative acts or the administration of justice, is represented by the existence of general and branch principles of law, some of which are enshrined in the Constitution.

The principles of law, by their nature, generality and depth, are topics of reflection primarily for the philosophy of law, only after their construction in the sphere of the metaphysics of law, these principles can be transposed into the general theory of law, can be normatively enshrined and applied in jurisprudence. Moreover, there is a dialectical circle because the "meanings" of the principles of law, after the normative consecration and jurisprudential elaboration, are to be elucidated also in the sphere of the philosophy of law. Such a finding nevertheless imposes the distinction between what we could call: constructed principles of law, and on the other hand metaphysical principles of law. The distinction we propose has as its philosophical basis the distinction shown above between "constructed" and "given" in law.

The constructed principles of law are, by their very nature, legal rules of maximum generality, elaborated by legal doctrine or by the legislator, in all situations explicitly established by the rules of law. These principles can constitute the internal structure of a group of legal relations, of a branch or even of the unitary system of law. The following features can be identified: 1) they are elaborated within the law, being, as a rule, the expression of the will of the legislator, enshrined in legal norms; 2) are always expressed explicitly by legal norms; 3) the work of interpretation and application of the law is able to discover the meanings and determinations of the constructed principles of the law which, obviously, cannot exceed their conceptual limits established by the legal norm. In this category we find principles such as: the publicity of the court session, the principle of contradiction, of the supremacy of the law and the Constitution, the principle of non-retroactivity of the law, etc.

Therefore, the constructed principles of law have, by their nature, first of all a legal connotation and only in the subsidiary a metaphysical one. Being the result of an elaboration within the law, the possible metaphysical meanings are to be after their consecration established by the metaphysics of law. At the same time, being rules of law, they are binding and produce legal effects just like any other normative regulation. It is necessary to mention that the legal norms that enshrine such principles are superior in legal force to the usual regulations of the law, because they usually target social relations considered to be essential in the first place for the respect of the fundamental rights and legitimate interests recognized by the subjects by law, but also for the stability and fair, predictable, transparent conduct of judicial procedures.

In the situation of this category of principles, the dialectical circle mentioned above has the following appearance: 1) the constructed principles are elaborated and normatively consecrated by the legislator; 2) their interpretation is carried out in the law enforcement work; 3) the value meanings of these principles are later expressed in the sphere of metaphysics of law; 4) metaphysical "meanings" can constitute the theoretical basis necessary for broadening the connotation and denotation of principles or for the normative elaboration of such new principles.

The number of constructed principles of law can be determined at a certain moment of legal reality, but there is no pre-constituted limit of them. The evolution of law is also manifested through the normative elaboration of such new principles. As an example, we mention the "principle of subsidiarity", a construction in European Union law, adopted in the legislation of many European states, including Romania.

The metaphysical principles of law can be considered as a "given" to legal reality and by their nature are external to law. At their origin, they do not have a legal, normative or jurisprudential elaboration. They are a transcendental and non-transcendent "given" of law, therefore, they are not "beyond" the sphere of law, but they are "something else" in the legal system. In other words, it represents the value essence of law, without which this constructed reality could not have an ontological dimension.

Since they are not constructed, but represent a transcendental, metaphysical "given" of law, it is not necessary to express them explicitly through legal norms. Metaphysical principles can also have an implicit existence, discovered or exploited in the work of interpreting the law. As an implicit given and at the same time as the transcendental essence of the law, these principles must be found, after all, in the content of any legal norm and in any act or manifestation that represents, as the case may be, the interpretation or application of the legal norm. It must be emphasized that the existence of metaphysical principles also underpins the teleological nature of law, because any manifestation in the legal sphere, in order to be legitimate, must be appropriate to such principles.

In the specialized legal literature, such principles, without being called metaphysical, are identified by their generality and that is why they were called "general principles of law". We prefer to emphasize their metaphysical, valuable and transcendental dimension, which is why we consider them metaphysical principles of legal reality. As a transcendental "given" and not constructed by law, the principles in question are permanent, limited, but with determinations and meanings that can be diversified in the dialectical circle that encompasses them.

In our opinion, the metaphysical principles of law are: *the principle of justice*; *the principle of truth*; *the principle of equity and justice*; *the principle of proportionality*; *the principle of freedom*. In a future study, we will elaborate on the considerations that entitle us to identify the principles mentioned above as having a metaphysical and transcendental value in relation to legal realities.

The metaphysical dimension of these principles is indisputable, but the normative dimension remains under discussion. A broader analysis of this problem exceeds the object of this study, which was intended to be a broad excursion on the philosophical dimension of the principles of law. However, some considerations are necessary. Contemporary ontology no longer considers reality by referring to the classical concepts of substance or matter. In his work, "Substamzbegriff und Funktionsbegriff" (1910), Ernest Cassirer opposes the modern concept of function to the ancient concept of substance. Not what the "thing" is or the concrete reality, but their way of being, their inner fabric, their structure interests the moderns. Concrete objects no longer exist in front of knowledge, but only "relations" and "functions". In a way, for scientific knowledge, but not for ontology, things disappear and give way to relationships and functions. Such an approach is cognitively operational for material reality, not for ideal reality, that "world of Ideas" of which Plato spoke of[60].

The normative dimension of legal reality seems to correspond very well to the findings formulated by Ernest Cassirer. What else is the legal reality than

---

[60] Constantin Noica, Becoming a being, Humanitas Publ.-house, Bucharest, 1998, pp.332-334

an ensemble of social relations and functions that are transposed into the new ontological dimension of "legal relations" through the application of the rules of law. The principles built by applying to a sphere of social relations through the legal norm transform them into legal relations, so these principles correspond to a legal reality, understood as a relational and functional structure.

But there is a deeper order of reality than relationships and functions. Constantin Noica said that we must call "element" this order of reality, in which things are fulfilled and which makes them be. Between the concept of substance and that of function or relationship, a new concept is imposed, which preserves a substantiality and, without dissolving in function, manifests functionality[61].

Taking this idea of the great Romanian philosopher, we can affirm that the metaphysical principles of law evoke not only legal relationships or functions, but "value elements" of legal reality, without which it would not exist.

The metaphysical principles of law have normative value, even if they are not explicitly expressed by legal norms. Moreover, as it follows from the jurisprudential interpretations, they can even have a super-normative meaning and, in this way, can legitimize jusnaturalist conceptions in law. These concepts and the doctrine of supra-legality supported by François Geny, Leon Duguit and Maurice Duverger, consider that justice and, in particular, constitutional justice must relate to supra-constitutional rules and principles. In our opinion, such standards are expressed precisely by the metaphysical principles to which I referred. Natural law concepts were also applied by some constitutional courts. The decision of January 16, 1957, of the Federal Constitutional Court of the Federal Republic of Germany regarding the freedom to leave the federal territory is famous in this regard. The Court declares: "Laws are not constitutional unless they were enacted in compliance with the prescribed forms. Their substance must be in accordance with the supreme values of the democratic and liberal order as a system of values established by the Constitution, but they must also be in accordance with the *unwritten elementary principles* (s.n.) and the fundamental principles of the

[61] Constantin Noica, *op.cit.*, pp.327-367

Basic Law, especially with the principles of the rule of law and the social state"[62].

A final aspect that we want to emphasize refers to the role of the judge in the application of constructed principles, but especially of the metaphysical principles of law. We believe that the fundamental rule is that of the interpretation and, implicitly, of the application of any legal regulation in the spirit and respecting the value content of the metaphysical and constructed principles of law. Another rule refers to the situation where there is inconsistency between the usual legal regulations and, on the other hand, the constructed and metaphysical principles of law. In such a situation, we appreciate, in the light of the jurisprudence of the German constitutional courts, that the metaphysical principles will have to be applied with priority, even at the expense of a concrete norm. In this way, the judge respects the essential feature of the legal system and not only the legal functions or relations.

[62] Andreescu Marius, op.cit., pp.34-38

Bibliography

Andreescu, Marius, The principle of proportionality in constitutional law, Bucharest: C.H. Beck, 2007;

Aristotle, Metaphysics, Book I, Bucharest: IRI Press, 1996;

Bolintineanu, Alexandru, Adrian Năstase, Bogdan Aurescu, Contemporary International Law, Bucharest: All Beck, 2000;

Ceterchi, Ioan, and Craiovan, Ion, Introduction to the general theory of law, Bucharest: All, 1993;

Craiovan, Ion, Introduction to the philosophy of law, Bucharest: All Beck, 1998;

Deleanu, Ion, Constitutional law and political institutions, Bucharest: Europa Nova, 1996;

del Vecchio, Giorgio, Lessons in legal philosophy, Bucharest: Europa Nova, 1995;

Djuvara, Mircea, General theory of law. Rational law, sources and positive law, Bucharest: All Beck, 1999;

Kant, Immanuel, Critique of pure reason, Bucharest: IRI Press, 1994;

Mihai, Gheorghe C., Radu I. Motica, Fundamentals of law. Theory and philosophy of law, Bucharest: All, 1997;

Murariu, Ioan, and Elena-Simina Tănăsescu, Constitutional law and political institutions. 1st Volume, Bucharest: All Beck, 2003;

Noica, Constantin, Becoming a being, Bucharest: Humanitas, 1998;

Platon, Opere, 5th Volume, Bucharest: Scientific and Encyclopedic Publ.-house, 1982;

Speranţia, Eugeniu, Fundamental principles of legal philosophy, Cluj: Transylvanian Institute of Graphic Arts, 1936.

3. ASPECTS OF SOCIAL AND LEGAL NORMATIVISM CONTEMPORARY

Abstract:

The most striking expression of the social fact is the social norm. Man's social existence cannot be conceived without norms, mainly moral, religious and legal, that regulate and even determine the behavior of the human person in the social environment. The existence of any individual as a social being presupposes a series of obligations exercised throughout his life cycle, materialized in a series of norms, some of which complement each other, others appear contradictory to others, being specific to different interest groups. .

This system of rules is a condition for the existence of society's life, a mechanism that requires good management of human relations and removes the imminent danger of chaos. Social norms are imposed, promoted and perpetuated by several methods that we will analyze in our study Regardless of the field they regulate, social norms contain rules addressed to individuals, describing and detailing the ways in which values must be translated into legitimate behaviors and accepted by society.

As social relations are extremely varied, a diversity of social norms that regulate these relations is also outlined. Thus, the system of social norms consists of the following groups: ethical norms, ordinary norms (customs), corporate norms, religious norms and legal norms.

There are also technical norms that are not part of social determinism because they do not regulate social relations.

Regarding the complex relationship between the normative legal system and, on the other hand, society, it can be seen that currently the legal system tends to have its own functional autonomy, apart from the objective or subjective determinations that society transmits. The autonomy of the judiciary tries to transform itself from a secondary, phenomenological and ideational structure, into one with its own reality, with the power to impose its order on the social and natural order.

In this study we also analyze aspects of the work of normative codification.

Key words:

Social fact, Social norms, Legal norms, Autonomy of the legal, Codification of legal norms

I. Determinism and social norms

Man is a social being because his own living environment, as opposed to the natural environment is society, the community. Isolation, a state that is not to be confused with loneliness and loneliness, is contrary to human nature because it involves removing the human person from his natural environment, the social one. Therefore, isolation applied as a criminal sanction, or more recently for an alleged prevention of the contagious disease that has haunted the world for two years can only be temporary and cannot destroy the social dimension of human existence.

The doctrine of social determinism, endorsed by both Marxists and the current politicians and rulers of capitalist democracy, supports the hypothesis of the primacy of society over individual behavior. Determinists say that social interactions determine individual human behavior. As a result, the individual does not choose his own action, but is forced to do so under the pressure of society; he is not really free to act as he wishes. Emile Durkheim, considered the father of modern sociology, uses the concept of social fact to explain the primacy of society over the human person. The social fact is characterized, among other things, by its exteriority and especially by its coercive power, i.e., it is imposed on individuals. In this capacity, it is the paradigm that justifies the primacy of society over individual behavior and thus validates social determinism.

The most striking expression of the social fact is the social norm. Man's social existence cannot be conceived without norms, mainly moral, religious and legal, which regulate and even determine the behavior of the human person in the social environment. Moreover, social norms represent the structure of the social system, orienting its dynamics, change and becoming.

The determinism and social normativism are at least in contradiction in a relationship contrary to human freedom. Freedom is constitutive for the human person. Man was created by God as a free being and aware of his freedom.

The essence of social determinism and social normativism is formed by the causal necessity and the normative imperative. Human social freedom can thus be conditioned, restricted or sometimes even abolished.

The relationship between determinism, social normativism and on the other hand the person's freedom in the social environment is particularly complex, requires a broad analysis and involves establishing the priority between social and human as well as between the social normative system and freedom.

II. Legal normativism

"Order", whatever its nature, expresses necessity, limit and even coercion, but which cannot be contrary to human freedom as existential data.

The relationship between freedom and necessity, between freedom and law, moral or legal, is recessive. Necessity as order, regardless of its nature and configuration, is the dominant term and freedom the recessive one. Of course, freedom does not flow from necessity, be it spiritual order, it is not determined by such a necessity as in the materialist conception. As existing, freedom is different from necessity, but in relation to the order whose expression is necessary, freedom is always recessive and unfulfilled.

In relation to the need for an existential order, as a recessive term, freedom is never complete, it is not fulfilled, but it is always in precariousness.

The approach to the issue of freedom that we encounter in the legal sciences has multiple conceptual features and, we would say, many times more important than philosophical conceptions of freedom, because the legal is a state of human existence, a characteristic of social status, distinct from the state natural, material. It is a contemporary state of human existence, respectively the "legal state", which includes an existential order based on two realities: the legal norm and freedom.

Law cannot be conceived outside the idea of freedom. The normative system, the most important aspect of law, has its meanings and legitimacy in human existence, the latter being based on freedom.

But what kind of freedom can we talk about in legal norms and in the categories and concepts of law? Inevitably, it is a freedom of the legal norm, a constructed freedom, and not an existential fact. We must emphasize that the legal norm also involves coercion, as well as any existential order applied to human phenomenology. There is an important paradox pointed out by some authors in the field of Christian metaphysics, namely the coexistence of legal constraints, and on the other hand of human freedom, both being essential for the specific order of the legal state in which contemporary man is.

Another aspect is interesting, namely that the legal norm does not show what freedom is, does not define it, does not show its meanings, but only the situations in which freedom is guaranteed or restricted. Moreover, it is good to note that, unlike metaphysics and ethics, the legal norm does not express or conceptualize freedom as such, but only freedoms or rights, i.e., the phenomenal aspects of human manifestations in the social environment, by its nature a relational environment. It is obvious that the legal normative system could not even define freedom as such, because it remains only with the phenomenological and social aspect of existence. Likewise, legal doctrine postulates human freedom and highlights the content of legal freedoms, but does not define freedom as a reality, as an essential feature of man as a person, including in the social environment.

The most important expression of social determinism is the social normative system. The standardization of social life is necessary and has an imperative character, but it is also a restriction of the exercise of man's natural freedom.

The existence of any individual as a social being presupposes a series of obligations exercised throughout his life cycle, materialized in a series of norms, some of which complement each other, others appear contradictory to others, being specific to different interest groups. Sorin M. Rădulescu considers that "the diversity of these norms, as well as their specific way of functioning in various life contexts, creates the so-called normative order of a society, based on which the rational development of social life is regulated".

The term "nomos" meaning from the Greek language natural law, norm, which implies the observance of the order established by the gods, has its counterpart in Asian spirituality, through "Dao", in several forms: Dao of heaven; Dao of man. Genoveva Vrabie defines the social norm as "a general pattern of behavior that regulates certain social actions of people, their conduct and activity, and thus the relationships between people. There is no kind of social activity to which no rules of development or exercise should be imposed or recommended". The social norm is a rule that determines the behavior of the individual in a concrete situation. Moreover, society as a complex set of structures imposes a developed and dynamic system of social norms.

This system of rules is a condition for the existence of society, a mechanism that requires good management of human relations and removes the imminent danger of chaos. Social norms are imposed, promoted and perpetuated by several methods, namely: those behaviors or conducts that are detrimental to the values of society or the social group are prohibited; those behaviors or conducts that preserve the order of that society are mandatory and those behaviors or conducts that help the integration of the individual as a member of the society are recommended, approved.

As emanations of the collective consciousness of society, social norms, in their entirety, represent the conditions for the rational organization of human behavior, directly contributing to ensuring the continuity of social life, by establishing patterns of behavior for certain conditions. Thus, social norms presuppose the organization of human actions in accordance with the rules, the values positively appreciated by the respective society. Through them, society, as a coherent set of social relations and actions, develops a normative reference system that allows members to behave intelligibly and normally.

As we have mentioned, social norms impose patterns of behavior on individuals, creating optimal conditions for achieving life in the social framework that determines their existence. The various fields of social activity, which are constantly developing, involve the continuous modernization of the system of social norms.

Regardless of the field they regulate, social norms contain rules addressed to individuals, describing and detailing the ways in which values must be translated into legitimate behaviors and accepted by society.

As social relations are extremely varied, a variety of social norms governing these relations are also outlined. Thus, the system of social norms consists of the following groups of norms: ethical norms, ordinary norms (customs), corporate norms, religious norms and legal norms.

There are also technical norms that are not part of social determinism because they do not regulate social relations.

Adherents of social contract theory argue that the transition of man from the natural state to the social state determines the need for social norms, especially moral and legal ones.

The social norm is imperative, obligatory, even if in law theorists also speak of the existence of supplementary norms and recommendations. Being an expression of social determinism, the norms condition and determine the social conduct of man. In relation to these rules, the responsibility and, as the case may be, the social responsibility of the persons are established. Failure to do so may result in moral, religious or legal sanctions.

Their imperative character is not a constitutive one but derives either from a social recognition or from a manifestation of will of a center of power, most of the times the state.

Where does the need for social norms come from? It is a question that theorists, including philosophers and sociologists, answer by referring to the characteristics of the state-organized society. We believe that this explanation is not enough. Proponents of the utopian Marxist view of man and society believed that a time would come when the state would disappear, that society would exist in itself without a state and without legal norms. This moment was marked by the complete victory of communism all over the world, the achievement of a general welfare and the removal of any social differentiation and the formation of the new man with a perfect social consciousness, fully integrated into the social environment whose conduct is harmonized with the requirements of good social coexistence. Therefore, there is no need for normative coercion.

This conception is a utopia because Marxists believed that in this world and form of existence the only possible happiness and full freedom can be achieved, but without God and for a man reduced to the stage of socially integrated individual without personality and without individual consciousness and freedom.

The very freedom and fundamental rights to be guaranteed and respected must be included in normative systems, but which are based on coercion often incompatible with the ontological freedom of man in the social environment.

It is a freedom that unites. In contrast, the social and implicitly legal state of man is based on the distinction between mine and yours that Kant mentioned, which divides, divides and limits. This is how the philosophical and legal concept of coexistence of freedoms and legal norms arose.

The limits of social normativism, especially the legal one, are obvious especially in relation to human freedom. Social normative determinism cannot comprehend or constrain the freedom of man as a person. The existential freedom of man in the social environment is manifested in its phenomenal forms, determined, guaranteed but also controlled by the power of the state, the creator of the social order through laws. It is therefore a freedom whose content is expressed through the forms of culture and civilization, a creative freedom, but a limited, conditioned freedom, possible to be subject to the restrictions imposed by the state. It is a freedom of the legal norm.

The constitutions enshrine the possibility of restricting the exercise of legal rights and freedoms. But also, in the legal sphere there is the principle that any restriction of a fundamental right cannot affect its very substance, cannot abolish it, which means that the origin and basis of legal freedoms are outside the law, is the existential freedom of man as a gift of God. Moreover, the doctrine, but also the judicial practice enshrines and recognizes natural rights, essential for the social existence of man whose exercise cannot be restricted or conditioned. We consider, among other things, the right to life or freedom of conscience.

Regarding the complex relationship between the normative legal system and, on the other hand, society, it can be seen that at the same time the legal system tends to have its own functional autonomy, apart from the objective or subjective determinations that society transmits. The autonomy of the judiciary tries to transform itself from a secondary, phenomenological and ideational structure, into one with its own reality, with the power to impose its order on the social and natural order. In this context, the legally established legal freedoms try to determine the existential freedom of man, explaining it, ordering it and conditioning it. It is a situation contrary to the natural reality; the phenomenology of the legal must be conditioned, determined, by the existence of man, as a person, and by the particularities of social existence and not vice versa. It is an expression of the dictatorship by law even in democratic societies, because the legitimacy of the legal norm is, in such a situation contrary to nature, only in the will and interests of the rulers who express themselves, paradoxically, on behalf of the people.

The reality described above, specific to contemporary society, has negative consequences, in the sense that man, as a person, the only holder of existential freedom, is no longer aware of his own freedom and expects the normative order, the state or even justice to give him freedom. he needs. It can be said that in such a situation, not realizing his own freedom, contemporary man does not exist authentically, but lives by delegation, his existence being determined externally by state and legal normativism, abstract, impersonal and often, meaningless.

The jus naturalistic conceptions consider freedom as an ontological data of the human being and try to realize the transition from freedom as an ontological essence to liberties as a social phenomenon, specific to the legal state of man and determined by the norm. We say that none of the forms of jus naturalistic conceptions succeeds in making such a transition fully, and the attempt to preserve within the legal liberties the immutability and prestige of liberty is often unsuccessful.

We note, in this ideological context, that legal freedoms, as a structural element of the legal state of man, have as a metaphysical basis the principle of coexistence of freedoms, postulated by jus naturalism, but also by the French Declaration of Human Rights of 1789. It is an expression natural of human social existence, understood by the limits and not by the absolute of existential freedom. In other words, in this phenomenal legal plan, man's freedom is up to the limit of his neighbor's freedom. It is about the specific distinction of the right between "mine" and "yours", through which legal freedom is not constituted as a spiritual opening, but as a closing within the limits of the individual. We believe that the legal norm, in this way, cannot be addressed to the person, focused on the ontological idea of freedom, but only to man as an individual, included in the multiple structures of the social scaffolding.

Obviously, such a reality is not in itself negative, because the dimension of human social phenomenality is a reality through which the human essence is manifested and the affirmation, recognition, normative consecration and guarantee of fundamental human rights and freedoms, a fact realized relatively late in history, it is a remarkable act of culture and civilization, which places the man in his social individuality in an equal relationship with the power of the state and places limits on the absolute and discretionary power of those who exercise state power. The constitutional statement of human freedoms and rights is the most important fact in the contemporary history of mankind, a re-establishment of the relationship between state and man, in the sense that man is not for the state, but the state for man. But this is also a gift from God. Unfortunately, in contemporary society this fundamental reality of the legal is altered and distorted by abusive manifestations of power, which cannot always be effectively controlled and eliminated by legal means.

The starting point that marks the legal and implicitly normative consecration of human rights is the "Declaration of the Rights of Man and of the Citizen" adopted on August 26, 1789. It is the starting point of Enlightenment rationalism in the field of law, rationalism that now culminates in human beings are unlimited, that man is the result of natural evolution, and legal rights and freedoms have their origin and basis in the legal norm and form what has been called "a new religion". This exacerbated rationalism excludes God and man's connection with God, believing erroneously, but with disastrous consequences for man and humanity, that existence has its cause and meaning in itself.

Article IV of the Declaration expresses the famous legal principle of the coexistence of freedoms: "Freedom is to do everything that does not harm others: thus, the right of every human being has no limits, except those that ensure the other members of society exercise the same rights. These limits can only be determined by law". In other words, my freedom extends to the beginning of another's freedom. Of course, this principle is valuable because it enshrines the legal rule that the exercise of my freedom cannot affect the similar freedom of others. In essence, the coexistence of freedoms, as conceived in legal doctrine, is a principle that divides and does not unite, because it is the expression of the same fundamental dichotomy for law and the legal status of man that I mentioned. It is a rational principle.

We believe that the principle of the coexistence of liberties, in order to overcome the mentioned legal dichotomy, to include in itself the fundamental truth that freedom is an invaluable gift from God, and God's gifts are offered to man from His boundless love, which unites and does not divide, should be stated differently: **I am free only if the other is also free**; **the exercise of my freedom is conditioned by the exercise of freedom by other people.** Such an approach, in our opinion, would change the way of consecration and legal guarantee of fundamental human rights and freedoms, because it would take into account the existential freedom as a gift of God and any legal interpretation would be directly or indirectly related to God. For now, this legal perspective is a mere ideal, but by God's will could become a reality.

The legal norm, especially in the conditions of the will of "legal normalization" that the contemporary society knows, is moving further and further away from human values. It is an abstract, general and impersonal structure whose legitimacy is not a value one, but of a formal recognition within the normative system considered. The abandonment of values, including Christian ones, results in normative relativism based almost exclusively on the pure will of the legislator.

The doctrine of legal normativism recognized and applied in almost all states is a concretization of those shown above.

The normative theory, as a current of legal positivism, is reflected in the main work of the American jurist Hans Kelsen "Pure Theory of Law". In this doctrine, the author aims to study law only in the context of its existence. According to Kelsen, the science of law must be limited to the study of law only in its pure state, apart from its links with politics, morality. Otherwise, it will lose its objective character and turn into an ideology.

Kelsen examines the rules of law in terms of validity, and then effectiveness, in a way that can be called "pure" because it leaves out any other extrinsic elements that are not strictly legal (for example, politics).

The theory of law aims to eliminate dualism subjective – objective law, arguing that the objective law is the legal normative framework through which subjective law is exercised. Kelsen also relativizes through his theory the dualism of private law - public law, stating that this dichotomy should not be seen as separating two branches of law in opposition. The noticeable difference between the two branches, Kelsen believes, can be analyzed ideologically, not theoretically.

The central place in the pure theory of law is occupied by the legal norm which, formally, has a pure character, as opposed to the moral norm, which has a content. Through his system of rules, Kelsen supports the theory of the creation of the right in cascade. Thus, the authority of a court decision originates in a presidential decree; this, in turn, in a law adopted by parliament, and this being claimed by the constitution. All legal norms belong to a given legal order; they justify their validity by referring to a fundamental norm.

In case of non-compliance with the higher legal norm, the legal regulation does not achieve its purpose. The theory of law has the task of deciphering the relationship between the fundamental norm and the inferior norms. It is not the science of law that has to assess whether the fundamental norm is good or bad, political science, ethics or religion rule in this regard.

Kelsen's normative theory purifies the right of all its foreign elements: psychology, ethics, sociology, theology. Thus, he determines the content of the law as totally normative. It can be deduced only from legal norms and not from social facts. The norms are broken by social life, by the relations between people.

One of the most controversial and important legal issues is the relationship between stability and innovation in law.

This issue can be addressed in two ways. From a historical perspective, legal norms as well as social and state organization are not immutable but constantly changing. The evolution of the legal normative system is marked by historical moments of progress but also by important involutions and contradictions. The evolutionary nature of norms and law is part of social determinism and is explained by the fact that they are an expression of the will of those who govern are created by the state and determined by multiple economic, social, cultural factors, the interests of the rulers. There are, however, fundamental principles of law with a special value and moral load, essential for the rational configuration of a legal system and whose stability is historically demonstrated. Most, such as the principles of justice, fairness, truth, human dignity, are external to law, in the sense that they are not a normative construction, an expression of the will of the legislator, but the rule of law only enshrines them. The evolutionary change, the becoming of the society and of the social normative system correspond to the nature of the human being, of the consciousness and of the thinking, unstable and always in change.

The relationship between stability and change in law can be analyzed in relation to a specific historical moment and the current state of a legal regulatory system and a company.

The stability of legal norms is an indisputable necessity for the predictability of the conduct of subjects of law, for the security and proper functioning of economic and legal relations as well as for giving substance to the principles of the rule of law and the Constitution.

On the other hand, it is necessary to adapt the legal norm and in general the right to the social and economic phenomena that follow one another so quickly. It is necessary for the legislator to be constantly concerned with eliminating everything that is "obsolete in law", of what does not correspond to reality. The relationship between stability and innovation in law is a complex and difficult issue that needs to be addressed carefully, taking into account a wide range of factors, which can lead to a favorable or unfavorable position for legislative change.

One of the criteria that helps to solve this problem is the principle of proportionality. Between the legal norm, the work of interpretation and its application, and on the other hand the social reality in all its phenomenal complexity, an adequate relationship must be made, in other words the right to be a factor of stability and dynamism of the state and society, to satisfy as best as possible the requirements of the public interest, but also to allow and guarantee the person the possibility of a free and predictable behavior, to realize himself in a social context. Therefore, the right, including in its normative dimension, to be viable and to represent a factor of stability but also of progress must be adequate to the social realities but also to the purposes for which the legal norm is adopted or, as the case may be, interpreted and applied. This is not a new finding. Centuries ago, Solon, being called upon to draw up a constitution, asked the leaders of his city the question, "Tell me for what time and for which people", for the same great sage would later say that he did not give the city a perfect constitution but only one appropriate to the time and place.

The relationship between stability and innovation in law is of particular importance when it comes to maintaining or amending a constitution because the constitution is the political and legal establishment of a state on which the entire scaffolding of the state and society is structured.

Essential for a constitution is its stability over time because only in this way can the stability of the entire normative system of a state, the certainty and predictability of the conduct of subjects of law, but also to ensure the legal, political and economic stability of the social system as a whole. Stability is a requirement for guaranteeing the principle of the supremacy of the constitution and its implications. In this sense, Prof Ioan Muraru stated that the supremacy of the constitution is not only a strictly legal category, but a politico-legal one, pointing out that the fundamental law is the result of economic, political, social and legal realities. "It marks (defines, outlines) a historical stage in the life of a country, it enshrines victories and gives expression, political and legal stability to the realities and perspectives of the historical stage in which it was adopted" (Muraru, Tănăsescu, 2004: 18).

We do not intend to analyze in this study all the components of the social normative system that we have identified and listed above. We stop by evoking some aspects of what we have called ethical norms. Many authors, philosophers, sociologists, jurists speak of moral norms as a component part of the social normative system. We believe that we must distinguish the ethical normative system from the moral one. Only ethics can be normalized and not moral. There are many codes of ethics applicable to different professions, organizations, activities or social and professional statutes. These ethical imperatives regarding the conduct of different social subjects in different situations also form a legal normative system because they are established by laws adopted by the state, more precisely those who exercise governance at a given time and are abstract impersonal and imperative like any legal norm and are subject to change.

Morality does not contain norms but only values that can become constitutive of man's existence and conduct as a conscious, free and responsible person both in relation to himself and to other members of society. Relevant in this respect is the conception of the great German philosopher Kant.

His moral system is based on the belief that reason is the highest instance of morality. From this point of view, there are two ways of making a decision dictated by the will: a conditioned or hypothetical imperative, which arises from a subjective inclination and pursues a certain individual purpose, and a "categorical imperative", which is subject to an objective law, universally valid and necessary. Kant thus formulates the principle of the "categorical imperative" considered the foundation of morality: "Act in such a way that the maxim of your actions can be imposed as a universal law". The philosopher's assertion that "duty is the necessity of performing an act of respect for the law" is a plea for the moral law and for the "epicenter" of the whole Kantian construction, that is, the concept of debt. The author operates with the distinction between debt-compliant actions and debt-related actions (Kant, 2013: 96).

In this context, moral values are necessary, universal and stable. Ethical norms expressed in law can contain perceptions and social values, which become phenomenal and applicable to social relations but without losing the character of moral values, independent of the ethical legislative norm.

III. Constitutional rules

The constitutional norms are provisions containing the formulation of the general principles of law or constitutional law. These norms legitimate the power of state, bases and organizing of the power, define some of the institutions or consecrate principles applicable to the fundamental rights. In this context we emphasize that the constitutional regulations containing the formulation of some law principles cannot be excluded from the sphere of the concept on judicial norm because here we find all features specific to them. (Burdeu, 1966: 71-90; Muraru, Tănăsescu, 2004: 20)

The compliance of entire law with the fundamental Law is an important consequence of supremacy of the Constitution, and it should be understood not only through the correspondence in content and form of the lower norms as legal force with the constitutional ones, but also through the need to translate the constitutional regulations and rules (within their spirit and letter) in other judicial regulations.

To note as an important feature of the constitutional norms that arises from the principle of supremacy of fundamental law, the possibility and even the necessity to be translated, concretized through normative regulations, in other branches of the unified system of law. In relation to this element of specificity of the constitutional law norms, is necessary for the constituent legislator to establish a synthetic content, generalizing these norms' content, and not an analytical, procedural one. In the event that, when in the normative content of a constitution would prevail the descriptive, procedural character of the norms, this would lose too much of its constitutionalism finality, the one of being an essence, generalizing factor, for the whole law system. However, the generality of the constitutional law norm's formulation, would not exclude its clarity and precision. Therefore, any codifying work in the matter of constitutional law, is difficult as it should combine dialectically the generality specific to some norms containing law principles, and on the other side the clarity and precision, the last one absolutely necessary to ensure their correct application and to avoid thus, the arbitrariness or possibility for asserting in the name of some constitutional values, of any partisan political interests. This requirement's fulfilling, can be verified in the practice for transposing and interpretation of the constitutional norms met in all state authorities.

One of the most important problems to elucidate the specific of the constitutional norms' aims the answer to the question if all constitutional provisions contain legal norms. The constitutional provisions that aim the economical, social or financial system are norms of constitutional law with the value of a principle, and not mere political goals, as they regulate the conduct of the law subjects taking part in specific social relations. Likewise, the constitutional norms in question establish genuine legal rights and obligations for the law subjects. For example the constitutional obligation for the derived legislator (Parliament or Govern) like in the process of law making to comply these constitutional regulations, otherwise may intervene the sanction of unconstitutionality of the normative acts in question. We note in conclusion that all constitutional provisions contain legal norms because they have the essential features of a norm of law: prescribe the conduct of the subjects to whom they address and generate legal obligations, and such obligations' breaching may attract legal sanctions specific to constitutional law.

The logical-formal structure of the constitutional law needs to contain all three elements: hypothesis-provision-sanction. The main feature of these norms lies in the way the sanction is being expressed. Thus, for several provisions a single sanction may be present. Also there are specific sanctions in the constitutional law, for instance declaring as unconstitutional a legislative act or revocation of a state body. Given the structuring role of constitutional law for the entire law system, the logical-formal appreciation of the constitutional norms must also be made by reference to other categories of legal regulations. For the regulations of principle or of maximum generality contained in the fundamental law, some sanctions are included in the norms of other branches of law (civil law, criminal law, administrative law). In this regard, the solution of principle was correctly mentioned into the doctrine: "I think that sanctions are to be found even in the constitutional norms for the violation of any provision provided that the obligation or entitlement is exactly identified, in other words the conduct of the subjects of law." (Muraru, Tănăsescu, 2004: 21)

Another element of particularity for the principles with legislative value of the constitutional law refers to the regulation subject. Without going into detail, we retain the idea contained in the contemporary doctrine, according to which the common element and proper only to social relations that form the regulation subject of the constitutional law norms, is that they appear in the process for establishing, maintaining and exercising of state power. (Muraru, Tănăsescu, 2004: 14)

All norms contained in the constitution are norms of constitutional law, and also principles of law, even if some of these regulate also the social relations specific to other law branches. Having into consideration that the constitutional law, in particular the constitution, contains norms with value of principle, referring not only to the organizing and functioning of state authorities but also referring to the social and economical system. In consequence, the subject for regulation of the constitutional law is formed by the social relations that appear during the process for the establishing, maintaining and exercising of state power, but also those referring to the bases of the power and bases for power organizing. These categories refer to the sovereignty of the people, characters attributed to the state, to the territory of population, included those referring to the fundamental features of social economical system.

From the technical, juridical point of view, the regulation object of the norms with principle value of the constitutional law and implicitly of a constitution, can be split into two categories of social relationships: a) specific relations of constitutional law that relate to the organizing and exercising of state power and cannot be a regulatory object for other juridical branches; b) double legal natured relationships, governed both by the constitutional law norms and by the norms of other law branches (Muraru, Tănăsescu, 2004: 16-18; Iancu, 2010: 12-15). The existence of such legal relationships justifies by because between the branches of the law there is no rigid demarcation. One needs to consider also the superior legal force of the constitutional law norms, the criterion differentiating them from other norms of law, which confers a structuring value for entire law system.

Constitution is a law, but at the same time through its juridical force and content distinguishes from all other laws. At the same time, the fundamental law supremacy confers to it the quality of a primary formal source for all other branches of law.

In a comparative analysis of the regulations contained in the contemporary constitutions is noticed that the historical, political, national, cultural, religious etc. diversity of the states, does not directly result in a diversity of the legislative content for the fundamental laws. The content of the modern states' constitutions present many resemblances and sometimes wordings almost identical with some of the institutions regulated (Ionescu, 2008: 208-209). This resemblance is determined mainly by the identity of the regulatory object of the constitutional norms.

On the other side, the diversity in the normative content removes the idea of uniform standards generally valid for the contemporary constitutions. The diversity of normative content is a consequence of the fact that the fundamental law of the state is determined in terms of the content of social, political and economical realities, on the characters and attributes of the respective state, historically expressed and at the same time on the will of the constituting legislator, essentially a political will, at a certain historical moment.

Along with other authors, we believe that the scientific definition of constitution is the main criterion for identifying the normative content. Such a criterion ensures the generality necessary to give a scientific character to the scientific elaborations in the matter and it explains at the same time the regulatory unit but also the constitutional normative diversity.

For the purpose of this scientific approach, we retain the essence of every attempt to define the fundamental law namely: "The Constitution is a political and legal fundamental establishment of a state" (Deleanu, 2008: 88). In the legal acceptance, the fundamental law is the act through which it is determined the power statute and therewith all legal rules, having as object the regulation of the bases of power and bases for power organizing.

The legal concept of constitution can be expressed in two different meanings, respectively in a substantial and a formal meaning. Analyzed separately, the formal and material acceptation cannot be a sufficient criterion for identifying the normative content of the fundamental law. Accepting the formal criterion has as a consequence that the fundamental law could regulate any social relationship, regardless of their importance or object of regulation. [63] The material criterion is also unilateral as it excludes the procedural elements, required for a scientific characterization of the fundamental law. The scientific approach regarding the identification of the normative content of the constitution must consider cumulatively both the formal and the material acceptation to which the political dimension referred above, is added. Therefore, we consider one may identify three criteria in order to establish the normative content of a constitution:

The establishing of the normative content of constitution is made according to the specific, importance and value of the social relation regulated.

---

[63] For example Swizerland Consitution, by article 25bis states rules for cattle sacrificing.

We share the view expressed in the literature that, unlike other categories of legislative acts, the norms contained in the constitution should regulate the fundamental social relations that are essential for the establishing, maintaining and exercising of power, but also those referring to the bases for the power, respectively the bases for power organizing. Therefore, the constitutional norms are always principles of law having a decisive role in establishing and functioning of the government bodies and in determining the form of the state, namely its character and attributes.

The normative expression of the constitutional principles, themselves simple as a normative form, but complex in nature and in the content determined by the object of regulation, constitutes a source and the normative-value ground of the unity and simplicity of entire legislative system of the state. The reporting of legislator to the constitutional principles, not only for guaranteeing the simple formal correspondence between the judicial norm and the fundamental law, but mainly to legislate in respect to these principles and having as a finality their content, is a prerequisite to eliminate the diversity of norms, a natural consequence of the governors' excess of power in legislative matters. There are therefore two ways through which the power can legislate: the first that is disregarding the teleological reporting to the constitutional principles and in general to the principles of law, aiming only the formal correspondence with the constitutional norms, and the second one teleological oriented to the content, meaning and limits imposed by the principles of law. In the first case, the result is the normative diversity, lacking a rational, unifying factor; in the second hypothesis there is at least the possibility of achieving the simplicity and unity of the normative system within the content's complexity.

It is important to underline the constitutional dynamism. The fundamental law is a dynamic, opened act, and in a continuous crystallization process. The constitutional status is achieved through a continuous and complex process of interpretation and application of the texts contained in the body of the constitution by state authorities. Furthermore, the constitutional norms cannot and must not provide definitions. For instance also in Romania's constitution exist such concepts, definable by way of interpretation and forming an object of analysis for the Constitutional Court: "spirit of tolerance and mutual respect" (article 29, paragraph 3); "identity" (article 30, paragraph 6); "private life" (article 30, paragraph 6); "lawful state principles" (article 48, paragraph 2); "public interest" (article 44, paragraph 3); "proportionality and public moral" (article 53) or "extraordinary situations" (article 115, paragraph 4).

The normative content of constitution needs to be understood and determined by having into consideration the teleological criterion highlighted in the above stated definition. Namely, the fundamental law's structuring role for entire social, political and state system, guarantor of fundamental rights and liberties. The fundamental law must achieve the social dynamic balance but also the stability and institutional harmony, the efficient guaranteeing of the fundamental rights, essentially the real constitutional democracy requirements based on the values of the lawful state, on institutional and social balance and on proportionality (Andreescu, 2007: 267-298).

IV. Conclusions

Law is a normative rule, a system of rules governing human conduct. This human conduct can have a legal content only on the basis of a legal norm. The law, unlike the moral, religious norms, has a constraining character, in case the subject refuses to comply with the normative provisions.

Public power imposes on individuals a normative conduct of law, because law is a reflection of the common interests of society. Law cannot be conceived without power.

The state, in Kelsen's view, identifies with law. It represents the legal order, and its reality is the content of positive law. The state and the law are two sides of the same phenomenon. In creating the law, the state must be subordinated to the law, and this, in turn, regulates its building process. Identifying the rule of law, according to Kelsen, any state is a rule of law, which obviously does not correspond to the current reality.

We appreciate that the "pure doctrine of law" as a theory is not convincing, as law cannot be broken by social reality, seen as objective reality and especially cannot be deprived of moral values by its foundation which is justice. The normative system cannot subordinate the individual.

Applying the principles of abstract and impersonal legal normativism in all democratic constitutions is enshrined the principle No one is above the law. It is valid only in man's formal relations with the law and in accordance with the social determinism in which freedom is a given of the law and conditioned by it. Law has many political, historical, economic and sociological implications that are intrinsic to it, arising naturally from interpersonal relations and the citizen-state relationship. Although the status of law as an autonomous science cannot be denied, a rule of law cannot be analyzed without being placed in a historical context, without being correlated with the political and economic factors that led to its promulgation, and without assessing the social impact. which it has produced among the population by its application.

We believe that Immanuel Kant's words are applicable to both social normativism: "Only the law of becoming really explains the permanence of existence, making it intelligible according to empirical laws".

Bibliography

Andreescu, M., 2007, The principle of proportionality in constitutional law, C.H. Beck Publishing House, Bucharest;

Burdeu, G., 1966, Droit constitutionnel et institutions politiques, LG "Constitutional Law and Public Institutions" DJ, Paris;

Deleanu, I., 2008, Institutions and constitutional procedures, C.H. Beck Publishing House, Bucharest;

Iancu, Gh., 2010, Constitutional law and political institutions, C.H. Beck Publishing House, Bucharest;

Ionescu, C., 2008, Treatise on contemporary constitutional law, C.H. Beck Publishing House, Bucharest;

Kant, I., 2013, Critique of pure reason, Antet Publishing House, Bucharest;

Muraru, I & Tănăsescu E. S., 2004, Constitutional law and political institutions, vol. I, C.H. Beck Publishing House, Bucharest.

4. THE PHILOSOPHICAL BASIS OF THE PRINCIPLE OF PROPORTIONALITY

Abstract:

The proportionality is a general principle of law, signifying the ideas of balance, justice, responsibility and the needed adequate suiting of the measures adopted by the State to the situation in fact and to the purpose aimed by the law.

The principle is expressly formulated in the European Union documents but also in the constitutions of other states. The normative or jurisprudential regulation of the principle explains the numerous preoccupations at scientific level to identify its dimensions. In this study, the principle of proportionality is analyzed from the perspective of the philosophy of the law, in order to try to identify its value dimensions that are to be found in the normative consecrations or in jurisprudence.

The normative of jurisprudential dimension of proportionality, as a law principle has its content in the concepts and philosophical categories that make up the contents of the principle of proportionality, in the law philosophy's main periods and currents.

We consider that such a scientific attempt is useful, having into consideration the importance of this principle for the contemporary law. The principle of proportionality is an important guaranty in the observance of the human rights, mainly in situations in which their exercising is being restricted by the actions ordered by state's authorities, being at the same time an important criterion to delimit the discretionary power from the power excess in the activity of state's authority.

In our opinion, only in the extent of our knowledge and understanding of the philosophical contents of this principle it is possible this one's correct applying in jurisprudence. This study is aiming to be a pleading for the possibility and usefulness of law's philosophy in this epoch dominated by juridical pragmatism and normativism.

Key words:

proportionality, equity, idea of justice, lawful state, rational law, adequate relationship, freedom of action, margin of appreciation, just measure, principle of law, human rights

I. Introduction

The legal understanding of the principle of proportionality presents difficulties, because its content depends on a certain philosophical conception of justice. The legal doctrine, from antiquity to the present, evokes proportionality as meaning the idea of order, balance, rational relationship, fair measure.

Proportionality is not exclusively a principle of rational law, but at the same time, it is a principle of positive law, a principle of normative value. Thus, proportionality is a legal criterion that assesses the legitimacy of the interference of state power in the field of exercising fundamental rights and freedoms.

This principle is explicitly or implicitly enshrined in international legal instruments, or by the majority of the constitutions of democratic countries. The Romanian Constitution expressly states this principle in art. 53, but there are other constitutional provisions that imply it.

In constitutional law, the principle of proportionality is applied especially in the field of protection of fundamental human rights and freedoms. It is considered an effective criterion for assessing the legitimacy of the intervention of state authorities in the situation of limiting the exercise of certain rights. Moreover, even if the principle of proportionality is not expressly enshrined in the constitution of a state, doctrine and jurisprudence consider it to be part of the notion of the rule of law[64].

This principle is applied in several branches of law. Thus, in administrative law it is a limit of the discretionary power of the public authorities and represents a criterion for exercising the judicial control of the discretionary administrative acts. Applications of the principle of proportionality also exist in criminal law or in civil law.

The principle of proportionality is also found in European Union law, in the sense that the legality of Community rules is subject to the condition that the means used correspond to the objective pursued and do not go beyond what is necessary to achieve that objective.

---

[64] Petru Miculescu, The Rule of Law (Bucharest: Lumina Lex Publishing House, 1998), pp. 87-88.

The jurisprudence has an important role in the analysis of the principle of proportionality, applied in concrete cases. Thus, in the case law of the European Court of Human Rights, proportionality is conceived as a fair, equitable relationship between the factual situation, the means of restricting the exercise of certain rights and the legitimate aim pursued or as a fair relationship between the individual interest and the public interest. Proportionality is a criterion that determines the legitimacy of the interference of the Contracting States in the exercise of the rights protected by the Convention.

In the same sense, the Constitutional Court of Romania, through several decisions, established that proportionality is a constitutional principle[65]. Our constitutional court stated the need to establish objective criteria, by law, for the principle of proportionality: "it is necessary for the legislature to establish objective criteria that reflect the requirements of the principle of proportionality"[66]. Therefore, the principle of proportionality is increasingly imposed as a universal principle, enshrined in most contemporary legal systems, explicitly or implicitly found in constitutional norms and recognized by national and international jurisdictions.

As a general principle of law, proportionality presupposes a relationship considered fair, between the legal measure adopted, the social reality and the legitimate aim pursued. The doctrine states that proportionality can be analyzed at least as a result of the combination of three elements: the decision taken, its finality and the factual situation to which it applies. Proportionality is correlated with the concepts of legality, opportunity and discretion[67]. In public law, a breach of the principle of proportionality is considered to be a violation of the freedom of action left to the authorities and, in the last resort, an excess of power. There is interference between the principle of proportionality and other general principles of law, namely: the principles of legality and equality, as well as the principle of fairness and justice. The essence of this principle lies in the relationship considered fair between the components.

---

[65] Decision no 139/1994 published in the Official Gazette of Romania no 353/1994; Decision no 157/1998 published in the Official Gazette of Romania no 3/1999; Decision no 161/1998 published in the Official Gazette no 3/1999.

[66] Decision no 71/1996 published in the Official Gazette of Romania no 13/1996

[67] M. Guibal, "De la proportionnalité", in *L'actualite juridique. Droit administratif 5* (Paris: Dalloz, 1978), 477-479

In summary, we can say that proportionality is a fundamental principle of the law enshrined explicitly or deduced from constitutional regulations, legislation and international legal instruments, based on the values of rational law, justice and fairness and which express the existence of a balanced or adequate relationship between actions. situations, phenomena as well as the limitation of the measures ordered by the state authorities to what is necessary to achieve a legitimate aim, thus guaranteeing the fundamental rights and freedoms, and avoiding the abuse of rights.

II. Content

Many contemporary authors consider the principle that ensures the unity, homogeneity, balance and capacity of the particular normative development of society to be the principle of justice[68]. In essence, the principle of fairness and justice supposes the existence of fundamental, a priori prescriptions derived from reason or from a superindividual order and whose purpose is to give security to social life.

Proportionality expresses the content of this principle through the idea of balance between situations and social phenomena, between state and individual, but also as a "fair measure", when comparing different situations or to assess the legitimacy of decisions of state authorities.

Justice is synonymous with justice and emphasizes the ideal of fairness, which must characterize any legal relationship. The balance that it supposes and that represents proportionality is not only an abstract notion, but it also has a concrete dimension that is achieved through the equivalent of benefits, or in other words "to give everyone what they deserve". Justice protects every natural or legal person, establishes the proportion of interests in order to ensure everyone's freedom in the context of achieving the freedom of all. In the literature it has been shown that: "Justice is an absolute victory over selfishness, and whoever says justice says subordination to a hierarchy of values"[69].

It is necessary to distinguish between the values of fairness, justice and proportionality, analyzed from antiquity to the present, of theology, philosophy and law, and on the other hand proportionality as a principle of established normative law and jurisprudence. Mircea Djuvara said: "There can be no immutable principles of law that are valid for any time and any place"[70]. The author wants to say that on the one hand there are principles and values of universal law, and on the other hand their capitalization is variable according to time and place. Indeed, one is the existence of fairness and proportionality, long since law existed, and another is their formulation as principles in contemporary law as an expression of justice and fairness, given that the

---

[68] Gheorghe Mihai, Radu Motica, Fundamentals of law. Theory and philosophy of law, (Bucharest: ALL, 1999), p. 127

[69] Nicolae Popa, General Theory of Law, (Bucharest: Actami, 1999), p. 129

[70] Mircea Djuvara, Law and Sociology (Bucharest: ISD, 1936), p. 11

modern legal meanings of the principle of proportionality contain the traditional and perennial value connotations of the idea of justice.

Since ancient times, the ideas of justice and justice have been well outlined, and their content is formed by the concept of proportionality, as a way to achieve the balance between the benefits of participants in legal relations. The purpose of justice is to exclude any discriminatory behavior between people.

Plato makes the issue of the nature, origin and purpose of the law the central issue of his political dialogues[71]. The fundamental principles of Plato's philosophy are: One, Good, Virtue, and Truth. Laws are created by people, not anyway, but as a reflection of these principles. The law is based on the rational principles, listed above, and its purpose is virtue and good, as moral realities, in the ideal state conceived by Plato. The law determines the social order, but in turn it is based on reason. Plato says that "...in a word, wherever the laws will endeavor, in all their power, to make the state as unitary as possible, it can be argued that the culmination of the political virtue has taken place there". The laws to which the state is subordinated, in Plato's philosophical doctrine, are imbued with the ideas of *justice* and *morality*. The great philosopher wants to apply the moral principles to society as a whole, but also to the behavior of each individual. In this context, the laws must be assessed from the point of view of correspondence with the principle of justice, ie on considerations superior to the legal order[72]. The laws are accompanied by a statement of reasons, which has the role of making citizens understand not only the existence of the norm, but also its necessity. The rulers, in the state conceived by Plato, are subject to the laws and cannot act arbitrarily. Platonic theory expresses an absolute confidence in law, the only one capable of limiting political power, thus preventing the formation of an authority too strong, "not temperate"[73] as a result of which the state must pursue the "union, science, and freedom"[74].

Plato argues for the need to moderate state power and subordinate the law to the principle of justice. The limitation of the power of the rulers by law,

---

[71] Plato, The Laws (Bucharest: IRI, 1995); "Republic" in *Works*, 5th Volume (Bucharest: Scientific and Encloclopedic Publishing-House, 1986)

[72] Plato, The Laws, p.155

[73] Plato, The Laws, p. 112

[74] Plato, The Laws, p. 112

the balance and the moderation in the exercise of state authority are forms of expression of proportionality, as an element of content of the principle of justice, as Plato conceived it. The rule of law is based on the concept of justice. However, Plato conceives of a state in which individuality is considered in the background. In Plato's ideal state, the individual will unconditionally submit to the law, everything being governed by the law, from intimate life to the highest political relationship. Therefore, in Plato's philosophical conception, which is part of the ancient traditional thinking of "state – city", there is no proportional relationship between individual and state, because man is fully integrated into the state, and material equality between members of a state represents the guarantee of social harmony.

The principle of justice and implicitly the idea of proportionality are well emphasized, in Antiquity, in the work of Aristotle, many of these considerations remain valid today.

In order to define justice and law, and then to explain the nature of the state, Aristotle started from the concept of sociability: "man is by nature a social being"[75]. In this context, "justice is a social virtue, for law is only the order of the political community"[76]. In another work, Aristotle states that "law is what creates and maintains for a political community happiness and its constituent elements, and happiness in the city is given by legality and equality"[77]. For the trainee, justice as well as the law is a medium term that ensures the balance between extremes, in other words justice and implicitly the principle of justice have in their content and express the idea of proportionality.

Justice is no longer for Aristotle, as for Plato, virtue in general, but that social virtue which consists in the harmonization of interests respecting proportionality, in social relations. The legislator who wants to introduce just laws must consider the public good. Justice is equality here, and this equality of justice takes into account both the general interest of the state and the individual interest of the citizens[78]. Unlike Plato, in whom the state represents the absolute, and the human individual a simple means in achieving his goals, Aristotle notes a greater attention paid to the human individual, according to a

[75] Aristotle, Politics (Bucharest: Antet, 1997), p. 29

[76] Aristotle, Politics, p. 7

[77] Aristotle, Nicomachean Ethics, Book I (Bucharest: IRI, 1998), p. 28

[78] Aristotle, Politics, p. 29

relationship of balance, proportionality, between state and citizens, a relationship that substantiates the principle of justice.

Aristotle distinguished between *distributive justice* and *corrective justice*[79]. The first presupposed the fact of attributing to each one what is due to him, of achieving not a formal equality but a concrete one, an equivalence of the benefits on the condition of observing the distribution criteria. Distributive justice is based on *proportion*, being conceived as an equality of relations. "The justice in question here is, therefore, a *proportion*, and the injustice is that which is out of proportion, assuming on the one hand more, on the other hand less, than what is proper. This also happens in practice because the one who commits the injustice owns a larger part of the distributed good, and the unjust one, a smaller part than he deserves"[80]. Aristotle considers that justice consists in reciprocity and the existence of a common standard by which to appreciate facts. Reciprocity ensures the connections between people, respectively the legal relations, it being based on proportion, and not on equality in the strict sense.

Justice or corrective justice intervened when disputes arose between people, and the judge determined the proportion, granting the necessary compensation. It is interesting that Aristotle conceived of justice as proportion, but not purely quantitative, but as an equality that is achieved between persons participating in legal relations, through various consideration: "Justice is therefore a kind of *proportion* (for proportion is not a property only of the abstract number, but of the number in general), the proportion being an equality of relations and assuming at least four terms"[81].

The Roman jurists also contributed to the definition and understanding of the principle of justice. The Latin adage is known, which defined law as "*Jus est boni et aequi*". The idea of equity, existing in this definition, represents a dimension of proportionality. not to hurt your neighbor; to live honestly[82]. The principle of "giving everyone what is their own" expresses distributive justice, which in turn imposes the idea of proportion between the performance of the participants in the justice reports.

---

79 Aristotle, Nicomachean Ethics, p. 128

80 Aristotle, Nicomachean Ethics, p. 115

81 Aristotle, Nicomachean Ethics, p. 114

82 Nicolae Popa, Ion Dogaru, Gheorghe Dănişor, Dan Claudiu Dănişor, Philosophy of law. The Great Currents (Bucharest: All Beck, 2002), p. 83

Proportionality, as a concept, appears in the doctrine of natural law, either by direct reference, as in the work of Jean Jacques Rousseau, or in the form of categories such as "right reason", which expresses the essence of law and signifies the idea of justice and fairness. Equality is a consequence of sociability resulting from natural law. Proportionality also appears in the analysis of the relations between the state and the citizen and of the way in which the freedom of the individual in relation to the authority of the state is conceived.

An important representative of this school is Montesquieu, who reveals in his work some ideas that involve the principle of proportionality. In Montesquieu's view, everything is subject to the action of universal laws, expressions of necessary relations which derive from the nature of things: "There is a primordial reason, and laws are the relations between it and different entities, and the relations between these entities"[83]. The author considers the law in general to be human reason, and the civil and political laws of a state are particular cases of human reason. The idea of "necessary relations" and especially the identification of the law with human reason means the principle of justice and implicitly the proportionality understood as a balanced relationship between the different entities.

One of Montesquieu's greatest contributions to legal doctrine is the theorizing of the principle of the separation of powers in the state. The essence of this theory, developed in his work "The Spirit of Law", is to prohibit the accumulation of state powers. At a first analysis it is found that the author promotes equality between powers. However, he argues that the judiciary does not play a very important role in relation to other powers. At the same time, in the author's conception, the separation of powers is achieved by reference to the law, or in this situation, the legislature becomes the dominant power in the state[84]. There is not so much equality between the powers of the state but especially a balance, based on the differentiation of roles, which is a form of the principle of proportionality. The activity of the executive and the judiciary aims at the sovereignty of the law and the assurance of the freedom of the citizen.

---

[83] Montesquieu, The Spirit of Law (1748), 1st Volume (Bucharest: Scientific Publishing-house, 1964), p.11

[84] Montesquieu, The Spirit of Law (1748), 2nd Volume, p. 200

Related to the idea of social justice, the principle of proportionality appears explicitly formulated, or through other concepts, in the work of Jean Jacques Rousseau[85]. The social pact gives the state authority full power over all members of society. This power is not unlimited, because the state must respect the natural rights of the citizens: "It is appropriate, therefore, that the respective rights of citizens and the sovereign, as well as the duties which citizens should perform in their capacity as subjects, should be clearly distinguished from the natural rights which they should enjoy as human beings"[86]. The author's effort to harmonize the rights of the individual with sovereign power is noted. Man transmits part of his rights to the sovereign, who is animated by the general will expressed by law. On the other hand, the general will cannot annul the natural rights of the individual. In this sense, Jean Jacques Rousseau said: "We have agreed that what alienates everyone from his power, from his goods, from his freedom – through the social pact – is only that part of whose use is important for the community"[87]. This relationship between the rights of the sovereign and the natural rights of the citizen evokes proportionality and, implicitly, the idea of limiting state power, but also of harmonizing it with the natural, inalienable rights of the individual. The author believes that there must be a balanced relationship between the power of a state and its extent: "The stronger the social bond, the weaker it becomes, otherwise a small state is generally proportionally stronger than a large one"[88].

The principle of proportionality is applied to the relationship between sovereign, executive power (government) and state. "So, what is government? An intermediate body placed between the subjects and the sovereign, for their mutual connection and in charge of the application of the laws and the maintenance of the freedom, both civil and political"[89]. In Jean Jacques Rousseau's view, government is the middle ground between a sovereign and a state in a mathematical relationship of "continuous proportion". This proportion is not arbitrary, but a necessary consequence of the nature of the political body. Failure to respect the proportionality between the three terms can have consequences in the author's conception, disturbing the balance and social harmony. If the power of government increases too much in relation to that of its subjects, the rule of law and that of private judgments will be

[85] Jean Jacques Rousseau, The Social Contract (Bucharest: Antet, 1999), p. 23
[86] Jean Jacques Rousseau, The Social Contract, p. 23
[87] Jean Jacques Rousseau, The Social Contract, p. 29
[88] Jean Jacques Rousseau, The Social Contract, p. 53
[89] Jean Jacques Rousseau, The Social Contract, p. 53

confused. This can lead to despotism. If the subjects become too strong, then anarchy prevails. "Moreover, says Jean Jacques Rousseau, none of these terms could be changed without the proportion immediately disappearing. If the sovereign wants to govern, if the magistrate wants to make the laws, or if the subjects refuse to obey, disorder instead of order, force and will no longer act in harmony, and the decomposed state falls into despotism or anarchy"[90]. Proportionality appears in this report, more in a mathematical, quantitative sense, but it is also a legal principle based on which the powers of the state are organized and the connection between the state and the individual is explained. The author reveals the nature of social relations with reference to the relationship between the individual, society and sovereign power, proportionality expressing balance and harmony, necessary for the stability of the state.

Proportionality as a way of expressing the principle of justice and fairness is also found in the work of the representatives of the rational school of law. This doctrine states that by law we must not only understand the positivist meaning, but we must also consider the rational dimension, which is the essence of law, meaning its understanding as "*jus-dike*", or in other words, as "*just measure*". This is the expression of proportionality as a rational principle of law. For rationalists, the application of proportionality to the legal norm means to give it meaning and value, while achieving the equivalence between law, understood as the totality of legal norms, and justice as a principle.

Immanuel Kant considers that law comes from reason and man can rise to the pure universal, intelligible through morality, whose fundamental concept is that of freedom[91]. For Kant, "law is therefore the set of conditions by which the arbitrator of one can agree with the arbitrator of the other following a general law of liberty"[92]. The conditions to which Kant refers impose limits on freedom in order to be able to correlate with the freedom of the other. It follows from the definition that freedom in law is a freedom of relationship, limited and constraining. Consequently, it is in accordance with the law, and therefore just any action that reconciles my freedom with the freedom of all, following a general rule. Exceeding these limits makes freedom an unjust act. A person's

---

[90] Jean Jacques Rousseau, The Social Contract, p. 54

[91] Immanuel Kant, Foundations of the Metaphysics of Morals (Bucharest: Antaios, 1999), p. 49

[92] Immanuel Kant, Foundations of the Metaphysics of Morals, p. 50

freedom must not harm the freedom of others but be in harmony with it. Although Kant does not explicitly refer to the principle of proportionality, *freedom as a relationship*, which is the basis of law, means balance, fairness, in a word an appropriate proportion between individual freedoms.

In the conception of Giorgio del Vecchio, who is an important representative of legal rationalism, neo-Kantian ideas constitute a reaction to legal positivism and empiricism. Giorgio del Vecchio constructs a philosophy of law starting from an a priori principle, which is the ultimate limit and on which the entire legal edifice rests. This fundamental principle is the *principle of justice*. The author makes an analysis of the Aristotelian conception of justice, criticizing the fact that in Aristotelian theory various species of justice appear, which are not deduced from a single principle. "What is essential – argues Georgio del Vecchio – in any kind of justice is the element of intersubjectivity, or correspondence in the relations between several individuals, which is found in the last analysis, even where it does not appear at first sight"[93]. The author considers that in a very general sense, justice implies a certain harmony, congruence and proportion, to which Leibnitz also referred[94]. At the same time, said the great jurist, "not every congruence or correspondence realizes – properly – the idea of justice, but only that which is verified or can be verified in the relations between several persons; not any proportion between objects (whatever they may be), but only that which, in Dante's words, is a *hominis ad hominem proportio*. Justice, in its own sense, is the principle of coordination between subjective beings"[95]. Proportion is the quality of relations between persons, which only insofar as it meets this requirement means justice as a principle. The author emphasizes other features of the principle of justice, one of the most important being that the prescriptions of positive law are subject to this principle[96]. Thus, laws can be unfair if they do not correspond to the concept of "Justice", understood as a balanced, harmonious proportion between the content of the norm and social reality. In this situation, it is necessary to change the existing laws and even the existing legal order in order to achieve the imperative of Justice.

The law, as a normative act, is general, impersonal, and the legal equality it implies is formal, because the generality of the law is categorical in nature.

---

[93] Georgio del Vecchio, Justiţia (Bucharest: Cartea Românească, 1936), p. 64
[94] Georgio del Vecchio, Justiţia (Bucharest: Cartea Românească, 1936), p. 33
[95] Georgio del Vecchio, Justiţia (Bucharest: Cartea Românească, 1936), p. 33
[96] Georgio del Vecchio, Justice (Bucharest: Romanian Book, 1936), p, 56

In contrast, equality, understood as a fair proportion, as required by the principle of justice, involves the reporting of concrete situations and legal assessments to be achieved according to rigorously established criteria. Equity, understood as legal proportionality, requires taking into account the factual situations, personal circumstances, the uniqueness of the case, the relationship between the legal means used and the appropriate legitimate purpose, thus completing the generality of the legal norm. For Giorgio del Vecchio, the rule of law corresponds to the principle of justice, only if it is appropriate to the diversity of social reality, but also to the ideal of justice, as a rational value. This appropriate report is the expression of proportionality as a general principle of law.

Mircea Djuvara analyzes the principle of justice from the perspective of rational law inspired by Kantian philosophy. For the representatives of the neo-Kantian school of law, justice is transcendental. It may be, or as the case may be, not insured by law enforcement. Law as a system of legal norms is not always equivalent to the principle of justice. Prof Mircea Djuvara divided the "characteristics of justice" into rational and factual elements. As rational elements he suggested: a) equality of the parties; b) the objective (rational) and logical nature of justice; c) the idea of equity, which establishes a balance of interests in essence; d) the idea of proportionality in the conduct of justice. Proportionality would operate primarily through qualities between which relationships are established. Second, it would operate on the idea of equivalence.

Analyzing the legal report and its applicable prescriptions, the author states that the ideal of justice refers to: "the rational equality of free persons, limited in their actions only by rights and debts"[97]. This is the basis in relation to which there is the possibility of normative generalization and the consecration of the formal equality of the law without any discrimination. However, equality in principle can be achieved only by taking into account factual situations, particular factors and individual cases. The author emphasizes that the administration of justice makes necessary the idea of proportion in any legal relationship, including the criminal one: "The idea of proportion proceeds through quantities between which relations are established"[98].

[97] Mircea Djuvara, General theory of law. Rational law, sources and positive law, p. 268
[98] Mircea Djuvara, op.cit., p., 271

Respect for the principle of proportionality is a general condition for a law to be "fair" or in other words, to be conform to the principle of justice and fairness. In this sense, the author states: "Why in the application of justice do we find the idea of proportion? The penalty must always be proportionate to the guilt. If the idea of proportion were not a rational idea, this assertion would make no sense. The idea of proportion proceeds through quantities, between which relationships are established. Rational appreciation always tends to quantify relationships. Science also aims to establish quantitative relationships; it is known that contemporary science, in any branch, is considered all the more advanced as it eliminates the subjective elements of experimental knowledge, reduces them to simple quantities and thus matures"[99]. It is obvious that for Mircea Djuvara, proportionality is a principle of rational law, which evokes the idea of justice and justice. In the desire to provide rigor and precision to the application of the legal norm, the author conceives the proportionality more, mathematically, as a quantitative ratio, between two quantities or values.

Eugeniu Speranţia, another representative of the neo-Kantian school of law, considers that the spirit is the one who leads the human activity. The need for normality and non-contradiction is realized in social life "by organizing the law, the norm and the sanction"[100]. In the author's opinion, coercion and sociability are the two elements that can define law, and both belong to rationality. Law is "a system of rules of social action, rationally harmonized and imposed by society"[101]. Normativity means that, in all his actions, man must follow certain directions and must strictly observe certain limits. The author does not refer to proportionality as a principle, but as we have noted in other situations, proportionality, even if not explicitly stated, is implicit in the idea of rationality which means a certain harmonious ordering of the constituent elements of society and compliance with the rules in order to achieve social order, and ultimately justice.

George Alexianu evokes the principle of proportionality, although he does not explicitly use this concept. Referring to the role of the state in contemporary society, the author points out that it must ensure social order and guarantee individual freedoms. Its power must be limited in relation to the

---

[99] Mircea Djuvara, General theory of law. Rational law, sources and positive law, p. 272

[100] Eugeniu Speranţia, Fundamental Principles of Legal Philosophy (Cluj: Institute of Graphic Arts Transylvania, 1937), p. 7

[101] Eugeniu Speranţia, Fundamental principles of legal philosophy, p. 8

exercise of individual freedoms. State authorities can restrict individual freedoms only if this measure is absolutely necessary for the preservation of society. The state is only a means of guaranteeing individual freedoms. The limitation of the power of the state, the fact that the actions of the state must not exceed the purpose of their exercise, as well as the existence of the "necessity" to justify the interference of the state in the exercise of fundamental freedoms implies the principle of proportionality[102]. "The state has a duty to ensure the social order without which the life of society is not possible. By ensuring the social order, it ensures and guarantees the individual life, because the individual can only live in a society. He must demand of individual freedom only those sacrifices which are absolutely necessary for the coexistence of individuals in society. The state is therefore a means of securing individual life. "The necessary strictness to which its intervention is limited is dictated by political science"[103].

The French jurist François Geny pointed out that the rule of law is guided by the ideal of justice and that this, beyond the inclusion of basic perceptions, not to harm, not to harm another person and to give everyone what they deserve, involves deeper thought. of establishing a balance between conflicting interests in order to ensure the essential order to maintain the progress of human society[104].

Paul Roubier noted that the rule of law that aspires to govern human societies must conform to a certain ideal of justice, otherwise it will be neither respectable nor respected if it rejects that ideal. The author proposes among the values that guide law "justice as an essential value of the good order of human relations with its own qualities of equality and proportionality"[105].

For Rudolf Stammler, the law is justified in so far as the aims pursued by him are just. "Fair law" must always be in line with social aspirations. "The basis of the justice of a legal system must be sought in the fundamental law of the will. We deduce the possibility that a legal will is fair exclusively from the highest concept of free will. "Justice will therefore be the harmonization of all

---

[102] George Alexianu, Constitutional Law Course (Bucharest: Casa Ţoalelor, 1930-1937), p. 149

[103] George Alexianu, Constitutional Law Course, p. 149

[104] François Geny, Science et technique en droit positif, 1st Volume (Paris: Sirey, 1925), p. 258

[105] Paul Roubier, Théorie générale du Droit, (Paris: L.G.D.J., 1986), p. 268.

social wills"[106]. In our opinion, the harmony that Stammler speaks of is the expression of proportionality as a value and principle of law.

In contemporary Romanian legal literature, there are characterizations of the principles of equity and justice that imply proportionality. Thus, for Radu Motica and Gheorghe Mihai "the principle of equity implies moderation in the prescription of rights and obligations by the legislator, in the process of elaborating legal norms... This principle and equity first appeared because experience has shown that there is no perfect equality between people, absolute, this must be covered"[107]. Proportionality is perceived by legal doctrine as a form of expression of the principle of justice and justice through the idea of an equivalent, balanced, harmonious relationship between two or more values or quantities. works of authors or law schools.

The question is whether the understanding of proportionality, in relation to the general principles of law, in particular, the idea of justice, justice and fairness is relevant to contemporary law and especially to constitutional law. We consider that the answer is in the affirmative, for the following reasons:

The end of the 18th century and the beginning of the 19th century marked the accentuation of preoccupations, both in terms of legal doctrine and in the elaboration of political declarations, or normative acts, which enshrine and guarantee human rights and normative continued previous rationalist traditions and at the same time meant an emphasis on the analysis of the limits of state power and the inalienable human rights.

The fundamental question that arises in the legal doctrine of this period is: how can man be a free being, whose fundamental rights and freedoms are recognized and at the same time live in an organized society? The answer to this question depends on how the law is considered and implicitly the content of its fundamental principles. The solution of this problem has meant and means an evolution of the legal doctrine, oriented more and more towards the conciliation of the law, as an instrument of affirmation of the human being through the freedoms that must be recognized and guaranteed by law.

---

[106] Rudolf Stammler, Theorie der Recktswissenschaft, (Chicago: University of Chicago Press, 1989), p. 58.

[107] Radu I. Motica and Gheorghe C. Mihai, General theory of law (Bucharest: ALL, 2001), p. 81

In the legal doctrine of the mentioned period, man is not only a citizen, a subject of law passively integrated into social relations, dominated by state power, but he is a person who has rights and freedoms essential for his existence, inalienable, which he can oppose to power. state. Law is increasingly understood as the "coexistence of freedoms" and not just a system of positive rules applied by the discretionary authority of the state. In this context, proportionality is found in legal doctrine both to characterize the principle of justice and to explain the increasingly complex social relations that require the recognition of individual freedoms in the context of the freedoms of all, but also to determine the limits of state power. in relation to the fundamental rights recognized to man. Proportionality is increasingly understood as a guarantee of respect for fundamental rights and a criterion for assessing the legitimacy of their restriction by the state authority.

The French Declaration of the Rights of Man and of the Citizen of 1789 enshrines the principle that people "are born and remain free and equal in rights. Freedom means being able to do everything that does not harm another". The documents with constitutional value from that period, evoke the idea according to which, if the man is born with some inalienable rights, from which no one can separate him, it means that the state power is not unlimited either. There is, therefore, a fair, proportionate relationship, on the one hand, between the recognized freedoms of each individual, and on the other hand between the liberties of the individual and state power.

The doctrine and the constitutions enshrined the principle of equality. The elimination of privileges and discrimination is a condition for any democratic state. However, the principle of equality has a formal, abstract dimension: equality before the law or equality of opportunity. Few legal concepts have supported material equality. The enshrinement of the principle of equality by the liberal doctrine in law did not mean ignoring the differences between social situations or between participants in social life. The law applied to social relations must take into account these differences, it must not be a simple uniforming factor, based on the abstract and general nature of the legal norm. Different normative regulation of different situations is an application of the principle of proportionality.

Although fundamental human rights are inherent in the human being and essential to his development, liberal legal doctrine holds that there is no equality between the private interest and the public interest, but only a fair balance, ie a relationship of proportionality, because the two social realities and legal, however, have a different nature. Therefore, the liberal doctrine in the field of law has led to the assertion of human individuality, constituted as a counterweight to statism. The liberal doctrine in law is based on the assertion of human rights, but does not support the abolition of any authority, but a society in which the power of the state is limited, only in drafting and enforcing the law, there is a balanced, proportionate relationship between the state and individuals.

An important representative of liberal doctrine, John Stuart Mill, evoked proportionality as the relationship between the fundamental rights of individuals and state power, or so to speak, between freedom and authority, two concepts which in a first analysis are mutually exclusive[108]. The author considers that a limit should be found beyond which the interference of the state in the sphere of individual independence is no longer legitimate. "Finding this limit and defending it against any violation is an indispensable condition for the smooth running of people's lives, an indispensable condition for protection against political despotism"[109]. As a result, there must be a balance between human rights and the right of the state to intervene in individual life. This balance actually means a relationship of proportionality. For the intervention of state authorities in individual life to be justified, there must be a legitimate purpose: "the only purpose which entitles men, individually or collectively, to interference in the sphere of the freedom of action of any of them is self-defense, the only purpose in which power may be legitimately exercised over any member of civilized society against his will is to prevent harm to others"[110]. The balance that the author is talking about is an application of the principle of proportionality and imposes the existence of limits for individual freedom, beyond which the authority of the state begins. The first limitation of individual liberty is not to infringe on the rights of others. The second restriction is to bear the burdens imposed by the existence of the company. This self-limitation of individual behaviors expresses proportionality in the relationships between members of society.

We also notice Alexis de Tocqueville's conception of democracy as a form of government. The basic principle of democracy, in the author's conception, is equality of conditions. Tocqueville believes that the ideal democracy is realized through the reciprocity of legal equality and political

---

[108] J. S. Mill, On Liberty (1859) (Bucharest: Humanitas, 1994), p. 7

[109] J. S. Mill, op.cit., p. 12

[110] J. S. Mill, op. cit., p. 17

freedom, the latter signifying the possibility and the right of all to participate in government. One danger in democratic society, the author says, is "the tyranny of the majority and the tendency to centralize power"[111]. The tyranny of the majority is the result of the equality and independence of every human being in society. If everyone is right, the disproportion of believing the mass increases, so that the opinion of the majority leads the world. This danger is an obvious disproportion between the power of the state and the freedom of individuals. In order to counteract this risk, the political freedom of man must be ensured, whose role is to limit the power of the state in its relationship with individuals and at the same time, to limit individual excesses. Consequently, a balance is achieved, i.e., a relationship of proportionality, between state power and individual freedoms, and man ultimately benefits from this balance.

Another representative of the liberal doctrine in law, in whose conception is found the principle of proportionality is John Rawls. His main objective is to theoretically establish a constitutional democracy. His whole conception of law is based on the principle of justice[112]. The theory of justice, in which equity plays a major role, supports the enshrinement and observance of human rights, the principle of just equality of opportunity and the principle of difference. In a democratic, pluralistic society, the idea of reasonableness plays a major role. Reasonable, in John Rawls's view, is that which brings together different situations, and which expresses "tolerance", the achievement of harmony and stability in a pluralistic society. The principle of "equal opportunities, the principle of difference, fairness and reasonableness" are categories that express, in our opinion, the proportionality in social relations. Democratic equality, in the author's conception, does not exclude the "differences", and social harmony is achieved through equitable, proportionate relations between participants in social life.

Once the state is created, it must intervene in the regulation of the social phenomena. This intervention must be well justified, it must serve a legitimate purpose, it must be done only to the extent necessary and by appropriate means that can be controlled. The existence of the state and its manifestation implies a "status of power" that creates its limits, prevents it from becoming discretionary. State power is institutionalized by law, but the law must

[111] Alexis de Tocqueville, On Democracy in America (1840) (Bucharest: Humanitas, 1994), p. 160

[112] John Rawls, Political Liberalism (1988) (Bucharest: Sedona, 1999), p. 8

legitimize its exercise, first and foremost by the constitution[113]. "The rule of law – said J. Chevallier – is inseparable from the representation of a minimal state, respectful of social autonomy and which does not go beyond its legitimate powers". The same author states that the doctrine of the rule of law is based on the fundamental idea of limiting power through threefold game: 1) the protection of individual freedoms; 2) the submission of power to the nation; 3) entrusting a restricted area of competence to the state. The structuring of the legal order is only a means to ensure and guarantee this limitation through the mechanisms of law creation. Thus, the rule of law covers a) a conception of public liberties; b) a conception of democracy; c) a conception of the role of the state, which constitutes the underlying basic foundation of the legal order.

The application of the principles of the rule of law posed the problem of finding a criterion for assessing the measures ordered by the state authority, in the situation when they are taken within the limits of the competence established by law. Thus, in order not to be arbitrary and discretionary, the measure ordered by a state authority must be in accordance with the law, but also adequate for the proposed legitimate purpose. The relationship between means and purpose is in the doctrine of the rule of law, but also in jurisprudence, one of the particular aspects of the principle of proportionality.

The rule of law is also based on the idea of harmony, balance between its constituent elements. This balanced relationship "is another aspect of the principle of proportionality, in fact a dimension of the general principle of fairness and justice. Thus, the analysis of fundamental rights or the perpetuation and preservation of human life, through the prism of the way of thinking of natural law, will reveal the principle of proportionality. Between the individual and the general, between the public and the private, there must be a fair measure, a balance, because "the exacerbated individual bears in himself the seal of absolutism and totalitarianism"[114], as the exaggerated and disproportionate power of the state in relation to fundamental human rights leads to same purpose: abuse of power and right. In the classical conception of natural law, taken over by the doctrine of the rule of law, law was only a "just measure", that is, proportionality.

---

[113] George Burdeau, Traite de science politique, 4th Volume (Paris: L.G.D.J., 1976); Ion Deleanu, Constitutional law and political institutions, 1st Volume (Bucharest: Ed. Europa Nova, 1996), p. 260

[114] Louis Dumont, Essay on Individualism (Bucharest : Anastasia, 1998), p. 27-35

The principle of proportionality represents in the doctrine of the rule of law the introduction of a new concept, namely legitimacy. The right that limits the power of the state is not only the "the rule of power", in the sense of "legislative power", i.e. to create legal norms as an expression of the will of the legislature, nor of "subjective rights", in the sense of human rights, as powers of the individual to claim something, even the state, only if these rights are recognized by objective law, as legal norms enacted by the legislator, but the law must be understood, in addition to these two meanings, which are real, and by the criterion of law as "fair measure", in the sense of giving each He deserves it, as Aristotle said. Legitimacy, conceived as an adequate and fair measure, is the expression of the principle of proportionality[115].

The role of the state is another area of application of the principle of proportionality. The state cannot do them all, nor is it good to do them. There are objective limits to state activity, which result from the nature of things. The most important criterion for determining these limits is the principle of proportionality. In this regard, J.J. Chevallier states that social activities must, as far as possible, escape the influence of the state, which must reduce its interventions to what is strictly necessary, which means the adequacy (proportionality) of the measures adopted by the state for the purpose pursued, namely maintaining order and ensuring law enforcement. At the same time, it is better for the market and the initiative to be diffuse, spreading throughout the social body, than to be concentrated in a single body that has an exorbitant power. The balance of the social system is all the better ensured as it results more from the free play of the natural laws of functioning and not from a state regulation that risks falsifying and distort them.

---

[115] Petru Miculescu, State of Law, p. 257

III. Conclusions

The application of the principle of proportionality results in the concretization of the legal norm, the legitimacy of which is given by the fair application to each particular case or situation. At the same time, by this principle the individual is not subsumed to the general, the latter expressed by the legal norm, but has its own legitimacy, which imposes a different relationship than the logical-formal one, which confers existence and necessity only to the general. Therefore, the principle of proportionality used in its philosophical meanings imposes the right adequacy of the rule of law (of the general) to the individual who is essentially man in all his existential determinations. Thus, the legal norm is not only "legal" but also legitimate.

The question is whether the understanding of proportionality, by reference to the general principles of law, in particular, the idea of justice, justice and fairness is relevant to contemporary law and especially to constitutional law. We consider that the answer is in the affirmative, for the following reasons:

Law cannot be reduced to a positivist or normative dimension, which, we must admit, dominates the contemporary legal reality. Not every right is expressed by the rules. Therefore, the reference to principles, including the principle of proportionality, is likely to give value to normative regulations. Moreover, the application of legal norms to the diversity of individual cases cannot ignore the idea of justice, of equity, in the sense that the application of the norm must be adequate to the concrete situation, which means the observance of the principle of proportionality.

From the perspective of the idea of justice, the principle of proportionality is also important for constitutional law. The constitution is "the political and legal establishment of a state"[116]. "Moreover – says Ioan Muraru – a constitution is viable and efficient if it achieves the balance between citizens (society) and public authorities (state) on the one hand, then between public authorities and of course even between citizens. It is also important that the constitutional regulations ensure that public authorities are at the service of the citizens, ensuring the protection of the individual against arbitrary attacks

[116] Ion Deleanu, Constitutional law and political institutions, p. 120

by the statute against his freedom"[117]. It does not limit itself to regulating only the exercise of power. It also regulates the principles that govern society. Thus, Art 1 Para3 of the Romanian Constitution enshrines justice as the supreme value of the state and society. The term "justice" is equivalent to the principle of justice and implies proportionality. Aristotle stated that "justice is a middle term"[118], which explains why the principle of justice has a regulatory role in the application of law.

Taking this idea into account in contemporary doctrine, it has been stated that: by limiting them. It therefore has a positive role, because it ensures social cohesion and a negative one, because it ensures that none of the other principles become predominant"[119].

Schleiermacher's words are still valid today, including for any actor in the field of law: "Every scientist must philosophize in order not to remain only a crossing point of a tradition that is transmitted through him, a collector of material, because whatever representation in which neither principles nor connections are seen, it is only a material".

---

[117] Ioan Muraru, Constitutional protection of freedom of opinion (Bucharest: Lumina Lex, 1999), p. 17

[118] Aristotle, Nicomachean Ethics, p. 112

[119] Nicolae Popa, Ion Dogaru, Gheorghe Dănişor, Dan Claudiu Dănişor, Philosophy of law. The great currents, pp.77-78

Bibliography

Alexianu, George. Constitutional law course. Bucharest: House of Schools, 1930-1937;

Aristotle. Politics. Bucharest: Antet, 1997;

Aristotle. Nicomachean Ethics. Book I. Bucharest: IRI, 1998;

de Tocqueville, Alexis. On Democracy in America (1840). Bucharest: Humanitas, 1994;

del Vecchio, Giorgio. Justice, Bucharest: Cartea Românească, 1936;

Deleanu, Ion. Constitutional law and political institutions, 1st Volume. (Bucharest: Europa Nova, 1996;

Mircea Djuvara, Law and sociology. Bucharest: ISD, 1936;

Dumont, Louis. Essay on individualism. Bucharest: Anastasia, 1998;

Geny, François. Science et technique en droit positif, 1st Volume. Paris: Sirey, 1925 ;

Guibal, M. "De la proportionnalité", in L'actualite juridique. Droit administratif 5. Paris: Dalloz, 1978;

Kant, Immanuel. Foundations of the Metaphysics of Morals. Bucharest: Antaios, 1999;

Miculescu, Peter. The Rule of Law (Bucharest: Lumina Lex Publishing House, 1998);

Mill, J. S. On Liberty (1859). Bucharest: Humanitas, 1994;

Montesquieu, The Spirit of Law (1748). Bucharest: Scientific Publishing-house, 1964 Motica, Radu I. and Gheorghe C. Mihai, *Teoria generală a dreptului*. Bucharest: ALL, 2001;

Muraru, Ioan. Constitutional protection of freedom of opinion. Bucharest: Lumina Lex, 1999;

Plato, *The Laws*. Bucharest: IRI, 1995;

Plato. "Republic" in *Works*, 5th Volume. Bucharest: Scientific and Encloclopedic Publishing-House, 1986;

Popa, Nicholas. General theory of law, Bucharest: Actami, 1999;

Popa, Nicolae and Ion Dogaru, Gheorghe Dănişor, Dan Claudiu Dănişor. Philosophy of law. Big Currents Bucharest: All Beck, 2002;

Rawls, John. Political liberalism. Bucharest: Sedona, 1999;

Roubier, Paul. Théorie générale du Droit. Paris: L.G.D.J., 1986;;

Rousseau, Jean Jacques. The Social Contract. Bucharest: Antet, 1999;

Eugeniu Speranţia, Fundamental principles of legal philosophy, Cluj: Institute of Graphic Arts Transylvania, 1937;

Stammler, Rudolf. Theorie der Recktswissenschaft. Chicago: University of Chicago Press, 1989;

***

Decision no 139/1994 published in the Official Gazette of Romania no 353/1994;

Decision no 157/1998 published in the Official Gazette of Romania no 3/1999;

Decision no 161/1998 published in the Official Gazette of Romania no 3/1999;

Decision no 71/1996 published in the Official Gazette of Romania no 13/1996.

5. CONTRIBUTIONS TO CONSTITUTIONAL JURISPRUDENCE IN THE CONSTRUCTION OF PRINCIPLES OF LAW

Abstract:

For the Romanian legal system, the jurisprudence does not have the quality of a formal source of law. Nevertheless, the legal reality, viewed from a historical perspective, has demonstrated the essential role of judicial practice in interpreting and enforcing the law, in constructing argumentative practices, in clarifying the will of the legislator and in discovering the less obvious meanings of legal norms and, last but not least, in unifying thought and legal practice. Therefore jurisprudence, along with doctrine, is an important component of the Romanian legal system.

Based on these considerations, in this study we intend to highlight some aspects of constitutional jurisprudence. We underline its contribution to the emergence and development of the constitutionality control of laws as well as the building of some principles of law. We mainly analyze the role of judicial practice in constructing the principle of proportionality in the constitutional law, of the principle of equality and the interference between the principle of proportionality and the principle of equality. In this respect, we support the role of jurisprudence not only in the correct interpretation and application of constitutional norms, but also in their construction, in the discovery of normative meanings which are often only implicit in the formal expression of the rule of law of the constitutional principles mentioned above. By doing this, the constitutional jurisprudence does not limit itself to the interpretation of the rules of the Fundamental Law in accordance with the classical methods, but also has an important contribution to the clarification and construction of some principles of law, to the constitutionalizing of the entire legal system and of the judicial practice from all the courts

Key words:

Constitutional principles / principle of proportionality / principle of equality of rights / contributions of case law

I. Some aspects regarding the interpretation of the law by constitutional jurisprudence

The normative law-making activity needs to be continued with the activity for norms enforcement; in view of implementation, the first logical operation to perform is their interpretation.

Both the Constitution and the law are presented as a set of legal norms, but these norms are expressed in the form of a normative text. That is why, what is the object of interpretation is not the legal norms, rather the text of the law or the Constitution. A legal text may contain several legal rules. From the constitutional norm can be deduced a constitutive text by way of interpretation. The text of the Constitution is drafted in general terms, which influences the degree of determination of the constitutional norms. By interpretation the constitutional norms are identified and determined.

It should also be emphasized that a Constitution may contain certain principles that are not clearly expressed *expresis verbis*, but they can be inferred through the systematic interpretation of other norms.

In the sense of the above, the specialized literature stated: "The degree of determination of the constitutional norms through the text of the fundamental law can justify the necessity of interpretation. The norms of the Constitution are very well suited to the evolution of their course, because the text is inexorably inaccurate, formulated in general terms. The formal superiority of the Constitution, its rigidity prevents its revision at very short intervals and then the interpretation remains the only way to adopt the normative content, usually older, to the constantly changing social reality. The meaning of the constitutional norms is by their very nature, that of maximum generality, its exact determination depends on the will of the interpreter."[120].

The scientific justification of interpretation results from the need to ensure the effectiveness of the norms contained in both the Constitution and the laws by means of some institutions which mainly carry out the activity of interpreting the norms enacted by the author.

[120] I. Muraru, M. Constantinescu, E.S. Tănăsescu, M. Enache, Gh. Iancu, Interpretation of the Constitution. Doctrine and Practice, Lumina Lex Publishing House, Bucharest, 2002, p. 67.

These institutions are firstly the law courts and constitutional courts.

Verifying the compliance of a normative act with the constitutional norms, institution that represents the constitutionality control of the laws, does not mean a formal comparison or mechanical juxtaposition of the two categories of norms, but a complex work based on the techniques and procedures for interpreting both the law as well as the Constitution.

Therefore, the necessity of interpreting the Constitution is a condition for its application and for the assurance of its supremacy. The constitutional control of laws is essentially an interpretation of both the Constitution and the law. It is necessary to have independent public authorities that have the competence to interpret the Constitution and in this way to examine the conformity of the law with the Constitution. Within the European model of constitutional justice, these authorities are the Constitutional Courts and Courts of Law.

II. Contributions of the constitutional jurisprudence on the construction and interference of the principles of proportionality and equality

The uniformity has been consistently rejected by the Constitutional Court's jurisprudence in relation to the interpretation and application of the principle of equality. The strict equality before the law implies that, in equal situations, the treatment is equal, without discrimination. If the situations are different, the treatment can only be differentiated, which implies the principle of proportionality. Consequently, the breach of the principle of equality arises when a different treatment is applied to similar situations or where the same legal treatment applies to situations which by their nature are different. Also, the breach of this principle may also occur in situations where there is no objective and reasonable reasoning for a differential treatment of identical situations, or if the unequal legal treatment is not appropriate to the purpose of the law.

The jurisprudence of the Constitutional Court has evolved in this respect, starting from accepting that different situations are to be treated differently, until recognizing new constitutional principles, namely the right to difference.[121] The Constitutional Court has ruled that a difference in legal treatment on social grounds or categories of officials is inadmissible, as it would be discriminatory.[122] It admitted that there may be situations that allow for such particularities, but not any such case justifies a difference in legal treatment, especially if the different legal treatment would be discriminatory. The Constitutional Court has established unconstitutional the provisions of the War Veterans Act concerning the conditioning of the veteran of war, to the circumstance of not being fighting against the Romanian army. In this case, the discrimination between Romanian citizens is unjustified, and therefore it is necessary to ensure "equal treatment of all those who have joined in foreign armies"[123]. These are identical situations, which require identical treatment. The Constitutional Court has also applied the principle of equality in other situations, considering either that the situations to be so similar that there is no

[121] Ioan Muraru, Mihai Constantinescu, *România's Constitutional Court*, Albatros Publishing House, Bucharest, 1997, pp. 113-114;

[122] Decision No.6/1993, published in the Official Gazette no. 01/1993

[123] Decision No.47/1994, published in the Official Gazette no.139/1994

justification for a difference in legal treatment or, if it exists, constitutes discrimination in relation to the criterion used.[124]

The Constitutional Court has held that the principle of equality of rights requires an equal treatment for situations which, depending on the purpose pursued, are not different.[125] It is also interesting to emphasize the fact that the appreciation of the identity or the difference between the situations in which legal treatment is applied is made from a teleological perspective with reference to the aim pursued by the legislator.

At the same time, the Constitutional Court has pointed out that the observance of the principle of equality of rights does not have the significance of reflecting in the legal norm a full uniformity of social situations but, on the contrary, the diversity of social situations can be corrected by the legislator in a proportionate way, to bring them to a common denominator.[126] The explicit reference to the principle of proportionality means the adequacy of the legal norm to the diversity of the reality to which it applies and, therefore, the general and abstract nature of the rule is concretized in relation to this diversity of situations.

The rejection of uniformity and the need to differentiate the legal treatment according to different objective situations, without being discriminatory, is reflected in the jurisprudence of the Constitutional Court. Referring to the different situation of students in private education, and on the other hand, those in state education, the Court found that, once they entered the chosen system, they are subject to the rules of each system. So, in reality, the contested provisions do not discriminate, but offer different solutions for different situations.[127] In other words, the necessary adequacy of the legal treatment to

[124] Decision No.124/1995, published in the Official Gazette no.293/1995; Decision No.35/1993, published in the Official Gazette no.218/1993; Decision No.3/1994, published the Official Gazette no.155/1994; Decision No.114/1994, published in C.D.H. – 1994, pp 324-328; Decision No.30/1998, published in the Official Gazette no.113/1998

[125] Decision No. 1 on February 8th, 1994, published in the Official Gazette no. 69 on March 16th, 1994

[126] Decision No. 349 on September 24th, 2013, published in the Official Gazette no. 708 on November 19th, 2013

[127] Decision No.70/1993, published in the Official Gazette no.307/1993. This Decision is invoked constantly by the Constitutional Court, in this matter.

the objective situation considered is an application of the principle of proportionality.

This rule is formulated in the jurisprudence of the Court of Justice with value of a principle: "The principle of equality before the law requires equal treatment for situations which, depending on the purpose pursued, are not different. Consequently, a different treatment cannot only be the expression of the judge's exclusive appreciation, but must be rationally justified in respecting the principle of equality of the citizens before the law and public authorities."[128]

The jurisprudence of our Constitutional Court confirms this interpretation of the principle of equality which refers to the equality of citizens before the law and the public authorities and not the equality of the legal treatment applied to a category of citizens compared to another. Since the fundamental rights "represent a constant of the personality of the citizen, an equal chance granted to any individual", article 16, paragraph (1) of the republished Constitution concerns the equality of rights between the citizens, not the identity of the legal treatment on the application of some measures, regardless of their nature. Thus, the Constitutional Court justifies not only the constitutionality of administering a different legal regime in relation to certain categories of persons, but also the need for such legal treatment.[129]

It has also been established in the jurisprudence that the principle of equality of rights does not imply uniform legal treatment of all offenses and the regulation of a sanctioning regime according to the coverage of the damage caused by the offense committed is the natural expression of the constitutional principle of equality which requires that in the same situations the same regime be applied, and in different legal situations the legal treatment should be differentiated.[130] The conduct of the investigated persons who can contribute to finding the truth, in certain cases, is a situation involving a differentiated legal treatment. This constitutes a measure of the criminal policy, caused by the recrudescence of some serious antisocial phenomena which require the

---

[128] Recital 5 of the Plenum of the Constitutional Court no.1/1994, published in the Official Gazette no.69/1994. In the same sense, see the Decision No. 85/1994, in C.D.H. – 1994, pp. 68 - 74

[129] See Decision No.213/2004, published in the Official Gazette no.519/2004 and Decision No.240/2004, published in the Official Gazette no.562/2004.

[130] See Decision No. 1214 on October 5th, 2010, published in the Official Gazette no. 808 on December 3rd, 2010

necessity for the establishment by the State of a system of special measures, which are not such as to prejudice the principle of equality.[131] The Constitutional Court has not held the existence of a discrimination between the persons committing the theft and benefiting from the possibility of reconciliation as a way of removing criminal liability and the persons committing theft of trees, because they are in different situations and the different legal treatment established by the legislator is based on the objective criterion of the importance of the social value protected by the rule of incrimination, the national forest fund constituting a good of national interest[132].

Also, in its jurisprudence, our Constitutional Court referred to the criterion according to which finds its application one or other legal regime: "When the criterion according to which, one or the other legal regime applies, is objective and reasonable, and not subjectively and arbitrarily, being constituted by a certain situation envisaged in the hypothesis of the norm and not by the personality or the quality of the person to whom it is applied, therefore *intuitu personne*, there is no basis for the qualification of the regulation deducted to the control as discriminatory, therefore contrary to the constitutional standard of reference[133].

At the same time, the jurisprudence of the Constitutional Court stated that: "one cannot talk about discrimination if, through the play of legal provisions – included also through the succession in time of some normative acts - certain persons may end up in unfavorable situations, thus appreciated subjectively in the light of their own interests[134].

Applying this reasoning of proportionality, the Constitutional Court has come to the recognition of a fundamental right: *the right to difference.* "Generally, it is appreciated that a violation of the principle of equality and non-discrimination exists when differential treatment is applied to equal cases, without the existence of objective and reasonable motivation or if there is a

---

[131] Decision No. 636 on May 18th, 2010, published in the Official Gazette no. 398 on June 16th, 2010.

[132] Decision No. 293 on April 28th, 2015, published in the Official Gazette no. 436 on June 18th, 2015.

[133] See Decision No. 192 on March 31st, 2005, published in the Official Gazette no. 327 on June 21st, 2005

[134] Decision No. 1038 on September 14th, 2010, published in the Official Gazette no 742 on November 5th, 2010

disproportion (s.n.) between the aim pursued by unequal treatment and the means used. In other terms, the principle of equality does not prohibit specific rules. That is why the principle of equality leads to the emphasizing on the existence of a fundamental right, *the right to difference (s.n.),* and to the extent that equality is not natural, the fact of imposing it would mean the establishing of discrimination."[135]

The applying of the principle of proportionality has as legal consequences the relativization of equality as a principle. The jurisprudence of the Court confirms that the principle of equality is a particular case of the general principle of proportionality, since the uniqueness of legal treatment can be justified only in a particular hypothesis, namely when the situations are the similar or identical. Starting from the need to differentiate the legal treatment for different situations, the Constitutional Court has consistently held that a protection measure applied to certain social or professional categories in special situations does not have the meaning of a privilege: "A measure of protection cannot have the meaning of a privilege neither of a discrimination, therefore it has been intended precisely to ensure, in certain specific situations, the equality of the citizens who would have been affected in its absence."[136] In these situations, the principle of proportionality imposes the necessary adequacy of the protection measures to the proposed purpose, namely, ensuring, in special situations, the equality of citizens.

Applying the same reasoning, which is based on the principle of proportionality, the Constitutional Court ascertained that a regime derogating from the common law regarding the enforcement of tax receivables is justified by the fact that it is foreseen the non - obsolescence to the forced enforcement of these debts (article 137, paragraph C. Fiscal Procedure). These special procedural rules are appropriate to special situations, namely the fact that the object of enforced enforcement is to collect the tax receivables, which are the sources of the state budget, "which is of general interest"[137]

In accordance with the principle of proportionality, applied in this area, the difference in legal treatment must have a rational and objective basis. The

---

[135] Decision No.107/1995, published in the Official Gazette no.85/1996. See Decision No.6/1996, published in the Official Gazette no.23/1996; Decision No.198/2000, published in the Official Gazette no.702/2000; Decision No.54/2000, published in the Official Gazette no.310/2000; Decision No.263/2001, published in the Official Gazette no.762/2001

[136] Decision No.104/1995, published in the Official Gazette no.40/1996

[137] Decision No.432/2004, published in the Official Gazette no.1176/2004.

provisions of Article II from O.U.G. No 22/2003[138] are constitutional because the difference in the legal treatment regarding the granting of compensatory payments introduced by the criticized text between the category exempted by state-owned companies and other companies is justified by the existence of a rational and objective criterion, consisting in the existence of different situations, but also by the real possibility of the Government to bear compensatory payments.[139] The different legal treatment, objectively and rationally determined by different situations, cannot create privileges or discrimination. The Constitutional Court rejected the objection of unconstitutionality of the provisions of Article 4, paragraph 2, letter a, point 12 of Law no. 543/2002[140], finding that, according to the legal provisions criticized, all culprits in the same situation benefit or are exempted from the pardon, "in relation to the nature of the offense and its content, in the legal form in force at the time of the offense." In the opinion of the Constitutional Court, the convicts who committed crimes at different times, when the criminal law regulated in different editing the content of the respective offenses, are in different situations, which justify the application of different legal treatment "according to the legislator's free choice, without being able to hold the establishment of privileges or discrimination."[141]

In the same sense, the Constitutional Court ruled that the withdrawal by the issuing authority of the endorsement, authorization or attestation, which results in the termination of the individual employment contract, for which concluding the existence of these documents is a mandatory condition, does not constitute a discriminatory legal treatment, but rather the application of a differentiated legal treatment in relation to the different situation of certain categories of employees who choose to exercise some occupations or trades.[142]

---

[138] Published in the Official Gazette no.252/2003

[139] Decision No.457/2003, published in the Official Gazette no.49/2004.

[140] Published in the Official Gazette no.72 /2002.

[141] Decision No.546/2004, published in the Official Gazette no.107/2005. See Decision No.200/2004, published in the Official Gazette no.420/2004, see also Decision No.240/2004, quoted previously, through which the Constitutional Court ascertained that the provisions of article 81, paragraph 3, article 86^1, paragraph3 şi article 86^7, paragraph 3 of the Criminal Code are constitutional. The legislator did not violate the provisions of article16 of the Constitution, as the different legal regime is justified by the different situation in which certain person categories are.

[142] Decision No.545/2004, published in the Official Gazette no.85/2005.

Unlike these cases where the principle of proportionality has been observed, in others, the Constitutional Court has found that the difference in legal treatment has no rational and objective justification, which fact has as consequence a disproportionate and discriminatory treatment between persons in the same situation.

Thus, our Constitutional Court ascertained as unconstitutional the provisions of Article 15, paragraph 1 of Law no. 80/1995 on the Status of Military Staff[143], which allows the granting of paid parental leave up to 2 years only to active military women, and not male military cadres.[144] The legislator may introduce derogating measures from the common rules, with respect to the following conditions: the existence of different situations; to exist a rational and objective justification; the different legal treatment does not create a clear disproportion between different categories of persons; that the derogating measures are not discriminatory. Or, in the present case, the Constitutional Court rightly found that the complete abolition of certain categories of persons from the benefit of a form of insurance prescribed by law for all insured persons violates the constitutional principle of equality, representing a discrimination, because military cadres in activity are not different from other categories of policyholders. Applying the same legal reasoning, the Constitutional Court noticed the unconstitutionality of article 362, paragraph 1 letter *d* of Criminal Procedure Code[145] the legal provisions criticized, which stipulate that the injured part can appeal the criminal side of the case and the civil part only in respect of the civil side, being contrary to the constitutional principle of equality. These two parts of the criminal proceedings are in an identical situation, namely in the situation of a person injured in his / her rights by committing the offense. As a consequence, the unequal treatment in access to redress is unjustified, including the proportionality criterion, since the

---

[143] Published in the Official Gazette no.155/1995.

[144] Decision No.90/2005, published in the Official Gazette no.245/2005. In exchange, the Constitutional Court ascertained the constitutionality of the provisions of article 38, paragraph 4, article 50, paragraph 1^1 şi article 194 of Law no.19/2000, because the right of the citizens to a pension is regulated both through general law as through special laws in regard to certain social-professional categories that are in a particular situation. Therefore, the regime instituted throughout the regulations criticized is reasonable and is justified, because the persons referring to are in different situations. (Decision No. 116/2005, published in the Official Gazette no. 228/2005).

[145] Decision No.482/2004, published in the Official Gazette 1200/2004.

defendant, the injured part, the civil part and the civilly responsible part are of the same quality and respectively are parties to the criminal proceedings.

The Constitutional Court has stated that the legislator is free to lay down conditions for the occupation of certain positions or for exercising of certain professions. If the legislator intends to introduce an exception to these conditions without complying with the constitutional requirements, it creates the premises of discrimination between persons who, although in the same objective situations, enjoy different legal treatment, which contravenes the provisions of article 16 paragraph 1 of the Constitution. [146]

The interference between the principle of equality and the principle of proportionality also exists in the case of protection of the national minorities.

As stated in the Explanatory Report on the Framework Convention for the Protection of National Minorities[147], the states may adopt special measures to promote full and effective equality between national minorities and those belonging to the majority. Such measures must be appropriate to the intended purpose. This requirement expresses the principle of proportionality, which is applied in order to avoid violating the rights of others or discriminating against others. The principle of proportionality requires that these safeguards are not extended, in time and in the sphere of application, beyond what is necessary, in view of achieving the intended purpose.

The Constitutional Court has applied the principle of proportionality by analyzing the constitutionality of some provisions of the Law on Education no. 84/1995[148]. The Romanian village in areas traditionally inhabited or in a substantial number of persons belonging to national minorities, if there is sufficient demand, should, as far as possible, endeavor to ensure the persons belonging to national minorities "the benefit of adequate learning opportunities for their minority language. The application of these measures shall be without prejudice to the learning of the official language or teaching in that language."

---

[146] Decision No. 117 on March 6th, 2014, published in the Official Gazette no. 336 on May 8th, 2014

[147] Adopted by the Committee of Ministers of the Council of Europe in Strasbourg at 10.11.1994

[148] Published in the Official Gazette no.167/1995 and republished in the Official Gazette no.1/1996. See Decision No.139/1999, published in the Official Gazette no.353/1999

The measures taken by the state for the protection of national minorities must not contravene the requirements of the principle of equality of rights of citizens and therefore there must be "a reasonable ratio of proportionality between demand and possibilities, between demand and the means used or between the means used and the aim pursued."[149]

The principle of equality, applied to the exercise of the right to vote, may also involve proportionality. The material conditions for exercising the right to vote may vary according to the diversity of situations. This reality involves a differentiated legal treatment, appropriate to every concrete solution, which is a proportionality relationship. The doctrine stated that "the legislator can set up so many different legal regimes, how many particular situations he encounters, without respecting the strict equality imposed on it regarding the right to vote."[150]

The constitutional principle of equality has applications in electoral, judicial, fiscal, etc.[151] In all these areas, the principle of proportionality, which implies the right to differentiation in legal treatment, applies if the situations in which are the citizens are different.

For our research we have chosen to analyze the application of the constitutional principle of proportionality in tax matters for two reasons: the constitutional text (Article 56 paragraph (2)), recalls the general principle of justice and equity, and secondly the jurisprudence of the Constitutional Court is richer in this field than in other areas, with regard to the interference between the principle of equality and the principle of proportionality.

The application of the principle of proportionality in the field of taxation arises from the provisions of Article 56 (2) of the revised Constitution. "The statutory system of taxation must ensure the *correct* settlement of tax burdens." These provisions must be analyzed through a systematic interpretation of the constitutional texts in the matter, namely the provisions of Article 56, paragraph (1), which establishes the obligation of citizens to contribute through fees and taxes on public expenditure and the provisions of Article 139, according to which taxes and duties can be established only by law or, in case of local taxes and duties, are set by local and county councils, according to the

---

[149] Ibidem

[150] Simina Elena Tănăsescu, Principiul egalităţii în dreptul românesc, The Principle of Equality in Romanian Law, All Beck Publishing House, Bucharest 1999., p. 219

[151] Simina Elena Tănăsescu, quoted works, p.169-253.

law. In accordance with the provisions of Article 56, paragraph (3), any other benefits shall be prohibited, except for those established in exceptional circumstances by the law.

The French Declaration on Human and Citizens Rights (1789)[152] consecrated the principle of equality before tax law and the need for proportionality between the possibilities of citizens and their contribution to public spending. The Romanian constitutional provisions in the field are similar to the regulations existing in the constitutions of other states. Thus, the provisions of Article 53 of the Constitution of Italy establish the obligation of each to participate in public expenditures, *proportionally* to their own capacity, and the fiscal system functions on principles of progressivity. Similarly, the Constitution of Spain establishes in Article 31, the obligation for all citizens to contribute to public spending, according to their possibilities, through a fair tax system, based on principles of equality and progressiveness.

The provisions of Article 56, paragraph (2) of the Romanian Constitution have the meaning of a principle of social justice and equity. As a principle of social justice, the correct setting of tax burdens corresponds to the social character of the state, taking into account the need to protect the most disadvantaged social strata. As a principle of fairness, is intended not to distort the equal opportunities that exclude any privilege or discrimination.[153] The Law on Public Finance (Law no. 10/1991)[154] states in Article 5 that at the elaboration and execution of the budget lie the principles of universality, balance and reality, which represent the concretization of the constitutional provisions above.

The provisions of Article 56, paragraph (2) of the Constitution imply a necessary adjustment between the contribution of each and his / her possibilities. This adequacy can be imagined either in the form of a strict equality of everyone's contribution, or in the form of a necessary proportionality between the income of each and his part of the tasks.[155] The proportionality ratio between the contribution of each and his / her possibilities

---

[152] Article13 stipulates that: "For the maintenance of public and administrative expenditure, a common contribution is needed. It must be shared among citizens equally in relation to their possibilities."

[153] Ibidem, quoted works, p. 127

[154] Published in the Official Gazette no.23/1991

[155] Simina Elena Tănăsescu, quoted works, p. 194

also involves the possibility of reducing or exempting from tax liability if their situation so requires.

The peculiarities of the principle of equality, applied in tax matters, were highlighted in the legal doctrine, as well as in the jurisprudence of the Constitutional Court. The equality before the tax law is based on the universality of participation in tax burdens, which is a specific principle of fiscal policy. According to the provisions of Article 56, paragraph (1) of the Constitution, all citizens are obliged to contribute to public expenditures. This obligation involves the idea of equality before tax law without any privilege or discrimination.

The expression of the principle of equality applied in this area is uniformity. The applying of the constitutional principle of equality in tax matters translates into a very simple exigency, though quite constraining for the legislator: "for the rule of universality to be strictly respected within the same category of taxpayers, both the privileges and discrimination are formally forbidden".[156]

The tax law may take into account the objective differences between the various categories of taxpayers, but any differentiated legal regime must be justified by an objective difference in the situation, in relation to the purpose of the law. In this sense, "the notion of category plays an important role in the principle of equality in tax matters"[157], and the uniformity is not contrary to a certain trans-category differentiation[158].

The tax may be proportional, progressively or regressively. In the literature in specialty it has been shown that the specificity of the tax, regardless of its form, "exists in the ratio of *proportionality* that is established between the taxable amount and the levy, because in terms of tax, proportionality is the true picture of the principle of equality.[159]" In this case, proportionality is a mathematical relation, which can realize the idea of social justice, which results in a fair distribution of tax burdens depending on the possibilities of each taxpayer. The progressivity of the tax is a particular aspect of the principle of proportionality applied in this matter in the sense that the fair distribution of tax burdens means: the higher a person's income is, the more his tax

[156] Ibid, quoted works, p. 175

[157] L. Favoreu and L. Philip, "Les grandes decisions du Conseil Constitutionnel," quoted works, pp. 551, quoted by Simina Elena Tănăsescu, quoted works, p. 182

[158] Simina Elena Tănăsescu, quoted works,p. 192

[159] Ibid, pg. 194

contribution increases. Accordingly, proportionality is an expression of material equality, "when the quota increases at the same time with the taxable mass, we find ourselves in the presence of a progressive rate, expression of the material equality that seeks to equalize the real income, through tax.[160]

The Court applies the provisions of Article 56, paragraph (2) of the Constitution, specifying the constitutional requirements which the law on taxes and charges must comply. "Taxation must be not only legal, but proportionate, equitable and not to differentiate taxes on the basis of groups or categories of citizens."[161] It is noted that the principle of proportionality is a condition of constitutionality of the law in tax matters but to be applied after the distinctions shown in the previous chapter. The Court applies the principle of proportionality, as expressed by the provisions of Article 56 (2) of the Revised Constitution, and notes that Article 7, paragraph (4) of amended Law No 32/1991 removes any inequality and discrimination in the field of taxation, being in line with constitutional provisions, according to which, "the higher the total income of a person, the more his tax contribution increases"[162].

The Constitutional Court has applied the principle of proportionality as a relationship between the taxation base and the tax. Regarding the provisions of article 7, paragraph 6 of the Law no. 32/1991, the Court finds that by indexing the taxation, the grid does not change, but the level of the taxable income is updated, correlated with the increase of the inflation index. "It is true that the tax increases, but only as a result of the increase of the taxation base."[163] In this respect, the doctrine stated: "As the taxpayer's criterion for equality before the tax law, the taxable amount is the criterion according to which vary the legal regime of the tax. But the principle of tax justice, imposed by Article 53, paragraph (2) of the Constitution (Article 56 (2) of the Revised Constitution *n.n.*), imposes the uniformity of the legal regime of taxation as soon as the taxable amount is the same".[164]

The principle of proportionality has also been applied by the Constitutional Court in other situations. Thus, proportionality implies a comparative reasoning that takes place between taxes and duties and, on the other hand, the

---

[160] Ibid, pg. 203

[161] Decision No.6/1993, previously quoted.

[162] Decision No.91/1994, published in C.D.H. – 1994, pp. 287 – 292.

[163] Decision No.53/1994, published in C.D.H. – 1994, pp. 222 – 225.

[164] Simina Elena Tănăsescu, quoted works, pp. 205.

income, salaries or benefits. A fee, in order to be legitimate, must be justified in the performance of a public authority. Otherwise, it is a financial impediment that restricts unconstitutionally the exercise of a right[165]. In the same sense, the Constitutional Court has established that the judicial stamp and the stamp duty are not a restriction of the free access to justice because justice is a public service of the state and it is fair that part of the expenses be borne by those who resort to this service.

However, the fees are not the price of the service, and the state has the possibility to determine the amount of the service. The Constitutional Court is not in measure of censoring the legislator's options and to replace its sovereign and full appreciation with its own appreciation, for it would thus turn itself into a legislator, practically a subsequent one.[166] Therefore, the introduction by the legislator of exceptions to the general rule for the payment of the judiciary fees for the stamp duty (tax exemptions) does not constitute discrimination or a violation of this constitutional principle[167]. The exclusive right of the legislator to determine taxes or duties and their amount or, as the case may be, tax exemptions or reductions in favor of certain categories of taxpayers, cannot be arbitrary. These measures must respect the principle of proportionality found in the content of the concept of fiscal justice, in that the measures adopted to favor certain categories of taxpayers must be appropriate to the conjectural situations and to the economic and financial situation of the country during that period[168]. The application of this principle results also from the fact that any differentiation must be justified by the purpose of the law or the economic and fiscal policy of the state.[169] "No constitutional rule prohibits the granting of fiscal facilities to categories of taxpayers for the purpose of the good realization of the economic, fiscal and social policy of the state." The Constitutional Court also objected to the idea of uniformity of the tax: "The legal regime of taxes is inevitably different, and it also involves an economic and financial strategy. The uniformity of the regulations in this area would result in the abolition of

---

[165] Decision No.179/1994, published in C.D.H. – 1994, pg. 78 – 86.

[166] Decision No.75/1997, published in the Official Gazette no.258/1997.

[167] Decision No.29/2000, published in the Official Gazette no.460/2000. In the same sense see Decision No.532/2004, published in the Official Gazette no.91/2005, by which the Constitutional Court rejected the exception of unconstitutionality of the provisions of article 40^1 of Law no.137/2002, published in the Official Gazette no.215/2002.

[168] Decision No.292/2000, published in the Official Gazette no.702/2000.

[169] Decision No.62/.1999, published in the Official Gazette no.308/1999.

all taxing criteria and of the purpose pursued by the legislator throughout the financial leverages."[170]

The Constitutional Court has determined that the tax should not be abusive. Thus, it must correspond to the objective pursued by the legislator and be appropriate to the taxable mass.[171] As we have seen, the taxable mass is the criterion by which the tax regime varies. Moreover, "the tax is based on a strict conception of proportionality, which refers exclusively to the notion of an arithmetical proportion. "Consequently, the establishing of a tax without existing a taxable mass in an objective sense, that is, an income that cannot be achieved, is an abusive taxation. "In order to eliminate any possibility of abusive taxation and taking into account the intention of the legislator ... it follows that the extension of the obligation to pay the tax, considering the non-utilitarian lands, is unconstitutional, contravening article 53, paragraph (2) of the Constitution (article 56, paragraph (2) of the revised Constitution *n.n.*), on which grounds one cannot establish a tax on an income that cannot be achieved."[172]

---

[170] Decision No.102/1995, published in C.D.H. 1995 – 1996, pp. 118 – 125.

[171] Simina Elena Tănăsescu, quoted works, p. 195.

[172] Decision No.49/1994, published in C.D.H. – 1994, pp. 40 – 52.

III. Conclusions

The supremacy of Constitution would remain a mere theoretical issue if there were no adequate safeguards. Undoubtedly, the constitutional justice and its particular form, the constitutionality control of the laws, represent the main guarantee of the supremacy of the Constitution, as expressly stipulated in the Romanian Basic Law.

The constitutionality control of laws is the main form of constitutional justice and is a basis for democracy guaranteeing the establishment of a democratic government that needs to respect the supremacy of law and Constitution.

George Alexianu considered that legality is an attribute of the modern state. The idea of legality in the author's conception is formulated as follows: all the state organs operate on the basis of an order of law established by the legislator and which must be respected.

The same author, referring to the supremacy of the Constitution, asserts itself in full regard to the realities of today: "When the modern state organizes its new appearance, the first idea that concerns it is to stop the administrative abuse, hence the invention of constitutions and by judicial means, the establishment of a legality control. Once this abuse is established appears a new, a more serious one, that of the Parliament. Then are invented the supremacy of the Constitution and various systems to guarantee it. The idea of legality thus gains a strong leverage."[173]

Verifying the compliance of a normative act with the constitutional norms, an institution that represents the constitutionality control of the laws, does not mean a formal comparison or mechanical juxtaposition of the two categories of norms, but a complex work based on the techniques and procedures for interpreting both the law as well as the Constitution.

Therefore, the necessity of interpreting the Constitution is a condition for its application and for the assurance of its supremacy. The constitutionality control of laws is essentially an activity for the interpretation of both the Constitution and the law.

---

[173] G. Alexianu, Constitutional Law, House of Schools Publishing House, Bucharest, 1930, p. 71

6. CONSTITUTIONAL PROTECTION OF FREEDOM OF EXPRESSION IN THE CONTEXT OF INFORMATION TECHNOLOGY

Abstract:

Few legal, philosophical, or theological categories have given rise to such a great interest as the issue of human freedom. It is natural to be so because freedom is not only a concept, but rather an ontological dimension of man viewed as a person but also in the social environment.

Freedom of expression is an important form of human freedom, which is transposed into a legal form and becomes a fundamental constitutional right.

In this study we analyze the main doctrinal and jurisprudence aspects of freedom of expression. As a novelty aspect to other similar studies, the correlations between the legal form and some theological and philosophical interpretations of freedom of expression are analyzed.

In the context of the development of information technology in the field of communication, important aspects of constitutional jurisprudence regarding the protection of freedom of expression are analyzed, especially in the situation where the exercise of this fundamental right could be conditioned or restricted.

Key words:

Significances of human freedom/ freedom of expression as a fundamental right/ theological and philosophical reflections on freedom of expression/ aspects of jurisprudence regarding the protection of freedom of expression

I. Reflections on the social phenomenality of man

The report and, moreover, the dialectics between "being" and "existence" do not overlap completely with the relation and dialectics of essence and the phenomenon, because the sense and meanings of the being, both in philosophy as in theology, are not identical to the category of essence. Without going into detail, we note that the being has an ontological dimension that manifests itself in its becoming, unlike the category of essence, accepted predominantly in the theory of knowledge in order to distinguish the phenomenal appearance of the profound reality on which relies the existential exteriority.

For our scientific approach, we note therefore the ontological dimension of the relationship between being and existence, so that on this basis to present briefly the correspondence between man in individuality and the depth of his being, and on the other hand, his existence as a sphere of his deeds and manifestations that would exteriorize the depth of being, which, in case of genuine Christian experiences, should be a natural continuation of what is deeper than ourselves.

It is an aspect that has long been accepted in the thinking that the social phenomenality of man, we would say of his being, is a reality and this cannot be ignored. We emphasize that the social dimension of man is one of its nature and not one built or imposed by historical factors in the evolution of the forms of sociability and socialization of man. The subject does not allow a wider discussion on this, but we believe that are relevant the ideas of the great philosopher Kant, which emphasized very well the social nature of man: "We admit that the impulse to society is natural to man; the aptitude and tendency toward that, that is, sociability, are necessary for man, a creature destined to live in society, therefore these are the attributes of humanity." (Kant, 2007: 243)

The "expression" and everything related to the guarantee of its freedom is nothing else but the social dimension of the human being, the way in which he builds oneself and becomes at the same time in relation to others, and not only in relationship to oneself. Therefore, this concept can be understood by what philosophy and theology refer to as "deeds" and "perpetration". The deeds of man, in the terminology we are referring to "its expression", are those that define the being in his social existence. In this sense, one can say that the social expression of the human being is the very individuality of man in his concreteness. Father Arsenie Boca very well synthesizes this reality in the famous and unique painting from Drăgănescu by saying: *"You are in us"*. There is therefore a continuation that should be natural between the inwardness of the human being, and on the other hand, the expression of man in the exteriority of his social existence. This continuity has the dimension of the natural, therefore it is "of the nature", as long as the social expression of man is a value that is constituted in the complex dialectic process of becoming into the spiritual personality of man, which he has inborn, as his first nature, as son of God, by grace. If man's social expressiveness is not a continuation of the depth of his spiritual being, then it is in contradiction with the authentic being of man, unable to contribute to his becoming into self-conscious, the man remains only in the precariousness of his social existence whose expression is inappropriate, not being included in a values sphere and not having as target the destination of man, which is his perfection. Man, in his ontological discontinuity between the depth of his being and his social expressiveness, is the man fallen into exteriority, the one for which there is no values meaning, nor the becoming from the state of individual to the spiritual person.

We also note that what we are able to know about man, otherwise said the scientific knowledge of man no matter how it is achieved through any of the social sciences, including legal or philosophical ones, remain at the level of his expressiveness in the social environment and cannot reach the deeper inner being of man, who remains outside any scientific conceptualization. The depth of the human being in its singularity and indefiniteness can be contemplated and intuited or can be revealed, but cannot be known by means of the usual approach belonging to the sensible or rational knowledge. This aspect was very well emphasized by Father Professor Dumitru Stăniloaie, who said that *"Man is mystery and light; is a mystery of light."* It is, in fact, the distinction that the great philosopher Kant realizes between the phenomenon that can be contained in the sensitive intuition in the concepts of intellect and in the concepts of reasoning, and on the other hand, the "thing in itself", which cannot be conceptualized and known. The depth of man's individual being and its reflection in self-consciousness express "the hidden man of the heart in his perfect purity." The existential depth of the human being, that "something deeper than ourselves" means the spiritual singularity, may mean loneliness, but in no way can lead to loneliness as an accepted ontological dimension for the existence of man. Even in the depth of his being, man's self-consciousness exists only in relation to another who is his fellow man and at the same time with God. This report progresses indefinitely by what characterizes it and represents its content, that is, the depth of love and humility.

A third aspect that we want to note is that only the expressiveness and social dimension of the human being can be the subject to the normative order, thus said, it denotes, inter alia, what we call the "legal status of man's existence."

It is noteworthy that in the legal concepts it is taken into consideration not only the freedom of speech, but the freedom of expression, that is, the ensemble of the social manifestations of man, which can form the object of normativity, but also of scientific knowledge. There is a natural continuity between consciousness and the forms of social expression of man, or, in other words, between freedom of conscience and freedom of expression. If the freedom of expression confirms what we can call the consciousness of the self, that is to say, of man who considers himself sufficient, then the man remains at the level of the individual in the inevitable fall into the exteriority of his existential precariousness. In case the human expressiveness is a natural continuation of his values self-consciousness, which is built only in the infinite and indefinite relationship of love for God and his fellow man, then the deeds and the perpetration of man are in their true value. Father Arsenie Boca notices this man's ontological sustainability, talking about the self-love of man sacrificing people, and on the other hand, the self-sacrifice that leads to the consciousness of the love of men.

These modest considerations we consider to be necessary to understand the freedom of expression in its legal phenomenality, not only at the level of formal structures and concepts with normative or jurisprudential character, also in the authenticity of the value that derives directly from the nature of man, from his existence which is, firstly, ontic, and later becomes ontological.

The deep connection, we call it even dialectical, between the inner and outer dimension of man's being outlines another truth, namely, the infinite opening towards the existence of man, including the supersensible existence and the unacceptability of non-existence and nothingness. This fact was noticed by the Greek antiquity philosophers who did not have a conscience of the non-existence, but also by the contemporary philosophy based on the truths of faith. Bergson notes in this sense that non-existence or nothingness are only "ontological" constructs and have no ontological significance, otherwise said they are forms of human consciousness and thinking that remain in his existential precariousness.

To be authentic, man's expressiveness at the level of his social being must be free, that is, not be subjected to constraints that are outside the natural order that social existence demands. However, human reasoning is inherently binding through the logical laws that it implies. The rational constraint together with the freedom of the reasoning is part of the natural order of the social dimension of human being. In this dialectical report the freedom of reasoning is the dominant term and the rational constraint is the recessive term. This is natural, because the being of man, both in his interiority and in his social expression, is self-evident only as freedom, only in an order whose foundation is freedom.

The freedom of expression, including at the level of the word, is not beyond the responsibilities. Father Arsenie Boca said, *"Prohibited words misinterpret or disorient. Therefore you must be above the words of men: neither praise nor reproach in them should touch you. The words are living beings, able to do the job to which they have been sent. And because they are living beings, life out of life, the one who created them, they accompany to the Last Judgment, as his children, with all their consequences."*

In the following we want to highlight some aspects of the juridical phenomenality of the freedom of expression, noting that the juridical state of man cannot exhaust all that means wealth and, we would say, the inexhaustibility of the forms and content of human expression within the natural and social environment.

II. Reflections on the legal significance of the freedom of expression

As stated in the literature in specialty, that tries to highlight the specificity of this right, the freedom of expression - as stated in Article 19 of the United Nations Universal Declaration of Human Rights in 1948 - constitutes an unusual legal phenomenon: equally a right in itself and an indispensable one or, as the case may be, prejudicial for the realization of the other rights. Thus, the freedom of expression and information is necessary for the freedom of meetings, but at the same time constitutes a threat to the right to respect private life, family life or intimate life, that is, all that represents the interiority of human being

It is also an individual right that pertains to the freedom of conscience or the spiritual freedom of each person, but also a collective right, because by its essence it exists only in the phenomenal, social manifestation of man. At the same time, it is the foundation of the structure of social existence, because only through the forms of expression and the guaranteeing of their freedom, man communicates with other peers, and at the same time constitutes the foundations of community and communion, including in the spiritual meaning of the latter one.

These realities have also been underlined since the 18th century when, in Article 11 of the French Declaration of Human and Citizen Rights adopted in 1789, the freedom of expression was "a democratic right by excellence and characterized as one of the most the valued rights of man".

Such ideas are also highlighted in the jurisprudence of the European Court in Strasbourg, since 1976 (The Handyside case against the United Kingdom) emphasizing that freedom of expression is "one of the essential foundations of a democratic society, one of the primordial conditions for its progress and the fulfillment of each person." At the same time, the freedom of information and freedom of expression "are the foundation stones of any free and democratic society."

The exercising of this right obviously implies duties and responsibilities. Therefore, as we shall see below, the freedom of expression, at least in the legal sense, is not absolute, intangible, but may be subjected to the conditions, limits, limitations or even derogations naturally arising from the limits of the human being in relationship with his fellow men. The social dimension of the human being is always legally defined, because it can be contained within quantifiable limits and determined by the legal order, unlike self-consciousness and interiority of the human being, characterized by depth, infinity, but only in a relationship of humbleness and love with God and others.

The modern legal theory reveals the complex content of the freedom of expression, which obviously does not reduce itself only to the freedom of speech. Without going into detail, there are three components of the legal content specific to the freedom of expression: *a. Freedom of opinion; b. Freedom of information; c. Freedom of the press.*

Romanian Constitution consecrates and guarantees this fundamental freedom in the provisions of art. 30 par. 1 - 8. The constitutional consecration and of the freedom of expression is based on the fact that any opinion, creation, idea, theoretical conception, etc. enter into the legal circuit only if they are communicated, expressed. Communication and expression of the thoughts is not only a possibility but at the same time a necessary condition of human existence, of society organized according to civilization criteria determined historically. That's why the freedom of expression is a natural right, to be found as such since the very first documents of constitutional value. The freedom of expression is the ability of man to express his or her thoughts aloud by writing, by images, by sounds or by other means of communication. Spiritual creations of any kind, thoughts, opinions, feelings, religious beliefs, etc. can be expressed.

From the perspective of the constitutional right, it is a fundamental right with a complex content and one of the highest values of citizens' freedom. The constitutional content refers to the following:

a. The content of communication: thoughts, opinions, religious beliefs, etc., as well as the means by which communication is realized, through live speech, sounds, images, writing.

b. The right is inviolable and cannot be arbitrarily restricted. The state authorities have the obligation to respect the right to expression of any subject of law, if realized under the conditions provided by the law.

c. The freedom of expression is interpreted in the sense of the concept of communication and must therefore be made public. The legal meaning of this notion is that conferred by the provisions of Article 152 of the Criminal Code.

d. It is forbidden the censure of any kind on the free communication in the sense that no publication can be suppressed and secondly that the state authorities cannot exercise a prior control over the content of the communication for political or other reasons. Romanian Constitution does not explicitly prohibit the suspension of publications. We consider that this restrictive measure could be taken only under the conditions of a special law expressing this possibility and the legal conditions for its exercise.

e. The freedom of expression also implies the freedom to set up publications and the freedom to set up organizational structures to support the possibility of communication: radio and television studios, publishers, editors, etc. The law may require such organizational structures to make the source of funding public, which is a guarantee of the freedom of expression.

f. The freedom of expression cannot be absolute, but is subjected to the principles of legal and moral responsibility. In this regard, the International Treaty on Civil and Political Rights establishes that the exercise of the freedom of expression entails special duties and special responsibilities and may be subjected to restrictions. The Constitution prohibits expressions that seek to prejudice the human dignity, the individual's private life and his right to his or her own image. It is also forbidden to defame the country, to indulge in war, to aggression, to national hatred, class or religious hatred, to discrimination, to territorial separations, to political violence or obscenities against good morals.

The legal responsibility for exceeding these limits can be civil or criminal, as the case may be, the civil liability, namely the obligation to pay material or moral damages to the injured person, is in the order stipulated by the Constitution: to the editor of to the publisher, the author, the organizer of the manifestation, the owner of the means of reproduction of the radio or television station under the law. The criminal liability is governed by the Criminal Code or other special laws. It is always personal and can intervene when crimes of insult, slander, outrage, offense to authority, the spread of obscene material, etc. are committed.

III. Some aspects of jurisprudence regarding the guarantee of the freedom of expression

The freedom of expression is a consecrated right guaranteed by Article 10[174] of the European Convention on Human Rights, adopted in Rome in 1950, according to which the jurisprudence of the European Court of Human Rights (CEDO) has contributed to the application and understanding of the conditions and limits of the exercise.

The constitutive elements of this freedom, as regulated in Article 10, are: the freedom of thinking, the freedom to seek information, the freedom to communicate ideas and information, without being restricted by borders and without any interference by the public authorities, freedom to benefit from information and ideas internally and internationally. The jurisprudence also established that art.10 guarantees also the artistic expression, the activities of the broadcasting companies, cinema or television and, of course, press. In summary, the European Court has emphasized that the freedom of expression includes the right to have and to express its opinion, but also the right to information. A democratic society is characterized by pluralism, tolerance and openness. Therefore, by protecting the freedom of expression, are protected not only the opinions or information received "favorably or indifferently, but also those that may offend or shock the state authorities or a part of the population"[175]. It is stated in the doctrine that the ability of each one to have and express a minority opinion is an essential component of a democratic society. (Sudre, 2006: 417)

The freedom of expression has an autonomous character, in the sense that it has a value unsubordinated to the general interest or determined by the state at a certain moment. (Micu, 2007: 94).

The autonomy is a guarantee for respecting the principle of pluralism and at the same time excludes the arbitrary interference of the state in the act of creation, information and expression of the individual.

The state has several categories of obligations to exercise this right: the obligation to refrain from limiting the freedom of expression in all its forms;

---

[174] The Dispositions of article 10 of the Convention are to be found in Romanian Constitution in the regulations of the two articles: article 30 – Liberty of expression and article 31 – The right to information.

[175] Case Lingens versus Austria, Decision on July 8th, 1986.

the positive obligation to ensure the exercise of this right by guaranteeing the existence of diversified means of information. In this regard, the state must oppose excessive media concentration and ensure the diversity of media, information and ideas.

The provisions of Article 10 paragraph 2 provide that exercise of the freedom of expression implies "duties and responsibilities". Also the freedom of expression may also be subjected to restrictions, but also to certain formalities or conditions. The European Court has held that Article 10 may be violated by a wide variety of measures ordered by the national authorities against persons who have exercised their freedom of expression. These measures, which constitute interference from public authorities, may consist of: civil and criminal actions, confiscation of goods, refusal to authorize publications or television stations, prohibition of dissemination of information, etc. (Harris, Gomien & Zwook, 1997:382).

In order not to constitute a violation of Article 10, these interferences must comply with the conditions imposed by paragraph 2: the restriction must be prescribed by law, pursue a legitimate aim, be necessary in a democratic society for the achievement of the aim pursued, which implies the compliance with the proportionality criterion.

The basic philosophy expressed in C.E.D.O. jurisprudence on freedom of expression can be synthesized through the following idea: Freedom of expression is one of the essential foundations of the democratic society, one of the primordial conditions for progress and flourishing of each one. Under the reserve of paragraph 2 of Article 10, it is used not only for information or ideas collected by favors or considered harmless or indifferent, but also for those who strike, shock or disturb the state or a part of the population. Therefore, they prove it: pluralism, tolerance and the spirit of openness, without which there is no democratic society. It follows, in particular, that any formality, condition, restriction or penalty imposed in the matter must be proportionate to the legitimate aim pursued.[176]

The observance of the principle of proportionality is an important condition which C.E.D.O. is examining in order to ascertain whether the restrictive measures ordered by the national authorities are appropriate to the

[176] See case Handyside versus United Kingdom, Decision on December 7th, 1976, paragraph 49.

legitimate aim invoked. The jurisprudence of the international Court reveals particular aspects of the principle of proportionality applied in the case of conditioning or restricting the exercise of the freedom of expression, particularities determined by the sphere and content of the forms of freedom of expression, the modalities of realization, the nature of the legitimate aim pursued and the concrete interests of the subjects involved.

The exceptions from the rule of guaranteeing the exercise of freedom of expression are interpreted restrictively, and the necessity and proportionality of certain limits must be established convincingly. The contracting States are recognized a certain margin of appreciation, which differs according to the legitimate aim pursued and the means of expressing of the freedom of expression. In this regard, C.E.D.O. concluded that it is impossible for the jurisprudence and law of the Contracting States to develop a uniform notion of morality and that the domestic authorities are better placed than the international judge to decide on the precise content of the requirements imposed by the morals of a society. Therefore, in these situations, C.E.D.O. has left to the national authorities a wide margin of appreciation, which also has consequences on respecting the principle of proportionality.

In the opinion of Strasbourg Court, the freedom of the press is one of the most effective means by which the public learns or forms opinions about the ideas and attitudes of political leaders and, in general, about social realities. Therefore, the restrictions on press freedom, including sanctions imposed on journalists, must be "rigorously proportional and centered on statements that have in fact exceeded the limits of an acceptable criticism." (Sudre, 2006: 425)

The analysis of the principle of proportionality respecting, in case of the restrictions on press freedom, also takes into account the fact that the press has the task to communicate information and ideas related to the issues debated in political life. To this obligation corresponds the right of the public to assume them. Consequently, the limits of admissible criticism are much broader toward a politician or government, rather than for a simple citizen. C.E.D.O. has set a high level of media protection, stating that the general interest is better served when providing the public with the most comprehensive information possible and therefore the proportionality ratio is strictly interpreted in the sense that there must be "an imperious social need" to justify a limitation of press freedom.

The Strasbourg Court also distinguished between facts and value judgments. If the materiality of the former ones can be proved, the value judgments are not capable of being demonstrated in terms of their accuracy. Therefore, it is not justified, including in terms of proportionality, a measure to condemn a journalist for expressing valuable judgments. However, even when it comes to a value judgment, the proportionality of the interference may depend on the existence of a sufficient factual basis, because a value judgment without any factual basis for its support may be excessive.[177]

A particular aspect of the freedom of expression refers to the activity of state officials in the performance of their professional duties. C.E.D.O. jurisprudence has determined that the State may restrict the right to freedom of expression of its officials to the extent that their views relate to their duties or professional duties. In this case too, the proportionality principle must be respected so that restrictive measures are not excessive.

In relation to these rules, the observance of proportionality, understood as an appropriate relationship between the restrictive measures adopted and the legitimate aim pursued, is analyzed in concrete terms by C.E.D.O. depending on the particularities of each case.

Thus, in Sunday Times versus the United Kingdom[178], C.E.D.O. found that the prohibition on the publication of an article relating to a case pending before a court, a ban ordered by the High Court and supported by the House of Lords, was a violation of Article 10 of the Convention because the principle of proportionality has not been respected. In order to determine whether the prohibition on publication is in this case proportionate to the legitimate aim pursued, the Strasbourg Court emphasizes the importance in a democratic society of press freedom, including for rendering the issue on justice administration: "Not only has the media the mission to communicate information and ideas on the issues that the tribunals judge, but the public also has the right to receive them." Consequently, satisfying the public's interest to be informed is essential to determine whether the interference by public authorities into the exercise of freedom of expression is justified. In relation to

[177] See case Unabhangige Initiative Informationsvielfalt versus Austria, Decision on May 26 th 2002; Dichand and others, versus Austria, Decision on May 26 th 2002; Krane Verlag Con & Co. K.G. versus Austria, Decisions on February 26th, 2002.
[178] Decision on April 26th, 1979. For the same meaning see case Barthold versus Germania, decision on March 25th, 1985.

these premises, C.E.D.O. notes that the interest in maintaining the authority of the judiciary was not such a pressing social need to counteract the public's interest in receiving information. Consequently, the restriction imposed on the applicants is not justified and is not proportionate to the legitimate aim pursued.

The convictions imposed on journalists for the articles published in the press, are a restriction on the freedom of expression. In these cases, the Court examines very rigorously the compliance with the condition of proportionality, especially if the sanctions have been applied to criticisms made against political people or state authorities.

The assessment of the observance of the principle of proportionality is carried out in relation to the following coordinates: "In a democratic system, the actions or omissions of the government must be placed under careful control, not only of the legislative and judicial powers, but also of the public opinion. Indeed, the dominant position it occupies requires that it shows restraint in the use of the criminal path, especially if having other means to respond to the unjustified attacks and criticisms of opponents."[179]

The competent authorities of the state have the possibility, as a guarantor of the public order, to apply criminal sanctions even in order to react appropriately and necessarily to such allegations. The national authorities have a broader margin of appreciation regarding the need to interfere in the exercise of freedom of expression, in situations where the discourse in litigation instigates to the use of violence against an individual, a representative of the State or a part of the population. In relation to those considerations, which are consistently settled in jurisprudence, C.E.D.O. ascertained the violation of the principle of proportionality in several cases where the national authorities have adopted criminal sanctions against some journalists[180].

---

[179] Case Seker Karatos versus Turkey, Decision on July 9th, 2002. For the same meaning see case Ayse Őztűrk versus Turkey, Decision on October 15th, 2002.

[180] See case Lingens versus Austria, Decision on July 8th, 1986; case Dalban versus Romania, Decision on September 28th, 1999; case Thargeirsan versus Ireland, Decision on 25 iunie 1992; case Jersild versus Denmark, Decision on September 23rd, 1994; case Castells versus Spain, Decision on April 23rd, 2002; case Lehideux and Isarni versus France, Decision on September 23rd, 1998; case Sabău and Pârcălab versus Romania, Decision on September 28th, 2004.

The freedom of the press is not absolute. The press should not exceed certain limits, particularly as regards the reputation and rights of others, as well as the need to prevent the disclosure of confidential information.[181] While it is accepted that journalistic freedom includes the possible use of a certain amount of exaggeration, even of provocation, the limits of admissible criticism are narrower for a simple individual rather than for a government or a political personality.

In such cases, in order to determine whether the principle of proportionality has been respected, the Court distinguishes between injurious expressions used by a journalist in the press and the criticisms that are acceptable. Thus, in the case Tammes v. Estonia, cited above[182], the complainant was convicted for using in the press terms that are offensive to the wife of a former prime minister and minister. In assessing whether the sanction applied is proportionate to the legitimate aim pursued - the protection of the reputation or the rights of others - C.E.D.O. notes that the offensive terms used by the journalist are value judgments expressed in an offensive manner that were not necessary to be used to express a negative opinion. At the same time, the use of these terms to qualify a person's private life is not justified by the public interest pursued. The nature and severity of the sanction applied is another criterion for assessing the respecting of proportionality. In the present case, the claimant was convicted to a modest fine. In relation to these elements C.E.D.O. has established that the principle of proportionality has been respected and consequently there is no violation of Article 10 of the Convention.

Obliging a journalist to disclose his sources of information and the application of a fine for refusal to comply is an interference with the exercise of freedom of expression which, in order to be justified, must also respect the criterion of proportionality[183]. In order to verify compliance with the principle of proportionality, in the quoted case, C.E.D.O. has taken into account the importance of the protection of journalistic sources for the freedom of the press and the negative effect that a disclosure ordinance is likely to produce. In this respect, it was stated that: "It is necessary to give greater importance to the democratic society's interest in assuming and maintaining the freedom of the

---

[181] Case Tammer versus Estonia, Decision on February 6th 2001.

[182] See case Constantinescu versus Romania, Decision on July 27th, 2000; case Chawy and others, versus France, Decision on 29 iunie 2004.

[183] Case Goodwin versus United Kingdom, Decision on March 27th 1996.

press when it comes to determining whether the restriction is proportionate to the legitimate aim pursued. The limits brought to the confidentiality of journalistic sources, demand the Court the most scrupulous exam. "In the cause was considered that the ordinance for disclosure of the sources of information used by the journalist was not a reasonable means proportionate to the legitimate aim pursued.

In the most recent jurisprudence C.E.D.O. has established that the time is a criterion for assessing whether the principle of proportionality has been respected in the event of a restriction on the exercise of the freedom of expression by prohibiting the publication of a work which is likely to reveal confidential data on the evolution of a disease suffered by an important political person[184]. The passage of time must necessarily be taken into account in order to examine the compatibility with the freedom of expression of such a grave measure as the absolute prohibition on the publication of a book.

The interdiction on the cable retransmission of broadcasts,[185] the refusal by the national authorities to authorize an electronic company to receive non-coded[186] television programs by help of a parabolic antenna or the impossibility of having and operating private radio or television stations due to the monopoly[187] of the State, constitute interference in the exercise of freedom of expression requiring consideration of compliance with the criterion of proportionality. The particularities of the freedom of expression, the necessity and pluralism in a democratic society, the margin of appreciation recognized by the national authorities, depending on the protected values, constitute in these cases criteria for assessing the observance of the principle of proportionality.

The principle of proportionality has particular features in C.E.D.O. jurisprudence when it is applied in order to establish whether the restriction of the freedom of expression of office clerk is justified.

The international Court in Strasbourg has consistently held that the State may restrict the right to the freedom of expression of its officials to the extent that their views relate to their professional duties or tasks. In such cases,

---

[184]Case Plan (Society) versus France, Decision on May 18th 2004.

[185] Case Groppero Radio A.G.and others, versus Switzerland, Decision on March 28th 1990.

[186] Case Autronic A.G. versus Switzerland, Decision on May 22nd 1990.

[187] Case Informationsverein Lentia and others, versus Austria, Decision on November 24th 1993.

C.E.D.O. jurisprudence also refers to other criteria for assessing whether the restrictive measure is proportionate to the legitimate aim pursued. Thus, in case of persons having military status, the Court examines the concept of "order". The idea of order refers not only to public order, but also covers the order that must prevail within the limits of a specific social group. In case of the armed forces, the "order" imposed by the regulations has a particularly important aspect and may require the military not to undermine military discipline, including throughout written materials. Consequently, the States have a broader margin of appreciation and the measures imposed on soldiers on the freedom of expression are appropriate to the legitimate aim pursued. [188]

The duty of political loyalty imposed on an official is of a particular importance for the constitutional order of a state. However, the dismissal of a teaching staff, due to lack of loyalty to the Constitution, was appreciated by C.E.D.O. for being disproportionate to the legitimate aim pursued, especially as the national authorities had other alternatives for lighter sanctions. [189]

The freedom of the political debate is a particular aspect of the freedom of expression. Maintaining and strengthening the pluralistic democracy requires constitutional safeguards restricting the freedom of exercise for some professional categories. Therefore, the interdiction by the Constitution for police officers to conduct political activities respects the principle of proportionality. [190]

In its jurisprudence, C.E.D.O. has determined that in cases where the freedom of expression of the high-ranking magistrates is at stake, the rights and responsibilities referred to in Article 10 paragraph 2 are of particular importance. "Thus, it is justified to expect the judicial clerks to use their freedom of speech with restraint, whenever it is susceptible to question the authority and impartiality of the judiciary power.[191] " Any breach of the freedom of expression of a magistrate requires careful consideration of the observance of the principle of proportionality. The premise of this analysis is the existence of a fair balance between the fundamental rights of the individual to the freedom of expression and, on the other hand, the legitimate interest of

[188] Case Engeland and others, versus The Nederlands, Decision on June 8th 1976.

[189] Case Vogt, versusGermany, Decision on June 8th 1976.

[190] Case Rekveny versus Hungary, Decision on May 20th 1999.

[191] Case Wille versus Lichtenstein, Decision on October 28th 1999.

a democratic state to ensure that the public office acts for the purposes stated in Article 10, paragraph 2.

In the above-mentioned case, the Court found that there had been a violation of the right of the claimant, a high magistrate, to exercise his freedom of expression, because the national authorities criticized the content of his speech and announced its intention to sanction him for expressing his opinion freely. C.E.D.O. considers that the reasoning of the national authorities, in order to justify the infringement of the claimant's right to the freedom of expression, is not sufficient to show that the interference was necessary in a democratic society, since the disputed litigation concerned constitutional law issues. Even if there is a certain margin of appreciation, the reaction of the national authorities, namely the removal from office of the magistrate, was not proportionate to the aim pursued and therefore Article 10 of the Convention was violated.

The freedom of expression also includes artistic expression. The Strasbourg Court found that Article 10 of the Convention "includes the freedom of artistic expression that allows the participation in the public of the exchange of cultural, political, and social information and ideas of all kind"[192].

In most cases, the restrictive measures adopted by the national authorities on the freedom of artistic expression have legitimately aimed at protecting the morals or protecting the rights of others. Applying the principle of proportionality in such cases implies also the characterization of the concept of morality and, implicitly, of the possibility for the States to adopt restrictive measures. In this regard, C.E.D.O. has constantly stated that contracting states have a greater margin of appreciation when regulating issues likely to offend intimate beliefs in morals and religion. "In terms of morality, European countries do not have a uniform conception on the protection requirements against attacks on religious beliefs."[193]

---

[192] Case Műller and others, versus Switzerland, Decision on May 24th 1988.

[193] Case Wingrove versus United Kingdom, quoted previously. For the analysis of the observance of the criterion of proportionality, in cases of restriction of the freedom of artistic expression, see the case Handyside versus United Kingdom previously quoted and case Műller and others, versus Switzerland, previously quoted.

The Romanian legal doctrine and the jurisprudence of the Constitutional Court have also contributed to the understanding and guarantee of the freedom of expression.

The doctrine states that, according to their more authoritarian or more liberal tendencies, the legal regulations on press can be grouped in the light of comparative law into two main systems: the preventive and repressive systems (Drăganu, 1998: 176). The legal regime applied in this area must comply with the principle of proportionality, in that the limits and conditions imposed on the exercise of that freedom must be appropriate to the aim pursued by the constituent legislator, namely the protection of the freedom of expression, but at the same time to prevent the abusive exercise of this right.

The Constitutional Court refers to the jurisprudence of C.E.D.O. and to the provisions of the Convention involving the principle of proportionality. In this respect, it has been stated that the freedom of expression is not absolute and, consequently, has certain legal limits. Thus, the establishing by law of the restrictions or sanctions are measures compatible with freedom of expression if they comply with the conditions imposed by Article 10, paragraph 2, of the Convention. "It is of principle that to a legal obligation, regarding the limiting of the freedom of expression, and even more so to a constitutional obligation must correspond a legal sanction in the event of its non-compliance."[194]

This interpretation is also confirmed by the recent jurisprudence of the Constitutional Court. By Decision no.183 / 2004[195] was established the constitutionality of the provisions of article 205 Criminal Code who incriminates the insult. In the recitals it was stated that the insult is an offense against dignity, and the dignity of man is a supreme value according to art.1,

---

[194] Decision no.51/1999, published in the Official Gazette no.262/1999; See Decision no.205/2000, published in the Official Gazette no.702/2000

[195] Published in Official Gazette no. 431 / 2004. See in the same meaning the Decision no.268/2004, published in the Official Gazette no.640 /2004, by which the objection of unconstitutionality of the provisions was rejected art.206 Criminal Code. In consideration of the decision it was stated that all the provisions of the Constitution and the international legal instruments by which is consecrated the freedom of expression, allowing the possibility of restricting this freedom, if the restrictive measures are necessary and appropriate for the defense of the rights and liberties of others. Incriminating of the defamation is such a measure appropriate to the legitimate purpose pursued, especially as the law allows the person who proves to have a legitimate interest, in whose defense he made the slanderous statement or imputation, to make the test of verity.

paragraph (3) of the Constitution. The limits of the exercise of freedom of expression are determined by the need to respect the dignity, honor, private life of the person and the right to their own image. The violation of these limits is sanctioned by incriminating the sanction of insult. The Court states that the determination of the limits of the exercise of a right or freedom can be made by the legislator in compliance with the provisions of Article 53 of the Constitution, implicitly respecting the proportionality criterion, although, as happened in other cases, the Constitutional Court does not analyze it. However, the cited judgment makes extensive references to C.E.D.O. jurisprudence to argue that the restriction of the freedom of expression, by incriminating by the lawmakers the insulting offence, is a necessary measure in a democratic society, appropriate to the legitimate aim pursued, namely "the protection of the reputation or the rights of others".

In the older jurisprudence, the Constitutional Court found, in our opinion on good grounds, the constitutionality of the provisions of Article 238, paragraph 1 of the Criminal Code, which incriminates the offense committed against authorities.[196] Although the principle of proportionality is not explicitly invoked, out of the constitutional judge's reasoning and from extensive references to C.E.D.O. jurisprudence it follows that the restrictive measure on the freedom of expression is necessary and appropriate to the legitimate aim pursued, namely the protection of the dignity and honor of a citizen who performs a public office. "Precisely the investing of a citizen with a public office attracts not only increased demands on the part of the official, but also the need for special legal protection, since the reputation of such a person indirectly affects the prestige of the authority in whose name he acts within the legal framework of the duties invested."

The freedom of expression implies "the right to reply", which in turn is considered to be a fundamental right. The Constitutional Court has applied the principle of proportionality to determine the limits of each of these rights. In this regard, the Court found that the statutory regulation of the right to reply "meets the constitutional requirements contained in the Constitution". By analyzing the limits of the right to reply, the Constitutional Court applies the principle of proportionality, expressed as a fair relationship between the allegedly defamatory information and the replica given to this information: "Even in case of pertinence of the right of reply, the question on its limits is questionable because it is natural that between the dimensions of the

[196] Decision no 140 /1996 published in the Official Gazette no 324 / 1996.

information allegedly defamatory and those of the injured person's reply, there is no *apparent disproportion* (s.n) in favor of the latter one, keeping the limits of a reasonable reply, focused on the defamatory aspects, fought by the replica whose publicity is required."[197] The limits of exercising the freedom of expression imply the principle of proportionality when determined by other values protected by the constitutional norms. The Court ruled that "the provisions of paragraph (6) of Article 30 of the Constitution have into regard *the limits* of the exercise of the freedom of expression, which cannot, through other supreme values of the lawful State, prejudice the right of the person to his own image." [198] In the same meaning is C.E.D.O. jurisprudence that refers to the principle of proportionality in situations where the exercise of the freedom of expression may be limited[199].

The protection of public morality is one of the legitimate purposes justifying the restriction of the freedom of speech. Having into consideration this legitimate purpose, the Constitutional Court has found the constitutionality of the provisions of Article 325 of the Criminal Code which incriminates the crime of spreading obscene material. [200] The restrictive measure is necessary in a democratic society, although the concepts of "public morality" and "good morals" have varying content according to collectivity and epoch. However, in all these cases, there is a limit to the tolerance of manifestations, the violation of which must be sanctioned by criminal law, since the constitutionally guaranteed fundamental rights and freedoms can not be exercised in a manner contrary to good morals or that would harm public morality. The principle of proportionality is a jurisprudential criterion for determining these limits.

---

[197] Decision no 8/1996, published in the Official Gazette no.129/1996

[198] Decision no.54/2000, published in the Official Gazette no.310/2000

[199] Case Handyside versus United Kingdom - 1976; Case Sunday Times versus United Kingdom - 1979; Case Lingens versus Austria - 1986; Case Dalban versus Romania - 1999, in decisions of the European Court of Human Rights, vol. I.

[200] Decision no. 19/2005 published in the Official Gazette no.153/2005. Nevertheless, this is our Constitutional Court constant jurisprudence on this matter. See the Decision no.108/1995, published in the Official Gazette no.8/1996.

IV. Instead of conclusions

The spiritual being of man in the depth and interiority of self-consciousness has something characteristically opposed to the expressiveness of the social dimension of the being, which also denotes the primacy of the spirit, as in essence the self-consciousness is spirit, against externality, against everything that is deeds and doing. It's about *silence*. The authenticity of expressing the self-consciousness is the silence, which in principle cannot be the subjected to the legal status or normative regulation, representing, by excellence, an area of the non-right. There are however exceptions.

The philosophers and theologians spoke about "the knowledge through silence." We will discuss in detail on this in another material with more reflections on the philosophical and theological conception of silence. Here we highlight some aphorisms that we consider important to appreciate silence as the self-discovery of man in the authentic of his being.

Saint Isaac Sirius said that *"Silence is the mystery of the future century, and the words are the instruments of this world."* The same wise man said, *"It is good to be friends with all, but alone in your conscience."* The loneliness of conscience is actually a silence that does not imply immutability or inactivity, but the immersion into the indefinite and infinite depth of being through continuous spiritual progress. Father Arsenie Boca identifies the ten commandments of wisdom: *"For nine times to shut up and once to talk and then only for a little."* And the Holy Saints Calist and Ignatius said: *"The prayer of the pure is the silence"*

Almost paradoxically, the phenomenality of the juridical status of man recognizes and even consecrates the "right to silence" - the right of the defendant not to make any statement. Moreover, "silence" can produce legal effects. For example, the adoption of a legal act through consensus by a collegiate body, or in some cases is recognized the value of consent to the conclusion of contracts or the acquiescence of a third party's claims. The legal meanings of "silence", however, require a separate study. In the context of the above, we limit ourselves to the emphasizing that by exception the human will in the legal plane can also be expressed by silence, therefore silence is also a phenomenal social reality, legally quantifiable, not only a dimension of self-consciousness, of interiority of the human being

Let us therefore acquire the power of silence in order to express ourselves in the authenticity of our being, in the freedom that it assumes, in all that is the social nature of our being.

Bibliography

Andreescu, M., 2016, Philosophy, Faith and Law, University Publishing House, Bucharest;

Andreescu, M. & Puran, A., 2017, Constitutional Law. General Theory and Constitutional Institutions, 2nd Edition, CH. Beck Publishing House, Bucharest;

Andreescu, M., 2017, Principles and Values of Law and Culture, Universul Juridic Publishing House, Bucharest;

Father Boca, A., 2012, A Life dedicated to the Change of Our Life, Agaton Publishing House, Fagaras;

Drăganu, T., 1998, Drept constitutional si instituţii politice, Constitutional Right and Political institutions vol. I, Lumina Lex Publishing House, Bucharest;

Harris, D.J., Gomien, D. & Zwook, L., 1997, Convention Europeénne des Droits de l'Homme et Charte Sociale Europeénne: droit et pratique, Editions du Conseil de l'Europe, Strasbourg;

Kant, I., 2007, Critique of the Faculty of Judgement, All Publishing House, Bucharest;

Micu, D., 2007, Human Rights Guarantee, All Publishing House, Bucharest;

Muraru, I & Tănăsescu, S., 2013, Constitutional Law and Political Institutions, C.H. Beck Publishing House, Bucharest;

Sudre, F., 2006, European and International Law on Human Rights, Polirom Publishing House, Bucharest.

7. CONSTITUTION AND CONSTITUTIONALISM CONTEMPORARY ISSUE

Abstract:

In a democratic society, the judicial legitimacy of the state and its power, of its institutions, but also the social and political grounds are generated and determined by the Constitution, defined as expressively as possible as being: "The fundamental political and judicial settlement of a people" (I. Deleanu)

The supremacy of the Constitution has as main effect the conformity of the entire system of law with the constitutional norms. Guaranteeing the compliance with this principle, essential for the state of law, is first of all an attribution of the Constitutional Court, but also an obligation of the legislative power to receive, through the adopted normative acts, in content and in form, the constitutional norms.

Altering the fundamental law of a state represents a political and judicial act extremely complex with major meanings and implications for the socio-political and national systems, but also for each individual. This is why such measure should be very well justified, to answer certain socio-political and legal needs well shaped and mainly to match the principles and rules specific to a democratic constitutional and state system, by insuring its stability and functionality.

These are a few aspects of the Romanian contemporary constitutionalism that this study shall critically analyse in order to differentiate between the constitutional ideal and reality.

Key words:

Constitution/ constitutional supremacy/ constitutional ideal and reality/ fundamental rights/ discretionary power of the state/constitutional reform

I. Political and judicial meanings of the Constitution

For any people, for any form of modern social state organization, the Constitution was and is an ideal given by the meanings and role of the fundamental law especially for each one's social existence.

In modern history, starting with the 18th century, the *constitution* has been imposed along with other major institutions created with the purpose of expressing the political, economic or legal structural transformations as the fundamental law of a state. Towards the importance and meanings of the Constitution, of the practices in this area, it is considered as the fundamental political and judicial settlement of a state. This is why the Constitution was and is created in a broader vision, exceeding the politics, not only as a fundamental law, but also as a political and state reality identifiable with the society it creates or shapes and for whom its adoption has the meaning of a true revolution.

The constitution states the fundamental principles of the economic, political, social and legal life, in accordance with the fundamental values promoted and protected by the state. The people, according to Hegel, must have, for his constitution, the feeling of his law and state of fact, thus it may exist, in an exterior form, but without meaning and value. How current are the words of the great philosopher saying that "The constitution of any given nation depends in general on the character and development of its self-consciousness".

The value, content and meanings of the constitution as an ideal of a democratic society were clearly stated by the constitutional acts and constitutions opening the way for the constitutional process. Thus, the French Declaration of the Rights of Man and of the Citizen of 1789 stated that "Any society, in which no provision is made for guaranteeing rights or for the separation of powers, has no Constitution". The United States Constitution, the first written constitution in the world, in 1787, stated in its preamble that "We the People of the United States, in Order to form a more perfect Union, establish Justice, insure domestic Tranquillity, provide for the common defence, promote the general Welfare, and secure the Blessings of Liberty to ourselves and our Posterity, do ordain and establish this Constitution for the United States of America". As stated by the American legalists the spirit of constitutionalism has found its climax in the American Constitution. Therefore, right from its apparition, the constitution has been considered and analysed in opposition to absolutism, as a limitation in the arbitrary performance of power. Once this purpose has been fulfilled, the constitutionalism continued to play an important and, most of all, progressive role in history, aiming the efficient guarantee of the fundamental rights and freedoms for citizen.

The ideal of constitutionalism is best expressed by the notion of the *state of law*. Moving from the state's law to the state of law was and still remains a long and difficult process enlisted between the poles of contradictory values. Conceptually, on the foundation of the construction of the state of law is the idea of rationalizing the system of law and of emphasizing its efficacy. The essential requirement of the constitutional ideal of the state of law is represented by the subordination of the state towards the law and the limitation of the state's power using the law. The supremacy of the law and, implicitly, of the constitution, forces the state authorities to comply with the fundamental rights and freedoms of the citizens, to withheld from any arbitrary interference in their performance, moreover to adopt politically and legally appropriate and necessary means for the preservation and affirmation of the fundamental rights.

Indeed, the constitutions, in a state of law which assumes the compliance of legality and the rule of law, the protection of the individual and of the citizen in his relations with the power, the performance of the entire state activity based on and within the strict limits of the law, are or might be an obstacle in the way of the arbitrary, if they express the general will and their respect becomes a "religion" for the governors.

The ideal of the constitution, as well as of the constitutionalism, is also expressed by the concept of the supremacy of the constitution. We may say that the supremacy of the constitution is one of its qualities placing it on top of the politico-legal institutions of a state and makes the constitution the source of all regulations in the political, economic, social and legal areas. The most important consequences of the supremacy of the constitution are the conformity of the entire legal system with the constitutional norms and the fundamental obligation of the state authorities to perform their attributions within the limit and in the spirit of the constitution.

Of course, the constitution's supremacy would represent only an ideal if there were not any specific guarantees which mainly allow the control of power and the avoidance of its evolution towards the arbitrary. Among these guarantees, only two of them are more important: the control of the constitutionality of the laws which represent an important counterweight to the parliamentary and governmental powers, while the second one refers to the establishment of the principle to free access to justice. In a constitutional system based on the constitution's supremacy, the control performed by the courts represent an important guarantee of the compliance with the citizens' rights and freedoms, especially in their relations with the executive authorities.

The essence and finality of the constitution, as well as of the constitutionalism as a historic process consists in the achievement of a balance between different realities and forces, but which must coexist and harmonize to insure the social stability, the individual freedom, but also the legitimacy and functionality of the state's authorities. In other words, the purpose of a democratic constitution consists in the achievement of a fair and rational balance between different realities, between individual and public interest. In the meaning of the above mentioned, Prof Ioan Muraru stated that "In socio-legal and contemporary state realities, the constitutionalism must be seen as a complex politico-legal status, expressing at least two aspects: a) on the one hand, the constitution must reflect the demands of the movement of ideas (originating in its evolution) on the state of law and the democracy, public freedoms, organization, functioning and balance of powers; b) on the other hand, the large reflection of the subjects of law regarding the constitutional provisions. This mutual reflection is the only one able to insure the efficiency and viability of the constitution; it may insure the concordance between the constitutional rules and the political practice".

We have discussed about what could be considered as the ideal of the constitution and the constitutionalism. The reality of a constitution mainly represents the interpretation and application of the fundamental law, but especially the compliance with its provisions by the public authorities. There cannot be an ideal, perfect and immutable constitution. The constitution, as fundamental law, in order to be efficient, must be adjusted to the social, economic and political realities of the state. The dynamic of these factors shall eventually determine alterations of the constitutional norms. The achievement of an adequate relation between the constitution and the political, ideological, economic and state's realities is a complex matter, which must not be formally understood. We emphasize the fact that strictly juridical, the constitution may define both a liberal regime, as well as dictatorial one. If in any type of state, either democratic, or totalitarian there is a constitution, one cannot state that there is a real constitutional regime everywhere. The features of the constitutional regime existing at some point in history in a state, but also the way in which is perceived and complied with, the constitution determines the reality of the fundamental law and of the constitutionalism.

The differences which may arise between the constitutional ideal above expressed, and on the other hand, the reality of the constitutionalism existing in every state is justified by objective and subjective factors. Among the objectives factors, we identify:

a) the dynamic of the social life in relation to the stability of the constitution. The inevitable transformations in the social, economic, political or legal life of a state led to a distance between these realities and the viability and efficiency of the constitutional norms. This situation is one of the factors determining the revision of the fundamental law;

b) the constitution has all the features of a normative act, therefore the application of the fundamental law requires an interpretation of the public authorities, which may imply a different reception of the constitution;

c) there may be cases in which the constitutional regulations, though democratic in their essence are in contrast with the socio-economic realities of the moment, inferior towards the democratic constitutional principles. Such situation inevitably leads to a reduced reception of the constitutional norms among the population and to its inefficiency. The history of the Romanian constitutionalism offers a conclusive example in this meaning, if we consider the period between 1866-1938, in which the reality of the Romanian constitutionalism was inferior to the values and principles stated by the Constitutions of 1866 and 1923.

There are also subjective factors we might determine a difference between the constitutional values, and on the other hand the way in which are respected and applied. The tendency of the central authorities to abuse the power, attempting to authoritatively exercise powers, sometimes in disregard with the constitutionals norms, represents an important subjective factor denaturising the norms and spirit of the constitution, with the consequence of building a political, economic and social reality obviously contrasting with the fundamental law.

We shall exemplify the above mentioned with brief mentions to the Romanian Constitutions of 1866, 1923 and 1991.

The Constitution of 1866 was mainly a liberal constitution which stated in the area of the legal and political practice the Romanian liberalism, emphasizing the "historical role and purpose" of the Romanian bourgeoisie in the creation of a form of government and of democratic institutions based on the creative valorisation of our traditions in this area. The functionality of the Constitution raised a controverted issue regarding the incapacity of the monarchy and of the central authorities of that time to adjust to the social realities of the country. From a socio-economic perspective, the Romanian society was polarized, the middle class being extremely thin as average (formed only by clerks and liberal professionals). In exchange, the majority of the peasantry recently released from servitude, mostly analphabetic, was in contrast with the reduced average of large landowners, many of them having received a good education in western schools. Under these conditions, the Romanian monarchy system and the Romanian state system were compelled to adjust the political parliamentary regime to the existent social and political structure, and from here on sprang most of the limits of the Romanian constitutionalism, because the general interests of society interfered and were contradictory with the interests of the landowners, amid a weak economic power of the bourgeoisie crumbled into several factions and political groups. To all these, were added the personal ambitions of the politicians who, often, have seriously complicated the nature of the political area, hardening the acceleration of reforms and the amplitude of the modernization.

Analysed from a historical-political perspective, the Constitution of 1923, as an expression of the real balance of forces during 1919-1923 has represented the main legal settlement on whose base functioned the fundamental institutions of the united Romania, offering the Romanian state the monarchism, but based on the democratic parliamentary regime. The Constitution of 1923 maintains most of the structure of the Constitution of 1866, taking and deepening a series of principles offering the feature of modernity, as well as the real possibility for democratizing the interwar Romanian state and society. In this meaning, under the empire of this Constitution, the principles of representativeness, the separation of powers, the principle of legality and legitimacy of the laws, of the control of constitutionality, as well as the principles regarding the elective system and of the regime of property were much stronger than the one mentioned by the settlement in 1866. So, the Constitution of 1923 has represented a progress in the democratization of the Romanian society.

The application of the Constitution of 1923 has beard the mark of two trends: on the one hand, a series of subsequent legislations have tried to develop the democratic content of some provisions, and on the other hand, certain laws have narrowed the rights and fundamental freedoms. The position of the monarchy in the political practice has led to the reality that the appointment of the Government by the king, followed by the dissolution of the legislative bodies and the organization of new elections was, first of all, the expression of certain deals between the monarch and the representatives of the main parties, consultations which in most cases were the result of subjectivism and personal ambitions represented by the governmental changes. During the interwar period, 11 legislative bodies succeeded, representing their development within half the legal time stated by the Constitution.

Undoubtedly, the Romanian Constitution in force, adopted on 1991 has represented the rebirth of the Romanian constitutional life. The fundamental law of the state represents the fundamental legislative framework for the organization and functioning of the Romanian state and society on democratic bases. Nevertheless, the reality of the contemporary Romanian constitutionalism proves, in most cases, an abandonment of the values and spirit of the Constitution from certain central authorities, through their obvious intent to evolve towards the discretionary performance of the attributions given to them by the law and the biased interpretation of certain constitutional norms. We shall present two examples :

- The right to a decent living is stated by Art 47 of the Romanian Constitution, which states that: "The State shall be bound to take measures of economic development and social protection, of a nature to ensure a decent living standard for its citizens". It is a fundamental human right based in the feature as "social state" of the Romanian state, mentioned by Art 1 Para 3 of the Constitution which entails constitutional obligations for the state, namely to adopt political and legislative decisions in the political, economic and social areas, whose finality to be represented not only by the guaranteeing, but also the achievement of this fundamental right. This obligation is more of a constitutional and political ideal, than a legal obligation, because there are no normative criteria based on which it could be evaluated by the constitutional court, if the legislative measures adopted by the state have as result the material, effective, and not theoretical, abstract insurance of decent living for all citizens. The only sanctions if the state does not comply with these positive obligations have a preponderant political nature, and indirectly a constitutional one, such as the adoption of a motion of no confidence for the Parliament.

- According to Art 80 of the Romanian Constitution, the President has the obligation to guard the observance of the Constitution and the proper functioning of the public authorities. In this purpose, the president is the mediator between the state's powers, but also between state and society. It is a constitutional provision which may remain in the area of the constitutional ideal, or a political principle, because it is not concretized under the aspect of the means and procedures for achievement, nor is accompanied by specific constitutional sanctions. The Romanian political practice of the last decade proved that there is the possibility of a discretionary manifestation of power from the Chief of state based on this constitutional text.

Obviously, the examples could continue. We aim to emphasize that the constitutional norm, even if in most cases it has the value of a principles, it imposes in its logic the compliance with the syllogism hypothesis – disposition – sanction, to not only stay within the area of the constitutional ideal.

The modification of the Constitution could be necessary if the social and political realities impose it. We consider that the state authorities should be more concerned by the appropriate application of the fundamental law and only in subsidiary by its possible modification. Further, we shall analyse certain legal aspects and aspects of other nature entailed by the initiatives to revise the Romanian Constitution.

II. Constitutional stability and reform

The decision to initiate the revision of the Constitution of a state is, without any doubt, a political one, but in the same time it must have legal basis and to correspond to a historical need of the social system organized as a state from the perspective of its subsequent evolution. Therefore, the revision of the constitution must not be subordinated to political interests at that time, no matter how beautiful they are wrapped, but to the social general interest, well-shaped and possible to be legally expressed.

The late Prof Antonie Iorgovan rightfully stated that "In terms of the revision of the Constitution, we dare to say that where there is a political normal life, one shall express cautious restraints, the imperfections of the texts in their confrontation with life, with subsequent realities are corrected by the interpretations of the Constitutional Courts, namely by the parliamentary customs or traditions, reason for which the western literature does not longer talks about the Constitution, but about the constitutional block" [1].

The revision of the Constitution cannot have as result the satisfaction of the political interests of the temporary holders of power. In the direction of strengthening the discretionary power of the state, with the inadmissible consequence of damaging certain democratic values and principles, unlike the political and institutional pluralism, the principle of the separation of powers or the principle of the legislative supremacy of the Parliament. Also, the limitations of the Romanian constitutional revision are stated by Art 152 of the Constitution, though the political interpretation of these constitutional provisions may denaturise their meaning and finality.

The two and a half decades of democratic constitutional life in Romania proved that the political power, by its decisions, numerous times it has denaturised the constitutional principles and rules using interpretations contrary to the democratic spirit of the fundamental law, for political purposes and the support of conjectural interests. The consequences were and still are obvious: the limitation or violation of certain rights and fundamental freedoms, the generation of social tensions, non-compliance with the constitutional role of the state's institutions, in other words political actions, some dressed with a legal aspect, contrary to the constitutionalism which must characterize the Romanian state of law.

Under these conditions, a possible step in revising the fundamental law should be focused on the need to strengthen and enhancement of the constitutional guarantees for complying with the requirements and values of the state of law, to avoid excessive power specific to the politics exclusively subordinated to group interests, mostly conjectural and contrary to the Romanian people's interests, which according to Art 2 Para 1 of the Constitution has the national sovereignty.

In our view, the concern among politicians and state authorities in the current period compared to the current content of the fundamental law should be guided not so much towards the change of the Constitution, but especially towards the correct interpretation and application of it and respect of the democratic purpose of the constitutional institutions. To strengthen the rule of law in Romania, it is necessary that political parties, especially those in power, all state authorities to act or perform their duties within a *loyal constitutional behaviour* involving respect for the democratic meanings and significance of the Constitution.

Some proposals to revise the Romania fundamental law aim to modification of the constitutional system of bicameralism to unicameralism and strengthen the executive power, especially the presidential institution.

We consider that the Romanian bicameralism is appropriate for the state and social system of this historic moment, better reflecting the need to achieve not only the efficiency of the legislative parliamentary procedures, but especially "norming" and the quality of the legislation. Bicameralism is a necessity for Romania, for the Parliament to represent a viable counterweight to the executive, in the context of the exigencies and balance of the powers in a democratic state. Rightfully, late Prof Antonoe Iorgovan pointed out: "It should represent a high political risk, in that post-revolutionary tension, that in Romania be projected a unicameral Parliament, such risk still being present at this hour, under the conditions in which we can no longer talk about a political life established on the normal aisles of the democratic doctrines accepted by the West (social-democratic doctrine, Christian-democratic doctrine, liberal doctrines and ecologist doctrines) [2].

Unicameralism in a semi-presidential constitutional system, such as the Romanian one, in which the powers of the head of state and generally of the executive are significant, also considering the current excessive politicking, would have as consequence the serious deterioration of the institutional balance between the legislative and executive, resulting in the increase of the discretionary power of the executive and the minimization of the Parliament's role as a supreme representative organ and of the Romanian people, as single legislative authority of the state, as stated by Art 61 Para 1 of the Constitution. The evolution to a unicameral Parliament must not be considered as a simple act as unfortunately it results from the project law on the revision of the Constitution drafted by the Government, but it requires a general modification of the Romanian constitutional system, a reconfiguration of the role and attributions of the state authorities, in order to preserve the balance between legislative and executive and to not create the possibility of an evolution towards an overrated preponderance of the institution of the head of state in relation to the Parliament. We emphasize the fact that all European states with a unitary structure which have a unicameral Parliament also have a constitutional parliamentary system in which the head of state has limited attributions regarding the governing.

We do not aim to perform a thorough analysis of this issue, underlining only the conclusion that the Romanian unicameralism could be justified both politically and constitutionally, and appropriate to the democratic values in a state of law only if the legitimacy and role of the Romanian Presidency, as constitutional institution, is fundamentally altered. The election of the President should be performed by the Parliament. Also, in the case of a unicameral parliamentary structure, it is necessary to significantly reduce the attributions of the President in relation to the executive. Such reconfiguration of the state institutions should increase the role and attributions of the Constitutional Court and of the justice, representing guarantees of the supremacy of the law and of the Constitution also avoiding the abuse of power of the other state institutions. In Romania, the unicameralism could only be associated with the existence of a constitutional system. The unicameralism has the nature to generate a disproportion between the Parliament and the executive, by that that a single chamber of the Parliament, in Romania, does not represent a satisfactory guarantee to represent an efficient counterweight for the executive, especially that the constitutional attributions of the President as participant in the governing are obviously significant. The dispute between bicameralism and unicameralism with application to the case of Romania is very well presented by the late Prof Antonie Iorgovan: "...any bicameral or unicameral parliamentary system could generate serious dysfunctionalities, as expressed by Prof Tudor Drăganu, no matter how good the constitutional solution might be, if the parliamentary practice shows politicking, demagogy and irresponsibility" [3].

Does the current Romanian parliamentary system corresponds to the exigencies of the democratic requirements of the bicameralism and is it fit for the performance of the role and functions of the Parliament? The late Prof Tudor Drăganu, in a large study of flawless argumentative logic answered this question: "The revised Constitution establishes a system claiming to be bicameral, but currently functioning as a unicameral one, convicted to break, by some of its aspects, certain elementary principles of the parliamentary regime and which embraces the danger of future serious dysfunctionalities in the performance of the legislative activity" [4]. The illustrious professor considered that the law amending the Constitution contains no explicit reference to the number of deputies and senators; it questions the substantial legitimacy of the two chambers because their members are appointed by the same body and by the same type of electoral system and electoral scrutiny; the chambers' legislative powers are not sufficiently differentiated; exercising the right for a legislative initiative by senators and deputies, as it is stated, generates constitutional contradictions.

We support that the prospect of a constitutional revision to regulate the differentiation between the two chambers using particular types of representation. The comparative law provides sufficient examples of this kind (Spain, Italy and France) and even the Romanian electoral Law of 27 March 1926 provides a benchmark in this regard. The Senate may represent the interests of the local communities. Thus, Senators could be elected by an electoral college consisting of the elected members of local councils. Interesting to note is that in the draft of the Constitution in 1991, the Senate was designed as a representative of the local communities, grouped in counties and in Bucharest.

The criticism of Prof Tudor Drăganu is fair, according to which the current constitutional regulation does not provide a functional difference between the two chambers. This aspect was also noticed by the Constitutional Court, which referring to the parliamentary legislative procedure inserted by the project for revising the Constitution underlined that: "The cascade examination of the draft laws, in a chamber of first lecture, and in the one the second lecture, transforms the bicameral Parliament into an unicameral one" [5]. Therefore a new initiative for the modification of the fundamental law should also consider this aspect and to perform a real and functional differentiation between the two Chambers.

The final part of this study shall refer to certain aspects that we consider necessary to be stated by a future procedure for revising the Constitution.

As above mentioned, unlike the excessive politicking and discretionary use of power from the executive contrary to the spirit and letter of the Constitution, with the consequence of violating certain rights and fundamental freedoms, manifested during the past two decades of democracy in Romania, we consider that the scientific approach and not only in the area of the revision of the fundamental law should be oriented towards solutions guaranteeing the values of the state of law, limiting the violations of the constitutional provisions for the purpose of particular interests and to avoid the excessive power of the state authorities.

1. Art 114 Para 1 of the current regulation states that: "The Government may assume responsibility before the Chamber of Deputies and the Senate, in joint sitting, upon a programme, a general policy statement, or a bill".

The responsibility of the Government has a political feature and is a procedural means by which it is avoided the phenomenon of the "*dissociation of majorities*" [6] for the case in which the in Parliament the majority necessary for the adoption of a measure proposed by the Government was not gathered. In order to determine the legislative forum to adopt its measure, the Government, using the procedure of assuming the responsibility conditions the performance of its activity by requesting a vote of trust. This constitutional procedure guarantees that the majority required for the dissolution of the Government, in the case of a censure motion to coincide with that for rejecting the law, the programme or the political statement to which the Government connects its existence.

Adjusting the laws as effect of invoking the political responsibility of the Government has as important consequence the absence of any parliamentary debates or deliberations on the draft law. If the Government is supported by a comfortable majority of the Parliament, this procedure could result in the adoption of the laws by "bypassing the Parliament", which could have negative consequences on the compliance with the principle of the separation of powers, but also regarding the role of the Parliament, as it is defined by Art 61 of the Constitution. As consequence, using such constitutional procedure by the Government for the adoption of a law must have an exceptional feature, justified by a political situation and a social imperative very well shaped.

This aspect of extreme importance for the compliance with the democratic principles of the state of law by the Government was well emphasized by the Romanian Constitutional Court: "This simplified means of legislation must be used *in extremis*, when the adoption of the draft law using the common or the emergency procedure is no longer available or when the political structure of the Parliament does not allow the adoption of the draft law using one of the above mentioned procedures" [7]. The political practice of the Government for the past years has been contrary to these rules and principles. The Executive frequently assumed its responsibility not only for a single law, but also for packages of laws, without any justification in the meanings stated by the Constitutional Court.

The Government's politicking clearly expressed by the frequency of using this constitutional procedure seriously harms the principle of the political plurality, which is an important value of the system of law stated by Art 1 Para 3 of the Constitution, but also of the principle of the parliamentary right stating that "the opposition shall express and the majority shall decide" [8]. "Denying the right of the opposition to express itself is synonym with denying the political plurality, which according to Art 1 Para 3 of the Constitution represents a supreme and guaranteed value". The principle "the majority shall decide, the opposition shall express itself" refers to that throughout the organization and functioning of the parliamentary Chambers be assured that the majority is not obstructed especially in the performance of the parliamentary procedure, and on the other hand that the majority rule only after the opposition has spoken" [8]. The censorship of the Constitutional Court proved to be insufficient and inefficient in order to determine the Government to comply with these values of the state of law.

III. Conclusions

In the context of these arguments, we propose that in the perspective of a constitutional revision to limit the right of the Government to entail its responsibility for a single draft law in a parliamentary session.

All post-December Governments have massively used the practice of the emergency ordinances, practice blamed by the literature.

The conditions and interdictions stated by the Law No 429/2003 for the revision of the Constitution of Romania regarding the constitutional regime of the emergency ordinances, proved to be insufficient in order to limit this practice of the Executive, also the control of the Constitutional Court proved insufficient and even inefficient. The consequence of such practice is the violation of the role of the Parliament as single "legislative authority of the state" (Art 61 of the Constitution) and the creation of an imbalance between executive and legislative by accentuating the discretionary power of the Government, which in most cases turned into excessive power.

We propose that in the perspective of a future revision of the fundamental law, Art 115 Para 6 be modified in the meaning of prohibiting the adoption of emergency ordinances in the area of the organic laws. In this meaning it is protected an important area of social relations considered by the constitutional legislator as essential for the social and state system, from the excess of power of the executive by issuing emergency ordinances.

In the current conditions characterized by the executive's trend to profit from the obvious politicking and to unduly and dangerously force the limits of the Constitution and of the democratic constitutionalism it is necessary to create mechanisms for the control of the executive's activity in order to really guarantee the supremacy of the Constitution and the principles of the state of law.

According to our opinion, it is necessary that the role of the Constitutional Court as guarantor of the fundamental law be amplified by new attributions with the purpose of limiting the excess of power of the state's authorities. We do not agree with the statements made by the literature that a possible amelioration of the constitutional justice could be achieved by reducing the attributions of the court of administrative contentious [9]. It is true that the Constitutional Court has ruled certain questionable decisions under the aspect of compliance with the limitations of its attributions according to the Constitution, by assuming the role as positive legislator [10]. The reduction of the attributions of the constitutional court for this reason is not a legally fundamental decision. Of course, the reduction of the attributions of a state authority has as consequence the elimination of the risk for deficient performance. This is not the way to achieve the perfection of the activity of a state authority in a state of law, but by the continuous search for legal solutions for better conditions for the performance of such attributions, which proved to be necessary for the state and social system.

The attributions of the Constitutional Court might as well include the one about ruling upon the constitutionality of the administrative acts exempted from the control for legality of the courts of administrative contentious. This category of administrative acts, to which Art 126 Para 6 of the Constitution and the Law No 544/2004 on the administrative contentious refer to, are extremely important for the entire social and state system. Therefore, it is necessary a control for constitutionality, because in its absence the discretionary power of the issuant administrative authority is unlimited with the consequence of a possible excessive limitation of the rights and fundamental freedoms or of the violation of certain important constitutional values. For the same arguments, our Constitutional Court should be able to control under the aspect of constitutionality the presidential decrees establishing the referendum.

The High Court of Cassation and Justice has the competence to adopt decisions using the procedure of the appeal in the interests of the law, which are mandatory for the courts. In the absence of any form of control for legality or constitutionality, the practice proved in numerous situations that the Supreme Court overcame its attribution to interpret the law, and by such decisions it modified or completed normative acts, acting as a real legislator, thus violating the principle of the separation of powers [11]. With the purpose of avoiding the excessive power of the Constitutional Court, we consider necessary the establishment for the Constitutional Court of the competence to rule upon the constitutionality of the decisions of the High Court of Cassation and Justice, adopted using the procedure of the appeal in the interests of the law.

The proportionality is a fundamental principle of the law expressly stated by constitutional and legislative regulations and international legal instruments. It is based on the values of the rational law of justice and equity and expresses the existence of a balanced or appropriate relation between actions, phenomena or situations, also being a criterion for limiting the measures ordered by the state authorities to what is necessary for the achievement of a legitimate purpose, thus guaranteeing the fundamental rights and avoiding the excessive powers of the state authorities. The proportionality is a basic principle of the European Union, being expressly stated by Art 5 of the Treaty on the European Union [12].

We consider that the express statement of this principle only by Art 53 of the Constitution, with application in the area of limiting the exercise of certain rights is insufficient for the valorisation of the entire meaning and importance of the principle for the rule of law.

It is useful the addition to Art 1 of the Constitution of a new paragraph stating that "*The performance of the state power must be proportionate and indiscriminate*". This new constitutional statement could represent a true constitutional obligation for all state authorities to perform their attributions so that the measures adopted to be within the limits of the discretionary power recognized by the law. Also, it is created the possibility for the Constitutional Court to sanction using the control for constitutionality of the laws and ordinances the excess of power in the Parliament's and Government's activities, using as criterion the principle of proportionality.

References

Iorgovan, A. (2001). The revision of the Constitution and bicameralism. Journal of public law (1), p. 23;

Iorgovan, A. (2001). The revision of the Constitution and bicameralism. Journal of public law (1), pp. 18-19;

Iorgovan, A. (2001). The revision of the Constitution and bicameralism. Journal of public law (1), p. 16;

Draganu, T. (2003). Some critical considerations on the bicameral system established by the Constitution revision law adopted by the Chamber of Deputies and in the Senate. Journal of public law (4), p. 55-66;

Decision No 148 of 16 April 2003, published in the Official Gazette No 317/12 May 2003;

Iancu, Gh. (2010). Constitutional law and public institutions. Bucharest: All Beck, p.482;

Decision No 1557 of 18 November 2009, published in the Official Gazette No 40/19 January 2010;

Muraru I., Constantinescu M. (2005). Romanian parliamentary law. Bucharest: All Beck, pp.55-69;

Sparrow, G. (2010). The legal nature of the constitutional courts and their place in the system of public authorities. Public Law Review (1), p. 33;

Decision No 356/2007, published in the Official Gazette No 322/14 May 2007; Decision No 98/2008, published in the Official Gazette No 140/22 February 2008;

Andreescu, M. (2011). The constitutionality of the appeal in the interest of the law and of the pronounced decisions. Judicial Courier (1), pp. 32-36;

Andreescu, M. (2010). Proportionality, a principle of European Union law. Judicial Courier (10), pp. 593-598; Andreescu, M., Puran, A. (2016);

Constitutional law. General theory and constitutional institutions. Bucharest: Ch. Beck, pp. 123-130.

8. THE LIMITS OF STATE POWER IN A DEMOCRATIC SOCIETY

Abstract:

The coding is not only the expression of the political will of the law maker, it firstly is a complex juridical technique for the choosing and systematization of the normative content necessary and adequate to certain social, political, economic, institutional realities. Since Constitution is a law, yet it nevertheless distinguishes itself from the law, the problem is to establish which juridical norms it contains. The solving of this problem needs to consider the specific of the fundamental law and also of the requirements of the coding theory. The determining with all scientific stringency of the normative content of the Constitution is indispensible both for the removal of any inaccuracy in delimiting the differences from the law, for the stability and predictability of the fundamental law and last, but not the least, for the reality and effectiveness of its supremacy.

In our study we realize an analysis based on compared criterions of the techniques and exigencies for the choosing and systematization of the constitutional norms with reference to their specific, to the practice of other states and within a historical context. The analysis is aiming to the actual proposals for the revising of the Constitution.

Key words:

Constitutional norms / constitutional norm establishing criterions / technical - juridical structure / supremacy of Constitution / normative content

I. Historic argument

From the beginning up to the present the human society is marked by two constants that have ontological value: *the struggle for power* and on the other hand *the fight against the power*, both in situations where it is illegitimate because it takes the form of dictatorship or tyranny, also in the versions of apparent legitimacy, especially in democratic societies, such as for example the legitimate political activity of the opposition to come to power or the actions of civil society and individuals against abuse of power.

These ontological constants of any human society are inevitable no matter of the social form of organization or characteristics of political regimes, including in democratic societies because the existential and functioning essence of any social system is the expression of the contradictory difference between governors and the governed, between society as a whole and on the other hand, the man in his concrete and personality, between the normative order and moral values, between law and liberty, between public interest and private interest and of course between the vocation of human intangible fundamental rights, and on the other hand the public interest of the state to condition, limit and restrict their exercise.

These contradictions, if they remain in their absolute form, by antagonist excellence can be destructive to an organized state society, as history has shown. History shows the political and legal solutions which, especially in the modern period, were devoted to avoid dictatorial forms of power exercising. Here are some of them established since the first written constitution in the world - the US Constitution, adopted in 1787 - Declaration (French) of human and citizen rights on 1789, up to the internal and international contemporary political and legal instruments: supremacy of the Law and Constitution, separation and balance of powers within the state, proclamation and guarantee of the fundamental rights and freedoms, constitutional and judicial control.

Incontestable these principles in fact and the features of the lawful right materialized and guaranteed constitutionally define the contemporary democratic societies and virtually eliminates totalitarian, dictatorial forms of state power.

However the differences and contradictions mentioned above, because they are ontological constants of society, they exist in any democratic society. In addition there is a subtle situation, namely the difference between the legality of state decisions and on the other hand the state legitimacy. These realities may cause or encourage excess of the power of authorities in societies built upon the principles of modern constitutionalism.

In this context remains a problem of essence, not only theoretical but also practical to determine the limits of state power in a democratic society in concrete in România and to find solutions in cases of excessive form of manifestation of state authority.

II. Ideality and reality of democracy. About the dictatorship in democracy

The doctrine, in its majority reveals an insurmountable contradiction that exists between the democratic political regimes and, on the other hand those considered to be dictatorial, or simply between dictatorship and democracy.

Dictatorship means centralization and concentration of power, denial of pluralism in all its forms, absolute or discretionary power of the governors, coercion and excessive limitations of individual liberties, rigid separation of the governors from the governed, inexistence or formal existence of constitutional guarantees of human rights, inexistence or fictitious, formal character of principles essential to the state organization of society, such as principle of supremacy of law and constitution. For a synthetic manner of speech, dictatorship represents the annulment, dissolution or in the best case, the minimizing of the individuality of the singular, of diversity and affirmation of unity as abstract and constraining generality.

Unlike this, democracy is associated with the idea of a lawful state, focused on the principle becoming real and applicable of the supremacy of law and constitution. The centralization and concentration of power is replaced, as a modality of organizing of state powers, with the principle for their separation and balance. Pluralism in all its forms is institutionalized and guaranteed. The individual freedoms are also consecrated and guaranteed, while their exercise is governed by the rule according to which: the limit of any individual freedom is the need to respect others' similar freedoms. The legitimacy of state power involves the distinction between the being or essence of power and on the other hand, its exercise. In a democratic regime is not necessary to demonstrate the legitimacy of power as such because the axiom according to which " the holder of power is the people or nation" does not require demonstration, being a prerequisite for the entire political and legal construction of the state organized society Instead, any democratic government must find ways through which the exercising of power, in other words, the phenomenality of power be legitimate and lawful. Such a legitimacy is achieved when between essence (power in itself owned by the people) and forms of exercising (the phenomenon of power) there are no irreconcilable contradictions. The legitimacy of the exercise of power in case of democratic political regimes means reflecting the essence of power in its phenomenality, respectively in the organizing and exercising manner. Therefore, in case of democracy there is always a conceptual distinction, and a real one between the legitimacy of the essence of power that requires no demonstration, this results as such by the mere proclamation of the principle that the power has as its holder the people and on the other hand, the phenomenal legitimacy of organizing and exercising of power, that is not a "given" but a construction, firstly constitutional, realized in the concrete forms of institutional organization and exercising of state power. The legitimacy of the organizing and exercising of power is outside the power's phenomenality, in the meaning that the phenomenality is not the source of its legitimacy, but this is constructed in a relation whose content is the correspondence between the essence of power and the manifestation forms.

The power, in its essence, can be considered a "thing in itself", in the Kantian sense, because the full knowledge of the essence will never be possible. Reality of the state power considered in the relationship between essence and phenomenon reveals another aspect: the phenomenality of power can never fully correspond to the essence of power. The object of knowledge for the legal or political science is the phenomenon of power and not its essence. Therefore, the legitimacy of power phenomenal manifestation represents an ideal of which, the concrete forms of organization and exercising of power, get closer without ever touching it.

The legitimacy of power's phenomenality lies among others in achieving the principle of representation. This principle highlights very well the distinction between the being or essence of power and on the other hand the phenomenon of power. The holder of power cannot exercise it directly, only in exceptional circumstances. The essence is not the manifestation of power. The exercise of power reflects the being of power without containing it. Thus, the state institutions exercise the power without holding it, therefore, they need a recognition of the legitimacy of the acts of power, actually conferred mainly by applying the principle of representation.

The power and its phenomenality are undoubtedly at the heart of democracy. If the phenomenal legitimacy of power is an ideal of which the concrete forms of institutional embodiment through the principle of representation can get closer, results thus that democracy in its essence is still an ideal related to which the social and political reality is constructed and manifested, without letting the democratic ideal to coincide with the social and political reality. It is relevant in this regard the statement of Professor Ion Deleanu: "Democracy is a form of moral perfection. It dimensions the organization and operation of a power to humanize it and also the way of life of citizens to shape it."

It is necessary to distinguish between the *ideal democracy* that is a purely speculative construction based on the possible coincidence between the essence and the phenomenality of power, but also an ethical imperative that should mean the unity of will between the individual and society, and on the other hand, the *real democracy*, characterized through the contradictory dichotomy between the essence and the phenomenality of power, between the individual and society. Real democracy takes concrete forms, multiple manifestations (such as the form of "parliamentary or representative democracy "), is not an immutable given, but is in a continuous evolutionary process, in considering the historical progress as a finality, never possible to be achieved, the ideal democracy. The science of law has as a study topic the real democracy, or more precisely its forms of manifestation and for its implementation. Paradoxically, however, the legitimacy of any form of real democracy is conferred by the values and principles of ideal democracy, the latter forming mainly the studying topic for metaphysics.

Unlike dictatorship, democracy involves the rehabilitation of the individual, of the particular that is no longer absorbed and dissolved into the social abstract general or of the concentrated power. In democracy the individual has ontological value and manifests into existential coexistence with the social general. In other words, the individual has the meaning and power of the general, the latter being legitimate, precisely because it recognizes to the individual the existential and ontological dimension. The power, even in its concrete manifestations is the expression of the general as such, reflected for example in the notion of "public interest". In a democratic society the legitimacy of the act of power lies not in reflecting own generality (of public interest) but in respecting the individuality of diversity in all forms specific to existential pluralism. In constitutional terms, this evokes the relation between "majority and opposition".

The issue of democracy cannot be reduced to the phenomenon of power as it seems to result from the constitutional definition of democracy that we find in Article 2 of the Constitution of French Republic: "government of the people by the people and for the people". The essence of democracy, in our opinion, is the forms and content of the concrete relation between society and individual. The relation expresses a unilateral contradiction because the society can contradict the individual (particularity and diversity), which is proper to dictatorship, but the individual does not contradict the society, situation particular to democracy. Furthermore, the dialectic report between the individual and society specific to democracy is an affirmative one, not containing a negation, such as Hegel argued. It is proper to democracy so that society asserts the individual (individuality and diversity), not to deny, therefore, to consecrate and guarantee the individuality and diversity. Any further analysis of the phenomenon of democracy involves references to the concepts of civilization and culture, the relationship between civilization, society and the individual.

In our opinion between dictatorship and democracy is obviously a contradiction, but one-sided: dictatorship is inconsistent and excludes democracy, yet democracy does not exclude the forms of dictatorship. The space and scope of this study do not allow further analysis of this interesting problem. However we mention that in doctrine are made referrals to forms of dictatorship that can characterize any democratic regime: parliamentary dictatorship, dictatorship of masses or the dictatorship of the majority. In all these situations the democratic reality, contradictions highlighted above become negative (majority excluded or ignoring the minority). Consequently, it gets to the exercising of authority in discretionary forms, which obviously contradicts the essential values of ideal democracy.

John Stuart Mill, in his works "Civilization," published in 1836 believes that civilization is contrary to the nature status or barbarism. A nation is civilized when the social conditions in which lives gives sufficient safety guarantees, so that social peace be a reality. Among consequences of higher civilization the most striking one, is the philosopher's opinion that the power tends to move from individuals and small communities to the masses. The importance of masses increases when that of individuals decreases. With the decreasing of individual's role, decreases the power of individual beliefs and the public opinion acquires supremacy. In this ideational context Stuart Mill pointed out that "the drawbacks of democracy lie precisely in this tyranny exercised by the masses, the majority of public opinion. Therefore, the political organization of representative governing must contain all guarantees for the individual against the tyranny of the masses. Among other measures, Stuart Mill suggested the representation of opinions minority in the Parliament.

The great philosopher findings are, in our opinion, fully valid also for the contemporary forms of real democracy or representative. That's why the realization of the principle of representation in any of the types of electoral system should allow as much as possible, the reduction or even elimination of the forms of dictatorship in a real democracy through enhancement of individualities, of the political minorities or otherwise. In this way, the progress of a democratic society becomes a balanced one based on a unilateral affirmative contradiction in which the masses affirm and do not deny individual, and the majority affirm the minorities. Thus, the *famous parliamentary principle "the minorities express and the majority decides"* should become*: legitimacy of the decision is given by the representativeness and power to express of minorities.*

III. Brief considerations regarding the concepts of "lawfulness" and "legitimacy"

Legality, as a feature that must characterize the legal acts of public authorities, has as central element the concept of "law". Andre Hauriou defined the law as a written general rule established by the public powers after deliberation, entailing direct or indirect acceptance of the governors[201]. Ion Deleanu defines just the "document that contains general and mandatory rules sanctioned through the coercive force of the state, when its application is not done out of conviction and is prone to produce application whenever arise the conditions foreseen in its hypothesis[202]."

In a broader meaning, the concept of law includes all legal acts that contain legal norms. The law in its restricted sense is the legal act of parliament drawn up in accordance with the constitution, according to an established procedure and which regulates the most important and general social rules. A special place in the legal system administered has the constitution defined as fundamental law, located on the top of legislative system, which includes legal rules of a higher legal force, which regulates fundamental and essential social relations, especially those concerning the establishment and exercising of state power.

The state of legality in the work of public authorities is based on the concepts of supremacy of the constitution and supremacy of law. The supremacy of constitution is a quality of the fundamental law that basically expresses its supreme legal force in the legal system. An important consequence of fundamental law supremacy is the compliance of entire law with the constitutional norms[203]. The notion of juridical supremacy of law is defined as "its feature that finds expression in the fact that the norms it establishes must not meet either of other norms, apart from the constitutional ones and the other legal acts issued by state bodies are subordinated to it in

[201] André Hauriou, Droit constitutionel et institution politiques, Ed. Montchrestien, Paris, 1972, p.137

[202] Ion Deleanu, Constitutional Law and Political Institutions, Europa Nova Publishing House, Bucharest, 1996, p.509

[203] For developments see Marius Andreescu, Florina Mitrofan, Constitutional Law, General theory, Publishing House of Pitești University, pp.61-68

terms of their legal effectiveness[204]".Therefore, the supremacy of law in the sense above is subsequent to the principle of supremacy of constitution. Important is that the legality, as a feature of the legal acts of state authorities involves the observance of the principle of supremacy of the constitution and law. The observance of these two principles is a fundamental constitutional obligation consecrated by the provisions of article 1 paragraph 5 of the Constitution. Failure to observe this obligation attracts the appropriate sanction of unconstitutionality or illegality of legal documents.

The legality of the legal acts of public authorities involves the following requirements: legal document to be issued in compliance with the competence prescribed by law; legal act to be issued in accordance with the procedure prescribed by law; legal act to respect the rules of law as superior legal force.

The "Legitimacy" is a complex category with multiple meanings and which is the topic for research for the general theory of law, philosophy of law, sociology and other disciplines. There are multiple meanings of this concept. We mention a few: legitimacy of power; the legitimacy of the political regime; legitimacy of governance; the legitimacy of the political system, etc. Referring to this concept Jean Leca said: "The term legitimacy designates the quality which enables the holder to a power to order or prohibit the ability to be heard without resorting to physical violence explicit or, what is meaning the same thing, an option recognized as normal to successfully use coercion if necessary[205]".The concept of legitimacy can be applied in case of legal acts issued by public authorities being related to the" margin of appreciation" recognized to them in the exercise of their prerogatives.

The application and observance of the principle of legality in the work of state authorities is a complex issue, because the exercise of state functions assumes the discretionary powers with which state bodies are invested or otherwise said, the right for appreciation of authorities regarding the moment of adoption and the contents of the measures ordered. What is important to note is that discretionary power cannot be opposed to the principle of legality, as a dimension of the lawful state.

---

[204] Tudor Draganu, Constitutional law and political institutions. Elementary Treaty, "Constitutional Law and political institutions, elementary Treaty, Lumina Lex Publishing House, Bucharest, 1999, volume II, p.362

[205] Dictionary of Sociological thinking, Polirom Publishing House, Bucharest, p.431

In our opinion, the legality represents a particular aspect of the legitimacy of the public authorities' legal acts. Thus, a legitimate legal act is a lawful legal act, issued within the margin of appreciation recognized by the public authorities, which does not generate discriminations, unjustified privileges or restrictions of the subjective rights and is appropriate to the situation in fact that determines its legal purpose. The legitimacy distinguishes between the discretionary power recognized by the state authorities, and on the other hand, the excess of power.

Not all legal documents which satisfy the legality conditions are legitimate. A legal act that complies with the formal legality, but is generating discriminations or privileges or unduly restricts the exercising of some subjective rights, or is not appropriate to the situation in fact, or to the purpose pursued by the law, is an illegitimate legal act. The legitimacy, as a feature of the legal acts of public administration authorities must be understood and applied in relation to the principle of supremacy of the Constitution.

IV. The discretionary power and power excess in a Democratic society

Antonie Iorgovan says that a problem of the essence of the lawful state is to answer the question: "where ends the discretionary power and where starts the abuse of law, where ends the legal behavior of administration, materialized through its right of appreciation and where it begins the infringement of a subjective right or a legitimate interest of the citizen? [206] "

Addressing the same issue, Leon Duguit in 1900 is doing an interesting distinction between the "normal powers and the exceptional powers" conferred by the Constitution and laws to the administration, and on the other hand the situations where state authorities act outside the legal framework. The latest situations, are divided by the author into three categories: 1) the excess of power (when the state authorities go beyond the legal powers); 2) misappropriation of power (when the state authority accomplishes an act which falls within its jurisdiction following another purpose, other than the one prescribed by law); 3) the abuse of power (when the state authorities act outside their powers, but through acts that have no legal character) [207].

Therefore, the application and observance of the principle of legality in the work of state authorities is a complex issue because the performance of the state's functions assumes the discretionary power with which the state bodies are invested, in other words "the right of appreciation" of the authorities regarding the moment of adoption and the contents of the measures ordered. What is important to highlight is that discretionary power cannot be opposed to the principle of legality, as a dimension of the lawful state.

In the administrative doctrine, that is primarily studying the issue of discretionary power, it was emphasized that the opportunity of administrative acts may not hinder their legality, and the conditions of legality can be divided into: general conditions of legality and specific conditions of legality on expediency[208]. Consequently, the legality is the corollary of validity conditions, and the opportunity is a requirement (size) of legality[209]. However,

---

[206] Anthony Iorgovan. Forward to: Dana Apostol Tofan, Discretionary Power and Power Excess of Public Authorities, All Beck Publishing House, Bucharest, 1999.

[207] Leon Duguit, Manuel de Droit Constitutionnel, Paris, 1907, pp..445-446.

[208] Antonie Iorgovan, "Treaty of Administrative Law", Nemira Publishing House, Bucharest 1996, vol I, pp. 301

[209] Ibidem, p.292.

the right of appreciation is not recognized by the state authorities in exercising all the prerogatives they have. One needs to remember the difference between the *competence* of state authorities that exist when the law imposes on them a certain strict behavioral decision, on the other hand the *discretionary power*, in which situation the state authorities may choose the means for achieving a legitimate aim or in general, when the state body can choose between several decisions, within the law and its jurisdiction limits. We will remember the definition proposed in the literature to the discretionary powers: "there is a margin of freedom at the discretion of the authorities, so in order to achieve the purpose indicated by the law maker to have the possibility of use any means of action within its jurisdiction. [210]"

Although the problematic of the discretionary power is studied mainly in the administrative law, the right of appreciation in exercising some prerogatives represents a reality that is encountered in the work of all state authorities. [211] The Parliament, as the supreme representative body and the sole legislative authority, has the broadest limits to manifest discretionary power, which identifies itself through the characterization of the legislative act. Since the period between the two world wars I.V. Gruia pointed out: "The need to legislate in a particular matter, the choosing of enactment timing, the choosing of the timing for implementation of the law by fixing by the legislator of the date of application of the law, revising of previous legislation, which may not restrict and compel the activity of future Parliament, limitations of the social activities from the free and uncontrolled way of carrying out and their subjecting to law rules and sanctions, the contents of the legislative act etc, prove the sovereign and discretionary appreciation of the legislative body's function." [212]

That is the case today, because every Parliament has the freedom to exercise its powers almost unlimited. The legal limit of this freedom is shaped only by

---

[210] Dana Apostol Tofan, quoted works p. 22.

[211] In doctrine, Jellinek and Fleiner claimed the thesis according to which the discretionary power is not specific only to the administrative function, but it appears in the activity of other functions of the state, under the form of a liberty of appreciation on the contents, on the opportunity and covering of the juridical act. (see Dana Apostol Tofan, *quoted works* p. 26)

[212] I.V.Gruia, Puterea discreţionară în funcţiunile Statului," The discretionary power in State's functions", in Weekly Pandectales, 1934, p.489.

the constitutional principles applicable to the legislative activity and the mechanism for controlling the constitutionality of laws.

The discretionary power exists also in court's activity. The judge is required to decide only when it is noticed, within the referral's limits. Beyond that is manifested *the sovereign right of assessment* of the facts, the right to interpret the law, the right to set a minimum or a maximum punishment, to grant or not extenuating circumstances to determine the amount of compensation etc. The exercise of these powers means nothing else but discretionary power.

Exceeding the limits of the discretionary powers means breaching of the principle of legality or what in legislation, doctrine and jurisprudence is called to be "abuse of power". The excess of power in the activity of state bodies is equivalent to the abuse of rights, as it means the exercising of some legal competences without any reasonable motivation or without any appropriate relation between the imposed measure, situation in fact and the legitimate aim pursued.

The problematic of the excess of power forms mainly the subject of the law doctrine and administrative jurisprudence. Thus, the jurisprudence of the administrative prosecution courts in other countries delimited the freedom of decision of the administration from the excess of power. French State Council uses the concept of "appreciation manifest error" to describe situations where the administration exceeds, by legal acts adopted, the discretionary power. German administrative courts can annul the administrative acts for abuse of power or "wrong use of power". In such cases the legal acts of the administration have the appearance of legality, since they are adopted within the scope prescribed by law, but the excess of power consists in the fact that the administrative acts are contrary to the purpose of the law.

The Romanian [213]Administrative Litigation Law uses the concept of "abuse of power of the administrative authorities", which it defines as "the exercise of the appreciation right belonging to public authorities, through the violation of the fundamental rights and freedoms of citizens consecrated in the constitution or by the law" (Article 2, paragraph 1, letter m). For the first time the Romanian legislator uses and defines the concept of abuse of power and also recognizes

[213] Law nr.554/2004, published in Official Gazette. no.1154/2004.

the competence of the administrative prosecution courts to sanction the exceeding of the limits of the discretionary powers through administrative acts.

The exceptional situations represent a particular case in which the state authorities, and especially administrative ones, may exercise their discretionary power, with existence of the obvious dangers of power excess.

In the doctrine there is no unanimous agreement on the legal significance of the exceptional situations. Thus, in the older French doctrine, the discretionary power is considered to be the liberty of decision of the administration within the law permitted framework, and the opportunity evokes an action in fact of the public administration, under exceptional circumstances, action not necessary (therefore advisable) but contrary to the law[214]. Jean Rivero believes that through exceptional circumstances means certain factual circumstances that have a double effect: suspending of the application of the ordinary legal system and triggering of the application of a particular law to which the judge defines the requirements. Another author identifies three specific elements for exceptional situations: 1) the existence of some abnormal and exorbitant situations or serious and unforeseen events; 2) inability or difficulty to act in accordance with the natural regulations; 3) the need to intervene quickly to protect a considerable interest, gravely threatened[215].

The excess of power can manifest itself in these circumstances at least by three aspects: a) an appreciation of a factual situation as being an exceptional case, although it has not this meaning (lack of a reasonable and objective motivation); b) the measures taken by the competent state authorities, by the virtue of the discretionary powers, exceed what is necessary for the protection of the public interest seriously threatened; c) if these measures restrict excessively, unjustified the exercise of the rights and freedoms constitutionally recognized.

The existence of an economic, social, political or constitutional - crisis does not justify the abuse of power. In this respect Professor Tudor Drăganu said: "the idea of the lawful state requires that they (the exceptional circumstances) to find adequate regulations in the constitution texts, whenever they have a rigid character. Such constitutional regulation is needed to determine the limits of the areas of social relations, in which the transfer of competence from the

---

[214] Antonie Iorgovan, quoted works, vol. I, pg. 294.

[215] Dana Apostol Tofan, quoted works, pg.81.

Parliament to the government may take place, to highlight the temporary character, by setting deadlines for application and by specifying the purposes in view of which it is carried out.[216]"

Of course, the excess of power is not only a phenomenon manifesting itself in the practice of the executive bodies, it can also be found in the work of Parliament or of the courts.

We appreciate that discretionary power recognized by the state authorities is exceeded, and the measures ordered represent an abuse of power, wherever the following situations occur:

1. The measures decided do not pursue a legitimate aim;

2. The decisions of public authorities are not adequate to the factual situations or the legitimate aim pursued, as they go beyond what is necessary to achieve that purpose;

3. There is no rational justification of the measures imposed, including the situations in which is established a different legal treatment for identical situations, or an identical legal treatment for different situations;

4. Through the measures ordered the state authorities restrict the exercise of fundamental rights and freedoms, without any rational justification to represent, in particular the existence of an appropriate relation between these measures, the situation in fact and the legitimate aim pursued.

[216] Tudor Drăganu, Drept constitutional si instituţii politice.Tratat elementar,"Constitutional Law and Political Institutions. Elementary Treaty", Lumina Lex Publishing House,1999,vol II,pp.131-132

V. Examples of power excess in the activity of state authorities. Possible constitutional solutions

In the final part of this study we will refer to some issues that we believe that need to be considered in a future proceeding for revising the Constitution.

As shown above in regard to the excessive politicianism and the power discretionary manifestations of the executive contrary to the spirit and even the letter of the Constitution, with the consequence of violation of fundamental rights and freedoms, manifested throughout the last two democracy decades in Romania, we consider that the scientific approach and not only in reviewing matters of the basic law should be directed to find solutions to guarantee the values of the lawful state, to limit the violation of the constitutional provisions in view of some particular interests and to avoid the excess of power by state authorities.

1. The provisions of art. 114, paragraph 1 of the current drafting state: "The Government may assume responsibility before the Chamber of Deputies and the Senate in joint session on a program of general policy statement or a bill."

The engagement of Government liability has a political nature and is a procedural instrument which avoids the phenomenon of *"dissociation of majorities"*[217] where the Parliament could not meet the required majority to adopt a certain action initiated by the Government. To determine the Legislative forum to adopt the measure, the government through the accountability procedure, conditions to continue its work requiring a vote of confidence. This constitutional process ensures that the majority required for the government dismissal, in case of submitting a motion of censure to dismiss to coincide with that for rejecting the law, program or political statement of which the government binds its existence.

The adapting of the laws as a result of the political liability engagement of the Government has as an important consequence the absence of any discussions or parliamentary deliberations on the bill. If the government is supported by a comfortable majority in the Parliament, through this procedure one can achieve the adoption of the laws by "bypassing the Parliament", which

[217] Gheorghe Iancu, Drept constituţional şi instituţii publice,"Constitutional Law and public Institutions", All Beck Publishing House, Bucharest, 2010, p. 482.

can have negative consequences on the principle of separation of powers in the State, but also in regard to the role of Parliament, as defined of Article 61 of the Constitution.

Consequently, the use of this constitutional procedure by government for adopting a law must be exceptional, justified by a political situation and a social imperative, well defined.

This particularly important aspect for respecting the democratic principles of the lawful state by the Government was well highlighted by the Constitutional Court of Romania: "To this simplified form of regulation one must reach *in Extremus*, when the adopting of bill in the ordinary procedure or emergency procedure is no longer possible or when the Parliament's political structure does not allow the adopting of the bill in the current or emergency procedure.[218]" The political practice of the Government in recent years is contrary to these rules and principles. The Executive frequently used the assuming of responsibility not only for a single law, but for packages of laws without a justification in the sense shown by the Constitutional Court.

The politicianism of the government clearly expressed by the high frequency of assuming such a constitutional decision seriously harms the principle of political pluralism which is an important value of the lawful system as consecrated in the provisions of article 1, par. (3) of the Constitution but also of the principle of parliamentary law that shows that "the opposition expresses and the majority decides"[219]. "To deny the right of the opposition to speak is synonymous with the denial of political pluralism which, according to Article 1, paragraph (3) of the Constitution is a supreme value and is guaranteed ... the principle the 'majority decides, opposition expresses "implying that in the entire organization and functioning of the Parliament's Chambers to ensure, on one hand that the majority is not obstructed, especially in the conduct of the parliamentary procedure and, on the other hand the majority to decide only after the opposition has voiced"[220]. The censorship of the Constitutional Court has not proved to be sufficient and effective to determine the Government to respect these values of the lawful state.

---

[218] Decision nr. 1557 on 18th of November 2009, published in the Official Gazette. Nr. 40 on 19,01,2010.

[219] Ioan Muraru, Mihai Constantinescu, Drept parlamentar românesc, "Romanian parliamentary Law", All Beck Publishing House, Bucharest, 2005, p. 55-69.

[220] Ioan Muraru, Mihai Constatinescu, quoted works, p.56

In the context of these arguments we support the proposal to revise these constitutional provisions that limit the right of the Government to use its liability for a single bill in a parliamentary session. However, in our opinion there is no justification to exclude from the limitation of Government's liability, situations aiming the government draft law on state budget and state social insurances.

2. All post-December governments have massively used the practice of Emergency ordinances, fact widely criticized in the literature.

The conditions and prohibitions established by revising law in 2003 on the constitutional regime of emergency ordinances, in practice proved to be insufficient to limit this practice of the Executive and the control of the Constitutional Court also proved insufficient and even ineffective. The consequence of such a practice is the violation of the Parliament's role as "the sole legislative authority of the country" (art. 61 of the Constitution) and creating of an imbalance between the executive and legislature by emphasizing the discretionary power of the Government, which most often turned into the abuse of power.

We propose in the perspective of a new revision of the Basic Law, that art. 115 par. 6 of the Constitution be amended so as to prohibit the adopting of emergency ordinances in the field of organic laws. In this way is protected an important area of social relationships as the constitutional legislature considers essential for the social and state system, the excess power of the executive through the practice of issuing emergency ordinance.

3. In our opinion is necessary that the Constitutional Court's role as guarantor of the Basic Law to be amplified by new responsibilities in order to limit the excess of power by the state's authorities. We disagree with the assertions in the literature that a possible improvement of constitutional justice could be achieved by reducing the powers of the constitutional court[221]. It is true the Constitutional Court ruled some questionable decisions regarding their compliance with the limits of exercising their duties according to Constitution,

[221] Genoveva Vrabie, Natura juridică a curţilor constituţionale şi locul lor în sistemul autorităţilor publice, în Revista de Drept Public" The Juridical nature of the constitutional courts and their place within the public authorities system", in the Review of Public Law, no..1/2010 p. 33

by assuming the role of a positive legislator[222]. Reducing the powers of the constitutional court for this reason is not a solution as a legal basis. Of course reducing the powers of the state authority has the consequence of eliminating the risk of improper exercise of those powers. This is not a way of doing things in a lawful state, but it should be done by seeking legal solutions to achieve better conditions of the tasks which prove to be necessary to the state and social system.

To the powers of the Constitutional Court may be included the one to rule on the constitutionality of administrative acts, exempted from the review of legality by the administrative courts. This category of administrative acts, to which refers Article 126 paragraph 6 of the Constitution and the provisions of Law no. 544/2004 of administrative litigation, are particularly important for the whole social system and state. Therefore it is necessary a constitutional scrutiny because in its absence, the discretionary power of the issuing authority is unlimited with the consequent possibility of restricting the excessive exercise of fundamental freedoms and rights or of breaching the important constitutional values.

For the same reasons our constitutional court should be able to control in terms of constitutionality also the Presidential decrees establishing the referendum procedure.

The High Court of Cassation and Justice has the power to take decisions in an appeal on points of law that are binding on the courts. In the absence of any control of legality or constitutionality, the practice has shown that in many cases the Supreme Court has exceeded its power to interpret the law, and such decisions amended or completed acts behaving as a genuine legislature thus violating the principle of separation of powers in the state[223].

In these circumstances, in order to avoid the excessive power of the Supreme Court, we consider it necessary to assign the Constitutional Court the

[222] We refer with the title for example to the Decision No.356/2007, published in the Official Gazette.no.322on 14th of May 2007 and to the Decision no..98/2008 published in the official gazette no. 140 on 22nd of February 2008.

[223] For developments see Andreescu Marius, Constituţionalitatea recursului în interesul legii şi ale deciziilor pronunţate, “The Constitutionality of appeal on point of law and of the decisions given in Juridical Courier no.. 1/2011, pp.32-36.

power to decide on the constitutionality of the decisions of High Court of Cassation and Justice adopted in the procedure of appeal on points of law.

4. The abuse of authority of all state authorities, paradoxically within the law limits, whenever, the normative documents recognize a marge of appreciation from the decider body (Parliament, administrative authorities or courts), on the moment of decision or on the measures decided. The State practice in Romania showed that in many instances the content of the decision which may materialize in: law, government ordinance, acts of administrative authorities at all levels, judicial documents of the prosecution or court orders, exceed through provisions, particularly the restrictive nature what is necessary to achieve the purpose of the law or inadequate to the situation in fact. Such manifestations of power can cause severe damages to fundamental human rights or public interest, in a word to the features of the lawful state. The criterion that could allow censorship by the courts of these forms of abuse of power is in our view *the principle of proportionality.*

Proportionality is a fundamental principle of law consecrated explicitly to the constitutional, legislation and international legal instruments regulations. It is based on the values of the rational right of justice and equity and expresses the existence of a balanced or appropriate relation between actions, situations, events, being a criterion for limiting the measures ordered by the authorities to what is necessary to achieve a legitimate aim, thus being guaranteed the fundamental rights and avoided the excess of power by the state's authorities. Proportionality is a fundamental principle of EU law being expressly consecrated by article 5 of the Treaty on European Union[224].

We consider that this principle's express regulation in the content of the provisions of Article 53 of the Constitution, with application in the restriction of certain rights, is not enough to highlight the full significance and importance of the principle of the lawful state.

It is useful that to article 1 of the Constitution to add a new paragraph stating that *"The exercising of state power must be proportionate and non-discriminatory"*. This new constitutional regulation would be a veritable constitutional obligation for all state authorities to conduct their duties in a way

---

[224] For developments see Marius Andreescu, Proporţionalitatea, principiu al dreptului Uniunii Europene," Proportionality, principle of European Union Law" in Juridical Courier no. 10/2010, pp. 593-598

that the measures adopted to enroll within the discretionary power recognized by law. At the same time it creates the possibility for the Constitutional Court to sanction by means of the constitutional reviewing control of the laws and ordinances, the excess of power in the work of Parliament and Government, using as criteria the principle of proportionality.

Of course, the existence of an institutional state viable, efficient qualitatively, well structured and harmonized, including under the aspect of moral and professional quality of the civil servants and magistrates dignitaries is obviously an ontological factor to eliminate or at least diminish the excess of power of state's authorities in all its forms, especially we would emphasize on the situation in which the measures decided by the political and legal manifestations will take the *form of legality* but are in obvious contradiction with the requirements of *the principle of legitimacy.*

Strengthening the judiciary power, the control of the courts and control of constitutionality, particularly, mainly in situations where being questioned the violation of human rights or of the principles of lawful state, particularly the separation and balance of powers, can be a viable solution to ensure not only the legality of the measures taken by the state authorities, but also of their legitimacy.

9. REASONS CONCERNING THE RESTRICTION OF SOME RIGHTS

Abstract:

An essential dimension of the lawful state is represented by the consecration and guaranteeing of the fundamental rights and liberties, the ensuring of the optimum conditions for their exercising. The state authorities have the negative obligation to restrain from any arbitrary or excessive requirement that may restrict or condition the exercise of the constitutional right. In order to be legitimate and constitutional, any restriction of the exercise of the fundamental rights and liberties through the measures prescribed by the state's authorities, needs to have the character of exemption, not to affect the substance of the law and to fulfill all conditions stipulated by article 53 of Constitution. In relation to these premises we analyze in this study the constitutional institution of restraining some rights' exercising and the relevant aspects of jurisprudence. The observance of the principle of proportionality is one of the constitutional requirements in order that such a restrictive measure be legitimate. The main particularities of the principle of proportionality applied in the matter of restraining some rights' exercising are analyzed with reference to the jurisprudence of the Constitutional Court and the European Court of Human's Rights.

Key words :

Lawful state/fundamental rights and liberties/restriction of the exercise of the fundamental rights/principle of proportionality/constitutional requirements

I. Limits, restrictions and derogations concerning the exercise of fundamental rights and freedoms

A Romanian author emphasized that freedom has a meaning provided the limit exists, as to manifest itself, it must depend on something, to circumscribe itself to certain coordinates. "Human freedom is construed in a bundle of limits that are the very condition of its exercise."[225]

Consecration and guaranteeing of human rights through domestic and international regulations does not exclude their limiting. Moreover, the existence of such unconditional, theoretical rights can not be accepted in a democratic constitutional system. The lack of the exercising limits and conditions prescribed by law, constitutions or international legal instruments can lead to arbitrariness or abuse of law, because it would not allow the differentiation of illegal behavior from the legal one. This idea is expressed by Article 4 of the French Declaration of Rights of Man and Citizen: "the exercising of each man's natural rights has no limits, others than those which provide every member of society the possibility to exercise those rights." Also, the legal doctrine noted that in the relationships between the rights holders „one's freedom begins where stops the other one's freedom, since the condition inherent to the person is its relationship with others."[226]

The social order and stability implies tolerance and mutual respect among the subjects participating to social relations. The exercising of fundamental rights and freedoms must not conflict with the order existing in social life: the coexistence of freedoms and social protection are the two commandments underlying the limits enacted by positive law."[227]The difficulty lies in finding the most suitable solutions that would balance the individual interests and public interest while guaranteeing the fundamental rights and freedoms in situations in which could be limited or restricted their exercising.

In the relationship between the rights and freedoms, on one hand, and society on the other hand, two extreme attitudes have been outlined: sacrificing of rights and freedoms in the interests of social order, or the preemitence of

[225] Gabriel Liiceanu, Despre limită, "About the limit", Humanitas Publishing House, Bucharest, 1994, p. 11.

[226] Ion Deleanu, Instituţii şi proceduri constituţionale,"Constitutional Institutions and Proceedings", Servo-Sat Publishing House, Arad, 1998 vol.I, pp. 269-270.

[227] Jean Rivero, Les Libertés publiques, P.U.F., (Ed.1973), p. 106.

rights and freedoms, even if thus are sacrificed the interests and order social.[228] None of these solutions is justified by the imperatives of authentic democracy and the requirement to achieve a balance and social harmony. The Constitutional regulations, to be effective, must achieve a balance between citizens and public authorities, then between public authorities and of course, citizens. It must also ensure protection to the individual against the arbitrary interference of State in the exercise of its rights and freedoms.[229] Therefore, the limits imposed to the fundamental rights and freedoms must be appropriate to a legitimate purpose, it can be: protection of society, social, economic and political order, of lawful order, or protection of the rights of others. The limits must not deprive of contents the rights themselves, but must ensure the exercise thereof in such situations.

The existence of certain limits on the exercise of fundamental rights is justified through constitutional protection or the protection through important international legal instruments or state human values. However, it is not acceptable that in the name of these values, the state authorities to limit discretionary and abusively the exercise of rights which in turn are constitutionally guaranteed. In this case one might come to destroying democracy under the pretext of defending it.

The principle of proportionality, understood as the appropriate relationship between the measures restricting the exercise of human rights and freedoms, the factual situation and the legitimate aim pursued represents a criterion for determining these limits, avoiding the excess power, but also a guarantee of the constitutional rights consecrated.[230]

In doctrine, the legal instruments and jurisprudence, the limits of the fundamental rights and freedoms were differentiated by several criteria.

---

[228] Ion Deleanu, quoted works, vol.I, p.205.

[229] Ioan Muraru, *Protecţia constituţională a libertăţilor de opinie*", "Constitutional Protection of the Right to Opinion" Lumina Lex Publishing House, Bucharest, *1999*, pp. 16-17.

[230] For developments see : Andreescu Marius,Principiul proporţionalităţii în dreptul constituţional,"Principle of proportionality in the Constitutional Right", CH.Beck Publishing House, Bucharest,2007

A first distinction is between the limit and limitation of fundamental rights.[231] Thus, the limit is a content item of the law and is necessary for its exercise. In contrast, the limitation (restriction) limits the exercise of a right by measures taken by the competent state authorities in view of a legitimate aim.

Another author[232] believes that there are limits imposed on the fundamental rights and freedoms in order to facilitate their implementation, and on the other hand, limits aiming at "the protection of society, its socio-economic and political and legal order." [233] The limits deriving from such a purpose may be *absolute*, imposed by the demands of social life, in all circumstances for the protection of the essential values of the state and society, and on the other hand may be *relative*, those that do not apply in a general and permanent manner, but only to some of the rights and freedoms, or only in a certain time or in a determined situation, or only to certain subjects.[234]

In our view we can distinguish: a) *Conditions* for the exercise of rights and freedoms that are found even in their legal and constitutional definition contents; b) *restrictions, exemptions, suspension, loss of rights*, which have an exception and temporary nature, being measures taken by the state authorities to protect or achieve a legitimate aim.

State interference in the exercise of the fundamental rights and freedoms can be realized in principle by restricting and suspending certain rights or by derogations. These modalities are regulated in constitutions and international legal instruments. Avoiding any misuse of state authorities and guaranteeing of the rights and fundamental freedoms in such situations requires constitutional regulation, but also in the international legal instruments of the conditions justifying such measures' enacting.

There are constitutions governing the institution of certain rights' restriction in certain circumstances, [235] the possibility of suspending certain

---

[231] Doina Micu, *Garantarea drepturilor omului, "Guaranteeing the Human Rights", All Beck Publishing House, Bucharest, 1998,*. p. 141.

[232] Ion Deleanu, *quoted works*, vol.I, p.205.

[233] Ibidem pg. 205.

[234] Ibidem pg. 205. See Jean Rivero, *quoted works,* p. 171-175.

[235] On this meaning to remember provisions of art.18 of Portugal Constitution; art.19, paragraph.1 and 2 of German Constitution and provisions of art.53 of România Constitution.

rights or freedoms[236] or in cases that due to the abusive exercising of a right, its exercise is being lost.[237]

Romania Constitution imposes *conditions* on the exercise of certain rights or freedoms. Thus, the freedom of movement is exercised under the conditions established by law (Article 25, para. (1)). Physical person may dispose of oneself, if not violating the rights and freedoms of others, public order or morals (Article 26, para. (2)); a person's right to access information of public interest can not be restricted, but should not be prejudicial to the protection of young people or national security. (Art. 31 paragraph (3)); the right to strike can only be exercised under law, which sets its limits (article 43, par. (2)); the content and limits of ownership right are determined by law (Article 44 para. (1)); the freedom of expression may not harm the dignity, honor, privacy of person or the right to own image (article 30, par. (6)); meetings may be organized and held only peacefully, without any kind of arms (39).

The restriction of certain rights or freedoms is governed by Article 53 of the Constitution. These are provisions of principle, which refer to the measures taken by state through law or government ordinance that represents interference with the exercise of constitutionally guaranteed rights. In order not to affect the substance of the right, such measures are temporary and also, in order to be constitutional, must comply cumulatively with the conditions provided by article 53. There are also constitutional provisions which restrict the exercise of some rights, the restrictions having a permanent character. The restrictions are usually specific to the legal content of the law constitutionally consecrated. Thus, the exercise of individual freedom may be restricted by search, detention or arrest (Article 23). Inviolability of home may be restricted under the terms of article 27, par. (2). The provisions of article 36, par. (2), prohibit to certain categories of persons the right to vote. The provisions of article 40, par. (3) prohibit such professional categories the right to join political parties.

There are differences between restrictions and derogations, and on the other hand, that can cover the exercise of rights and fundamental freedoms.

[236] Art. 55 of Spain Constitution.

[237] Art.18 of German Constitution.

Restrictions are measures considered needed in a democratic society, inflicted in order to achieve public interest or to protect the rights and freedoms of others. In this respect, the provisions of article 18 of the Convention states that: "... restrictions... can not be applied unless on the purpose for which they were intended."

With all specific aspects, arising from Constitution or international legal instruments, can be identified common conditions for the legitimacy of restrictions: be prescribed by law, be necessary in a democratic society, not be discriminatory, be appropriate at least to one of purposes provided by law and justifying circumstance. Compliance with these conditions must be achieved cumulatively. In this way the fundamental rights are guaranteed and is removed the arbitrary interference of state authorities in their pursuit.

Exemptions are wider restrictions of rights and fundamental freedoms and can be decided by States in emergencies. Restrictions may aim, in principle, any fundamental right, as opposed to derogatory measures that may concern only some human rights guaranteed by the international legal instruments.

From the international legal instruments, to which I referred, results that the derogations, in order not to be arbitrary, must meet the following conditions: must be applied only in exceptional circumstances; be strictly appropriate to the facts; be compatible with other obligations that States members adjusted to the international law; not be discriminatory; the states that make use of the right of derogation to announce the relevant international fora.

There are also absolutely guaranteed rights (absolute rights) in that no restrictions or derogations are being allowed. Obviously, we are referring to the right to life; the right not to be subjected to torture or to any kind of inhuman or degrading treatment or punishment.

The principle of proportionality is a guarantee in all circumstances when the exercise of a right or fundamental freedom is subjected to a condition, restriction, suspension or exemption. The principle of proportionality, applied in this matter has into consideration the achieving of a fair balance between individual interests and the public interest or private interests which corresponds to the fundamental subjective rights, consecrated and guaranteed constitutionally.

II. Particular aspects of proportionality under the provisions of Article 53 of Romania Constitution

Ragarding the Romanian constitutional provisions related to the restriction of fundamental rights and freedoms in the literature in specialty, a distinction is made between the common circumstances to restrict the exercising of certain rights that form the subject for the regulation of provisions of article 53 of the Constitution, and secondly the special circumstances, specific to certain rights and freedoms. The common restriction circumstances are of temporal nature, are essentially fortuitous, while the special circumstances are permanent[238]. The quoted author stresses that such circumstances should be expressly recognized as "not being the product of conventionalism "[239].

Although these circumstances are common, they can justify the restriction having into consideration the nature of the right or freedom. Thus, no circumstances can justify the restriction of the right to life or the right not to be tortured.

România Constitution uses a simple and efficient method for regulating the restriction of exercising certain rights and freedoms (common circumstances) by provisions in one single article. The provisions of Article 53 allow the restriction of certain rights and freedoms, but only conditioned.[240] The issue of interpretation and application of the provisions of Article 53 is particularly complex because the restrictions can aim the exercise of any right or fundamental freedom consecrated and guaranteed by the Constitution, except those regarded as absolute. The complexity is due to the diversity of concrete situations justifying the restriction of certain rights.

The rules imposed by the provisions of Article 53 have the value of a constitutional principle, because they are applicable to all fundamental rights and freedoms of citizens.

---

[238] Ion Deleanu, *quoted works*, vol. II, p.123. Jurisprudence consecrates this difference also. See decision no.13/ 1999 of Constitutional Court, published in the Official Gazette no.178/1999.

[239] Ibidem, *quoted works,* vol.II, p.123.

[240] Ioan Muraru, Simina Elena Tănăsescu, Drept constituţional şi instituţii politice,"Constitutional Right and Political Institutions, All Beck Publishing House, Bucharest, 2003, vol.I, p.174-176.

In the version prior to revision of Constitution, the provisions of article 49 indicated that the restraints can be achieved only by law, if necessary, according to the following purposes: "protection of national security, public order, health or morals, rights and freedoms of citizens, the conduct of criminal investigation, preventing of consequences of a natural disaster, or of any extremely severe catastrophe."At the same time, the restriction should not affect the existence of the right or freedom and must be proportional to the situation that caused it.

Through the Law amending the Constitution on September 18, 2003, were modified the provisions of Article 49, and by the republication of Constitution was given a new numbering of the Articles, Article 49 becoming Article 53. The initial rules in place for the restriction of some rights exercising have been maintained but two more conditions have been added: the restriction must be "necessary in a democratic society" and another condition is that the restrictive measure be applied "nondiscriminatory". In this way, the Romanian Constitution perceived in this matter the most important rules in the international legal instruments in the matter and capitalized C.E.D.O jurisprudence.

If making a comparative analysis between the Romanian constitutional provisions and those contained in certain international legal instruments governing the conditions for the restriction of certain rights and freedoms exercising, some differences can be found. For our study is of interest that the provisions of Article 53. (2) of Constitution expressly consecrates proportionality as a condition that must be met in case of restriction of certain rights exercising, while in most international legal instruments this condition results implicitly out of the regulations content and is deduced by way of interpretation, by the jurisprudence of international courts.

To identify the peculiarities of the principle of proportionality, applied in this matter, it is useful to highlight some aspects of doctrine and jurisprudence on the interpretation and application of Article 53 of the Constitution.

The doctrine asserted that, in case the legislator restricts the exercise of certain rights without indicating expressly the constitutional background, it "does not remove the obligation of a verification within the procedure for monitoring the legitimacy of the constitutional law, if the measure thus established constitutes a limitation of a right."[241] In recitals of Decision No. 4/1992 of Constitutional Court results that under the assumption that the legal provision subjected to a control, constitutes a limitation of a constitutional right, it is legitimate only in cases falling within the limiting situations expressly provided by Article 53 of Constitution.[242]

The Constitutional Court held that the provisions of Article 53, have into consideration the fundamental rights and freedoms contained in Chapter II, Section I of Constitution, and no other rights.[243] Our Constitutional Court, interpreting the provisions of Article 53 in relation to the provisions of article 5 of the Convention for the Protection of Human Rights and Fundamental Freedoms, the distinction was made between the loss and restriction of a right. The last situation is envisaged by the provisions of Article 53. "The Court finds that the invoking of provisions of article 5 of the Convention for the Protection of Human Rights and Fundamental Freedoms has no bearing in the cause because these provisions apply to deprivation of liberty and not to restriction of freedom."[244]

At the same time, our Constitutional Court decided that the restriction of a right must be temporary, being instituted only for the time period the causes that led it are acting, which are limitative consecrated by para (1) of Article 53 of the Constitution. [245]

Whenever the restriction of a right exercising is realized in order to defend the rights of citizens, restrictive measures are legitimate only in consideration of a particular law, as without this restriction, that right would be affected.[246] The restrictions brought upon the right exercising should not bring touch to the substance of this right. The Constitutional Court has established that through the law can be disposed certain restrictions of ownership, but they should not bring touch to this very right substance. These restrictions can be established in regard to the object of the right or other

---

[241] Ioan Muraru, Restrângerea exercițiului unor drepturi sau libertăți, "Restraining the exercise of some rights or freedoms", in Constitutional studies, Actami Publishing House, Bucharest,1995, p. 199.

[242] Decision no 4/1992, published in the Official Gazette no192/1992.

[243] Decision no 19/1999, published in C.D.H., 1999, pg.308

[244] Decision no 239/2001, published in the Official Gazette no 838/2001.

[245] Decision no 83/1999, published in C.D.H., 1999, p.582.

[246] Decision no 139/1994, publicată C.D.H., 1994, p.84.

attributes of law, for the protection of the rights of persons or the general social and economic interests.[247]

Constitutional Court jurisprudence distinguishes the restriction of certain rights related to the circumstances in which the legislator conditions the exercise of a right. In this regard it was decided that the seniority requirements established by article 19 of Law No.51 / 1995[248] on the legal profession, are seeking to enforce the right of defense in terms of competence, professional responsibility and practice experience, related to hierarchical level of the courts and to the complexity of the cases, so it is natural that they involve certain conditions, which cannot be regarded as affecting the right to work, but as measures to protect both the interests of the litigant and lawyer's.[249]

Also, the exemption by law of certain categories of citizens of the benefit of rights granted to others, who are in a different situation, does not represent a limitation on the exercise of these rights. Therefore the provisions of Article 53 of Constitution are not applicable.[250]

Proportionality is a condition of constitutionality of the measures ordered by law or by ordinances, through which is restricted the exercise of some fundamental rights and freedoms, condition expressly stipulated by provisions of article 53, par. (2) of Constitution. The Analysis of the particularities of this principle must be carried out systematically in the context of the Article 53. Express consecration of a particular aspect of principle of proportionality, through the provisions of article 53, par. (2) changes the proportionality, from a rule of moral or opportunity into a law's constitutionality condition, while the Constitutional Court has the power to check the compliance with this principle.

Restriction of certain rights or freedoms by law represents a requirement of the state in the exercising of those rights and freedoms, justified by achieving a legitimate aim. To avoid arbitrariness or excess of power by state authorities that adopt such measures, it is necessary to exist guarantees provided by the state, which need to be adequate to the constitutional purpose pursued, namely for the protection of the fundamental rights and freedoms in

---

[247] Decision no19/1993, published in C.D.H., 1992-1993; Decision no147/1997, published in C.D.H., 1998.

[248] Republished in the Official Gazette no 113/2001.

[249] Decision no 256/1997, published in the Official Gazette no 134/1998.

[250] Decision no 115/1999, published in the Official Gazette no 522/1999.

the concrete situations in which prejudice might be brought to them. The principle of proportionality is thus a constitutional guarantee that allows sanctioning by the constitutional court of the arbitrary interferences of Parliament or Government in those rights exercising.[251]

Therefore, the measures taken by the State through which is restricted the exercise of fundamental rights or freedoms, in order not to be abusive must be not only legal, ie disposed by law, or by a normative act equivalent as legal force to the law, but also legitimate (fair) that is necessary in a democratic, non-discriminatory society, proportionate to the situation causing them and not affect the substance of the law. The proportionality and necessity in a democratic society are criteria of evaluation, both for the legislator as for the judge, of the legitimacy of the restriction of certain rights and freedoms.

In the doctrine was pointed out that whenever the legislator brings a limitation in the exercise of a right or freedom, shall state expressly in the wording of that disposition, the provision, under constitutional article 53.[252] This statement aims implicitly the respecting of the principle of proportionality and corresponds to the principle of supremacy of Constitution: "The law is an enactment act, in the meaning that the legislator's will necessarily finds limits in the supremacy of Constitution, as a fundamental law of state and society.[253]" In such cases, the assessment made by the legislator or constitutional judge, is based on a proportional reasoning. The restriction of certain rights exercising is justified by the existence of diverse interests and in some cases, even contradictory. On one hand, the subjective interest of the fundamental rights holders, and on the other hand, the public interest or the need to guarantee the fundamental rights of other persons. In such circumstances, one of the interests backgrounds its constitutional legitimacy on a provision and the other one, on another constitutional provision. The proportional reasoning involves the comparing of interests, so as the limiting of the exercise of a right or fundamental freedom does not exceed what is strictly necessary to satisfy the public interest or the rights of others.

The principle of proportionality, applicable in the matter of restriction of certain rights, is concretely determined by the meaning of the elements being

---

[251] Ioan Muraru, Protecţia constituţională a libertăţilor de opinie, "Constitutional Protection of the liberties of opinion, quoted works, p. 22-23.

[252] Ioan Muraru, quoted works, pg.200-201.

[253] Ibidem, p.201.

compared, pending on which can be established whether the respective measure is either appropriate or not to the situation and intended purpose. Proportionality of the restrictive measures must be assessed in relation to a well defined legitimate aim, whose significance is given where applicable, by the doctrine, statute or case law. The restrictive measure violates the condition of proportionality if the purpose for which it was prepared is generic, and does not indicate a particular right or fundamental freedom as legitimate aim.[254]

The purposes justifying the restriction of certain rights and related to which is appreciated the respecting of the principle of proportionality are expressly and limitating provided by article 53, par. (1) of Constitution. Their meaning is important to determine the proportionality of the restrictive measures.

Astfel, prin "securitate naţională", expresie nou introdusă ca urmare a revizuirii Constituţiei şi care înlocuieşte termenul de "siguranţa naţională", se înţelege: "starea de legalitate, de echilibru şi de stabilitate socială, economică şi politică existentă şi dezvoltării statului naţional român, ca stat suveran, unitar, independent şi indivizibil, menţinerii ordinii de drept, precum şi a climatului de exercitare neîngrădită a drepturilor, libertăţilor şi îndatoririlor fundamentale ale cetăţenilor, potrivit principiilor şi normelor democratice, statornicite prin Constituţie.

Thus, by "national security", a newly introduced expression following the revision of Constitution, which replaces the term "national security" means "the existing state of legality, balance and social, economic and political stability and development of the Romanian national state, as a sovereign, unitary, independent and indivisible, for the maintenance of public order and the climate for unrestrained exercise of rights, freedoms and fundamental duties of citizens, according to democratic principles and norms settled by the Constitution."[255]

---

[254] See Decision no 139/1994 published in the Official Gazette. No 353/1994, Decision no75/1994, published in the Official Gazette. No 190/1994 and Decision no 21/2000, published in the Official Gazette. No 159/2000.

[255] Dispositions of art.1 of Law no51/1991 regarding the national safety of România, published in the Official Gazette. No 163/1991.

"Public order" is the set of rules that ensures the safety of society, public welfare, social harmony, respect for law and for the legitimate decisions of public authorities.

"Public health" means health protection of whole population or part thereof.

"Public Morals" is all precepts of conduct, dependent on individual conscience and values of the community to which he belongs.

Ensuring the respecting of citizens' "rights and freedoms" is a requirement mainly due to the fact that the person belongs to a social collectivity, aspect implying the fact that the rights and freedoms of others require the same protection as their own rights and freedoms.

The "Criminal Instruction" is a component of lawful order and implies the succession of acts and deeds that form the criminal proceedings in all its phases and stages.[256]

Depending on the legitimate aim pursued is determined the "margin of appreciation" which the public authorities have to impose limitations to the exercise of fundamental rights and freedoms, as provided by Article 53 of Constitution. The limits of the right of appreciation of the competent state authorities and also the respecting of principle of proportionality, are established in our constitutional jurisprudence court, including by reference to C.E.D.O. jurisprudence.

Thus, the proportionality of the interference of state authorities is considered by the international court against the requirements of a democratic society, a concept found in the jurisprudence of the Constitutional Court.

Also, our constitutional court invoked other aspects of C.E.D.O jurisprudence: the restrictive measures are: proportionate to the legitimate aim pursued if national and institutional legislative system has adequate and sufficient guarantees against abuses.[257] There is a distinction between facts and valuable judgments. If the materiality of the first one can be proved, the value judgments are not able to be demonstrated in terms of their accuracy.[258]

---

[256] For developments see Ion Deleanu, quoted works, vol.II, p.121-122.

[257] See Case Leander versus Suedia. ,1999

[258] Case Lingens versus Austria, 2002

Therefore, the compliance with the condition for proportionality of the restrictive measures imposed on freedom of expression is appreciated differently depending on the nature of allegations. The proportionality can be regarded as a strict fitness unto the purpose of the restrictive measure, or there may be a greater margin of appreciation of authorities when the legitimate aim pursued is public morality, for instance.[259]

These are just some aspects of C.E.D.O. jurisprudence, invoked in the jurisprudence of the Constitutional Court of Romania, in case are to be analyzed the restrictive measures imposed by Parliament or Government, regarding the exercise of fundamental rights and freedoms.

The jurisprudence of the Constitutional Court of Romania contributed to identifying the features of proportionality principle applied in relation to guaranteeing the fundamental rights and freedoms, including in situations in which the competent state authorities have restrictive measures which must meet the conditions of Article 53.

In this matter, the Constitutional Court jurisprudence reveals defining characteristics of the constitutional principle of proportionality, which assumes the necessary adequacy of the constitutional guarantees conferred to fundamental rights and freedoms, to the finality pursued, namely the protection of the exercise of rights in concrete situations that could be restricted. The applying of the principle of proportionality has a dual significance: state guarantees on human rights become effective in specific situations; It is removed the arbitrary interference of public authorities in the exercise of these rights or in applying the measures for restricting their exercise, measures which constitute abuse of power.

Proportionality is a fundamental guarantee for exercising the fundamental right, subjected to a limit or circumstance. The existence of some limits or conditions for the exercise of some fundamental rights is justified by the idea of constitutional protection of some important human or state values.

In the meaning of those above Romania's Constitutional Court held: "The legislation, doctrine and jurisprudence have rejected and reject constantly the existence of absolute rights and liberties."[260] Given this premise, the court

---

[259] Case Wingrove versus United Kingdom, 2001.

[260] Decision no 13/1999, M.Of. no 178/1999.

identifies the Romanian constitutional provisions that set limits, conditions or restrictions in exercising of some rights.[261]

Although not expressly referring to the principle of proportionality, the decision No.13 / 1999 is important because it reveals the peculiarities of this principle applied in the matter of fundamental rights and freedoms protection. The need for a proper balance expresses the general principle of proportionality. At the same time, the conditions, limitations or restrictions imposed on some fundamental rights must be appropriate to the objective pursued by the constituent legislator, that of protection of the fundamental rights in situations in which it can be conditioned or limited.

By several decisions, the Constitutional Court ruled that it has jurisdiction to verify the compliance with the proportionality requirement in case of certain rights' restriction. The Constitutional Court assumes this jurisdiction only if the proportionality is a condition of constitutionality of the law instituting the restriction of the right. "Unquestionably, the checking of proportionality is within the competence of Court's control, while the proportionality of restricting with the situation that has caused, it is a constitutionality prerequisite of the law that established the restriction of the right".[262]

This finding of the Constitutional Court is important for several aspects: proportionality is regarded as a requirement of constitutionality which the law, setting up the restriction of the right, must follow. In this way the principle of proportionality is not only a simple state of fact, closed to opportunity, but is a *legal* requirement within the Court's controlling jurisdiction. The Court draws a distinction between the general principle of proportionality, the proportionality applied in other branches of law and the constitutional principle of proportionality applicable in matter of certain rights' restriction. The Constitutional Court competence refers only to the constitutional principle of proportionality, consecrated by Article 53 para (2) provisions. To be noted the interpretation of our Constitutional Court on the content of the principle of proportionality applied in this matter: the appropriateness of restriction to situation that caused it.

---

[261] Decision no 13/1999 quoted previously.

[262] Considerent no3 of Decision no71/ 1996, published in the Official Gazette. No 131/1996.

The Constitutional Court pointed out that proportionality must be analyzed and understood pending the legitimate purpose aimed for which is applied the restricting measure. This purpose has to be one of the stipulated limiting set of article 53, par. (1). Moreover then this, because the law through which is ordered the restriction of a right's exercising, to respect the principle of proportionality, the reference to the legitimate aim must not be generic, but it needs to be determined. Analyzing the restricting of the right to free movement, the Government Ordinance no.50 / 1994, the Constitutional Court held that the restriction of a constitutional right is possible, in accordance with Article 53 of the Constitution "solely on account of a certain law, as a measure that is being imposed whereas without that restriction, that right would be severely undermined and, according to the principle of proportionality, only to the extent necessary, so that this right be not at least partly compromised ... or, in the absence of specifying in whose service the restriction takes place, from the simple reference to the social protection right (Article 1 of the Ordinance) or to social rights existing (Article 7 of the Ordinance) does not result neither that this restriction is imposed - as required by Article 53 of the Constitution - nor that it is proportional the situation that caused it - as required by paragraph 2 of the same Article"[263]

The argumentation of proportionality reasoning, which in the matter of certain rights' restriction involves the adequacy of the restrictive measure to the situation in fact, but also to the legitimate aim pursued, is used in the jurisprudence of Constitutional Court. Analyzing the respecting of principle of proportionality, in the event of exceptions of unconstitutionality regarding the provisions of Article 148, paragraph 1, letter h of the Criminal Procedure Code, our Constitutional Court found that principle of proportionality is satisfied, having into consideration both the provisions of article 18 of the Convention and the provisions of article 53, par. (2) of Constitution. It was found that the preventive arrest measure is necessary for conducting a criminal investigation and proportional to the situation that has caused it.[264]

In the jurisprudence of Constitutional Court, the argumentation of proportionality is revealed under the form of a fair balance analysis that should

[263] Considerent no16 of Decision no 139/1994, published in the Official Gazette. No 353/1994. See Decision no 75/1994, published in the Official Gazette no 190/1994; Decision no 21/2000, published in the Official Gazette no 159/2000.

[264] Decision no 26/2000, published in the Official Gazette no 232/2000.

exist between two constitutionally protected rights, balance which determines simultaneously their limits of their exercising[265].

The Constitutional Court stressed that the principle of proportionality, under article 53, par. (2) of Constitution, has as objective only the rights and fundamental freedoms. [266] In this regard, the Constitutional Court stated that the ratio between the offense committed and the penalty imposed, which must be a just one, exceeds the regulation sphere of Article 53, para. (2) of Constitution. "It is undeniable that the verification of proportionality belongs to the controlling powers of the Court, as long as the restriction has as objective the exercise of certain fundamental rights or freedoms.[267]

The Constitutional Court jurisprudence contributes to the understanding and explaining of the principle of proportionality in cases in which it is noticed its interference in the principle of equality.

To be noted that the jurisprudence of our Constitutional Court, in matters of interpretation and applying of the principle of equality has evolved, from the admitting that different situations must be treated differently up to the recognition of new constitutional rights, respectively "the right to difference"

The uniformity has been consistently rejected in the jurisprudence of the Constitutional Court, in connection to the interpretation and applying of the principle of equality. To situations, which by their nature are different, must be applied a different treatment. The principle of proportionality means, in this case the required adequacy of legal regulation to the objective situation considered. Also, the proportionality requires the existence of a motivation "objective and reasonable" for a differentiated legal treatment applied to identical situations.

These rules are formulated in the jurisprudence of the Constitutional Court: "The principle of equality before the law requires the establishment of

---

[265] Decision no 57/1998, published in the Official Gazette no 167/1998. On the same meaning see Decision no110/1995, published in the Official Gazette no74/1996.

[266] Decision no 24/1997, published in C.D.H./1998, pg.99-101; Decision no 157/1998, published in the Official Gazette. No 3/1999.

[267] Decision no 25/1999, published in the Official Gazette no 3/1999. See Decision no 13/1999 previously quoted, by which the Constitutional Court ascertains that in the present case, it is not applied the principle of proportionality, stipulated by art.53 of Constitution, Since the right to hunger strike is a fundamental right protected by constitutional norms.

equal treatment for situations, which pending on the purpose aimed, are not different. Accordingly, a different treatment may not be only the exclusive appreciation expression of the judge, but must be rationally justified, in observing the principle of equality of citizens before the law and public authorities."[268]

Applying the reasoning of proportionality, the Constitutional Court has reached to the recognition of a fundamental right: "the right to difference". "In general, it is estimated that the violation of the principle of equality and non discrimination exists when applying a differential treatment to equal cases, without the existence of an objective and reasonable motivation or if there is a disproportion between the aimed purpose by unequal treatment and means used. In other words, the principle of equality does not prohibit specific rules. Therefore the principle of equality leads to underline the existence of a fundamental right, the right to difference, and as far as equality is not natural, the fact to impose it would mean to establish a discrimination.[269]

The jurisprudence issues discussed above lead to the conclusion that the understanding and applying of the principle of proportionality by the Constitutional Court is consistent with the meanings conferred to this principle, applied in the field of human rights' guaranteeing by C.E.D.O.

However, the jurisprudence of our Constitutional Court is not generous nor edifying in the application and interpretation of the principle of proportionality in ensuring fundamental rights and freedoms, which demonstrates that proportionality, as a principle of law in general and constitutional law in particular, does not represent another object of major concern of jurisprudence.

Most times, the Constitutional Court refers to the criterion of proportionality generically, invoking the provisions of article 53 of

---

[268] Considerent no 5 of the Decision of Constitutional Court Plenum no 1/1994, published in the Official Gazette. No 69/1994. On the same meaning see Decision no 85/27th July 1994, published in C.D.H./1994, pp. 68-74.

[269] Decision no 1071995, published in the Official Gazette No 85/1995. See Decision no 6/1996, published in the Official Gazette No 23/1996; Decision no 198/2000, published in the Official Gazette No 702/2000; Decision no 54/2000, published in the Official Gazette No 310/2000; Decision no 263/2001, published in the Official Gazette no762/2001;

Constitution. There are relatively few decisions of our Constitutional Court to include elements of proportionality analysis. It is true that the interpretation and understanding of the principle of proportionality, considered to be one of the guarantees of fundamental rights and freedoms in situations where it is possible to limit or restrict their exercising, presents serious difficulties, given the diversity of concrete situations, the appreciation margin recognized by legislator, the nature of the right protected and not least the interpretative reasoning of Constitutional Court, which must be maintained to a high level of abstraction, setting the constitutionality of a provision by relating to the provisions of Constitution.

Summarizing, we can say that in the matter of fundamental rights and freedoms' protection, the principle of proportionality is explicitly or implicitly invoked by the Constitutional Court in the following forms:

a) necessary appropriateness of constitutional and legal guarantees conferred to fundamental rights and freedoms, on pursued finality, namely the protection of the exercise of rights in concrete situations in which could be restricted;

b) adequate relationship between the restrictive measures ordered by law, the situation in fact and the legitimate aim pursued, in accordance with Article 53 of Constitution;

c) "argumentation of proportionality" as a means of interpretation used by the Constitutional Court to establish the existence of a fair, equitable ratio, between categories of rights and interests constitutionally protected.

10. THE SIMPLICITY OF THE FORM AND COMPLEXITY OF NORMATIVE CONTENT OF CONSTITUTION

Abstract:

The coding is not only the expression of the political will of the law maker, it firstly is a complex juridical technique for the choosing and systematization of the normative content necessary and adequate to certain social, political, economical, institutional realities. Since Constitution is a law, yet it nevertheless distinguishes itself from the law, the problem is to establish which juridical norms it contains. The solving of this problem needs to consider the specific of the fundamental law and also of the requirements of the coding theory. The determining with all scientific stringency of the normative content of the Constitution is indispensable both for the removal of any inaccuracy in delimiting the differences from the law, for the stability and predictability of the fundamental law and last, but not the least, for the reality and effectiveness of its supremacy.

In our study we realize an analysis based on compared criterions of the techniques and exigencies for the choosing and systematization of the constitutional norms with reference to their specific, to the practice of other states and within a historical context. The analysis is aiming to the actual proposals for the revising of the Constitution.

Key words:

Constitutional norms / constitutional norm establishing criterions / technical - judicial structure / supremacy of Constitution / normative content

I. Principles of law, a possible solution to the requirement for simplicity in the juridical domain

Simplicity is a concept that is constantly to be found in the theoretical elaborations of theology, but in most philosophical doctrines, is associated to the idea of unity of rationality, and generally, of the existence. Understanding the concept of simplicity, involves a comparative report with contradictory accents: simplicity opposes to diversity and composed realities that do not shelter under a law or order. Simplicity does not exclude, however, the complexity of the content, be it rational, of an idea or an objective reality. Simplicity is contrary to uniformity: it is the expression "of one diverse in itself". In the reality plan, the concept of "person", for instance, expresses, in our opinion, the dialectical coexistence between simplicity of the form and the inexhaustible depth of the existential content complex.

We consider as significant in philosophical thinking plan, the philosophical ideas of the great Romanian philosopher Constantin Noica: "The pace of history, in philosophical thinking. The simplicity of pre-Socratic *element* (that gives the composition of world), the simplicity of *self-knowledge*, with Socrate, of *Idea*, with Platon, of *the form*, logical and substantial, with Aristotel, of *subjectivity*, with the Christianity, of *divine,* with medieval philosophy, of *simple natures*, with Descartes, of *perception and representation*,

with the empiricists, of *the monad*, with Leibniz, of *transcendental conscience,* with Kant, of *the Self*, with Fichte, of *the Spirit*, with Hegel. The pulsations of history"[270].

In the meanings given above, the simplicity can be accepted as a fundamental aspect of law, mainly in the form imposed by contemporary realities. In the sphere of juridical, the diverse, opposed to simplicity, is mainly made of a multitude of normative regulations that do not answer to a unifying idea and to the unity of the principle expressing the essence. The requirement of simplicity in the sphere of juridical, in our opinion, is best expressed and may be accomplished by the principles of law, as their normative form, simple, preserves at the same time the complexity of the content.

[270] C. Noica, Carte de înţelepciune, "Book of Wisdom", Humanitas Publishing House, Bucharest, 2009, p.71.

In the followings, we try to make a brief analysis of the notion of principle of law associated both to the idea of simplicity, as to the idea of complexity of content. The normative act that by its nature can highlight better this blend between simplicity of the form and complexity of the content, specific to the principle of law, is the Constitution. That's why we will customize the analysis on the principles of law with referral to the normative content of Constitution.

In philosophy and, in general in science, the principle has a theoretical and explanatory value as it is meant to synthesize and express the foundation and unity of human being, of the existence in general and knowledge, in their manifesting diversity. The discovery and assertion of the principles in any science gives the certitude to knowledge, both by expressing the *prime element* that exist by itself, without the need to be inferred or demonstrated, both by accomplishing the cohesion of system, without which no knowledge or scientific creation may exist. The principle has multiple meanings in philosophy and science, but for our scientific approach, to remember this one: fundamental element, idea, basic law on which is grounded a scientific theory, a political, juridical system, a behavior norm or the totality of laws and basic concepts of a discipline". [271] The common place for all meanings of the term of principle, is the *the essence*, an important category for philosophy and law.

A good systematization of the meanings which the notion of principle has is done in a monography[272] : a) the founding principle of this domain of existence; b) what would be hidden to the direct knowledge and requires logical-epistemological processing; c) logical concept that will allow knowing the particular phenomenon." This systematization, applied to law means: a) discussion on the essence of law; b) whether and how we may know the essence of law; c) operability of settlement in the phenomenality of law, correlated or not with the essence."[273] The need of the spirit to climb up to the principles is natural and particularly persistent. Any scientific construction or normative system need to relate to principles to guarantee or substantiate them.

The law, as it implies a very complex ratio, between essence and phenomena, and a specific dialectic to each of the two categories in terms of

[271] Dicționar explicativ al limbii române, "Romanian Language Explanatory Dictionary", The Socialist Republic of Romania, Bucharest, 1975, p.744.
[272] Ghe. C. Mihai, R I. Motica, Fundamentele dreptului. Teoria şi filozofia dreptului,"The Fundamentals of Law. Theory and Philosophy of Law", All Beck Publishing House, Bucharest, 1997, p.19
[273] Ibidem, quoted works, p.20

theoretical reality, normative but also social one, cannot be outside the principles. Mircea Djuvara states: "All science of law consists not in reality, for a serious and methodical research, other then in releasing from the multitude of law provisions, of their essential, meaning just the ultimate principles of justice from which the other provisions derive. Thus the entire legislation becomes of a greater clarity and what is called the juridical spirit, is being captured. Only then is done the scientific development of the law."[274] The words of the great philosopher Kant are still actual, which we propose for meditation to any contemporary legislator: "It's old the desire, which, who knows when?, will it ever be fulfilled: to be discovered for once, instead of the infinite variation of the civil laws, *their principles,* as only in this will reside, as one says, the secret to simplify the legislation."[275] In our opinion this is the starting point for understanding the principles of law.

In the literature in specialty, there is no unanimous explanation with regard to the definition and significances of the principles of law[276]. One can identify a series of common elements which we emphasize in the followings: a) the principles of law are general ideas, guiding postulates, fundamental requirements or foundations of the law system; b) The general principles of law configure the structure and development of the law system, ensure its unity, homogeneity, balance, coherence and developing capacity; c) The authors distinguish between the fundamental principles of law, which characterize the entire law system and reflect what is essential within the respective law system and the valid principles for certain branches of law or juridical institutions.

[274] Mircea Djuvara, Teoria generală a dreptului. Drept rațional, izvoare și drept pozitv, "General Theory of Law. Rational law, sources and positive law" All Beck Publishing House, Bucharest, 1999, p.265.

[275] I. Kant, Critica Rațiunii Pure, "Critique of Pure Reason" Gold Encyclopedic Universe Publishing House, Bucharest, pp.276 – 277.

[276] On this meaning please see: I. Ceterchi, I. Craiovan, Introducere în teoria generală a dreptului, "Introduction into General Theory of Law" All Publishing House, Bucharest, 1993, p.30; Ghe. Boboș, Teoria generală a statului și dreptului, "General Theory of the State and Law", Didactical and Pedagogical Publishing House, Bucharest, 1983, p.186; N. Popa, Teoria generală a dreptului, "General Theory of Law", Actami Publishing House, Bucharest, 1999, p.112-114; I. Craiovan, Tratat elementar de teorie generală a dreptului,"Elementary Treaty of General Theory of Law" All Beck Publishing House, Bucharest, 2001, p.209,; R. Motica, Gheorghe Mihai, Teoria generală a dreptului, "General Theory of Law", Alma Mater Publishing House, Timișoara, 1999, p.75.

One of the great problems of juridical doctrine is the ratio between the principles of law, law norms and social values. The views expressed are not unitary they differ depending on the legal concept. The natural law school, rationalists, Kantian and Hegelian philosophy of law admit the existence of some principles outside the positive norms and superior to them. The principles of law are grounded on human reason and configure in term of values, the entire juridical order. Contrary, the positivist law school, Kelsian normativism considers that the principles are expressed by the law norms and in consequence there are no law principles outside the juridical norms' system. Eugeniu Speranţia established a correspondence between the law and the principles of law: "If the law appears as a total of social norms, mandatory, the unity of this totality is due to the consistency of all norms related to a minimum number of fundamental principles, they themselves having a maximum of logical affinity between them."[277] In connection to this problem, in Romanian literature in specialty is stated the idea that the principles of law are fundamental prescriptions of all juridical norms.[278] In another opinion, was considered that the principles of law orientate the elaboration and applying of juridical norms, they have the force of superior norms, to be found in the normative act texts, but can be inferred from the "permanent social values" when they are not expressly formulated by the positive law norms .[279]

We consider that the general principles of law are delimited by the positive norms of law, but undoubtedly there is a relation between the two realities. For instance, equality and freedom or equity and justice are foundations of the values of social life. They need to find their juridical expression. In this way appears all kind of juridical concepts that are expressing these values, which concepts become foundations (principles) of law. From these principles the juridical norms derive. Unlike the other normative regulations, the general principles of law have an explanatory value as they contain the grounds of the existence and evolution of law. [280]

---

[277] E. Speranţia, Principii fundamentale de filozofie juridică,"Fundamental principles of Juridical Philosophy", Cluj, 1936, pg.8. On this meaning see N. Popa, quoted works p.114.
[278] N. Popa, quoted works, p.114.
[279] I. Ceterchi, I. Craiovan, quoted works, p.30
[280] N. Popa, quoted works p.116-117.

Alongside other authors[281], we assert our opinion, that the juridical norms are related to the principles of law in two ways: the norms contain and describe most of the principles; the principles are then accomplished by putting into practice the conduct prescribed by the norms. In relation to the principles, the juridical norms have a teleological, explanatory value, more restricted, the scope of the norms being the preservation of the social values, not to explain the causal reasoning of their existence. We may say that the most general principles of law coincide with the social values promoted by the law.

One can identify several most important features of the principle of law:

A) Any principle of law must be of the order of essence. It cannot be identified with a specific case or an individual appreciation of the juridical relations. The principle needs to represent the stability and balance of judicial relations, regardless of the variety of normative regulations or particular aspects specific to judicial reality. Consequently, the principle of law must be opposed to randomness and express the need as essence. Being of the essence order, the principles of law have a generalizing character, both on the variety of judicial relations, as well as for the norms of law. At the same time by expressing the essential and general of judicial reality, the principles of law are the grounds for other normative regulations.

There are important principles of law that do not depend on their consecration through judicial norms, yet the norm of law determines their definite content, in relation to the reference historical time.

B) The principles of law are consecrated and recognized through constitutions, laws, customs, jurisprudence, international deeds or formulated in the judicial doctrine.

With all variety of ways of consecration and recognition of the principles of law, it is obvious the necessity of at least of their recognition in order to be characterized and applied to the law system. This consecration or recognition is not enough to be doctrinaire, yet it must accomplish itself through norms and jurisprudence. It should however be applied a distinction between the

[281] N. Popa, quoted works pp.116-117, R.I. Motica, Ghe. C. Mihai, Teoria generală a dreptului. Curs universitar, "General Theory of Law. Academic course", Alma Mater Publishing House, Timişoara, 1999, p.78.

consecration and recognition of law principle, and on the other side, on their application.

C) The principles of law represent values for the law system, as they express both the judicial ideal, as the objective requirements of society, have a regulatory role for the social relations. In case the norm is unclear or it does not exist, the solving of litigations can be achieved directly based on the general or special principles of law. As an ideal, they represent a basis for the coordination of the work for lawmaking.

The principles of law, by their nature, generality and depth, are themes for reflection, primarily for law's philosophy. Only according to their construction in the sphere of metaphysics of law, these principles can be applied in the general theory of law, can be normatively consecrated and applied to jurisprudence. Moreover, there is a dialectic cycle as the "meanings" of the principles of law, after the normative consecration and jurisprudential development, are to be elucidated also within the law philosophy.

Such a finding imposes nevertheless the distinction between what we may call: *constructed principles of law,* and on the other side *"metaphysical principles of law.* The distinction we propose has as philosophical substantiation, the distinction between 'constructed" and "given" in the law.

The constructed principles of law are by their nature, judicial rules of maximum generality, elaborated by the judicial norm or legislator, in all situations explicitly consecrated by the law norms. These principles can establish the internal structure of a group of judicial relationships, of a branch or even of the unitary law system. The following features can be identified: 1) are developed within the law, being as rule, the expression of manifestation of the will of legislator, consecrated in the norms of law: 2) are always expressed explicitly by judicial norms; 3) the work of interpretation and application of law is able to discover the meanings and determinations of law constructed principles, which obviously cannot exceed their conceptual limits, established by the legal norm. In this category we will find principles such as publicity of the hearing, the contradictoriness principle, of law and Constitution's supremacy, principle of law non-retroactivity, etc.

The metaphysical principles of the law may be considered as a "given" related to the judicial reality and by their nature are outside the law. At their origin they don't have a legal, normative, respectively jurisprudential, drafting.

They are a transcendental 'given" and not transcendent of the law, therefore they are not "beyond" the sphere of law, but are "something else" in the justice system. In other words, they represent the essence of values of the law, without which this constructed reality cannot have an ontological dimension. Not being constructed, but being a metaphysical, transcendental 'given" of the law, they need not be explicitly expressed through judicial norms. The metaphysical principles may have an implicit existence, discovered and exploited in the work for interpretation of law. As an implicit "given" and at the same time as a transcendental essence of law, these principles need to be found, at last, within the content of each judicial norm and in any act or manifestation that represents, where appropriate, the interpretation or application of the legal norm. It should be emphasized that the existence of the metaphysical principles grounds also the teleological nature of law, as any manifestation in the legal sphere, in order to be legitimate, needs to be adequate to such principles.

In our opinion, the metaphysical principles of the law are: *principle of justice; principle of truth; principle of equity and justice; principle of proportionality; principle of freedom.* In a future study, we will expose extensively the general considerations that allow us to identify the principles above mentioned as having a metaphysical and transcendental value in relation to the legal realities.[282]

[282] For development see M. Andreescu, Scurte considerații despre principiile dreptului şi filosofia dreptului. Brief considerations about the principles of law in Review "The Law" no. 12/2012 pp 71-86

II. Constitutional principles and norms

The constitutional norms are provisions containing the formulation of the general principles of law or constitutional law. These norms legitimate the power of state, bases and organizing of the power, define some of the institutions or consecrate principles applicable to the fundamental rights. In this context we emphasize that the constitutional regulations containing the formulation of some law principles cannot be excluded from the sphere of the concept on judicial norm because here we find all features specific to them. [283]

The compliance of entire law with the fundamental Law is an important consequence of supremacy of the Constitution, and it should be understood not only through the correspondence in content and form of the lower norms as legal force with the constitutional ones, but also through the need to translate the constitutional regulations and rules (within their spirit and letter) in other judicial regulations.

To note as an important feature of the constitutional norms that arises from the principle of supremacy of fundamental law, the possibility and even the necessity to be translated, concretized through normative regulations, in other branches of the unified system of law. In relation to this element of specificity of the constitutional law norms, is necessary for the constituent legislator to establish a synthetic content, generalizing these norms' content, and not an analytical, procedural one. In the event that, when in the normative content of a constitution would prevail the descriptive, procedural character of the norms, this would lose too much of its constitutionalism finality, the one of being an essence, generalizing factor, for the whole law system. However, the generality of the constitutional law norm's formulation, would not exclude its clarity and precision. Therefore, any codifying work in the matter of constitutional law, is difficult as it should combine dialectically the generality specific to some norms containing law principles, and on the other side the clarity and precision, the last one absolutely necessary to ensure their correct application and to avoid thus, the arbitrariness or possibility for asserting in the name of some constitutional values, of any partisan political interests. This

[283] I.. Muraru, E. S. Tănăsescu, Drept constituţional şi instituţii politice, "Constitutional Law and Public Institutions". C.H, Beck Publishing House, Bucharest, 2004, vol. I, p. 20; G. Burdeu, Droit constitutionnel et institutions politiques, LG "Constitutional Law and Public Institutions". DJ, Paris, 1966, pp. 71-90.

requirement's fulfilling, can be verified in the practice for transposing and interpretation of the constitutional norms met in all state authorities.

One of the most important problems to elucidate the specific of the constitutional norms' aims the answer to the question if all constitutional provisions contain legal norms. The constitutional provisions that aim the economical, social or financial system are norms of constitutional law with the value of a principle, and not mere political goals, as they regulate the conduct of the law subjects taking part in specific social relations. Likewise, the constitutional norms in question establish genuine legal rights and obligations for the law subjects. For example the constitutional obligation for the derived legislator (Parliament or Govern) like in the process of law making to comply these constitutional regulations, otherwise may intervene the sanction of unconstitutionality of the normative acts in question. We note in conclusion that all constitutional provisions contain legal norms because they have the essential features of a norm of law: prescribe the conduct of the subjects to whom they address and generate legal obligations, and such obligations' breaching may attract legal sanctions specific to constitutional law.

The logical-formal structure of the constitutional law needs to contain all three elements: hypothesis-provision-sanction. The main feature of these norms lies in the way the sanction is being expressed. Thus, for several provisions a single sanction may be present. Also there are specific sanctions in the constitutional law, for instance declaring as unconstitutional a legislative act or revocation of a state body. Given the structuring role of constitutional law for the entire law system, the logical-formal appreciation of the constitutional norms must also be made by reference to other categories of legal regulations. For the regulations of principle or of maximum generality contained in the fundamental law, some sanctions are included in the norms of other branches of law (civil law, criminal law, administrative law). In this regard, the solution of principle was correctly mentioned into the doctrine: "I think that sanctions are to be found even in the constitutional norms for the violation of any provision provided that the obligation or entitlement is exactly identified, in other words the conduct of the subjects of law."[284]

Another element of particularity for the principles with legislative value of the constitutional law refers to the regulation subject. Without going into detail, we retain the idea contained in the contemporary doctrine, according to

[284] Ibidem, quoted works p. 21.

which the common element and proper only to social relations that form the regulation subject of the constitutional law norms, is that they appear in the process for establishing, maintaining and exercising of state power. [285]

All norms contained in the constitution are norms of constitutional law, and also principles of law, even if some of these regulate also the social relations specific to other law branches. Having into consideration that the constitutional law, in particular the constitution, contains norms with value of principle, referring not only to the organizing and functioning of state authorities but also referring to the social and economical system. In consequence, the subject for regulation of the constitutional law is formed by the social relations that appear during the process for the establishing, maintaining and exercising of state power, but also those referring to the bases of the power and bases for power organizing. These categories refer to the sovereignty of the people, characters attributed to the state, to the territory of population, included those referring to the fundamental features of social economical system.

From the technical, juridical point of view, the regulation object of the norms with principle value of the constitutional law and implicitly of a constitution, can be split into two categories of social relationships: a) specific relations of constitutional law that relate to the organizing and exercising of state power and cannot be a regulatory object for other juridical branches; b) double legal natured relationships, governed both by the constitutional law norms and by the norms of other law branches.[286] The existence of such legal relationships justifies by because between the branches of the law there is no rigid demarcation. One needs to consider also the superior legal force of the constitutional law norms, the criterion differentiating them from other norms of law, which confers a structuring value for entire law system.

[285] I. Muraru, E. S. Tănăsescu, quoted works, p. 14

[286] A se vedea I. Muraru, E. S. Tănăsescu, quoted works, pp.16-18; Ghe. Iancu, Drept constituţional şi instituţii politice, "Constitutional Law and Political Institutions" Editura C.H.Beck. Bucharest, 2010 pp. 12-15

III. Normative content of constitution

Constitution is a law, but at the same time through its juridical force and content distinguishes from all other laws. At the same time, the fundamental law supremacy confers to it the quality of a primary formal source for all other branches of law.

In a comparative analysis of the regulations contained in the contemporary constitutions is noticed that the historical, political, national, cultural, religious etc. diversity of the states, does not directly result in a diversity of the legislative content for the fundamental laws. The content of the modern states' constitutions present many resemblances and sometimes wordings almost identical with some of the institutions regulated.[287] This resemblance is determined mainly by the identity of the regulatory object of the constitutional norms.

On the other side, the diversity in the normative content removes the idea of uniform standards generally valid for the contemporary constitutions. The diversity of normative content is a consequence of the fact that the fundamental law of the state is determined in terms of the content of social, political and economical realities, on the characters and attributes of the respective state, historically expressed and at the same time on the will of the constituting legislator, essentially a political will, at a certain historical moment.

Along with other authors, we believe that the scientific definition of constitution is the main criterion for identifying the normative content. Such a criterion ensures the generality necessary to give a scientific character to the scientific elaborations in the matter and it explains at the same time the regulatory unit but also the constitutional normative diversity.

For the purpose of this scientific approach, we retain the essence of every attempt to define the fundamental law namely: "The Constitution is a political and legal fundamental establishment of a state"[288]. In the legal acceptance, the fundamental law is the act through which it is determined the

---

287 A se vedea C. Ionescu, Tratat de drept constituţional contemporan, "Treaty of Constitutional Law and Political Institutions" C.H.Beck Publishing House, Bucharest, 2008, p.208-209.

288 I Deleanu, Instituţii şi proceduri constituţionale,"Institutions and Constitutional Procedures" C.H. Beck Publishing House, Bucharest ,2008 p.88

power statute and therewith all legal rules, having as object the regulation of the bases of power and bases for power organizing.

The legal concept of constitution can be expressed in two different meanings, respectively in a substantial and a formal meaning. Analyzed separately, the formal and material acceptation cannot be a sufficient criterion for identifying the normative content of the fundamental law. Accepting the formal criterion has as a consequence that the fundamental law could regulate any social relationship, regardless of their importance or object of regulation. [289] The material criterion is also unilateral as it excludes the procedural elements, required for a scientific characterization of the fundamental law. The scientific approach regarding the identification of the normative content of the constitution must consider cumulatively both the formal and the material acceptation to which the political dimension referred above, is added. Therefore, we consider one may identify three criteria in order to establish the normative content of a constitution:

The establishing of the normative content of constitution is made according to the specific, importance and value of the social relation regulated. We share the view expressed in the literature that, unlike other categories of legislative acts, the norms contained in the constitution should regulate the fundamental social relations that are essential for the establishing, maintaining and exercising of power, but also those referring to the bases for the power, respectively the bases for power organizing. Therefore, the constitutional norms are always principles of law having a decisive role in establishing and functioning of the government bodies and in determining the form of the state, namely its character and attributes.

The normative expression of the constitutional principles, themselves simple as a normative form, but complex in nature and in the content determined by the object of regulation, constitutes a source and the normative-value ground of the unity and simplicity of entire legislative system of the state. The reporting of legislator to the constitutional principles, not only for guaranteeing the simple formal correspondence between the judicial norm and the fundamental law, but mainly to legislate in respect to these principles and having as a finality their content, is a prerequisite to eliminate the diversity of norms, a natural consequence of the governors' excess of power in legislative matters. There are therefore two ways through which the power can legislate:

---

[289] For example Swizerland Consitution, by article 25 bis states rules for cattle sacrificing.

the first that is disregarding the teleological reporting to the constitutional principles and in general to the principles of law, aiming only the formal correspondence with the constitutional norms, and the second one teleological oriented to the content, meaning and limits imposed by the principles of law. In the first case, the result is the normative diversity, lacking a rational, unifying factor; in the second hypothesis there is at least the possibility of achieving the simplicity and unity of the normative system within the content's complexity.

It is important to underline the constitutional dynamism. The fundamental law is a dynamic, opened act, and in a continuous crystallization process. The constitutional status is achieved through a continuous and complex process of interpretation and application of the texts contained in the body of the constitution by state authorities. Furthermore, the constitutional norms cannot and must not provide definitions. For instance also in Romania's constitution exist such concepts, definable by way of interpretation and forming an object of analysis for the Constitutional Court: "spirit of tolerance and mutual respect" (article 29, paragraph 3); "identity" (article 30, paragraph 6); "private life" (article 30, paragraph 6); "lawful state principles" (article 48, paragraph 2); "public interest" (article 44, paragraph 3); "proportionality and public moral" (article 53) or "extraordinary situations" (article 115, paragraph 4).

The normative content of constitution needs to be understood and determined by having into consideration the teleological criterion highlighted in the above stated definition. Namely, the fundamental law's structuring role for entire social, political and state system, guarantor of fundamental rights and liberties. The fundamental law must achieve the social dynamic balance but also the stability and institutional harmony, the efficient guaranteeing of the fundamental rights, essentially the real constitutional democracy requirements based on the values of the lawful state, on institutional and social balance and on proportionality[290].

---

[290] For development regarding the application of the principle of constitutionality and proportionality in state organization of power, see M. Andreescu, *Principiul proporționalității în dreptul constituțional, "Principle of proportionality and Constitutionality"* C.H. Beck Publishing House, Bucharest, 2007, pp.267-298.

11. STABILITY AND CONSTITUTIONAL REFORM. NORMATIVE CONTENTS OF CONSTITUTION

Abstract:

The modification of the fundamental law of a state represents a very special political and juridical act with major significances and implications in the political social system as in the state's one, but also at each individual level. That's why such an approach needs to be well justified, to answer to some juridical and political social needs well defined, but mainly to correspond to the principles and rules specific to a constitutional and state's democratic system providing to the state the stability and functionality it needs.

In this study we analyze the necessity of such a constitutional reform in Romania, and also some provisions from the report of the Presidential Commission for the analysis of the political and constitutional regime in our country. We formulate our opinions in relation to the justifying some constitutional regulations. In this context, we consider that there are arguments for the maintaining of the bicameral parliamentary system and an eventual revising of the fundamental law needs to consider the measures needed to guarantee the political and constitutional institutions specific to the lawful state.

Key words:

Revising of the Constitution / limits of the constitutional revising / bicameral system/ power excess/ guaranteeing of the fundamental liberties /constitutional norms

I. Stability and constitutional innovation

One of the most controversial and important juridical problems is represented by the relationship between the stability and innovation in law. The stability of the juridical norms is undoubtedly a necessity for the predictability of the conduct of the law topics, for the security and good functioning of the economical and juridical relationships and also to give substance to the principles of supremacy of law and constitution.

On the other hand it is necessary to adapt the juridical norm and in general the law to the social and economical phenomenon that succeed with such rapidity. Also the internal juridical norm must answer to the standards imposed by the international juridical norms in a world in which the 'globalization" and "integration" become more conspicuous and with consequences far more important in the juridical plan also. It is necessary that permanently the law maker be concerned to eliminate in everything that it is "obsolete in law", all that do not correspond to the realities.

The report between stability and innovation in law constitutes a complex and difficult problem that needs to be approached with full attention having into consideration a wide range of factors that can determine a position favorable or unfavourable to legislative modification[291]

One of the criterions that help in solving this problem is the principle of proportionality. Between the juridical norm, the work of interpretation and its applying, and on the other hand the social reality in all its phenomenal complexity must be realized with an adequate report, in other words the law must be a factor of stability and dynamism of the state and society, to correspond to the scope to satisfy in the best way the requirements of the public interest but also to allow and guarantee to the individual the possibility of a free and predictable character, to accomplish oneself within the social context. Therefore, the law included in its normative dimension in order to be sustainable and to represent a factor of stability, but also of progress, must be adequate to the social realities and also to the scopes for which a juridical norm is adapted, or according to the case to be interpreted and applied. This is not a new observation. Many centuries ago Solon being asked to elaborate a

[291] Victor Duculescu, Georgeta Duculescu, „Constitution's revising" „Revizuirea Constituţiei", Lumina Lex Publishing House, Bucureşti, 2002 p. 12

constitution he asked the leaders of his city the question:" Tell me for how long and for which people" then later, the same wise philosopher asserted that he didn't give to the city a constitution perfect but rather one that was adequate to the time and place.

The relationship between stability and innovation has a special importance when the question is to keep or to modify a constitution because the constitution is the political and juridical foundation of a state[292] based on which is being structured the state and society's entire structure. On the essence of a constitution depends its stability in time because only thus will be ensured in a great extent the stability of the entire normative system of a state, the certitude and predictability of the law topics' conduct, but also for ensuring the juridical, political stability of the social system, on the whole. [293]

The stability is a prerequisite for the guaranteeing of the principle for the supremacy of constitution and its implications. On this meaning, professor Ioan Muraru asserts that the supremacy of constitution represents not only a strictly juridical category but a *political-juridical* one revealing that the fundamental law is the result of the economical, political, social and juridical realities. "It marks (defines, outlines) a historical stage in the life of a country, it sanctions the victories and gives expression and political-juridical stability to the realities and perspectives of the historical stages in which it has been adopted" [294].

In order to provide the stability of the constitution, varied technical modalities for guaranteeing a certain degree of rigidity of the fundamental law, have been used, out of which we enumerate: a) the establishing of some special conditions for exercising of an initiative to revise the constitution, such as the limiting of the topics that may have such an initiative, the constitutionality control ex officio upon the initiative for the constitution's revising; b) the interdiction of contitution's revising by the usual legislative assemblies or otherwise said by the recognition of the competence for the constitution's revising only in favour of a Constituent assembly c) the establishing of a special procedure for debating and adopting of the revising initiative; d) the

---

[292] Ion Deleanu, ","Constitutional Law and Public Institutions", Europa Nova Publishing House, Bucharest, 1996, vol. I, p. 260.

[293] Elena Simina Tănăsescu, în Romania's Constitution , Comments on articles, coordinators I. Muraru, E.S. Tănăsescu, All Bach Publishing House, Bucharest, 2008, pp.1467-1469.

[294] Ioan Muraru, Simina Elena Tănăsescu, "Constitutional Law and the Political Institutions" XI th edition, All Bach Publishing House, Bucharest, 2003, p.80.

necessity to solve the revising by referendum; e) the establishing of some material limits for the revising, specially by establishing of some constitutional regulations that cannot be subjected to the revising [295].

On the other hand a constitution is not and cannot be eternal or immutable. Yet from the very appearance of the constitutional phenomenon, the fundamental laws were conceived as subjected to the changes imposed inevitably with the passing of time and dynamics of state, economical, political and social realities. This idea was consecrated by the French Constitution on 1971 according to which "A people has always the right to review, to reform and modify its Constitution, and in the contemporary period included the "International Pact with regard to the economical, social and cultural rights" as well as the one regarding the civil and political rights adopted by U.N.O. in 1966 - item 1 - is stipulating:"All nations have the right to dispose of themselves. By virtue of that right they freely determine their legal status.

The renowned professor Constantin G. Rarincescu stated on this meaning:" A constitution yet is meant to regulate in future for a longer or a shorter time period, the political life of a nation, is not destined to be immobile, or perpetuum eternal, but on the other hand a constitution in the passing of time can show its imperfections, and no human work is being perfect, imperfections to whose some modifications are being imposed, on the other side a constitution needs to be in trend with the social necessities and with the new political concepts, that can change more frequently within a state or a society". [296] Underlying the same idea the professor Tudor Drăganu stated: "The constitution cannot be conceived as a perennial monument destined to outstand to the viccisitudes of the centuries, not even to the ones of the decades. Like all other juridical regulations, the constitution reflects the economical, social and political conditions existing in a society at a certain time of history and aims for creating the organizational structures and forms the most adequate to its later development. The human society is in a continuous changing. What it is valid today tomorrow can become superannuated. On the other side, one of

[295] For the development see : Ioan Muraru,Simina Tănăsescu, quotted works pp.52-55,Tudor Drăganu,, „Constitutional Law and the Political Institutions. Elementary Treaty" Lumina Lex Publishing House, Bucharest,1998,Vol I,pp. 45-47, Marius Andreescu, Florina Mitrofan, „Constitutional Law. General Theory" Publishing House of Piteşti University, 2006,pp. 43-44,Victor Duculescu ,Gergeta Duculescu, quotted works. pp.28-47, Ion Deleanu , quotted works.,pp.275-278.

[296] Constantin G. Rarincescu,, « Constitutional Law Course » Bucharest, 1940, p. 203.

the characteristics of the juridical regulations consists in the fact that they prefigure certain routes meant for chanelling the society's development in one or another direction. These directions as well as the modalities to accomplish the targeted scopes may prove to be, in their confronting with the realities, inadequate. Exactly for this very reason, the constitutions as all other regulations, cannot remain immutable but must adapt to the social dynamics"[297].

In the light of those considerents we appreciate that relationship between the stability and the constitutional revising needs to be interpreted and solved by the requirements of principle of proportionality[298]. The fundamental law is viable as long as it is adequated to the realities of the state and to a certain society at a determined historical time. Much more – states professor Ioan Muraru – "a constitution is viable and efficient if it achieves the balance between the citizens (society) and the public authorities (state) on one side, then between the public authorities and certainly between the citizens. Important is also that the constitutional regulations realize that the public authorities are in the service of citizens, ensuring the individual's protection against the state's arbitrary attacks contrary to one's liberties"[299].In situations in which such a report of proportionality no longer exists, due to the imperfections of the constitution or due to the inadequacy of the constitutional regulations to the new state and social realities, it appears the juridical and political necessity for constitutional revising.

Nevertheless in the relationships between the stability and constitutional revising, unlike the general relationship stability – innovation in law the two terms have the same logical and juridical value. It is about a contrariety relationship (and not a contradiction one) in which the constitution's stability is the dominant term. This situation is justified by the fact that the stability is a requirement essential for the guaranteeing of the principle of constitution supremacy with all its consequences. Only through the primacy of the stability against the constitution's revising initiative one can exercise its role to provide the stability, equilibrium and dynamics of the social system's components, of the stronger and stronger assertion of the principles of the lawful state. The

---

[297] Tudor Drăganu, quotted works pp. 45-47

[298] For development see Marius Andreescu „The Principle of Proportionality in the Constitutional Law" CH Beck Publishing House ,Bucharest,2007.

[299] Ioan Muraru, "The Constitutional Protection of the Liberties for Oppinion" Lumina Lex Publishing House, Bucharest, 1999, p.17.

supremacy of the constitution bestowed by its stability represents a guarantee against the arbitrary and discretionary power of the state's authorities, by the pre-established and predictable constitutional rules that regulate the organization, functioning and tasks of the state authorities. That's why before putting the problem of constitution's revising, important is that the state's authorities achieve the interpretation and correct applying of the constitutional normative dispositions in their letter and spirit. The work of interpretation of the constitutional texts done by the constitutional courts of law but also by the other authorities of the state with the respecting of the competences granted by the law, is likely to reveal the meanings and significances of the principles for regulating the Constitution and thus to contribute to the process for the suitability of these norms to the social, political and state reality whose dynamics need not be neglected. The justification of the interpretation is to be found in the necessity to apply a general constitutional text to a situation in fact which in factum is a concrete one"[300].

The decision to trigger the procedure for revising a country's Constitution is undoubtedly a political one, but at the same time it needs to be juridically fundamented and to correspond to a historical need, of the social system stately organized from the perspective of its later evolution. Therefore, the act for revising the fundamental law needs not be subordinated to the political interests of the moment, no matter how nice they will be presented, but in the social general interest, well defined and possible to be juridically expressed. Professor Antonie Iorgovan specifies on full grounds:" in the matter of Constitution's revising, we dare say that where there is a normal political life, proof is given of restraining prudence, the imperfections of the texts when confronting with life, with later realities, are corrected by the interpretations of the Constitutional Courts, respectively throughout the parliamentary usance and customs, for which reason in the Western literature one does not speak only about the Constitution, but about the block of constitutionality" [301].

The answer to the question if in this historical moment is justified the triggering of the political and juridical procedures for the modifying of the fundamental law of Romania can be stressed out in respect with the reasons

---

[300] Ioan Muraru, Mihai Constantinescu, Simina Tănăsescu, Marian Enache, Gheorghe Iancu, „Interpreting of the Constitution" Lumina Lex Publishing House, Bucharest, 2002, p.14

[301] Antonie Iorgovan, „The Revising of Constitution and Bicameralism" in the l the Public Law Journal no. 1/2001, p. 23.

and purpose targeted. The revising of Constitution cannot have as finality the satisfying of the political interests of the persons holding the power for a moment, in the direction of reinforcing of the discretionary power of the Executive, with the inacceptable consequence of harming certain democratical constitutional values and principles, mainly of the political and institutional pluralism, of the principle of separation of powers in the state, of the principle of legislative supremacy of the Parliament.

On the other hand, such as the two decades lasting history of democratical life in Romania has shown, by the decisions taken for many times, were distorted the constitutional principles and rules by the interpretations contrary to the democratical spirit of the fundamental law, or worse, they didn't observe the constitutional dispositions because of the political purposes and their support in some conjunctural interests. The consequences were and are obvious: the restraining or violation of some fundamental rights and liberties, generating some political tensions, the nonobservance of the constitutional role of the state's institution, in a single word, due to political actions, some dressed in juridical clothes, contrary to the constitutionalism that needs to characterize the lawfull state in Romania. In such conditions, an eventual approach of the revising of the fundamental law should be centered on the need to strengthen and enhance the constitutional guarantees for respecting the requirements and values of the lawfull state, in order to avoid the power excess specific to the politician subordinated exclusively to a group interests, many time conjunctural and contrary to the Romanian people, which in accordance to Constituion item 2 paragraph (1) of the one who is the holder of the national sovereignity.

In our opinion, the preoccupation of the political class and state's authorities in the current period, in relation to the actual contents of the fundamental law, should be oriented not so for the modification of the Constitution, but especially into the direction of interpreting and correct applying and towards the respecting of the democratical finality of the constitutional institutions. In order to strengthen the lawfull state in Romania, it is necessary that the political formations, mostly those that hold the power, all authorities of the state to act or to exercise its duties within the limits of a *loyal constitutional behavior* that involve the respecting of the meaning and demoratical significances of the Constitution.

Currently, the political and juridical reality in Romania is confronting with an extensive political approach for the revising of the fundamental Law, substantied throughout the results of the referendum organized on 2009 having as objective the reducing of the number of parliamentarians and with the passing to a unicameral parliamentary system, in the "Report of the Presidential Commission for the Analysis of the Political and Constitutional regime in Romania"[302] that was published on April 28th 2010, the initiative of the President of Romania for revising the fundamental law at the Government proposal and the decision no. 799/17.06.2011 of the Constitutional Court targeting the law draft for Romania's Constitution revising[303].

This is up to now the only political initiative that has been materialized in a legislative draft for revising the fundamental law that was submitted to the Parliament. In the present social and political context other proposals, ideas for the modifying of the Constitution are being expoxed by the governing ones yet without being materialized in a new legislative initiative.

Our scientific approach has into consideration, from a critical perspective, mostly the political initiative for the Constitution revising that has already the form of a legislative project, though it is not on the Parliament 's roll for debating. We wish at the same time to underline few important themes which in our opinion need a more serious consideration, included in regard to the normative contents of the Constitution. In this epoch of political class' intense preoccupations for the modifying of the fundamental law it is important to reflect in the light of the political exigencies of the constitutional law, upon the normative content of the Constitution. The establishing based on some scientific criterions to what exactely needs to contain the fundamental law of a state, is essential to avoid that throughout political enthusiasm be ignored the basic aspects regarding the specific of the normative contents of the Constitution that explains thus last one's supremacy.

The proposals for the Constitution's revising have as an obvious finality the passing of Romania's constitution system from bicameral to unicameral and the strengthening of the executive power, mostly of the presidential institution.

The doctrine in specialty underlines the fact that in the unitary states, such as Romania, both the unicameral system, as the bicameral system have

---

302 Published by C.H. Beck Publishing House, Bucharest, 2009.

303 M.Of. no. 440/23.06.2011.

advantages and disadvantages [304]. There is no ideal constitutional solution on this meaning. Important is the fact that the Parliament's structure which the Constitution consecrates be adequate to the social, political and economical realities of a country, be functional and to integrate harmoniously within the system of authorities of the state with the observance of the principle of constitutional democracy principles and of the lawfull state. Nevertheless, prestigious authors such as professor Herbert Schambeck remark the importance of the parliamentary system: "From the second chamber of this type, it is expected to emanate *auctoritas*, which in a specific way grants personal fame, in plus to *potestas* or the political power. The second Chamber or the superior chamber has always existed in the area of tensions between the tradition inherited and the present political reality. It represents a part of the basic constitutional organization and a political reality of the state"[305].

Coming back to the essence of the problem, besides other authors[306] , we appreciate that in Romania, the bicameralism is adequate to the state and social system at this historical moment, corresponding better to the necessity to achieve not only the efficiency of the parliamentary legislative procedures but also the "norming ponderation" and quality of the legislative act. The bicameralism is a necessity for Romania because the Parliament represents a valid counterpondering against the Executive, in the context of the exigencies and balance of the powers in a democratic state. With good reason the regretted professor Antonie Iorgovan underlined: " It would have been a very high political risk, in that post revolutionary tension, that in Romania to have designed a unicameral Parliament and such a risk exists still at present, considering that one cannot speak about a political life settled on natural pathes of the democratical doctrines accepted in Occident (the social-democratic doctrine, the democratic-Christian doctrine, liberal doctrines and ecologist doctrines)"[307]. The unicameralism in a semi-presidential constitutional system such as the one of Romania, in which the powers of the head of the state and

[304] For development see Ioan Muraru, Mihai Constantinescu, „Romanian Parliamentary Law" All Beck Publishing House, Bucharest, 2005, pp. 72-79.

[305] Herbert Schambeck, „Reflections on the Importance of the Bicameral Parliamentary System" in the Public Law Review no. 1/2010 p. 3.

[306] Ioan Muraru, Mihai Constantinescu, quotted works., pp. 2-37; Antonie Iorgovan, quotted works., pp. 3-7; Florian Vasilescu, „Questions about Bicameralism" in the Romanian Public Law Review no. 3/2010 pp. 28-51; Ioan Alexandru, ,"Reflections regarding the bicameralism and asymmetry of the distribution of competences" in the Public Law Review no.. 3/210 pp. 51-60;

[307] Antonie Iorgovan, quotted works., pp. 18-19.

in general those of the Executive are significant, having into consideration the excesive politicianism of the moment, would have as a consequence the severe deterioration of the institutional balance between the Legislative and Executive, with consequence the increase of the discretionary power of the Executive and the minimizing of the role of Parliament as a supreme representative organism of the Romanian people, as a unique law maker authority of the country, such as the provisions of item 61 paragraph (1) of the Constitution foresee.

The transition to a unicameral Parliament needs not be treated simplistic such as unfortunately comes out from the contents of the Law draft regarding the revising of Constitution elaborated by the Government, it rather needs a general modification of the Romanian constitutional system, a reconfiguring of the role and duties of the state authorities so that the balance between the Legislative and Executive be maintained and not create the possibility of an evolution towards an exaggerated preponderance of the institution of the head of the state in respect to the Parliament.

We underline the fact that all states with a unitary structure of Europe that have a unicameral Parliament have at the same time a constitutional system of parliamentary type in which the duties of the head of the state regarding the governing are being reduced. We do not wish to do a thorough analysis of this constitutional problem, we stress only the conclusion that the unicameralism may have be political and constitutionally justified in Romania and adequate to the democracy values in a lawfull state only if the legitimacy and the role of Romania's President as a constitutional institution, will be fundamentally be changed. The election of the President needs to be by the Parliament. At the same time in case of a unicameral structure of the Parliament it is necessary to reduce significantly the responsibilities of the President in respect to the Executive and the governing ones. In such a reconfiguring of the institutions of the state needs to be increased the role and duties of the Constitutional Court and those of the Justice, these ones being guarantees of the supremacy of the law and Constitution and for avoiding the power excess coming from the other authorities of the state. In one word, in our opinion the unicameralism cannot be associated in Romania other than with the existence of a constitutional system of parliamentary type.

The legislative proposal for the Constitution revising is of a nature to create a disproportion between the Parliament and Executive by the fact that the unicameral structure of the Parliament does not represent a guarantee sufficient to make an efficient counterponderance in respect to the Executive, mainly as the responsabilities of the President are obviously enhanced. The dispute between unicameralism and bicameralism with applying to the conditions of Romania is well characterized by the regretted professor Antonie Iorgovan: „...any bicameral or unicameral parliamentary system can lead into severe disfunctionalities such as professor Tudor Drăganu states, no matter how successful may be the constitutional solutions, if in the parliamentary practice evidence is given of politicianism, demagogy and lack of responsibility"[308].

Does the present Parliamentary system of Romania correspond to the exigencies of the democratic traditions of bicameralism and is it really adequate to the fulfilling of the role and functions of the Parliament? Professor Tudor Drăganu, in a flawless argumenting logic, in an extensive study answered to this question:"The revised Constitution establishes a system that claims to be bicameral but it functions currently like a unicameral system, condemned being to violate by certain of its aspect the most elementary principles of the parliamentary regime and which contains in itself the danger of producing in future of severe disfunctionalities in accomplishing the legislative activity"[309].The illustrious professor had into consideration that the law for the Constitution's revising does not contain references with regard to the number of deputies and senators it sets the matter of legitimacy of substance of the two chambers, because their members are appointed by the same election body and by the same type of system and election ballot; the responsibilities of the chambers in legislative matter are not sufficiently well differentiated; the exercising of the right to the legislative initiative of the senators and deputies, such as regulated, generates constitutional contradictions.

Together with other authors[310], we state that in the perspective of a future constitutional revising, to regulate the differentiation between the two chambers also by special types of representation. The law compared offers sufficient examples of this kind (Spain, Italy, France) and even the election law of Romania on March 27th 1926 offers a landmark on this meaning. The Senate

---

308 Antonie Iorgovan, quotted works., p. 16.

309 Tudor Drăganu, Few critical remarks about the bicameral system established by the Law for Constitution's revising adopted by the Deputies Chamber and in the Senate, in the Public Law Review no. 4/2003 pp. 55-66.

310 Dan Claudiu. Dănişor, quotted works, p. 23-24.

may represent the interests of the local collectivities. Thus, the senators may be elected from an electoral college made of the local councils' chosen members. Interesting to underline is the fact that in the Constitution draft on 1991 the Senate was designed as a representant of the local collectivities, grouped on the country's counties and Bucharest municipality.

It is reasonable the critic of Professor Tudor Drăganu according to which the current constitutional regulation does not achieve a functional differentiation between the two chambers. This aspect was also noticed by the Constitutional Court that, referring to the parliamentary legislative procedure introduced in the draft for the Constitution revising, stressed: "The examining in cascade of the law drafts, in a chamber in the first lecture, and in the other one in the second lecture transforms the bicameral Parliament in a unicameral one"[311]. Therefore a new initiative for the modification of the fundamental law should have into consideration this aspect also and should achieve a real functional differentiation of the two chambers.

[311] Decision no. 148/16.04.2003 (M.Of. no. 317/12.05.2003).

II. Brief Considerations regarding the normative contents of the Constitution

The Constitution is a law, but in the same time through it juridical force and its contents it distinguishes itself from any other laws. At the same time, the supremacy of the fundamental law grants to this one the quality of a main formal spring for all other law branches. Consequently, there are specific features of the normative contents of the Constitution in respect to the other normative acts, included compared to the existing codes. The normative specific of the Constitution makes an important criterion for explaining scientifically this one's supremacy and the structurant role of the fundamental law, not only by the system of law but also for the entire social, political and economical system of a state. Thus such as it is mentioned in the literature in specialty, the supremacy of the Constitution is a quality of the last one expressed throughout the supreme juridical force but also through its normative contents. As a first observation we specify that the norms forming the content of a constitution have the features of the constitutional law which I analyzed above. This observation is not enough to determine the normative content of the fundamental law because the sphere of the constitutional law norms is wider, including other formal sources specific to this branch of law.

The constitutional contemporary reality that is stressing also the diversity of the normative content removes the idea of general uniform standards valid for the contemporary constitutions. In this regard it is enough to remember that there are some states and constitutions whose provisions are inspired by the religious precepts. The diversity in the normative content is a consequence of the fact that the fundamental law of a state is determined in view of the aspect of the content of the social, political and economical realities, by the characters and attributes of the respective state historically expressed and in the same time by the will of the constituent law maker, in essence the political will, at a certain historical moment.

Besides other authors, we consider that the scientifical definition of the constitution is the main criterion for the identifying of the normative content. Such a criterion provides the generality necessary to give a scientific character to the scientific elaborations in the matter and at the same time it explains the existence of the differences between the fundamental laws of the contemporary states. The space allocated to this study, does not allow an extensive analysis of the definitions proposed in the literature in speciality. For the purpose of this scientific approach we bear in mind the essence of any attempt to define the fundamental law, namely "The constitution is the political and juridical fundamental foundation of any state"[312].

In juridical acceptation, the fundamental law is the act through which it is determined the statute of the power and at the same time all the juridical rules, having as regulating objective the establishment of exercising and maintaining of the power, as well as the regulation of the basis of the power, of the bases for power organizing. The juridical concept on the constitution can be expressed in two different meanings, respectively in the material meaning and in the formal one.

In the "material" acceptation, the constitution contains all the law rules, no matter of their nature and form, having as regulating objective the organizing and functioning of state power, the relations between the state's organs and society. Therefore they are part of the constitution body not only the so called constitutional regulations but also the norms contained in the ordinary laws and normative acts of the executive powers if through these are being regulated the social relations specific tó state power. In such a conception has preeminence the regulating objective of the constitutional norm and not its form of expression. The theory above stated was accepted by the Constitutional Council of France which elaborated the concept of "the constitutionality block".

In the formal acceptation, the constitution is all the law rules, no matter of their regulating objective, elaborated in a form different from other normative acts, by a state authority namely established (the constituent assembly) following a specific procedure, derogatory from the usual legislative procedure. This way of defining the constitution starts from the correct idea that a certain "procedure" defines a juridical form or a normative category. Consequemtly the categories of normative acts can be differentiated by the adopting procedures.

Analyzed separately, the formal acceptation and respectively the material one cannot be a criterion enough to identify the normative content of the fundamental law. The accepting of the formal criterion has as a consequence the fact that the law fundamental may regulate any kind of social

---

[312] Ion Deleanu, quotted works p.88

relations, no matter of their importance or regulating objective. [313] The material criterion is also unilateral because it excludes the procedural elements, necessary for a scientific characterization of the fundamental law.

The scientific approach regarding the identifying of the normative content of the constitution needs to have into consideration cumulated both the formal acceptation as the material one to which adds the political dimension to which we referred to above. Therefore, we consider that three critera can be identified in view to establish the normative contents of a constitution:

A. The establishing of the normative content of the constitution is fulfilled depending on the specific, importance and value of the regulated social relations. We concur to the opinion stated by the literature in speciality according to which, unlike other normative act categories, the norms contained in the constitution must regulate the fundamental social relations that are essential for the establishment, maintaining and exercising of the power, but also those referring to the bases of the power, respectively the power organizing bases. There are three such categories of social relations, that can form the regulating objective of the norms contained in the constitution that allow their identification such as follows:

- The constitutional norms, some having values of principle, having a determining role in the establishing and functioning of the governing organs and in the establishing of the form of the state, respectively of its characters and attributes;
- the norms for the consecration and guaranteeing of the fundamental righs and liberties and those that regulate the citizens' fundamental duties;
- constitutional dispositions that have no direct connection with the governing process and regulate the bases for power organizing (sovereignity, territory, population) and the bases of the power (economy, social and cultural aspects etc)

B. The form for adopting the constitution or of the constitutional laws have a solemn character and are achieved according to a procedure derogatory from the usual legislative procedure and by a state authority specially established or by the Parliament, that acts as a constituent power and not as a usual legislative power;

[313] For example the Switzerland Constitution , by item. 25 bis establishes rules for cattle cutting.

C. The significance of the constitution as a fundamental poitical document determines the concrete content of some constitutional regulations, expressing the will of the legislator constituted at the historical time for adopting or as the case may be, for the revising of the fundamental law. The political dimension of the constitution evokes the complex and multiple characters of its exterior determinations, respectively the historical particularities of the society organized at state level, the development degree and corresponding to the political will of the constituent legislator.

It is important to underline the constitutional dynamism. The fundamental law is a dynamic and opened act, in a continuous crystallization process. The constitutionality status is achieved in a continuous and complex process for interpreting and applying by state's authorities of the texts contained in the body of the constitution. A special role in this wide process of interpretation and concrete fulfilling of the constitutional provisions is in the charge of the constitutional authorities. The activity for interpreting the fundamental law texts is justified because in the normative content of the constitution there are categories and concepts whose sphere cannot be defined by the constituent law maker. Thus, the constitutional norms cannot and must not offer definitions. For example in Romania's constitution there are such concepts that are defining by interpretation way and have formed the objective of analysis of the Constitutional Court: " spirit of tolerance and mutual respect" (item 29, paragraph 3); "identity" (item 30, paragraph 3); "private life" (item 30, paragraph 6), " the principles of the lawfull state" (item 48 paragraph 2); "public utility" (item 44, paragraph 3); "public and moral proportionality" (item 116, paragraph 4).

The interpreting and applying of the constitutional norms involve what in the literature in speciality is called the "loyal constitutional behavior", namely the authorities of the state have the obligation in the work of interpreting of the constitutional text to respect the spirit and mainly the finality of the juridical norm. That's why the work for interpreting and applying of the fundamental law is not legitimate if by such an activity the finality aimed consists in fulfilling the supporting interests of political nature. The juristprudential interpreting of the constitutional text can reveal new constitutional norms. For example, the jurisprudential interpretation of the Constitutional Court underlined a new fundamental law that has no express formulation in the Constitution, respectively "the right to one's image".The normative contents of the constitution must be understood and determined with having into consideration the teleological criterion emphasized in the above stated definition. Namely the fundamental law's structuring role for the entire social, political and state system, guarantor of the fundamental rights and liberties.Noticing a political and juridical reality yet present, G. Bourdeau stated:" The written constitution is the work of the theoreticiens preoccupied more by the elegance and juridical balance of the mechanism they construct, than by its political efficiency [314]" Such a finding, we consider valid also for the Constitution, respectively the contemporary Romanian constitutionalism.

The fair determination of the normative contents of a constitution is expressed by its political and juridical efficiency. The fundamental law must achieve the social dynamic balance but also the stability and institutional harmony, the efficient guaranteeing of the fundamental rights, in essence the requirements of a real constitutional democracy based on the values of the state, of the institutional and social balance and of the proportionality[315]. Ion Deleanu noticed very well that: "the success of the constitution and constitutionalism is always a political one as far as it is the result of a transaction, of a relationship between what the constitution offers in a formalizing and objectiving term of the political matters and what the political actors ask or search for at a certain time in order to fulfill their own objectives. [316]

---

[314] George Bordeau, Traite de science politique, LGDJ, 1969, p.59.

[315] For developments regarding the applying of the constitutional principle of proportionality at the state power organizing see. Andreescu Marius, Principle of proportionality in the constitutional law, quotted works, pp.267-298.

[316] Ion Delenu, quotted works p.89.

Bibliography

1. Victor Duculescu, Georgeta Duculescu, „Constitution's revising" ,„ Lumina Lex Publishing House, Bucureşti, 2002;

2. Ion Deleanu, "Constitutional Law and Public Institutions" Europa Nova Publishing House, Bucharest, 1996;

3. Romania's Constitution, Comments on articles, coordinators I. Muraru, E.S. Tănăsescu,CH.Beck , Publishing House, Bucharest, 2008;

4. Ioan Muraru, Simina Elena Tănăsescu, "Constitutional Law and the Political Institutions" XI th edition, All Bach Publishing House, Bucharest, 2003;

5. Marius Andreescu, „The Principle of Proportionality in the Constitutional Law", CH Beck Publishing House, Bucharest, 2007;

12. PRINCIPLE OF PROPORTIONALITY, CRITERION OF LEGITIMACY IN THE PUBLIC LAW

Abstract:

A problem of essence of the state is the one to delimit the discretionary power, respectively the power abuse in the activity of the state's institutions. The legal behavior of the state's institutions consists in their right to appreciate them and the power excess generates the violation of a subjective right or of the right that is of legitimate interest to the citizen.

The application and nonobservance of the principle of lawfulness in the activities of the state is a complex problem because the exercise of the state's functions assumes the discretionary powers with which the states authorities are invested, or otherwise said the 'right of appreciation" of the authorities regarding the moment of adopting the contents of the measures proposed. The discretionary power cannot be opposed to the principle of lawfulness, as a dimension of the state de jure.

In this study we propose to analyze the concept of discretionary power, respectively the power excess, having as a guidance the legislation, jurisprudence and doctrine in the matter.

At the same time we would like to identify the most important criterions that will allow the user, regardless that he is or not an administrator, a public clerk or a judge, to delimit the legal behavior of the state's institutions from the power excess. Within this context, we appreciate that the principle of proportionality represents such a criterion.

The proportionality is a legal principle of the law, but at the same time it is a principle of the constitutional law and of other law branches. It expresses clearly the idea of balance, reasonability but also of adjusting the measures ordered by the state's authorities to the situation in fact, respectively to the purpose for which they have been conceived.

In our study we choose theoretical and jurisprudence arguments according to which the principle of proportionality can procedurally be determined and used to delimit the discretionary power and power abuse.

Key words:

Discretionary power/ power excess/ subjective right / principle of lawfulness / principle of proportionalityconstitutional la

I. Introduction

The lawfulness, as a feature that needs to characterize the juridical acts of the public authorities, has as a central element the concept of "law". Andre Hauriou defined the law as a written general rule established by the public powers, after the deliberation and involving the direct or indirect acceptance of the governors[317]. In a wide meaning, the concept of law includes all juridical acts that contain the law norms. The law in a restricted acceptance is the juridical act of the Parliament elaborated in compliance with the constitution, according to some pre-established proceedings, that regulates the most general and most important social rules. A special place in the administered legislative system is owned by the constitution defined by the fundamental law that is placed on top of the hierarchy of the legislative system which contains juridical norms with a superior juridical force regulating the fundamental and essential social relationships, mostly those regarding the installing and exercising of the state power.

The lawfulness status in the public authorities' activity is founded on the concept of supremacy of the constitution and supremacy of the law.

The supremacy of the constitution is a quality of the fundamental law which in essence expresses its supreme juridical force in the law system. An important consequence of the supremacy of the fundamental law is the compliance of the entire law with the constitutional norms[318]. The concept of juridical supremacy of the law is defined like "its characteristic that is seeking its expression in the fact that the norms it establishes should not correspond to neither of the norms, except for the constitutional ones, and the other juridical acts issued by the state bodies, are subordinated to it, from the point of view of their juridical efficacy"[319].

Therefore, the supremacy of the law, in the above given acceptance is subsequent to the principle of supremacy of constitution. Important is the fact that the lawfulness, as a feature of the juridical acts of the state authorities involves the observance of the principle of supremacy of constitution and

[317] André Hauriou, Droit constitutionel et institution politiques, Ed. Montchrestien, Paris, 1972, p.137

[318] For development see Marius Andreescu, Florina Mitrofan, Constitutional Law. General Theory, Printing House of the University of Pitești, p.61-68

[319] Tudor Drăganu, Constitutional Law and Political Institutions. Elementary Treaty, Lumina Lex Publishing House, Bucharest, 1999, vol. II, p.362

supremacy of the law. The observance of the two principles is a fundamental obligation of constitutional nature consecrated by the provisions of item 1 paragraph 5 of the Constitution. The non observance of this obligation results, as the case might be, into sanctions of non-constitutionality or unlawfulness of the juridical acts.

The lawfulness of the juridical acts of the public authorities involves the following requirements: the juridical acts should be issued with the observance of the competence stipulated by the law; the juridical act should respect the superior law norms as a juridical force.

The "legitimacy" is a complex category with multiple significances that forms the search topic for the general theory of the law, philosophy of law, sociology and other branches of instruction. The significances of this concept are multiple. To remind a few: the legitimacy of the power, the legitimacy of the political regime; the legitimacy of a governing, the legitimacy of the political system, etc.

The legitimacy concept can be applied also in the case of the juridical acts issued by the public authorities being linked to the "appreciation margin" recognized to them in the exercising of the duties.

The applying and observance of the principle of lawfulness in the activity of state's authorities is a complex problem because the exercise of the state's powers implies also the discretionary power with which the state's bodies are invested, or otherwise said the right of appreciation of the authorities regarding the adopting moment and the contents of the disposed measures. What it is important to underline is the fact that the discretionary power cannot be opposed to the principle of lawfulness, as a dimension of the rightful state.

In our opinion, the lawfulness represents a particular aspect of the legitimacy of the juridical acts of the public authorities. Thus, a legitimate juridical act is a legal juridical act, issued outside the appreciation margin recognized by the public authorities, that does not generate unjustified discriminations, privileges or restraints of the subjective rights and is adequate to the situation in fact, which is determined by the purpose of the law. The legitimacy makes distinction between the discretionary power recognized by the state's authorities, and on the other side, the power excess.

Not all the juridical acts that fulfill the conditions of lawfulness are also legitimate. A juridical act that respects the formal conditions of lawfulness, but which generates discriminations or privileges or unjustified restrained to the exercising of the subjective rights or is not adequate to the situation in fact or to the purpose aimed by the law, is an un-legitimate juridical act. The legitimacy, as a feature of the juridical acts of the public administration authorities should be understood and applied in relation to the principle of supremacy of Constitution.

II. Paper content

Antonie Iorgovan asserted that a problem of essence of the rightful state is that of answering to the question: "where ends the discretionary power and where begins the law abuse, where ends the legal behavior of the administration, materialized by its right of appreciation and where begins the subjective law or the legitimate interest of the citizen? "[320]

Approaching the same problem, Leon Duguit in 1900 makes an interesting distinction between the "normal powers and the exceptional powers" conferred to the administration by the constitution and the laws, and on the other side the situations in which the state's authorities act outside the normative framework. The last situations are split into three categories by the author: 1) the power excess (when the state authorities exceed the limits of the legal mandates; 2) the embezzlement of the power (when the state's authority fulfils an act that enters its competence aiming a different scope, other than the one the law stipulated), 3) the power abuse (when the state's authorities act outside their competence, but through acts that don't have a juridical character)[321].

In the administrative doctrine, that studies mainly the problematic of the discretionary power, it was underlined that the opportunity of the administrative acts cannot be opposed to their lawfulness, and the conditions of lawfulness can be split in general lawfulness conditions and respectively in lawfulness specific conditions on opportunity criterions[322]. As a consequence, the lawfulness is the corollary of the conditions of validity, and the opportunity is a requirement (a dimension) of the lawfulness.[323] Nevertheless, the right of appreciation is not recognized by the authorities of the state in the exercising of all duties they have. One must remember the difference between the *linked competence* of the state's authorities that exists when the law imposes them a certain strict decisional behavior, and on the other side the *discretionary competence*, situation in which the state authorities can choose between more decisions, within law limits and its competences. To remember the definition proposed in the literature in specialty to the discretionary power: "it is the margin of liberty that is let to the free appreciation of the authorities, so that in

[320] Antonie Iorgovan. Forward to: Dana Apostol Tofan, Discretionary power and the power excess of the public authorities, All Beck Publishing House, Bucharest, 1999.

[321] Leon Duguit, Manuel de Droit Constitutionnel, Paris, 1907, p. 445-446.

[322] Antonie Iorgovan, Treaty of administrative law, Nemira Publishing House, Bucharest 1996, vol I,p.301

[323] Ibidem, pg.292.

view of fulfilling the purpose indicated by the law maker, to use any means of action within its limits of competence."[324]

Yet the problematic of the discretionary power is studied mainly in the administrative law, the right for the appreciation in the exercise of some duties represents a reality met in the activity of all state's authorities.[325] The Parliament, as a supreme representative organ and with a unique law making authority, disposes of the largest limits in order to show its discretionary power, which is identified by the characterization of the legislative act. The discretionary power exists in the activity of the law courts. The judge is obliged to decide only when it is noticed for, within this notification limit. Beyond these it is manifested the sovereign *right of appreciating* the facts, the right to interpret the law, the right to fix a minimum punishment or a maximum one, to grant or not extenuating circumstances, to establish the quantum of the compensations etc. The exercising of such competences means nothing else but the discretionary power.

Exceeding the limits of the discretionary power signifies the violation of the principle of lawfulness and of legitimacy or, of what in legislation, doctrine or jurisprudence is named to be the "excess of power".

The power excess in the activity of state's organs is equivalent with the law abuse because it signifies the exercising of the legal competences without the existence of a reasonable motivation or without the existence of an adequate relation between the disposed measures, the situation in fact and the legitimate purpose aimed at.

The law of the Romanian administrative prosecution[326] uses the concept of "power excess of the administrative authorities" which is defined to be the "exercising of the right of appreciation belonging to the public administration, by the violation of the fundamental rights and liberties of the citizens stipulated by the Constitution or by the law" (item 2, paragraph 1, letter m). For the first time the Romanian law maker uses and defines the concept of power excess

---

[324] Dana Apostol Tofan, quoted works. p. 22.

[325] In the doctrine, Jellinek and Fleiner sustained the thesis according to which the discretionary power is not specific only to the administrative function, but also it appears in the activity of the other functions of the state, under the form of a liberty of appreciation upon the content, on the opportunity and the extent of the juridical act. (see Dana Apostol Tofan, *quoted works*. pg. 26)

[326] Law no.554/2004, published in the Official Gazette no..1154/2004.

and at the same time acknowledges the competence of the administrative prosecution instances to sanction the exceeding of the discretionary power limits throughout the administrative acts.

The exceptional situations represent a particular case in which the Romanian authorities, and mainly the administrative ones, can exercise the discretionary power, obviously existing the danger of the power excess.

Certainly, the power excess is not a phenomenon that manifests itself only in the practice of the executive organs it can be seen in the Parliament activity or in the activity of the law courts.

We appreciate that the discretionary power acknowledged by the state's authorities is exceeded, and the measures disposed represent a power excess, anytime it is ascertained the existence of the following situations:

The measures disposed do not aim to a legitimate purpose;

The decisions of the public authorities are not adequate to the situation in fact or to the legitimate purpose aimed, in the meaning that everything that is needed in order to reach the aimed purpose, is exceeded;

There is no rational justification of the measures disposed, included the situations in which it is established a juridical treatment that is different for identical situations, or a juridical treatment identical for different situations;

By the measures disposed the state's authorities limit the exercise of some fundamental rights and liberties, without the existence of a rational justification that would represent, mainly, the existence of an adequate relationship between those measures, the situation in fact and the legitimate purpose aimed at.

The essential problem remains that for the identification of criterions through which are to be established the limits of the discretionary power of state's authorities and to differentiate them from the power excess, that should be sanctioned. Of course there is the problem of using some criterions in the practice of the law courts or in the constitutional prosecution.

In connection to these aspects, in the literature in specialty it is expressed the opinion according to which the "purpose of the law will be then the legal limit of the right to appreciate (the opportunity). Therefore the discretionary power does not mean a liberty outside the law but one allowed by the law." [327]

Of course, "the purpose of the law" represents a condition of lawfulness or, as the case may be, of constitutionality of the juridical acts of the state bodies and that's why it can be considered as a criterion to delimit the discretionary power from the power excess.

Such as results from the jurisprudence of some national and international law courts, in relation to our search topic, the purpose of the law cannot be the only criterion to delimit the discretionary power (synonymous with the margin of appreciation, term used by C.E.D.O.), because a juridical act of the state can represent a power excess not only in the situation in which the measures adopted do not aim to a legitimate purpose, but also in the hypothesis in which the measures disposed are not adequate to the purpose of the law and are not necessary in relation to the situation in fact and with the legitimate purpose aimed at.

The suitability of the measures disposed by the state authorities to the aimed legitimate purposes represents a particular aspect of the principle of proportionality. Significant is the opinion expressed by Antonie Iorgovan which considers that the limits of the discretionary power are established by the: "written positive rules, the general law principles subscribed, the principle of equality, the principle of non retroactivity of the administrative acts, the right to defense and the principle of contradictoriality , *the principle of proportionality" (s.n.).*[328]

Therefore, the principle of proportionality is an essential criterion that allows the delimiting of the discretionary power from the power excess in the activity of state's authorities.

---

[327] Rozalia Ana Lazăr, The Lawfulness of the administrative act. Romanian law and the compared law, quoted works p. 165.

[328] Antonie Iorgovan, quoted works vol. I, p.296.

This principle is consecrated explicitly and implicitly in the international[329] juridical instruments or by the majority of the constitutions of the democratic[330] countries. Romania's Constitution regulates explicitly this principle in item 53, but there are other constitutional dispositions that imply it.

In the constitutional law, the principle of proportionality finds its use mainly in the field of protection of human fundamental rights and liberties. It is considered as an efficient criterion of appreciation of legitimacy of the interventions of the state authorities in a situation limiting the exercise of some rights.

Much more, even if the principle of proportionality is not consecrated expressly in the constitution of a state, the doctrine and jurisprudence considers it as being a part of the notion of a rightful state[331].

This principle is applied in many branches of the law. Thus, in the administrative law it is a limit of the discretionary[332] power of the public authorities and represents a criterion in the exercising the jurisdictional control of the discretionary administrative acts. Applications of the principle of proportionality exist in the criminal law[333] or in the civil law[334].

---

[329] To remind on this topic item.29, paragraphs.2 and 3 of the Universal Declaration of Human Rights items 4 and 5 of the International Pact regarding the economical, social and cultural rights, item 5, paragraph 1, item 12 paragraph 3, item 18, item 19 paragraph 3 and item 12 paragraph 2 of the International pact regarding the protection of the national minorities; item G Part V of the European Social Chart – revised; items 8, 9, 10, 11 and 18 of the European Convention for the defense of human rights and the fundamental liberties or item B13 of the Treaty regarding the European Economical Community.

[330] For example, item 20, point.4; item 31 and item 55 of Spain Constitution; items 11,13.14,18,19 and 20 of the German Constitution or the provisions of items.13,14,15,44 and 53 of Italy Constitution.

[331] For the development see Petru Miculescu, The Lawful State, Lumina Lex Publishing House, Bucharest, 1998, pg.87-88 and Dana Apostol Tofan quoted works., p.49.

[332] On this meaning see Dana Apostol Tofan, quoted works pg.46-50; Iulian Teodoroiu, Simona Maya Teodoroiu, Lawfulness of opportunities and the constitutional principle of proportionality in: Law no. 7/1996, p.39-42.

[333] The provisions of item 72 of the Criminal Code refer to the proportionality as a general criterion of judicial individualization of the punishments or the provisions of item 44, paragraph 3 of the Criminal Code considers the proportionality as a condition of legitimate defense.

[334] The provisions of items 951 and 1157 of the Civil Code, allow the cancellation of a contract for the obvious disproportion of the service conscriptions (lesion).

The principle of proportionality is found also in the community law, in the meaning that the lawfulness of the community rules is subject to the condition that the means used to be adequate to the aimed objective and not to exceed what it is necessary to reach this objective.

The jurisprudence has an important role in the analysis of the principle of proportionality, applied in concrete cases. Thus, in the jurisprudence of the European Court of the Human Rights, the proportionality is conceived as a just, equitable ratio, between the situation in fact, the restraining means of the exercise of some rights and the aimed legitimate purpose, or as an equitable ratio between the individual interest and the public interest. The proportionality is a criterion that determines the legitimacy of state interference of the contracting states in the exercising of the rights protected by the Convention.

In the same meaning, the Constitutional Court of Romania, by several decisions established that the proportionality is a constitutional principle[335]. Our constitutional instance asserted the necessity to establish some objective criterions, by the law, for the principle of proportionality: "it is necessary that the legislative institutes objective criterions that should reflect the exigencies of the principle of proportionality" [336].

Therefore, the principle of proportionality is imposed more and more as a universal principle consecrated by the majority of the contemporary law systems, to be found explicitly or implicitly in constitutional norms and acknowledged by the national and international jurisdictions[337].

In the literature in specialty were identified three jurisdictional levels of the administrative acts: "a) the minimum control of the procedure rules (form); b) normal control of the juridical appreciation of the facts; c) the maximal control, when the judge asserts upon the necessity and proportionality of the administrative measures".[338]

---

335 The Decision no 139/1994, published in the Official Gazette no 353/1994, decision no.157/1998, published in the Official Gazette no 3 /1999; the decision no. 161 / 1988 published in the Official Gazette no 3 / 1999.

336 The decision no. 71/1996, published in the Official Gazette no.13/1996

337 For development see Marius Andreescu, Principle of proportionality in the constitutional law, Publishing House C.H. Beck, Bucharest 2007

338 Antonie Iorgovan, *quoted works.* Vol I, p. 296.

The maximal control, to which the quoted author refers to, represents the correlation between the legality and the opportunity, otherwise said, between the exigencies of the principle of lawfulness and the right of appreciation of the public authorities, the proportionality couldn't be considered as a super legality criterion, but as a principle of law, whose main finality is to represent the delimiting between the discretionary power and the power excess in the activity of the public authorities.

There are situations in which the Constitutional Court used a "proportionality reasoning" as an instrument for the interpretation of the correlation between the legal contested dispositions and on the other side the constitutional dispositions, and in situations in which the proportionality, as a principle, is not explicitly expressed by the constitutional texts. Self evident in this meaning are two aspects: invoking in the Constitutional Court's jurisprudence of C.E.D.O. jurisprudence, which, in the matter of restraining the exercise of some rights, analyzes also the proportionality conditions, and the second aspect, the use of such a principle in situations in which it is raised the question of respecting the principle of equality.

Declaring as non constitutional a normative disposition on the ground of non observance of the principle of proportionality, applied in this matter, signifies in essence the sanctioning of the power excess, manifested in the activity of the Parliament or of the Government. Also excess of power, sanctioned by the Constitutional Court, using the criterion of proportionality, are the situations in which the principle of equality and non discrimination are violated, if by the law or by the Government ordinance it is applied a differentiated treatment to equal cases, without the existence of a reasonable justification or if exists a disproportion between the aimed purpose and the means used.

III. Conclusions

There are two most important finalities of the constitutional principle of proportionality: the control and the limiting of the discretionary power of the public authorities and respectively the granting of the fundamental rights and liberties in situations in which their exercising could be conditioned or restricted.

The proportionality is a constitutional principle, but in several cases there is no explicit normative consecration, the principle being deducted by different methods of interpretation from the normative texts. This situation creates some difficulties in the application of the principle of proportionality.

In relation to these considerations we propose that in the perspective of a reviewing of Romania's Constitution, that at item 1 having as a side denomination "Romanian state" to be added a new paragraph that will stipulate that :"*the exercising of the state power must be proportional and non discriminatory*".

In such a manner many of requirements have been answered:

a) The proportionality is consecrated expressly as a general constitutional principle and not only with a restrained application in case of restraining of the exercise of fundamental rights and liberties, such as it may be considered presently, when having into consideration the provisions of item 53 in the Constitution:

b) This new constitutional provision corresponds to some similar regulations contained in the "Treaty instituted by the European Community" or in the draft for the Treaty for the establishment of a Constitution for Europe, which is very important in the perspective of Romania's adhering to European Union.

c) This new regulation would represent a genuine constitutional obligation for all state authorities to exercise their duties in such a way that the measures adopted, to subscribe within the limits of the discretionary power limits acknowledged by the law and not to represent a power excess;

d) To create the possibility for the Constitutional Court to sanction, by the means of control of constitutionality of the laws and ordinances, the power excess in the activity of the Parliament and the Government, using as criterion the principle of proportionality;

To make a better correlation between the principle of proportionality and the principle of equality.

Bibliography

André Hauriou, Droit constitutionel et institution politiques, Ed. Montchrestien, Paris, 1972;

Ion Deleanu, Constitutional law and political institutions, Europa Nova Publishing House, Bucharest, 1996;

Marius Andreescu, Florina Mitrofan, Constitutional law. General theory, Publishing House of the University of Pitesti;

Tudor Drăganu, Constitutional law and political institutions. Elementary treaty, Lumina Lex Publishing House, Bucharest, 1999;

Dana Apostol Tofan, Discretionary power and the power excess of the public authorities. All Beck Publishing House, Bucharest, 1999;

Marius Andreescu, Principle of proportionality in the constitutional law, C.H. Beck Publishing House, Bucharest, 2007.

13. EVOLUTION AND PERSPECTIVES OF CONSTITUTIONAL JUSTICE

Abstract:

The supremacy of Constitution is a reality also due to the role of the Constitutional Court, as defined in article 142 paragraph (1) of the Constitution. The Constitutional Court's powers contribute essentially to the achievement of the lawful state and, therefore, a historical analysis of the evolution of this important constitutional institution is likely to highlight the legitimacy of the constitutionality control of the laws in Romania,but also its perspectives.

In our analysis, we are debating for the concept of constitutional justice, regarded from a historical point of view, which includes the main attribution of a constitutional court, namely that of controlling the constitutionality of the laws. From this perspective, we point out the main evolution moments of the constitutionality control of the laws in Romania, analyzing briefly the particularities of the constitutional regulations during the evolution of constitutional justice in our country. At the same time, we emphasize the contemporary features of the control of constitutionality of the laws in Romania, and we argue that guaranteeing the supremacy of the Constitution, through constitutionality control, must be seen in the broad sense and in terms of the attributions of the courts in this field.

We believe that the role of the Constitutional Court must be amplified by new powers, including through future revisions of the Fundamental Law, as this creates new guarantees regarding the reality of the principle of separation and balance of powers in the state, and obviously the guaranteeing of the supremacy of the Basic Law.

Key words:

Constitutional justice / control of constitutionality of the laws / historical stages of the control of constitutionality of the laws in Romania / contemporary features of constitutional justice / new proposals for ferenda law

I. Introduction

The supremacy of Constitution would remain a mere theoretical issue if there were no adequate safeguards. Undoubtedly, the constitutional justice and its particular form, the control of constitutionality of laws, represent the main guarantee of the supremacy of Constitution, as expressly stipulated in the Fundamental Law of Romania.

Professor Ion Deleanu appreciated that "the constitutional justice can be considered, in addition to many others, a paradigm of this century."[339] The birth and evolution of constitutional justice is determined by a number of factors to which the doctrine refers, among which we mention: the man, as a citizen, becomes a cardinal axiological reference of the civil and political society, while the fundamental rights and freedoms only represent a simple theoretical discourse, but a a normative reality; it is done a reconsideration of democracy in the sense that the protection of the minority becomes a major requirement of the lawful state and, at the same time, a counterpart to the principle of majority; "the parliamentary sovereignty" is subjected to the supremacy of the law and, in particular, to Constitution, therefore the law is no longer an infallible act of Parliament, yet is it conditioned by the norms and values of the Constitution; and not the least, the reconsideration of the role and place of the constitutions in the sense of their qualification, especially as "fundamental foundations of the governed ones and not of the governors, as a dynamic act, in a continuous modeling and act of society".[340]

[339] Ion Deleanu, Constitutional justice, Lumina Lex Publishing House, Bucharest, 1995, p.5
[340] For developments see Ion Deleanu, Quoted works., p. 5,6

II. Content

The term "constitutional justice" or "constitutional jurisdiction" are controversial in the literature in specialty, the control of constitutionality of laws being preferred in particular. However, the notion of "constitutional justice" appears in Kelsen's work as "the jurisdictional guarantee of Constitution"[341]. Eisenmann also considers it to be "that form of justice or, more precisely, the jurisdiction that pertains to constitutional laws", without which the Constitution would be but a mere "political program, only binding morally". The same author makes the distinction between constitutional justice and constitutional jurisdiction. The "Constitutional justice" is the form through which the distribution of prerogatives between ordinary legislation and constitutional law is guaranteed, and the "constitutional jurisdiction" refers to the authority through which the constitutional[342] justice is achieved.

In Romanian literature, the notion of "constitutional justice" has come about mainly due to the contribution made by Professor Ion Deleanu[343] in this field. Without a thorough analysis of this concept, we consider that the constitutional justice is a legal category of special significance whose constitutional constituents are as follows:

a) designates all the institutions and procedures through which the Constitution supremacy is achieved.

b) a state body competent to carry it out with the duties provided by the Constitution and the law;

(c) a set of technical means and forms of implementation with specific and exclusive features;

d) the purpose of the constitutional justice is to ensure the supremacy of Constitution.

---

[341] H.Kelsen, La garantie jurisdictionnelle de la Constituion, în Revue de Droit publique, 1928, p.197 and the nexts.

[342] For development see Ch. Eisenmann, La Justice constitutionnelle de la Haute Cour Constitutionnelle d'Autriche, Paris, 1928, reed. PUAM et Economica, 1986

[343] For developments see Ion Deleanu, quoted works. p. 9-126

There is no identity between the concepts of constitutional justice and, respectively, the constitutionality control of laws. The latter one is only a part of the first.

In the sense of the above definition, the general features of the constitutional justice can be identified:

- it is a genuine jurisdiction but having some peculiarities over other forms of jurisdiction having in view this one's purpose;

- it may use common procedural rules, but also the own procedural rules consecrated in the Constitution, laws and regulations determined by the nature of the constitutional litigation;

- can be done by a specialized state body (political, judicial, or dual-nature), or by the common law courts;

- it is an exclusive justice because it has the monopoly of the constitutional litigation.

- it is not always concentrated because the common law courts may have perspectives in the area of constitutional litigation:

- the independence of the constitutional justice consists in the existence of a "constitutional statute" of the body implementing this type of jurisdiction, consisting in the independent statutory and administrative autonomy vis-à-vis of any public authority; the verification of its own competence, the prevalence of abuses of constitutional justice over any other judicial decisions: the independence and immovability of the judges and, in some cases, their designation using criteria other than those relating to the recruitment, appointment and promotion of career magistrates;

The control of constitutionality of the laws is the main form of constitutional justice and is a basis for democracy guaranteeing the establishment of a democratic government that respects the supremacy of the law and Constitution.

George Alexianu considered that legality is an attribute of the modern state. The idea of legality in author's conception is formulated as follows: all the state organs operate on the basis of a lawful order established by the legislator, which one must be respected.

The same author, referring to the supremacy of Constitution, fully affirmed and in relation to today's realities: "When the modern state organizes its new appearance, the first idea that concerns it is to stop the administrative abuse, hence the invcention of the constitutions and by judicial means the establishing of the legality control. Once this abuse is established appears a new one, a more serious one, that of the Parliament. Then are invented the supremacy of Constitution and various systems for guaranteeing it. The idea of legality thus gains a strong strengthening leverage"[344].

An important aspect is also to define the notion of control of the constitutionality of laws. In the legal doctrine[345] was emphasized that the issue of this attribution must be included in the principle of legality. Legality is a fundamental principle of organizing and operating the social and political system. This principle has several coordinates: the existence of a hierarchical legal system on top of which is the Constitution. Therefore, the ordinary law must comply to Constitution in order to fulfill the condition of legality; the state bodies must carry out their duties in strict compliance with the observance of the competences established by the laws; the elaboration of the normative acts should be done by competent bodies, after a predetermined procedure in compliance with the provisions of the higher normative acts with legal force and with the observance of the law and Constitution by all state bodies.

In the doctrine, the constitutionality control of the laws was defined as: "The organized activity for verifying the conformity of the law with the constitution, and from the point of view of the constitutional law it contains rules regarding the authorities competent to make this verification, the procedure to follow and the measures that can be taken after this procedure[346] has been completed."

The analysis of the definition shows the complex significance of the constitutionality control of the laws. This is an institution of the constitutional law, which is the set of legal norms relating to the organization and functioning of the authority competent to exercise the control, as well as the set of legal

---

344 G. Alexianu, Constitutional Law, Schools' House Publisher, Bucharest, 1930, p. 71

345 On this meaning see Ion Deleanu, Constitutional institutions and procedures, C.H.Beck Publishing House, Bucharest, 2006, p.810; I.Muraru, E.S. Tănăsescu, Constitutional law and political institutions, Vol. II, C.H.Beck Publishing House, Bucharest, 2014, p.191; Marius Andreescu, Andra Puran, Constitutional law. General theory of the State, Second edition , C.H.Beck Publishing House, Bucharest, 2017, p.p. 205-206

346 I. Muraru, E.S. Tănăsescu, quoted works p.191

rules having a procedural nature that regulate which ones may be disposed by a constitutional court.

At the same time, it is also an organized activity guaranteeing the supremacy of Constitution by verifying the conformity of the norms contained in the laws and other normative acts with the constitutional regulations.

In essence, the control of the laws' constitutionality requires the verification of laws' compliance as a legal act of the Parliament, but also of other categories of normative acts with the norms contained in the Constitution. The compliance must exist both formally (the competence of the issuing body and the elaboration procedure) as well as from the material point of view (the competence of the norm in the ordinary law must be in line with the constitutional norm).

There are several factors that explain the emergence and evolution of the constitutionality control of laws, of which we mention:

a) *The inconsistency between Constitution and the laws*. This compliance of the law with the Constitution is not a given or an absolute presumption. Both theory and practice have shown that due to the dynamics and peculiarities of the legislative process, there may be inconsistencies between the law and Constitution. Thus, by giving effect to groups of political interests, which usually belong to the majority, the Parliament can adopt a law that contravenes the constitutional norms. For the same reason, the government could adopt unconstitutional normative acts.

In other cases, the legislative technique regulated by the Constitution may not be respected by the Parliament, which would lead to inconsistencies between the law and Constitution.

b) *The necessity of interpreting the Constitution and the laws in view of establishing the conformity of the right with the constitutional norms.*

The normative law-making activity must be continued with norms implementing work; in view of their application, the first logical operation to perform is their interpretation.

Both the Constitution and the law are presented as a set of legal norms, but these norms are expressed in the form of a normative text. Therefore, what is the object of interpretation are not the legal norms, but the text itself of the law or Constitution. A legal text may contain several legal rules. From a constitutional text a constitutional norm can be deduced by interpretation. The text of Constitution is drafted in general terms, which influences the degree of determination of the constitutional norms. By interpreting are identified and determined the constitutional norms.

It should also underline that a Constitution may contain certain principles which are not clearly expressed *expresis verbis*, but they can be inferred through the systematic interpretation of other norms.

In the sense of the above, the specialized literature stated: "The degree of determination of the constitutional norms through the text of the fundamental law can justify the necessity of interpretation. The norms of the Constitution are well suited to the evolution of their course, because the text is inexorably inaccurate, formulated in general terms. The formal superiority of Constitution, its rigidity, prevents its revision at very short intervals, and then interpretation remains the only way to adapt the normative content, usually older, to the constantly changing social reality. The meaning of the constitutional norms being by their very nature, that of maximum generality, its exact determining depends on the will of the interpreter." [347]

The scientific justification of interpretation results from the need to ensure the effectiveness of the norms contained both in Constitution and the laws, by means of the institutions which carry out mainly the activity of interpreting the norms enacted by the author.

These institutions are primarily the judging courts and constitutional courts.

Verifying the conformity of a normative act with the constitutional norms, institution that represents the constitutionality control of the laws, does not mean a formal comparison or a mechanical juxtaposition of the two categories of norms, but a complex work based on the techniques and procedures for interpreting both the law and Constitution.

Therefore, the necessity of interpreting the Constitution is a condition of its application and for ensuring its supremacy. The constitutionality control of the laws is essentially an activity for interpretation of both the Constitution and the law. It is necessary to have independent public authorities that have the

[347] I. Muraru, M. Constantinescu, E.S. Tănăsescu, M. Enache, Gh. Iancu, Interpretation of Constitution, Doctrine and Practice, Lumina Lex Publishing House, Bucharest, 2002, p. 67.

competence to interpret the constitution and in this way to examine the conformity of the law with the Constitution. Within the European model of constitutional justice, these authorities are the Constitutional Courts and tribunals.

c) *The applying of the principle of separation and balance of powers in the state. Avoiding the abuse of parliamentary power*

The limits of Parliament's power to legislate are determined by the constitutional norms determining the competence and the legislative procedure. Another limit is the need to respect the supremacy of Constitution in terms of the contents of the norms enacted by the Parliament.

Consequently, the constitutionality control of the laws is the practical way for verifying the compliance with the Constitution's supremacy by the Parliament and it constitutes a counterpart to its powers in the legislative matter.

The constituent legislator and the ordinary legislator must find the most appropriate procedures to respond to two major requirements: first, the need not to obstruct the exercise of the legislative function of the Parliament by conferring exaggerated powers in matter to other state authorities, and, on the other hand, the need to ensure, within strictly defined limits, the compulsoriness of the decisions of some constitutional courts for the Parliament.

The necessity of the control of constitutionality of the laws is in fact the expression of the need to guarantee the supremacy of Constitution in relation to the activity of the Parliament.

If the chronological character is concerned, the constitutionality test was first made in England by Eduard Cohe through his judgment decision in 1610 in Bonham case, as chief justice. The usefulness of constitutionality control was then demonstrated by Alexander Hamilton in the U.S. in 1780: "If there were to be a pre- reconcilable difference between the laws and Constitution, it would of course be preferable to the one that has a superior validity and compulsoriness or, in other words, the constitution must be preferred to the law ... No legislation act contrary to Constitution can be valid."[348]

---

[348] G.Alexianu, quoted works p.72

The one who frequently raises the issue of controlling the constitutionality of laws by a political body is the famous French lawyer and politician Siéyes. In his speech in the 1791 Convention of France, he called for the creation of a political body that would cancel out of office or at the request of those concerned, of any act or any law that would be contrary to Constitution. Moreover, this organ even had a Constituent Assembly role.

From a historical perspective, it is of particular importance the judicial control of constitutionality established in the United States at the beginning of the nineteenth century, although the Constitution does not regulate procedural rules.

The evolution of the constitutionality control of the laws in the U.S. can be divided into two periods. The first period begins with the adoption of the Constitution in 1787 and ends in 1886.

During this period, in the matter of constitutionality, the judges verified in particular whether the ordinary legislator respected the competence conferred by Constitution in the sense of not being legally enforced on matters prohibited through constitutional norms. The judges could not annul a law as unconstitutional, but could only to implement its application in the case before the court.

The Supreme Court pronounces in the *Marbury affair vs. Madison*, for the first time in a case of this nature, declaring the federal Constitution to be the supreme law of the state and removing an act of the Congress contrary to the federal Constitution. The decision of the Court is written by Judge John Marshall and forms the basis on which is based the American jurisprudence on constitutionality control.

The reasoning attributed by the American judge is the following: the judge is meant to apply and interpret the laws. The Constitution is the supreme law of a state that must be applied with priority to any other law. The Constitution, being a law, is to be interpreted and applied by the judge, including to a particular case forming the subject of the judgment.

In case the law does not comply with constitutional norms, the latter ones will be applied because of the supreme character of the Constitution.

The second period begins in 1883 with a famous decision of the Supreme Court in Massachussets in the Wiegman litigation. The judges' powers increase in matter of constitutionality. The Supreme Court is no longer confined to verifying a law in terms of respecting the legislature's constitutional competence or in regard to the observance of procedures. Starting with this moment, and until now, the justice in the matter of constitutionality control examines the law in terms of its opportunity, its rationality and its economic and social justification. Thus, through the procedure of constitutionality control, the judiciary power examines the entire activity of the Parliament and removes all measures that are deemed to be contrary to the legal order in the state. In this way, justice is a guarantor of the supremacy of Constitution and of the observance of the principle of separation of powers in the state, "as the control and mutual supervision of the powers are the very essence of the existence of a state"

But the American model of constitutional justice is not without criticism. Among the most significant ones we mention:

a) verifying the compliance of the law with the constitutional norms is a constitutional litigation that differs from the ordinary legal disputes, the latter ones being the object of settling of the common or specialized courts of law. In contrast to these, a constitutional litigation can only be solved by a constitutional judge;

b) the legal effects of the constitutionality control occur only between the parties involved in the process. In the absence of a parliamentary procedure of law reviewing, we reach the paradoxical situation to let in force an unconstitutional law;

c) the ordinary jurisdictional procedure is incompatible with the specificity of a constitutional litigation;

d) There is the danger of transforming the justice into a judges' ruling, and thereby breaking the principle of separation of the powers in the state. "The judiciary authorities become, unwillingly a branch of the legislative power, or even worse, a real governing power, an authority above the others." [349]

[349] I. Deleanu, Constitutional Justice, Lumina Lex Publishing House, Bucharest, 1995, p. 38.

Therefore, several theoretical, institutional and political considerations have led to the establishment of a control of constitutionality of the laws through a specialized body, which is the European model in this field.

From these considerations, shown in the literature in specialty[350] we can mention two:

a) the political regime of a parliamentary or semi-presidential type existing in most European countries leads to a dominant position of the parliamentary majority, that fulfills the governing. The judicial reviewing of the constitutionality of laws is not a genuine counterpart related to the power of the Parliament. It is necessary to carry out the constitutionality control of the laws through a specialized body, which is, as the case may be, either a counterbalance to a parliamentary majority too strong – expressively, volunteering or a substitute for a non-existent parliamentary majority.

b) the control of constitutionality of the laws through a specialized body ensures the correct acceptance and application of the principle of separation of the powers in the state. In this sense, Hans Kelsen[351] said: "The guaranteeing of the Constitution implies the possibility of canceling the acts contrary to it, and not by the body that adopted them, which is considered a free-creator of law, and not a law-enforcement body, but by another organ, different and independent of the legislative one and any other authority".

The European model of constitutional justice is institutionally characterized in the constitutional courts or tribunals.

In the interwar period, this model was noted in Austria (1920), Czechoslovakia (1979), Spain (1931) and Ireland (1938).

After the Second World War are established the constitutional courts and tribunals in most European countries: Italy (1948), Germany (1949), Turkey (1961), Portugal (1976), Spain (1978) etc.

---

[350] See I. Deleanu: Constitutional Institutions and Procedures; C.H. Beck Publishing House; Bucharest, 2006, pg 805; I. Muraru, E.-S. Tănăsescu, Constitutional Law and political institutions, , vol. II, C.H. Beck Publishing House , Bucharest, 2013, p. 269

[351] H. Kelsen, The pure doctrine of the law, Humanitas Publishing House, Bucharest, 2000, pp. 110-111

Among the Eastern European countries that have this model of constitutional justice we mention: Romania, Poland, Hungary, Czech Republic, Croatia, Macedonia, Russia, Ukraine, Lithuania, etc.

In case of France, the constitutionality control is carried out by a dual, political and judicial body, the French Constitutional Council. This is made up of the former presidents of the republic, still living, as well as of nine members appointed for a 9 years unique mandate. The members of the Constitutional Council shall be appointed as follows: three members by the President of the State, three by the Senate President and other three by the President of the National Assembly. The President of the Constitutional Council is appointed by the decision of the President of the Republic. In the competence of this Council fall other responsibilities outside the control of constitutionality of the laws.

In our country, the control of the constitutionality of laws has developed marked by the national particularities and the successive application of the two models presented above.

Thus, Cuza's statute established in article 12, that the state and constitutional laws are placed under the protection of the weighing body. Therefore, this Chamber of Parliament could verify the conformity of a law with the Constitution.

The 1866 Constitution did not regulate the control of constitutionality of the laws.

However, the provisions of Article 93 of the Constitution, according to which the Lord "sanctions and promulgates the laws" and that, he "may refuse his sanction." Consequently, the head of state could refuse to promulgate a law if he considered it unconstitutional. Obviously, it is not a genuine control of constitutionality of the laws, but it is a precursor to such verification. As long as the 1866 Constitution was in force, the head of state never made use of this procedure.

The control of constitutionality of the laws done by a judging court rather than by a specialized institution, different from the judiciary power, has also been accepted on the European continent. The constitutional history mentions a Romanian priority in this case. Thus, during the period 1911-1912, the Ilfov Tribunal and then the High Court of Cassation and Justice had the right to verify the constitutional conformity of the laws in the litigation known as the "trams affair" in Bucharest.

Interestingly, the reasoning used by Ilfov Tribunal and by the High Court of Cassation and Justice in motivation of the possibility to carry out the Constitutionality control on a pretorian basis. In essence, the recitals were the following: (1) The court did not of its own motion take the jurisdiction to rule on the constitutionality of a law and to annul it, since such a procedure would have constituted an interference of the judicial power into the powers of the legislature. As a consequence, the court assumed this competence because it was asked to verify the constitutionality of a law; 2) On the basis of the attributions that are given, the judiciary power has as its main mission the interpretation and application of all laws, whether ordinary or constitutional.

If a law invoked is contrary to the Constitution, the court can not refuse to settle the case; 3) There is no provision in the 1866 Constitution which specifically prohibits the right of the judiciary power to check whether a law is in conformity with the Constitution. The provisions of Article 77 of the Constitution are being invoked, according to which a judge, according to the oath, is obliged to apply the laws and the Constitution of the country; 4) unlike ordinary laws, the Constitution is permanent and can only be revised exceptionally. Being the law with supreme power, the Constitution is imposed by its own authority and therefore the judge is obliged to apply it with priority, including in case where the law on which the litigation is settled is contrary to the Constitution[352].

The decisions of Ilfov Tribunal and the High Court of Cassation and Justice were well received by the experts of the time. Here's a short comment: "This decision was a great satisfaction for all people of law. It is a great step forward in advancing this country towards progress, because it consecrates the principle that the Constitution of this state, its foundation, the palace of our rights and freedoms, must not be despised by anyone. We are proud that it has been given to our justice the privilege to show even to the justice of the Western countries the true way of progress in the matter of public law."[353]

[352] See the „Judicial Courier", No. 32, on April 29th , 1912, p.p.373-376

[353] N.D.Comşa, The notifications in the „Judicial Courier", No.32, on April 29th , 1912, p.378

For the first time, the constitutionality control of the laws was regulated by the Romanian Constitution in 1923, by article 103, adopting the American model. "Only the Court of Cassation in unified sections has the right to judge the constitutionality of the laws and to declare inappropriate those that are contrary to the Constitution. The judgment on the unconstitutionality of laws is limited to the case alone."

Consequently, the control of constitutionality of the laws was the exclusive competence of the Court of Cassation in unified sections. It could be exercised only by way of the exception of unconstitutionality invoked during the trial of the litigation. At the same time, the pronounced ruling had legal effects only between the parties in the trial and had the power of a rex judecata only in the case solved.

Also, the constitutionality of laws is judged after the litigation has passed all levels of jurisdiction. This procedure was an extraordinary way to appeal a judgment. The provisions of article 29 of the Law of the Court of Cassation stipulated only one exception when the applicant accepted the suspension of the trial of the case matter so that for the Cassation Court to decide in advance on the constitutionality of the law whose application was required.

At the same time, through these constitutional regulations, the transition from the "diffuse" judicial control, assumed by all courts, to a "concentrated" judicial control, assigned to a single court, namely the Court of Cassation, was made in unified sections. Also, the decision given in that procedure has effects only on the case and between the parties in litigation, and could not have legal effects *"erga omnes"*.

The constitutionality control of the laws was governed identically by the Romanian Constitution in 1938, by the provisions of article 75.

In the post-war period, the constitutionality control of the laws was practically no longer regulated. The provisions of article 24 letter j) of the 1952 Constitution stated that the supreme representative body, the Grand National Assembly, has in its competence "the general control over the implementation of the Constitution", which included the right to examine the law's compliance with Constitution.

Similarly, the provisions of Article 43 (point 5) of the Constitution adopted in 1965 established the competence of the Grand National Assembly to exercise general control over the implementation of Constitution, but these provisions regulated more specifically the competence of the supreme representative body in respect of the constitutionality control of laws: "Only the Grand National Assembly decides on the constitutionality of the laws ".

The constituent lawmaker of the post-war period of the totalitarian state renounces the American model, as well as to the principle of separation of the powers in the state and entrusts the constitutionality control to a political body.

The Romanian Constitution in 1991, that restores the values of democracy and of the lawful state, regulates initially the constitutionality of laws in Article 140-145, according to the European model, the competence being entrusted to the Constitutional Court, this one being constituted as an independent public authority.

In Romania, the constitutional justice is carried out by the Constitutional Court. The core of the matter are the provisions of article 142-147 of Constitution and those contained in the Law no. 47/1992 on the organization and functioning of the Constitutional Court[354]. However, as we shall see below, the constitutional justice is not an exclusive attribute of the Constitutional Court, being only its most important component the constitutionality control of laws, to which are added the exclusive competencies conferred by Constitution and special laws.

The constitutional provisions through which the Constitutional Court of Romania became a reality were accepted after extensive parliamentary debates during the discussion of the Constitution draft. It is useful for our scientific approach to succinctly mention the maturity of these parliamentary talks, as a result of which the Constitutional Court has become a reality. The Parliamentary Committee on the Drafting of the Basic Law has made Title IV to be consecrated to the "Constitutional Council" under the influence of the French constitutional system.

The debates in the constituent assembly can be systematized, as shown in the literature in speciality, into four great ideas: "namely, a) the elimination of the institution, without any variant; b) the abolition of the constitutional council, with the entrusting of its controlling mission to the courts; c) entrusting a constitutional review to a commission; d) acceptance of the control

---

[354] Republished in the Official Gazette no. 807 on December 3rd , 2010

of the laws' constitutionality, exercised by a distinct authority, council, court or constitutional court".[355]

Finally, the Constituent Assembly decided to create a specialized judicial body, namely the Constitutional Court. The essence of the reasoning behind this decision was as follows: "The Constituent Assembly has decided to institutionalize this form of control of constitutionality of the laws. Such control is inherent to the lawful state and democracy. In the post-war period, all the European states that have adopted constitutions have entrusted the control of constitutionality of the laws, not to the courts, but to a special and specialized body, so that the model offered in the project is a European model. By its makeup and its attributions, the Constitutional Court is not a "superpower", nor is it expensive – in relation to other institutions - through its nine members. Entrusting the control of constitutionality of the laws of the Supreme Court of Justice would result in the transformation of the jurisdictional body into a political body, the overordination of the judicial authority, the stimulation of arbitrariness on its part, the return to a form of desuet control, long time outdated in most of the democratic countries world "[356].

The doctrine has synthesized the following features and functions of the Constitutional Court:

a) *It is no other power in the state nor does it take any of the functions of the three powers*. The Constitutional Court is a typical example of non-formal and non-rigid interpretation of the theory of separation of powers in the state. The Constitutional Court cannot formally be classified into any of the three classical powers of the state but it contributes to the balance between them.

b) *It has a dual nature: political and jurisdictional*. The political nature derives from the way of designation of judges and from some attributions concerning the verification of the observance of Constitution in the procedure for appointing the President of Romania, the organization of the referendum, the mediation of the constitutional conflicts between the public authorities, the verification of Constitution's observance by the political parties, or in general, to verify the compliance with Constitution by some public authorities.

---

[355] I. Muraru, E. S. Tănăsescu (coordinators), România Constitution. Comments on the article, C.H.Beck Publishing House , Bucharest, 2008, p.1370

[356] Ibidem, p.1373

It has a jurisdictional nature because the members of the Constitutional Court act as veritable judges. At the same time, in the exercise of its functions, the Court applies a number of jurisdictions governed by the framework law for the organization and functioning which is supplemented by some regulations of the Civil Procedure Code. Also, the jurisdictional nature arises from the attributions of the Constitutional Court, especially in the field of constitutionality control of the laws and other normative acts.

c) *The role of the Constitutional Court as a public authority is to be the guarantor of the supremacy of Constitution*. This feature expressly results from article 142 paragraph (l) of Constitution. The Constitutional Court is not the only guarantor of Constitution, a very broad category that also characterizes the function of the Head of State. Thus, the provisions of article 80 paragraph (2) of Constitution show that the President of Romania is watching over the observance of Constitution. Our Constitutional Court is the guarantor of the supremacy of Constitution, an expression that underlines the foundation of the Court's functions.

d) It is the public authority that supports the good functioning of the public authorities in constitutional relationships, of separation, balance, collaboration and mutual control. In the sense of this feature, by amendments to the Constitution as a result of a new revision a new attribution was introduced to the Constitutional Court, namely: it solves the legal conflicts of constitutional nature between the public authorities [article 146 letter e) of the Constitution]. In order to achieve this, the Constitutional Court is independent of any other public authority; it only obeys the Constitution and its organic law (article 1 paragraph. (3) of Law no. 47/1992, republished]. The independence of the Court implies its right to decide on its competence and, moreover, the jurisdiction of the Constitutional Court cannot be challenged by any public authority. Therefore, there can be no positive or negative conflict of competence between the Constitutional Court and another public authority.

e) *The Constitutional Court is the only authority of constitutional jurisdiction in Romania* [article 1 paragraph. (2) of Law no. 47/1992, republished]. The Romanian constituent lawmaker has adopted the European model in the sense that constitutional justice is carried out by a single authority. The courts have some attributions that materialize in the right of appreciation of the admissibility of some unconstitutionality exception, but this does not invalidate the Court's monopoly on the constitutional justice, since only this public authority has the competence to resolve the constitutional disputes.

f) *The organization, operation and exercise of the duties shall be carried out in compliance with the principle of legality.* Our constitutional court exercises exclusively the powers provided by article 146 of the Constitution and those regulated by the organic law. The Court is not a supra constitutional court, its role is to interpret and apply the constitutional and law provisions.

In the same meaning, the provisions of Article 2 of Law no. 47/1992, republished, shows that the Constitutional Court ensures the constitutionality control only of the laws, international treaties, regulations of the Parliament and ordinances of the Government. The unconstitutionality can only be ascertained if the procedures of these normative acts violate the provisions or principles of the Constitution [article 2 paragraph (2) of the Law no. 47/1992, republished].

g) *The structure of the Constitutional Court is determined by the Constitution and the Law no. 47/1992.* As the Constitutional Court is independent in regard to any public authority, in a particular case only this institution can decide whether or not has the competence to resolve the constitutional dispute. Moreover, its competence cannot be challenged by any public authority (article 3 paragraph (3) of Law no. 47/1992, republished]. The Code of Civil Procedure regulates the resolution of negative or positive conflicts of jurisdiction between the courts. Taking into consideration the normative norms mentioned above between the Constitutional Court of Romania and, on the other hand, a court or other public authority, conflicts of jurisdiction cannot arise, because the exclusive competence in the matter of constitutional verification of the laws is in the right of the Constitutional Court, and this monopoly of constitutional jurisdiction cannot be challenged. The Constitutional Court has the power to decide on its jurisdiction in a specific case, but it cannot decline its jurisdiction in favor of another public authority in case the Constitutional Court is noticed with a request under conditions other than those stipulated by the Constitution or the organic law, the petition will be dismissed as inadmissible.

h) *In the exercise of its powers, the Constitutional Court regulates a work of interpretation of the law and Constitution.* The Constitutional Court cannot amend, complete or abrogate a law.

In its old drafting, before the revision of the Constitution, the Law no. 47/1992 prohibited the Constitutional Court to interpret the normative acts that are subject to constitutionality control. Naturally, the current regulation has removed this ban because the activity of verifying the compliance of normative regulations with the provisions of the Constitution made by the constitutional judge is in essence also a work for the law enforcement based on the interpretation of the legal norms.

The Constitutional Court participates in the achievement of the legislative function in the state, but not as a positive legislator, yet as a negative legislator whose purpose is to eliminate the "unconstitutionality venom" from a normative act. Therefore, by its attributions, the Court is not subrogated to Parliament's activity, because the amending, supplementing or abolishing of a law is an exclusive attribute of Parliament

i) *The Constitutional Court "supports the good functioning of the public authorities in constitutional relationships of separation, balance and mutual control".* The principle of separation and balance of the powers in the state with all the criticisms expressed by some authors remains the foundation of the democratic exercise of state power and the main constitutional guarantee for avoiding the excess or abuse of power by any state authority.

The relationships between the state authorities are complex, but they must also ensure their proper functioning while respecting the principle of legality and supremacy of Constitution. In achieving this goal, it is very important to maintain the state balance in all its forms and variants, including as a social balance.

The separation and equilibrium of the powers no longer concern only the classical powers (legislative, executive and judicial). To these powers are added others that give new dimensions to this classic principle. The relationships between the participants to the state and social life can also generate conflicts that need to be resolved to maintain the balance of powers. Some constitutions refer to public law litigations (German Constitution - Article 93), to conflicts of jurisdiction between the state and autonomous communities, or conflicts of powers between state powers, between the state and regions and between regions (Constitution of Italy - Article 134).

România's Constitution speaks about the legal conflicts of constitutional nature between public authorities [(art. 146 lit. c)] and regulates the mediation function between the powers of the state exercised by the President.

The Constitutional Court is an important guarantor of the separation and balance of state power because it solves the constitutional legal conflicts between public authorities and through its attributions in the matter of the constitutionalilty control previous to the laws and the verification of constitutionality of the Chamber's regulations, it intervenes in ensuring the balance between the majority and the parliamentary minority, assuring effectively the right of the opposition to express itself.

j) *The Constitutional Court is a guarantor of the observance of the fundamental rights and freedoms*. In principle, three are the essential constitutional guarantees of the citizens' rights and freedoms established by Constitution:

a) the supremacy of Constitution;

b) the rigid nature of Constitution

c) citizens' access to the control of constitutionality of the law and to the control of lawfulness of the acts subordinated to the law.

In Romania, the procedure for the unconstitutionality exception provides the indirect access of the citizens to constitutional justice.

The judicial control is an important way of guaranteeing the supremacy of the fundamental law, because by the nature of the attributions of the courts, it interprets and enforces the law, which also implies the obligation to analyze the conformity of judicial acts subjected to the judicial control with the constitutional norms. The courts therefore have competences in ther matter of constitutional justice. We are considering not only the general obligation of the judge to observe and apply the constitutional norms or the powers conferred by the law to notify the constitutional court with an exception of unconstitutionality but in particular the possibility to censure a legal act in terms of constitutionality.

The recent doctrine and jurisprudence in the matter examines the jurisdiction of the courts to verify certain legal acts in terms of compliance with the constitutional rules. An unconstitutional legal act is an act issued with excess power.

The unconstitutionality of a legal act can be ascertained by a court if the following conditions are met cumulatively:

1. the court to exercise its powers within the limits of competence provided by law;

2. the legal act may be individual or normative, may be mandatory or optional;

3. that in the case does not exist the exclusive jurisdiction of the Constitutional Court to rule on the constitutionality of the legal act;

4. the settlement of the case depends on the legal act that is criticized for nonconformity;

5. there is a reasonable, sufficient and pertinent reasoning of the court regarding the unconstitutionality of the legal act.

In case of the cumulative fulfillment of these conditions, the limits of the courts' attributions are not exceeded, but, on the contrary, the principle of supremacy of the Constitution is applied and efficiency is given to the role of the judge to apply and interpret the law correctly. Such a solution is also justified in relation to the role of the judge in the lawful state: to interpret and enforce the law.

The accomplishment of this constitutional mission, which is particularly important and difficult at the same time, requires the judge to apply the law in accordance with the principle of the supremacy of Constitution, therefore to control the constitutionality of the legal acts that form the subject of the litigation brought to justice or that is applied to the settlement of the case. The application of legal acts shall be carried out by the judge taking into account their legal force and observing the principle of the supremacy of Constitution. In this respect, worth mentioning the provisions of Article 4 paragraph (1) of Law no. 303/2004 obliging the magistrates that through their entire activity to ensure the supremacy of the law .

Another issue is to know what solutions the courts can issue, in compliance with the above conditions, when they ascertain the unconstitutionality of a legal act. There may be two situations: *In a first hypothesis*, the courts may be directly invested in verifying the legality of a legal act, as is case for the administrative litigation. In this case, the courts can determine by decision the absolute nullity of the legal acts on the grounds of unconstitutionality. *The other situation* concerns the hypothesis that the courts are not directly invested with verifying the legal act criticized for unconstitutionality, but that legal act applies to the settlement of the case brought to the court. In this case, the courts can no longer dispose the annulment of the unconstitutional legal act, but they will no longer apply it for the settlement of the case.

III. Conclusions

In our opinion, it is necessary that the role of the Constitutional Court as guarantor of the Fundamental Law to be amplified by new powers in order to limit the excess power of state authorities. We disagree with what has been stated in the literature in speciality that a possible improvement of the constitutional justice could be achieved by reducing the powers of the constitutional[357] litigation court. It is true that the Constitutional Court has made some controversial decisions regarding the observance of the limits of exercising its attributions in its charge, according to Constitution, by assuming the role of a positive legislator.[358] Reducing the powers of the Constitutional Court for this reason is not a legal solution. Of course, reducing the powers of a state authority has as consequence the elimination of the risk of misconduct of those attributions. Not in this way it is achieved within a lawful state the improvement of the activity of a state authority, but by seeking legal solutions for better performing of the duties that prove to be necessary to the state and social system.

Proportionality is a fundamental principle of the law explicitly consecrated in the constitutional, legislative regulations and international legal instruments. It is based on the values of the rational justice and equity and expresses the existence of a balanced or appropriate relationship between actions, situations and phenomena, being a criterion for limiting the measures disposed by the state authorities to what is necessary to achieve a legitimate aim, thus being guaranteed the fundamental rights and avoided the excess power of state authorities. Proportionality is a basic principle of the European Union law being explicitly consecrated in the provisions of Article 5 of the Treaty on the European Union. [359]

We consider that the express regulation of this principle only in the content of the provisions of Article 53 of Constitution, with applying on the restriction

[357] Genoveva Vrabie, The juridical nature of the Constitutional Courts and their place within the public authorities system, in the Journal of Public Law no.1/2010 p. 33

[358] We are referring for exemplifying to the Decision no.356/2007, published in the Official Gazette no.322 on May 14th 2007 and to the Decision no. 98/2008 published in the Official Gazette no. 140 on February 22nd, 2008.

[359] For developments see Marius Andreescu, Proportionality, principile of European Union law, in the Judicial Courier no. 10/2010, pp. 593-598

of the exercise of some rights, is insufficient to give full meaning to the significance and importance of the principle for the lawful state.

It is useful, in a future revision of the fundamental law that, at article 1 of the Constitution to be added a new paragraph stipulating that *"The exercise of state power must be proportionate and non-discriminatory"*. This new constitutional regulation would constitute as a genuine constitutional obligation for all state authorities, to exercise their powers in such a way that the measures adopted be within the limits of discretionary power recognized by law. At the same time it is created the possibility for the Constitutional Court to sanction the excess of power in the activity of the Parliament and Government, by the constitutionality control of the laws and ordinances, using as a criterion the principle of proportionality.

In the attributions of the Constitutional Court may also be included the one to rule on the constitutionality of administrative acts exempted from the legality control of the administrative litigation courts. This category of administrative acts, to which Article 126 paragraph 6 of the Constitution refers to and the provisions of Law no. 544/2004 of the administrative litigation, are of great importance for the entire social and state system. Consequently, a constitutional review is necessary because, in its absence the discretionary power of the issuing administrative authority is unlimited with the consequence of the possibility of an excessive restriction on the exercise of the fundamental rights and freedoms or with the violation of some important constitutional values. For the same reasons, our Constitutional Court should be able to pronounce on the constitutionality and the decrees of the President for establishing the referendum procedure.

The High Court of Cassation and Justice has the power to take decisions in the appeal procedure in the interest of the law that are binding on the courts. In the absence of any verification of legality or constitutionality, the practice has shown that in many situations the Supreme Court has exceeded its duty to interpret the law, and through such decisions has amended or supplemented the normative acts by acting as a true legislator, violating the principle of separation of powers in the state[360]. In these circumstances, in order to avoid the excess power of the Supreme Court, we consider that it is necessary to

---

[360] For developments see Andreescu Marius, Constitutionality of appeal in the interest in the name of the law and other decisions pronounced, in the Judicial Courier no. 1 /2011, pp.32-36.

assign to the Constitutional Court the power to rule on the constitutionality of the decisions of the High Court of Cassation and Justice adopted in the appeal procedure in the interest of the law.

Bibliography

Andreescu M., The Competence of courts to censure unconstitutional legal acts, in Judicial Courier no. 3/2009;

Andreescu M., The constitutionality of the appeal in the interest of the law and of the pronounced decisions, in the Judicial Courier no. 1/2001;

Deleanu I., Deleanu S., Jurisprudence and jurisprudential revival, Juridical Universe Publishing House, Bucharest, 2013;

Deleanu I., Constitutional Institutions and Procedures, C.H. Beck Publishing House, Bucharest, 2006;

Deleanu I., Constitutional Justice, Lumina Lex Publishing House, Bucharest, 1994;

Drăganu T., Constitutional Law and Political Institutions. Elementary treaty, vol I, Lumina Lex Publishing House, Bucharest, 1998;

Iancu Gh., Constitutional Law and Political Institutions. Revised and Added Edition, Juridical Universe Publishing House, Bucharest, 2015;

Iancu Gh., Constitutional Procedures. Constitutional trial law, Official Gazette Publishing House, Bucharest, 2010;

Ionescu Treaty on Contemporary Constitutional Law, C.H. Beck Publishing House, Bucharest, 2008;

Muraru I., Constantinescu M., Constitutional Court of Romania, All Publishing House.

14. SOCIAL AND LEGAL NORMATIVISM.TRADITION AND PRESENT

Abstract:

The most striking expression of the social fact is the social norm. Man's social existence cannot be conceived without norms, mainly moral, religious and legal, that regulate and even determine the behavior of the human person in the social environment. The existence of any individual as a social being presupposes a series of obligations exercised throughout his life cycle, materialized in a series of norms, some of which complement each other, others appear contradictory to others, being specific to different interest groups. .

This system of rules is a condition for the existence of society's life, a mechanism that requires good management of human relations and removes the imminent danger of chaos. Social norms are imposed, promoted and perpetuated by several methods that we will analyze in our study Regardless of the field they regulate, social norms contain rules addressed to individuals, describing and detailing the ways in which values must be translated into legitimate behaviors and accepted by society.

As social relations are extremely varied, a diversity of social norms that regulate these relations is also outlined. Thus, the system of social norms consists of the following groups: ethical norms, ordinary norms (customs), corporate norms, religious norms and legal norms.

There are also technical norms that are not part of social determinism because they do not regulate social relations.

Regarding the complex relationship between the normative legal system and, on the other hand, society, it can be seen that currently the legal system tends to have its own functional autonomy, apart from the objective or subjective determinations that society transmits. The autonomy of the judiciary tries to transform itself from a secondary, phenomenological and ideational structure, into one with its own reality, with the power to impose its order on the social and natural order.

In this study we also analyze aspects of the work of normative codification

Key words:

Social fact and social norms / Evolution and classification / Legal norms / Norms, principles and values / Social order and legal order

I. Introduction

Man is a social being because his own living environment, as opposed to the natural environment is society, the community. Isolation, a state that is not to be confused with loneliness and loneliness, is contrary to human nature because it involves removing the human person from his natural environment, the social one. Therefore, isolation applied as a criminal sanction, or more recently for an alleged prevention of the contagious disease that has haunted the world for two years can only be temporary and cannot destroy the social dimension of human existence.

The doctrine of social determinism, endorsed by both Marxists and the current politicians and rulers of capitalist democracy, supports the hypothesis of the primacy of society over individual behavior. Determinists say that social interactions determine individual human behavior. As a result, the individual does not choose his own action, but is forced to do so under the pressure of society; he is not really free to act as he wishes. Emile Durkheim, considered the father of modern sociology, uses the concept of social fact to explain the primacy of society over the human person. The social fact is characterized, among other things, by its exteriority and especially by its coercive power, i.e., it is imposed on individuals. In this capacity, it is the paradigm that justifies the primacy of society over individual behavior and thus validates social determinism.

The most striking expression of the social fact is the social norm. Man's social existence cannot be conceived without norms, mainly moral, religious and legal, which regulate and even determine the behavior of the human person in the social environment. Moreover, social norms represent the structure of the social system, orienting its dynamics, change and becoming.

The determinism and social normativism are at least in contradiction in a relationship contrary to human freedom. Freedom is constitutive for the human person. Man was created by God as a free being and aware of his freedom.

The essence of social determinism and social normativism is formed by the causal necessity and the normative imperative. Human social freedom can thus be conditioned, restricted or sometimes even abolished.

The relationship between determinism, social normativism and on the other hand the person's freedom in the social environment is particularly complex, requires a broad analysis and involves establishing the priority between social and human as well as between the social normative system and freedom.

II. Content

There are philosophical theories or conceptions that support the primacy of determinism over freedom and even deny the possibility of man being free. The theory of causality is based on the theory of natural and causal determinism. According to causality, no act or event in the universe, taken as an effect, can arise and exist, by itself, but only motivated by one or more causes. Since all acts and choices of a man are generated by a cause, it means that they are not free choices, but the result of a causal constraint. In turn, the effect automatically becomes the cause for another effect and so on.

Some ancient philosophers, followers of Stoicism, such as Marcus Aurelius and especially Epictetus, sought to discern human realities quite boldly by dividing them into those that are in the power of man and those that are not in his power. Those that are in our power, said Epictetus, are desire, impulses, aversion, opinion, soul, etc., and those that are not in our power are body, death, fame, poverty, and so on. In order to be free, Epictetus believed, we must only maneuver with the realities over which we have power, for if we try to remove death, fame, or oppose the laws of the body, we will plunge into misery. "Being free, said Marcus Aurelius, does not mean being able to get everything you want, but not wanting what you can't get, aspiring to what is achievable. The secret of freedom lies not in the domination of necessity, but in the domination of one's own desires and aspirations", (Marcus Aurelius, Meditations).

Another important term for the determinism-freedom relationship is that of free will. The concept of this term presupposes the freedom of man to choose, to arbitrate all things according to his will, unconstrained by anyone. Saint Augustine wrote about free will, but also the French philosopher Voltaire, who argues in favor of determinism and contradicts the Stoics. The French thinker rhetorically wonders at one point how it is possible that in nature there are effects that have a cause and effects that do not have a cause? According to Voltaire, there is absolutely no effect without a cause. Moreover, he states that man can never be free, because he is not born when he wants and does not die when he wants (although a Dostoevsky character defies this second principle and, constantly carrying on him a revolver, declares that he is an absolutely free man, because he can die whenever he wants and no one else!).

Voltaire adds that man is not even the master of his own ideas, because no one, he said, can guarantee that in an hour or five minutes he will not radically change his ideas.

These conceptions that support the primacy of determinism in all its forms over freedom, or even deny the freedom of man.

Free will was also criticized by the German philosopher Friedrich Nietzsche, who finds other weaknesses: "Today we have no mercy for the concept of *free will*; we know all too well what it really is — the most wicked of all the theologians' artifices, meant to make mankind "responsible" in their sense, that is, dependent on them. [...] Wherever responsibilities are sought, what usually works is the instinct to want to judge and punish. [...] The doctrine of free will was essentially invented for the purpose of punishment, that is, because it was intended to impute guilt. The whole ancient psychology, the psychology of the will, was conditioned by the fact that its initiators, priests, and leaders of the old communities, wanted to create their right to punish — or wanted to create that right for God. People were considered "free" so that they could be judged and punished; [...] Therefore, every act was to be regarded as intentional, and the origin of every act was to be regarded as a matter of conscience. (Friedrich Nietzsche, Twilight of the Idols).

A Romanian thinker who studied and wrote about "human freedom" is Vasile Conta; he uses another term specific to our topic in question, namely fatalism. "[...] The causal link between the environment and man is so close that all its manifestations of life reflect the former. Thus, he cannot feel, nor think, nor believe, nor you, nor work other than as commanded by the environment".

Any attempt in the field of humanities to characterize and explain man in his individuality or in social relations, also refers to the problem of freedom. It is natural for this to happen, because freedom is essentially linked to the human being but also to the existential phenomenality of man. The existence of man does not make sense without considering the freedom through which man becomes from the individual a person and creator of meanings and meanings. The importance of this existential reality also lies in the fact that man is the only created being whose fundamental ontological dimension is freedom. By this he is not only a natural being, but also a spiritual being. Freedom, as an ontological determination, makes the difference between an individual and a person. Only man, as a person, is a free being, not the individual. Constantin Noica said in this sense that "where there is no freedom is number", because the number is the conceptual expression of the abstract and indeterminate generality that characterizes any human existential structure, based only on the existential phenomenality of the "I", not on the deep "self" of the human being.

Undoubtedly, philosophy, first of all, but also other sciences, make an important contribution to the conceptual understanding of human freedom, an understanding that remains in the sphere of rationality of abstract concepts be they moral or utilitarian and less existentially engages the human being. Freedom is thought of by philosophy as a dimension of ethics, which is obviously correct because indisputably freedom is both a principle and a value of human ethics. Kant remains of course one of the main thinkers who made an essential contribution to the phenomenology of human freedom, in its moral dimension.

The philosopher concluded his Critique of Pure Reason summing up his entire thought and work: "Two things fill the soul with ever new admiration and increasing veneration, the more often and perseveringly the reflection deals with them: the starry sky above me and the moral law in me".

The Kantian perspective on freedom, in our opinion, forms a distinct note in relation to all other metaphysical systems that address this issue of freedom because it is related to the practical transforming reason of man, the vocation and ability of the human being to manifest creatively in existence. natural, to create and impart meanings and values.

Realistic and materialistic philosophical thinking and pragmatism conceive of freedom in relation to necessity. Freedom is understood not so much as an essential, defining aspect, completely different from current and temporary determinism, but especially as a consequence of this determinism. In other words, in ontological realism and materialism, freedom is only a form of necessity, of determinism, which it can overcome, but cannot transform or transfigure spiritually. The consequence is the subordination of freedom and, implicitly, of man to natural determinism. The materialist conception of freedom as "understood necessity" is famous in this sense.

This understanding of freedom as being determined by value, spiritual or legal order is also found in more refined forms of theological or philosophical thinking and indisputably proper to legal thinking.

"Order", whatever its nature, expresses necessity, limit and even coercion, but which cannot be contrary to human freedom as existential data.

The relationship between freedom and necessity, between freedom and law, moral or legal, is recessive. Necessity as order, regardless of its nature and configuration, is the dominant term and freedom the recessive one. Of course, freedom does not flow from necessity, be it spiritual order, it is not determined by such a necessity as in the materialist conception. As existing, freedom is different from necessity, but in relation to the order whose expression is necessary, freedom is always recessive and unfulfilled.

In relation to the need for an existential order, as a recessive term, freedom is never complete, it is not fulfilled, but it is always in precariousness.

The approach to the issue of freedom that we encounter in the legal sciences has multiple conceptual features and, we would say, many times more important than philosophical conceptions of freedom, because the legal is a state of human existence, a characteristic of social status, distinct from the state natural, material. It is a contemporary state of human existence, respectively the "legal state", which includes an existential order based on two realities: the legal norm and freedom.

Law cannot be conceived outside the idea of freedom. The normative system, the most important aspect of law, has its meanings and legitimacy in human existence, the latter being based on freedom.

But what kind of freedom can we talk about in legal norms and in the categories and concepts of law? Inevitably, it is a freedom of the legal norm, a constructed freedom, and not an existential fact. We must emphasize that the legal norm also involves coercion, as well as any existential order applied to human phenomenology. There is an important paradox pointed out by some authors in the field of Christian metaphysics, namely the coexistence of legal constraints, and on the other hand of human freedom, both being essential for the specific order of the legal state in which contemporary man is.

Another aspect is interesting, namely that the legal norm does not show what freedom is, does not define it, does not show its meanings, but only the situations in which freedom is guaranteed or restricted. Moreover, it is good to note that, unlike metaphysics and ethics, the legal norm does not express or conceptualize freedom as such, but only freedoms or rights, i.e., the phenomenal aspects of human manifestations in the social environment, by its nature a relational environment. It is obvious that the legal normative system could not even define freedom as such, because it remains only with the phenomenological and social aspect of existence. Likewise, legal doctrine postulates human freedom and highlights the content of legal freedoms, but does not define freedom as a reality, as an essential feature of man as a person, including in the social environment.

The most important expression of social determinism is the social normative system. The standardization of social life is necessary and has an imperative character, but it is also a restriction of the exercise of man's natural freedom.

The existence of any individual as a social being presupposes a series of obligations exercised throughout his life cycle, materialized in a series of norms, some of which complement each other, others appear contradictory to others, being specific to different interest groups. Sorin M. Rădulescu considers that "the diversity of these norms, as well as their specific way of functioning in various life contexts, creates the so-called normative order of a society, based on which the rational development of social life is regulated".

The term "nomos" meaning from the Greek language natural law, norm, which implies the observance of the order established by the gods, has its counterpart in Asian spirituality, through "Dao", in several forms: Dao of heaven; Dao of man. Genoveva Vrabie defines the social norm as "a general pattern of behavior that regulates certain social actions of people, their conduct and activity, and thus the relationships between people. There is no kind of social activity to which no rules of development or exercise should be imposed or recommended". The social norm is a rule that determines the behavior of the individual in a concrete situation. Moreover, society as a complex set of structures imposes a developed and dynamic system of social norms.

This system of rules is a condition for the existence of society, a mechanism that requires good management of human relations and removes the imminent danger of chaos. Social norms are imposed, promoted and perpetuated by several methods, namely: those behaviors or conducts that are detrimental to the values of society or the social group are prohibited; those behaviors or conducts that preserve the order of that society are mandatory and those behaviors or conducts that help the integration of the individual as a member of the society are recommended, approved.

As emanations of the collective consciousness of society, social norms, in their entirety, represent the conditions for the rational organization of human behavior, directly contributing to ensuring the continuity of social life, by establishing patterns of behavior for certain conditions. Thus, social norms presuppose the organization of human actions in accordance with the rules, the values positively appreciated by the respective society. Through them, society, as a coherent set of social relations and actions, develops a normative reference system that allows members to behave intelligibly and normally.

As we have mentioned, social norms impose patterns of behavior on individuals, creating optimal conditions for achieving life in the social framework that determines their existence. The various fields of social activity, which are constantly developing, involve the continuous modernization of the system of social norms.

Regardless of the field they regulate, social norms contain rules addressed to individuals, describing and detailing the ways in which values must be translated into legitimate behaviors and accepted by society.

As social relations are extremely varied, a variety of social norms governing these relations are also outlined. Thus, the system of social norms consists of the following groups of norms: ethical norms, ordinary norms (customs), corporate norms, religious norms and legal norms.

There are also technical norms that are not part of social determinism because they do not regulate social relations.

Adherents of social contract theory argue that the transition of man from the natural state to the social state determines the need for social norms, especially moral and legal ones.

The social norm is imperative, obligatory, even if in law theorists also speak of the existence of supplementary norms and recommendations. Being an expression of social determinism, the norms condition and determine the social conduct of man. In relation to these rules, the responsibility and, as the case may be, the social responsibility of the persons are established. Failure to do so may result in moral, religious or legal sanctions.

Their imperative character is not a constitutive one but derives either from a social recognition or from a manifestation of will of a center of power, most of the times the state.

Where does the need for social norms come from? It is a question that theorists, including philosophers and sociologists, answer by referring to the characteristics of the state-organized society. We believe that this explanation is not enough. Proponents of the utopian Marxist view of man and society believed that a time would come when the state would disappear, that society would exist in itself without a state and without legal norms. This moment was marked by the complete victory of communism all over the world, the achievement of a general welfare and the removal of any social differentiation and the formation of the new man with a perfect social consciousness, fully integrated into the social environment whose conduct is harmonized with the requirements of good social coexistence. Therefore, there is no need for normative coercion.

This conception is a utopia because Marxists believed that in this world and form of existence the only possible happiness and full freedom can be achieved, but without God and for a man reduced to the stage of socially integrated individual without personality and without individual consciousness and freedom.

The very freedom and fundamental rights to be guaranteed and respected must be included in normative systems, but which are based on coercion often incompatible with the ontological freedom of man in the social environment.

It is a freedom that unites. In contrast, the social and implicitly legal state of man is based on the distinction between mine and yours that Kant mentioned, which divides, divides and limits. This is how the philosophical and legal concept of coexistence of freedoms and legal norms arose.

The limits of social normativism, especially the legal one, are obvious especially in relation to human freedom. Social normative determinism cannot comprehend or constrain the freedom of man as a person. The existential freedom of man in the social environment is manifested in its phenomenal forms, determined, guaranteed but also controlled by the power of the state, the creator of the social order through laws. It is therefore a freedom whose content is expressed through the forms of culture and civilization, a creative freedom, but a limited, conditioned freedom, possible to be subject to the restrictions imposed by the state. It is a freedom of the legal norm.

The constitutions enshrine the possibility of restricting the exercise of legal rights and freedoms. But also, in the legal sphere there is the principle that any restriction of a fundamental right cannot affect its very substance, cannot abolish it, which means that the origin and basis of legal freedoms are outside the law, is the existential freedom of man as a gift of God. Moreover, the doctrine, but also the judicial practice enshrines and recognizes natural rights, essential for the social existence of man whose exercise cannot be restricted or conditioned. We consider, among other things, the right to life or freedom of conscience.

Regarding the complex relationship between the normative legal system and, on the other hand, society, it can be seen that at the same time the legal system tends to have its own functional autonomy, apart from the objective or subjective determinations that society transmits. The autonomy of the judiciary tries to transform itself from a secondary, phenomenological and ideational structure, into one with its own reality, with the power to impose its order on the social and natural order. In this context, the legally established legal freedoms try to determine the existential freedom of man, explaining it, ordering it and conditioning it. It is a situation contrary to the natural reality; the phenomenology of the legal must be conditioned, determined, by the existence of man, as a person, and by the particularities of social existence and not vice versa. It is an expression of the dictatorship by law even in democratic societies, because the legitimacy of the legal norm is, in such a situation contrary to nature, only in the will and interests of the rulers who express themselves, paradoxically, on behalf of the people.

The reality described above, specific to contemporary society, has negative consequences, in the sense that man, as a person, the only holder of existential freedom, is no longer aware of his own freedom and expects the normative order, the state or even justice to give him freedom. he needs. It can be said that in such a situation, not realizing his own freedom, contemporary man does not exist authentically, but lives by delegation, his existence being determined externally by state and legal normativism, abstract, impersonal and often, meaningless.

The jus naturalistic conceptions consider freedom as an ontological data of the human being and try to realize the transition from freedom as an ontological essence to liberties as a social phenomenon, specific to the legal state of man and determined by the norm. We say that none of the forms of jus naturalistic conceptions succeeds in making such a transition fully, and the attempt to preserve within the legal liberties the immutability and prestige of liberty is often unsuccessful.

We note, in this ideological context, that legal freedoms, as a structural element of the legal state of man, have as a metaphysical basis the principle of coexistence of freedoms, postulated by jus naturalism, but also by the French Declaration of Human Rights of 1789. It is an expression natural of human social existence, understood by the limits and not by the absolute of existential freedom. In other words, in this phenomenal legal plan, man's freedom is up to the limit of his neighbor's freedom. It is about the specific distinction of the right between "mine" and "yours", through which legal freedom is not constituted as a spiritual opening, but as a closing within the limits of the individual. We believe that the legal norm, in this way, cannot be addressed to the person, focused on the ontological idea of freedom, but only to man as an individual, included in the multiple structures of the social scaffolding.

Obviously, such a reality is not in itself negative, because the dimension of human social phenomenality is a reality through which the human essence is manifested and the affirmation, recognition, normative consecration and guarantee of fundamental human rights and freedoms, a fact realized relatively late in history, it is a remarkable act of culture and civilization, which places the man in his social individuality in an equal relationship with the power of the state and places limits on the absolute and discretionary power of those who exercise state power. The constitutional statement of human freedoms and rights is the most important fact in the contemporary history of mankind, a re-establishment of the relationship between state and man, in the sense that man is not for the state, but the state for man. But this is also a gift from God. Unfortunately, in contemporary society this fundamental reality of the legal is altered and distorted by abusive manifestations of power, which cannot always be effectively controlled and eliminated by legal means.

The starting point that marks the legal and implicitly normative consecration of human rights is the "Declaration of the Rights of Man and of the Citizen" adopted on August 26, 1789. It is the starting point of Enlightenment rationalism in the field of law, rationalism that now culminates in human beings are unlimited, that man is the result of natural evolution, and legal rights and freedoms have their origin and basis in the legal norm and form what has been called "a new religion". This exacerbated rationalism excludes God and man's connection with God, believing erroneously, but with disastrous consequences for man and humanity, that existence has its cause and meaning in itself.

Article IV of the Declaration expresses the famous legal principle of the coexistence of freedoms: "Freedom is to do everything that does not harm others: thus, the right of every human being has no limits, except those that ensure the other members of society exercise the same rights. These limits can only be determined by law". In other words, my freedom extends to the beginning of another's freedom. Of course, this principle is valuable because it enshrines the legal rule that the exercise of my freedom cannot affect the similar freedom of others. In essence, the coexistence of freedoms, as conceived in legal doctrine, is a principle that divides and does not unite, because it is the expression of the same fundamental dichotomy for law and the legal status of man that I mentioned. It is a rational principle.

We believe that the principle of the coexistence of liberties, in order to overcome the mentioned legal dichotomy, to include in itself the fundamental truth that freedom is an invaluable gift from God, and God's gifts are offered to man from His boundless love, which unites and does not divide, should be stated differently: I am free only if the other is also free; the exercise of my freedom is conditioned by the exercise of freedom by other people. Such an approach, in our opinion, would change the way of consecration and legal guarantee of fundamental human rights and freedoms, because it would take into account the existential freedom as a gift of God and any legal interpretation would be directly or indirectly related to God. For now, this legal perspective is a mere ideal, but by God's will could become a reality.

The legal norm, especially in the conditions of the will of "legal normalization" that the contemporary society knows, is moving further and further away from human values. It is an abstract, general and impersonal structure whose legitimacy is not a value one, but of a formal recognition within the normative system considered. The abandonment of values, including Christian ones, results in normative relativism based almost exclusively on the pure will of the legislator.

The doctrine of legal normativism recognized and applied in almost all states is a concretization of those shown above.

The normative theory, as a current of legal positivism, is reflected in the main work of the American jurist Hans Kelsen "Pure Theory of Law". In this doctrine, the author aims to study law only in the context of its existence. According to Kelsen, the science of law must be limited to the study of law only in its pure state, apart from its links with politics, morality. Otherwise, it will lose its objective character and turn into an ideology.

Kelsen examines the rules of law in terms of validity, and then effectiveness, in a way that can be called "pure" because it leaves out any other extrinsic elements that are not strictly legal (for example, politics).

The theory of law aims to eliminate dualism subjective – objective law, arguing that the objective law is the legal normative framework through which subjective law is exercised. Kelsen also relativizes through his theory the dualism of private law - public law, stating that this dichotomy should not be seen as separating two branches of law in opposition. The noticeable difference between the two branches, Kelsen believes, can be analyzed ideologically, not theoretically.

The central place in the pure theory of law is occupied by the legal norm which, formally, has a pure character, as opposed to the moral norm, which has a content. Through his system of rules, Kelsen supports the theory of the creation of the right in cascade. Thus, the authority of a court decision originates in a presidential decree; this, in turn, in a law adopted by parliament, and this being claimed by the constitution. All legal norms belong to a given legal order; they justify their validity by referring to a fundamental norm.

In case of non-compliance with the higher legal norm, the legal regulation does not achieve its purpose. The theory of law has the task of deciphering the relationship between the fundamental norm and the inferior norms. It is not the science of law that has to assess whether the fundamental norm is good or bad, political science, ethics or religion rule in this regard.

Kelsen's normative theory purifies the right of all its foreign elements: psychology, ethics, sociology, theology. Thus, he determines the content of the law as totally normative. It can be deduced only from legal norms and not from social facts. The norms are broken by social life, by the relations between people.

One of the most controversial and important legal issues is the relationship between stability and innovation in law.

This issue can be addressed in two ways. From a historical perspective, legal norms as well as social and state organization are not immutable but constantly changing. The evolution of the legal normative system is marked by historical moments of progress but also by important involutions and contradictions. The evolutionary nature of norms and law is part of social determinism and is explained by the fact that they are an expression of the will of those who govern are created by the state and determined by multiple economic, social, cultural factors, the interests of the rulers. There are, however, fundamental principles of law with a special value and moral load, essential for the rational configuration of a legal system and whose stability is historically demonstrated. Most, such as the principles of justice, fairness, truth, human dignity, are external to law, in the sense that they are not a normative construction, an expression of the will of the legislator, but the rule of law only enshrines them. The evolutionary change, the becoming of the society and of the social normative system correspond to the nature of the human being, of the consciousness and of the thinking, unstable and always in change.

The relationship between stability and change in law can be analyzed in relation to a specific historical moment and the current state of a legal regulatory system and a company.

The stability of legal norms is an indisputable necessity for the predictability of the conduct of subjects of law, for the security and proper functioning of economic and legal relations as well as for giving substance to the principles of the rule of law and the Constitution.

On the other hand, it is necessary to adapt the legal norm and in general the right to the social and economic phenomena that follow one another so quickly. It is necessary for the legislator to be constantly concerned with eliminating everything that is "obsolete in law", of what does not correspond to reality. The relationship between stability and innovation in law is a complex and difficult issue that needs to be addressed carefully, taking into account a wide range of factors, which can lead to a favorable or unfavorable position for legislative change.

One of the criteria that helps to solve this problem is the principle of proportionality. Between the legal norm, the work of interpretation and its application, and on the other hand the social reality in all its phenomenal complexity, an adequate relationship must be made, in other words the right to be a factor of stability and dynamism of the state and society, to satisfy as best as possible the requirements of the public interest, but also to allow and guarantee the person the possibility of a free and predictable behavior, to realize himself in a social context. Therefore, the right, including in its normative dimension, to be viable and to represent a factor of stability but also of progress must be adequate to the social realities but also to the purposes for which the legal norm is adopted or, as the case may be, interpreted and applied. This is not a new finding. Centuries ago, Solon, being called upon to draw up a constitution, asked the leaders of his city the question, "Tell me for what time and for which people", for the same great sage would later say that he did not give the city a perfect constitution but only one appropriate to the time and place.

The relationship between stability and innovation in law is of particular importance when it comes to maintaining or amending a constitution because the constitution is the political and legal establishment of a state on which the entire scaffolding of the state and society is structured.

Essential for a constitution is its stability over time because only in this way can the stability of the entire normative system of a state, the certainty and predictability of the conduct of subjects of law, but also to ensure the legal, political and economic stability of the social system as a whole. Stability is a requirement for guaranteeing the principle of the supremacy of the constitution and its implications. In this sense, Prof Ioan Muraru stated that the supremacy of the constitution is not only a strictly legal category, but a politico-legal one, pointing out that the fundamental law is the result of economic, political, social and legal realities. "It marks (defines, outlines) a historical stage in the life of a country, it enshrines victories and gives expression, political and legal stability to the realities and perspectives of the historical stage in which it was adopted".

We do not intend to analyze in this study all the components of the social normative system that we have identified and listed above. We stop by evoking some aspects of what we have called ethical norms. Many authors, philosophers, sociologists, jurists speak of moral norms as a component part of the social normative system. We believe that we must distinguish the ethical normative system from the moral one. Only ethics can be normalized and not moral. There are many codes of ethics applicable to different professions, organizations, activities or social and professional statutes. These ethical imperatives regarding the conduct of different social subjects in different situations also form a legal normative system because they are established by laws adopted by the state, more precisely those who exercise governance at a given time and are abstract impersonal and imperative like any legal norm and are subject to change.

Morality does not contain norms but only values that can become constitutive of man's existence and conduct as a conscious, free and responsible person both in relation to himself and to other members of society. Relevant in this respect is the conception of the great German philosopher Kant.

His moral system is based on the belief that reason is the highest instance of morality. From this point of view, there are two ways of making a decision dictated by the will: a conditioned or hypothetical imperative, which arises from a subjective inclination and pursues a certain individual purpose, and a "categorical imperative", which is subject to an objective law, universally valid and necessary. Kant thus formulates the principle of the "categorical imperative" considered the foundation of morality: "Act in such a way that the maxim of your actions can be imposed as a universal law". The philosopher's assertion that "duty is the necessity of performing an act of respect for the law" is a plea for the moral law and for the "epicenter" of the whole Kantian construction, that is, the concept of debt. The author operates with the distinction between debt-compliant actions and debt-related actions.

In this context, moral values are necessary, universal and stable. Ethical norms expressed in law can contain perceptions and social values, which become phenomenal and applicable to social relations but without losing the character of moral values, independent of the ethical legislative norm.

III. Conclusions

Law is a normative rule, a system of rules governing human conduct. This human conduct can have a legal content only on the basis of a legal norm. The law, unlike the moral, religious norms, has a constraining character, in case the subject refuses to comply with the normative provisions.

Public power imposes on individuals a normative conduct of law, because law is a reflection of the common interests of society. Law cannot be conceived without power.

The state, in Kelsen's view, identifies with law. It represents the legal order, and its reality is the content of positive law. The state and the law are two sides of the same phenomenon. In creating the law, the state must be subordinated to the law, and this, in turn, regulates its building process. Identifying the rule of law, according to Kelsen, any state is a rule of law, which obviously does not correspond to the current reality.

We appreciate that the "pure doctrine of law" as a theory is not convincing, as law cannot be broken by social reality, seen as objective reality and especially cannot be deprived of moral values by its foundation which is justice. The normative system cannot subordinate the individual.

Applying the principles of abstract and impersonal legal normativism in all democratic constitutions is enshrined the principle No one is above the law. It is valid only in man's formal relations with the law and in accordance with the social determinism in which freedom is a given of the law and conditioned by it.

Law has many political, historical, economic and sociological implications that are intrinsic to it, arising naturally from interpersonal relations and the citizen-state relationship. Although the status of law as an autonomous science cannot be denied, a rule of law cannot be analyzed without being placed in a historical context, without being correlated with the political and economic factors that led to its promulgation, and without assessing the social impact. which it has produced among the population by its application.

We believe that Immanuel Kant's words are applicable to both social normativism: "Only the law of becoming really explains the permanence of existence, making it intelligible according to empirical laws".

Bibliography

Andreescu, Marius. The principle of proportionality in constitutional law. Bucharest: C.H. Beck, 2007;

Berdiaev, Nikolai. Spirit and freedom. Christian Philosophy Essay. Bucharest: Paideia, 2009;

Cassirer, Ernst. Kant. Life and work. Pitesti: Parallel 45, 2013;

Deleanu, Ion. Institutions and constitutional procedures in Romanian and comparative law. Bucharest: C.H. Beck, 2006;

Deleanu, Ion. Constitutional law and political institutions. Bucharest: Europa Nova, 1996;

Draganu, Tudor. Treaty of Constitutional Law. Bucharest: Lumina Lex, 1997;

Duculescu, Victor, and Georgeta Duculescu. Revision of the Constitution. Bucharest: Lumina Lex, 2002;

Kant, Immanuel. The Critique of Pure Reason. Bucharest: Antet, 2013;

Murariu, Ioan, and Elena-Simina Tănăsescu. The Constitution of Romania, Comments on articles. Bucharest: All Beck, 2008;

Murariu, Ioan, and Elena-Simina Tănăsescu. Constitutional law and political institutions. 11th Edition, Bucharest: All Beck, 2003.

15.THE JUDGE AND JUSTICE. CONTRADICTIONS OF CONTEMPORARY JUSTICE

Abstract:

This essay represents an attempt to highlight, from a philosophical perspective, the most significant contradictions that can affect the justice throughout a period of social crisis. The object of our analysis consists of the contradictions between: the law and justice; the justice and society and the act to fulfill the justice and what we have just called "the fall in exteriority" of justice. Within this context we refer to some aspects that characterize the person and personality of the judge. This essay is a pleading to refer to the principles, in the work for the law's creation and applying.

Starting with the difference between "given" and "constructed" we propose the distinction between the "metaphysical principles" outside the law, which by their contents have philosophical significances, and the "constructed principles" elaborated inside the law. We emphasize the obligation of the law maker, but also of the expert to refer to the principles in the work of legislation, interpretation and applying of the law. Arguments are brought for the updating, in certain limits, the justice – naturalistic concepts in the law.

Key words:

Justice, normative order, law and justice, the contradictions of the justice, the fall in exteriority, the loneliness of the judge, metaphysical principles, constructed principles

I. Judicial power

The development of modern constitutionalism in relation to the theory of the separation of powers in the state was achieved by affirming and consecrating justice with a distinct function and a distinct system in the state. The constitutionalists emphasized the need to separate the jurisdictions in relation to the governors to allow their control by independent judges.

Justice, as a state authority and institutional system, expresses judicial power as one of the forms of manifestation of the unique and sovereign power of the state. Thus, justice with judicial power has two meanings:

a) the system of judicial bodies;

b) the activity of solving civil, commercial, criminal, administrative processes;

Both meanings know a historical evolution, but the essential element is the guarantee of realization and respect by justice of the principles of legality in the activity of state bodies, legal entities and citizens. This means that the judiciary must be the main guarantor of respect for the Constitution and the law, for fundamental citizen rights and freedoms.

Unlike the other state powers, this activity has numerous points of interference. In achieving the goals, their judicial power must be independent and impartial to any state authority[361]. Therefore, the judge is obliged to resolve the case, pronounce the law and obey only the Constitution and the law. In all forms of state organization, except in dictatorial regimes, the magistrate is an independent[362] and impartial person, vested with the power of the state to resolve disputes brought to court. In the contemporary period, the law recognizes the right of other state bodies to carry out some jurisdictional activities, an example can be the administrative bodies with jurisdictional activity. In this case, the mentioned state bodies do not administer justice and

---

[361] For developments see Florina Mitrofan, "Reflecting the principles of judicial independence and impartiality in doctrine and jurisprudence", in Proceedings of the International Scientific Conference History, Culture, Citizenship In The European Union. In Memoriam Prof. Eugen CHELARU, 15th Edition, 26 May 2023, C.H. Beck Publishing House, pp. 242-249.

[362] For developments regarding the independence of the judge see Florina Mitrofan, " The Independence of Judge – a guarantee of the rule-of-law state", in Journal of Law and Administrative Sciences, Special Issue/2015, pp. 93-102.

are not part of the judicial power, because they are not absolutely independent, being part of an administratively organized system, a system that resolves disputes between legal entities that are part of it (commercial arbitrations) or whose activity violates the specific rules of the authority in question. Also, the Constitutional Court is not part of the judicial power system due to its dual nature: political and legal. As a result of the dispute settlement activity, judgments are pronounced which, once they have become definitive, are binding and must be respected by all legal subjects.

The specificity of the jurisdictional activity with state power can be concretized in the following aspects:

- the achievement of justice requires the existence of an institutional organization and the application of general principles. The organization of justice is done according to the principle of degrees of jurisdiction[363];

- in his activity, the judge interprets the law and applies it, but does not create the law. That is why jurisprudence is usually not considered a source of law, except for the Anglo-Saxon system;

- the competence of the courts is established by the Constitution and laws and, consequently, the judicial activity will be carried out in strict compliance with these competences;

- justice is an activity for resolving disputes, the term conferred by the Constitution, law and sometimes by "jurisprudence". The judge, resolving the case, must find out the truth in the respective process, apply the law to the factual situation and establish, as the case may be, the legal responsibility, responsibilities, causality of the litigation subject to judgment, in order to pronounce the most equitable solution. Justice is an instrument of repression or social revenge. At the same time, the court cannot refer itself and it is

---

[363] For the organization of the judicial system in Romania see Viorica Popescu, " The analysis of the human resources management in the Romanian legal system from the perspective of the cooperation and verification mechanism", in Proceedings of the International Conference Challenges of the Knowledge Society, 17th Edition, ProUniversitaria Publishing House, Bucharest, 2013, p. 624.

necessary to always be referred by another subject of law, this being a requirement of the principle of impartiality[364].

- court decisions represent the act by which the judge pronounces the right and the dispute is resolved. They are pronounced in the name of the law and can be enforced by state coercion. In the Constitution of Romania, the seat of the matter is represented by chapter VI art. 124-134.

The Constitution uses the phrase "authority", and not judicial power. However, from the interpretation of the constitutional norms, it follows that the Fundamental Law makes the distinction between the judicial power exercised exclusively by the courts and the judicial authority, an attribute that belongs to the Public Ministry and the Superior Council of Magistracy.

[364] Andreea Tabacu, Drept procesual civil, Legislaţie internă şi internaţională. Doctrină şi jurisprudenţă (Civil procedural law. National and international legislation. Doctrine and jurisprudence), Universul Juridic Publishing House, Bucureşti, 2019, p. 45.

II. Constitutional justice

The supremacy of the Constitution would remain a mere theoretical matter if there were no adequate guarantees.

In this sense, the term constitutional justice appears in the work of H. Kelsen[365], meaning the "constitutional guarantee of the Constitution" and in the work of Ch. Eisenmann[366], who defined it as: "that form of justice or more precisely jurisdiction that concerns the laws constitutional, without which the constitution is only a political program, binding only morally". Constitutional justice designates the set of institutions and procedures through which the supremacy of the Constitution is achieved.

The components of constitutional justice are:

a) a state body competent to carry it out with the attributions provided by the Constitution and the law;

b) a set of technical means and forms of performance that present specific and exclusive elements;

c) the purpose of constitutional justice is to ensure the supremacy of the Constitution.

In the specialized literature[367] the attributions of constitutional justice have been emphasized:

a) ensuring the authenticity of the manifestations of will of the sovereign people;

b) vertical and horizontal respect of the competences conferred by the Constitution on the various public authorities;

c) protection of the fundamental rights and freedoms of citizens;

---

365 Hans Kelsen, "La garantie jurisdictionnelle de la Constitution" (The jurisdictional guarantee of the constitution), Revue de Droit publique (1928), 197 and next.

366 Charles Eisenmann, "L'espirit des lois et la separation des pouvoirs" (The spirit of law and the separation of the powers), Cahiers de philosophie politique, no. 2-3/1984, Ousia Publishing House, Bruxelles, p. 50.

367 Ion Deleanu, Instituții și proceduri constituționale (Institutions and constitutional procedures), C.H. Beck Publishing House, Bucharest, 2006, p. 810-817.

d) the resolution of some of the contentious issues given by the Constitution in the competence of the constitutional justice.

There is no identity between the concepts of constitutional justice and, respectively, constitutional control of laws. The latter is only a component part of the former.

In the sense of the definition proposed above, the general features of constitutional justice can be identified:

- it is a genuine jurisdiction, but having some particularities compared to other forms of jurisdiction considering its purpose;

- can use common procedural rules but also its own procedural rules inscribed in the Constitution, laws and regulations determined by the nature of the constitutional litigation;

- it can be carried out by a specialized state body (political, jurisdictional, or with a dual nature), or by common law courts;

- it is an exclusive justice because it has a monopoly on constitutional disputes.

It is not always focused because common law courts can have perspectives in the field of constitutional litigation:

- the independence of the constitutional justice consists in the existence of a "constitutional statute" of the body that exercises this type of jurisdiction, consisting in the statutory and administrative autonomy independent of any public authority; the verification of one's own competence, the preeminence of abuses of constitutional justice over any other jurisdictional decisions: the independence and immovability of judges and, in some cases, their designation using criteria other than those regarding the recruitment, appointment and promotion of career magistrates;

- the constitutional control of laws represents only one part of constitutional justice, the other component refers to attributions regarding the assurance of the authenticity of the manifestations of will of the sovereign people and the jurisdictional guarantee of respect for the Constitution. Therefore, not all the attributions belonging to the constitutional judge are carried out within jurisdictional procedures.

George Alexianu believed that legality is an attribute of the modern state. The idea of legality in the author's conception is formulated as follows: all state organs operate on the basis of a legal order established by the legislator and which must be respected.

Referring to the supremacy of the Constitution, George Alexianu affirms with full reason and in relation to today's realities: "When the modern state organizes its new appearance, the first idea that concerns him is that of curbing administrative abuse, hence the invention of constitutions and the judicial establishment of a control of legality. Once this abuse is established, a new one appears, much more serious, that of the Parliament. The supremacy of the Constitution and different systems to guarantee it are then invented. The idea of legality thus acquires a powerful lever of strengthening"[368].

The constitutionality control of laws is the main form of constitutional justice and constitutes a basis of democracy, guaranteeing the realization of a democratic government, which respects the supremacy of the law and the Constitution.

The first problem is to define the notion of control of the constitutionality of laws. In legal doctrine, it was emphasized that the issue of this attribution must be included in the principle of legality.

Legality is a fundamental principle of organization and functioning of the social and political system.

This principle has several coordinates: the existence of a hierarchical legal system at the top of which is the Constitution. Therefore, the ordinary law must be in accordance with the Constitution in order to fulfill the condition of legality; state bodies must carry out their duties in strict compliance with the competence established by law; the development of normative acts to be done by competent bodies, following a pre-established procedure with compliance with the provisions of higher normative acts with legal force and compliance with the law and the Constitution by all state bodies.

In essence, the control of the constitutionality of the laws involves the verification of the conformity of the law as a legal act of the Parliament, but also of other categories of normative acts with the norms included in the

[368] George Alexianu, Drept constitutional (Constitutional law), Casa Şcoalelor Publishing House, Bucharest, 1930, p. 7.

Constitution. Conformity must exist both from a formal point of view (the competence of the issuing body and the drafting procedure), and from a material point of view (the content of the norm in the ordinary law must be in accordance with the constitutional norm).

In the doctrine, the constitutionality control of laws was defined as: "the organized activity of verifying the conformity of the law with the constitution, and from the point of view of constitutional law, it includes rules regarding the competent authorities to make this verification, the procedure to be followed and the measures that can be taken after the completion of this procedure".[369]

The analysis of the definition reveals the complex significance of the constitutionality control of laws. This is an institution of constitutional law, respectively the set of legal rules relating to the organization and functioning of the authority competent to exercise control, as well as the set of procedural and regulatory legal rules that can be ordered by a constitutional court.

At the same time, it is also an organized activity through which the supremacy of the Constitution is guaranteed by verifying the compliance of the norms contained in laws and other normative acts with the constitutional regulations.

---

[369] Marius Andreescu, Andra Puran, Drept constitutional. Justiția constituțională-garant al supremației Constituției. Doctrină și jurisprudență (Constitutional law. Constitutional justice-guarantor of the supremacy of the Constitution. Doctrine and jurisprudence), C.H. Beck Publishing House, Bucharest, 2023, p. 58.

III. The ailing contradictions of the justice

Justice should be a harmonious system in order to be in its truth and reality. "The truth is real only as a system"[370] said Hegel and by confirming this statement, justice is in its truth only if it satisfies this condition. The system means coherent order, functionality, suitability to the real and its purpose, but mainly unity in its diversion, a concrete universal in which each part to express the whole and this one to legitimize through the created order, the component parts. The system, including the justice one manifests itself dialectically, transforms itself, become a historical being, without losing the harmony and coherence. The thinker of Jena pointed out that "Truth is the whole. The whole is only the essence that fully accomplishes itself through its development"[371]. Like any other system, justice has its components or subsystems: ideal, value, normative, jurisprudential subsystem (the act of justice), institutional and perhaps the most important component, man as a producer, but also as a beneficiary of the act of justice. The truth of the judiciary system involves the making in its wholeness but also by each component of own existential purpose, which is at the same time its being, namely the *righteousness* as a value ideal but transposed into reality's concrete.

To the extent that the functions, we may say, the mission of justice, fulfill and express at the same time the functional harmony of a system, which at any time attempts the adequacy to its purpose as a value, the fulfilling of justice, justice finds itself in its truth, otherwise said, it gives its own legitimacy without waiting for it to be given, in forms sometimes inadequate, from outside.

The contradictions and in general any malfunction in the coherence of the system or inadequacy to the purpose are maladies, deficiencies of the justice, that departs it from its role and truth. When the maladies of the justice become chronical but with manifestations which lead towards aggravation, one may speak about a crisis of the system of justice. Our justice is obviously in such a chronical crisis with tendencies towards aggravation. The main cause is the ailing contradictions of the system. In contrast to the beneficial contradictions that give the becoming, the unhealthy ones tend to depart more and more the justice from its reality and truth. In the followings we try to emphasize the

[370] Georg Wilhelm Friedrich Hegel, Fenomenologia spiritului (Phenomenology of the Spirit), Academy Publishing House, Bucharest ,1965, p. 18.
[371] Hegel, quoted work, p. 18.

sickly contradictions of the justice system specific to the crisis in which this is located:

1. The fundamental contradiction of the justice, expression of the profound crisis in which this is between law and justice, and on the other side the constructive order of the norms and jurisprudence. The *law,* the justice don't represent the purposes and truth of justice, substituting these values, the law, norms and jurisprudence, that will find legitimacy in itself, in the abstract forms, the ephemeral realities, interests and precarious purposes but not in the ideal and reality of justice. Ofcourse even when a judicial system is harmonious functional and does not have this malady, there isn't always a formal overlapping between law and justice. In the healthy justice system, between the justice and law there is a unilateral contradiction in the meaning that the law may contradict the justice, but this one does not contradict the law. The crisis of the judiciary system expresses sometimes in aggravated forms the inadequacy in absolute terms between the justice and law.

The abovementioned contradiction unleashed the "will of power" of the governors to impose their own order and legitimacy to justice by norming and legislating in the meaningless and illusory attempt to create an "order of the norms" that will replace the being and truth of justice: *the righteousness.* Reality shows that this false order proves itself inconsistent, contradictory and mostly inadequate to the realities it is destined for. The mere accumulation of rules, laws even codified, does not lead to the settlement into their being and purpose of the man, the "social" and justice if the norms do not express as a phenomenon the essence: the superior order of the values of justice, equity, truth, proportionality, tolerance. Jurisprudence is manifested the same in the exclusive concern to correspond to itself or to the norms, to be sufficient in itself and not be related to the higher order of the values named above. The act of justice accomplished by the magistrate obstinately seeks for exclusive legitimation only by the rules of law and not through the value order that should be its own.

This ailing contradiction is confirmed, but not made aware by the judicial technique and formalism. A judgement is not pronounced in the name of the justice but in the "name of the law". That is in the name of an order constructed by a temporary political will for the fulfilling of some temporary interests steeped into their particularity and often contrary to the common good and not, as it should naturally be done, in the name of the order *given* and not *constructed* of the values outside the justice but which represent its truth and purpose.

The doctrine asserts that the judge pronouncing a decision "is saying the law". It would be good to be so. In fact, most of times, the magistrate by the judgment pronounced "is saying the law" – when he is not doing it – trying to include his sentence in the order of law, which is not necessarily the order of justice, the judge if having the conscience of achieving an act of justice, respecting his moral and professional statute, does not contradict the law, yet there are situations when he should and could do so in the name of a superior order formed out of the values subsumed to the justice concept. For such an act, that is not only an act of justice but also an act of righteousness, courage is needed. The magistrate must assume the risk to exceed the constructed imperfect order of the law in order to legitimate the act of justice achieved in the superior values reality of the metaphysical principles of law. Such an exiting from the normality of the inadequate forms of the concrete reality is risky for the judge, because the order constructed of the law can impose its coercive force.

The contemporary justice is dominated by the order of normativity, of forms that are not abstracted from reality but ignores it.

The sickly rupture between the law and justice (the law as expression of the will of the legislator, of the temporary power, the only one seeking such a separation) should be reflected in the legal education plan. For a correct suitability to the crisis of justice emphasized by this contradiction, but also in order to reflect the order of law and not of righteousness, taught to the students, the faculties in speciality shouldn't be called "Law" Faculties but "Faculties of Laws", as it once was.

2. The contradiction between the justice and "world', throughout "world" we understand both the human in his individuality as the society as a whole. It seems it is increasingly present in the actuality of justice and placed in a place of honour the dictum „ *Fiat justiţia et pereat mundus*." It is not a simple dictum but a tragic reality, a disease of the justice consisting in the inauthentic legitimizing of the separation of justice from the world and man. Justice cannot live, triumph, *be* if the world dies. Bteween justice and the world there is a unilateral contradiction: justice can contradict the world, but the world cannot contradict the justice, because the world is the medium, the element that justifies the manifestations of justice. The righteousness through justice involves he man, both as a performer of the act of justice and as a beneficiary.

In its contemporary manifestations, the justice in crisis is increasingly making the dictum „Fiat justiţia et pereat mundus", tring to become a closed system, existing for itself and in some cases, even worse, directed against human, the only beneficiary of the act of justice, denying its own reason for being. The crisis of justice, by this disease, is also found in the meaningless rethoric of proclamation of the "abstract man" through rights equally abstract with the intention to give teleological form to its manifestations. But the true existential meaning of justice and its finality at the same time is the man considered in his human dignity. The rhetoric specific to the separation between the justice and world in favour of the abstract man, impersonal has obvious manifestations. Before the court, in a judgment, man is no longer in the concrete of his dignity as a person, but he becomes the "named" at most identified through a locus standing equally impersonal.

The existential rupture between the justice and world, further more the attempt of justice to deny its own medium that justifies its own reason to be, cannot confirm the natural dialectical order that should characterize a good placing of justice in its truth, but may have at the end of the road the nothingness, justice as an empty form, void of the fullness which only the "just" is offering when existing in relation to human's dignity.

3. The contradiction between the justice understood and even in the acception of the normative order of law, and on the other side, the act of justice and the magistrate performing it. In philosophy one speaks about an autonomous world of the values existing per se and for itself independent even to man. As stated, justice is undeniable a reality and a normative institutional system but also a system of values. Unlike other systems of moral, religious values and in general cultural ones, the essence of justice consists also in its achieving and fulfilling through the act of justice of the magistrate without which the justice system does not close. One can speak at most about the autonomy of the right understood as an order of values, but not about the autonomy of justice outside the act by which it gets concretized. Unlike other systems of values or by other nature, justice is a clear example of a universal concrete fulfilled through the act of justice whose expression is firstly the decision of the judge.

Therefor the act of justice may confirm or refute the normative order of justice and equally as much the right as a system of values. It is a situation similar with the relation between the experiment and the scientific theory "the first being able to confirm or refure the theory, according to the case. Only that in the sphere of scientific theories an experiment may invalidate a theory legitimizing a new, superior order, that will include the old one such as it once happened with Einstein's relativity theory. In contrast, the act of justice, if contrary to the normative order or the value order of law is only but a mere judiciary error, willfully, unintentionally or accidental of the magistrate which denies even the justice itself and implicitly the right abolishing thus the order of juridical and the lawful order having as finality not another order but the disorder, the chaos. How many judicial errors are now known or unknown.

One needs to emphasize the fact that the act of justice cannot dissociate the person of the one performing it from the magistrate. A judgment even anonymized is not anonymous: the act of justice contains in itself the person but also the personality of the magistrate. We can say that not only the magistrate is the author of the act of justice, but also the act of justice "makes" the magistrate. When the judiciary errors become obvious – the cause being the abandonment by the magistrate of the moral, social, professional statute, he being at peace with the disorder that is specific to the existential non-values – it is customary to say that these are isolated cases that do not characterize the justice system and lawful order. This is not true. Justice as a system of values needs to be confirmed in its own being, coming to truth by each act of justice, by each court judgment. A single judiciary error, a single corrupted or immoral magistrate "denies it by sending the judiciary and lawful order into nothingness, into non-existence. The contemporary reality still provides too many examples for such situations so that you wonder if there's anything left into the value being of justice. Here is an acute manifestation and not only a chronical one of crisis of justice.

Justice located into its being and truth imposes the magistrate, as a fact of conscience, the object of judgment: the deeds of the man and not the man, meaning the phenomenal that is specific to the humanity of man. Being aware at the principles of law and implicitly the justice as a value specific to an order higher than the normative one, the judge, by fulfilling the act of justice, must although to teleologically relate to the concrete man even if he will rule only over the deeds (actions and omissions) thereof. Unlike this, in case of a sickly justice, the judge imagines that he has the power to judge the man.

4. The falling in exteriority. Of course, the justice made by man and for man is profane, to the "measures of man", but the sacred values are part of his being.

Being a component of the human temporary reality, the justice understood in its value dimension involves the relationship between transcendent and transcendental to which Kant[372] and Heidegger referred to. As a reality of man and society, justice should not be transcendent, meaning "beyond" the man and the world and neither beyond his own reason for being. If this happens, we are in the presence of a sickly manifestation specific to the crisis of justice, firstly by its separation from the "world" as mentioned above. Justice must be and remain in its *transcendental* being respectively "on this side" of the existential precariousnesses of this world and outside the conflicts and political interests of all kinds, without implications in the struggle for power or power games. The transcendental of justice is this one's being in its values dimension, is the right as justice manifested phenomenally through the act of justice.

The contemporary crisis of justice means falling from the immutability of the own existential and values transcendental into the social and political exteriority with the consequence of diminishing or even losing the very being of the "right as value". Unfortunately the examples are too numerous: conflicts and contradictions inside the institutional system of justice; transformation of justice into a tool for the political actors or of another kind; involving into the struggle for temporary power or into the power games both of the whole justice system and of the magistrates; shifting from the publicizing of the acts of justice, to the media justice, done by the prime mass media; magistrates' abandonment of the moral and professional statute for the illusory gain conferred by the involvement into the precariousnesses, sometimes miseries of the world; arrogarnt and aggressive rhetoric without substance by random using, and mainly for the satisfaction of some selfish interests many times immoral, in the sacred name of justice and law: "in the name of law", "in the name of the right" which become simple formulas for legitimizing of what is lacking legitimacy. The falling into exteriority is a painfull manifestation of the crisis of justice which is sensed not so much by the judiciary system itself but mainly by the system's beneficiaries: the man, people and society.

---

[372] Immanuel Kant, Foundations of the Metaphysics of Morals, Antaios Publishing House, Bucharest, 1999, p. 50.

We discussed about the crisis of justice. There is a justice of the crisis consisting in the illusion of the system to exist through the sickly contradictions presented above in a world which is not in the realization of the "progress in the conscience of liberty" such as Hegel believed, but mainly in a process of abolition, abandonment of the values cultural being and its replacing through civilization elements, excessive technicization, in a single word through the domination of the forms of civilization over the culture and not vice versa like normal. In social and political plane, the world's *dissolution* process is manifested through *mass democracy* and the *democratic individualism* with the consequence of ignoring the man as person and personality, man becoming an individual in a political and economical normative, social order in which he does not confirm his *self* as he has become a mere number taken over by the rhetoric of forms and void ideals.

The crisis of justice cannot have a being as it is outside truth and its purpose like the society of crisis to which is trying to adapt itself. There can be no proper relation between the justice that is in serious sickly contradictions and a society that is in crisis with the purpose to legitimize the existence of a justice of crisis. The justice of crisis can however be a reality but devoid of truth, of being, because not all that exists it really *is*.

IV. The Judge and the justice

It is spoken, somehow with bewilderment about the lonliness and intransigence of the judge. The judge, the magistrate in general, cannot be lonely, he cannot isolate himself, cannot alienate himself. But he can be *a secluded one*. Living in community he must be in communion with the others and at the same time he can take in his being and mainly in his conscience as much of the feelings, values, aspirations of others, of course if all these bear the mark of the being, they are beneficial and not ailing. The common good, but only as a Christian value, must become the own good. The seclusion, the withdrawal in oneself does not imply abandoning the social environment on the contrary it implies its regaining and evaluation by one's own self: "is something deeper in us than ourselves", said Holly Augustin. Only by seclusion in own self, the judge may understand man, he can assimilate him, he may understand a few about the world's self. Seclusion but not loneliness: to be with you in deeper own self, but in communion with yours' another one.

The judge must relate to the concrete man, not to the abstract one, the latter as Goethe understood the sum of all people. He must bring closer to his being Eminescu's words" "in every man a world starts its existence", discovering and understanding this world in every man that comes before the judgment seat. In his solitude the joy of the judge must be that to which Kant is referring to: "two things fill the soul with ever newer and growing admiration and veneration: the starry sky above me and the moral law inside me".

Of course, the judge is looking down the ground or (at the earth), such as Aristotel's hand is pointing to in Rafael's painting. Only thus can he take the real, the concrete, the existing, so that together with Plato, to rise up to the idea. The judge is looking down the earth naturally in order to feel, to know not only the rational in the real, but also the real as a rational and to be aware of piety's meanings." Taller is the man kneeling than standing" – pointed our priest Arsenie Boca.

Intransigence can not be in the nature of a judge's being, because it implies the impersonal authority, manifested in the name of the law and justice, but in fact without man and without justice. Intransigence means being placed in the exclusive plan of the formal logic with its categoric distinction between the true and false, between "yes' and "no". Yet, how many senses, how much richness of meanings life is offering between these extreme values to which judicial needs be identified.

Not the intransigence, but piety, mercy should characterize the judge because only thus can he see and understand something of every person's humanity. Noica said:"one needs to have mercy for the insignificant ones to see their meaningness"[373].The piety of the judge is the piety of justice. How well the being and meaning of justice was described on 1919 by the great legal expert Matei Cantacuzino, and how far we depart today from the truth of justice to immerse ourselves into the unauthentic of the "other justice", of the crisis: "In a small church in Rome I saw the painting with a woman holding the black earth into her hands. She warmly embraced it; her expression showed she was a mother, with her eyes turned up to the sky she seemed she was trying to pull the light out of the sky's blue. I was expecting to be written underneath: Charity or Justice or Philanthropy. It was not. It was *Justice*! A justice unblindfolded and understaning all pains, and not the other justice, blind with the sword in one hand and holding a scale with the other hand, so little, that it couldn't contain any of our miseries".

[373] Constantin Noica, Devenirea întru ființă (Becoming within being), Humanitas Publishing House Bucharest,1998, p. 257.

V. Justice and the principles of law

In the above we supported the higher order, in the sphere of values, which the concept of justice should confer on justice and the act of justice so that they do not remain only in the formal order of the normative. Justice as a value is legally expressed primarily through the principles of law that must be found in the rules of law.

An argument for which the philosophy of law must be a present reality not only in the theoretical sphere but also for the practical activity of drafting normative acts or the administration of justice, is represented by the existence of general and branch principles of law, some of which are enshrined in the Constitution.

The principles of law, by their nature, generality and depth, are topics of reflection primarily for the philosophy of law, only after their construction in the sphere of the metaphysics of law, these principles can be transposed into the general theory of law, can be normatively enshrined and applied in jurisprudence. Moreover, there is a dialectical circle because the "meanings" of the principles of law, after the normative consecration and jurisprudential elaboration, are to be elucidated also in the sphere of the philosophy of law. Such a finding nevertheless imposes the distinction between what we could call: constructed principles of law, and on the other hand metaphysical principles of law. The distinction we propose has as its philosophical basis the distinction shown above between "constructed" and "given" in law.

The constructed principles of law are, by their very nature, legal rules of maximum generality, elaborated by legal doctrine or by the legislator, in all situations explicitly established by the rules of law. These principles can constitute the internal structure of a group of legal relations, of a branch or even of the unitary system of law. The following features can be identified: 1) they are elaborated within the law, being, as a rule, the expression of the will of the legislator, enshrined in legal norms; 2) are always expressed explicitly by legal norms; 3) the work of interpretation and application of the law is able to discover the meanings and determinations of the constructed principles of the law which, obviously, cannot exceed their conceptual limits established by the legal norm. In this category we find principles such as: publicity of the court session, the principle of adversariality, of the supremacy of the law and the Constitution, the principle of non-retroactivity of the law, etc.

Therefore, the constructed principles of law have, by their nature, first of all a legal connotation and only in the subsidiary a metaphysical one. Being the result of an elaboration within the law, the possible metaphysical meanings and meanings are to be after their consecration established by the metaphysics of law. At the same time, being rules of law, they are binding and produce legal effects just like any other normative regulation. It is necessary to mention that the legal norms that enshrine such principles are superior in legal force to the usual regulations of the law, because they usually target social relations considered to be essential in the first place for the respect of the fundamental rights and legitimate interests recognized by the subjects by law, but also for the stability and fair, predictable, transparent conduct of judicial procedures.

In the situation of this category of principles, the dialectic circle mentioned above has the following appearance: 1) the constructed principles are elaborated and normatively consecrated by the legislator; 2) their interpretation is carried out in the law enforcement work; 3) the value meanings of these principles are later expressed in the sphere of metaphysics of law; 4) metaphysical "meanings" can constitute the theoretical basis necessary for broadening the connotation and denotation of principles or for the normative elaboration of such new principles.

The number of constructed principles of law can be determined at a certain moment of legal reality, but there is no pre-constituted limit of them. The evolution of law is also manifested through the normative elaboration of such new principles. As an example, we mention the "principle of subsidiarity"[374], a construction in European Union law, adopted in the legislation of many European states, including Romania.

The metaphysical principles of law can be considered as a "given" in relation to legal reality and by their nature are external to law. At their origin, they do not have a legal, normative or jurisprudential elaboration. They are a transcendental and non-transcendent "given" of law, therefore, they are not "beyond" the sphere of law, but they are "something else" in the legal system. In other words, it represents the value essence of law, without which this constructed reality could not have an ontological dimension.

---

[374] For development see Elise Vâlcu, "Brief considerations regarding the supremacy of the Union regulation in relation to national acts", in International Journal of Legal and Social Order, No. 1 (2022), pp. 368-374.

Since they are not constructed, but represent a transcendental, metaphysical "given" of law, it is not necessary to express them explicitly through legal norms. Metaphysical principles can also have an implicit existence, discovered or exploited in the work of interpreting the law. As an implicit given and at the same time as the transcendental essence of the law, these principles must be found, after all, in the content of any legal norm and in any act or manifestation that represents, as the case may be, the interpretation or application of the legal norm. It must be emphasized that the existence of metaphysical principles also underpins the teleological nature of law, because any manifestation in the legal sphere, in order to be legitimate, must be appropriate to such principles.

In the specialized legal literature, such principles, without being called metaphysical, are identified by their generality and that is why they were called "general principles of law".

We prefer to emphasize their metaphysical, valuable and transcendental dimension, which is why we consider them metaphysical principles of legal reality. As a transcendental "given" and not constructed by law, the principles in question are permanent, limited, but with determinations and meanings that can be diversified in the dialectical circle that encompasses them.

In our opinion, the metaphysical principles of law are: the principle of justice; the principle of truth; the principle of equity and justice; the principle of proportionality; the principle of freedom. In a future study, we will elaborate on the considerations that entitle us to identify the principles mentioned above as having a metaphysical and transcendental value in relation to legal realities.

The metaphysical dimension of these principles is indisputable, but the normative dimension remains under discussion. A broader analysis of this problem exceeds the object of this study, which was intended to be a broad excursion on the philosophical dimension of the principles of law. However, some considerations are necessary. Contemporary ontology no longer considers reality by referring to the classic concepts of substance or matter. In his work[375], "Substamzbegriff und Funktionsbegriff", Ernest Cassirer opposes the modern concept of function to the ancient concept of substance. Not what the "thing" is or the concrete reality, but their way of being, their inner fabric,

---

[375] Ernest Cassirer, Substamzbegriff und Funktionsbegriff (Concept of substance and concept of function), Verlag Von Bruno Cassirer, Berlin, 1910, p. 54.

their structure interests the moderns. Concrete objects no longer exist in front of knowledge, but only "relations" and "functions". In a way, for scientific knowledge, but not for ontology, things disappear and give way to relationships and functions. Such an approach is cognitively operational for material reality, not for ideal reality, that "world of Ideas" that Plato spoke of.

The normative dimension of legal reality seems to correspond very well to the findings formulated by Ernest Cassirer. What else is the legal reality than an ensemble of social relations and functions that are transposed into the new ontosogical dimension of "legal relations" through the application of the rules of law. The principles built applying to a sphere of social relations by means of the legal norm transform them into legal relations, so these principles correspond to a legal reality, understood as a relational and functional structure.

But there is a deeper order of reality than relationships and functions. Constantin Noica said that we must call "element" this order of reality, in which things are fulfilled and which makes them be. Between the concept of substance and that of function or relationship, a new concept is imposed, which preserves a substantiality and, without dissolving in function, manifests functionality.

Bibliography

Alexianu George, Drept constitutional (Constitutional law), Casa Ţoalelor Publishing House, Bucharest, 1930;

Andreescu Marius, Puran Andra, Constitutional law. Constitutional justice-guarantor of the supremacy of the Constitution. Doctrine and jurisprudence (Constitutional law. Constitutional justice-guarantor of the supremacy of the Constitution. Doctrine and jurisprudence), C.H. Beck Publishing House, Bucharest, 2023;

Cassirer Ernest, Substamzbegriff und Funktionsbegriff (Concept of substance and concept of function), Verlag Von Bruno Cassirer, Berlin, 1910;

Deleanu Ion, Institutions and constitutional procedures, C.H. Beck Publishing House, Bucharest, 2006;

Eisenmann Charles, "L'espirit des lois et la separation des pouvoirs" (The spirit of law and the separation of the powers), Cahiers de philosophie politique, no. 2-3/1984, Ousia Publishing House, Brussels;

Hegel Georg Wilhelm Friedrich, Phenomenology of the Spirit, Academy Publishing House, Bucharest, 1965;

Immanuel Kant, Foundations of the Metaphysics of Morals, Antaios Publishing House, Bucharest, 1999;

Kelsen Hans, "La garantie jurisdictionnelle de la Constitution" (The jurisdictional guarantee of the constitution), Revue de Droit publique, Paris, 1928;

Mitrofan Florina, "Reflecting the principles of judicial independence and impartiality in doctrine and jurisprudence", in Proceedings of the International Scientific Conference History, Culture, Citizenship In The European Union. In Memoriam Prof. Eugen CHELARU, 15th Edition, 26 May 2023, C.H. Beck Publishing House;

Mitrofan Florina, "The Independence of Judge - a guarantee of the rule-of-law state", in Journal of Law and Administrative Sciences, Special Issue/2015;

Noica Constantin, Becoming within being, Humanitas Publishing House Bucharest, 1998;

Popescu Viorica, "The analysis of the human resources management in the Romanian legal system from the perspective of the cooperation and verification mechanism", in Proceedings of the International Conference Challenges of the Knowledge Society, 17th Edition, ProUniversitaria Publishing House, Bucharest, 2013;

Tabacu Andreea, Civil procedural law, Domestic and international legislation. Doctrine and jurisprudence (Civil procedural law. National and international legislation. Doctrine and jurisprudence), Universul Juridic Publishing House, Bucharest, 2019;

Vâlcu Elise, "Brief considerations regarding the supremacy of the Union regulation in relation to national acts", International Journal of Legal and Social Order, No. 1 (2022), pp. 368-37.

16. THE RULE OF LAW AND PRINCIPLE OF THE SUPREMACY LAW

Abstract:

The doctrine of the rule of law originates from German theory and jurisprudence, but is now a requirement and a reality of constitutional democracy in contemporary society. At present, the rule of law is no longer a simple doctrine but a fundamental principle of democracy consecrated by the Constitution and international political and legal documents. In essence, the concept of the rule of law is based on the supremacy of the law in general and of the Constitution in general. Essential for the contemporary realities of the rule of law are the following fundamental elements: the moderation of the exercise of state power in relation to the law, the consecration, the guarantee and the observance of the constitutional rights of man especially by the state power and, last but not least, the independence and impartiality of justice.

In this study we analyse the most important elements and features of the rule of law with reference to the contemporary realities in Romania. An important aspect of the analysis refers to the separation, balance and cooperation of the state powers, in relation to the constitutional provisions. The most significant aspects of the jurisprudence of the Constitutional Court on the rule of law are being analysed.

Key words:

Conditions of the rule of law / powers separation and balance / law supremacy / guarantee of fundamental rights / contemporary realities and aspects of constitutional jurisprudence

I. Brief consideration on the notion of the rule of law

The notion of state attributes means its defining dimensions as they result from constitutional provisions, as an expression of the political will and determined by the political regime and at the same time values of principle of constitutional order.

The rule of law, pluralism, democracy, civil society are unquestionable universal values of contemporary political thinking and practice and are found to be expressed in the Constitution of Romania as well as in international documents. The state attributes configure its quality as constitutional law subject and define the power, but also the complex reports between the state and citizens and the other constitutional law subjects. The attributes of the Romanian state regulated by the provisions of art. 1 paragraph (3) of the Romanian Constitution: 1. rule of law; 2. social state; 3. pluralist state; 4. democratic state.

The rule of law is one of the most discussed concepts of constitutional law and is unquestionably related to the transition from the state law to the rule of law. In the literature, contradictory opinions were sometimes affirmed, according to which the rule of law corresponds to an anthropological necessity or is a myth, a postulate and an axiom, and on the other hand, the rule of law is a pleonasm, a legal nonsense.

The concept of the rule of law is a constitutional reality whose foundation is found in the mechanisms of the exercise of state power, in the relations between power and liberty of every individual of society and in the application of the principle of legality to the entire state activity, but also in the behaviour of each member of society.

The rule of law has formed and spread over three major models:

1. The English model of "Rule of Law" is characterized by the limitation of the monarch's power and, on the other hand, by preserving the power of the parliament, which in terms of constitutional law means:a) the restriction of the powers of the monarch and their recognition of a power constituted by the norms of positive law, b) the necessity to found acts of the executive directly or indirectly on the authority of the Parliament, c) the obligation of all subjects of law to submit to the law of jurisdiction. 2. The German concept emphasizes the need to ensure the legality of the administration and its judicial control; 3.

The French conception regards the rule of law as a legal state, proclaiming and maintaining the principle of legality. 3. The French concept considers the rule of law as a legal state that proclaims and defends the principle of legality.

In the expression rule of law there are two aspects of the legal, seemingly contradictory but still complementary: normativism and ideology. In the normative plane, the rule of law appears as a structural principle of the Constitution along with other essential attributes of the state, materializing the fundamental values on which the existence of society and state are based.

From the normative point of view, the requirements of the rule of law are manifested in a double sense: a) the formal meaning expresses the requirement that the state and its organs observe the laws, strictly subordinate to the juridical rules regarding the composition of the state bodies, their attributions and their functions. and b) the material meaning - the requirement that the state bodies, exercising their functions, comply with the legal guarantees concerning the exercise of citizens' fundamental rights and freedoms.

In the field of ideology, the rule of law confers a logical system of ideas by which people represent their society, the state, in all its manifestations, and which confer the legitimacy of the state.

The term "rule of law" is not a simple logical concept but it expresses a fundamental constitutional necessity according to which: a) the state is indispensable for the law in order to create for it its norms and to ensure the finality and effectiveness of the legal norms; b) the law is indispensable for the state to express power by establishing a general and binding behaviour.

In essence, the rule of law expresses a condition of power, a movement to rationalize it, but also a new conception of law, its role and functions. Professor Tudor Draganu, in his paper "Introducere în teoria şi practica statului de drept" (Introduction to the Law and Practice of the Rule of Law), proposes an interesting and comprehensive definition of this concept of constitutional law: "The rule of law is considered to be that state which was organized on the basis of the principle of separation of powers of the state, the application of which justice acquires real independence and pursues through its legislation the promotion of the rights and freedoms inherent in human nature, ensures the strict observance of its regulations by all its organs in all their activity. "

The definition defines the main elements of the rule of law - the separation of powers as a reality of the state activity, in the application of which justice acquires real independence and pursues through its legislation the promotion of rights and freedoms inherent in human nature, ensures the strict observance of its regulations by all its organs, in their entire activity".

This definition renders the basic features of the rule of law – separation of powers, as reality of the state activity, the application of the principle of legality in the activity of all the state bodies, the observance and the guarantee of fundamental human rights. Also, from the same definition result the basic features of the rule of law, respectively: a) the freedoms of the human being require guarantees of security and justice through the primacy of law and in particular the Constitution; b) the moderation of the execution of the power requires the organization and adaptation of the functions of the erratic organisms and a hierarchical normative system.

II. Conditions of the rule of law

In the final document of the Copenhagen Summit in 1990 was stated that *the rule of law* does not simply mean a formal legality, and in the Charter of Paris from 1990 *the rule of law* is prefigured not only in terms of human rights but also of democracy, as the only governing system.

From the corroboration of the principles written in international documents, as well as in relation to the constitutional law doctrine, we consider as conditions or characters of the rule of law the following: 1. the accreditation of a new concept concerning the state, especially under the following aspects: the voluntary or consensual nature of the state, the delimitation of the state from the civil society, the responsibility of the state and the authorities that make it, and the moderation of constraint as a means of intervention of the state in society by appropriate and reasonable forms; 2. capitalization of the rations and mechanisms of the principle of separation of powers in the state; 3. the establishment and deepening of an authentic and real democracy; 4. Institutionalization and guaranteeing of the rights and freedoms of man and citizen; 5. the establishment of a coherent and hierarchical legal order and of an area of law.

The systematic functionality and consistency of the rule of law must be ensured by a number of regulatory systems, namely: *a)* political control by Parliament as one of its essential functions through various institutional means *b)* administrative control that is carried out in the system public authorities, either on their own initiative or at the initiative of citizens; *c)* judicial review of the legality of administrative acts entrusted to either the courts of common law or the specialized courts; *d)* control of the constitutionality of laws; *e)* control of the observance of fundamental rights and freedoms through the bodies of the authority and the judiciary; *f)* the conciliation and control procedure, which is carried out through the institution of the "ombudsman" or the People's Advocate; g) free access to justice and organizing the court activity in several degrees of jurisdiction.

The consecration of the rule of law in the Constitution of Romania is achieved not only by art. 1 paragraph 3 of the 1st thesis, but also by many other constitutional provisions expressing the content of this principle of organization and exercise of power in a democratic society. In this respect we reiterate the provisions of art. 16 paragraph (2), which provide that no one is above the law and those of art. 15 paragraph (2) proclaiming the principle of the unretroactivity of the law, principles essential to the entire construction of the rule of law. The content of the rule of law is expressed in particular in the constitutional provisions regarding the separation and balance of state powers as well as those regarding the organization, functioning and attributions of the state institutions. The provisions refer to the fundamental rights, freedoms and duties of the citizens, to the mechanism of the separations of powers, pluralism, free access to justice, independence of courts, and the organization and functioning of parliamentary, administrative and judicial control. They can be considered as a constitutional normative expression of the content and requirements of the rule of law

The rule of law is not a state whose essence is exhausted by constitutional regulations and other normative acts at a given moment. The rule of law is not exclusively an institution of constitutional law but must become a reality found at the level of the conduct of each subject of law, whether it is a state organ or a simple citizen. This means and implies a complex evolutionary process in which all the structures of society participate, and at the same time a process of perfection on the ideological and moral level in order to improve the activity of the organs of state and to effectively establish the principle of legality, to form a civic behaviour in the spirit of observance the law and the fundamental values of democratism.

The Constitution of Romania establishes, in its normative content, the main guarantees of the rule of law:

a) the constitutional regime, that is, the establishment in the Constitution of the fundamental principles of organization and activity of the three powers. Establishing the legal regime applied to the revision of the Constitution;

b) the direct or indirect popular legitimacy of state and public authorities;

c) ensuring the supremacy of the Constitution through political or judicial control, as well as ensuring the rule of law, over other normative acts;

d) the exercise of fundamental rights and freedoms may be restricted only temporarily, only in cases expressly determined in proportion to the circumstance justifying the restriction and without suppressing the very right or fundamental freedom;

e) independence and impartiality of justice.

Therefore, art. 21 paragraph (2) of the Constitution of Romania stipulates that no law may impede the free access of a person to justice for the protection of legitimate rights, freedoms and interests.[376]

[376] To develop, see: Andreescu M., Puran A., Constitutional law. General theory of the state, 3rd edition, Ed. C. H. Beck, Bucharest, 2018, pp. 65-75.

III. Application of the principle of proportionality in terms of state organization of power

From the complexity of the issue of the rule of law, we further on refer to the implicit application of the principle of proportionality in the constitutional provisions on the state organization of power.

This principle is explicitly expressed in the Constitution of Romania only in the provisions of art. 53, but it is implicitly found in other constitutional regulations as it has been emphasized in the specialized literature. The constitutional principle of proportionality is a synthesis of other principles of law and expresses the ideas of fairness, and the correctness of the state's dispositions to the intended purpose. We consider it a criterion in relation to which the powers of the state are organized in a state of law because by its application a dynamic and functional balance is realized in the institutional diversity of the state system. We also underline the fact that this principle confers legitimacy and not only the legality of state decisions and is a criterion already used in jurisprudence which establishes the demarcation between the exercise of power within the limits of the Constitution and laws and on the other hand the excess of power in the activity of the organs of the state in situations where state decisions have the appearance of legality but are also not legitimate because they are not appropriate to the intended purpose defined by constitutional or secondary legislation We believe that the constitutional principle of proportionality can be considered a requirement of the rule of law.

Further on, briefly analyze the application of the principle of proportionality to the state organization of power in our country, as it results explicitly or implicitly from the constitutional provisions applicable.

The principle of the separation of powers in the state, considered to be a foundation of democracy, is at the same time a reflection on the moderation and rationalization of state power. "Balancing these powers by judiciously distributing the powers and equipping each of them with effective means of control over the others, thus defeating the inherent tendency of the human power to grasp the whole power and to abuse it is the condition of social harmony and the guarantee of human freedom". In its classical form, as it is known by the decisive contribution of Montesquieu, the principle of separation of powers in the state affirms that in any society there are three distinct powers: legislative, executive and judicial power. These three powers must be exercised by separate organisms independent of each other. The purpose of this division is that power should not focus on a single state organ, which would naturally tend to abuse the prerogatives entrusted to it. " In order that power not be abused, it is necessary that by the arrangement of things power stop power" -says Montesquieu. At the same time, the division of state power is necessary to respect individual rights and freedoms, so that one power opposes the other and creates itself instead of a single force, a balance of force.

In order to achieve these goals, the organs of the state must be independent of one another in the sense that no one can exercise the function entrusted to the other. Consequently, it is not possible for an organ of the state to be subordinated to another, if it exercises a separate power.

The doctrine states that: "The theory of separation of powers is in fact an ideological justification of a very concrete political purpose: weakening the power of the governors as a whole, limiting one another. It is considered that the separation of powers has two well-defined aspects: a) separation of parliament from the government; b) separation of jurisdictions against the governors, which allows them to be controlled by independent judges[377]. The theory and principle of the separation of powers in its classical form were criticized in doctrine. "Montesquieu's error", wrote Carré de Malberg, "is certainly to have thought it possible to regulate the game of the public powers by their mechanical separation and, in a certain way, mathematical, as if the problems of the state organization were susceptible to be solved by procedures of such rigor and precision"[378].

In the doctrine, other inaccuracies and limitations were noted as well, among which we recall: from the terminology used, it is not clear whether a "state body" or a "function" is to be understood by power; power is unique and indivisible and belongs to a single titular - the people. That is why we cannot speak of the division of powers, but, possibly, the distribution of the functions involved in the exercise of power; the separation of powers, conceived in the form of opposition between them, is likely to block the functioning of state authorities. It is not possible for the sovereign exercise of the completeness of each of the static functions to be assigned to a separate authority or group of authorities. None of the state organs perform a function in integrity, and

---

[377] Muraru I., Tănăsescu E.-S., Constitutional law and political institutions, vol. II, Ed. All Beck, Bucharest, 2003, p. 121.

[378] Carré de Malberg, Contribution á la théorie géneral de l'Etat, vol. II, Tenin, Paris, 1922, p. 35.

consequently the steady organs cannot be rigidly and functionally separated; in most constitutional systems, as a result of the existence of political parties, the real problem is not the separation of powers, but the relationship between the majority and the minority or, in other words, between the governors and the opposition. There is no antagonistic relationship between parliament and government. A government that has a parliamentary majority will work in close association with the parliament, which is considered a modern state of their efficiency; the legislative function is not equal to the executive function. Execution of the law is by definition subject to legalization. If the two functions are in hierarchical relations, then the organs that perform those functions are in the same ratios.

It should also be underlined that, in doctrine, there is more and more talk of a decline of legislative power in favour of the executive; the separation of powers does not solve the issue of guaranteeing fundamental human rights. Constitutional justice is the main guarantor of respect for fundamental rights, but it does not find its place in the classic scheme of separation of powers in the state[379].

In the case of the theory of separation of powers in the state it was said that "the myth" far exceeds the reality. In fact, it is the dogmatic confidence to impose on a concrete reality a pre-established theoretical and abstract framework[380]. The criticisms formulated and the modernization tendencies cannot result in the abandonment of this principle. "The great force of the theory of separation of powers in the state - said Professor Ioan Muraru - lies in its fantastic social, political and moral resonance[381]. It should not be forgotten that the principle is enshrined, explicitly or implicitly, in the constitutions of the democratic states. From the perspective of our research theme, it is important to consider the autonomy of the state authorities and the relations between them in order to prevent separatism and rigidity.

The myth of absolute separation of powers is in fact, Carré de Malberg says, irreconcilable, "with the principle of unity of the state and its powers"[382].

---

[379] See also: Eisenmann Ch., L'espirit des lois et la separation des pouvoirs, in Cahiers de philosophie politique, Ed. Ousia, no. 2-3, 1984, p.198; Rousseau D., Droit du contentiux constitutionnel, Paris, 1990, p. 365; p. 256-265; Muraru I., Tănăsescu E.S., op. cit., vol. II, p. 9-11.

[380] See Duhamel O., Meny I., Dictionnaire constitutionnel, PUF, Paris, 1992, p. 972-975.

[381] Muraru I., Tănăsescu E.S., op. cit., vol. II, p. 11.

[382] Carré de Malberg, op. cit., vol. II, p. 23.

The will of the state, he continues, being necessarily a single one, must be maintained between the authorities that held a certain cohesion, without which the state would risk being harassed, divided and destroyed by the opposite pressures to which it would be subjected. It is thus impossible to conceive that the powers in the state are equal. "That is why, in any state, even in those whose Constitution is said to be based on Montesquieu's theory and pursues a certain equalization of powers, invariably will find a supreme organ that will dominate all the others and thus achieve the unity of the state".[383] As the author states, it is not so much about separation, but rather about the "gradation of powers". There would then be a single power that would first manifest through acts of initial will - the legislative power - and would be exercised at a lower level through law enforcement acts - the executive power.

It follows that the powers of the state are unequal, but this cannot have the significance of subordination, nor can allow for excess power. "State means also force, hence the risk of escaping from the control of the holder, of considering himself being the owner of the power"[384]. At the same time, a coherent functioning of the organs of the state is not possible, nor can it be conceived, unless there are some relations between them.

It was said that, given the existence of political parties and their access to power, "the real problem is not that of the relations between the institutionalized powers but of the relations between the majority and the minority, between the government and the opposition, especially when the government comes from a parliamentary majority, comfortable and homogeneous and leaning on it".[385]

In a wider sense, it must be stressed that democracy generates a majority that leads, imposing its will and values to minorities, but they also have the opportunity to express themselves and their rights have to be respected. Achieving the democratic and functional balance between the majority and the minorities is the solution to avoid what the doctrine is called the "tyranny of the majority". Undivided power - says Giovani Sartori - is always an excessive and dangerous power. Thus, the tyranny of the majority, relevant from a constitutional point of view, is defined according to the rights

---

383 Carré de Malberg, op. cit., vol. II, p. 52.

384 Muraru I., Tănăsescu E.S., op. cit., vol. I, p. 19.

385 Deleanu I., Constitutional law and political institutions, vol. I, Ed. Europa Nova, Bucharest, 1996, p. 95..

of the minority, especially if the right to opposition is complied with or not[386]. The main problem in this context is that the minority or the minorities have the right to oppose, have the right to opposition.

The relationship between the majority and the minority involves the analysis of the very complex interaction between those that govern and the ones that are governed. Interaction consists of a multilevel process in which majorities and minorities are materialized in different ways and at different levels. The rule that allows the functioning of such a complex system of democracy is the application of the principle of majority in decision-making. However, Hamilton observed very well: "Give all the power to many, and they will oppress the few. Give all the power of the few, and they will oppress the many".[387] Therefore, the problem is to avoid giving all or most of the power to all, by distributing it, alternately and/or at the same time to the majority and minority.

Therefore, in order to avoid dogmatism, in order to respond to these problems of social, political and state realities, it is necessary to reconsider the theory of the separation of powers in the state from the point of view of the principle of proportionality. The fundamental idea has already been stated: the moderation of power and the balance in the exercise of power that actually reflects, to a certain extent, the balance of social forces[388]. When discussing the content and meanings of the separation of powers, it is less about separation, but especially about the balance of powers[389]. Balancing the powers in the state by judiciously distributing the powers and equipping each with effective means of control over the others, thus stabilizing the tendency to capture the whole power and to abuse it, is essentially the application of the principle of proportionality to the organization of state power. This is the condition of social harmony and the guarantee of human freedom [even though, until now, an explicit reference to the principle of proportionality has not been made in the specialized literature, it results from the context of supporting some authors: "So, weight and counterweights in the power tiles so that none of them dominates the others. It would not be so much a separation of powers, but especially about their relative autonomy and their mutual dependence: the

---

[386] Sartori G., Theory of democracy reinterpreted, Ed. Polirom, Bucharest, 1999, p. 137.
[387] Elliot J., Debates on the Adoption of the Federal Constitution, Philadelphia, Lippincott, 1941, p. 203.
[388] Grewe C., Fabri H.R., Droit constitutionnels europeans, PUF, Paris, 1995, p. 361 and next.
[389] Deleanu I., op. cit., vol. I, p. 80.

balance of powers ".[390]

Rethinking the separation of powers in terms of the constitutional principle of proportionality can be answered, in our opinion, to all the problems listed above.

The principle of the separation of powers in the state was not explicitly enshrined in the Constitution of Romania before its revision in 2003, but from the analysis of the constitutional texts, the doctrine ascertained that the balance of state powers as a principle was found in the content of the norms of the Constitution Through the Review Law, the Romanian derived constituent expressly enshrined this principle, referring not only to the separation of powers but also to the balance between them: "The State is organized according to the principle of separation and balance of powers - legislative, executive and judicial - within constitutional democracy"[Art. 1 paragraph (4)].

The necessary balance between state authorities is the expression of the principle of proportionality applied in the matter of organizing the institutional system of power in Romania. State authorities are neither equal nor independent in the absolute sense. The balance that a proportionality relationship implies is based on differences but also on interrelations that allow the functioning of the institutional system so as to avoid excessive concentration of power or exercise of the same, as well as the excess of power, especially by violating human rights and fundamental freedoms. The finality of the proportionality ratio between public authorities is "the establishment of balanced correlations between the governors and the ones that are governed, complying with the public freedoms" (I. Muraru, M. Constantinescu, Rolul Curţii Constituţionale în asigurarea echilibrului puterilor în stat, in Dreptul no. 9/1996).

We will refer to some of the constitutional regulations concerning the Romanian state institutional system, which reflects the principle of proportionality:

A. Elements of difference between state authorities, meaning the autonomy of each category of organs and their position within the system:

public authorities are governed distinctly by the rules contained in Title III

[390] Ibidem.

of the Constitution. These are the "three classic powers" in the traditional order: legislative, executive and judicial power.

The Constitution confers a certain degree of prerogative to Parliament in relation to the other state authorities: "Parliament is the supreme representative body of the Romanian people and the sole legislator authority of the country" (art. 61 paragraph (1)];

Besides the classic scheme of the separation of powers in the state, the Constitutional Court achieved constitutional power (art. 142 and subsequent of the Fundamental Law), which is the guarantor of the supremacy of the Constitution, the only constitutional jurisdictional authority of Romania, independent of the any other public authority [art. 1 paragraph (3) of the Law no. 47/1992 on the organization and functioning of the Constitutional Court, republished]. The People's Advocate is also independent of any other public authority. He is appointed by the Parliament in the joint session of the Chambers [art. 65 paragraph (2) letter i)]. Ex officio or at the request of persons injured in their rights or freedoms, the People's Advocate may refer the matter to the public authorities in order to take measures to eliminate acts or facts that affect subjective rights or legitimate protected legal interests (article 58 and subsequent). It has the power to notify the Constitutional Court, in the situations provided by art. 146 letters a) and d);

The bicameral structure of Parliament is an expression of the balance involved in the principle of proportionality. Thus, Chambers are equal but are functionally differentiated in the exercise of their legislative powers. The distinction between the Chamber referred first (of reflection) and the Decision Chamber, made by article 75, expresses the "quasi-perfect" bicameralism, which is a proportionality ratio. We agree with the opinion expressed in the literature, according to which "the system of parliamentary bicameralism in Romania must be preserved, but it must be transformed into a differentiated bicameralism. Thus, to the law of democratization and efficiency can be ensured, and to the legislative organ a representativeness and responsibility increment." (I. Muraru, A. Muraru, Scurtă pledoarie pentru un bicameralism parlamentar diferenţiat, in Revista de drept public no. 1/2005, page 8).

The difference between the length of the term of office of some state authorities contributes to a proportionate ratio between the powers of the state, is the expression of the balance and not of the formal equality, in order to ensure the good functioning of the Romanian institutional system. Thus, the duration of Parliament's mandate is 4 years (Article 63), of the President of Romania is 5 years (Article 83), of the members of the Superior Council of Magistracy is 6 years (Article 133), the mandate of the judges at the Constitutional Court is 9 years, and the president of this institution is elected for a period of 3 years (Article 142), the judges of the courts appointed by the President of Romania have practically an indefinite mandate in time because they are irremovable under the law (art. 125). The People's Advocate mandate is 5 years (Article 58).

B. The specialty literature highlighted the particularities of the relations between the state authorities, which in our opinion materialize the principle of proportionality, because the relational balance also implies the difference. In this respect, it was stated that:

"The election of the President of Romania by the people, an essential feature of the presidential republics, combines in our country with the pre-eminence of the Parliament, as a result, mainly, of the parliamentary origin of the government, thus defining a semi-presidential political regime" [391].

The set of interrelations between the different categories of organs of the state is the form of achieving the balance and mutual control of the powers These relations, which form the "identity card of the state power system"[392], presuppose the autonomy of the state authorities and the differences between them. The complex structure of the state power system is a concretisation of the principle of proportionality, in other words, it strikes a balance between the powers of the state, which are based on autonomy, differentiation and interrelations. The more the constitutional regulations in the field manage to materialize the requirements of the principle of proportionality, the more exists the guarantee of avoiding some forms of concentration of the state powers, the tyranny of the majority or minorities and obviously the excess of power.

The concern of the Romanian constituent legislator to achieve a functional balance between the powers of the state, between these and society, is obvious, if we refer to the provisions of art. 80, according to which: "The President exercises the function of mediation between the powers of the state as well as between state and society", but also to the provisions of art. 146 letter

---

[391] Constantinescu M., The balance of powers in the constitutional regime in Romania, in Law no. 3/1993, p. 3.

[392] Deleanu I., op. cit., Vol. II, p. 201.

e) according to which our constitutional court has the competence to resolve constitutional legal conflicts between public authorities. We also need to remember the role of mediator and balance factor for the powers of the state, but also for the society that justice has. In this respect, the provisions of art. 124 of the Constitution consecrate the general "uniqueness, impartiality and equality" of justice, which represents important guarantees for the achievement of the functions of the judicial power in society.

Of course, the system of state power is an open, dynamic one, implying not only the multiplication of its constituent elements or their reorganization, but also of the functions that correspond them and of the interrelationships between the elements of the system. Within the internal system, the social-political system, and externally the system of the international community of states represent the "environment" with which the state authorities interact. Therefore, the balance, as a particular aspect of the principle of proportionality, between the powers of the state must be understood in its dynamics, including in the continuous process of interpreting and applying the constitutional provisions in the matter.

Proportionality, as a principle of constitutional law, has a concrete dimension. The existence of a proportionate, balanced relationship between the state authorities, between them and society, is verified in practice through the functioning of the political and social system, the avoidance of crises, or, when they occur, through the capacity of the state authorities to manage these, complying in any situation with the principles of the rule of law. Essential for the fulfilment of the requirements of separation and balance between the powers of the state, but also for stability, in its social and political system dynamics, from the perspective of pluralism in society, there is the existence of a proportionate balance between the majority and the minorities between the government and the opposition.

IV. Aspects of the Constitutional Court jurisprudence on guaranteeing and complying with the requirements of the rule of law

At the end of this analysis we shall refer to some decisions of the Constitutional Court which we consider relevant to the rule of law.

The Constitutional Court identifies the fundamental feature of the rule of law, namely the supremacy of the Constitution and the obligation to observe the law. See to that effect[393].

At the same time, it has been stated in the jurisprudence of the constitutional court that the rule of law, ensuring the supremacy of the Constitution, also realizes "the correlation of all laws and all normative acts with it"[394] .

The requirements of the rule of law concern the major purposes of state activity, namely the supremacy of law, which implies the subordination of the state to the law. In this respect, the law provides the means by which the political options or decisions can be censored and performs the abolition of any abusive and discretionary tendencies of the state structures. Further on, the rule of law ensures the supremacy of the Constitution, the existence of the regime of separation of the public powers and establishes guarantees, including of a judicial nature, that ensure the observance of citizens' rights and freedoms, primarily by limiting the state authority, which represent the framing of the public authorities' activities within the limits of the law.

The jurisprudence of the Constitutional Court expresses the main requirements of the rule of law in relation to the goals of the state activity. Thus, by jurisprudence is achieved a very eloquent synthesis of the doctrine on the notion and features of the rule of law. It is significant in this respect the Decision no. 17 of January 21st 2015[395], by which the Constitutional Court gives an explanation concerning the state of law, enshrined in art. 1 paragraph (3) thesis I of the Constitution: "The requirements of the rule of law concern

---

[393] Decision no. 232 of July 5th 2001, published in the Official Gazette no. 727 of November 15th 2001, and Decision no. 53 of January 25th 2011, published in in the Official Gazette no. 90 of February 3rd 2011.

[394] Decision no. 22 of January 27th 2004, published in the Official Gazette no. 233 of March 17th 2004.

[395] Published in the Official Gazette no. 79 of January 30th 2015.

the major purposes of its activity, prefigured in what is commonly called the reign of law, a phrase involving the subordination of the state to the law, the guarantee of the means to allow the law to censor political choices and, in this context, to weigh the potential abusive, discretionary tendencies of the static structures. The rule of law ensures the supremacy of the Constitution, the correlation of laws and all normative acts with it, the existence of the regime of separation of the public powers that must act within the limits of the law, namely within the limits of a law expressing the general will. The rule of law enshrines a series of safeguards, including jurisdictional, to ensure that citizens' rights and freedoms are complied with by the state's self-restraint, namely the involvement of public authorities in the coordinates of law".[396]

The principle of stability and security of legal relations is not explicitly enshrined in the Constitution of Romania, but, like other constitutional principles, it is involved in the constitutional normative provisions, respectively art. 1 paragraph (3), which enshrines the rule of law. In this way, our constitutional court accepts the deduction, by way of interpretation, of the principles of law implied by the express rules of the fundamental Law. In this respect, by means of the Decision no. 404 of April 10th 2008[397], the Constitutional Court stated that: "The principle of stability and security of legal relations, although not explicitly enshrined in the Romanian Constitution, is deduced both from the provisions of art. 1 paragraph (3), according to which Romania is a state of law, democratic and social, and from the preamble to the Convention for the Protection of Human Rights and Fundamental Freedoms, as interpreted by the European Court of Human Rights in its jurisprudence". See also Decision no. 685 of November 25th 2014[398]. Furthermore, our Constitutional Court has considered that the principle of security of civil legal relationships is a fundamental dimension of the rule of law[399]

Constitutional Court decides constantly for clarity and predictability of law, which are requirements of the rule of law. Thus, "the existence of contradictory legislative solutions and the annulment of legal provisions

---

[396] See also Decision no. 70 of April 18th 2000, published in the Official Gazette no. 334 of July 19th 2000.

[397] Published in the Official Gazette no. 347 of May 6th 2008.

[398] Published in the Official Gazette no. 68 of January 27th 2015.

[399] See Decision mo. 570 of May 29th 2012, published in the Official Gazette, no. 404 of June 18th 2012, Decision no. 615 of June 12th 2012, published in the Official Gazette no. 454 of July 6th 2012.

through other provisions contained in the same normative act lead to the violation of the principle of security of legal relations, due to the lack of clarity and predictability of the norm, principles which constitute a fundamental dimension of the rule of law, as it is expressly enshrined in the provisions of art. 1 paragraph (3) of the fundamental Law [400]

Concerning the rule of law, the Constitutional Court has shown that justice and social democracy are supreme values. In this context, the militarized authorities, in this case the Romanian Gendarmerie, exercise, under the law, specific powers regarding the defense of public order and tranquillity, of citizens' fundamental rights and freedoms, of public and private property, of prevention and detection of crimes, and other violations of applicable laws, and the protection of state institutions and the fight against acts of terrorism. Consequently, the Constitutional Court ruled: "By the possibility of militarized authorities to find contraventions committed by civilians, art. 1 paragraph (3) of the Constitution is not affected in any way, regarding the Romanian state, as a rule of law, democratic and social"[401]

Human dignity, together with the freedoms and rights of citizens, the free development of human personality, justice and political pluralism, are supreme values of the rule of law (art. 1 paragraph (3)). In the light of these constitutional regulations, it has been stated in the Constitutional Court's jurisprudence that the state is forbidden to adopt legislative solutions that can be interpreted as being disrespectful of religious or philosophical beliefs of parents, which is why organizing school activity must achieve a fair balance between the process of education and teaching religion, and on the other hand with respect for the rights of parents, to ensure education in accordance with their own religious beliefs. Activities and behaviours specific to a certain attitude of belief or philosophical, religious or non-religious beliefs must not be subject to sanctions that the state requires for such behaviour, regardless of the person's motivation for faith. "As part of the constitutional system of values, freedom of religious conscience is attributed to the imperative of tolerance, especially to human dignity, guaranteed by art. 1 paragraph (3) of the fundamental Law, which dominates the entire value system as a supreme

---

[400] Decision no. 26 of January 18th 2012, published in the Official Gazette no. 116 of February 15th 2012.

[401] Decision no. 1330 of December 4th 2008, published in the Official Gazette no. 873 of December 23rd 2008.

value"[402]

It is also interesting to note that our constitutional court considers human dignity as the supreme value of the entire system of values constitutionally consecrated, value that is found in the content of all human rights and fundamental freedoms. At the same time, it is an important aspect that requires the state authorities in their entire activity to first consider respecting the human dignity.

It should be noted that in its jurisprudence the Constitutional Court also identifies the content components of human dignity, as a moral value but at the same time constitutional, specific to the rule of law: "Human dignity, in constitutional terms, presupposes two inherent dimensions, namely the relations between people, which refers to the right and obligation of the people to be respected and, in a correlative way, to respect the fundamental rights and freedoms of their peers, as well as the relation of man to the environment, including the animal world".[403]

---

[402] Decision no. 669 of November 12th 2014, published in the Official Gazette no. 59 of January 23rd 2015.

[403] Decision no. 1 of January 11th 2012, published in the Official Gazette no. 53 of January 23rd 2012. See also Decision no 80 of February 16th 2014, published in Official Gazette no. 246 of February 7th 2014.

V. Conclusions

Antonie Iorgovan said that an essential problem of the rule of law is to answer the question: "where discretionary power ends and where the abuse of law begins, where the legal behaviour of the administration ends, materialized in its right of appreciation and where the violation of a subjective right or legitimate interest of the citizen begins?" Therefore, the application and observance of the principle of legality in the activity of state authorities is a complex issue because the exercise of state functions presupposes the discretionary power with which the organs of the state are invested, or in other words the authorities' "right of appreciation" regarding the moment of adoption and the content of the measures imposed. What is important to emphasize is that discretionary power cannot be opposed to the principle of legality, as a dimension of the rule of law.

The excess of power can be manifested in these circumstances by at least three aspects: a) the appraisal of a factual situation as an exceptional case, although it does not have this significance (lack of objective and reasonable motivation); b) the measures ordered by the competent authorities of the State, by virtue of discretion, to go beyond what is necessary to protect the publicly threatened public interest; c) if these measures unduly and unjustifiably restrict the exercise of fundamental rights and freedoms constitutionally recognized.

The key issue for the practitioner and the theorist is to identify criteria by which to establish the limits of the discretionary power of the state authorities and to differentiate it from the excess of power that must be sanctioned. Of course, there is also the question of using these criteria in court practice or constitutional litigation.

Concerning these aspects, the opinion of the specialized literature was that the purpose of the law will be the legal limit of the right of appreciation (of opportunity). For discretionary power does not mean a freedom beyond the law, but one permitted by law. Of course, "the purpose of the law" is a condition of legality or, as the case may be, the constitutionality of the legal acts of the organs of the state, and can therefore be considered a criterion for delimiting discretionary power from excess of power.

As can be seen from the case law of some international and domestic courts in relation to our research theme, the purpose of the law cannot be the only criterion to delimit discretionary power (synonymous with the margin of appreciation, term used by the ECHR) of the State may be an excess of power not only in the case where the measures adopted do not pursue a legitimate aim but also in the case that the measures ordered are not appropriate to the purpose of the law and are not necessary in relation to the factual situation and the legitimate aim pursued.

The adequacy of the measures ordered by the state authorities to the legitimate aims pursued is a particular aspect of the principle of proportionality. Significant is the opinion expressed by Antonie Iorgovan, who considers that the limits of discretionary power are set by: "positive written rules, general principles of law, principle of equality, principle of nonretroactivity of administrative acts, right to defense and principle of contradictory, principle of proportionality" Therefore, the principle of proportionality is an essential criterion that allows the discretionary power to delimit excess of power in the work of state authorities. And by this is an essential principle of the rule of law.

Bibliography

Andreescu M., Puran A. (2018), Constitutional law. The general theory of the state, 3rd Edition, Bucharest: C.H. Beck Publishing House;

Constantinescu M. (1993), The balance of powers in the constitutional regime in Romania, in Law no. 3/1993;

Deleanu I. (1996), Constitutional law and political institutions, vol I., Bucharest: Europa Nova Publishing House;

Eisenmann Ch. (1984), *L'espirit des lois et la separation des pouvoirs*, in Cahiers de philosophie politique no. 2-3, Paris: Ousia Publishing House;

Muraru I., Tănăsescu E.S., (2003), Constitutional law and political institutions, vol. II, Bucharest: All Beck Publishing House;

Sartori G. (1999), Theory of democracy reinterpreted, Bucharest: Polirom Publishing House;

17. CONTROL OF CONSTITUTIONALITY OF LAW IN ROMANIA. CONTRIBUTIONS TO JURISDUDENCE

Abstract:

To the Romanian system of law, jurisprudence does not have the quality of a formal source of law. Nevertheless, a legal reality, viewed from a historical perspective, has demonstrated the essential role of judicial practice in interpreting and enforcing the law, in constructing argumentative practices, in clarifying the will of the legislator, and in discovering the less obvious meanings of legal norms and, last but not least, in unifying thought and legal practice. Therefore jurisprudence, along with doctrine, is an important component of the Romanian system of law.

Based on these considerations, we intend to highlight some aspects of constitutional jurisprudence in this paper. We underline its contribution to the constitutional review of laws in Romania. Under the Constitution of 1866, which did not regulate institutionally such a control, the courts have assumed this competence by interpreting the law and by way of jurisprudence.

Important aspects of the Constitutional Court jurisprudence and of the courts in the development of constitutional review in our country are presented and analysed. We support the idea that jurisprudence currently plays an important part in the interpretation of constitutional norms, including with regard to deepening the constitutional review forms.

Key words:

The emergence of constitutional review in Romania / jurisprudential reasoning / the interpretation of the Constitution by case-law/ the role of jurisprudence in the calibration and development of constitutional review

I. Meanings and traits of constitutional justice

Constitutional supremacy would remain just a theoretical matter if not for proper guarantees. Indisputably, constitutional justice and its particular form, constitutional review is the main guarantee of Constitution's supremacy, as is expressly stipulated by the Basic law of Romania.

Teacher Ion Deleanu believed: "*Constitutional justice may be deemed, alongside many other things, a paradigm of this century*"[404]. The emergence and evolution of constitutional justice is determined by several factors to which the doctrine refers; of these, we mention: man, as a citizen, becomes a cardinal axiological benchmark of civil and political society, and the fundamental rights and freedoms are no longer just a theoretical speech, but a normative reality as well; democracy is reconsidered, within the meaning that minority's protection becomes a key requirement of the rule of law and, at the same time, a counterweight to the principle of majority "parliamentary sovereignty" is submitted to the primacy of law and especially to the Constitution; as a consequence, the law is no longer an infallible act of Parliament, but conditional upon the Constitution's norms and values; last, but not least, reconsideration of the role and place of constitutions, within the meaning of qualifying them, especially as: "fundamental establishments of the governed, not of the governing people, as a dynamic act, as a continues shaping and as an act of society"[405].

The terms of "constitutional justice" or "constitutional jurisdiction" are controversial in the specialty literature; constitutional review is the more preferred term. However, the "constitutional justice" notion arises in Kelsen's work under the form of "Constitution's jurisdictional guarantee"[406]. Also, Eisenmann believes it to be "that form of justice or more specifically, jurisdiction which concerns the constitutional laws" without which the Constitution would be nothing but a "political programme, compulsory just from a moral standpoint". The same author makes the distinction between constitutional justice and constitutional jurisdiction. "Constitutional justice" is the form by which prerogatives are distributed between ordinary law and

---

[404] I. Deleanu, Justiţia constituţională, Lumina Lex Publishing House, Bucharest, 1995, p.5

[405] For more information, see Ion Deleanu, Op. cit., pp. 5-6

[406] H. Kelsen, La garantie jurisdictionnelle de la Constituion, în Revue de Droit publique, 1928, p.197 and the following

constitutional legislation, and "constitutional jurisdiction" refers to the authority by which constitutional justice is fulfilled[407].

The notion of "constitutional justice" has established in the Romanian literature especially thanks to the contribution in the field of professor Ion Deleanu[408]. Without thoroughly analysing this concept, we believe that constitutional justice is a legal category with particular meaning, whose constitutional components are the following:

a) Designates the totality of institutions and proceedings whereby Constitutional supremacy is achieved.
b) A competent state body has to achieve it by the duties set out by Constitution and by law;
c) An assembly of technical means and forms of accomplishment presenting specific and exclusive elements;
d) The purpose of the constitutional justice is to ensure Constitutional supremacy.

There is no identity among the concepts of constitutional justice and constitutional review, respectively. The latter is just a component of the first.

Within the meaning of the definition proposed above, the general traits of constitutional justice may be identified as follows:

- it is genuine jurisdiction, but it consists of a few particularities as opposed to other forms of justice, considering its purpose;

- it can use common procedural rules, but also own procedural rules registered in the Constitution, laws and regulations determined by the constitutional dispute's nature;

- it can be achieved by a specialized state body (political, jurisdictional or with double nature) or by the general law courts;

- it is an exclusive jurisdiction because it has monopoly over constitutional litigations.

---

[407] For more information, see Ch. Eisenmann, La Justice constitutionnelle de la Haute Cour Constitutionnelle d'Autriche, Paris, 1928, reed. PUAM et Economica, 1986

[408] For more information, see I. Deleanu, op.cit. pp. 9-126

- it is not always concentrated, because general law courts may have perspectives in the constitutional litigations field:

– constitutional justice's independence consists in the existence of a "constitutional status" of the body achieving this type of jurisdiction, consisting of the statutory and administrative autonomy, independent of any public authority; checking own competency, pre-eminence of constitutional justice's abuses toward any jurisdictional decisions: independence and the security of judges' tenure and in some cases, assigning them using other criteria than those concerning the recruitment, appointing and promoting career magistrates.

Evaluation of the constitutionality of the laws is the constitutional justice's main form and it is the basis for democracy, guaranteeing a democratic government is to be accomplished, complying with the Constitutional and law supremacy.

George Alexianu thinks legality is an attribute of modern state. The idea of lawfulness in the author's conception is formulated as follows: all state bodies operate based on a rule of law decided by the lawmaker, which needs to be complied with.

When referring to the Constitutional supremacy, the same author claimed with full justification and in relation to today's realities: "When modern state organizes its new look, the first idea with which it is preoccupied is to crack down the administrative abuse; hence the intervention of constitutions and jurisdictionally, the establishment of an examination of legality. Once this abuse established, another one arises, much more serious, that of Parliament. Constitution's supremacy is then invented and various systems to guarantee it. The idea of legality thus acquires a strong strengthening leverage"[409].

An important aspect is also that of defining the notion of evaluation of the constitutionality of the laws. The legal doctrine[410] has underlined that this duty's problematic should be included in the principle of legality. Legality is a

---

409 G. Alexianu, Drept constituţional, Ed. Casei Şcoalelor, Bucharest, 1930, p. 71

410 See, in that regard, I. Deleanu, Instituţii şi proceduri constituționale, C.H. Beck Publishing House, Bucharest, 2006, p.810; I.Muraru , E.S. Tănăsescu, Drept constituţional şi instituţii politice, Vol. II,C.H.Beck Publishing House, Bucharest, 2014, p.191; M. Andreescu, A. Puran, Drept constituţional. Teoria generală a statului, Ed. a II-a, C.H.Beck Publishing House, Bucharest, 2017, pp. 205-206

fundamental principle for the organization and operation of the social and political systems. This principle has several coordinates: existence of a hierarchized legal system, on top of which lies the Constitution. Consequently, the ordinary law should be compliant with the Constitution in order to meet the legality condition; State's bodies should carry out their duties by strictly complying with the competency set out by law; normative acts' drafting should be made by competent persons, by a predetermined procedure, complying with the provisions of the superior normative acts with legal force and by complying with the law and the Constitution by all State bodies.

The doctrine has defined constitutional review as: "*Organized activity of checking the conformity of the law with the constitution and from the point of view of the constitutional right, it comprises rules about the competent authorities making this check, the procedure to follow and the measures which can be taken after this procedure has been fulfilled*"[411].

It follows, from the definition's examination that the constitutional review has a complex meaning. This is an institution of the constitutional law, i.e. the assembly of legal norms on the organization and operation of the competent authority of exercising control, as well as the assembly of legal norms with procedural character, which regulate and may be ordered by a constitutional court.

At the same time, there is also an organized activity whereby Constitutional supremacy is guaranteed, as compliance of the norms comprised by laws and other normative acts with constitutional regulations.

Essentially, constitutional review supposes checking compliance of the law as a legal act of Parliament, but also of other categories of normative acts with the rules comprised by the Constitution. Compliance should exist both in terms of a formal aspect (competency of the issuing body and the drafting procedure), as well as from a material standpoint (content of the norm in the ordinary law should be compliant with the constitutional requirements).

---

[411] I. Muraru, E.S. Tănăsescu, op.cit., p.191

II. Brief considerations about the case-law's role in the constitutional review's appearance

Historically, the judicial review of constitutionality established in the U.S.A. in the beginning of the 19th century holds particular importance, although the Constitution does not regulate procedural rules.

The progress of the constitutional review in the U.S.A. may be divided into two periods. The first period begins with the moment Constitution was adopted in 1787 and it ends in 1886.

During this period, judges would especially check, with regard to constitutionality, whether the ordinary lawmaker has complied with the competency conferred by the Constitution, within the meaning of not legislating on the matters prohibited by the constitutional rules. Judges could not cancel a law as unconstitutional, but only fulfil its enforcement to the case referred to trial.

The Supreme Court ruled on the case of *Marbury v. Madison* for the first time in a case of this nature, declaring the Federal Constitution as a supreme law of the state and removing an act of Congress contrary to the Federal Constitution. The Court's decision is drawn-up by Judge John Marshall and is the basis on which the American case-law is founded in the matter of constitutional review.

The rationale that the American judge employed was as follows: the judge should enforce and construe laws. Constitution is the supreme law of a state which should be enforced with priority towards any other law. As Constitution is a law, it shall be construed and enforced by the judge, including to a particular case being the subject matter referred for trial.

If the law is not compliant with the constitutional rules, the latter shall be enforced given the Constitution's supreme character.

The second period commences in 1883 with a famous decision made by the Supreme Court of Massachusetts in the Wiegman dispute. The powers of the judges increase with regard to constitutionality. The Supreme Court nowadays does not just limit itself to checking a law from the point of view of complying with the constitutional competency of the lawmaker or in terms of compliance with procedures. As of that time until now, justice has begun, in the matter of constitutional review, examining the law from the point of view of opportunity, celerity and its social and economic justification. Thus, judicial power examines, via constitutional review procedure, the Parliament's whole activity and removes all the measures deemed as contrary to the legal order in a State. This way, justice is a guarantor of the Constitution's supremacy and compliance with the principle of separation of powers in a State, "for mutual review and supervision of powers refer to the existence of a state".

The European template of constitutional justice is characterized from an institutional point of view in constitutional courts or district courts. During the inter-war period, this template was noticed in: Austria (1920), Czechoslovakia (1979), Spain (1931) and Ireland (1938).

After World War Two, constitutional courts and district courts were founded in most European States: Italy (1948), Germany (1949), Turkey (1961), Portugal (1976), Spain (1978) etc. Among the Eastern- European countries to have this constitutional justice template, we mention: Romania, Poland, Hungary, Czech Republic, Croatia, Macedonia, Russia, Ukraine, Lithuania etc.

In the case of France, the constitutional review is achieved by a double nature body- political and jurisdictional- the French Constitutional Council. It is made up of former presidents of the republic who are still living, as well as 9 members appointed for a sole term of 9 years. Appointing the Constitutional Council's members occurs as follows: three by the Presidents of the State, three by the President of the Senate and three by the president of the National Assembly. The president of the Constitutional Council is appointed by the decision of the President of the republic. This council also has other duties in its competency apart from constitutional review.

III. Case-law's role in the emergence and development of constitutional review in Romania

In our country, constitutional review has evolved, being marked by the national particularities and successive application of the two templates presented above.

The Constitution from 1866 did not regulate the constitutional review. However, the provisions of Art. 9 of the Constitution may be mentioned, according to which the Lord "punishes and promulgates the laws" and that He "can refuse its punishment". Consequently, the head of State could refuse to promulgate a law if they believed it to be unconstitutional. Obviously, this wasn't exactly an evaluation of the constitutionality of the laws, but it is a precursor means to such a check. During the period in which the Constitution of 1866 was in force, the head of State never resorted to such a procedure.

The constitutional review made by a court of law, not by a specialized institution, different from the judicial power, was accepted on the European continent as well. The constitutional history mentions a Romanian priority in this case. Thus, during the period 1911/1912, first Ilfov County Court, then the High Court of Cassation and Justice extended their powers to check the constitutional compliance of laws in the dispute known as "the tramway matter" from Bucharest.

What is interesting is that the rationale employed by Ilfov County Court and by the High Court of Cassation and Justice in arguing the possibility to achieve, using a pretorian way, constitutional review. Essentially, the considerations were the following: 1) the Court did not assume competency ex officio to rule on the constitutionality of a law and to cancel it, since such procedure would have constituted a mixture of the judicial power in the law making powers' duties. Consequently, the court undertook this competency, since it had been referred to check the constitutionality of a law; 2) based on the duties given, judicial power's main mission is to construe and enforce all the laws, either ordinary or constitutional. If an invoked law contravenes the Constitution, the court may not refuse to settle the matter; 3) There is no provision in the Constitution of 1866 by which to expressly prohibit the judicial power's right to check whether a law is compliant or not with the Constitution. The provisions of Art. 77 of the Constitution are invoked; according to them, a judge, as per the oath taken, is under the obligation to enforce the laws and the country's Constitution; 4) Unlike ordinary laws, the Constitution is permanent and it can only be revised as an exceptional measure. As it is the supreme force law, Constitution is imposed by its authority on everybody and this is why the judge is obligated to enforce it with priority, including in the hypothesis where the law based on which the dispute is settled is contrary to the Constitution[412].

Decisions ruled by Ilfov County Court and by the High Court of Cassation and Justice have been well received by the specialists of that time. Here is a brief comment: "*This decision was a great satisfaction to all the people of law. It is a big step in the advancement of this country toward progress, for it enshrines the principle that this country's Constitution, its foundation, the palladium of our rights and freedoms, and no one should disobey them. We are proud our justice is showing even to the justice in the Western countries what is the true path to progress in the matter of public law*"[413].

[412] See "Judicial Courier", No. 32, of 29 April 1912, pp. 373-376

[413] N. D. Comşa, Notes from „ "Judicial Courier",", Nr.32, of 29 April 1912, p.378

IV. Contemporary aspects of constitutional case-law. Case-law of the courts

The regulatory activity of law elaboration should continue by the activity of enforcing the rules; in order to enforce them, the first logical operation to carry out is to construe them.

Both the Constitution, and the law come as an assembly of legal rules, but these rules are expressed under the form of a legislative text. This is why it is not the legislative texts that constitute an object of interpretation, but the legal texts or the one of the Constitution. A legal text may comprise several legal rules. By way of interpretation, a constitutional rule can be deduced from a constitutional text. The Constitution text is drawn-up into general terms, which influences the determination degree of the constitutional rules. The constitutional rules are identified and determined via interpretation.

What also needs to be underlined is that a Constitution may comprise certain principles that are not clearly expressed *expresis verbis*, but they can be deduced by systematically interpreting other rules.

Within the meaning of the above, the speciality literature stated: "The determination degree of constitutional rules using the basic law text may justify the need for interpretation. The Rules in the Constitution are very suited for a progress of their course, because the text is par excellence imprecise, formulated into general terms. Constitution's formal superiority, its rigidity prevent its review under very short time-spans and then the interpretation remains the only way to adopt the normative content, usually older, to the social reality which is permanently changing. As the meaning of constitutional rules is by their very nature of outmost generality, its precise determination depends on the interpreter's will"[414].

The scientific justification of the interpretation arises from the need to ensure the effectiveness of the rules comprised both by the Constitution, and by the laws via institutions mainly carrying out the activity of interpreting the rules provided by the author.

---

414 John. Muraru, Mihhai Constantinescu, Elena Simina Tănăsescu, Mihai Enache, Gheorghe. Iancu, Interpretation of the Constitution. Doctrine and practice, Lumina Lex Publishing House, Bucharest, 2002, p. 67..

These institutions are first the courts of law, and the constitutional ones.

Checking compliance of a normative act with constitutional rules, institution which represents the constitutional review is not a formal comparison or mechanical juxtaposition of the two categories of rules, but a complex work relying on the interpretation techniques and procedures both of the law, and the Constitution.

Consequently, the need to construe the Constitution is a condition of applying it and securing its primacy. The constitutional review is essentially an activity of construing the Constitution, and the law. There need to be independent public authorities competent to construe the Constitution and to examine in this manner compliance of the law with the Constitution. These authorities are the Courts and the Constitutional Courts within the European template of constitutional justice.

In exercising its duties, the Constitutional Court regulates a work of interpreting the law and the Constitution. The constitutional court cannot amend, complete or repeal a law.

In its former drafting, before the Constitution's review, Law no. 47/1992 prohibited the Constitutional Court to construe those normative acts making the subject matter of the constitutional review. Naturally, the current regulation has removed this ban, since the activity of checking compliance of the normative regulations with the provisions of the Constitution the constitutional judge carries out is essentially a work of enforcing the law relying on the interpretation of the legal rules.

The Constitutional Court participates in the fulfilment of the legislative function in the State, but not as a positive lawmaker, but as a negative lawmaker, whose purpose is to remove the "unconstitutionality venom" from a normative act. This is why the Court, by its duties, is not subrogated to the Parliament's activity, since the amendment, completion or repealing of a law is an exclusive attribute of the Parliament.

The Constitutional Court's constructive interpretation by case- law of the Basic Law also arises from this institution's role to "support the good operation of public powers in the constitutional reports of separation, balance and mutual control". The principle of separation and balance of powers in the State is still, despite all the critiques some authors expressed, the fundament of democratic exercise of state power and the main constitutional guarantee of avoiding excess or abuse of power from any of the State's authorities.

The relationships between State's authorities are complex in nature, but they must also secure their proper operation, by complying with the principle of Constitution's legality and supremacy. To carry out this desideratum, it is very important that a state balance is maintained between all its forms and variants, including as social balance.

The separation and balance of powers no longer concerns just the classical powers (legislative, executive and judicial). Other powers are added to these, rendering new dimensions to this classical principle. The relationships between the participants in the state and social life can also cause conflicts which need to be settled in order to preserve the balance of powers. Some constitutions refer to disputes of public law (Constitution of Germany- Art. 93), to conflicts of jurisdiction between the State and autonomous communities or conflicts of duties between the State's powers, between the State and regions and between regions (Constitution of Italy – Art. 314).

Romania's Constitution speaks of judicial conflicts of constitutional nature between the public authorities [Art. 146 sub-par. c)] and regulates the mediation function between State powers that the President exercises.

The Constitutional Court is an important guarantor of the separation and balance of the State's powers, since it settles legal conflicts of constitutional nature between public authorities and by the duties it has in the matter of control of constitutionality prior to laws and checking constitutionality of regulations of chambers, it intervenes in ensuring balance between the parliamentary majority and minority, effectively ensuring the opposition's right to express itself.

The Constitutional Court is a guarantor that the fundamental freedoms and rights are complied with. This fundamental part the constitutional court plays in the rule of law is accomplished by interpreting Constitution's case-law and of the laws. As a general rule, there are three key guarantees from a constitutional point of view on the rights and freedoms of citizens established by the Constitution:

a) Constitutional supremacy; b) Constitution's rigid character; c) citizens 'access to the constitutional review and to the control of legality for the acts subordinated to law.

In Romania, the procedure of the exception of unconstitutionality ensures citizens 'indirect access to the constitutional justice.

Judicial review is an important way to guarantee the Basic Law's supremacy, since the courts, by the nature of their duties, they construe and enforce the law, which also implies the obligation to analyse compliance of the legal acts subjected to judicial review with the Constitution's rules. Consequently, the courts have competency in the matter of constitutional justice. We are taking into consideration not only the general obligation of the judge to comply with and enforce the Constitution rules or the duties conferred by law to refer the constitutional court by an exception of unconstitutionality, but particularly the possibility to censure a legal act in terms of constitutionality.

Recent case-law and doctrine in the matter look into the competency of the courts to check some legal acts in terms of compliance with the constitutional rules. An unconstitutional legal act is an act issued with misuse of power.

The unconstitutionality of a legal act may be ascertained by a court if the following conditions are cumulatively met:

1. the court exercises its duties within the limits of the competency set out by law;

2. the legal act may be individual or normative; it may be binding or elective;

3. not to have to the case the exclusive jurisdiction of the Constitutional Court to rule over the constitutionality of a legal act;

4. settlement of the case should depend on the legal act being criticized for its unconstitutionality;

5. there is a pertinent, sufficient and reasonable motivation of the court on the legal act's unconstitutionality.

If these conditions are cumulatively met, the boundaries of the courts 'duties are not exceeded, but on the contrary, the principle of the Constitutional primacy applies and effectiveness is given to the judge's role of applying and interpreting the law correctly. Such a solution is justified in relation to the judge's role in the rule of law as well: to construe and enforce the law.

Fulfilment of this constitutional mission, particularly important and difficult at the same time, requires the judge to enforce the law by complying with the principle of Constitutional primacy; consequently, to evaluate the constitutionality of legal acts forming the object of the dispute referred for trial or which apply to the settlement of the case. Enforcement of the legal acts is made by the judge taking account of their legal force, by complying with the principle of Constitutional primacy. In this regard, the provisions of Art. 4 par. (1) of Law no. 303/2004 also need to be mentioned, which force the magistrates to ensure the supremacy of law through their entire activity.

Another problem is that of knowing what are the solutions that the courts can rule, by complying with the conditions shown above, where they find the unconstitutionality of a legal act. There can be two situations: In a *first hypothesis,* the courts can be directly vested with checking the legality of a legal act, as is the case of the courts of administrative disputes. In this case, the courts can find by making a decision, the absolute nullity of legal acts, on grounds of unconstitutionality. *The other situation* takes into consideration the hypothesis in which the courts are not vested directly with checking the legal act criticised for unconstitutionality, but that legal act applies for settling the case referred for trial. In this case, the courts can no longer order the cancellation of the unconstitutional legal act; however, they shall no longer enforce it to settle the case.

V. Matters related to the Constitutional Court's case-law. On the material competence

Our constitutional court's case-law brings its contribution to the constitutional review in Romania by several aspects. We would like to analyse some relevant decisions in this matter next.

The Constitutional court has construed the notion of "law" in order to determine the scope of competency of the constitutional review on normative acts. The case-law has mentioned that the term of "law" provided under Art. 146 sub-par. b) of the Constitution is not widely used consisting of all normative acts, but only in its strict meaning, of law, by which the normative act is understood, adopted by the Parliament and promulgated by the President of Romania. At the same time, this scope also includes ordinances which are normative acts adopted by the Government based on a legislative delegation. "The concept of law arises from the combination of the formal criterion to the material one, since the content of law is determined by the importance paid by the lawmaker to the regulated aspects...settlement of the exception of unconstitutionality concerning other normative acts is not of the Constitutional Court's competency, as these acts are controlled in terms of legality by the administrative disputes courts" [415]. This decision of the Constitutional Court is important, particularly because it follows that the courts, particularly the administrative disputes ones, in relation to the legal rules of competency, may check the legality of a normative act, including in terms of its constitutionality.

The Court has determined that its role is to set out that the provisions of law criticised are constitutional and, at the same time, if the interpretation given to them abides by the Constitution's requirements, as such that, to the extent the legal text criticised may be conferred a constitutional interpretation, the Court shall find the legal provision's constitutionality in this interpretation and shall exclude any other possible interpretations from this application[416]. This solution of our constitutional court is important because it identifies, from a constitutional point of view, the so-called interpretative decisions of the Court, by which the legal text criticised for unconstitutionality is not removed,

[415] Decision no. 435 of 13 September 2005, published in the Official Journal no.924 of 17 October 2005

[416] Decision no. 223 of 13 March 2012, published in the Official Journal no.256 of 18 April2012; Decision no. 448 of 29 October 2013, published in the Official Journal no .5 of 7 January 2014

but interpreted within the meaning of the constitutional rules to produce legal effects.

The Constitutional Court has constantly, in its case- law, decided that it does not have the competency to control facts materialized into actions or inactions, but only the "extrinsic and intrinsic conformity of the normative act adopted with the Constitution"[417] in connection with the scope of the Constitutional Court's competency to exercise constitutional review *a priori* on the laws, especially if the constitutionality check is required by a normative act amending a law whereby it was decided by the case-law that "In accordance with Art. 146 sub-par. a) of the Constitution, the a priori constitutional review s exercised by the Constitutional Court only on the laws before they are promulgated, not on the provisions of laws in force. Irrespective of the connections that can be made between the amending text and the amended text, the Constitutional Court, on grounds of Art. 146 sub-par. a) of the Constitution, cannot make a ruling within the a priori control over the law-amending text to be submitted to promulgation and it cannot expand constitutional review over the amended text from a law in force"[418].

Decision no. 799 of 17 June 2011 made by the Constitutional Court is important, because it established competency of this court of ruling over the constitutionality of the review law, adopted by the parliament before being subjected to referendum. In this regard, it decided that: "The review law adopted by the Parliament needs to be submitted to referendum, under the conditions of Art. 151 par. 3 of the Basic Law to be examined by the Constitutional Court to find out, on the one hand, whether the Court's decision on the law draft or proposal for review of the Constitution was respected or not and, on the other hand, whether the changes and completions made to the draft or proposal for review in the procedure for parliamentary debate and adoption complies with the constitutional provisions concerning the review." [419] .

More decisions have been ruled by our constitutional court in connection with the determination of its competency of ruling on the constitutionality of decisions made by the Parliament. In this regard, we refer to an important

---

[417] Decision no. 1237 of 6 October 2010, published in the Official Journal no.785 of 24 November 2010

[418] Decision no. 498 of 8 June 2006, published in the Official Journal no.554 of 27 June 2006

[419] Decision no. 799 of 17 June 2011 on the law draft concerning the review of Romania's constitution published in the Official Journal no.440 of 23 June 2011

matter arising from the case-law in connection with the scope of constitutional review in this matter. In this regard, the Constitutional Court has constantly ruled that only decisions made by the Parliament can be subjected to the constitutional review, adopted after this competency has been conferred by the lawmaker, affecting constitutional values, rules and principles or, as applicable, the organization and operation of authorities and institutions with a constitutional rank.[420].

At the same time, the Constitutional Court stated that the task of controlling the decisions made by the Parliament "is an expression of the Rule of Law's requirements and a guarantee of the fundamental rights and freedoms… lack of jurisdiction control is equal to a transformation of the parliamentary majority into judges of own acts"[421] In the same regard, it was claimed that accepting the contrary thesis, leading to the exclusion of the exercise of constitutional review of the decisions made by the Parliament, made by violating the express provisions of the law, would lead to the placement of the supreme representative body of the people- the Parliament- above the law and accepting the idea that it is precisely the authority which legitimately adopts the laws constitutionally may breach them without any sort of punishment.[422]

One of the most important problems to have made the object of analysis by the Constitutional Court refers to the competency of this court of ruling on the conformity of a normative act with a legal act of the European Union institutions. In this regard, the case-law has constantly stated that the constitutional court has no competency to carry out a conformity control between a directive and the national normative act whereby it is transposed. A potential non-conformity of the national act to the European one does not

---

[420] Decision no. 53 of 25 January 2011, published in the Official Journal no.90 of 3 February 2011. See also: Decision no. 54 of 25 January 2011, published in the Official Journal no.90 of 3 February 2011; Decision no. 307 of 28 March 2012 , published in M.Of.no.293 of 4 May 2012; Decision no. 783 of 26 September 2012, published the Official Journal no.684 of 3 October 2012

[421] Decision no. 727 of 9 July 2012, published in the Official Journal no.477 of 12 July 2012; Decision no. 80 of 16 February 2014, published the Official Journal no. 246 of 7 April 2014

[422] Decision no. 251 of 30 April 2014, published in the Official Journal 376 of 21 May 2014

implicitly draw the unconstitutionality of the national act of transposition. The competency of conferring greater protection in the national law towards the legal instruments of the European Union devolves on the lawmaker.[423]

In connection with the constitutionality check of the decisions ruled by the High Court of Cassation and Justice in settling appeals in the interest of the law, the Constitutional Court has ruled in its case-law that according to the legal rules in force, it has not such competency[424]). However, if, by a decision ruled in an appeal for the interest of the law, a legal text is given a certain interpretation, it cannot exclude the competency of the Constitutional Court of analysing the respective text, in the interpretation given by the court of last instance. "From the perspective of relating to the Constitution's provisions, the Constitutional Court checks the constitutionality of the applicable legal texts, in the interpretation enshrined in the interest of the law. Admitting a contrary thesis contravenes to reason of existence itself of the Constitutional Court, which would deny its constitutional role, accepting that a legal text is applied under the limits which would collide with the Basic Law[425]."

The case-law has established that the constitutional disputes court may rule in connection with the constitutionality of a repealing rule, seeing as, on the one hand, the presumption of constitutionality of the law is a relative presumption and, on the other hand, the provisions of Law no. 24/2000 lay down that it is impossible to reinstate the initial normative act by repealing of an prior repealing act.[426]

With regard to the competency of the Constitutional Court of settling legal disputes of constitutional nature, several relevant decisions have been ruled.

A first aspect is the definition given by the Constitutional Court to the legal dispute of constitutional nature: "The legal conflict of constitutional nature implies specific acts or actions whereby one or more authorities assign themselves powers, duties or competencies which, according to the

---

[423] Decision no. 415 of 7 April 2011, published the Official Journal no.471 of 5 July 2011

[424] Decision no. 778 of 16 June 2011, published the Official Journal no.668 of 20 September 2011

[425] Decision no. 854 of 23 June 2011, published the Official Journal no.672 of 21 September 2011

[426] Decision no. 20 of 2 February 2000, published the Official Journal no.72 of 18 February 2000

Constitution, belong to other public authorities or the omission of public authorities, consisting in the declination of their jurisdiction or refusal to carry out certain acts falling within their obligations". Consequently, according to the court's case-law, legal disputes of constitutional nature are not limited to just disputes of positive or negative jurisdiction, which could create institutional blockages, but aim at any conflicting legal situations whose occurrence reside directly in the Constitution's text.[427].

The case- law has set out that political parties, public persons of public law are not in the category of public authorities that are susceptible of being parties involved in a legal dispute of constitutional nature which, according to the provisions of Art. 8 par. 2 of the Basic Law, contributes to the definition and expressing of the public will of the citizens. Hence, it is the Constitutional Court's opinion that political parties are not public authorities. Also, parliamentary groups as well are not public authorities, but structures of the chambers of Parliament. "A potential conflict between a political party or a parliamentary group and a public authority does not fall within the category of conflicts that can be settled under the jurisdiction of the Constitutional Court, as per Art. 146 sub-par. a) of the Constitution".[428]

By the same decision, the Constitutional Court ruled that opinions, judgments of value or allegations of a public dignity mandate holder- as is the President of Romania, or the leader of a public authority- concerning other public authorities cannot, by themselves, constitute legal disputes between public authorities, because they cannot trigger institutional blockages, if not followed by actions or inactions which may prevent these public authorities from carrying out their constitutional tasks

[427] Decision no. 901 of 17 June 2009, published the Official Journal no. 503 of 21 July 2009

[428] Decision no. 53 of 28 January 2005, published the Official Journal no. 144 of 17 February 2005

VI. Some conclusions

In our opinion, the Constitutional Court's role as a guarantor of the Basic Law should be enhanced by new duties aiming at limiting the excess of power of the State's authorities. We do not agree to what the specialty literature states, i.e. that a potential improvement of constitutional justice could be achieved by reducing the constitutional disputes court's duties[429]. It is true that the Constitutional Court ruled some questionable decisions in terms of abiding by the limits of exercising the duties incumbent upon it under the Constitution, by undertaking the positive lawmaker role.[430]. Reduction of the duties of the constitutional court for this reason is not a solution as legal basis. Surely, reducing the duties of a state authority leads to the removal of the risk of faultily exercising such duties. This is not how the activity of a state authority is improved in a rule of law, but by searching for legal solutions of carry out the duties which turn out to be necessary to the state and social system under better conditions.

Proportionality is a fundamental principle of the law explicitly enshrined by constitutional, legislative regulations and international legal tools. It is based on the values of the rational law of justice and equity and it expresses the existence of a balanced or suitable relationship between actions, situations, phenomena; it is a criterion for limiting the measures set out by the state authorities to what is necessary to reach a legitimate goal, this way guaranteeing the fundamental rights and avoiding the abuse of power by the state's authorities. Proportionality is a basic principle of the European Union's law, being expressly enshrined by the provisions of Art. 5 of the Treaty on the European Union[431].

We estimate that this principle's express regulation just in the contents of the provisions of Art. 5 of the Constitution, applied in the field of narrowing the exercise of rights is insufficient to emphasize the principle's entire meaning and significance for the rule of law.

---

[429] Genoveva Vrabie, The legal nature of constitutional courts and their place in the system of public authorities, in Public Law Review, no. 1/2010 p. 33

[430] As an eample, we refer here to the Decision no. 356/2007, published the Official Journal no. 322 of 14 May 2007 and to the Decision no. 98/2008 published the Official Journal no. 140 of 22 February 2008.

[431] For more information, see Marius Andreescu, Proportionality, a principle of European Union law, in Judicial Courier no. 10/2010, pp. 593-598

In a future review of the basic law, it would be useful to add another paragraph at Art. 1 of the Constitution, foreseeing that "*The exercise of State power should be proportional and non-discriminating*". This new constitutional regulation would become a genuine constitutional obligation for all State authorities, and they would exercise their duties as such that the measures adopted would register within the limits of the discretionary power recognized by law. At the same time, the possibility is created for the Constitutional Court to penalize the abuse of power in the Parliament and Government's activities, via the constitutional review of laws and ordinances, using the principle of proportionality as a criterion.

Among the Constitutional Court's duties can be included the one of ruling on the constitutionality of those administrative acts exempted from the legality control of the administrative disputes court. This category of administrative acts, to which Art. 126 par. 6 of the Constitution refers, along with the provisions of Law no. 544/2004 of administrative-disputes are particularly important to the whole social and state system. Consequently, constitutionality review is necessary since, in lack thereof, discretionary power of the issuing administrative authority is limitless and it may lead to the excessive narrowing of the exercise of the fundamental rights and freedoms or to the breach of important constitutional values. Our constitutional court should, for the same arguments, be able to review the President's decrees instituting the proceedings of referendum, in terms of their constitutionality.

The High Court of Cassation of Justice has the competency to adopt decisions in the appeal procedure for the interest of the law, which are binding for courts. If there is no legality or constitutionality control, practice has demonstrated that the court of last resort has, in numerous situations, exceeded its duty of construing the law and, by such decisions, has amended or completed normative acts, acting like a genuine lawmaker, thus violating the principle of separation of powers in the State[432]. We believe that, under these circumstances, the Constitutional Court must be given the competency to rule on the constitutionality of the decisions made by the High Court of Cassation and Justice adopted in the appeal proceedings for the interest of the law, in order to avoid the abuse of power from the court of last instance.

---

[432] For more information, see Marius Andreescu, The constitutionality of the appeal in the interest of the law and of the pronounced decisions, in the Judicial Courier no. 1/2011, pp. 32-36.

18. THE LAWFUL STATE IN THE CONTEXT OF THE NORMATIVE AND INSTITUTIONAL REQUIREMENTS OF EUROPEAN UNION

Abstract:

The doctrine of the lawful state comes from the German theory and jurisprudence, but is now a requirement and a reality of the constitutional democracy in contemporary society. Presently, the lawful state is no longer merely a doctrine but a fundamental principle of democracy consecrated in the Constitution and international political and legal documents. In essence, the concept of the lawful state is based on the supremacy of law in general and of Constitution in particular. Essential for the contemporary realities of the lawful state are the following fundamental elements: the moderation of the exercise of state power in relation to the law, the consecration, guaranteeing and observance of the constitutional rights of man especially by the state powers and, last but not least, the independence and impartiality of justice.

In this study we analyze the most important elements and features of the lawful state with reference to the contemporary realities in Romania in the context of the requirements expressed in the political and legal instruments of European Union. An important aspect of the analysis is the separation, balance and cooperation of the state powers, in relation to the constitutional provisions.

The excess of power of the public authorities, the excessive politicking and failure to respect the independence of justice are aspects of contemporary social and state reality that contravene to the requirements of the lawful state. Are analyzed the most significant aspects of the Constitutional Court jurisprudence and the jurisprudence of administrative courts in regard to the guaranteeing of the lawful state attribute in Romania, as well as, regarding the power excess.

Key words:

Conditions of the lawful state / separation and balance of the powers / the supremacy of law / guaranteeing of the fundamental rights / contemporary realities and aspects of the constitutional and administrative jurisprudence

I. Brief considerations on the notion of the rule of law

The notion of state attributes means its defining dimensions as they result from constitutional provisions, as an expression of the political will and determined by the political regime and at the same time values of principle of constitutional order.

The rule of law, pluralism, democracy, civil society are unquestionable universal values of contemporary political thinking and practice and are found to be expressed in the Constitution of Romania as well as in international documents. The state attributes configure its quality as constitutional law subject and define the power, but also the complex reports between the state and citizens and the other constitutional law subjects. The attributes of the Romanian state regulated by the provisions of art. 1 para. 3 of the Romanian Constitution: 1. rule of law; 2. social state; 3. pluralist state; 4. democratic state.

The rule of law is one of the most discussed concepts of constitutional law and is unquestionably related to the transition from the state law to the rule of law. In the literature, contradictory opinions were sometimes affirmed, according to which the rule of law corresponds to an anthropological necessity or is a myth, a postulate and an axiom, and on the other hand, the rule of law is a pleonasm, a legal nonsense.

The concept of the rule of law is a constitutional reality whose foundation is found in the mechanisms of the exercise of state power, in the relations between power and liberty of every individual of society and in the application of the principle of legality to the entire state activity, but also in the behaviour of each member of society.

The rule of law has formed and spread over three major models:

1. The *English model of* "Rule of Law" is characterized by the limitation of the monarch's power and, on the other hand, by preserving the power of the parliament, which in terms of constitutional law means:a) the restriction of the powers of the monarch and their recognition of a power constituted by the norms of positive law, b) the necessity to found acts of the executive directly or indirectly on the authority of the Parliament, c) the obligation of all subjects of law to submit to the law of jurisdiction. **2.** The *German concept* emphasizes the need to ensure the legality of the administration and its judicial control; 3. The

French conception regards the rule of law as a legal state, proclaiming and maintaining the principle of legality. **3.** The *French concept* considers the rule of law as a legal state, which proclaims and defends the principle of legality.

In the expression rule of law there are two aspects of the legal, seemingly contradictory but still complementary: normativism and ideology. In the normative plane, the rule of law appears as a structural principle of the Constitution along with other essential attributes of the state, materializing the fundamental values on which the existence of society and state are based.

From the normative point of view, the requirements of the rule of law are manifested in a double sense: a) the formal meaning expresses the requirement that the state and its organs observe the laws, strictly subordinate to the juridical rules regarding the composition of the state bodies, their attributions and their functions, and b) the material meaning - the requirement that the state bodies, exercising their functions, comply with the legal guarantees concerning the exercise of citizens' fundamental rights and freedoms.

In the field of ideology, the rule of law confers a logical system of ideas by which people represent their society, the state, in all its manifestations, and which confer the legitimacy of the state.

The term "rule of law" is not a simple logical concept but it expresses a fundamental constitutional necessity according to which: a) the state is indispensable for the law in order to create for it its norms and to ensure the finality and effectiveness of the legal norms; b) the law is indispensable for the state to express power by establishing a general and binding behaviour.

In essence, the rule of law expresses a condition of power, a movement to rationalize it, but also a new conception of law, its role and functions. Professor Tudor Draganu, in his paper (Draganu, 1993), proposes an interesting and comprehensive definition of this concept of constitutional law: "The rule of law is considered to be that state which was organized on the basis of the principle of separation of powers of the state, the application of which justice acquires real independence and pursues through its legislation the promotion of the rights and freedoms inherent in human nature, ensures the strict observance of its regulations by all its organs in all their activity."

The definition defines the main elements of the rule of law - the separation of powers as a reality of the state activity, in the application of which justice acquires real independence and pursues through its legislation the promotion of rights and freedoms inherent in human nature, ensures the strict observance of its regulations by all its organs, in their entire activity".

This definition renders the basic features of the rule of law – separation of powers, as reality of the state activity, the application of the principle of legality in the activity of all the state bodies, the observance and the guarantee of fundamental human rights. Also, from the same definition result the basic features of the rule of law, respectively: *a)* the freedoms of the human being require guarantees of security and justice through the primacy of law and in particular the Constitution; *b)* the moderation of the execution of the power requires the organization and adaptation of the functions of the erratic organisms and a hierarchical normative system.

II. Conditions of the rule of law

In the final document of the Copenhagen Summit in 1990 was stated that *the rule of law* does not simply mean a formal legality, and in the Charter of Paris from 1990 *the rule of law* is prefigured not only in terms of human rights but also of democracy, as the only governing system.

From the corroboration of the principles written in international documents, as well as in relation to the constitutional law doctrine, we consider as conditions or characters of the rule of law the following: 1. the accreditation of a new concept concerning the state, especially under the following aspects: the voluntary or consensual nature of the state, the delimitation of the state from the civil society, the responsibility of the state and the authorities that make it, and the moderation of constraint as a means of intervention of the state in society by appropriate and reasonable forms; 2. capitalization of the rations and mechanisms of the principle of separation of powers in the state; 3. the establishment and deepening of an authentic and real democracy; 4. institutionalization and guaranteeing of the rights and freedoms of man and citizen; 5. the establishment of a coherent and hierarchical legal order and of an area of law.

The systematic functionality and consistency of the rule of law must be ensured by a number of regulatory systems, namely: *a)* political control by Parliament as one of its essential functions through various institutional means *b)* administrative control that is carried out in the system public authorities, either on their own initiative or at the initiative of citizens; *c)* judicial review of the legality of administrative acts entrusted to either the courts of common law or the specialized courts; *d)* control of the constitutionality of laws; *e)* control of the observance of fundamental rights and freedoms through the bodies of the authority and the judiciary; *f)* the conciliation and control procedure, which is carried out through the institution of the "ombudsman" or the People's Advocate; g) free access to justice and organizing the court activity in several degrees of jurisdiction.

The consecration of the rule of law in the Constitution of Romania is achieved not only by art. 1 para. 3 of the 1st thesis, but also by many other constitutional provisions expressing the content of this principle of organization and exercise of power in a democratic society. In this respect we reiterate the provisions of art. 16 para. 2, which provide that no one is above the law and those of art. 15 para. 2 proclaiming the principle of the unretroactivity of the law, principles essential to the entire construction of the rule of law. The content of the rule of law is expressed in particular in the constitutional provisions regarding the separation and balance of state powers as well as those regarding the organization, functioning and attributions of the state institutions. The provisions refer to the fundamental rights, freedoms and duties of the citizens, to the mechanism of the separations of powers, pluralism, free access to justice, independence of courts, and the organization and functioning of parliamentary, administrative and judicial control. They can be considered as a constitutional normative expression of the content and requirements of the rule of law.

The rule of law is not a state whose essence is exhausted by constitutional regulations and other normative acts at a given moment. The rule of law is not exclusively an institution of constitutional law but must become a reality found at the level of the conduct of each subject of law, whether it is a state organ or a simple citizen. This means and implies a complex evolutionary process in which all the structures of society participate, and at the same time a process of perfection on the ideological and moral level in order to improve the activity of the organs of state and to effectively establish the principle of legality, to form a civic behaviour in the spirit of observance the law and the fundamental values of democratism.

The Constitution of Romania establishes, in its normative content, the main guarantees of the rule of law:

a) the constitutional regime, that is, the establishment in the Constitution of the fundamental principles of organization and activity of the three powers. Establishing the legal regime applied to the revision of the Constitution;

b) the direct or indirect popular legitimacy of state and public authorities;

c) ensuring the supremacy of the Constitution through political or judicial control, as well as ensuring the rule of law, over other normative acts;

d) the exercise of fundamental rights and freedoms may be restricted only temporarily, only in cases expressly determined in proportion to the circumstance justifying the restriction and without suppressing the very right or fundamental freedom;

e) independence and impartiality of justice.

Therefore, art. 21 para. 2 of the Constitution of Romania stipulates that no law may impede the free access of a person to justice for the protection of legitimate rights, freedoms and interests (Andreescu & Puran, Drept constitutional. Teoria generala a statului, 2018).

III. Application of the principle of proportionality in terms of state organization of power

From the complexity of the issue of the rule of law, we further on refer to the implicit application of the principle of proportionality in the constitutional provisions on the state organization of power.

This principle is explicitly expressed in the Constitution of Romania only in the provisions of art. 53, but it is implicitly found in other constitutional regulations as it has been emphasized in the specialized literature. The constitutional principle of proportionality is a synthesis of other principles of law and expresses the ideas of fairness, and the correctness of the state's dispositions to the intended purpose. We consider it a criterion in relation to which the powers of the state are organized in a state of law because by its application a dynamic and functional balance is realized in the institutional diversity of the state system. We also underline the fact that this principle confers legitimacy and not only the legality of state decisions and is a criterion already used in case-law which establishes the demarcation between the exercise of power within the limits of the Constitution and laws and on the other hand the excess of power in the activity of the organs of the state in situations where state decisions have the appearance of legality but are also not legitimate because they are not appropriate to the intended purpose defined by constitutional or secondary legislation. We believe that the constitutional principle of proportionality can be considered a requirement of the rule of law.

Further on, briefly analyze the application of the principle of proportionality to the state organization of power in our country, as it results explicitly or implicitly from the constitutional provisions applicable.

The principle of the separation of powers in the state, considered to be a foundation of democracy, is at the same time a reflection on the moderation and rationalization of state power. "Balancing these powers by judiciously distributing the powers and equipping each of them with effective means of control over the others, thus defeating the inherent tendency of the human power to grasp the whole power and to abuse it is the condition of social harmony and the guarantee of human freedom". In its classical form, as it is known by the decisive contribution of Montesquieu, the principle of separation of powers in the state affirms that in any society there are three distinct powers: legislative, executive and judicial power. These three powers must be exercised by separate organisms independent of each other. The purpose of this division is that power should not focus on a single state organ, which would naturally tend to abuse the prerogatives entrusted to it. "In order that power not be abused, it is necessary that by the arrangement of things power stops power" - says Montesquieu. At the same time, the division of state power is necessary to respect individual rights and freedoms, so that one power opposes the other and creates itself instead of a single force, a balance of force.

In order to achieve these goals, the organs of the state must be independent of one another in the sense that no one can exercise the function entrusted to the other. Consequently, it is not possible for an organ of the state to be subordinated to another, if it exercises a separate power.

The doctrine states that: "The theory of separation of powers is in fact an ideological justification of a very concrete political purpose: weakening the power of the governors as a whole, limiting one another. It is considered that the separation of powers has two well-defined aspects: a) separation of parliament from the government; b) separation of jurisdictions against the governors, which allows them to be controlled by independent judges (Muraru & Tanasescu, 2003). The theory and principle of the separation of powers in its classical form were criticized in doctrine. "Montesquieu's error", wrote Carré de Malberg, "is certainly to have thought it possible to regulate the game of the public powers by their mechanical separation and, in a certain way, mathematical, as if the problems of the state organization were susceptible to be solved by procedures of such rigor and precision" (Malberg, 1992).

In the doctrine, other inaccuracies and limitations were noted as well, among which we recall: from the terminology used, it is not clear whether a "state body" or a "function" is to be understood by power; power is unique and indivisible and belongs to a single titular - the people. That is why we cannot speak of the division of powers, but, possibly, the distribution of the functions involved in the exercise of power; the separation of powers, conceived in the form of opposition between them, is likely to block the functioning of state authorities. It is not possible for the sovereign exercise of the completeness of each of the static functions to be assigned to a separate authority or group of authorities. None of the state organs perform a function in integrity, and consequently the steady organs cannot be rigidly and functionally separated; in most constitutional systems, as a result of the existence of political parties, the real problem is not the separation of powers, but the relationship between the majority and the minority or, in other words, between the governors and the opposition. There is no antagonistic relationship between parliament and government. A government that has a parliamentary majority will work in close association with the parliament, which is considered a modern state of their efficiency; the legislative function is not equal to the executive function. Execution of the law is by definition subject to legalization. If the two functions are in hierarchical relations, then the organs that perform those functions are in the same ratios.

It should also be underlined that, in doctrine, there is more and more talk of a decline of legislative power in favour of the executive; the separation of powers does not solve the issue of guaranteeing fundamental human rights. Constitutional justice is the main guarantor of respect for fundamental rights, but it does not find its place in the classic scheme of separation of powers in the state, as (Eisenmann, 1984), (Rousseau, 1990), (Muraru & Tanasescu, Drept constitutional si institutii politice, 2003) develop in their papers. In the case of the theory of separation of powers in state it was said that "the myth" far exceeds the reality. In fact, it is the dogmatic confidence to impose on a concrete reality a pre-established theoretical and abstract framework (Duhamel & Meny, 1992). The criticisms formulated and the modernization tendencies cannot result in the abandonment of this principle. "The great force of the theory of separation of powers in the state - said Professor Ioan Muraru - lies in its fantastic social, political and moral resonance (Muraru & Tanasescu, Drept constitutional si institutii politice, 2003). It should not be forgotten that the principle is enshrined, explicitly or implicitly, in the constitutions of the democratic states. From the perspective of our research theme, it is important to consider the autonomy of the state authorities and the relations between them in order to prevent separatism and rigidity.

The myth of absolute separation of powers is in fact, Carré de Malberg says, irreconcilable, "with the principle of unity of the state and its powers" (Malberg, Contribution á la théorie géneral de l'Etat, 1992). The will of the state, he continues, being necessarily a single one, must be maintained between the authorities that held a certain cohesion, without which the state would risk being harassed, divided and destroyed by the opposite pressures to which it would be subjected. It is thus impossible to conceive that the powers in the state are equal. "That is why, in any state, even in those whose Constitution is said to be based on Montesquieu's theory and pursues a certain equalization of powers, invariably will find a supreme organ that will dominate all the others and thus achieve the unity of the state" (Malberg, 1922). As the author states, it is not so much about separation, but rather about the "gradation of powers".

There would then be a single power that would first manifest through acts of initial will - the legislative power - and would be exercised at a lower level through law enforcement acts - the executive power.

It follows that the powers of the state are unequal, but this cannot have the significance of subordination, nor can allow for excess power. "State means also force, hence the risk of escaping from the control of the holder, of considering himself being the owner of the power" (Muraru & Tanasescu, Drept constitutional si institutii politice, 2003). At the same time, a coherent functioning of the organs of the state is not possible, nor can it be conceived, unless there are some relations between them.

It was said that, given the existence of political parties and their access to power, "the real problem is not that of the relations between the institutionalized powers but of the relations between the majority and the minority, between the government and the opposition, especially when the government comes from a parliamentary majority, comfortable and homogeneous and leaning on it" (Deleanu, 1996).

In a wider sense, it must be stressed that democracy generates a majority that leads, imposing its will and values to minorities, but they also have the opportunity to express themselves and their rights have to be respected. Achieving the democratic and functional balance between the majority and the minorities is the solution to avoid what the doctrine is called the "tyranny of the majority". Undivided power - says (Sartori, 1999)- is always an excessive and dangerous power. Thus, the tyranny of the majority, relevant from a constitutional point of view, is defined according to the rights of the minority, especially if the right to opposition is complied with or not. The main problem in this context is that the minority or the minorities have the right to oppose, have the right to opposition.

The relationship between the majority and the minority involves the analysis of the very complex interaction between those that govern and the ones that are governed. Interaction consists of a multilevel process in which majorities and minorities are materialized in different ways and at different levels. The rule that allows the functioning of such a complex system of democracy is the application of the principle of majority in decision-making. However, Hamilton observed very well: "Give all the power to many, and they will oppress the few. Give all the power of the few, and they will oppress the many" (Elliot, 1941).Therefore, the problem is to avoid giving all or most of the power to all, by distributing it, alternately and/or at the same time to the majority and minority.

Therefore, in order to avoid dogmatism, in order to respond to these problems of social, political and state realities, it is necessary to reconsider the theory of the separation of powers in the state from the point of view of the principle of proportionality. The fundamental idea has already been stated: the moderation of power and the balance in the exercise of power that actually reflects, to a certain extent, the balance of social forces (Grewe & Fabri, 1995). When discussing the content and meanings of the separation of powers, it is less about separation, but especially about the balance of powers (Deleanu, 1996). Balancing the powers in the state by judiciously distributing the powers and equipping each with effective means of control over the others, thus stabilizing the tendency to capture the whole power and to abuse it, is essentially the application of the principle of proportionality to the organization of state power. This is the condition of social harmony and the guarantee of human freedom [even though, until now, an explicit reference to the principle of proportionality has not been made in the specialized literature, it results from the context of supporting some authors: "So, weight and counterweights in the power tiles so that none of them dominates the others. It would not be so much a separation of powers, but especially about their relative autonomy and their mutual dependence: the balance of powers"(Deleanu, 1996).

Rethinking the separation of powers in terms of the constitutional principle of proportionality can be answered, in our opinion, to all the problems listed above.

The principle of the separation of powers in the state was not explicitly enshrined in the Constitution of Romania before its revision in 2003, but from the analysis of the constitutional texts, the doctrine ascertained that the balance of state powers as a principle was found in the content of the norms of the Constitution Through the Review Law, the Romanian derived constituent expressly enshrined this principle, referring not only to the separation of powers but also to the balance between them: "The State is organized according to the principle of separation and balance of powers - legislative, executive and judicial - within constitutional democracy" [Art. 1 para. 4].

The necessary balance between state authorities is the expression of the principle of proportionality applied in the matter of organizing the institutional system of power in Romania. State authorities are neither equal nor independent in the absolute sense. The balance that a proportionality relationship implies is based on differences but also on interrelations that allow the functioning of the institutional system so as to avoid excessive concentration of power or exercise of the same, as well as the excess of power, especially by violating human rights and fundamental freedoms. The finality of the proportionality ratio between public authorities is "the establishment of balanced correlations between the governors and the ones that are governed, complying with the public freedoms" (Muraru & Constantinescu, 1996).

We will refer to some of the constitutional regulations concerning the Romanian state institutional system, which reflects the principle of proportionality:

A. Elements of difference between state authorities, meaning the autonomy of each category of organs and their position within the system:

Public authorities are governed distinctly by the rules contained in Title III of the Constitution. These are the "three classic powers" in the traditional order: legislative, executive and judicial power.

The Constitution confers a certain degree of prerogative to Parliament in relation to the other state authorities: "Parliament is the supreme representative body of the Romanian people and the sole legislator authority of the country" (art. 61 para. 1);

Besides the classic scheme of the separation of powers in the state, the Constitutional Court achieved constitutional power (art. 142 and subsequent of the Fundamental Law), which is the guarantor of the supremacy of the Constitution, the only constitutional jurisdictional authority of Romania, independent of the any other public authority [art. 1 para. (3) of the Law no. 47/1992 on the organization and functioning of the Constitutional Court, republished]. The People's Advocate is also independent of any other public authority. He is appointed by the Parliament in the joint session of the Chambers [art. 65 para. (2) letter i)]. Ex officio or at the request of persons injured in their rights or freedoms, the People's Advocate may refer the matter to the public authorities in order to take measures to eliminate acts or facts that affect subjective rights or legitimate protected legal interests (art. 58 and subsequent). It has the power to notify the Constitutional Court, in the situations provided by art. 146 letters a) and d);

The bicameral structure of Parliament is an expression of the balance involved in the principle of proportionality. Thus, Chambers are equal but are functionally differentiated in the exercise of their legislative powers. The distinction between the Chamber referred first (of reflection) and the Decision Chamber, made by art. 75, expresses the "quasi-perfect" bicameralism, which is a proportionality ratio. We agree with the opinion expressed in the literature, according to which "the system of parliamentary bicameralism in Romania must be preserved, but it must be transformed into a differentiated bicameralism. Thus, to the law of democratization and efficiency can be ensured, and to the legislative organ a representativeness and responsibility increment" (Muraru & Muraru, 2005).

The difference between the length of the term of office of some state authorities contributes to a proportionate ratio between the powers of the state, is the expression of the balance and not of the formal equality, in order to ensure the good functioning of the Romanian institutional system. Thus, the duration of Parliament's mandate is 4 years (art. 63), of the President of Romania is 5 years (art. 83), of the members of the Superior Council of Magistracy is 6 years (art. 133), the mandate of the judges at the Constitutional Court is 9 years, and the president of this institution is elected for a period of 3 years (art. 142), the judges of the courts appointed by the President of Romania have practically an indefinite mandate in time because they are irremovable under the law (art. 125). The People's Advocate mandate is 5 years (art. 58).

B. The specialty literature highlighted the particularities of the relations between the state authorities, which in our opinion materialize the principle of proportionality, because the relational balance also implies the difference. In this respect, it was stated that: "The election of the President of Romania by the people, an essential feature of the presidential republics, combines in our country with the pre-eminence of the Parliament, as a result, mainly, of the parliamentary origin of the government, thus defining a semi-presidential political regime" (Constantinescu, 1993).

The set of interrelations between the different categories of organs of the state is the form of achieving the balance and mutual control of the powers. These relations, which form the "identity card of the state power system" (Deleanu, 1996), presuppose the autonomy of the state authorities and the differences between them. The complex structure of the state power system is a concretisation of the principle of proportionality, in other words, it strikes a balance between the powers of the state, which are based on autonomy, differentiation and interrelations. The more the constitutional regulations in the field manage to materialize the requirements of the principle of proportionality, the more exists the guarantee of avoiding some forms of concentration of the state powers, the tyranny of the majority or minorities and obviously the excess of power.

The concern of the Romanian constituent legislator to achieve a functional balance between the powers of the state, between these and society, is obvious, if we refer to the provisions of art. 80, according to which: "The President exercises the function of mediation between the powers of the state as well as between state and society", but also to the provisions of art. 146 letter e) according to which our constitutional court has the competence to resolve constitutional legal conflicts between public authorities. We also need to remember the role of mediator and balance factor for the powers of the state, but also for the society that justice has. In this respect, the provisions of art. 124 of the Constitution consecrate the general "uniqueness, impartiality and equality" of justice, which represents important guarantees for the achievement of the functions of the judicial power in society.

Of course, the system of state power is an open, dynamic one, implying not only the multiplication of its constituent elements or their reorganization, but also of the functions that correspond them and of the interrelationships between the elements of the system. Within the internal system, the social-political system, and externally the system of the international community of states represent the "environment" with which the state authorities interact. Therefore, the balance, as a particular aspect of the principle of proportionality, between the powers of the state must be understood in its dynamics, including in the continuous process of interpreting and applying the constitutional provisions in the matter.

Proportionality, as a principle of constitutional law, has a concrete dimension. The existence of a proportionate, balanced relationship between the state authorities, between them and society, is verified in practice through the functioning of the political and social system, the avoidance of crises, or, when they occur, through the capacity of the state authorities to manage these, complying in any situation with the principles of the rule of law. Essential for the fulfilment of the requirements of separation and balance between the powers of the state, but also for stability, in its social and political system dynamics, from the perspective of pluralism in society, there is the existence of a proportionate balance between the majority and the minorities between the government and the opposition.

IV. Aspects of the constitutional court case-law on garanteeing and complying with the requirements of the rule of law

At the end of this analysis we shall refer to some decisions of the Constitutional Court which we consider relevant to the rule of law.

The Constitutional Court identifies the fundamental feature of the rule of law, namely the supremacy of the Constitution and the obligation to observe the law[433].

At the same time, it has been stated in the case-law of the constitutional court that the rule of law, ensuring the supremacy of the Constitution, also realizes "the correlation of all laws and all normative acts with it"[434].

The requirements of the rule of law concern the major purposes of state activity, namely the supremacy of law, which implies the subordination of the state to the law. In this respect, the law provides the means by which the political options or decisions can be censored and performs the abolition of any abusive and discretionary tendencies of the state structures. Further on, the rule of law ensures the supremacy of the Constitution, the existence of the regime of separation of the public powers and establishes guarantees, including of a judicial nature, that ensure the observance of citizens' rights and freedoms, primarily by limiting the state authority, which represent the framing of the public authorities' activities within the limits of the law.

The case-law of the Constitutional Court expresses the main requirements of the rule of law in relation to the goals of the state activity. Thus, by case-law is achieved a very eloquent synthesis of the doctrine on the notion and features of the rule of law. It is significant in this respect the Decision no. 17 of January 21st 2015[435], by which the Constitutional Court gives an explanation concerning the state of law, enshrined in art. 1 para. (3) thesis I of the Constitution: "The requirements of the rule of law concern the major purposes of its activity, prefigured in what is commonly called the reign of law, a phrase

---

[433] Decision no. 232 of July 5th 2001, published in the Official Gazette no. 727 of November 15th 2001; Decision no. 53 of January 25th 2011, published in in the Official Gazette no. 90 of February 3rd 2011.

[434] Decision no. 22 of January 27th 2004, published in the Official Gazette no. 233 of March 17th 2004.

[435] Decision no. 17 of January 21st 2015, published in the Official Gazette no. 79 of January 30th 2015.

involving the subordination of the state to the law, the guarantee of the means to allow the law to censor political choices and, in this context, to weigh the potential abusive, discretionary tendencies of the static structures. The rule of law ensures the supremacy of the Constitution, the correlation of laws and all normative acts with it, the existence of the regime of separation of the public powers that must act within the limits of the law, namely within the limits of a law expressing the general will. The rule of law enshrines a series of safeguards, including jurisdictional, to ensure that citizens' rights and freedoms are complied with by the state's self-restraint, namely the involvement of public authorities in the coordinates of law".[436]

The principle of stability and security of legal relations is not explicitly enshrined in the Constitution of Romania, but, like other constitutional principles, it is involved in the constitutional normative provisions, respectively art. 1 para. (3), which enshrines the rule of law. In this way, our constitutional court accepts the deduction, by way of interpretation, of the principles of law implied by the express rules of the fundamental Law. In this respect, by means of the Decision no. 404 of April 10th 2008[437], the Constitutional Court stated that: "The principle of stability and security of legal relations, although not explicitly enshrined in the Romanian Constitution, is deduced both from the provisions of art. 1 para. (3), according to which Romania is a state of law, democratic and social, and from the preamble to the Convention for the Protection of Human Rights and Fundamental Freedoms, as interpreted by the European Court of Human Rights in its case-law[438]. Furthermore, our constitutional court has considered that the principle of security of civil legal relationships is a fundamental dimension of the rule of law[439]

Constitutional Court decides constantly for clarity and predictability of law, which are requirements of the rule of law. Thus, "the existence of contradictory legislative solutions and the annulment of legal provisions through other

---

[436] Decision no. 70 of April 18th 2000, published in the Official Gazette no. 334 of July 19th 2000.

[437] Decision no. 404 of April 10th 2008, published in the Official Gazette no. 347 of May 6th 2008.

[438] Decision no. 685 of November 25th 2014, published in the Official Gazette no. 68 of January 27th 2015.

[439] Decision no. 570 of May 29th 2012, published in the Official Gazette no. 404 of June 18th 2012; Decision no. 615
of June 12th 2012, published in the Official Gazette no. 454 of July 6th 2012.

provisions contained in the same normative act lead to the violation of the principle of security of legal relations, due to the lack of clarity and predictability of the norm, principles which constitute a fundamental dimension of the rule of law, as it is expressly enshrined in the provisions of art. 1 para. (3) of the fundamental Law [440]

Concerning the rule of law, the Constitutional Court has shown that justice and social democracy are supreme values. In this context, the militarized authorities, in this case the Romanian Gendarmerie, exercise, under the law, specific powers regarding the defense of public order and tranquillity, of citizens' fundamental rights and freedoms, of public and private property, of prevention and detection of crimes, and other violations of applicable laws, and the protection of state institutions and the fight against acts of terrorism. Consequently, the Constitutional Court ruled: "By the possibility of militarized authorities to find contraventions committed by civilians, art. 1 para. (3) of the Constitution is not affected in any way, regarding the Romanian state, as a rule of law, democratic and social"[441]

Human dignity, together with the freedoms and rights of citizens, the free development of human personality, justice and political pluralism, are supreme values of the rule of law (art. 1 para. (3)). In the light of these constitutional regulations, it has been stated in the Constitutional Court's case-law that the state is forbidden to adopt legislative solutions that can be interpreted as being disrespectful of religious or philosophical beliefs of parents, which is why organizing school activity must achieve a fair balance between the process of education and teaching religion, and on the other hand with respect for the rights of parents, to ensure education in accordance with their own religious beliefs. Activities and behaviours specific to a certain attitude of belief or philosophical, religious or non-religious beliefs must not be subject to sanctions that the state requires for such behaviour, regardless of the person's motivation for faith. "As part of the constitutional system of values, freedom of religious conscience is attributed to the imperative of tolerance, especially to human dignity, guaranteed by art. 1 para. (3) of the fundamental Law, which

---

[440] Decision no. 26 of January 18th 2012, published in the Official Gazette no. 116 of February 15th 2012.

[441] Decision no. 1330 of December 4th 2008, published in the Official Gazette no. 873 of December 23rd 2008.

dominates the entire value system as a supreme value"[442]

It is also interesting to note that our constitutional court considers human dignity as the supreme value of the entire system of values constitutionally consecrated, value that is found in the content of all human rights and fundamental freedoms. At the same time, it is an important aspect that requires the state authorities in their entire activity to first consider respecting the human dignity.

It should be noted that in its case-law the Constitutional Court also identifies the content components of human dignity, as a moral value but at the same time constitutional, specific to the rule of law: "Human dignity, in constitutional terms, presupposes two inherent dimensions, namely the relations between people, which refers to the right and obligation of the people to be respected and, in a correlative way, to respect the fundamental rights and freedoms of their peers, as well as the relation of man to the environment, including the animal world".[443]

---

[442] Decision no. 669 of November 12th 2014, published in the Official Gazette no. 59 of January 23rd 2015.

[443] Decision no. 1 of January 11th 2012, published in the Official Gazette no. 53 of January 23rd 2012; Decision no. 80 of February 16th 2014, published in Official Gazette no. 246 of February 7th 2014.

V. Conclusions

Antonie Iorgovan said that an essential problem of the rule of law is to answer the question: "where discretionary power ends and where the abuse of law begins, where the legal behaviour of the administration ends, materialized in its right of appreciation and where the violation of a subjective right or legitimate interest of the citizen begins?" Therefore, the application and observance of the principle of legality in the activity of state authorities is a complex issue because the exercise of state functions presupposes the discretionary power with which the organs of the state are invested, or in other words the authorities' "right of appreciation" regarding the moment of adoption and the content of the measures imposed. What is important to emphasize is that discretionary power cannot be opposed to the principle of legality, as a dimension of the rule of law.

The excess of power can be manifested in these circumstances by at least three aspects: a) the appraisal of a factual situation as an exceptional case, although it does not have this significance (lack of objective and reasonable motivation); b) the measures ordered by the competent authorities of the State, by virtue of discretion, to go beyond what is necessary to protect the publicly threatened public interest; c) if these measures unduly and unjustifiably restrict the exercise of fundamental rights and freedoms constitutionally recognized.

The key issue for the practitioner and the theorist is to identify criteria by which to establish the limits of the discretionary power of the state authorities and to differentiate it from the excess of power that must be sanctioned. Of course, there is also the question of using these criteria in court practice or constitutional litigation.

Concerning these aspects, the opinion of the specialized literature was that the purpose of the law will be the legal limit of the right of appreciation (of opportunity). For discretionary power does not mean a freedom beyond the law, but one permitted by law. Of course, "the purpose of the law" is a condition of legality or, as the case may be, the constitutionality of the legal acts of the organs of the state, and can therefore be considered a criterion for delimiting discretionary power from excess of power.

As can be seen from the case law of some international and domestic courts in relation to our research theme, the purpose of the law cannot be the only criterion to delimit discretionary power (synonymous with the margin of appreciation, term used by the ECHR) of the State may be an excess of power not only in the case where the measures adopted do not pursue a legitimate aim but also in the case that the measures ordered are not appropriate to the purpose of the law and are not necessary in relation to the factual situation and the legitimate aim pursued.

The adequacy of the measures ordered by the state authorities to the legitimate aims pursued is a particular aspect of the principle of proportionality. Significant is the opinion expressed by Antonie Iorgovan, who considers that the limits of discretionary power are set by: "positive written rules, general principles of law, principle of equality, principle of nonretroactivity of administrative acts, right to defense and principle of contradictory, principle of proportionality" Therefore, the principle of proportionality is an essential criterion that allows the discretionary power to delimit excess of power in the work of state authorities. And by this is an essential principle of the rule of law.

Bibliogaphy

Andreescu M., Puran A. (2018) Constitutional Law General Theory of the State, 3rd Edition, Bucharest, Ed. Ch Beck;

Carré de Malberg (1922) Contribution á la théorie général de l'Etat, vol. II, Paris, Tenin;

Constantinescu M. (1993) The balance of powers in the constitutional regime in Romania, Law no. 3/1993;

Deleanu I. (1996) Constitutional law and political institutions, vol. I, Bucharest, Ed. New Europe;

Draganu T. (1993) Introduction to the theory and practice of the rule of law, Cluj-Napoca, Dacia;

Duhamel O., Meny I. (1992) Dictionnaire constitutionnel, Paris, PUF;

Eisenmann Ch. (1984) L'espirit des lois et la separation des pouvoirs, Cahiers de philosophie politique, Ed. Ousia;

Elliot J. (1941) Debates on the Adoption of the Federal Constitution, Philadelphia, Lippincott;

Grewe C., Fabri H. (1995) Droit constitutionnels europeans, Paris, PUF;

Malberg C. (1992) Contribution a la theorie general de l'Etat, Paris, Tenin;

Muraru I., Constantinescu M. (1996) The role of the Constitutional Court in ensuring the balance of powers in the state, Law 9/1996;

Muraru I., Muraru A. (2005) Short plea for a differentiated parliamentary bicameralism, Journal of Public Law;

Muraru I., Tănăsescu E.S. (2003) Constitutional law and political institutions, vol. II, Bucharest, Ed. All Beck;

Rousseau D. (1990) Droit du contentieux constitutionnel, Paris;

Sartori G. (1999) Theory of democracy reinterpreted, Bucharest, Ed. Polyrom.

19. FROM LEGAL LIBERTIES TO ONTOLOGICAL FREEDOM

Abstract:

Any attempt in the sphere of humanities to characterize and explain man in his individuality, but also in the social existential context, relates to the issue of freedom. Freedom is essentially related to the human being, but also to the existential phenomenality of man. Man is the only created being whose fundamental ontological dimensions are freedom and spirit.

In this study we briefly look onto the concept of freedom not only as a moral value or category, but also as an ontological dimension of man. In this way we make the distinction between ontological freedom and the legal freedoms established or recognized by the legal norms. The legal liberties are a phenomenal expression of human existence whose legitimacy and motivation is conferred by the ontological dimension of human freedom. In this context, the main features of the legal freedoms and the practical importance of the ontological meaning are to be found in the freedoms consecrated in the law.

Key words:

Freedom as moral value / Characteristics of ontological freedom / The features of the legal freedoms / The ontological basis of legal freedoms

I. Introduction

Any attempt in the sphere of humanities to characterize and explain man in his individuality or in social relations also relates to the issue of freedom. It is natural to do so, because freedom is essentially related to the human being, but also to the existential phenomenality of man. The existence of man makes no sense without considering the freedom by which man becomes from the individual person also a creator of meanings and senses. The importance of this existential reality also lies in the fact that man is the only being created whose fundamental ontological dimension is freedom. By this he is not only a natural being, but also a spiritual being. Freedom, as ontological determination, makes the difference between an individual and a person. Only man, as a person, is a free being, not the individual. Constantin Noica said in this sense that "where freedom is not there is a number", because the number is the conceptual expression of the abstract and undetermined generality that characterizes any human existential structure based solely on the existential phenomenality of the "ego", and not on the "self" down deepest of human being.

Father Dumitru Stăniloaie said that man "is secrecy and light, it is a mystery of light." We might try to say that man is also a mystery of freedom, because by this own feature of him, to be free, he differentiates and opposes to the natural and temporary determinism, to the necessity of the repeating laws of nature, transfigures the existence from "what is" to what "must be" adding value and meanings to it. Through freedom as an existential given one can conceive and understand all the majesty and splendor of human existence, both in relation to himself, in relation to society, in relation to God, and to the whole universe.

II. On Liberty and Legal Freedoms

Although philosophy, legal sciences, anthropology, morals, and other disciplines abound in conceptualizations and theories and descriptions of human freedom, one cannot say that a full understanding of the meanings and senses of liberty has been reached, especially if regarded not only from the perspective of rationality, but as an existential given, as an ontological determination of man. That is why freedom is a mystery of man, but which does not mean skepticism or the inability of the reasoning to understand, but rather the fact that the capacity and vocation to deepen more and more in the deepest senses of ontological freedom. Although it is an existential given of the human being, freedom is alive, is not frozen into abstract structures it rather relates to the becoming of man and society.

There is an indissoluble connection between freedom and love because, as Orthodox theology shows, the true freedom is determined by the love communion between man and God and through God, between man and his fellowmen, and the whole universe. Undoubtedly, philosophy first of all, but also other sciences, make an important contribution to the conceptual understanding of human freedom, an understanding which remains, in the sphere of rationality of abstract concepts, either moral or utilitarian, and is engaging less existentially the human being. Freedom is thought by philosophy as a dimension of ethics, which is obviously correct because undeniably freedom is both principle and value of human ethics.

Kant, of course, remains one of the main thinkers who made an essential contribution to the phenomenology of human freedom in its moral dimension. The philosopher concluded the *Critique of Practical Reason* with a conclusion that synthesized his entire thinking and work: "Two things fill the soul with ever-new admiration and growing reverence, the more often and more persistently our reflection is concerned with them: the starry sky above me and the moral law inside me"[444].

This profound and beautiful diction is, in fact, a rational basis for the unification of the two areas of human investigation, but also for the existence of man, respectively of nature and morality. It is also a basis for the entire moral conception of the philosopher from Konigsberg. For a moral built on the basis of three postulates, two of which lie above the interpersonal relationships - *God and the immortal soul* - can be interpreted as uniting the high of the "starry sky" in which these ideas are projected with *the liberty* of the deepest

---

[444] Immanuel Kant, Critique of Practical Reason, Antet Publishing House Bucharest, 2013, p. 214

self of man, there is a need for a different conceptual structure other than the one used to investigate nature, which means, as Kant points out, that concepts of practical reasoning are needed, which have an existential constitutive value. In this construction, the concept of freedom proves to be indispensable, due to its association with the rational being, the core of the deepest self of man. The Romanian philosopher, Constantin Noica, said that in order to reach freedom "he must be unfaithful to own self on his way towards himself". The moral ascendant of the liberty makes that through it the other *two rational ideas*, namely the existence of God and the existence of the immortal soul, to leave one's state of transcendental ideas, finding oneself in the moral immanence through which these can be understood also within certain proven limits. That is why Kant calls freedom the "keystone" of the whole system of pure reasoning. We have emphasized that in Kantian thinking and even in philosophical rationalism also in Christian Protestant orientations, including in the pantheistic or deist ones, God is not conceived as a person, and soul and freedom are not as realities but as rational ideas.

The Kantian perspective on freedom, in our opinion, forms a distinct note in relation to all other metaphysical systems that addresses this issue of freedom because it is connected to the practical transforming reasoning of man, to the vocation and capacity of human being to manifest itself in natural existence , to create and confer meanings and values.

The realistic and materialist philosophical thinking and pragmatism conceive freedom in relationship to necessity. Freedom is understood not as an essential aspect, defining, totally different from the current and temporary determinism, but rather as a consequence of this determinism. In other words, in the realism and ontological materialism, freedom is only a form of the necessity, of determinism, which it can overcome, but cannot transform or transfigure spiritually. The consequence is the subordination of freedom and, implicitly, of man to natural determinism. It is the materialist conception of freedom as a "necessity understood". This understanding of freedom as determined by the value, spiritual or juridical order is also found under more refined forms of the theological or philosophical thinking and indisputably is proper to legal thinking. The "order," no matter of what kind, expresses necessity, limitation and even coercion, all of which are contrary through meanings, to human freedom as existential given.

The relationship between freedom and necessity, between freedom and law, moral or legal is a recessive one. Necessity as order, no matter of its nature and configuration, is the dominant term and freedom is the recessive one. Of course, freedom does not result out of necessity, be it the spiritual order, it is not determined by such a necessity as in the materialist conception. As existence freedom is different from necessity, but in relation to the order whose expression is the necessary, freedom is always recessive and unfulfilled In relation to the necessity of an existential order, as a recessive term, freedom is never full, it is not fulfilled, but it is always in precariousness.

In the previous studies dedicated to freedom we have talked about such precariousness specific to the existential order in which man is. We refer to different forms and disappointments of human freedom, but which do not have a pejorative meaning, they are the expression of freedom and not of the natural determinism. Here are some of these forms: natural freedom, moral, cultural freedom, social and legal freedoms.

In this context, the question is whether there are fulfillments of liberty, even in an absolute sense without a recessive relationship with the order of any nature, without limit and with an infinite opening towards existential absolute. Our answer is affirmative: *it is the freedom of spirit human, who, by paraphrasing Father Arsenie Boca, is in this world and always above it. It is the true ontological freedom, which, as we shall see below, has its basis not in the necessity of an outer order but in love communion between God and man, the inexhaustible fountain of freedom and love is God.*

The approach of the issue of freedom that we encounter in the legal sciences, has multiple conceptual particularities and, we would say, often more important than the philosophical concepts on liberty, since the legal is a status of human existence, a characteristic of the social status, distinct from the natural, material status. It is a contemporary status of human existence, namely the "juridical status", which comprises an existential order based on two realities: *the juridical norm and freedom*.

Law cannot be conceived beyond the idea of freedom. The normative system, the most important aspect of law, has its meanings and legitimacy in human existence, the latter having freedom as existential given.

But what kind of freedom can be said in the legal normativism and in the categories and concepts of the law? Inevitably, it is about the freedom of the legal norm, a liberty built, not an existential given. We must emphasize that the legal norm implies the constraint, as any other existential order applied to human phenomenology. Appears then an important paradox that some authors in the field of Christian metaphysics noticed, namely the coexistence of the legal constraints and the freedom of man, on the other way, both of which are essential for the order specific to the legal status in which the contemporary man is.

Another aspect is interesting, namely that the legal norm does not show what freedom is, it does not define it, it does not show its meanings, but only the situations in which freedom is restricted. Moreover, it is good to notice that, unlike metaphysics and ethics, the legal norm does not express or conceptualize freedom as such, but only as *freedoms or rights*, which is the phenomenal aspects of human manifestations in the social environment, by its nature a relational environment. It is obvious that the legal normative system cannot define freedom as such, because there is existential incompatibility between normative constraint and on the other hand, liberty as an ontological given. This is also reflected in the doctrine, in the legal concept on liberty. A closer analysis of the legal theory on liberty, even of the just-naturalist conceptions, one notes the absence of the definition of freedom. The legal doctrine postulates the freedom of man and highlights the content of the legal freedoms, their limits, but it does not define freedom as an ontological given. The law, including the Constitution, or, in a wider sphere, the international treaties and conventions do not explain, characterize and define freedom, but only the *freedoms of man* which they consecrate.

It can be said that the legal normative system, which has as a component the necessity as a normative order and on the other hand the human liberties consecrated by this order, has the following characteristics:

1. There is no consecrated existential freedom, impossible to analyze by the legal norm, but only the freedoms built by the juridical norm, as an expression of the legislator's will at a determined historical moment. In this context, it is interesting to note, however, that the first Constitution of the world, namely that of the United States of America, in its original form, does not consecrate and, therefore, does not normatively express any of the legal freedoms. The doctrinaires said at that time that the Basic Law cannot regulate freedoms because it expresses the liberty itself. Subsequently, through the amendments adopted, this situation has also changed with respect to the United States' Basic Law. In the sphere of liberties and constitutional rights, of course, the individual freedom is the keystone. If we study the Constitution of Romania, we notice the same things that I mentioned above, namely the impossibility of the normative definition or the rational explanation of individual freedom. Article 23 paragraph (1) of the Constitution of Romania consecrates the individual freedom, individual safety and these ones' inviolability: "The individual freedom and individual safety are inviolable." Inviolability remains, however, the sphere of the legal phenomenological relativism, because the very legal norm constrains the freedom and, moreover, the exercise of individual freedom can be restricted by the state means;

2. The legal freedoms, which, we say, have their source in the ontological freedom of man, are characterized by negative expressions, that is, the general obligation of state not to restrain them and, more rarely, the positive obligations of state to promote them. Sometimes there are also concrete situations where freedom is restricted. In other words, the legitimate situations in which state, in accordance with the law, may restrict the exercise of certain rights or freedoms.

3. The legal freedoms are always limited and conditional. The whole construction of the system of legal freedoms is based on the concept of the "coexistence of liberties" which is natural to the phenomenology of the legal order and at the same time to social one.

4. The normatively consecrated legal liberties are the expression of the human dignity within state-organized society. Their owner, the man, or the "individual," as they call it in the doctrine, can oppose these freedoms to the state power, may demand for their observance. The effectiveness of such a behavior specific to human dignity in the social environment is conditioned by two major aspects: a) the degree of awareness of the legal freedoms by their owner; b) the efficiency of the legal means for guaranteeing these freedoms.

5. There is also an important aspect that we find especially in the international legal instruments on human rights and freedoms, namely the expression used in their preamble, in the sense that the signatory states "recognize" the rights and freedoms they consecrate. This expression is very important because it evokes the idea of man's existential freedom, previous to the legal freedoms, and in relation to which the rights and freedoms specific to the legal status of man, find their legitimacy. "To recognize" is to admit that freedom is a given of the human being, and not just a legal construction;

6. The legal norm, especially in the conditions of the "juridical normative" will, which the contemporary society knows, is moving further away from the human values. It is an abstract, general and impersonal structure whose legitimacy is not a value one, but one of a formal recognition within the normative system contemplated. Abandoning the values results in the normative relativism based almost exclusively on the legislator's pure will at a decisive historical moment.

7. There is, however, an aspect that the philosophical concepts or other concepts of freedom cannot realize; freedom united with the legal norm can do it. It is about guaranteeing the legal freedoms, obviously not the ontological freedom. The legal norms, which consecrate liberties, together with justice, have this purpose to be able to guarantee the individual freedoms in relation to the interferences or abuses of all kinds that may exist in a state-organized

society. Only the normative system, and in particular the constitutional one, can guarantee to every man that the freedoms recognized or consecrated by the law can be defended, first of all before the power of the state, which at any time can become discretionary, but also against the interferences of other lawful subjects in the sphere of their own freedom. The guarantee of the individual freedoms by the legal norm is a requirement of the lawful state. The reality of the guarantees and the efficiency of the legal means, for the defense of the subjective rights and liberties, is a matter that depends on the particularities of each state, the system of government, the concrete forms of achievement of the state power, the relationships between state and citizens and, last but not least, the efficiency of the act of justice.

Regarding the complex relationship between the legal normative system and society, on the other hand, can be noticed that in the contemporaneity the legal system tends to have its own functional autonomy, in addition to the subjective or objective determinations which society transmits. The autonomy of the juridical tries to transform itself from a secondary, phenomenological and ideological structure into one with its own reality, with the power to impose its order to the social and natural order. In this context, the normatively consecrated legal liberties seek to determine the existential freedom of man by explaining, arranging and conditioning it. It is a situation contrary to natural reality; the phenomenology of the juridical must be conditional, determined by the existence of man, as a person, and by the particularities of social existence and not the other way round. It is an expression of dictatorship through law even in democratic societies, because the legitimacy of the legal norm lies, in such a situation contrary to nature, only in the will and interests of the governors, which paradoxically expresses on behalf of the people.

The reality described above, which is specific to contemporary society, has negative consequences in the sense that man, as a person, the only holder of ontological freedom, is no longer aware to his own freedom and expects that the normative order, state or even justice to confer the freedom that he needs. It can be said that in such a situation, the contemporary man not being aware to his own freedom, does not exist genuinely, but he lives throughout delegation, his existence being determined externally by the state and legal normativism, as mentioned above, abstractly, impersonally and most often deprived by the value meaning.

Of course, the just-naturalist views emphasize on freedom as ontological given of the human being and try to achieve the transition from freedom as an ontological essence to liberties as a social phenomenon, specific to the juridical status of man, normatively determined. We say that none of the forms of just-naturalist views fully succeeds in making such a transition, and the attempt to preserve the immutability and prestige of ontological freedoms within the legal freedoms, is most often unsuccessful.

In this ideological context, we keep in mind that the legal freedoms, as a structural element of the juridical status of man, are based on the metaphysical principle of the coexistence of liberties, postulated also by just-naturalist, but also by the 1789 French Declaration of Human Rights. It is a natural expression of the social existence of man, understood through the limits and not through the absolute of the existential freedom. In other words, in this phenomenal legal plan the freedom of man, as individual, approaches up to the freedom limit of his neighbor. It is about the distinction specific to law between "mine" and "yours", through which the legal liberty is not a spiritual opening but a closure within individual's limits. We believe that the legal norm, in this way, cannot address to the person, focused on the ontological idea of freedom, but only to man as individual, contained in the multiple structures of the social scaffolding. Obviously, such a reality is not by itself negative, because the dimension of the social phenomenality of man is a reality in which the human essence manifests itself.

III. Aspects of the ontological dimension of freedom

In earlier studies, we recalled the so-called precariousness of freedom, that is, forms of human freedom, unfulfilled, but which have existence and manifest themselves. We were talking about natural freedom, moral freedom, cultural freedom and obviously, not least, the legal and social freedom. It is a matter of knowing, which is the source and, at the same time, the legitimacy of these forms of freedom.

There are two explanations. First one, the normativist, according to which the normative order, as the case may be, of the natural determinism, moral or cultural values or legal norms, represent sources of the freedom in precariousness.

The second conception attempts to explain all forms of human freedom, not by the order created by the necessity of any kind of a natural and social determinism, but through profoundness and essence aspects that belong only to the being and the reality of man as a person. To this explanation, we mean to go through some modest references.

The ontological freedom is the freedom of the spirit, is the original freedom of man. In the world of the spirit, freedom is not a recessive term related to necessity, for the simple reason that the necessity in any form of the natural determinism specific to this world no longer manifest itself, it was overcome and transfigured by the boundless wealth of values of the spirit Freedom as fullness and spiritual fulfillment is no longer the freedom of an order, it has no limits imposed by the law, nor the existential conditions specific to this world. The only order compatible with the freedom of the spirit is the order of love and commandments of God. Fulfilling God's commandments is the condition of the freedom of spirit when man sets himself steadily, existentially into good and truth. The facts of the freedom of spirit, even if defined and outlined, are openings to the infinity of the spiritual truths. The freedom of spirit is not a freedom of the law it is a *freedom of grace*, working together with man and Holy Spirit. In a single word, the freedom of the spirit is the freedom of man as a person in this world, but not within the boundaries of this world, which spiritualizes itself and the whole universe. It should also be emphasized that the spirit is not always the reasoning, always abstract, limited and impersonal, but the authentic living through the understanding feeling in truth and in life. Lord Jesus said, "I am the way, the truth, and the life (John 14: 6). Being with God this is the freedom of spirit as a fulfillment, as fullness.

The truths of faith, found in all Orthodox theological thinking, affirm and claim that "man was created as a free being." It is about the ontological freedom, inherent to human being, and not the freedom of value of the rational categories or legal norms.

The meanings of ontological freedom or spirit are also illustrated in Orthodox theological thought. In his works, Saint Augustine distinguishes between the so-called minor freedom and, on the other hand, the major liberty of man. The ontological freedom has two different meanings: "By freedom is meant both the initial, irrational freedom that precedes good and evil, determining their choice, as the intelligent freedom, the final freedom in good and in truth." [445] It is the freedom of man to choose between good and evil, between truth and lie, between value and non-value, and ultimately, to choose between the world, subjected to natural and biological determinism, with all its precariousness, and on the other hand, the true and eternal life in God.

The second form of ontological freedom expresses a supreme spiritual principle: which is the freedom of truth and good, the natural order in which man should be. "And ye shall know the truth, and the truth shall make you free" (John 8:32). And the spiritual knowledge, God's knowledge, does not have the boundaries of thinking, as Professor Galeriu pointed out.

The Savior also said, "So if the Son will make you free, you will be free indeed" (John 8:36). This freedom is the one given by the incarnated Logos, as a gift of God, and at the same time, the man's vocation to know God, which is "the way, the truth, and the life." It is the absolute spiritual freedom of life in communion of love with God and, at the same time, of the life full with the uncreated energies of divinity. St. Paul the Apostle stated that "where the Spirit of the Lord is, there is freedom" (II Cor. 3:17).

The theological thinking has presented many aspects regarding the relationship between the two forms of ontological freedom, which is: the freedom of choice, involving the freedom of human conscience, and discernment of distinguishing good from evil and, on the other hand, the supreme, ontological freedom as the ultimate goal of human existence, that is to live effectively in good and in truth.

It has been said that accepting the freedom of choice, including choosing evil, and refusing the good given by God, is contrary to human nature and, as a result, cannot be accepted. It is the theological conception promoted in particular by the Catholic thinking and some forms of Protestantism.

[445] Nikolai Berdiaev, Spirit and Freedom. The Christian Philosophy Test, Paideia Publishing House, Bucharest, 2009, p.145

Criticizing this conception, Nikolai Berdiaiev notes that "human freedom is not only the freedom in God, but also the freedom related to God. Man must be free in regard to God, to the world and to his own nature"[446]. Therefore, the possibility of choosing between good and evil as a determination of the human being is essential to explain the communion between man as a person and God. This connection between man and God is not imposed it is not a result of an inexorable normative determinism, or of an order in which man participates as a simple element. If so, there would be no possibility of a connection and, moreover, of a communion of faith and love between man and God, and man would be a simple element subjected to an absolute determinism, be it spiritual and not a free person, endowed with conscience.

The same author I mentioned above emphasized: "If we only admit the liberty given through truth, given through God, and reject the freedom of choice and acceptance of truth, we are fatally engaged into tyranny and the freedom of the spirit is replaced by its determination"[447]. In fact, the idea of a single freedom of the order of good and truth had consequences in the plan of philosophical and theological thinking. It is, in fact, the expression of a freedom that arises from necessity, either of a divine order imposed on man or of a social order, also imposed, in the idea of good and full happiness. We have to notice that the Communist order wished to impose on man its own order, which it considered to be of the good, truth and absolute happiness. Therefore, any attempt to understand the spirit, through coercion and normative necessity, cannot be accepted as a way of ontological freedom. "Catholic and Byzantine theocracy, like atheist socialism, are naturally inclined to deny human freedom, to coerce and organize human life in good, that is, to identify freedom, either with the necessity of a divine organization or with the necessity of a social organization of life."[448] The consequence is that man becomes a simple element of natural determinism in which his consciousness is basically annihilated by the desire to consider freedom only in the sphere of good and truth and to exclude the possibility of evil as a free choice of man. It is true that the same author quoted above notices that "man deprived of the freedom of evil is but an automaton of good." [449]

In this context, we try to highlight some meanings of the ontological freedom by combining its two forms: the freedom to choose and, respectively,

---

[446] Quoted works, p.147

[447] Quoted works., p.146

[448] Quoted works., p. 160

[449] Quoted works., p. 150

the freedom to live in good and indeed, the fulfillment and the fullness of freedom.

Undoubtedly, freedom of choice cannot be denied as a dimension specific to the human being, through which man can complete oneself. The devoutly Varsanufie and John stated in this regard: "God has made man free, so that he may surrender towards good. But inclining towards good, by free will, he cannot do it without the help of God. For it is written, "It is not from he that pleases, neither from he that executes, but from the God who mercifully pleases" (Romans 9:16). If, then, man surrenders his heart onto good and calls God for help, God, having his good will in regard, gives strength to his work. Thus they both meet; freedom of man and power of God. For good comes from God, but it is fulfilled by His saints. And so God is glorified in them all, and He glorifies them "[450].

This is the synthetic, dogmatic and rational explanation of the unity of human ontological freedom, namely the freedom to choose and the freedom to live in good and truth. It is, in fact, the explanation of the theandric work between man and the Holy Spirit to reach the experience of freedom in truth. It also means the dynamic character of freedom, which is, in essence, the becoming of man in Christ, with Christ and towards Christ. This becoming involves a most important aspect of the freedom specific to the freedom of spirit and which we do not encounter in the existential precariousness of man. It is the *liberation* as the constituent moment of ontological freedom. It is the liberation from passions, the cutting of your own will, and the unconditional obedience to God's will, is the liberation proper to the man who has replaced his own thoughts with the thoughts of God. Liberation is synonymous with the acquisition of the virtue of humility as a foundation for the other virtues.

---

[450] Teodosie Paraschiv, Maximes and Philocalic Thoughts, Adenium Publishing House, 2013; Varsanufie and John, Spiritual Writings, p.281

IV. Conclusions

Father Dumitru Stăniloae said: "for man has a liberty that can be let enslaved, to which one can more or less give up. God gave man a freedom related to his own being, left to grow inside himself, as his own being, towards perfection or union with God. He also let man the dignity to preserve himself free, to strengthen himself in it. Man can say, "I am free when I want to be free." But he can be free through the will to be free because it has freedom also as a gift related to his being (ontological). Freedom is also a gift, but also a work of it. Therefore, any time in the earthly life, man can lose and regain his freedom. But because the absolute freedom only God has, the created beings can only have, maintain and regain it in union with Him"[451].

As a conclusion, we emphasize that any form or precariousness of human freedom, philosophically, ethically or theologically thought, has its source in the ontological freedom about which we have spoken. This is also our conclusion on the legal freedoms of man, source of legal normativism, but whose legitimacy is not the legal normativism itself, but the ontological freedom of man.

The question arises, in relation to these considerations, how free are we today, even in the precariousness of the social freedom? It is a question that we will try to answer in a future study.

The measure of freedom, in its ontological meaning, is given by culture and faith. Marin Voiculescu said: "The slaves of culture are the sons of liberty," and Father Arsenie Boca emphasized that "a man praying is a free man," also the Father said, "Christianity has made people aware of their freedom." We must remember what Saint Isaac Sirius says: "Watch for freedom that leads to evil slavery." Thus we will be able to find out how we are placed in relationship to freedom, which is the measure of the freedom of each of us.

---

[451] Dumitru Stăniloare, Philokalia Humanitas Publishing House, Bucharest, 2009, Vol. 11, p.357

Bibliography

ImmanuelKant, Critique of Practical Reason, Antet Publishing House, Bucharest, 2013;

Nikolai Berdiaev, Spirit and Freedom. The Christian Philosophy Test, Paideia Publishing House, Bucharest, 2009;

Teodosie Paraschiv, Maximal and Philokalia Thoughts, Adenium Publishing House 2013; Varsanufie and John, Spiritual Writings, page 281;

Dumitru Staniloaie, Philokalia, Vol. 11, Humanitas Publishing House, Bucharest, 2009.

20. CONSTITUTIONAL SUPREMACY IN THE CONTEXT OF THE PRINCIPLE OF PRIMACY OF EUROPEAN UNION LAW

Abstract:

The relation between constitutional rules and European Union Law is construed differently, as there are several doctrinaire concepts and different case-law solutions. There is a school of thought claiming the Constitution's supremacy, including over European Union law, albeit it accepts the latter's enforcement priority in its compulsory rules over all the other rules of national law, and another one claiming the unconditional enforceability priority of all provisions in European Union law over all rules of national law, including over constitutional rules.

There are European constitutional jurisdictions to have set out they have the legal power to conduct the review of constitutionality of European Union law, incorporated into national legal order, by virtue of the principle of the Basic Law's supremacy.

This study addresses the interferences between the principle of primacy of European Union law and the principle of Constitution's supremacy with regard to doctrine and case-law pertinent to the matter.

Key words:

Principle of primacy of European Union law/ principle of Constitution's supremacy/ binding nature of European Union's legal standards/review of constitutionality of European Union's legal acts incorporated into domestic law/ Conformity of domestic law with European Union law.

I. Relationship between national law and European Union law

One of European Union's major hallmarks is the existence of a system of its own made up of principles, written rules and standards established by the case-law. Therefore, clarification of relations between European Union law and national law is important. This issue may be resolved by resorting to a set of rules that are not laid down explicitly by the Constitutional Treaties, but they have been developed by the Court of Justice via several decisions, some of which are controversial. The constitutions of the European Union Member States comprise principle-value rules as regards the relation between European Union law and national law.

In practical terms, the interference between European Union law and national law occurs especially when there are contradictions between legal standards belonging to systems of law. Surely, the issue of relation between the two categories of legal standards is of interest not only in such a case, but also in cases where a court of law may enforce a standard of European Union's law. One of the most important aspects of this issue is the relation between Constitution's supremacy and, on the other hand, the principle of primacy of European Union law, as well as constitutional jurisdiction's competences with regard to enforcement and interpretation of the rules comprised by the European Union's legal acts.

We believe this issue may be analysed on two directions: 1/ relation between the domestic law (other than the constitutional one) and European Union law; 2/ relation between constitutional rules of Member States and, on the other hand, European Union law.

One of the most interesting discussions, from a case-law and doctrinal sense, involving European Union Member States' constitutional courts refers to the cooperation mechanisms to the Court of Justice of the European Union, Court of Justice of the European Union's case-law, doctrine but also national legislation deals with the principle of primacy or supremacy, precedence, pre-eminence of the European Union law over national systems of law.

The relation between constitutional rules and European Union law is construed differently, as there are several doctrinaire concepts. There is a school of thought claiming the Constitution's supremacy, including over European Union law, albeit it accepts the latter's enforcement priority in its compulsory rules over all the other rules of domestic law, and another one claiming the unconditional enforceability priority of all provisions in European Union law over all rules in the domestic law, including over constitutional rules. Some old-established European constitutional jurisdictions have reached, in certain historic moments and contexts, to the conclusion that it falls within their competence to review the constitutionality of European Union law, incorporated into domestic legal order, by virtue of the principle of the Basic Law's supremacy (for instance the Constitutional Court of Germany).

The Court of Justice has come to develop the principle of primacy of European Union law having regard to the rule of international public law, according to which "A party may not invoke the provisions of its domestic law as justification for its failure to perform a treaty". Another source was represented by the provisions of Art. 10 of the Treaty Establishing the European Community, as amended by the Treaty of Lisbon. The rule included in the provisions of Art. 10 is still unchanged to this date and it lays down the Member States' obligation to take any and all steps necessary in order to make sure the obligations arisen from the Community's treaties and acts are complied with. The same provisions impose the negative obligation of Member States to refrain from taking any measures which would jeopardize the attainment of the Treaty's objectives. These are not the only regulations from the European Union Treaties which underlie the principle of primacy of European Union law over national law: the provisions of Art. 3 a) of the Treaty on European Union.

The principle of primacy and binding nature of the European Union Law was mainly constructed by case-law basis. The historical case-law of the Court of Justice of the European Union is pertinent to the matter, marking a step towards asserting this principle in relation to national law.

A significant moment is represented by the case of Costa v. Enel[452]. The Italian court submitted two applications for interpretation: one to the Italian Constitutional Court and another to the Court of Justice of the European Union. The Constitutional Court held that T.C.E. may not have normative value, except in so far as it is incorporated into national law by way of a law. At the same time, it was acknowledged that a national law may derogate from the Treaty's provisions.

[452] 6/64 Costa v. Enel (1964) ECR 585

The Court of Justice had a different opinion, expressed in its ruling: "These considerations show that the legal system arisen from the Treaty, independent source of law, may not be due to its special and original nature, overtaken by the domestic legal standards irrespective of their legal force, without lacking its community law characteristic and without the Community's legal foundation itself be called in question".

Another moment of the Court of Justice case-law's progress in this matter is represented by the cases "Internaţionale H[453]"; „Simmenthal I[454] and Simmenthal II[455]". The following considerations in the decision ruled to the case Simmenthal II are pertinent to our research theme: "as such it is incompatible with the requirements inherent to the community law's nature, any provision of national legal order or any practice – legislative, administrative or judicial, which would result in diminishing the community law's effectiveness in that denying the competent judge from enforcing it, the competency to do, at the precise moment of such enforcement, all that is necessary to remove the national legal provisions which, eventually would represent an obstacle to community rules' full effectiveness...Consequently, the answer to the first question is that the national judge in charge of, as per his/her competence, enforcing the provisions of community law, is obliged to ensure full effectiveness of such rules, declining to apply, ex officio if needed, any provision to the contrary of the national legislation, even subsequent, without seeking to or expecting its previous removal by law or by any other constitutional procedure" (considerations 22 and 24 of the decision).

Moreover, the Court found that national courts have the power to compel and even punish the legislative and executive power for the purposes of guaranteeing full effectiveness of the principle of primacy of European Union law over national law[456].

This principle should be understood in the light of the rule of Community acts binding nature as well. The *regulation* has general application and is compulsory in all its elements. Unlike it, a *directive* is addressed to all Member States and is compulsory with regard to the outcome to be reached

---

453 11/70, Internationale H., (1970) ECR 1125

454 35/76, Simmenthal SpA (1976) ECR 1871

455 106/77, Simmenthal (1978) ECR 629

456 For more information, see Ştefan T, Andreşan-Grigoriu B., Drept comunitar, C. H. Beck, pp. 196-202

leaving the national authorities competence with regard to form and means they resort to so as to achieve the objectives set out. *Decision* is compulsory in all its elements for addressees referred to.

Direct application rule characterizing some of the European Union's law legal acts concerns the manner of understanding and application of the principle of primacy of European Union law. Regulations are directly applied since they require no transposition into national law. As the Court held in its case-law, Member States must not adopt national legislation whereby to implement regulations. Their provisions may be invoked by natural persons or legal entities directly before national courts. Unlike it, directive has no direct enforceability. It must always be transposed into the system of law of every Member State it is addressed to. The domestic normative act for transposing the directive is that whereby directive's substance shall enter the national system of law.

The principle of primacy of European Union law over national law is to be understood by the criterion of the possibility to directly invoke community acts before national courts. The "direct effect" phrase designates the attribute of a community normative act of creating in natural persons and legal entities' patrimony rights they can invoke directly before national courts. Without entering into details, we highlight that regulations, directives and decisions may, under certain circumstances, have direct effect[457].

---

[457] Ştefan T., Andreşan-Grigoriu B., *quoted work*, p. 214-234

II. National courts' obligation to construe domestic law in accordance with European Union law

One of the consequences of the principle of primacy of European Union law is also national courts' obligation to construe domestic law in accordance with European Union law. In trying to ensure European Union law's effectiveness and uniformity, the Court of Justice of the European Union has laid down several means as an incentive for the states to implement directives correctly and in a timely manner and in order to ensure their enforcement. One of these means is creating the doctrine of directives' direct vertical outcome.

In so far as the provisions of a non-implemented or inadequately implemented directive may not lead to a vertical direct effect since they do not comply with the requirement to be clear enough, accurate and unconditional, in order to infer the law, the citizen seeking justice wishes to exploit before national courts, the Court has instituted the obligation, devolving upon the national judge, to construe national legislation in relation to directive's substance.

One of the first cases to have had this obligation expressly formulated was the case of Van Colson. The Court held, in considerations of the decision ruled, that national legislation limits the right to legal redress of persons to have been discriminated against while exercising the right to work. Such an instance is not in line with the requirements of effective transposition of Directive 76/207. As a consequence, the court of Luxembourg ruled: "It follows that, in applying national law and especially provisions of a national law specifically adopted with a view to applying Directive 76/207, the national court called upon to interpret it is required to do so, in the light of the wording and the purpose of the directive in order to achieve the result pursued by it and thereby comply with paragraph 3) of Art. 189 of TC.E. (*Treaty on the Establishment of European Community*). Consequently, the Court stated: "It is for the national court to pass laws adopted with a view to applying the directive, in so far as national law gives a margin of discretion, interpretation and application in agreement with the community law's requirements".

The judgment of the European Union's Court of Justice, ruled in the case of Seda Kücükdeveci v. Swedex GmbH & Co[458] is also enlightening. The Court reiterates the existence of the principle of non-discrimination on grounds

[458] Judgment in the case C-555/07

of age, as well as the role of the national court in applying it. The German legislation providing that the period of employment completed before the employee reaches the age of 25 is not taken into account for calculating the notice period is contrary to the principle of non-discrimination on grounds of age, as laid down by Directive 2000/78. In this situation, the national court should disapply, if necessary, any contrary internal regulation, even in the case of legal proceedings between private individuals.

The considerations of this judgment show that Directive 200/78 gives expression to the principle of equal treatment in the field of employment and occupation. The principle of non-discrimination on grounds of age is a general principle of Union's law. It is therefore for the national court, hearing a dispute involving the principle of non-discrimination on grounds of age as given expression in Directive 2000/78 to provide, within the limits of its jurisdiction, the legal protection which individuals derive from European Union law and to ensure the full effectiveness of that law, disapplying if need be any provision of national legislation contrary to that principle.

In accordance with these conclusions of the European Union's Court of Justice, Romanian courts also, where there are to apply the provisions of a national law for implementing a directive, shall interpret it in accordance with the directive's wording and purpose. The Court's case-law in the matter shows that national court is obliged, where it has to apply a law for implementing a directive, to take account not only of such law, but of the totality of rules of national law and to interpret them in accordance with the respective directives' requirements, in order to deliver a solution compliant to the purpose pursued by the community act.

Having regard to the fact that Romanian law consists of excessive procedural formalism and more particularly of significant inconsistencies and contradictions, national courts are going to have difficulties in fulfilling this obligation.

Furthermore, the European Union's Court of Justice considers, in its case-law, this obligation of national courts to be subject to limitations. The obligation to interpret the domestic law to take account of the directive's wording and purpose exists only in so far as national law gives the court a margin of discretion. Within this meaning, the Court held the following in the case of Papino: "The principle of conforming interpretation cannot serve as the basis for an interpretation of national law *contra legem*"[459].

We believe that every time national law confers "related jurisdiction" on the court, which excludes the existence of a margin of discretion, the national judge does not have the above-stated obligation. By way of example, this category may include some of the procedural nature normative provisions. Also, national courts may not, in criminal matters, aggravate liability in criminal law of persons committing an act falling within the provisions of a directive, if it has not been implemented in the domestic law.

---

[459] Judgment C-105/03

III. Brief considerations on the principle of Constitution's supremacy

In order to understand the relation between the two principles, i.e. Constitution's supremacy on the one hand, and primacy of European Union law on the other hand, there are a few considerations that are useful in connection to this quality of the Basic Law of being supreme in the rule of law, internal and social policy.

Constitution's supremacy expresses the upstream position of Basic law both in the system of law, as well as in the entire political and social system of every country. In the narrow sense, constitution supremacy's scientific foundation results from its form and content. Formal supremacy is expressed by the superior legal force, procedures derogating from common law on adopting and amending the constitutional rules, and material supremacy comes from the specificity of regulations, their content, especially from the fact that, by constitution, premises and rules for organization, operation and duties of public authorities are set out.

In that connection, it has been stated in the literature that the principle of Basic law's supremacy "Can be considered a *sacred,* intangible precept (...) it is at the peak of the pyramid of all legal acts. Nor would it be possible otherwise: Constitution legitimizes power, converting individual or collective will into State will; it gives power to the government, justifying its decisions and ensuring their implementation; it dictates the functions and duties incumbent on public authorities, enshrining the fundamental rights and duties, it has a leading role in relations between citizens, them and public authorities; it indicates the meaning or purpose of State activity, that is to say political, ideological and moral values under which the political system is organized and is functioning; Constitution is the fundamental background and essential guarantee of the rule of law; finally, it is the decisive benchmark for assessing the validity of all legal acts and facts. All these are substantial elements converging toward one and the same conclusion: *Constitution's material supremacy.* However, Constitution is supreme in a *formal sense* as well. The adoption procedure for the Constitution externalizes a particular, specific and inaccessible force, attached to its provisions, as such that no other law except a constitutional one may amend or repeal the decisions of the fundamental establishment, provisions relying on themselves, postulating their supremacy"[460].

The concept of Constitution supremacy may not, however, be reduced to a formal and material significance. Professor Ioan Muraru stated that: "Constitution's supremacy is a complex notion in whose content are comprised political and legal elements (values) and features expressing the upstream position of the Constitution not only in the system of law, but in the whole socio-political system of a country"[461]. Thus, Constitution's supremacy is a quality or trait positioning the Basic law at the top of political and juridical institutions in a society organized as a State and expresses its upstream position, both in the system of law and in the social and political system.

The legal basis for Constitution's supremacy is contained by provisions of Art. 1 paragraph 5) of the Basic law. Constitution supremacy does not have a purely theoretical dimension within the meaning it may be deemed just a political, juridical or, possibly moral concept. Owing to its express enshrining in the Basic law, this principle has a normative value, from a formal standpoint being a constitutional rule. The normative dimension of Constitution's supremacy involves important legal obligations whose failure to comply with may result in legal penalties. In other words, in terms of constitutional principle, enshrined as legislation, supremacy of Basic law is also a constitutional obligation having multiple legal, political, but also value meanings for all components of the social and State system. In this regard, Cristian Ionescu would highlight: "From a strictly formal point of view, the obligation (to respect the primacy of the Basic law n.n,) is addressed to the Romanian citizens. In fact, observance of Constitution, including its supremacy, as well as laws was an entirely general obligation, whose addressees were all subjects of law – individuals and legal entities (national and international) with legal relations, including diplomatic, with the Romanian State"[462].

---

[460] Deleanu I., Institutions and constitutional procedures - in Romanian law and in comparative law, Ed. C. H. Beck, Bucharest 2006, pp. 221-222

[461] Muraru I., Tănăsescu E.S., Romanian Constitution - Commentary on articles, Ed. C.H. Beck, Bucharest, 2009, p.18

[462] Ionescu C., The Constitution of Romania. Title I. General principles art. 1-14. Comments and explanations, Ed. C.H. Beck, Bucharest, 2015, p. 48

The general significance of this constitutional obligation relates to compliance of all law to the Constitution's rules. It is understood by "law" not just the legal system's component, but also the complex, institutional activity of interpretation and enforcement of legal rules, beginning with those of the Basic Law. "It was the derived Constituent Parliament's intention in 2003 to mark the decisive importance of the principle of Constitution supremacy over any other normative act. A clear signal was given, particularly as regards the public institution with a governing role to strictly respect the Constitution. Compliance with the Constitution is included in the general concept of lawfulness, and the term of respecting Constitution supremacy requires a pyramid-like hierarchy of normative acts at the top of which is the Basic law"[463].

[463] Ionescu C., quoted work, p. 48

IV. Relation between European Union law and constitutional rules

The constitutional courts in some of the Member States – above all, Germany, Italy and France- have consistently considered that the principle of primacy of European Union law does not apply in relation to the regulations contained in a constitution, since a State's Basic Law expresses national sovereignty and identity. This solution was particularly concerned with regulations on fundamental human rights and freedoms. By 1 December 2009, date on which the Treaty of Lisbon and the European Union Charter of Fundamental Rights became effective, European Union law did not include a coherent normative system whereby fundamental human rights would be guaranteed. Therefore, the courts of Member States called upon internal constitutional regulations in such cases.

Furthermore, the practice of European Union Member States' courts does not offer much examples of conflict between the European Union law's regulations and constitutional regulations. This is explained by the fact that, in the course of accession to the European Union, Member States have adapted their constitutional regulations as a principle to the requirements specific to the European Union law and they have enshrined, in one way or another, the principle of primacy of this system of law over domestic law every time there is an inconsistency between the rules of the two categories of legal standards. Needless to say, this issue remains open and is far from being resolved. It should be noted that in recent years the Constitutional Council and the State Council of France have developed the concept of "*constitutional national identity*" in their case-law. According to this principle, national courts shall always enforce the internal constitutional regulations, but also the rules laid down by usual legislation each time they lack correspondence in the European Union law.

The Romanian Constitution makes the distinction between the principle of supremacy of the Basic Law and the principle of primacy of European Union law over national law. Thus, the provisions of Article 1 par. (5) of the Constitution enshrines the principle of supremacy of the Basic Law: "Compliance with the Constitution, its supremacy and with the laws is mandatory in Romania". This principle cannot be confused with that of primacy of the European Union law over regulations contrary to the domestic laws, enshrined in Article 148 par. 2 of the Constitution.

The Constitutional Court of Romania's case-law reflects this gap.

Our constitutional court clearly makes, by decision 148 dated 16 April 2003 on the constitutionality of the legislative proposal to review the Constitution of Romania[464], the distinction between Constitution's supremacy and the principle of primacy of European Union law, stating: "The consequence of accession starts from the fact that European Union Member States have understood to place the Community acquis, European Union constitutive treaties and regulations thereof on an intermediate position between the Constitution and the other laws when it comes to mandatory European legal acts". Referring to the provisions of Art. 148 of the Constitution and in accordance with decision no. 148 dated 16 April 2003, the academic legal literature stated: "Therefore, it could be affirmed that in the domestic legal order, the legal act whereby Romania accedes to the European Union has legal force lower than the Constitution and constitutional laws, but higher than the ordinary and organic laws"[465].

The Constitutional Court seems, in its subsequent case-law, to have waived this distinction, basing decisions only on the principle of primacy of European Union law[466].

However, the Court found, by Decision no. 1258 delivered on 8 October 2009[467], that we believe it to be of historical significance in the subsequent constitutional case-law, that an internal law whereby a European Union directive is translated into domestic law is unconstitutional. In our opinion, such a solution enshrines the principle of Constitution supremacy and the requirement of compliance with it in relation to the principle of primacy of European Union law.

---

[464] Published in the Official Journal no. 317 of 12 May 2003

[465] Constantinescu M, Iorgovan A, Muraru I, Elena Simina Tănăsescu E.S., Constituția României revizuită - comentarii şi explicații, Editura All Beck, Bucureşti, 2004, p. 331; Muraru I., Tănăsescu E.S. (coordonatori), Constituția României. Comentariu pe articole, pp. 1432-1433

[466] See in this regard: Decision no. 308/2006 published in the Romanian Official Journal no. 390 of 5 May 2006; Decision no. 59/2007 published in the Romanian Official Journal no. 98 of 8 February 2007; Decision no. 1042/2007 published in the Romanian Official Journal no. 12 of 8 February 2008 and Decision no. 1172/2007 published in the Romanian Official Journal no. 54 of 23 January 2008

[467] Published in the Romanian Official Journal no. 798 of 23 November 2009

By the above-mentioned number decision, the constitutional court found that provisions of Act 298/2008[468] were unconstitutional. It follows from the decision's considerations that Act no. 298/2008 was passed so as to transpose Directive 2006/24/EC of the European Parliament and of the Council on 15 March 2006 on the retention of data generated or processed in connection with the provision of publicly available electronic communications services or of public communications networks into the national legislation. The Court refers to the legal regime of such community acts, emphasizing that: "(...) imposes its obligation to the European Union Member States as regards the legal solution regulated, not with regard to specific means by which this result it achieved, states having a wide margin of discretion for the purposes of adapting them for the legislation's specificity and national realities". The Court found, after having examined the content of Act 298/2008, that this normative act is liable to affect the exercise of fundamental rights or freedoms, i.e. the right to privacy and family, right to secrecy of correspondence and freedom of speech. The constitutional court holds that restricting the exercise of such rights does not comply with the requirements set forth by Art. 53 of the Romanian Constitution. Similarly, also see decision no. 17 dated 21 January 2015[469], by which the law on Romania's cyber security was ruled unconstitutional by our constitutional court.

Decision no. 80 of 16 February 2014[470] on the legislative proposal as regards the review of the Constitution of Romania is relevant to our research theme. With regard to interpretation of the provisions of Art. 148 on integration with the European Union, the Court notes that: "constitutional provisions are not declarative in nature, but they are binding constitutional rules without which the rule of law's existence cannot be conceivable, as set forth by Art. 1 par. 3 of the Constitution. At the same time, Basic Law represents the framework and extent to which the legislator and the other authorities may act; thus, interpretations that may be made to the legal norm should take account of this constitutional requirement as well, contained precisely in Art. 1 par. 4 of the Basic law, according to which in Romania, the respect of the Constitution and its supremacy shall be mandatory".

It is the opinion of our constitutional court that to consider the European Union law applies with no differentiation within the national legal

[468] Published in the Romanian Official Journal no. 780 of 21 November 2008
[469] Published in the Romanian Official Journal no. 79 of 30 January 2015
[470] Published in the Romanian Official Journal no. 246 of 7 April 2014

order, not making a distinction between the Constitution and the other domestic laws is to place the Basic Law at a second level in regard to the European Union's legal order. The legitimacy of the Constitution is the will of the people itself, meaning it cannot lose its binding force, even in the hypothesis that there would be disparities between its provisions and the European ones. Moreover, the fact that Romania's accession to the European Union cannot affect Constitution's supremacy over the entire domestic legal order was stressed.

The Constitutional Court has held that binding European Union acts are rules interposed between the constitutionality's control.[471] At the same time, lack of constitutional relevance of the European rule of law, interposed between reference constitutional rules within the constitutionality control was pointed out. In this instance, the referral of the Court based on non-compliance with the provisions of Art. 148 par. 4 of the Constitution was found to be inadmissible[472]. The Court ruled by the same decision that the legal standard of the European Union law needs to fall within a certain level of *constitutional relevance*, as such that its normative content could support the possible breach of the Constitution by the national law – "the sole direct reference rule within the control as to constitutionality". The constitutional court has enshrined, just like the French Constitutional Council, the concept of "national constitutional identity", whereby it understands the relevance of constitution's supremacy every time there is a question of compliance of domestic laws with European Union acts.[473]

Another issue examined by the constitutional case-law refers to the application, within the control as to constitutionality, of the European Union Charter of fundamental rights. Our constitutional court ruled that in principle it is applicable within the control as to constitutionality, "in so far as it safeguards, guarantees and develops the constitutional provisions in respect of fundamental rights; in other words, in so far as their protection level is at least at the level of the constitutional rules in the field of human rights".[474]

---

[471] See decision no. 668 of 18 May 2011, published in the Romanian Official Journal no. 487 of 8 July 2011

[472] See decision no. 157 of 19 March 2014, Romanian Official Journal no. 296 of 23 April 2014

[473] See in that respect, Decision no. 64 of 24 February 2015, Romanian Official Journal no.286 of 28 April 2015

[474] Decision no. 871 of 25 June 2010, Romanian Official Journal no. 433 of 28 June 2010

Also concerning the European Union rules 'enforcement with regard to human rights within the control as to constitutionality, it has been argued that the provisions contained in an act with legal force similar to the European Union's constitutive treaties should be referenced to the provisions of Art. 148 of the Constitution, not to those contained in Art. 20 of the Basic Law, which refer to the international treaties on human rights, other than those of the European Union.[475] Our constitutional court has ruled that provisions of Art. 41 of the European Union Charter of Fundamental Rights in regard to the right to good administration may be invoked via Art. 148, not Art. 20 of the Constitution[476].

Moreover, it has been established in constitutional case-law that analysis of compliance of a constitutional right provision with the Treaty's wording on the functioning of the European Union does not fall on the competence of the Constitutional Court, in light of Art. 148 of the Constitution. Such jurisdiction, i.e. to determine whether there is any contradiction between national law and treaty, is vested exclusively on the court, which also has the possibility to ask a preliminary question to the Court of Justice of the European Union. It is interesting to note that the constitutional court considers it has no jurisdiction to verify compliance of a national law provision with the wording of European Union's constitutive treaties and, if it were to assign itself such a competence, a possible conflict of interests would arise between the Constitutional Court of Romania and the European Union Court of Justice, which, at that level, is deemed inadmissible[477].

With regard to the cooperation between the Constitutional Court and the European Union Court of Justice, our constitutional court stated that the manner of application, in the case of control as to constitutionality, of decisions made by the European Union Court of Justice or formulation of preliminary questions by the Court in order to establish the content of the European rule is left to its discretion. "Such attitude takes account of the cooperation between the national constitutional court and the European one, as well as of the judicial

---

[475]See in that respect, Decision no. 967 of 20 November 2012, Romanian Official Journal no. 853 of 18 December 2012 and decision no. 206 of 6 March 2012, Romanian Official Journal no. 254 of 17 April 2012

[476] See Decision no. 12 of 22 January 2013, Romanian Official Journal no. 114 of 28 February 2013

[477] See in that respect, Decision no. 1249 of 7 October 2010, Romanian Official Journal no. 764 of 16 November 2010 and Decision no. 137 of 25 February 2010 Romanian Official Journal no. 182 of 22 March 2010

dialogue between them, without calling into question matters relating to setting a hierarchy between these courts."[478]

[478] See Decision no. 668 of 18 May 2011, published in the Romanian Official Journal no. 487 of 8 July 2011

V. Conclusions

We believe that the principle of pre-eminence or primacy of the law is not equivalent to the principle of supremacy of a rule of law, since *supremacy* is a trait belonging to the domestic constitutional rules. For that purpose, provisions of Art. 148 par. 2 of the Constitution of Romania enshrines *primacy,* not supremacy of the European Union's constitutive treaties provisions, as well as the other community regulations that are binding towards the provisions to the contrary from the domestic legislation. Therefore, there is not only a difference as to terminology between the terms "primacy" or "pre-eminence" on the one hand, and "supremacy" on the other hand, but also one of legal nature, which could impact the relation between European Union law and national law.

We claim that there is a juridical type of difference between the principle of primacy of European Union law and the principle of Constitution's supremacy. The supremacy of a state's Basic Law essentially expresses its higher legal force over any legal act which produces effects and applies on the territory of the state. The outcome of the principle of supremacy of a constitution is the compliance of the whole domestic law with the Basic Law's rules. To consider that on the territory of a state, even one member of the European Union, a rule of law contrary to the domestic constitutional regulations could produce legal effects is to limit that State's sovereignty in an impermissible manner, leading to the system of law being jeopardized, which is built on constitutional rules and principles.

Some theoretical conclusions can be drawn from the case-law analysis of our constitutional court: a) there is a judicial nature difference between the principle of Constitution's supremacy and the principle of primacy of European Union law. The first draws its legitimacy from the sovereign will of the people itself, which also holds constituent power based upon which Constitution exercises its supreme force in the national rule of law. The principle of primacy of European Union law is enshrined by the international laws to which Romania has adhered based upon the principles of national sovereignty and constitutional rules. Therefore, this principle cannot be countered against the Basic law's supremacy; b) if provisions of Art. 148 of the Constitution are enforced, the control as to constitutionality takes account of domestic law's compliance with the Constitution's rules, not with the European Union law's rules. In this regard, the Constitutional Court argued and developed the concept of "national constitutional identity"; c) European

Union acts may be invoked in the procedure of control as to constitutionality in so far as they have some degree of constitutional relevance; d) European Union Charter of Fundamental Rights can be applied within the control as to constitutionality, in reference, however, to Art. 148 of the Constitution, not to provisions of Art. 20 of the Basic Law, which refer to international treaties on human rights. Such a solution is just, having regard to the fact that the provisions of Art. 148 applicable to human rights are special in nature, in relation to provisions of Art. 20 which constitutes the general rule; e) the constitutional court established that it has the power to ask the European Union Court of Justice preliminary questions with a view to setting the European rule's content without, however, such a procedure being compulsory for the Constitutional Court. At the same time, enforcement of judgments delivered by the European Union's Court of Justice is not binding by reference to the constitutional jurisdiction.

We believe the principle of primacy of European Union law cannot aim at the constitutional rules also. One of the arguments to support this allegation is derived from the provisions of Art. 148 par. 2 of the Constitution. The constitutional rule links the due regard for the principle of primacy of community law to the "compliance with the provisions of the Act of Accession". The Accession Treaty cannot be contrary to the constitutional rules, since it couldn't have been ratified by the Parliament. The provisions of Art. 11 par. (3) of the Constitution are enlightening in this regard: "if a Treaty Romania is to become a party to comprises provisions contrary to the Constitution, its ratification shall only take place after the revision of the Constitution".

Bibliography

Ştefan T, Andreşan-Grigoriu B.(2008) Community law, Bucharest: C.H.Beck Publishing House;

Deleanu I., Institutions and constitutional procedures - in Romanian law and in comparative law (2006), Bucharest: C.H.Beck Publishing House;

Muraru I., Tănăsescu E.S., (2008) Romanian Constitution - Commentary on articles Bucharest: C.H.Beck Publishing House;

Ionescu C (2015) The Constitution of Romania. Title I. General principles art. 1-14. Comments and explanations, Bucharest: C.H. Beck Publishing House;

Andreescu M, Puran A(2016) Constitutional Law-General Theory of the Bucharest State, C.H.Beck Publishing House;

Dragoş C (2014) The Constitutional Court of Romania and the law of the European Union - Collection of jurisprudence, Bucharest, University Publishing House.

21. GUARANTEE HUMAN RIGHTS IN CONTEMPORARY SOCIETY. CONDITIONS, LIMITATIONS, RESTRICTIONS

Abstract

The enshrining in modern democratic constitutions and international legal instruments of some human rights and freedoms is the result of a long historical process that includes philosophical, legal and political conceptions, theories, doctrines, but also different forms of recognition, normative consecration of them. The normative affirmation of human rights is the legal recognition of the human being in his existential individuality, man becomes a person in legal relations, the holder of rights and freedoms that he can oppose to the state and demand their guarantee and respect.

The scientific research of fundamental rights and freedoms must be carried out on three levels: legal, philosophical, sociological.

The constitutional evolution of human rights was characterized by the existence of two large categories of regulations: internal, of each state, and international. In constitutional law, the question of their correlation was raised and two principles were affirmed: 1. The application of conventions related to human rights must be done taking into account the need to harmonize international cooperation with the principle of state sovereignty and 2. International documents are the main means for their application, the assumption in good faith by the states parties of their obligations according to their normative content.

Given the undeniable social and legal importance of enshrining human rights, one can speak of a new "religion" of fundamental rights enshrined by law. Is this conception justified; what are the theological, philosophical and legal meanings of human rights; Are freedoms and human rights really guaranteed by the states, including in Romania; To what extent are the rights of persons in special situations constitutionally guaranteed: foreigners, stateless persons, migrants, refugees? - these are some of the topics we want to address in this study, with reference to the relevant doctrine and jurisprudence.

Key words:

Fundamental rights and freedoms/ national and international normative consecrations and guarantees/ limits, restrictions, exemptions, Migrants and refugees.

I. General considerations regarding fundamental human constitutional rights and freedoms

The fundamental rights and freedoms of man and citizen are a constitutional reality, with deep implications in the existence of each person, in his relations with the state. It also represents an existential reality of each person, of society as a whole and a dimension of democracy. Modern constitutionalism is based on the affirmation, recognition and guarantee of fundamental rights and freedoms, against which the notions of state, law, civil society, democratic regime, sovereign power would be inconceivable. Therefore, this institution has an important philosophical dimension, which characterizes the existence of every human being, but also one of constitutional law and international law, expressing both conceptually and normatively the complex relations between man and the state.

The scientific research of fundamental rights and freedoms must be carried out on three levels: conceptual, philosophical, political. And, last but not least, legal, being at the same time a problem of the international constitution.

In the specialized literature, the terminology and conceptual approach is not uniform, different solutions are proposed.

1. J. Rivero, in the work "Public Liberties" (Paris, 1973), considered that human rights and freedoms are not on the same plane, thus:

- human rights reveal the concept of natural law and refer to the inert rights of human nature, which is a transcendental nature, they are universal and permanent, located above positive law;
- public liberties are real, recognized and legally guaranteed categories and are situated on the level of positive law.

2. G. Burdeau considers fundamental rights to have a different nature from fundamental freedoms because:

- human rights are abstract prerogatives recognized by human nature;
- freedoms are effective prerogatives, susceptible to realization in society.

3. Theories that treat them in a synonymy relationship, as being indivisible. In accordance with these theories, human rights, as well as fundamental freedoms, are not outside the positive law and, therefore, outside the state bodies that regulate and normatively guarantee the conditions for their realization. Public liberties are the necessary corollary of human rights and only their recognition can ensure the correct status of man in relation to power in society.

4. Professor Ion Deleanu's conception starts from the indivisible character of the two notions and considers that:

- by "human rights" are meant the rights of any person who is in the area of a state's sovereignty, regardless of his relationship with that state;

- "citizen's rights" are the rights specific to that person who, by virtue of citizenship, belongs to the respective state and, consequently, has the right to choose and be elected, to hold public positions, etc.

From the point of view of their legal nature, they are subjective rights, and the term of freedom assigned to those rights in the exercise of which the appreciation of the holder is strictly exclusive, only he can decide on the possibility of doing or not doing something.

Rights and freedoms are fundamental because they are enshrined and guaranteed by the Constitution and at the same time represent the nucleus with a determining character for all other subjective rights.

In essence, all the authors recognize that democracy and human rights form an indestructible unity that mutually conditions each other. Democracy marks the emancipation of the people, their becoming as a subject of the government, the emancipation that presupposes the power of determination of each person, therefore the endowment of them with the rights that are inherent to them as human beings and citizens.

For the constitutional definition of this institution, several aspects must be considered:

a) Fundamental rights are subjective rights, they are the faculties of the subjects of the legal relationship to act in a certain way or to ask the other subjects for an appropriate attitude and to benefit from the protection of the state in realizing legitimate claims;

b) Fundamental rights are essential rights for citizens. It is the feature that distinguishes the fundamental rights from the usual subjective ones, being decisive for the legal status of the citizen;

The delimitation criterion between subjective and subjectively essential rights is a value one, but also a concrete historical one.

From a value point of view, the rights that refer to life, freedom and the personality of each person are essential.

From a concrete historical perspective, the same subjective right can be considered a fundamental right or a simple subjective right, according to the concrete, economic, social, political conditions and according to the will of the rulers expressed by law.

c) Due to their importance, the fundamental rights are registered in separate documents, such as the declarations of rights and fundamental, constitutional laws.

The constitutional regulation of these rights is the result of the application of the value criterion, thus recognizing them as essential for citizens. Enshrined in the constitution, they are recognized as fundamental rights and guarantees are established for their protection and guarantee.

We can define the essential rights and freedoms as those subjective rights of citizens, essential for their life, freedom and dignity, indispensable for the free development of the human personality, rights established by the constitution and guaranteed by the constitution and laws.

The following consequences result from this definition:

a) There are no legal distinctions between the notions of rights and freedoms, even if sometimes they are used in nuanced meanings and interpretations. Th right is a freedom, and freedom is a right, even if from a historical point of view liberties appeared as human demands in opposition to public authorities, and these liberties did not presuppose on the part of the other subjects of law any attitude of abstinence;

b) The notion of public liberties evokes fundamental rights and liberties and in particular the fact that they belong to public law, respectively constitutional law, being subject to a special legal regime;

c) The notions of human rights and citizen's rights are in a close correlation, but from a legal point of view they are not confused.

Thus, human rights evoke the rights of the human being, endowed with rationality and conscience, to whom natural rights are recognized as imprescriptible and inalienable. On the level of legal reality, man becomes a citizen, integrates into a certain social and political system, regulated by moral and legal rules. Consequently, from this point of view, citizens benefit from all the rights enshrined in the constitution, while foreigners and stateless persons benefit from only some of them and especially those indispensables to the human being.

In conclusion, human rights, from the plane of universal and existential realities, become the rights of the citizen at the plane of the internal realities of each state.

The notion of fundamental duties is imposed, because it is inconceivable that the members of a society have only rights, without fundamental duties towards the society in which they live.

The fundamental duty is a legal obligation to which society, at a certain historical moment, assigns a greater value, a value that is reflected in the legal, respectively social regime that is attributed to them. Their realization is ensured either through persuasion, or if necessary, through the coercive force of the state.

The fundamental duties are those obligations of citizens considered essential, at a given historical moment, by the people, as the holder of sovereignty, for the achievement of general interests, inscribed in the constitution and guaranteed in their assurance by persuasion, or if necessary, by coercive force of the state.

The issue of fundamental rights and freedoms and their constitutional regulation is a consequence of the evolution of the state and its functions, and on the other hand, it is the result of the social, economic and political demands of society.

At the same time, there is a constant preoccupation in the legal sense of consecrating and especially guaranteeing fundamental rights, an aspect that also generates a variety of legal solutions with implications in terms of public international law as well.

Thus, in the 19th century, under the influence of the French Declaration of Human and Citizen Rights, the emphasis was placed on the consecration of civil and political rights, namely the equality of people before the law, freedom of conscience and expression, property rights, religious freedom, the right to resistance against oppression, the right to association, the right to vote, etc. These fundamental rights were of a nature to limit the absolute power of the state, to eliminate the status of inequality before the law, to ensure the exercise of sovereignty by its holder, the people. In this stage, fundamental rights and freedoms were initially institutionalized in declarations of rights and later in written constitutions, being thus guaranteed by the state.

The first documents with constitutional value that enshrine fundamental rights and freedoms with a civil and political character are: the French Declaration of the Rights of Man and Citizen from 1789, the Constitution of Philadelphia from 1787, the French Declaration of Fundamental Rights from 1793.

The fundamental rights and freedoms contained in these important international documents were considered by the doctrine to be rights of the first generation, because they directly targeted the human being in his relations with society and aimed to limit the power of the state by affirming the individual freedom.

From the second half of the 19th century, a wider social movement for the economic emancipation of some disadvantaged social categories is manifested in Europe. Consequently, the rulers accept economic and social concessions to the working class in the form of accepting their trade union demands.

After the First World War, under the influence of economic and social progress, but also due to the need to ensure the population a better material condition, access to culture and personality development, as well as effective control over the respect of fundamental rights and freedoms, in various constitutions are proclaimed economic and social rights, respectively: the right to work, the right to strike, freedom and trade union association, social equality, the right to social security, to job security, free access to justice, the guarantee of individual freedom, the right to education, etc.

In the constitutional doctrine, they are called rights and freedoms of the second generation.

In contrast to civil and political rights, which in principle do not presuppose concrete actions on the part of the state, apart from refraining from personal freedom, social, economic and cultural rights and freedoms involve actions, measures and guarantees on the part of the state.

Social and economic rights were imposed especially after the adoption by the UN of the Universal Declaration of Human Rights - 1948 and the Pacts adopted in 1966.

Although in some international documents, fundamental political rights and freedoms, on the one hand, and social and economic rights, on the other hand, are treated differently, modern constitutional doctrine has affirmed the indivisibility and close connection between rights, regardless of the specifics them.

In the 7th decade of our century, new human rights were imposed, rights from the third generation, also known as rights of solidarity, respectively: the right to peace, to development, the right to the environment, specific rights for young people, the rights of cohabiting minorities, the right of nations or peoples to self-determination, the right of the people to exploit natural wealth, the right to a decent standard of living, the right to privacy and respect for personal life.

These new fundamental rights emphasize the idea of promoting human personality and valuing the complex relationships between the individual and the collective. In this context, a particular theoretical and practical interest raises the right of nations to dispose of themselves or the right to self-determination.

This fundamental right does not appear inscribed in the Universal Declaration of Human Rights from 1948, but it is enshrined in the two international Pacts from 1966 and was considered by the doctrine as a synthesis of the possible fundamental human rights and freedoms.

The right to self-determination of nations highlights the connection between the freedom of nations and those who make them up. Most international declarations refer to this fundamental right.

That is why some doctrinaires considered this fundamental right as the most important of human rights and freedoms. It was also considered that a fundamental principle of international law is also the equality of rights of nations and, together with the right to dispose of themselves, constitutes an essential condition for the exercise of all human rights and freedoms. Cannot be exercised except collectively, self-determination is to nations what freedom is to individuals.

However, in modern constitutional doctrine it has been stated that self-determination cannot be an individual right of man, but it is the necessary condition of human rights, in the sense that where it does not exist, man cannot be free, because it is forbidden for him to break free.

The inclusion of fundamental rights and freedoms among the major international issues is the natural result not only of their special importance, but also of their close interdependence with the cardinal issues of humanity.

The evolution of this institution is permanent and involves the joint efforts of all states in the international community, through actions such as the regulation and criminalization of terrorism, retroactive legislation, the tendency to minimize opposition by bringing political disagreement under the criminal law, criminalizing the use of forms of detention without trial, of torture and humiliating and degrading treatment etc.

At the worldwide level, concerns for the promotion of human rights have been concretized in several documents of real value, among which we mention: The Universal Declaration of Human Rights - December 10, 1948; The International Pact on Economic and Social Rights, the International Pact on Civil and Political Rights, adopted at the UN in 1966; European Convention on Fundamental Human Rights and Freedoms - Rome, 1950; The final act of the Conference for peace, security and cooperation in Europe - Helsinki, 1975; Final Document of the Vienna Meeting, 1989; The final document of the Copenhagen Meeting, 1984 and the Paris Charter of 1990 and of course the European Union Charter of Human Rights entered into force in 2009.

There are also a number of regional international documents, such as the African Charter of 1981 or the Inter-American Convention of 1969.

The international control mechanism intervenes only in case of failure of the national guarantee regarding the respect of fundamental rights and freedoms.

In this sense, art. 20 of the Romanian Constitution establishes that: the constitutional provisions regarding the rights and freedoms of citizens will be interpreted and applied in accordance with the Universal Declaration of Human Rights.

This regulation is the concrete expression of the correlation between internal and international regulations, in the sense that both the consecration and the guarantee of fundamental rights and freedoms represent a manifestation of national sovereignty, a reality of internal law, but their concrete application and interpretation must be made in relation to the Universal Declaration, with international pacts and treaties ratified by Romania, which are part of domestic law.

According to the provisions of art. 20 para. (2) of the Romanian Constitution, if there is inconsistency between the pacts and treaties regarding fundamental human rights, to which Romania is a party, and the internal laws, the international regulations have priority.

This stipulation does not represent a violation of the principle of national sovereignty, because the constitutional priority concerns only the treaties and pacts ratified by Romania and which, through this procedure, are part of the internal law.

In the sense of respecting the third principle mentioned above, the provisions of art. 35 of Protocol no. 11 to the European Convention from 1950, which stipulates the following: "The European Court of Human Rights can only be referred to after the exhaustion of domestic appeals, as established, according to the generally recognized principles of international law and within a period of 6 months, starting with the date of the final internal decision".

In the legal literature it is specified that international control procedures have a limited and derogatory nature. At the same time, the moral force of international regulations is noted, the fact that they can be imposed and accepted by domestic law, if they defend human values understood even from the point of view of the theory of natural law.

II. Limits, restrictions and derogations regarding the exercise of fundamental rights and freedoms

A Romanian author emphasized that freedom only makes sense under the conditions of the existence of a limit, because in order to manifest itself it must depend on something, be circumscribed by some coordinates. "Human freedom is interpreted in a bundle of limits that are the condition of its exercise." (Liiceanu, 1994: 11)

Consecrating and guaranteeing human rights through domestic and international regulations does not exclude the possibility of limiting them. Moreover, the existence of unconditional rights, theoretically, cannot be admitted in a democratic constitutional system. The absence of limits and conditions of exercise, provided by law, constitutions or international legal instruments, can lead to arbitrariness or abuse of law, because it would not allow the differentiation of legal behavior from illegal behavior. This idea is expressed by art. 4 of the French Declaration of the Rights of Man and Citizen: "the exercise of the natural rights of each person has no other limits than those that ensure the other members of society the possibility of exercising these rights." Also, the legal doctrine stated that in the relations between the rights holders "the freedom of one stops where the freedom of other begins, because the condition inherent to the person is his relationship with others". (Deleanu, 1998: 269-270).

Social order and stability presuppose tolerance and mutual respect between subjects participating in social relations. The exercise of fundamental rights and freedoms must not contradict the existing order in social life: the coexistence of freedoms and social protection are the two commandments that underlie the limits dictated by positive law." (Rivero, 1973: 106)

The difficulty lies in finding the most appropriate solutions that harmonize individual interests and the public interest and at the same time guarantee fundamental rights and freedoms in situations where their exercise could be limited or restricted.

In the relationship between rights and freedoms, on the one hand, and society on the other, two extreme attitudes have emerged: the sacrifice of rights and freedoms in the interest of social order, or the pre-emission of rights and freedoms, even if in this way the interests and social order are sacrificed. (Deleanu, 1998: 105)

None of these solutions is justified by the imperatives of an authentic democracy and the requirement to achieve social balance and harmony. The constitutional regulations, to be effective, must achieve a balance between citizens and public authorities, then between public authorities and, of course, citizens. The individual must also be protected against arbitrary state interference in the exercise of his rights and freedoms. (Muraru, 1999: 16-17)

That is why the limits imposed on fundamental rights and freedoms must be appropriate to a legitimate purpose, which could be: the protection of society, the social, economic and political order, the rule of law, or for the protection of the rights of others. The limits must not deprive the rights themselves of content, but guarantee their exercise in such situations.

The existence of limits for the exercise of fundamental rights is justified by the constitutional protection or the protection by international legal instruments of important human or state values. However, it is not admissible that in the name of these values, the state authorities limit the discretionary and abusive exercise of the rights which in turn are constitutionally guaranteed. In this case, it could lead to the destruction of democracy under the pretext of its defense.

The principle of proportionality, understood as an appropriate relationship between the measures that limit the exercise of human rights and freedoms, the factual situation and the legitimate goal pursued, represents a criterion for determining these limits, avoiding excess power, but also a guarantee of constitutionally enshrined rights. (Andreecu and Puran, 2016: 132-137)

In doctrine, legal instruments and jurisprudence, the limits of fundamental rights and freedoms have been differentiated according to several criteria. A first distinction is that between the limit and the limitation of fundamental rights. (Micu, 1998: 141)

Thus, the limit is an element of the content of the right and is necessary for its exercise. In contrast, the limitation (restriction) restricts the exercise of a right through measures ordered by the competent state authorities for a legitimate purpose.

Another author (Deleanu, 1998: 205) considers that there are limits imposed on fundamental rights and freedoms to facilitate their achievement, and on the other hand, limits that aim at "the protection of society, its socio-economic and political order, as well as the rule of law". The limits deriving from such a purpose can be *absolute*, imposed by the exigencies of social life, in all situations for the protection of the essential values of the state and society, and on the other hand *relative*, those that are not applied in a general and permanent manner, but only to some of the rights and freedoms, or only in a certain time or in a certain situation, or only to certain subjects. (Rivero, 1973: 171-175)

In our opinion, we can distinguish: a) conditions for the exercise of rights and freedoms that can be found in the very legal content and their constitutional definition; b) restrictions, derogations, suspensions, loss of the right, which have an exceptional and temporary character, being measures ordered by the state authorities in order to protect or achieve a legitimate goal. State interference in the exercise of fundamental rights and freedoms can be achieved in principle by restricting and suspending the exercise of certain rights or through derogations. These methods are regulated in constitutions and international legal instruments. Avoiding any abuse of state authorities and guaranteeing fundamental rights and freedoms in such situations requires the constitutional regulation, but also in international legal instruments, of the conditions that justify the application of such measures.

There are constitutions that regulate the institution of restricting the exercise of certain rights in certain situations[479], the possibility of suspending certain rights or freedoms[480], or the cases in which due to the abusive exercise of a right, its exercise is lost[481]. The Romanian Constitution imposes conditions regarding the exercise of certain rights or freedoms. Thus, freedom of movement is exercised under the conditions established by law (art. 25, paragraph (1)). The individual can dispose of himself, if he does not violate the rights and freedoms of others, public order, or good morals (art. 26, paragraph (2)); the right of the person to have access to information of public interest cannot be limited, but it must not prejudice the measures for the protection of young people or national security (art. 31 paragraph (3)); the right to strike can only be exercised under the conditions of the law, which establishes its limits (art. 43, paragraph (2)); the content and limits of the property right are established by law (art. 44); freedom of expression cannot prejudice the dignity, honor, private life of the person or the right to one's own image (art. 30, paragraph (6)); meetings can be organized and held only peacefully, without any kind of weapons (art. 39).

The restriction of the exercise of certain rights or freedoms is regulated by the provisions of art. 53 of the Constitution. These are provisions of principle, which refer to the measures ordered by the state by law or government ordinances, which represent interferences in the exercise of constitutionally guaranteed rights. In order not to affect the substance of the

---

[479] In this regard, we recall the provisions of art. 18 of the Constitution of Portugal; art.19, par.1 and 2 of the German Constitution and the provisions of art.53 of the Romanian Constitution.

[480] Art. 55 of the Spanish Constitution.

[481] Art. 18 of the German Constitution.

right, these measures are temporary and also, in order to be constitutional, they must cumulatively comply with the conditions provided by the provisions of art.53. However, there are also constitutional provisions that restrict the exercise of certain rights, the restrictions having a permanent character. The restrictions are usually specific to the legal content of the constitutionally enshrined right. Thus, the exercise of individual freedom can be restricted by search, detention or arrest (art. 23). The inviolability of the domicile can be restricted under the conditions provided by art. 27, paragraph (2). The provisions of art. 36, paragraph (2), prohibit certain categories of persons from the right to vote. The provisions of art. 40, paragraph (3), prohibit certain professional categories from the right to be part of political parties.

There are differences between restrictions, and on the other hand, derogations that can target the exercise of fundamental rights and freedoms. Restrictions are measures considered necessary in a democratic society, applied in order to achieve a public interest or to protect the rights and freedoms of others. In this sense, the provisions of art. 18 of the Convention show that: "restrictions ... can only be applied for the purpose for which they were provided."

With all the particular aspects, resulting from the Constitution or from international legal instruments, common conditions for the legitimacy of restrictions can be identified: they must be provided by law, they must be necessary in a democratic society, they must not be discriminatory, they must be appropriate to at least one of the purposes expressly provided by law as well as the situation that justifies them. Compliance with these conditions must be achieved cumulatively. In this way the fundamental rights are guaranteed and the arbitrary interference of the state authorities in their exercise is removed.

Derogations are broader limitations of fundamental rights and freedoms and can be ordered by states in exceptional situations. Restrictions can, in principle, target any fundamental right, unlike derogatory measures that can have as their object only some of the human rights, guaranteed by international legal instruments. From the international legal instruments, it follows that the derogations, in order not to be arbitrary, must comply with the following conditions: to be applied only in exceptional situations; to be strictly appropriate to the actual situation; to be compatible with the other obligations that the party states have according to public international law; not to be discriminatory; states that make use of the right of derogation to notify the competent international forums.

There are also absolutely guaranteed rights (absolute rights) in the sense that no restrictions or derogations are allowed. Obviously, we are referring to the right to life; the right not to be subjected to torture, any kind of punishment or inhuman or degrading treatment. The principle of proportionality represents a guarantee in all situations where the exercise of a right or a fundamental freedom is subject to a condition, restrictions, suspensions or derogations. The principle of proportionality, applied in this matter, also aims to achieve a fair balance between individual interests and the public interest or between the various private interests that correspond to fundamental subjective rights, enshrined and constitutionally guaranteed.

Regarding the Romanian constitutional provisions regarding the restriction of the exercise of fundamental rights and freedoms, in the specialized literature a distinction was made between common circumstances of restriction of the exercise of certain rights that form the object of regulation of the provisions of art. 53 of the Constitution and, on the other hand, special circumstances, specific to certain rights and freedoms. The common limiting circumstances have a temporal character, they are essentially fortuitous, while the special circumstances have a permanent character. (Deleanu, 1998, vol II: 123) The cited author emphasizes that these circumstances must be expressly consecrated "not being the product of conventionalism". (Deleanu, 1998, Vol II: 123)

Although these circumstances are common, they may justify the restriction taking into account the nature of the right or freedom. Thus, no circumstance can justify restricting the exercise of the right to life or the right not to be subjected to torture.

The Romanian Constitution uses a simple and effective procedure to regulate the restriction of the exercise of certain rights and freedoms (common circumstances), through the provisions of a single article. The provisions of art. 53 allow the restriction of the exercise of some fundamental rights and freedoms, but only conditionally. (Muraru and Tănăsescu, 2003: 174-176; Andreescu and Puran, 2016: 254-256) The issue of interpretation and application of the provisions of art.53 presents a particular complexity because the restrictions may concern the exercise of any right or fundamental freedom enshrined and guaranteed by the Constitution, except for those considered as absolute. The complexity is also due to the diversity of concrete situations that justify restricting the exercise of certain rights.

The rules established by the provisions of art. 53 have the value of a constitutional principle, because they are applicable to all the fundamental rights and freedoms of citizens. In the case of a comparative analysis between the Romanian constitutional provisions and those contained in some international legal instruments, which regulate the conditions for restricting the exercise of certain rights and freedoms, some differences can be found. It is of interest for our study that the provisions of art. 53 paragraph (2) of the Constitution expressly enshrine proportionality as a condition that must be respected in the case of restricting the exercise of certain rights, while in most international legal instruments this condition results implicitly from the content of the regulations and is deduced, by way of interpretation, from the jurisprudence of international courts.

The general aspects analyzed above are necessary for the legal analysis of the rights and obligations that foreigners and migrants have on the territory of Romania.

III. Rights and limits of their exercise for foreigners, stateless persons and migrants on the territory of Romania

1.8 million years ago, Homo Erectus migrated from Africa to Eurasia in search of better survival conditions. Man settles in the environment that offers him the best conditions, which should not give rise to any controversy. It is absolutely essential not to ignore the effects produced when migrants are not received properly, we must always be prepared and aware of this, so that history does not repeat itself and migration does not again become a phenomenon that breeds fear.

Today, our globalized society is the result of countless migrations. Such movements were essential factors in the formation of mankind: from the beginning, man has known nothing but migration: one could say that after so much cultural diversity, citizenship, ethnicity or skin color should no longer matter. However, this is only a dream that has not yet come true. However, it can be achieved if we understand the advantages of migration, but also its inherent disadvantages. Thus, the following questions become relevant: What are the factors that affect our perception of migration? After all, if we take these factors into account, how should we actually relate to migration?

Numerous studies have shown that migration is indeed a means of mutual development, which disproves the myths that have been circulating so far. Immigrants can breathe new life into society and enrich their host countries through cultural diversity. "Migrants are not only a burden...the labor force, new citizens or simply young people can make a significant contribution to the prosperity of the population of the adoptive country, in many European states often aging. These are some of the benefits that migration brings to destination countries - and I'm sure there are many more." (Böhmer, on goethe.de)

Lately, the international community has been facing unprecedented waves of migration, and the situation of people who are forced to leave their homes due to armed conflicts, poverty, desertification or extreme climatic phenomena must be understood and managed effectively and responsibly. The countries where these people seek shelter out of the desire and need to start a better life have the obligation to provide them with protection according to international law. In the search for viable strategies, it must be taken into account that precisely these people are vulnerable members of society, and their rights can be easily violated.

Migrants can leave their country of origin for economic, educational reasons, but also as a result of the violation of the fundamental rights and freedoms guaranteed to them by international documents. These documents ensure the protection of the rights of all persons with a high degree of vulnerability, including the rights of migrants, refugees, asylum seekers, regardless of their status.

It is necessary to create communication bridges, understand cultural diversity, combat discrimination, ensure access to justice, but above all respect for all fundamental rights and freedoms.

It is shown that people can benefit from emigration, provided they can enjoy the same rights in the host country. When we talk about the rights of migrants, the focus must be on the well-being of the individual, not on the interest of the state. Thus, migration is an advantage when, through it, the individual is motivated to reach his potential.

The fundamental democratic rights and freedoms of foreigners and stateless persons are provided both in the Romanian Constitution and in domestic legislation as well as in international documents.

The constitutional provisions are supplemented with provisions contained in special internal regulations. Government emergency ordinance no. 194/2002 takes over and develops the constitutional framework regulations, enshrining the following rights of foreigners in Romania:

- general protection of persons and assets;
- the right of foreigners who are legally in Romania to move freely and to establish their residence or, as the case may be, their domicile anywhere on the territory of the country;
- the rights of foreigners legally residing in Romania to re-enter the country during the validity of the residence permit;
- the right to benefit from social protection measures for those who have their domicile/residence in Romania;
- the right to request and benefit from the correct registration of personal data in the documents issued by the Authority for Foreigners;
- the right to benefit from training of foreigners included in all levels of education.

The Romanian Constitution also includes provisions for the case of regulatory conflict between domestic law and international treaties regarding human rights. In the situation where there are inconsistencies between the pacts and treaties regarding fundamental human rights and the domestic law, the international regulations have priority, with the exception of the case where the Constitution or the law includes more favorable provisions.

An exception to the national regime applicable to foreigners is that they do not benefit from political rights. Thus, they do not have electoral rights and cannot be elected to public positions and dignities.

We underline the fact that the exception does not apply to persons with dual citizenship, Romanian and foreign, who can hold public offices, civil and military dignities, under the conditions of article 16 par. 3 of the Romanian Constitution. As an exception to this prohibition, art. 16 par. 4 of the Romanian Constitution stipulates that, under the conditions of Romania's accession to the EU, citizens of the Union who meet the requirements of the organic law have the right to elect and be elected in local public administration authorities. Foreigners cannot organize on Romanian territory parties or organizations with a political purpose.

We also mention that foreign citizens have all the civil rights provided by the Constitution and internal laws, such as the right to property (art. 44 paragraph 2 of the Constitution), the right to inheritance (as testamentary heirs), etc.; procedural rights, regulated by art. 1084 of Civil Procedural Code (rights and obligations identical to those of Romanian citizens); but also other rights related to the commercial activity, such as various commercial documents (having the quality of merchants), they can be employed based on a work permit issued by the competent authorities and can conclude legal documents.

According to art. 20 of Law no. 122/2006, refugee status confers the following rights:

a) to stay on the territory of Romania and obtain a residence permit and travel document for crossing the state borders. The beneficiary of a form of protection is assigned a personal numerical code, which is entered in the residence permit and in the travel document for crossing the state borders;

b) to choose his place of residence and to move freely, under the conditions established by law for foreigners;

c) to be employed by natural or legal persons, to exercise unpaid activities, to exercise free professions and to perform legal acts, to perform commercial acts and deeds, including economic activities independently, under the same conditions as Romanian citizens;

d) to transfer his goods that he introduced in Romania to the territory of another country, with a view to resettlement;

e) to benefit from the most favorable treatment provided by law for foreign citizens regarding the acquisition of movable and immovable properties;

f) to benefit from the protection of intellectual property, under the conditions established by law;

g) to benefit from social insurance, social assistance measures and social health insurance, under the conditions provided by law for Romanian citizens;

h) to have access to all forms of education, under the conditions provided by law for Romanian citizens;

i) to benefit from treatment equal to that granted to Romanian citizens in terms of the freedom to practice one's religion and the religious training of one's children;

j) to benefit from the right to protection of personal data and any other details related to his case;

k) to benefit from the right to association with regard to associations with apolitical and non-profit purposes and professional unions, under the conditions provided by law for Romanian citizens;

l) to have free access to the courts and to administrative assistance;

m) to receive, upon request, within the limits of the state's financial availability, under conditions established by Government decision, a non-refundable monthly aid, the amount of which is related to the reference social indicator, for a maximum period of 12 months, if, for objective reasons, he is deprived of the necessary means of subsistence;

n) to participate, upon request, in the integration programs and to be accommodated in the centers of the Romanian Immigration Office, under the conditions established by law;

o) to establish their legal domicile in Romania, according to the legislation on the legal regime of foreigners;

p) to be able to benefit, upon request, from assistance with a view to voluntary repatriation;

q) to have access to the acquisition of a home, under the conditions provided by law for Romanian citizens;

r) to benefit from equal treatment with Romanian citizens in terms of the equivalence of studies or study periods, the recognition of diplomas, attestations and certificates of competence, as well as professional qualifications that give access to regulated professions in Romania, in accordance with the regulations in force.

IV. Conclusions

The constitutional evolution of human rights was characterized by the existence of two large categories of regulations: internal, of each state, and international. In constitutional law, the question of their correlation was raised and two principles were affirmed: the application of conventions relative to human rights must be done taking into account the need to harmonize international cooperation with the principle of state sovereignty; international documents have as the main means for their execution the assumption by the party states of the fundamental obligation provided in their content.

Summarizing, it can be found that dominant in the set of theoretical, legislative and practical concerns regarding human rights is the idea that their effective proclamation and guarantee rests with internal legal regulations, as an expression of the recognition of states' sovereignty and their quality as equal members of the international community. Only from this perspective should the correlation with the international regulations in the matter be understood.

Bibliography

Andreescu, M., 2007, The principle of proportionality in constitutional law, CH. Beck Publishing House, Bucharest;

Andreescu, M. & Puran, A., 2016, Constitutional law. General theory and constitutional institutions, CH. Beck Publishing House, Bucharest;

Deleanu, I, 1998, Institutions and constitutional procedures, Servo-Sat Publishing House, Arad;

Liiceanu, G., 1994, About the limit, Humanitas Publishing House, Bucharest;

Micu, D., 1998, Guaranteeing human rights, All Publishing House, Bucharest;

Muraru, I., 1999, Constitutional protection of freedom of opinion, Lumina Lex Publishing House, Bucharest;

Muraru, I & Tănăsescu, S., 2003, Constitutional law and political institutions, vol. I, All Beck Publishing House, Bucharest;

Rivero, J., 1973, Les Libertés publiques, P.U.F., Paris.

22. MAN, SOCIETY AND CHRISTIANITY IN THE AGE OF POSTMODERNISM

Abstract:

More and more ideological currents are appearing and influencing society which, until recently, had a lasting vein in Christian culture and spirituality. In this context, there is more and more talk of postmodernism.

Postmodernism is the reference term applied to a wide range of developments in the fields of critical theory, philosophy, architecture, art, literature and culture. The various expressions of postmodernism originate from, transcend, or are a reaction to modernism. If modernism sees itself as a culmination of the search for a scientific and rational Enlightenment aesthetic, a rationalized and normative legal ethics and humanism, all of universal value, postmodernism is concerned with how the authority of these ideal entities (called metanarratives) is undermined by the process of fragmentation, consumerism and deconstruction.

In this study we analyze the social, cultural, religious ideological implications of postmodernism

Key words:

Postmodernism/ideologies/man and society

I. Argument

The evolution of humanity from the beginning until now, the history of culture and civilization have been divided into eras according to several criteria, among which we mention: the relationships between man, society and the universe, the relationship between reason and sensitivity, the specifics of knowledge, the sphere of values, the characteristics of creation human, but also the way man understood his relationship with God. There are no unanimous opinions in this periodization of the history of culture and civilization, but most authors identify: ancient culture and civilization, the medieval era, the Gothic, the Renaissance, classicism, the Enlightenment, modernism, and the era in which we seem to be, postmodernism.

Synthesizing and grouping these features, in our opinion we believe that the history of human culture and civilization can be grouped into three large periods:

ancient times,classicism which includes Gothic, Baroque Revival and Enlightenment

modernism and postmodernism (about the latter we will make some brief considerations).

From the perspective of natural and supernatural revelation, of the right faith, together with other authors, such as Mircea Eliade, we believe that the history of humanity can be divided into the pre-Christian era and the Christian era. Currently, there are numerous religions, religious confessions, sects, but which do not have the vocation of universality, including from a rational and value aspect, as Christianity has, they do not express and do not include the Absolute ontological Truth, they do not recognize God, unique in being and triune In Persons who is the One who is, the Way, the Truth and the Life, I do not know and do not recognize the mysteries of the Holy Spirit and the Church, nor the saving role of the Cross of the Lord, nor the holiness of the Mother of God as Mother of God, of the Son of God, Who was made man, out of his unfathomable love he also took human nature, sacrificed himself and rose again for our salvation, so that we too could become sons of God according to grace.

I speak at most of relative truths of existence, of an impersonal divine transcendent, without distinguishing between uncreated and created, as is the case with mystical pantheistic conceptions. What's worse is that, except for the three monotheistic beliefs and the beliefs on which the oriental culture is based, all the others, confessions, sects or even "religions", directly or indirectly deny God, refuse Him, even ridicule Him, so as it happens in the postmodern period and are therefore nonvalue human ways of thinking.

Adherents of this way of thinking and understanding man and society forget some existentially demonstrated truths. Nothing is possible without God, except sin and nonsense, the absurd, the unnatural, all created by man distancing himself from God and by men preferring absolute personal selfishness and the existential limits of this world. Although the cry of the philosopher Nietzsche "God is dead" is the basis of contemporary postmodernism, the truth is quite different. God does not die, only the righteous faith of man. Christianity does not fall, but only we fall from Christianity, as Father Arsenie Boca well said. God has no one to lose, his love for people is boundless, he is not of this world, but it is also true that God does not allow himself to be mocked.

Therefore, there is no, evolutionarily speaking, a continuous progress of culture, civilization and history that configures valuable, rational meanings to existence, to transfigure it, on an upward path towards perfection in God, towards deification through grace to which man is called by our Savior Jesus Christ, and by man the whole Universe. Regress, involution are also present at the individual and social level, being dimensions of history. Passage, change, becoming are characteristics of the created world, whose meaning can be for individual and collective spiritual perfection in Christ, or meaningless, involutive. And this because man was endowed with freedom, reason, will and sensitivity, being able to choose between good and evil. It does not mean that the destiny of mankind is determined solely by the will of man. God and His grace work unceasingly towards the fulfillment of God's revealed will to us. Without God's grace, regardless of whether man is aware of its presence or not, receives it or rejects it, the universe, creation would dissipate, would turn into nothing.

As we will show, unfortunately, contemporary postmodernism is a regressive era in the history of human and world salvation.

II. What is postmodernism?

More and more ideological currents are appearing and influencing society which, until recently, had a lasting vein in Christian culture and spirituality. In this context, there is more and more talk of postmodernism.

Postmodernism is the reference term applied to a wide range of developments in the fields of critical theory, philosophy, architecture, art, literature and culture. The various expressions of postmodernism originate from, transcend, or are a reaction to modernism. If modernism sees itself as a culmination of the search for a scientific and rational Enlightenment aesthetic, a rationalized and normative legal ethics and humanism, all of universal value, postmodernism is concerned with how the authority of these ideal entities (called metanarratives) is undermined by the process of fragmentation, consumerism and deconstruction. Jean-Francois Lyotard[1] described this current as a "distrust of metanarratives"; in his view, postmodernism attacks the idea of universal, monolithic, stable conceptions of man and monolithic existence and instead encourages fractured, fluid and multiple perspectives, promoting value relativism of a scientific, artistic or moral nature. Nothing makes sense, therefore everything is allowed. Existence is individual, concrete, without universals.

Therefore, postmodernism is an ideology, specific to the era we live in or to the present "eon" as Blaga would say, with consequences on the way man understands the world, relates to the world, to values, but also to divinity.

Postmodernism represents a set of intellectual, cultural, artistic, academic or philosophical responses to the condition of man and the created world. One term used is postmodernity, which refers to all the phenomena that succeeded modernity.

To better understand what postmodernism is, what it means to be postmodern, it is good to first characterize modernism and what it means to be modern. The word "modern" has its origin in the Latin "modo", which means "right now". Postmodern therefore literally means "after right now". Modernism is always, historically speaking, in a struggle with what was immediately before it. Modernism ends up fighting itself and thus inevitably becomes postmodernism. Therefore, postmodernism appears as a consequence, respectively as a continuation of modernism, but also as a reality that opposes modernism through some of its own aspects; therefore, continuation of modernism, but also a deconstructivist reaction to modernism. On the road from modernism to postmodernism, the "displacement" replaced the hierarchy of cultural and spiritual values in dissension and continues to proliferate; the geography of the conflict expanded, and the present was devastated by "culture wars", which led to the pressing need to reaffirm the social order of things[2].

Essentially postmodernism is defined by philosophers and sociologists as a trend in the culture of recent decades that has affected a variety of fields of knowledge, including philosophy. Postmodern discussions cover a wide range of socio-philosophical issues related to the external and internal life of the individual, politics, morality, culture, art, etc. The main characteristic of the postmodern situation was a decisive break with traditional society and its cultural stereotypes. Everything is subject to a reflexive review, evaluated not from the point of view of traditional values, but from the point of view of efficiency. Postmodernism is seen as the era of a radical revision of basic attitudes, the rejection of the traditional worldview, the era of breaking with all previous culture.

All representatives of postmodernism are united by a style of thinking, in which preference is not given to the constancy of knowledge, but to its instability; abstract results of knowledge are not valued, but concrete results of experience; it is stated that reality itself, i.e. the "thing in itself" of which Kant speaks is inaccessible to our knowledge. Contrary to the Kantian conception, even phenomenal reality cannot be known, it cannot be said what reality is. The focus of postmodernist ideology is not on the objectivity of truth, but on its relativity. Therefore, no one can claim to know what the truth is, and moreover, neither a person nor God is the Truth. Every understanding is a human interpretation, which is never definitive. In addition, it is significantly influenced by facts such as social class, ethnicity, race, tribe, etc. belonging to the individual.

A characteristic feature of postmodernism is negativism, "the apotheosis of groundlessness"[3] (L. Shestov). Everything that before postmodernism was considered established, reliable and certain: man, mind, philosophy, culture, science, progress - everything was declared unstable and undefined, everything turned into words, reasonings and texts that can be interpreted, understood and 'deconstructed' but untenable in human knowledge, existence and activity.

However, some philosophers also identify positive aspects of postmodernism. The concern for the philosophical understanding of the problem of language, in its appeal to the humanitarian roots of philosophy: literary discourse, narrative, dialogue, etc., is appreciated as positive. His priority attitude towards the issue of conscience is also considered positive. In this sense, postmodernism is consistent with the development of the entire philosophy of the modern world, which takes into account the problems of cognitive science (including cognitive psychology). However, the positive aspects of postmodernism should be understood in their worldliness, in the essential characteristics of this ideology that refuses the Absolute, the universal, objectivity and above all any reference to God. The positive elements of this way of being and existing are marked by the boundary that closes without opening to meaning and the authentic.

For a better understanding of what postmodernism represents, especially as an ideology, we will mention some historical aspects:

Because postmodernism has been the subject of partisan debates, there are as many definitions of the current as there are theorists. The difficulty of being able to establish its object is reinforced by an ethos of anti-label. Paradoxically, even if someone formulated a definition for it, a postmodern philosopher would want to deconstruct that too. Form relativism: everything is possible, there is no affirmation, only negation, there are no certainties, neither in existence nor in knowledge.

The chronology of postmodernism as an ideology and later as a way of life, begins in 1920 with the spread of the Dada movement, which proposed collage and emphasized the form, the edge, as the most important, more important than the work itself. Form was not abstracted from content, but form can determine any content. It is the transition from form in relation to a content, to formalization, without value meaning, sufficient in itself.

This idea was later taken up and developed by the philosopher Jacques Derrida[4]. Another movement that had a great impact on postmodernism was existentialism, which believes that there are no universal values, but the individual discourse of each man as the source of morality and understanding. However, it was only at the end of the Second World War that postmodern attitudes began to appear. Postmodernism begins to characterize a lifestyle, it is not only an ideology, but is taking shape as an era in the history of humanity.

Theorists and proponents of postmodernism quickly developed a vocabulary of anti-Enlightenment rhetoric, argued that rationality was never as certain as the rationalists claimed, and that knowledge itself was tied to place, time, social position, or other factors with with the help of which an individual constructs the points of view necessary for knowledge and life.

Rather than basing your knowledge on particular cases or texts, the basis of knowledge was seen as generated by the free play of discourse, an idea rooted in Wittgenstein's theory of language games[5]. This emphasis on the permissiveness of free play in the larger context of conversation and discourse leads postmodernism to adopt irony, paradox, textual manipulation, references or tropes.

Armed with this process of questioning the social bases of this assertion, postmodern philosophers began to attack the unity of modernism and that unity rooted in the Enlightenment.

Perhaps the most striking example of this skepticism is found in the works of the French cultural theorist, Jean Bauddrillard. In his essay, Simulations and Simulacra, he recognized that social reality does not exist in the conventional sense, but that it has been replaced by an endless process of producing simulacra[6]. Mass media cultural productions without any value significance, constantly generate processes of re-appropriation and re-contextualization of some cultural symbols or images, fundamentally shifting our experience from "reality" to a purely subjective "hyper-reality" , whose existence is built in the virtual space specific to artificial intelligence.

Postmodernism is reluctant to face the claims of some to hold the secrets of truth, ethics, or beauty that are rooted in anything other than individual perception or group construction. Truth can be understood if all connections are perpetually deferred, never being able to reach a point of knowledge that could be called truth. Therefore there are no truths demonstrated by science.

The concept of postmodernism is used in a very broad sense, denoting almost all currents of thought from the end of the 20th century and the current beginning of the century, but also the social and philosophical realities of this period. Marxist critics polemically believe that postmodernism is a symptom of "late capitalism" and the decline of institutions and then of the nation state. Other thinkers state that postmodernity is the natural reaction to media transmissions in society, of contemporary technologies that generate technological civilization, based on artificial intelligence and the play of forms without the need for a value universe or culture in the contemporary sense. In the vision of these philosophers, the fundamental questions of knowledge, including those concerning the meaning of this world, have no point.

The ability of knowledge to be endlessly copied stops attempts to constrain interpretation or establish its originality through simple means such as the production of a work.

We dwell in a few lines on the expression of postmodernism in philosophical thought.

Some personalities of the philosophy of the 20th century and the beginning of this century are considered as postmodern, because they claim that mathematics and natural sciences are not objective. Among them are two philosophers of science, Thomas Samuel Kuhn. And David Bohm The last expression of the mixture of philosophy and mathematics is "cognitive mathematics", which wants to demonstrate that, like all human sciences, mathematics is totally subjective, formal. The philosopher Wittgenstein I mentioned, through his authoritative, paradoxical, disordered, contradictory discourse, is a pioneer of philosophical postmodernism[7].

Postmodernism represents the philosophy of contemporary Western society. We mention that the representatives of postmodernism nowadays, such as: G. Pracasch, J. Latuz, J. Walerstain, B. de Souse Santus, D.R. Griffin, H. Smith, P. Rosneau, J. Derrida, J.F. Lyotard, J. Culler, M. Poster, G. Wattimo, R. Robertson et al. I am talking about the destruction of the social-cultural matrix of the old type of consciousness, where science was represented as the core and dominant force in society.

Postmodernists deny the existence of general and universal truths in science, noting only the local, singular, particular ones. Postmodernists, mentions L.A. Mikeşina avoids any form of monism and universalization, critically treats the positivist (logical) representations, the ideals and modes of classical science, of the modern era, in general.

The mentioned philosophers proclaim the multiplicity and diversity, the variety and competition of paradigms, the coexistence of heterogeneous elements, the recognition and stimulation of a variety of contemporary life projects, social interactions, philosophical teachings and scientific conceptions. This implies the re-evaluation of fundamentalism, the recognition of the multidimensional aspect of reality and a multitude of types of relations of the same essence, the recognition of the inevitable multiplicity of descriptions and points of view, the relations of complementarity and interaction between them. These ideas, originally coming from the sphere of art (literature, architecture, etc.), in the current stage, have a general-cultural character and are transformed into principles of intellectual, creative activity.

As an important consequence of postmodernist ideas, it is also considered necessary to shake the binary thinking of the type "either / or", good or bad, male and female and replace it with attitudes of thinking, when not two, but three or several variants, all justified. Instead of opposition, they propose systemicity, harmonization, complementarity, simultaneity, etc.

Artificial intelligence is a strong point of post modernist philosophy. M. Poster states that scientists project intelligent subjectivity onto the computer, and the computer becomes the criterion by which intelligence is defined. He, like Lyotard, talks about the transformation of information into a commodity, sees in postmodern society the expansion of elements of social control, and in new technologies he sees a great potential for domination. Radio, television and print media are considered by him as elements of the conception of the world. The real world is understood in the sense that our understanding of reality is composed of multiple images, interpretations and reconstructions, put into circulation by the means of communication, in competition with each other, and without any "central" coordination. This emancipation does not consist in the perfect knowledge of someone who knows how things are in reality, but in freedom within plurality, in the erosion of the very principle of reality.

The beginning of postmodernity could be represented by the emergence of "technologies of the self", as Michel Foucault called them, which "allow individuals to carry out, alone or with the help of others, a certain number of operations on their own body and soul, on their thoughts, behaviors, on their way of being; to transform himself in such a way as to reach a certain state of happiness, purity, wisdom, perfection or immortality".

As predecessors of postmodernism can be considered F. Nietzsche, S. Freud, M. Heidegger, as well as the neopositivists[8]. The postmodernist ideology is also present in architecture, art, linguistics.

But there are other facets of postmodernity that denote tolerance, egalitarianism, creativity, autonomy, the desperate search for personal happiness, obviously, absolute subjectivity, which can make us believe that all is not lost. In fact, the most complicated thing is to analyze the new world by reference to the old values[9].

III. Postmodern society. Postmodern man

We believe that postmodern society can be characterized by five ideologies and at the same time ontological realities:

systems convergence

zero economic growth

the ideology and practice of globalization

gender ideology

the ideology of the superman.

the ideology of artificial intelligence

Of course, they are not the only aspects. For example, another characteristic of postmodern society is the dominance of technologies over man and humanist values, including Christian ones.

In the following we will make a brief presentation of some realities of contemporary society in the era of postmodernism. The problems of contemporary state and social integration and globalization processes bring into question the viability of the theory of system convergence and zero economic growth elaborated in the 70s of the last century.

The term "convergence" itself comes from the Latin word "approach". Convergence theory suggests that, under modern conditions, the two antagonistic social systems of capitalism and socialism are in the process of convergence, being synthesized into a kind of "mixed society". It combines the positive characteristics of each of the systems.

The initial provisions of the theory of convergence were borrowed from the field of biological science, which proves that in the process of evolutionary interaction, similar anatomical features begin to possess groups of living organisms that are far from each other in origin, but forced to live together in the same environment.

The fathers of convergence theory are considered P. Sorokin, J. Golbraith, U. Ros-tou (USA), J. Fourastier and F. Perru (France), K. Tinbergen (Netherlands), X. Shelsky and O. Flecht-heim (Germany). These and other scientists of the era of the acute economic confrontation between capitalism and socialism proved that the capitalist system is historically irreversible and can continue to exist through transformations and reforms that are borrowed from socialist methods in the scientific management of the economy and society, in state planning of all fields of activity.

Convergence theory combines a wide range of ideas from the fields of sociology, economics and politics. It is based on reformist and social-democratic aspirations, aimed at improving state monopoly processes and attempts at assimilation in the form of reforms expressed by a market economy, political pluralism and the liberalization of the social system.

Starting from theoretically correct principles, the "convergence of systems" could have become beneficial in an honest world, animated by humanistic principles, of non-belligerent coexistence, presuming a certain balance between two entities, which coexisted bipolar, before 1989 , but assuming the assumption and implementation of a sustained policy of cohesion and mutual adjustment.

This, since, in the conditions of an undisguised euphoria, after the fall of the Berlin Wall, and despite a political pessimism or some nostalgic thoughts, both the East and the European left wanted a regenerating ideological infusion.

In reality, the process was completed by a perversion of the two entities, producing a confusion of the original values, a break in the balance between the initial project and the final one, which transformed convergence into emergence, balance into subordination. In this way, the "convergence of systems" became a channel of mutual contamination, with dangerous viruses, giving rise to a pandemic disease, for which we can hardly find the antidote.

We have in mind the abandonment of humanist culture in favor of a technocratic pseudo-culture or even increasingly extensive forms of sub-culture, the generalization of consumerism and ignoring or even repudiating spiritual values. Man is no longer a person, but an individual subordinate to the state, which sometimes provides him with bread and the political and social circus he needs. We also observe: the dominance of the great economic monopolies and the widening of the gaps between the rich and the poor, the alarming decrease in the quality of life and the serious damage to the natural environment, the abandonment of national identity expressed in national history, faith and culture, the phenomenon of population migration in search of a better job in terms of income that can be achieved, the breakdown of traditional families and the disregard of the traditions and values of the Christian family, the emergence of very dangerous and difficult forms of cross-border criminality to stop, such as corruption, money laundering, human and drug trafficking, various forms of violence. The list could go on. In essence, we are witnessing on the one hand the destruction of traditional humanist values and national identity, and on the other hand an abstract uniformity based on the domination of those who hold power and control over the world. Everything becomes appearance, demagoguery and nonsense.

It can be said that, in Romania, capitalism has taken over everything that was bad in socialism, becoming a "capitalism of balance", and through mutual miscegenation, a "mixtum compositum" has resulted so that the Romanians no longer enjoy a society post-industrial, as they were promised, but a programmed destruction of the economy and industry, under the conditions of a wild, ruthless, harmful capitalism in the truest sense of the word.

The theory of convergence of systems, especially with regard to governance models based on domination and spiritual, cultural uniformity and the promotion of abstract humanism that does not have man as a free person at its center, today finds its materialization in the supranational and suprastate organization, the European Union.

In the sphere of religion, ecumenism is an expression of the attempt to apply this theory. The ecumenical movement can be considered as having a positive role only in terms of dialogue between confessions and Christian churches, as a possibility for the right Orthodox faith to make its teachings and values known, to support them. Ecumenism cannot be accepted as an attempt by the Catholic church to subordinate the Orthodox believers to the primacy of a single bishop, the Pope, the bishop of Rome, nor as a renunciation or modification of Orthodox traditions and teaching of faith. Father academic professor dr. Dumitru Stăniloae emphasized these aspects very well: "We must first of all be concerned with strengthening our right faith and living according to it. Through our participation in the ecumenical movement we must aim primarily to make known our true faith in ways accessible to the understanding of those who belong to other Christian formations. It seems to me that the ecumenical movement has increased bureaucracy and the vested interests of its officials. It is not a real strength of faith and unity in it... But I do not know if the relativism that dominates it does not extend as a weakening of faith throughout the Christian world. "

Zero economic growth

In the era of the 70s and 80s, the "ZEG Theory" (Zero Economic Growth) was defined as a philosophical-economic theory of a limiting neo-Malthusian essence, according to which the world's population, the demand for food products and pollution would increase in a progressive way, threatening, while the globe's resources would be in limited quantities, the world thus rapidly moving towards self-destruction, total collapse.

This theory was supported by the Club of Rome, created in 1968, at the initiative of the Italian economist dr. Aurelio Peccei, who gathered around him 70 futurologists, from 25 countries, to study solutions to a crisis that was seen on the horizon since then.

The Club of Rome asked American professor Jay Forrester to mathematically model economic growth trends on a global scale for the next seven decades. Thus was born the first report of the Club of Rome, a study document coordinated by Donella and Dennis Meadows, Jorgen Randers and W. Behrens of the Massachusetts Institute of Technology. These specialists are asked to "examine the complex of problems that concern people everywhere; poverty in the midst of plenty, environmental degradation, loss of trust in institutions, uncontrolled expansion of robotization, job insecurity, alienation of youth, removal of traditional values, inflation and other monetary and economic crises".

Calling on a methodology established by this collective, a model was analyzed with the help of electronic computers that presented the evolution of the following indicators: population, industrial production, agricultural production, pollution of natural resources, in the period 1950-2030.

The basis were the ideas issued by Jay Forrester in his book "Industrial Dynamics", in which attention was drawn to the fact that the population grew from 1.6 billion in 1900 to 3.5 billion in 1970, but that it will double exponentially , in a smaller number of years, which will affect the entire world system, while the increase in the accumulation of industrial capital will know limits.

Since those years, Sicco Mansholt declared: "I made a very simple calculation: if we wanted the entire population of the globe to enjoy a standard of living comparable to that we have in the West, given the global global income, do you know what figure it should be reduced to? To a billion individuals".

The same calculations showed that an exponential increase in population and industrial development would dramatically reduce natural resources and, together with increased pollution, cause the growth curve of agricultural and industrial production to decline. The result can only be disaster, the closer we get to the material limits of the planet, which will be reached in the 21st century. In conclusion, the authors proposed the concept of "replacement family", with at most two children.

The same mathematical model led Chinese leaders to similar conclusions, reducing the number of children a family could have, but developing an economy at phenomenal rates, also appealing to the principle of "convergence of systems", a successful experiment, it seems, but with harmful repercussions on energy reserves, pollution and the economic balance of the planet.

Everyone's attitude towards the limits of growth is a matter of culture, free will, reason, but above all, being in the right Orthodox faith. There is no force or law of nature that pushes humanity towards free trade, irrational exploitation of the environment, depletion of resources and ultimately a war of all against all (Hobbes) for control of the last remnants.

Perhaps we should once again read the original message of this grim but realistic theoretical model: "In the last hundred years life on earth has been dominated by growth. Growth in population, production, income, capital, garbage and pollution . This growth will stop, but the question is by what means? Voluntarily, through the care of the governments and the goodwill of the people, or through a natural process which means collapse, decline and ultimately disaster?"

A very important amendment is necessary to this conclusion. The increase in the population of the planet is not and will not be a cause of decline for humanity. On the contrary, the multiplication of people is a command of God. "And God blessed them, saying: Increase and multiply and fill the earth and subdue it; and rule over the fish of the sea, over the birds of the sky, over all the animals, over all the living things that move on the earth and over all the earth!" (Genesis 1,28). Every man conceived and born is created by God with an immortal soul and called to a great destiny, to multiply the talents and gifts he received from God, according to his commands, to contribute to the transfiguration and spiritualization of nature, of the whole In a broader sense, it is not growth itself and industrial, scientific, economic, social and cultural progress, not existential growth, because God himself commands people to multiply the gifts they receive, but the ways and especially the goal of progress oriented towards distancing oneself from God, people and nature, towards material accumulation and consumption and the distorted use of soul powers.

We are talking about the fundamental change in our way of life. But this cannot happen without the right Orthodox faith and changing economic and governance models. The goal of economic and social development should not be unlimited growth and accumulation, but the preservation of harmony, the balance of the world created by God for man, the realization of man as a free, spiritual person created in the image and likeness of God, the fulfillment of the great values of Orthodox virtues and of wisdom, of which in the first place should be the humility and faith of the rulers towards God, merciful love, brotherhood and solidarity, discernment and right calculation, the spirit of individual and social justice in managing the resources entrusted to man by God. The problem is that no one wants temperance and austerity, no one wants to "return and live," as the Savior asked.

People riot and take to the streets because they want to consume more, not less. "If they were given the choice between a new cutlery set and the survival of humanity, I have a feeling that the vast majority would choose the cutlery set" (George Monibot - The Bottom of the Barrel, published in the "Guardian" December 2003).

Those who wrote "Limits" posed, perhaps for the first time, the problem of the global testament that we leave to posterity. Today we can no longer talk about what we were leaving and for whom. The man-made law of growth, accumulation and consumption in unlimited proportions will lead mankind to disaster. But God's will and law is different, man and the world through the work of holy grace must grow spiritually, transfigure themselves and the entire creation. Divine providence is our hope. But man has been endowed with freedom, and therefore he will have to choose as soon as possible between the inevitable disaster for man and mankind of the law of irrational and unlimited growth, accumulation and consumption, or receive the saving hand of God, return to the purpose for which man and existence were created, the fulfillment of God's will and commandments.

Ideology and practice of globalization

What does the contemporary globalization process mean and how useful or harmful is it for Romania and Romanians to participate in this process with an integrative purpose whose main exponent in Europe is the European Union? These are topical questions that can be answered with historical and contemporary realities.

History shows that social and state realities such as globalization and integration have existed since the state organization of society. All the empires of the world from antiquity to the present are the expression of the imposition of the dominance of a powerful state on other states or forms of social organization and their integration into the political, legal, economic or cultural and religious order of the state that thus constitutes its empire. The empires of the world, as many as there have been in history, are forms of globalization and integration.

Contemporary political ideas and theories materialized in political actions with the aim of achieving social and state universalism, in essence do not differ from the universalism of empires of another time. There is, however, one fundamental difference: the empires of the world that have existed in past historical epochs were, without exception, created by acts of armed conquest, by force. Globalization and contemporary social and state integration are much more subtle social realities, built on the principles of democracy, the rule of law in order to achieve a declared noble goal, social and economic progress, collaboration, assistance, the affirmation and guarantee of human rights.

There are also forms of spiritual, religious globalization present in contemporary postmodernism. The best example is the universalism imposed by Catholicism. The proclaimed principle is that of compelling Christians to come under the authority of the Pope. Many times in history Catholicism was imposed on peoples by force, not by persuasion, which had tragic consequences for many. This form of spiritual globalization is contrary and alien to the true Orthodox faith.

Contemporary globalization is no longer based on armed force (at least not directly), but on the free adherence of states and societies to a supra-state institutional, political and legal system.

The empires of old achieved the integration of the conquered states in the political, economic, legal order of the conquering state. The social and political status of those integrated into the empire was always inferior to the state and society of the conquering state. In contrast, the contemporary forms of globalization and integration are not related, at least declaratively and procedurally, to the political and social order of a dominant state, but to organizational structures with a supranational political and legal character, without them having their own social basis, as the states have.

The methods and procedures of contemporary state and social integration, specific to postmodern society, are different from the past and, as I said, much more subtle, but all of them are forms of domination of the economically, militarily and politically powerful over the integrated. As examples, we refer to the economic, social but also political integration carried out by large companies and economic trusts, to the monopolization of production and trade, to IT integration, to the emphasis placed in development programs on consumerism, on having and not on being, utilitarianism and moral pragmatism with the exclusion of the values of Christianity and especially the right Orthodox faith, the exclusive belief in the power of capital and technologies, the construction of a rationalized and impersonal humanism, the abolition of the national, cultural, religious particularities of those who freely adhere to globalization and the examples could continue.

With all these differences, we affirm that the historical empires of the world, as well as the modern forms of globalization and integration, have the same essence and existential purpose: the dominance of the politically, economically and socially powerful over integrated states and societies.

The European Union, a supranational organization, has all the characteristics that I have briefly listed. It is obvious that the member states are not equal politically, economically and socially. The states, the powerful political and economic forces within this organization are dominant, they create the political, economic and legal order that they impose on the other states under the guise of interstate equality, collaboration and assistance.

The political, economic and legal order of the European Union is not created by this organization, as it apparently, declaratively and theoretically appears, but by the states, the political and economic forces that dominate. The political and social pragmatism is clear. Through this apparent equality and aid provided, the states that dominate this organization have easy access to cheap labor, the natural resources of the dominated states, and above all, they control the entire state, economic and social activity of the dominated.

The national sovereignty attributes of the dominated states are restricted, and their own existential features: economic, state, political, cultural, faith are affected by the abstract state order created and imposed by those who dominate the European Union. The European Union is not a charity organization but a supranational institutional instrument of domination.

Globalization is a complex system or phenomenon, sometimes ambivalent, even contradictory, which has been viewed and analyzed differently by those who have assumed this risk or this responsibility. Beyond these analyses, globalization remains a real, living fact that we must face, regardless of our will or choice. It is believed that the greatest danger that globalization can involve is the dehumanization of some of those whom its wave simply swallows. Conquered by the market, doped by television, sports or the Internet, the postmodern globalized world, against the background of a general crisis of the meanings of life, a global cultural and educational disaster, a worrying but sure symptom of the barbarization of the society of the future.

The traditional culture of societies is disappearing or turning into spectacle and commodification. Humanist culture is increasingly eliminated by the invading techno-science and transformed into a pseudo-science. The world or globalized man, the man centered only economically, risks becoming the atomized man who lives only for production and consumption, emptied of culture, faith, politics, meaning, consciousness, religion and any transcendence.

Globalization in all its variants characterizes society in the era of postmodernism. Is this the last stage in the evolution of humanity? What does the European Union as a supranational organization represent for Romania and for Romanians?

Many Romanians forget that joining the European Union in 2007 is not the same as integration into the Union. Joining an organization, of any kind, does not necessarily mean integrating into that organization.

However, despite all the unfavorable aspects for Romania, the accession to the European Union was achieved. The Romanian state has given up important attributes of its sovereignty. We consider the most important to be political, economic and legislative independence. The legislation of the European Union is mandatory for Romania and the most important normative acts to be adopted by the Parliament must be approved in advance by the institutions of the European Union. Integration was also achieved by the fact that values of our culture and civilization were abandoned and European social standards foreign to our Romanian life appeared in their place.

The Romanian economy and agriculture, as much as is left, is dominated by the multinational trusts that also control the European Union.

The right Orthodox faith of the Romanian people, its values are blamed by the European Union and attempts are being made to integrate the Romanian society - in part it was succeeded through a rationalized and Protestant or atheistic humanism, which disregards man as a person and of course the right Orthodox faith of apostolic origin of the people Romanian. Many so-called politicians of the moment, who exercise the government, declare themselves atheists, behave like infidels and persecute the Orthodox Church and the Orthodox cult through unconstitutional prohibitions and restrictions, which are also sacrileges, acts of serious damage to the dignity of the Romanian people, who are overwhelmingly Orthodox .

Integration has not been achieved and will not be achieved regarding our status in the European Union. In reality we are not and will not be considered equal to the great European powers. We are and will be a second-rate country, providing cheap labor, important raw materials, but also cheap agricultural land that can be easily acquired by foreigners. Social and economic disparities are and will remain significant.

Romania is and will remain one of the poorest countries in the European Union, which is waiting and will continue to wait for the mercy of the masters from Brussels. The standard of living, the guarantee of a dignified life, health in Romania will never be at the level of the European Union countries. In fact, the political and economic forces that control the European Union do not want the integration of Romania and under these aspects as declaratively claimed.

What is worse, politicians and the population of European countries disregard and marginalize Romanians. In no case are Romanians considered equal to the citizens of these countries, but at most tolerated and treated as such. It is true that this reality is also the cause of the behavior of some of the Romanians in other countries of the European Union, the lifestyle far below the standards of Western civilization and, what is more serious, an increased rate of criminality caused by the Romanians.

According to the most recent Eurobarometer for Romania, published at the beginning of March last year, the free movement of citizens, goods and services within the Union European Union is considered by a significant part of Romanians to be the greatest achievement of the Union.

The future of the European Union is viewed optimistically by two thirds of the population, well above the European average. Also, over 50% of Romanians believe that the European Union is heading in a good direction, 20 percent above the European average!!! Romanians' optimism regarding the relationship with the European Union, insofar as the statistical data reflect reality, is not justified upon a closer analysis of the situation in Romania.

The financial and material aid of the European Union towards Romania is insignificant, almost an illusion in relation to the taxes and annual financial contributions of Romania to the budget of the European Union. Thus, the annual financial contribution of Romania is almost six times higher than the funds allocated by the European Union for Romania. Added to this is the burdensome bureaucracy imposed by European legislation for accessing European funds.

The priority areas in which the investments from the European Union budget allocated to Romania should increase are considered by Romanians to be employment, education, culture and mass media, agriculture and rural development. It is incomprehensible why health, infrastructure, climate change or environmental protection and Justice are not among the priorities, as things are at the level of the European Union.

In the 14 years since accession, Romania's social and economic situation has worsened. The poverty in which the majority of the population struggles has intensified. The average annual income per inhabitant does not exceed 400 euros in Romania. Social disparities have grown alarmingly.

There is no real economic growth and therefore jobs are few and unemployment is relatively high. The migration of a large number of Romanians to the countries of the European Union, approximately 5 million, had disastrous consequences for many of the families remaining in the country and especially for the children.

Romanian education suffers severely due to the so-called repeated reforms and the application of European standards foreign to national traditions and values. Statistics show that in Romania there are the most intellectual illiterates in the countries of the European Union, i.e. people who know how to read and write, but do not understand the meaning and significance of words.

The health system is disastrous, in a continuous involution due to the lack of interest of the governors, the non-allocation of the necessary funds, including from the European Union, and the wrong and harmful political and legislative measures applied. Professionally trained Romanian doctors and health personnel are forced to emigrate to European Union countries, where they can generally work and are recognized for their true professional value.

Moreover, life expectancy in Romania is the lowest among the countries of the European Union.

The judiciary is troubled by the multiple so-called reforms, but also by the bad legislation, appropriate to the European legislation that it has to apply. The Control and Verification Mechanism (MCV) imposed on Romania for justice and internal affairs, a true institutional system of domination and violation of the independence of the judiciary, did not have beneficial consequences for the judiciary in Romania, on the contrary, it did not lead to guaranteeing the independence of judges, but to the establishment of a system of excessive administrative control of their activity, accompanied by burdensome rules regarding the disciplinary liability of magistrates.

Legal postmodernism can be characterized by formalism and positivism, but also by the dominance of supranational systems and organizations and supranational law over the domestic legal order. This reality leads to the drastic limitation of national sovereignty, the supremacy of the Constitution and the entire domestic legal order. The Court of Justice of the European Union has shown unequivocally in several recent decisions that the legal order of the European Union is superior and applies as a priority to the internal legal order, including the Constitution.

European Union legislation is mandatory for Romania, a fact that has not happened in our history. The legislation of the empires that dominated the Romanian countries was never imposed on their territory. The more important normative acts to be adopted by the Parliament must now first be approved by the bodies of the European Union. Romania's political independence is limited because Romania's internal and external policy is carried out in relation to the political decisions of this supranational organization.

Here are some historic moments of our freedom. Through the Constitution of 1864, ruler Ioan Cuza conquered Romania's legislative freedom from the neighboring empires. In 1877 Romania became an independent and sovereign state from a political point of view, and in 1918 a unitary national and free state.

What the European empires and powers of those times failed to do throughout the millennial history of the people, neither by force of arms nor by political force, i.e. to abolish the right Orthodox faith and the freedom of the Romanian people, has now succeeded, not by force but by the freely assumed act of accession of the Romanian state to the European Union, an act that restricted national sovereignty, political and legislative freedom until its abolition.

Gender ideology

It became popular in the Western academic space in the 90s. It is a specific cultural model of contemporary postmodernism whose ideology asserts that anything is possible for man and his thinking, especially in a destructive sense, against the traditional values of humanity and contrary to the right faith. It's something not just new and trendy, it's something extremely radical.

The gender ideology, in reality, is a theory completely lacking in scientific basis and is disavowed not only by the Orthodox Church but also by numerous scientists, culture, philosophers and theologians.

This postmodernist theory argues that a distinction should be made between two concepts: a person's "biological sex" and their "gender". In other words, if a child is born with male sex organs, it does not necessarily mean that he is a boy, but can be gender-wise a boy, but gender-wise a girl. Gender ideology states that biological sex is a natural given, but gender must be chosen by each person according to their preferences and does not necessarily correspond to biological sex. So biological sex doesn't matter anymore. Everyone, since childhood, can declare for themselves the gender, and this declaration must be recognized by the state institutions, by society and produce legal consequences.

Theory is an aberration, a monstrosity of mind against nature. Goya's paintings are current and express the truth: "The sleep of reason gives birth to monsters." Unfortunately, the theory is supported even by church leaders, but also in the political environment, being affirmed by the so-called European ideologues and promoted by the Parliament of the European Union.

The Vatican has supported this ideology in recent years. In 2019 he published a 30-page paper on "gender ideology". It consists mostly of quotes from Pope Francis. "This ideology leads to educational programs and normative acts that promote a personal identity and emotional intimacy radically separate from the biological difference between male and female. Consequently, human identity becomes the individual's choice, which can also change over time."

In Romania, gender ideology has proliferated among some politicians, it was imposed in the Parliament as a consequence of our country's accession to some international conventions that support it. In 2016, the ratification of the Istanbul Convention on Combating Violence against Women accepted the difference between the concept of biological sex and gender. By ratifying this Convention, which according to the Constitution is part of the domestic normative system, it is admitted that a person's gender is no longer a biological fact (as it was defined in the Rome Statute where the term gender was used in its natural sense of biological sex), but it is a social construct, he meaning "the socially constructed behavioral roles, activities and attributes that a given society considers appropriate for women and men" (according to art. 3 letter c of the Istanbul Convention).

The social consequences of this theory are absurd, but also dramatic, as happened in Western Europe and the United States of America. For example, in the U.S. there have been cases of boys, born with male sexual organs and who, by simply declaring that they consider themselves to be of the female gender, received, under the Obama administration, the right to participate in female sports competitions. The Trump administration banned this theory, but it has returned under the new US administration.

As a result of social pressures and the opinions stated and publicly argued by the representatives of the Romanian Orthodox Church, renowned scientists and non-governmental organizations, the legislative proposal was formulated which prohibits gender studies in educational institutions or in any activity. The legislative initiative was adopted by the Romanian Parliament on June 16, 2020. The draft law proposed the following regulation: In all educational institutions and spaces intended for education, activities aimed at spreading the theory or opinion of gender identity, understood as the theory or opinion that gender it is a different concept from biological sex and that the two are not always the same." The project to amend the National Education Law, in the sense of the above, was voted by the Senate, the decision-making chamber, with 81 votes "for", 22 "against" and 27 abstentions. However, postmodernist ideology unfortunately triumphed through the intervention of President Klaus Iohannis at the Constitutional Court, i.e. at the very institution which, according to the Constitution, is the guarantor of the Fundamental Law, therefore also of the millennial traditions and values of the Romanian people, of the values of the right faith orthodox. The Constitutional Court admitted the referral made by President Klaus Iohannis to the law for the amendment of Article 7 of the National Education Law 1/2011, which prohibited the reference to gender identity in educational institutions. The law I referred to was declared unconstitutional. In essence, the Constitutional Court assessed that this draft law violates the provisions of art. 29 of the Constitution regarding freedom of conscience.

In our opinion, the solution of our constitutional court, the arguments invoked are clearly contrary to the provisions of art. 1 paragraph 3 and even of art. 29 and 30, regarding freedom of conscience and freedom of expression in the Constitution. In another study we will elaborate our arguments.

A derivative aspect of gender ideology, in postmodernism, is the acceptance, including legal, of marriages between people of the same sex, including their right to family, with the consequence of the possibility of adoptions.

The Romanian state and civil society in our country are faced with an important problem, namely the refusal to recognize marriages between homosexuals concluded in other countries, the refusal to consider that these couples form a family in the sense regulated by Romanian legislation and to grant rights to partners to such couples identical to those recognized by members of traditional families.

Unfortunately, there are decisions of the Court of Justice of the European Union (CJEU) and even of the Constitutional Court of Romania (CCR), which oblige the Romanian authorities to recognize in our country the marriages between homosexuals concluded abroad, to accept that they form a family and have the rights that the law gives to traditional families based on marriage between a man and a woman.

Together with renowned theologians, representatives of the Romanian Orthodox Church, Non-Governmental Organizations we support the following: Marriage, the act of freely consented union between a man and a woman through which a family is founded, is not a simple social fact or a legal creation, as came to be considered in the West by Protestants, atheists and atheist rulers.

For the true Orthodox faith, the wedding is a Sacrament of the Holy Spirit. By performing the Sacrament of the wedding, the priest notes not the performance of some impersonal social fact, but the direct work of Christ on the man and woman who unite through love, or the personal meeting of those who receive this Sacrament with Christ. The actual performer of the Sacrament of Marriage and the other Sacraments is Christ Himself invisibly.

This is the essential and radical difference between marriage and the traditional Orthodox family and on the other hand any other form of civil partnership between homosexuals or heterosexuals conceived as exclusively legal forms by atheists and atheist rulers who disregard and persecute the true Orthodox faith. That is why there can be no compatibility between marriage and the traditional Romanian Orthodox family and civil partnerships, nor can they be recognized as forming a family. In order to have ontological legitimacy, legal and moral norms cannot and must not be contrary to orthodoxy's dogma and truths of faith.

It is a serious mistake of the rulers of our days at all levels and from all structures to consider that the legal can have autonomy and be separated from the meanings and reasons of existence in general, of human existence in particular from the orthodox truths of belief revealed to us by God and contained in the Holy Gospel, dogmas of the Church, Holy Tradition and the writings of the Holy Fathers. It is erroneous to believe that state power exercised abusively by atheist rulers can create a social reality contrary to nature. Unfortunately the rulers and atheists of our day are deeply anchored in this error and what is even worse is that they want to impose the existential unnaturalness, the nothingness of meaninglessness on everyone.

"The Orthodox Church considers that salvation is not completed in the death of Christ on the cross, as the legal equivalent of the offense brought by mankind to God, but in the union of the crucified and risen Christ with the people who believe in him, so that they too can die sin and rise again. Consistent with this, it gives the Mysteries a place of great importance in the economy of salvation as means by which this union of people with Christ is accomplished... At the basis of the conception of the Mysteries of the Orthodox Church is the trust in the power of the work of the divine Spirit of Christ through one man on another man, through the mediation of the body and the matter between them, in the ambience of the Church, as the mystical body of Christ. It is the trust that the divine Spirit can work through the mediation of the human spirit on cosmic matter in general and on other people "[10].

Father academician Dr. Dumitru Stăniloae shows that: "The Sacrament of Marriage is a holy act, of divine origin, in which, through the priest, the grace of the Holy Spirit is shared with a man and a woman freely united in marriage, which sanctifies and elevates the natural bond of marriage to the dignity of representing the spiritual union between Christ and the Church "[11].

The sacrament of marriage and family was instituted by God Himself in the Garden of Eden when God blessed Adam and Eve saying, "Be fruitful and multiply, fill the earth and subdue it" (Genesis 1:28). From that moment the two (the man and the woman) became one body, being together in good times but also in bad, in joys but also in troubles, in prayer, but also in moments of wandering and weakening of faith, helping each other for strengthening it.

The family is not a civil partnership between heterosexuals or homosexuals. It is not and cannot be a simple social relationship that can become a legal relationship. It is a union by grace and love of two different human hypostases, a man and a woman.

As we have stated in other studies, we appreciate that in Romania, from a legal perspective, the family based on same-sex marriage cannot be recognized or admitted. We present the following arguments:

- According to natural law and legislation in force, the marriage and family of a homosexual couple cannot be recognized in Romania. Such a union, regardless of its source, cannot be identical to the family.

- The marriage between homosexuals concluded in another state cannot be recognized in Romania, nor can it generate the right to a family.

- Since the family is not only a right, but also a legal institution of a constitutional nature, the adoption by the Parliament of a law on the right to the family for homosexuals, or partnerships based on the distinction between family and family life would be possible in my opinion only after amending the Constitution in this regard. Neither the Constitution nor the subsequent legislation enshrines and guarantees such forms of partnership in Romania, in fact they prohibit them.

It would also be necessary to repeal art. 277 of the Civil Code, a fact that can only be achieved after a derogatory legislative procedure from common law because the Civil Code is an organic law.

- The constitutional and subjective rights of homosexual couples are not violated in Romania and can be exercised under the conditions provided by law.

- No special normative regulation is necessary for the different forms of civil partnership between heterosexuals or homosexuals, partnerships that currently exist in Romania. The moral and legal principle of tolerance allows their existence without being assimilated to the family, provided they do not contravene the legislation in force, the legal order or good morals.

- The last attempt to revise the Constitution took place in 2018, when, based on a citizens' initiative, it was proposed to revise art. 48 paragraph 1, in the sense that "The family is based on the freely consented marriage between a man and a woman". All procedural steps were successfully completed, but the final act of approving the revision, the National Referendum, failed, as the validation threshold was not reached. According to the Central Electoral Bureau, 21.1% of Romanians with the right to vote went to the polls during the two days dedicated to the consultation. The referendum on 6 and 7 October 2018 thus recorded the lowest voter turnout since 1990 to date. The amendment of the Constitution was supported by 91.56% of those present at the polls. It is the first citizens' initiative to revise the Constitution launched in Romania since the fall of communism in 1989.

This Referendum is an eloquent example of the indifference of the majority of the Romanian electorate towards the Constitution and especially for the inclusion in the normative content of the Fundamental Law of a principle regarding the formation of the family focused on the traditions and values of the right Orthodox faith of the Romanian people, whose validity and viability are approaching for 2000 years.

But it is worth continuing to affirm, in doctrine (or in other forms, and especially in fact) the traditional millennial Romanian family based on the Orthodox faith[12].

The superman theory

Along with the majority of authors who have studied this subject, the ideology of postmodernism begins with the philosophy of Nietzsche, Schopenhauer, Heidegger, continued by existentialist philosophy. The common notes consist in the distrust and disavowal of the classical values of rationalism and bourgeois morality, the preaching of atheism and even the antagonistic spirit especially towards orthodoxy and the Church, the affirmation and support of the thesis that this world is the last reality and therefore, man and the world are finite and meaningless, "man is thrown into the world", into a hostile existence that permanently causes him deep experiences of fear, anguish and despair. Man, in order to be happy in this existential state, must free himself from principles and values, act instinctually, express himself freely because everything is possible in a finite, meaningless world that inevitably ends in death and nothingness for which "God died," as Nietzsche says.

The reality is different. Even if postmodern man separates himself from God, He does not forget man. God does not die, only the belief in God of postmodern man because he was created by his Creator with freedom and can choose between good and evil, between believing and not believing, in the will and work of giving meaning to life, or to live in fear and anguish.

The words of the Savior, the Lord Jesus Christ, are eternally relevant: You have heard that it was said: 'Love your neighbor and hate your enemy.' But I say to you: Love your enemies, bless those who curse you, do good to those who curse you. that hate you, and pray for those who oppress you and persecute you, that you may be sons of your Father who is in heavens; for He makes His sun rise on the bad and on the good and sends rain on the just and on the unjust (Matthew 5, 43-45).

The secularization of man and society, the exponential progress of science and technology have led to man's immeasurable confidence in his own being, in his reason. Man became his own god, more precisely the person became an individual, each man considering himself to be his own god.

Man's power to know and give meaning, his aspiration to the high, to the transcendent, the scientific and technological progress that has as a result the improvement of life, comfort, communication, are priceless gifts of God. It is not knowledge, science and technology that is bad, but the way in which it is used, the finality conferred by man against nature, regarding himself as the sole creator.

Father Professor Dumitru Stăniloae stated in this regard: "It is only an opinion that man has lost God in our age. God cannot be completely lost by man. I saw that even man's fight against God is a sign that he has not lost and cannot lose God completely. He wants to remain with the attributes of God (infinity, perfection, meaning, immortal life, rationality), but without their bearer. When man remains only with these attributes, but without a bearer of them, they lose their form, their meaning, they become an indistinct and inconsistency pile when they no longer clothe someone"[13].

In this context, postmodernist ideology and those who support it promote the philosophy of the superman as conceived by Nietzsche. The moral relationship between man and the superman is a central theme in Nietzsche's works, particularly in The Genealogy of Morals. The German philosopher considers the existence of two fundamental patterns in morality: the morality of the herd man, of the slave, and the morality of the superman, of the master, of the free man. The characteristics of the herdman are kindness, humility and sympathy, more precisely the basic elements of Christianity, while the superman has the characteristics of pride, power and ennobling. Man and superman quantify moral actions differently. The term "morality" has a different meaning than its proper one in Nietzsche's philosophy; a particular morality is intrinsic to a particular culture, that is, language, practices, institutions are contained between the value conflict between the two patterns.

Utility and pleasure are the only value criteria for the existence of man who has become an individual. “The free man, possessor of a vast and untamed will, finds in this possession his standard of value: relying on himself to judge others, he reveres or despises; and just as he fatally honors those who resemble him, the strong who can be counted on (those who can promise)..."[14]. The free man or master sees himself in a certain sense as a measure of all things: "The aristocrat is self-confident, valuing all that is his own, he helps the unfortunate, but not from pity but from the impulse of an abundance of power, he is proud of his condition, hostile and ironic towards altruism, he considers that he has obligations only to those of his kind"[15].

However, for most people the superman condition in society is only an illusion. In fact, in the postmodern era, fundamental human rights and freedoms are claimed, but transformed by the rulers into an abstract, technological humanism, without people and above all without God.

The illusion that public liberties are no longer necessary is generated by rulers in order to dominate, to reduce man from person to individual. There is the concept that the state and European rulers are the ones who know what is good for man and society. That is why individual rights and freedoms in the public space no longer have a purpose.

Ovidiu Hurduzeu speaks in this sense of the happy slaves. The Westerner and not only feels more and more vulnerable today. Panic, insecurity, social apathy, the avoidance of drastic security measures have replaced the daring spirit, the desire to experiment and overcome the limits, the desire for freedom. Everything has become subordinate to the notion of safety, security. Now no one asks you - "do you feel free?" " Now the question is - "do you feel safe? "Safety should not be seen in a narrow, technical sense, but in its profound truth as a worldview. The perception of reality through the idea of vulnerability is a cultural phenomenon closely related to the status of the individual in our era of hyperglobalization and institutionalized postmodernity.[16] And the communist state wanted the same thing and had the same policy of annihilating man's liberties and giving him social security in return.

It is an illusion of the rulers that man created in the image and likeness of God could abandon his freedom, accept drastic restrictions and limitations of his rights, and accept the domineering tutelage of the state, accompanied by safety in the social environment. The personality, dignity and freedom of man cannot be abolished by the rulers because they are gifts of God and therefore man in social environment will never be satisfied with the status of "happy slave. "

Man, postmodern, endowed with freedom, can choose whether to remain in communion with God or separate from Him. Man today, like our forefathers, wants to be God, he cannot and therefore falls, becomes a prodigal son. Man today creates his own idols in which he believes and through which he falls into the finitude of this world in the repetitiveness of natural laws and determinism.

If we were to choose as a term of comparison the phenomena of physics, for the so-called postmodern superman the reflection in the mirror applies, just like in the myth of Narcissus. In this game we sense the metamorphosing power of the mirror. The self-image (projected in the personal mirror), takes control of the self, still anchored in the reality of nature, and gives it new perspectives. From now on, there are no more limits to nature in terms of evolution, of becoming. There is only my truth about myself. And in the personal mirror I can imagine myself without any restrictions. And whatever I can imagine, means it exists in reality.

The idols of our times through which the secularized society and the contemporary man are separated from God are selfishness, pride, vain glory, the consideration of this world as the only one that exists, the absolutization of the power of human reason, the idol of technology that substitutes for humanism and Christian virtues, consumerism that has distorted existence social, this becoming a society of consumption, of the desire for material accumulation, and man no longer wants to be but to have, the will to power and to dominate, vain glory, the replacement of fundamental rights and liberties with social security, the proliferation of sects and Protestantism through which man creates his own gods.

"Take heed, brethren, that none of you have an evil and unbelieving heart, which separates you from the living God." (Hebrews 3: 12) God, the Creator of all things, upholds all things in His hand and in His goodness. He is close to us. He is everywhere and He contains everything. Never, not even for a moment, does He want and does not want to be far from His works and His creation. He is the author of all things and all things were made through Him. His imprint is found everywhere, so that there is no place where He is not present.

He created men in His image and likeness, to make them masters of His creation and to have eternal and uninterrupted communion with them. Humans were to be His stewards on earth and the doers of His plan here on earth.

Unfortunately, people fell into sin and it took His Son Himself to come and die for our sins and mistakes and thus reconcile us to God again.

The people who would receive the Word of Jesus Christ became again like Adam and Eve were at the beginning of the beginning. That is, pure and without sin, in uninterrupted communion with God. Through Jesus Christ, sin and death, separation and distance from God have been defeated forever.

Separation from God is the tragic alienation of man not only from his Creator but also from himself, from society, from nature from the authentic nature of his nature, which he consents to, desires, seeking an illusory happiness in the idols of our times and the precarities of this world finite that it considers the only possible. Man becomes the slave of his own illusions, of all kinds of ideologies, the slave of his passions, of his ego that closes itself off, refusing to open up to another through love, kindness, doing good for one's neighbor. "We are exclusivists," said Father Teofil Părăian.

Contemporary man also endures another tragic alienation. The state separates from society and man. The rule of law, the social contract, in its supreme legal form which is the constitution, fundamental rights and freedoms are rhetorically proclaimed, but in fact refuted by the contemporary rulers through the decisions they impose.

Fundamental rights and freedoms have been drastically restricted in the last two years without any constitutional or rational justification, the independence of justice has become an illusion, contemporary globalization turns man into an anonymous individual lost in the social mass. The welfare state ceases to exist because the rulers do not respect their social contract obligations to guarantee a decent standard of living for all, jobs, free and efficient education, effective social insurance, a truly efficient health care system.

The contemporary state, contrary to its purpose and the social contract, promotes social existence based on consumerism, which generates ephemeral pleasures and satisfactions, on free competition, which leads to alienation, to social exclusivism. Liberty has been replaced by social security and implies the total submission of the individual to those who exercise power. The contemporary domestic and international rulers concerned solely with their patrimonial interests and domination and not with the public interest, are turning contemporary man into a "happy slave". What accentuates even more the tragedy of this form of alienation is the fact that man often accepts it, more or less consciously.

Today we are witnessing an unprecedented form of social separation, social abandonment. The state has abandoned man, turning him into an anonymous individual, completely subject to the power of the rulers, the guarantee of fundamental rights and freedoms becomes mere rhetoric or even an illusion, mass poverty and social discrepancies become a common place, instead of freedom it is given an ephemeral and illusory social security, and governance is based on constraints and restrictions of all kinds,

The separation of the state from man means the unilateral breaking of the social contract by the rulers, and the rule of law, so much praised, has become an instrument of coercion of the rulers, and for man an illusion. The sociability of man, the social dimension of his existence cannot be annulled or abolished. That is why man must find himself in other forms of social existence than the legal one.

Separation from God, the forms of social alienation that man today endures, cannot be and are not irreversible. The return to God, the reconstruction of the deeper self of man in its purity and beauty, given by the Creator, the return to the right Orthodox faith are still possible. God is waiting for each of us to return to Him, to the original beauty of his nature. The Savior Himself said this in the parable of the "Loving Father and the Prodigal Son."

The social alienation of postmodern man can be overcome. There are two conditions: for man to know himself and to realize that the gift of freedom is from God and not from the rulers, that he is not a simple anonymous individual in a mass of people, but a created person in the image and likeness of God; and a new paradigm of social existence to restore the values of the social dimension of human existence.

The ideology of artificial intelligence

Artificial intelligence (AI) is the intelligence of intelligent machines, robots, that perceive their environment and take actions that maximize the chance of successfully achieving their goals. It is defined as ""the ability of a system to correctly interpret external data, to learn from such data, and to use what it has learned to achieve specific goals and tasks through flexible adaptation"(Kaplan Andreas) . The existential risk posed by strong artificial (or general) intelligence is the assumption that substantial progress in artificial (or general; abbreviated AGI in English) could one day lead to human extinction or some other unrecoverable global catastrophe.

In the era of postmodernism, within the framework of this ideology, there is already talk of the superiority of artificial intelligence over human intelligence, of the competition between man and machine, of the need for legal regulation of social relations that have artificial intelligence as their object, even of a unitary legal regulation of natural intelligence of man and artificial intelligence, considering them to be phenomenologically equivalent.

The ethical aspects involved in computer systems, their use, storage and use of information are also topical. Many scientists, lawyers, people of culture, but also politicians are concerned about the risks for humans and society, the vulnerabilities and the elements of progress of artificial intelligence. We can talk about the ideology or philosophy of artificial intelligence because it is a component part of postmodernist thinking and realities and the implications of artificial intelligence are profound for man, society, for the meaning and purpose of existence.

We do not intend in this study to analyze all these aspects of artificial intelligence. In the following, we briefly present our opinion:

Definition of the notion of "intelligence":

- natural intelligence (there are authors, scientists who speak of an intelligence of matter)

- human intelligence. The concept is studied mainly by psychology than applied science. Philosophy and theology rarely use this concept. Human intelligence is understood by psychology either as a function of the neural activity of the brain or as a behavioral aptitude as stated by behaviorist theories.

In popular parlance intelligence is an aptitude of the resourceful enterprising man who adapts easily.

Human intelligence, both at the level of common sense and in philosophical or theological theories, is not assimilated to human reason or the cognitive capacity of man. The latter are attributes of man as a spiritual being, endowed with an immortal soul, rational, affective, cognitive and volitional capacity.

Research in the field of neural biology has demonstrated that neither rational capacities nor human intelligence can be fully explained by human neural functions alone. This is an objective limit of human knowledge, not a subjective one. In other words, human intelligence and reason are more and something else than the set of biological functions. At the same time, life is not the set of biological functions that support it. No scientific theory or hypothesis explains the origin of life or what life is, much less substantiates the possibility of artificial creation of life.

I personally believe that psychologism should not be absolutized because its explanations regarding reason, intelligence and human conduct are either incomplete or do not take into account much deeper realities than the phenomenality of psychological theories.

The concept of "artificial intelligence" must be defined, which in my opinion is much older than the time it was proposed. Thus the ancient civilizations of Egypt, Sumer or the Mayan civilization used tools and calculation techniques with the help of which they could create (see pyramids), or they could make long-term calendrical and astronomical predictions.

The notion of "artificial", corresponds philosophically to the idea of inauthentic, reality lacking existential hypostasis. See Plato, Aristotle, Kant, Hegel, but also contemporary rationalist and existentialist philosophy.

Undeniably artificial intelligence, in the form of computer systems, robotics, digitalization, etc., in my opinion, is nothing more than a technology, like so many others, created by man, in the service of man and obviously of great utility in achieving goals, cognitive rational and even volitional of man, excluding the affective ones. I think this aspect should also be emphasized.

I don't think comparisons can be made between human intelligence and artificial intelligence.

The two realities have a different nature. Aristotle in "Organon - Definitions", says that only realities that have the same existential nature can be compared, a truth found today in all sciences.

Man's intelligence is an existential attribute of him, while artificial intelligence is a technology, of indisputable utility for man, but in no case is it of the same nature as man's intelligence.

It is the absolute difference and separation between the creator and the created. In this case man is the creator of artificial intelligence.

It is true that the expansion of artificial intelligence today has led to the strengthening of atheism and the refusal of faith (not always of religion). This phenomenon has its beginning not now but in the 18th century when man thought he could replace his reason with God. Since then, new "religions" have appeared, such as the "religion of human rights or artificial intelligence". It is a drama of contemporary man. I think this aspect should be approached critically. Notions of religion or theology are not confused with faith. Man relates to God through faith, not through religion or theology, much less through technology in the conditions in which it is considered sufficient by itself.

Perhaps it is good to discuss the limits of artificial intelligence as well. No system considered to be an artificially intelligent system can subrogate the creative reason of man, his affective and volitional faculties. Any form of artificial intelligence must remain for man only a tool, a means and not an end. Kant says that man must always be considered as an end and never as a means.

Moreover, philosophy and science have highlighted the objective limits of human reason considered by its cognitive capacity. I don't go into details, but I have in mind Heisenberg's uncertainty principle, Plank's constant or the theory of the incomplete or contradictory nature of any axiomatic system, formalized by the mathematician Goodel.

I do not agree with the statements of politicians that the future will mean the digitization of education, democracy, decisions. Such a reality would be a great tragedy for man.

I think the risks of artificial intelligence should be better spelled out.

In my opinion, they are particularly aimed at trying to compare and replace human intelligence with artificial intelligence, man could become a mere means and not an end, weakening and even distorting social and legal humanism. Einstein pointed out very well that technology has taken the place of humanism

That is why it is not artificial intelligence that is bad or harmful, but how people understand how to use it.

IV. Postmodernism and Christianity

Postmodern man is not lost. Man and contemporary society unfortunately go through the crisis generated by postmodernist conceptions, which they accept knowingly or unknowingly. Man is created in the image of God and this gift is not lost, even if the image of divinity in man has faded.

Unlike other religions, and postmodernist ideology, Orthodox Christianity recognizes the special value of the world and man as God's creation. The world and man are not (only) fallen existences, as Origen considered them, but carry within themselves the love of God, because the world and man were created out of love. The world (universe) has a special value; it is a truth that results from the words of the Savior: "God so loved the world, that he gave his only begotten Son, that whoever believes in him should not perish, but have eternal life (John 3: 16).

We resort to the words of Father Professor Dumitru Stăniloae to emphasize this conception of the value of the world and of man according to Orthodox theological thinking: "The Creator gave man through creation such a great value and capacity to become a Brother with man, to speak and work through human nature. This is the great mystery of man: that God makes himself the Son of Man, but by totally descending into human boundaries - for this would be one with pantheism - showing a weakness of God, but also remaining God, above the limits of humanity. The birth as a man from Virgo shows both the glorification of God and the glorification given to man by his mate, by nature of his person. He becomes the Son of Man par excellence, for he raises man to his state of man with an undiseased nature. The new, healthy beginning of humanity is being made. Those who remain in it no longer fall from true humanity. And true humanity is only the one strengthened in God[17]".

In order to achieve a perfect communion with God, according to the inspired teaching of the Holy Apostle Paul, man must first of all have faith. Through faith, Christ comes into the storehouse of the human heart: "so that Christ may dwell in your hearts through faith; having the root and foundation laid in love..." (Ephesians 3:17) Thus man will receive the Spirit promised by God and by faith we can become sons of God (Galatians 2:15-21; 3; 14; 3:23-29; Philippians 3:8-11).

Man's approach to God is possible kenotically, through humility, through self-emptying, of the false, unspiritualized "I". Saint Paul teaches the Philippians that Christ Himself took the form of a servant and that "For this reason God also exalted Him beyond words and gave Him the Name that is above every name; so that in the Name of Jesus, everything should bow knee of those in heaven, on earth, and under the earth, and let every tongue confess, to the glory of God the Father, that Jesus Christ is Lord..." (Philippians 2:5-11).

Also, in order to know God, we must first love God, because He loved us before, so that we share the same love through which Christ brought us to the Father: "Whom no man knew sin, he made him to be sin for us, that we might become the righteousness of God in him" (II Corinthians 5:21). Through his victory over sin, death, and the devil, Christ defeated and destroyed that which separated man from God.

Through the Church we live in Christ sharing His life and death, and "Because we are baptized into the death of Christ" we have been buried with Him and ... "united with Him in a death like His ... " so that " The wages of sin is death, but the free gift of God is eternal life in Christ Jesus our Lord" (Romans 6). Death in the likeness of Christ's death is death in resurrection "And all these things are from God, who reconciled us to himself through Jesus Christ and entrusted us with the ministry of reconciliation". (II Corinthians 5:14-18)

References

[1] See, Jean-Francois Lyotard, The Postmodern Condition. A Report on Knowledge, Publisher, Manchester University Press, USA, 1984;

[2] For developments, see Gheorghe Cristian-Popa, Postmodernism does not deny God, it ironizes Him, published in https://ziarullumina.ro/educatie-si-cultura/interviu/postmodernismul-nu-l-neaga -he-ironizes-God-35933.html;

[3] See, Lev Sestov, All things are possible, 1905;

[4] See Jacques Derrida, The Beast and the Sovereign Volume II (Seminar 2002-2003), Tact Publishing House, Bucharest, 2014; Jacques Derrida Dissemination, Bloomsbury Publishing Plc., London, 2016;

[5] Ludwig Wittgenstein, Philosophical Researches, Humanitas Publishing House, Bucharest, 2013;

[6] Jean Bauddrillard, Access words, ART Publishing House, Bucharest, 2008;

[7] See, Postmodernism – philosophical openings. Cluj-Napoca: Dacia Publishing House, 1995;

[8] For developments see, Hutcheon L. The politics of postmodernism. Bucharest: Univers Publishing House, 1997 and Hutcheon L. The politics of postmodernism. Bucharest: Univers Publishing House, 1997;

[9] For developments, see Dorin Bodea, The mirror revolution and the birth of the postmodern man, published at https://dilemaveche.ro/sectiune/societate/revolutia-oglinzii-si-nasterea-omului-postmodern-620820.html;

[10] Dumitru Stăniloae, Orthodox Dogmatic Theology, Vol. III, Basilica Publishing House, Bucharest, 2003;

[11] Dumitru Stăniloae, op. quote p. 183;

[12] For developments, see Marius Andreescu, From the Romanian Orthodox family to the Western civil partnership, published in the magazine Porunca Iubirii, Editura Agaton, Făgăraş, 31. 01,2022;

[13] Dumitru Stăniloae, in, Protos Ioanichie Bălan, Spiritual Conversations, Publishing House of the Episcopiei Romanului si Huşilor, 1990, Vol. II, p. 98;

[14] Friedrich Wilhelm Nietzsche, Genealogia moralei, Editura Ideea Europeană, Iasi, 2020, p. 68;

[15] Marina Seredovschii, The concept of superman in Nietzsche's philosophy, published on https://ibn.idsi.md/sites/default/files/imag_file/61-63;

[16] See, Ovidiu Hurduzeu, Happy slaves. The world seen from Silicon Valley, Timpul Iaşi Publishing House, 2005, p. 5;

[17] Dumitru Staniloae, Jesus Christ. The light of the world and the deification of man, Complete Works, Vol. 6, Publishing House Basilica, Bucharest, 2014, p. 64.

Bibliography

Stăniloae D., Jesus Christ. The Light of the World and the Deification of Man, Complete Works, Vol. 6, Basilica Publishing House, Bucharest, 2014;

Foucault M. Words and things. Bucharest: Univers Publishing House, 1996;

Hutcheon L. The politics of postmodernism. Bucharest: Univers Publishing House, 1997;

Lyon D., Postmodernity. Bucharest: Du Style Publishing House;

Nicolescu B., We, the particle and the world. Iasi: Polirom, 2002;

Postmodernism – philosophical openings. Cluj-Napoca: Dacia Publishing House, 1995;

Ovidiu Hurduzeu, Happy slaves. The world seen from Silicon Valley, Timpul Iaşi Publishing House, 2005.

23. FREEDOM OF CONSCIENCE LEGAL AND RELIGIOUS IMPLICATIONS

Abstract:

Conscience is a defining existential reality of man, whose meaning can be seen only through an interdisciplinary unceasing effort of thinking and knowledge. In this study, we propose to make such an analysis of the conscience as an ontological foundation and characteristic of man, in its individual and social dimension, whose basis is made up of philosophical, theological and legal ideas, concepts and theories. Freedom of conscience is the main feature of the manifestations of man as a person within the specific environment of his/her existence. From the legal point of view, freedom of conscience is a complex fundamental right requesting a wide legislative system in order to establish and guarantee it. In our opinion, both the basis and the legitimacy of the legal system protecting the freedom of conscience are given by the philosophical truths and the truths of faith, as expressed in theological writings and meditations. In this study, we identify the theological and philosophical bases of the freedom of conscience and their reflection in the legal field.

Key words:

Self-conscience /Conscience of inner self / Social conscience /Freedom of conscience as a fundamental right / theological, philosophical and legal meanings of conscience and freedom of conscience /constitutional guarantees

I. About conscience, law and liberty

Conscience is the essence and particularity of man by which he relates to the nature, society, but also to his own being and, especially, to the Supreme Being. The blessed Augustine also said that "there is something inside of us deeper than ourselves", referring also to human conscience, especially inner self-conscience.

Important to underline is that before being transposed into legal norms, conscience is a natural dimension by which man becomes what he is and he definitely differentiates from any other existential form. Thus, the natural reality in its existential manifestations transforms under the laws of causality, as Kant would say. Unlike this, man through his conscience and in his supreme form, the inner self-conscience is not transformed, he rather becomes according to the laws of freedom, as the great philosopher said. So we can understand the thoughts of Father Theophilus Părăian: the man becomes to what he is, which is to his own self discovery and inner self-conscience achieving.

Man is the only creature that through rational senses can contemplate on existence, but also on his own thoughts, in other words possess the ability *to reflect and question*, on himself and the outside world, seeking answers and, if possible, certitudes to his questions.

The reflections on thoughts give existential meanings through which man conceives himself and sometimes defines himself, recognizes and asserts his place into the world and universe. We try to say that the contemplation on the thought, the returning of the thought on itself, or as rationalist philosophers say "the thinking that thinks on itself" is more than a philosophical meditation or a simple logical construction because the reflection has not a purely formal character, but an existential one. The thought which thinks on itself is aiming not only to the reason, but to the existence or being, as such. This is the *conscience* as ontological peculiarity of the being that is based on the reflective capacity of the reason. Through conscience I can state my own existence as a rational being by that "I am", not so much by the existential uncertitudes, as Descartes was saying, neither by the formal certainties of the reason, but through the compassionate, rational feeling, which reveals to me my inner self and meanings conferred by the reflection on the self, upon the world and universe.

The conscience is proper to the human being, distinguishing it of any other existential form, through which man is understood in his individuality, but also through his fellowship to all humanity. Conscience is the result of man's relationship, through the rational faculties and the understandable feelings with oneself, with nature, with society and with the Supreme Being. The existential meanings are not to be found in the simple consciences, but rather in the facts of the conscience that represent its content. Conscience is not an existential void, but is always the conscience of "something" or "through something". Content determinations generate two forms or sizes: the ego-conscience and inner self conscience.

In general, the philosophical and psychological thinking that emphasized the *inner self* is wider than - ***I***, integrates it and is much more than **I**: "And the inner self who broke the circle of the ego, is always proned to enlargement, as being the moving horizon in which you sooth yourself into the deep"[482]. For Carl Gustav Jung, "the self" refers to an entity that does not replace the designated one until now by the concept of "**I**", it rather includes this one within its scope as a superconcept. In the great psychologist's vision, **"I"** means that complex factor to which relates all contents of conscience. It is the centre of the field of conscience, and to the extent this one includes the empirical personality in its sphere, **I** is the subject of all personal acts of conscience. "The relating of the psychical content to **I** represents the criterion of this one's conscience, because no contents is aware whether not represented to *a subject*"[483].

We notice, as a matter that is common to philosophical and psychological thinking, the understanding of conscience through the idea of subject, we may say, through the idea of person conferred to the man.

For Jung, although the **I** is based on the entire "field of conscience", it is not this field, is rather the reference point defined by the somatic, psychological factor. Through the "**I**" is obtained an image of the established personality, but the total personality is more complex. The "inner self" is for the **"I"** an objective given which the liberty of will of **"I"** in the field of conscience, cannot change. Jung says: "That's why I suggested to name with **self**, the *total personality* which, though not entirely noticeable, is still present. **I** is, by definition, subordinated to the self and is related to it as part of the wholeness."[484]

---

[482] Constantin Noica, Cuvânt împreună despre rostirea românească, "Oration together on Romanian Wording" Humanitas Publishing House, Bucharest1996, p. 15.

[483] C.G. Jung, Puterea sufletului. Antologie, psihologia analitică, "The Power of Soul. Anthology, Analytical Psychology", Anima Publishing House, Bucharest1994, p. 129.

[484] C.G,Jung, quoted works p.133.

In Noica's concept, the understanding of the relationship between *self* and ***I*** is done on three levels: 1) the understanding the self in the passivity of I, "as a deeper conscience of this", one can understand that the self related to **I** is an archetype; 2) the self can be an active expression of the **I**: as ideal, ethical conscience, freedom. Here the self is a modeler of the **I**; 3) The self as an expression of lucidity of **I**, is determined by "the liberty that found the necessity". Under the term of lucidity hides the one of conscience, meaning the field of onscience, as it is called by Jung[485]. For Noica, the **"I"** is a dialectical process of elevation to innerself. In this becoming, the man and his creation are the expression of liberty of superior inner self that represents the being. Therefore, the becoming is understood by Noica as oriented towards the being, through a progressive transition from **I** to the deeper self.

Related to these brief philosophical reflections, one can notice that philosophy and psychology highlight the complexity of conscience, as a fundamental ontological dimension of human being. This complexity and profoundness of content does not exclude, but rather involves the unity of conscience, based at its turn, on the unity of being. The conscience, which only man as a rational being is possessing, is unitary, but manifestes itself in two forms: the *conscience of **I***, whose content is the existential phenomenality of man, as a finite being, in nature and society, subjected to the material and temporarily determinism and through this, to existential precariousness, and, on the other hand, the *inner self-conscience* specific to the man that found himself and the true meaning of existence that is beyond the finitude and natural determinism, transfiguring through this knowledge and conscience, the being and thus becoming what is through the nature, a person and spiritual personality, and as such, free.

Yet man can remain a simple individual constrained by the laws of nature and society, whether through will, faith and culture, he does not transcend the limits of **I** and he does not discover its true meaning in the Supreme Being and in eternal life, thus reaching to the conscience of inner self, inexhaustible in its depths. The transition from the conscience of **I** to inner self-conscience is, essentially, the becoming of man from individual to spiritual person, free, in an infinite and indefinite relationship of love with God, with people and whole creation. The philosophical concepts too, notice such a differentiation between man as a finite being, and on the other hand, the human personality defined by his freedom. Where there is no freedom, ie where there

---

[485] For development see Constantin Noica, Cuvânt împreună despre rostirea românească, "Oration together on Romanian Wording" pp. 17 – 35.

is only the finite conscience of **I** and not of the person, it is a number, such as Noice said ".

It is discussed in politology and philosophy about a social conscience, too. In our opinion, this concept is a gnoseologic construction, whose existence is theoretically and ontologically derived and conditioned by a single ontological form of conscience, namely the human conscience in his individuality and personality. Interesting to notice that the Juridical expresses this fact, meaning that it guarantees not the social conscience as an abstract and theoretical structure, but only the individual conscience inextricably linked with the person. It is remarkable that the law has more or less elaborately taken the theological and philosophical fundamental values regarding the understanding of man as a person throughout his social existence, in that as it constantly states the thesis according to which the holder of the fundamental rights can only be but the man in his individuality, I would say as a person and not as an individual, and not as a group, nor as a community or society as such. Certainly, since the legal status of man is his exterior existence in the social and natural environment, the holder of any fundamental right can exercise it, if we have into consideration this legal status, in the social environment in which he is located. Thus, any social individual liberty is also social through the legal existence of man in his social externality.

One should also notice that the freedom of conscience is part of the so-called natural rights of man, pre-existing, according to some authors, to the consecrations in the constitutional norms, or of a different type. This thesis, which the limited space does not allow us to develop, is worthy to be remembered in order to clarify, to some extent, the relationship between the liberties (rights) of man and, on the other hand, the juridical norms (positive law). It's not the law that determines and gives the content of individual freedoms and fundamental rights, but conversely, the legitimacy of any law stems directly from the way the fundamental rights and freedoms, pre-existing, are being reflected in the juridical norm. We appreciate that this is a social imperative to outline in this way, the possibility of man's liberty within the social environment. Assuming that the freedom is determined by the law, understood as a normative act rather than as a moral law, the dominant reality in which freedom manifestes is the non-authentic and constraining, because any juridical law, by its nature, is a form of limitation and restriction or conditioning, in a word of constraining the human freedom. In such a situation a distructive contradiction can manifest between the law, in its legal meaning and man's freedom, including the freedom of conscience.

If it comes to a situation where the law is a construction that reflects the preexisting natural rights of man, then we can speak of a genuine freedom, guaranteed by the legal enactment and not constructed by the juridical norm. It worth emphasizing that in the classical, universal legal instruments regarding the human fundamental rights and freedoms, usually there is a formula according to which the "States *recognize* the fundamental rights and freedoms", therefore they are normatively constructing them and do not impose them as a juridical given. This is not only a mere simple legal formula, but one expressing a fundamental thought of the derivative character of the law from the previous fundamental existential values, I would say, included in the truths of faith.

There is a unilateral contradiction such as Constantin Noica says, between law and liberty, if we accept the idea of the law's derived nature related to the values of freedom. Thus, the law can not contradict human freedom, yet the freedom of man can contradict the law.

II. Theological meanings of conscience

The issue of the unity of conscience and being is oviously a goal for theological meditation. Here is what the pious hermit Isaiah was saying, in this respect: "Let's persevere, beloved ones, in fear of God, guarding and keeping the doing of virtues, not causing lunacies to our conscience, but taking heed to ourselves in fear of God. Let's do it till this will be freed with us, to produce between it and us a union, so that it will reach to be our guardian, showing in everything the danger to fall. But if we do not listen to it, it will split from us, letting us to fall into the hands of our enemies and will no longer be helping us"[486].

Commenting on this text, the priest Professor Dumitru Stăniloae remarked the duality between our conscience and our being. The conscience is the one through which we can guard our being against the existential precariousness attractions, while the purpose of existence is to achieve the unity between the conscience and our being. In this regard priest Professor Dumitru Stăniloae said: "there are three in a man, different from the Supreme Third. The conscience that the third in man (different from **I** and from the own being) is strong in man, mostly when it has in itself the supreme Third, or God"[487].

The man who has reached to the inner self-conscience is a person and through it, is free to communicate with God and with others. Rev. Prof. Dumitru Stăniloae said that man, as a person, is "spirit and freedom" and at the same time, mystery and light, is a "mystery of light". The inner self-conscience of man is a depth of love and humbleness because is the infinite and indefinite link of the human person with the Supreme Person. This communion is however the higher order of the natural determinism, because it is neither constraining nor finite, is yet infinite in love, is the order revealed by the Savior in His commandments and mainly through *the commandment to love, and the commandment to perfection and commandment to holiness*.

One can say that the genuine philosophical reflection about the conscience is supported by the truths of faith in the natural and supernatural revelations, truths so beautifully expressed in many patristical writings.

One of the most beautiful reflection about the conscience , we see at Ava Dorotheos: "When God created man, planted in him something divine, like the hottest and brightest thought, having the quality of a sparkle to

---

486 Isaia Pustnicul, Word IV, Philocalia, Vol.XII, Publishing House Humanitas, Bucharest2009, p. 60.

487 Priest Professor Dumitru Stăniloaie, Philocalia Vol. XII, quoted works p.60.

enlighten the mind and to show to it the distinction of good from evel. This is called conscience and it is the law of His nature"[488].

Likewise, Mark the Ascetic refers to the conscience as man's own nature: "Conscience is a natural book. He who reads it with the deed makes the divine help's experience. The good conscience is known through prayer and the pure prayer through conscience. For one has need of another by nature"[489].

Should we examine the relationship between conscience and knowledge, we can say that there is no identity between the two faculties of human nature, but they presume each other. The amount of scientifical knowledge, or of any type, forms the conscience. Through inner self conscience the knowledges get their natural meaning. On the other hand, conscience is something else than the discursivity of reason or sensitivity of the intellect. Is the reflection on thought, on concept, categories built by the intellectual sensibility or the connoisseuring reason and is, in essence, the profound existential communion between the persons. In inner self-conscience, as defined by Philocaly parents, is disappearing the dichotomy of own rational knowledge between subject and object. Through knowledge, understood in the interpersonal communion relationship, the knowledges acquire their unity and meaning, because the conscience of **I,** mostly the conscience of inner self can belong, but only to the person. Such an idea is brilliantly built by Rev. Prof. Dumitru Stăniloae: "The same thing it attested by the word con-science. I do not know myself without a relationship with others. Ultimately, I know or am aware of myself in my relationship with God. The light of my knowledge related to the work or to myself, is projecting over the human face, communitarily, in the supreme personal communion. We are not aware of ourselves other than in relationship with another, and ultimately, before God. **I** alone would not have conscience; through conscience he is a spiritual "place" of his own in relationship with others. In his self-conscience he grows along with his self conscience growing, and this grows along with his growing in his knowledge of God and his neighbors, and also of the things"[490].

Unlike the conscience of **I**, bordered by the existential finitude, the self-conscience has its own freedom in the order given by the divine commandments. The man who has become a person is aware that he depends

[488] Avadoriotei, Teachings, III, 1, In Philocalia, Vol. X.

[489] Mark the Ascet, About the Spiritual Law, in 200 items, 186 şi 198.

[490] Priest Professor Dumitru Stăniloaie, The Orthodox Dogmatic Theology, vol. I, The Romanian Orthodox Church Biblic and Mission Institute Publishing House, Bucharest 2003, p. 243.

on God and through it, he is master on himself, being mastered by God and then from a slave of the sin he becomes "a slave of freedom", through equity, the work of virtues and through the Holy Grace. He is a slave of freedom because he lives through an infinite loving communion with God and with others and this is part of an order which the philosophers call "the law of freedom".

Conscience is a natural dimension through which man becomes what he is and he definitely differentiates from any other existential form. Thus, the natural reality in its existential manifestations transforms according to the laws of causality, as Kant says. In contrast, man through his conscience and in the supreme form, the self conscience, does not transform, he rather becomes according to *the laws of freedom*, such as the great philosopher said. Priest Theophilus Părăian said that man becomes what he is, which is that his existence meaning being oriented on the achieving and discovery of self-conscience.

Consequently, the freedom is distinctive to self-conscience. There cannot be conceived a self-conscience in the natural determinism's borders or subjected to some constraints, conditionings or any legal limitations imposed by the law and, in general, by the social law.

This is highly emphasized in the Patristic writings, which reveal that the freedomof the man that became a spiritual person is inherent to self-conscience. For the depth of thought we quote one of the most beautiful philocalia meditations on human freedom, as a self-aware person, in his love communion with God and with others, "God made man free, so that he is proned to good. But being proned to good, through his free will, he is not able to achieve it without the help of God. Therefore it was written: it is not from he who is willing, neither from the he who is running, but from God that is full of mercy (Rom. 9, 16). Therefore, if man orientes his heart to good, and calls God's name for help, God paying attention to his good desire, gives strength to his work. Thus, the two of them meet; man freedom and God power. For the good comes from God but is accomplished through His saints. Thus glorifies God in everyone and he glorifies them all"[491].

The juridical status of man narrows and even constraints to phenomenal limits the inexhaustibility of self-conscience, but also of the own freedom, proper to human nature as a spiritual person, because the law, no

---

[491] Devoutedly Varsanufie and Ioan. "Spiritual writings", Scrisori duhovniceşti, 763, Philocalia, vol. X.

matter how generous it may be, remains within the limits of human finitude, even when is trying to conceptualize, to recognize and guarantee this preciousless human divine gift, that is the freedom of conscience, about which Priest Arsenie Boca said that "it is the deepest spiritual good that man has in his hand throughout his life." Therefore, the freedom of conscience being a spiritual good, more than the material goods, must be cultivated, developed and mostly defended against any kind of constraints and interference, some coming precisely from the distorted application in relation to the profound existential meanings of the principles and norms of law.

III. Legal meanings of the freedom of conscience

This fundamental right is stipulated and recognized in most of the international declarations and treaties referring to the human fundamental rights and freedoms, starting with the Universal Declaration in 1948. It is at the foundation of other fundamental rights, such as the freedom of speech, freedom of association, freedom of mass media. At its core is a natural law that provides for the individual to be able to express, in private or in public, a certain conception about the world, to have or not have a religion, to belong or not to a religious faith or an organization of any kind, recognized by the existing constitutional order at a given time. It expresses at the same time the freedom to think, to have opinions, theoretical concepts, feelings, ideas expressed publicly, privately or not, so that no one can interfere or censorship, or know without the person's will, these thoughts. It is a natural right, because man distinguishes from other forms of life by the very existence of conscience and freedom to think, to have feelings.

Human conscience must not be directed by administrative means, though it must be the result of his freedom to think and to share his own thoughts expressed. The freedom of conscience involves also the moral and conscience responsibility for the thoughts expressed. The responsibility, including the juridical one, intervenes only when the thought or opinion are being expressed, in which case they may harm the dignity, honor and freedom of thought of another subject of law or even the social order or lawfull order, therefore the freedom of conscience is closely related to the freedom of expression, the latter one representing precisely the possibility acknowledged to man to express his thoughts. Consequently, the freedom of conscience has a complex content, whose legal content is expressed in three dimensions: freedom of thought, freedom of conscience and freedom of religion.

The freedom of religion, as a matter of content of the freedom of conscience, means the exteriorizing of a faith, religions and, secondly, the freedom to join a religious organization and the ritual practiced. It is necessary that religion or religious organization be known by the state through the law and the activity of a certain religious cult not be considered as contrary to the lawfull order or good morals. The organizing of the religious cults recognized by the State, is free and reflected in their own statutes. Over time, the relations between the state and the religious authority can be categorized into three types: 1. State is mistaken to the religious authority; 2. State supports the religious authority, but differentiates from it; 3. State takes a position of indifference towards the religious authority.

Romania's Constitution consecrates the separation of state from the authority, but obliges the state authorities to support religions cults recognized by law, including by financial means. It also proclaims the religious autonomy, meaning that each denomination is free to organize the form of the ritual, education, relations with the cult followers, the relationship with the state. The religious autonomy must be exercised only by respecting the human rights, morals and lawfull order. Art. 29 of the Constitution referrs to the relationships between religions, according to the following principles: equality between believers and nonbelievers; it requires cultivating tolerance and mutual respect; are forbidden all forms, means or acts of religious enmity.

The doctrine in specialty reveals some interesting aspects about the legal content of the freedom of conscience, sometimes called the freedom of thought.

Thus, an important dimension of the juridical content is *"the right to have a belief"*. This is a right with a general character, protecting the interior citadel, ie the domain of the personal opinions and religious beliefs. It is important to notice that, legally, the right to have an opinion may not be subjected to restrictions, conditioning, limitations or exceptions. The European Court of Human Rights in Strasbourg emphasizes that the freedom of religion is "one of the vital elements that contributes to forming the identity of believers and their conception of life" - Decision on 20th of September 1994 A.295 - A. Understood in a wider sense by the European Court, this right is used both by believers and by the atheists "agnostics, skeptics and neutral people."

According to the Strasbourg Court, "the belief" - a term used by the international legal instruments - distinguishes from the mere "opinions and ideas" and denotes the "views that reach a certain degree in intensity, seriousness, consistency and relevance" – Decision on 25th of February 1982, A.48. We emphasize an interesting statement in this regard of the Court: a faith that is essentially or exclusively in the cultivation and distribution of a narcotic drug can not enter the scope of a legal protection given by the European Convention on Human Rights.

The right to have opinions relates, therefore, to the practicing of spiritual or philosophical opinions that have a valuable, identifiable content and thus may be subjected to the juridical protection. The right to have an opinion involves state neutrality in regard to the moral and political beliefs. This obligation of neutrality excludes any assessment of state authorities regarding the legitimacy of beliefs and ways of expressing them. Understood thus, the right to have an opinion takes a triple aspect in legal terms. It represents, firstly, the freedom of every person to have or adopt a belief or religion in its sole discretion, without involving the freedom to deny the validity of the compelling legislative provisions, backed on objections arising from certain religious beliefs.

A second issue concerns *the freedom of not having a belief or religion*. In this way, in legal terms, the individual is protected against "any duty to directly participate in religious activities against his will" (see, on that regard the Court decision on May 9th, 1989, A187).

Finally, *the right to express an opinion expresses the legal guarantee of individual's freedom to change his belief or religion without suffering any coercion or prejudice*. In this spirit, the United Nations General Assembly adopted on 25th of November 1981 the Declaration on the Elimination of all forms of intolerance and of discrimination based on religious faith or beliefs, international document which prohibits "any distinction, exclusion, restriction or preference based on religious faith or belief".

Another aspect is the "*human right to manifest one's beliefs*". This right includes every person's freedom to manifest one's beliefs, individually or collectively, in public or private. The right has to do with the freedom of expression and refers in particular to the manifestation of religious beliefs. It is interesting to notice that in the European Court's opinion, the freedom to manifest the religious beliefs includes also "the right to try to convince your neighbor."

Social expression of freedom of thought, conscience and religion, with very diverse consequences, the freedom to manifest the beliefs may be subjected to some restrictions within law provisions. The European jurisprudence provides many examples of restrictions on the right of the individuals to express one's beliefs, justified by the protection of public order, lawfull order or moral order, or even health.

As highlighted in a decision delivered on 25th of May 1993, the European Court held that: "In a democratic society where several religions coexist within the same population, the limiting of the right of individuals to express their beliefs may prove to be necessary to reconcile the interests of different groups and ensure that everyone's beliefs are respected". The 'public order' clause allows in these situations the protection of the freedom of thought, conscience and religion and condemns the "poor quality" proselytism, characterized by abusive pressure which take the harassment form, or the abuse of power. In the same spirit, the protection of children's right to education, where conflicting with the right of parents to respect their religious, prevails on the latter one.

The freedom of individuals to manifest one's religion includes the participation in religious community life and assumes that the latter one "can function peacefully, without the state arbitrary interference" (see the Decision on 26th of October 2000, A.78). The state has the obligation to guarrantee not only the religious pluralism, but the internal pluralism within a particular religious denomination; on this purpose, it must not arbitrate in matters of dogma conflicts within a religious community and must not interfere in favor of a community or other religion.

The freedom of religion must be interpreted so that the religious communities have the opportunity to ensure their own legal protection, of their members and assets and in particular, of its legal personality, in case where under the national law only the recognized religious denominations can be practiced (see the Metropolitan Church of Bassarabia and others against Moldova, the Decision on 13th of December 2001: The refusal of the authorities to officially recognize a Church).

IV. Freedom of thought, conscience and religion in European jurisprudence

The three concepts, namely: thought, conscience and religion, which are the topic for the protection in Article 9 of European Convention on Human Rights, the most important European legal instrument in this area, are closely interlinked. The notions of "thinking", "conscience" and "religion" that appear in the content of the Convention emphasize the broader content attributed to the freedom of thought. The European Court of Human Rights (hereinafter ECHR) has estimated that the notion of philosophical belief" designate the ideas based on knowledge and reasoning with regard to the world, life and society ... which a person adopts and applies in accordance with own conscience requirements. These ideas can be described briefly as an individual concept about life, about human behavior in society.[492]

The freedom of thought, conscience and religion is one of the foundations of a democratic society in the sense of Convention, "it appears, in its religious dimension, among the essential elements of identity of believers and conceptions of life, but it is also a precious asset for atheists, agnostics, skeptics and the indifferent ones. This stems from the pluralism paid dearly along centuries, yet necessary to such a society"[493]

C.E.D.O jurisprudence reveals two major aspects of the right guaranteed by Article 9: a) the freedom of the individual to adopt a belief that he manifests; b) the freedom of the individual to be or not part of a group, including to another religious cult and defend it when deemed necessary[494].

Most cases related to the infringement of provisions of Article 9 of the Convention debated on religious freedom. The international Court in Strasbourg emphasized the importance of respecting the pluralism and tolerance between different religious groups. In its relations with various religions, denominations and beliefs, the state must be neutral and impartial

---

[492] Decisions and Reports of the European Commission for Human Rights no.25. Report on 16th of May 1980.

[493] Case of Basarabia Mitropoly and others versus Moldova, Decision on December 13th 2001.

[494] Doina Micu, *quoted works*, p..91.

"the role of authorities in this case is not to eliminate tensions, by eliminating pluralism, but to ensure that conflicting groups tolerate each other." [495]

The freedom of thought, conscience and religion requires the state's obligation to restrain from exercising any constraint on individual's conscience. The European Commission has shown that Article 9 protects what is called "interior forum" of the person, ie areas of strictly personal beliefs and closely related deeds. However, this text does not protect any social behavior based on certain beliefs. The right guaranteed in Article 9 is not absolute, because in a democratic society, where many religions co-exist in the same population, it is necessary that this freedom be accompanied by limits to reconcile the interests of different groups and ensure the respecting of everyone's beliefs. Furthermore, Article 9 paragraph 2 stipulates the possible restrictions of freedom of conscience, thought and religion. In accordance with these provisions, the liberties consecrated in Article 9 may be subjected to some restrictions if they are prescribed by law and are necessary in a democratic society and aim one of the legitimate purposes expressly and restrictively set out in the Convention.

The compliance with the proportionality condition, as appropriate relationship between the restrictive measures and the legitimate aim pursued form the International Court topic of analysis. Of course, in this case the European Court of Human Rights considers the proportionality related to the nature of protected right, the situation in fact, the legitimate aim pursued, the kind and intensity of the restrictive measures imposed, having in consideration the respecting of the principle of pluralism and the two procedural criteria: "the necessity in a democratic society" and "the appreciation margin" recognized by the Contracting States.

The Court in Strasbourg acknowledges that states have a certain appreciation margin in regard to the requirements for the exercising of this freedom, but their power can not be discretionary. The jurisprudence is oriented towards a strict interpretation of limiting of the freedom of conscience and religion, related to the specific circumstances of the case and the legitimate aim pursued. To determine the extent of the margins of appreciation of the respondent State, the international Court emphasizes the importance of the

[495] Case of Basarabia Mitropoly and others versus Moldova, quoted previously.

deed for the recognition of the national authorities. Only a denomination recognized has a legal personality, therefore it may organize and operate, can stay in court to protect its heritage. In relation to these criteria C.E.D.O. considers that the refusal to recognize the applicant church has such implications on the religious freedom, so that it can neither be considered proportionate to the legitimate aim pursued, nor necessary in a democratic society, therefore, Article 9 of the Convention has been violated.

In connection with the guarantee of freedom of conscience, thought and religion, we can say that the principle of proportionality is an essential criterion to limit the discretionary power of public authorities and to eliminate abuses by unduly restricting of the exercising of a right protected by the Convention. Thus, in any case, an administrative procedure can not be used to impose rigid conditions and even prohibitive, to the exercising of certain denominations. Proportionality is not an abstract condition, but is determined by each case peculiarities but as results from the jurisprudence of the Court in Strasbourg, there are important value premises that determine the assessment of the proportionality relations between the restrictive measures ordered and the legitimate aim pursued.

V. Some conclusions

Conscience is an ontological dimension of the human being, a *given* that is an existential feature of man. *Inner self-conscience* is a divine *gift* that every man carries within himself as a vocation since the baptism, but which is actual through the theandric work of the grace and human. The *freedom of conscience* is constituted and accomplished not in a relationship with the material world subjected to determinism and natural causality and implicitly to all existential precariousness, but by being related to the authentical values universe, which follows naturally out of man's love relationship with God and his fellowmen.

The legal status of the freedom of conscience has as essence the freedom of self-conscience in its theological meaning. Priest Professor Dumitru Stăniloaie says that "man in his essence is spirit and freedom." Man's freedom has as foundation the freedom of conscience which, through faith, becomes *self-conscience*. This way is surpassed the individualism, egotism, the "ego" and everything meaning the existence of man thrown into the world according to Heidegger and Sartre.

The freedom of conscience is the long path, but the only tranquil way of man towards himself, towards his deeper self, to found himself in the infinity of love for God and people.

Noica said: "You need to be unfaithful to your ego on the way to innerself".

Bibliography

Frederic Sudre, European and International Law of Human Rights, "The European and International Law of Human Rights", Polirom Publishing House, Bucharest, 2006;

Corneliu Bârsan, European Convention on Human Rights. Comment on the articles, "The European Convention of Human Rights. Comments on the Articles", volume I, C.H. Beck Publishing House, Bucharest, 2010;

Ioan Muraru, Constitution and constitutionalism in the constitutional studies, "Constitution and constitutionalism in the constitutional studies", Actami Publishing House, Bucharest, 1995;

Doina Micu, Guaranteeing human rights, "Guaranteeing human rights", All Beck Publishing House, Bucharest, 1998;

Constantin Noica, Jurnal de idei, "Journal of Ideas", Humanitas Publishing House, Bucharest, 2013;

Marius Andreescu, The Principle of Proportionality in the Constitutional Law, "The Principle of Proportionality in the Constitutional Law", C.H. Beck Publishing House, Bucharest, 2007;

Marius Andreescu, Andra Nicoleta Puran, Constitutional Law, "Constitutional Law", Sitech Publishing House, Craiova, 2012;

24. HOW IS DICTATORSHIP POSSIBLE IN A DEMOCRACY? LEGAL, PHILOSOPHICAL AND THEOLOGICAL ASPECTS

Abstract:

Dictatorship and democracy have as their common essence the content and manner of manifestation of state power and human freedom. Dictatorship can have absolute forms, as history demonstrates, in which state power is exercised most of the time by a single person, and civil liberties are significantly reduced, formally proclaimed or annihilated. Conversely, no form of democratic organization of society in which social freedoms and fundamental rights are recognized, enshrined and guaranteed can be outside the power of the state exercised by the rulers in the name of and for the ruled. Any form of state organization of society, be it democratic or not, implies this distinction or separation between the rulers and the ruled, the former exercising the power of the state on behalf of the people, which in the forms of constitutional democracy is the owner of it and of national sovereignty.

This is why, in our opinion, state power being a constant in any political regime, including the democratic one, its exercise can take dictatorial forms including in democracy and especially in contemporary state democracies. The dictatorship of power in democracy can be expressed essentially in state practices that represent excess power especially in relation to the exercise of fundamental rights and freedoms. This idea we want to develop and argue in what follows from a legal, philosophical and theological perspective.

Key words:

Political power/ dictatorship/ democracy/ secularization/ excess of power/ exceptional situations/ dictatorship in democracy

I. Power and freedom

The history of state-organized society and political and governing regimes is contained in the dialectic of the relationship between state power and human freedom on the other. In the historical moments when the power of the state predominates, it manifests itself in accentuated forms, sometimes on the part of a single man, and civil liberties are formally proclaimed, fenced or limited, it is said that we are in the presence of a dictatorial, totalitarian political regime

In the situation where the political regime is constitutional and is based on the reality of the principle of the supremacy of the law and of equality before the law including for the holders of state power, human freedom has a predominant character over power, it is enshrined by constitutions and laws, the limits of freedom are those determined by the need for social coexistence and mutual respect between the holders of these freedoms, and the restrictions, conditions and restrictions on the exercise of individual freedoms have an exceptional character, there is a democratic political regime

Therefore, dictatorship and democracy have as their common essence the content and the way of manifestation of state power and human freedom. Dictatorship can have absolute forms, as history demonstrates, in which state power is exercised most of the time by a single person, and civil liberties are significantly reduced, formally proclaimed or annihilated. Conversely, no form of democratic organization of society in which social freedoms and fundamental rights are recognized, enshrined and guaranteed can be outside the power of the state exercised by the rulers in the name of and for the ruled. Any form of state organization of society, be it democratic or not, implies this distinction or separation between the rulers and the governed, the former exercising the power of the state on behalf of the people, which in the forms of constitutional democracy is the owner of it and of national sovereignty.

This is why, in our opinion, state power being a constant in any political regime, including the democratic one, its exercise can take dictatorial forms including in democracy and especially in contemporary state democracies. The dictatorship of power in democracy can be expressed essentially in state practices that represent excess power especially in relation to the exercise of fundamental rights and freedoms. This idea we want to develop and argue in what follows from a legal, philosophical and theological perspective.

From the beginning until now, human society is marked by two constants that have an ontological value: the struggle for power and, on the other hand, the struggle against power, both in situations where it is illegitimate because it takes the form of dictatorship or even tyranny, and in the variants of apparent legitimacy, especially in democratic societies, such as for example the legitimate political activity of the opposition to access power or the actions of civil society and natural persons against the abuse of power.

These ontological constants of any human society are inevitable whatever the form of social organization or the characteristics of political regimes, including in democratic societies, because the existential and functional essence of any social system is the expression of the contradictory difference between the rulers and the ruled, between society as a whole and on the other hand, man in his concreteness and personality, between the normative order and the moral value order, between law and freedom, between public interest and private interest and of course between man's vocation to intangible fundamental rights, and on the other hand the public interest of the state of to condition, limit and restrict their exercise.

These contradictions, if they remain in their absolute form, through excellent antagonism can be destructive for a state-organized society, as history has demonstrated. All history reveals the political and legal solutions that, especially in the modern period, were consecrated to avoid dictatorial forms of exercising power. Here are some of them consecrated starting with the first written Constitution of the world - the US Constitution, adopted in 1787 -, the (French) Declaration of of human and citizen rights since 1789, up to contemporary domestic and international political and legal instruments: the supremacy of the law and the Constitution, the separation and balance of powers in the state, the proclamation and guarantee of fundamental human rights and freedoms, judicial and constitutional control.

Undeniably, these principles are in fact features of the rule of law, consecrated and constitutionally guaranteed, they define contemporary democratic societies and practically eliminate the totalitarian, dictatorial forms of state power.

However, the differences and contradictions mentioned above, because they are ontological constants of society, exist in any democratic society. In addition, there is a subtle situation, namely the difference between the legality of state decisions and, on the other hand, their legitimacy. These realities can determine or favor the excess of power of the authorities in societies built on the principles of modern constitutionalism.

In this context, there remains an essential problem, not only theoretical but also practical, namely that of determining the limits of state power in a democratic society, specifically in Romania, and of finding solutions in cases of excessive manifestation of state authority.

II. The secularization of the state and contemporary civil society, premises of dictatorship in democracy

The modern period of world history imposed the principle of separation of the state from the Church in relation to the activity of government. This principle was established by the Savior Jesus Christ himself when he said: "Give therefore to Caesar the things that are Caesar's and to God the things that are God's" (Matthew 22,21). Therefore, the Church must not get involved in the activity of governance, both as an institution and through its servants. At the same time, the state authorities must respect and guarantee the freedom of organization and operation of the Church, enshrine normatively, including in constitutions, and respect freedom of conscience and religious freedom, as fundamental human rights.

The separation of the state and the Church is necessary because the institutions of the state on the one hand and the Church on the other hand have different natures, goals and different activities. The Church, with special reference to the Orthodox Church, is the Body of Christ and the communion of believers united in the Holy Spirit, but also each believer is the member of the Body of Christ. The Church was established by the Lord Jesus Christ at the descent of the Holy Spirit. The Orthodox Church is a divine and human institution at the same time.

In contrast, the state and state authorities are human institutions, constituted by human political will enshrined in laws and constitutions. There is, however, an order of preference between the authority of the Church, which expresses the very authority of the Savior always present in his Church, and on the other hand the authority of state institutions, an order of preference expressed by the Holy Fathers through the phrase "We obey Caesar, and we worship God" '.

The application of this principle in the government activity carried out by the state through the institutions and dignitaries who are invested with power attributions and the realization of the entire state management activity in accordance with the truths of the Orthodox faith would have particularly beneficial consequences for the state, society and each person , would radically transform the meaning and realities of contemporary democracy, which in this way would be built not only on the political will of the state and not only on legal rules and principles, but at the same time would be based on the values and truths of faith, established not by human activity, but by divine, natural or supernatural revelation.

The realization of this form of social democracy, unlike all other forms and variants based on the political will of the rulers and the law, must start not only from the duty imposed by law on the rulers to exercise their powers in accordance with the law and for the purposes established by this, but also from their own conscience that would lead them to apply the power with which they were invested in a Christian, Orthodox sense. The principle of such a government was established by our Savior Jesus Christ when he said that: "And whoever wants to be first among you, let him be servant of all" (Mark, 10,44). The implementation by the rulers of this great principle of democracy focused on Christian values, to which the worthy Metropolitan Bartolomeu Anania also refers in one of the sermons on the Sundays of the Triod, would lead to radical transformations in the content and ways of exercising power state by those invested with such powers. The exercise of governance would fully correspond to the public interest and would no longer be confused with personal interest. The notion of public interest would receive a concrete, real content and would not only have an abstract, legal meaning as it happens now. The public good would become a real goal of government activity, as they say in law, a "good government" would be reached. Last but not least, democracy would no longer be exclusive to the law and its supremacy, but would become a democracy of the person and human freedom, in which man is not for the law but the law is for man. It thus moves from the forms of global democracy, such as the democracy of the masses, or from the democratic individualism of the present, focused on human rights considered in themselves as absolute legal values, but without God, to the democracy of freedom, in which the power of the law is subordinated the superiority of the person and the freedom of man. The essence of such a democratic reality of society was well expressed several centuries ago by Thomas Aquinas: "The individual is for the state, the state is for the person, and the person is for God".

In the current conditions of the state and society, we are far from such a reality regarding the exercise of power in a democratic society. A democracy built on Christian values cannot be established by law, but requires a deep transformation of the conscience of those who govern, of those at the top of state power, in the sense that they consider themselves dependent in everything they do on God and responsible in relation to it, It is necessary to refute the selfishness and the immeasurable pride that the feeling of power gives and which leads to the confusion between public interest and personal interest, to the ignorance of man as a person created in the image and likeness of God, a rediscovery of oneself is necessary true which gives the governed the conscience that they must fulfill the law and exercise their power as the servant of all and not as the master of all. The worthy of mention, Archbishop Justinian Chira emphasized the way of being of the contemporary man, of the rulers who believe themselves sufficient: "The stage to which we have risen through civilization gives the contemporary man the feeling of omnipotence. It seems to him that no one has ever been like him. But he is still an unfulfilled man, even if he is an enlightened man, a smart man, a learned man. We are very little aware of the mysteries that are around us. We are still very limited."

The consciousness of a person who holds powers and is invested with high dignities and functions, that he depends on God and in everything he does is related to God is the expression of the humility of the statesman, of the dignitary who fears God and is ashamed of man . The Savior told the parable of the merciless, unjust, proud and arrogant judge who did not fear God and was not ashamed of man (Luke, 18,1-8). This is the current prototype of many heads of state, politicians, dignitaries and magistrates.

If the dignitary or the politician has the consciousness of humility that I talked about above, then their activity can lead to a democracy built on Christian values. Humility also implies thanksgiving and gratitude for the gifts received from God, including for the public dignities and responsibilities that a statesman has. In this sense, we want to exemplify what Archbishop Justinian Chira said: "And then, enjoying the dowry that God has given us, we cannot declare ourselves omnipotent. But we are always grateful to God for giving us this gift of creative thinking, of reason, of thinking, with which we were able to create and with which we will continue to create. Thinking in this way and seeing in everything the work of God, rejoicing, you know how to appreciate."

This state of consciousness of dignitaries and heads of state, if it existed, would be a sure guarantee for their avoidance of excess power, of any form of dictatorial manifestation in a democracy.

As I said, the current society, the state and its leaders are far from such a reality of self-awareness, a fact that leads to the existence and existential manifestation including of state power without God, which favors the excess of power and the dictatorial manifestations of the leaders of state and those who hold and exercise positions of authority in the state.

Contemporary society and the state want to be without God, without Christianity and above all without the true faith which is Orthodoxy. Currently, we are witnessing a real fight against the Christian faith, the Church, especially the Orthodox Church in attempts to denigrate and fight them. This reality is also present at the legal level.

European democratic constitutions, including Romania's, do not enshrine the separation of the state from the Church, but the autonomy of the Church vis-à-vis the state (See in this sense also the Constitution of Romania, art. 29 paragraph 5). The concept of autonomy implies a lower degree of legal and decision-making freedom and implicitly the possibility of state intervention in the activity of the Church. Laws, decisions and any state measures can affect, based on the concept of autonomy and the conduct of the Church's activity, which means, if not a subordination, a lower position of the Church vis-a-vis the state. The Church and all believers must respect the laws of the state, obey the orders of the leaders and dignitaries of the state, but only God is to be worshipped. This truth would at least mean a position of legal equality between the Church and the state, which is obviously not possible today, given that the constitutions enshrine a freedom of the Church and the cults only within the limits of the concept of autonomy. The state has the predominant position and can intervene in the exercise of freedom of conscience and belief. This right of the state established by law allows those who exercise state power, heads of state, parliaments, governments and sometimes even the judiciary to impose unjustified, often contrary, limits, conditions, restrictions on the exercise of religious freedom and especially the freedom to exercise the right Orthodox faith the principles and values of the rule of law and always contrary to the divine nature of the Church, of what Orthodoxy represents for the Romanian people.

By Law no. 489/2006 on religious freedom, amended and republished this year, it is provided in art. 2 para. 2 that the freedom of persons to manifest their religious faith can be restricted by measures ordered by the state, under the law, if these measures are necessary in a democratic society, for the purposes that are listed, including for the protection of order, health or public morality. It is an almost faithful reproduction of the provisions of art. 53 of the Constitution which regulates the conditions under which the exercise of fundamental rights and freedoms can be restricted. This legal text no longer refers to the principle of proportionality as a condition for restricting the exercise of certain rights, a principle mentioned in art. 53 of the Constitution, which means that the discretionary power of the state authorities can manifest itself even more when it is desired to restrict freedom of conscience and religious freedom. We also emphasize the aspect that in modern philosophical and constitutional doctrine, freedom of conscience and religious freedom are natural rights, properties of human nature, and therefore they are immutable, they are intangible. It seems that the doctrine of natural rights is ignored by the current rulers.

Based on these legal provisions and the measures ordered as a result of the establishment of the state of emergency on the territory of Romania with the aim of combating and preventing the spread of the pandemic that affects all of human society, Churches and Monasteries were closed to the faithful. Religious services can be held in the Church, but without the presence of the faithful.

In our opinion, through these normative measures, the freedom of belief, as a fundamental human right, was not only restricted, but was abolished, abolished. The exercise by every Orthodox Christian of the right faith presupposes participation in the holy services of the Church and in particular the Holy Liturgy, the possibility of performing the Holy Mysteries of the Church, in particular the Mystery of Holy Confession and the Mystery of Holy Communion With the Holy Blood and Body of the Saviour, involves the possibility to worship and pray individually or in a group in front of the holy icons of the holy relics located in Church. By closing the Churches, the faithful cannot exercise these holy practices of the Orthodox cult, they no longer have religious freedom.

Based on these restrictive and illegitimate normative provisions, in some situations the police and the gendarmes forcefully removed the believers from the Church, they did not allow those who wanted to submit a prayer to a priest in the Church or to light a candle in the Church and pray for the living or for those who have passed to the Lord. They are examples of serious abuses committed by state authorities, abuses that unfortunately cannot be censured or sanctioned by any court.

These measures represent an abusive and discretionary exercise of state power, an example of the fact that dictatorship is also possible in a democracy. All this is a consequence of the secularization of the state, but also of society. The communion of believers in the Church is considered a mere gathering, similar to any other grouping of people, and the divine nature of the Church is ignored. We remind you that in the history of the Christian life of the Romanian state there was no similar situation. On the contrary, during the great epidemics or calamities that passed over our people, the leaders of the state at that time, less from the communist and contemporary period, encouraged prayer in the Church, participated with believers in religious services. Historical documents testify that the prayer of the Church and the faithful saved the Romanian people from the disaster, made the mercy of God and the Mother of God return to us.

The restrictive measures dictated by the state on religious freedom, under the pretext of protecting the health of the population, are unconstitutional. All legal doctrine in the matter of restricting the exercise of certain rights and freedoms, as well as domestic and international jurisprudence, clearly and consistently states that such restrictive measures, under no circumstances, nor in exceptional situations, can affect the substance of fundamental rights and freedoms and cannot abolish them . The normative provisions by which the closure of Churches for the faithful was ordered affect the very substance of freedom of belief, they practically abolish this fundamental right. The transmission of religious services on TV, radio or the Internet cannot represent the effective exercise by each person of the freedom of belief. The mentioned technical means can reflect religious freedom, but they cannot replace it.

As I have stated before, in such situations of major danger to the health of the population, measures are necessary, including those of a restrictive nature, which allow the prevention of the spread of diseases and the protection of people's health, but it is not allowed to abolish the freedom of belief itself. Many representatives of the clergy and others state with good reason that we are currently witnessing a real persecution against the Church and especially against the true Orthodox faith.

It is the culmination of multiple and repeated attempts by many important politicians and statesmen, by many governments, to denigrate Christianity and especially the right Orthodox faith, under the pretext of promoting some principles of human rights, principles that were formulated, understood and applied rationally according to Protestant criteria and without taking into account the Christian values that imposed themselves and characterized European culture and civilization for almost 2000 years.

The separation of the state from the Church, was understood and applied, not by reference to God, but by human measures and reasonings, it has dire consequences. The most obvious consequence is the secularization of the state and society, expressed expressly in the refusal to relate to God and in the refusal to accept Christianity and the true faith. Moreover, this secularization also materializes through the non-recognition of Christian culture and civilization as dominant in Europe, even through measures against the Church and the true faith. What is worse is that more and more people are moving away from God, from the Christian faith, from the right Orthodox faith, falsely considering that they can exist by themselves, without God and without the right faith or through all kinds of Protestant innovations that deviate from to Orthodox values and truths, because they are not creations of human reason but realities revealed by Our Lord Jesus Christ, contained in the Holy Gospel and transmitted through apostolic tradition uninterrupted until today. The words Savior and the holy Orthodox faith are more relevant than ever.

In the provisions of art. 29 of the Constitution, which legally enshrines freedom of conscience, does not expressly mention the Christian faith and the Orthodox Church. Paragraph 1 of this article stipulates: Freedom of thought and opinion, as well as freedom of religious beliefs cannot be restricted in any way. No one can be forced to adopt an opinion or adhere to a religious belief, contrary to his convictions". Paragraph 2 of the same article shows that:" Freedom of conscience is guaranteed; it must manifest itself in a spirit of tolerance and mutual respect". The other paragraphs of the article enshrine the freedom of religious cults, the relations between cults and between them and the state, as well as the right of parents or guardians to ensure the education of minor children according to their own beliefs.

Of course, all these constitutional regulations are valuable, in accordance with the current democratic standards, but we believe that more is needed than that, because it is necessary to be constitutionally consecrated that Romania is an Orthodox Christian country, as many of the high ministers of the Orthodox Church testify, theologians and scholars, and the Orthodox Church, through the community of Orthodox believers, is the majority compared to all other cults or denominations existing on the territory of Romania.

The pre-war and inter-war constitutional tradition represents an argument in this sense. Thus, in the Constitution of Romania from 1866, in art. 5 par. 2, it was expressly mentioned that: "The Orthodox Christian religion being the religion of the vast majority of Romanians, the Orthodox Church is the dominant church in the Romanian state". A similar text also existed in the 1923 Constitution at art. 22, paragraph 3 as well as in the 1938 Constitution at art. 19 paragraph 2.

These Romanian constitutional traditions have not been taken over by the contemporary constitutional legislator. It is a regrettable legal fact in our opinion, but which is in accordance with the secularized state society in which we live, with the accentuated secularization of the state and society Thus, consistently the atheist politicians, who hold power in Europe and not only refused any reference in the basic legal and political instruments of the European Union, as well as in the constitutions of the countries of this continent, to the Christian spiritual traditions and reality of Europe and refused to record the truth according to which the Christian faith and culture are dominant in this space. It is a serious error that tries to be justified on the idea that the reference to Christianity would be offensive to non-Christians or atheists and would not respect the principle of tolerance. These arguments are an obvious expression of the rationalized humanism of human rights falsely considered by some to be a new religion.

The rejection of Christianity in legal and constitutional terms is an important cause that favors the dictatorial manifestations of politicians in a democratic society.

The evidence, which overwhelms the mind and the power of understanding of man, but which should be consecrated and respected also on a legal level is completely different. Not only is the Christian religion dominant, even in these times of secularization of society and the state, but the evidence above this world shows that the Orthodox Church is the only one of all the existing cults and confessions that preserves whole and unaltered the apostolic tradition, in which The Holy Spirit is present and working in all His fullness, and which expresses the right faith.

Dictatorship is favored by the social context, the deficiencies of the legal and constitutional system, the state of man, society and the political class, and last but not least, the lack of a clean and good conscience of the politicians who live too much in the pride of power. An important aspect that favors the dictatorship is the refusal of the true faith, the ignorance or indifference towards it. There is a lot to say. I think, however, that the vast majority of Romanian voivodes and princes professed and lived in the Orthodox faith, some are recognized as saints and martyrs, they built churches. The kings of Romania, although originating from Catholic families, were Orthodox, manifested their faith in many ways, encouraged Orthodoxy and supported the Church. The motto of Charles I, but also of the royal house, inscribed on the royal flag is "Nihil sine Deo" - (Nothing without God).

I think the motto of today's politicians is Everything without God. Romanian politicians, especially those who hold important public dignities live in their own pride, ignore God, the true faith and the Church. I have not seen any Romanian head of state or prime minister participating in Orthodox services, except for some events that also had political significance. The communist leaders from other times and the current leaders with some exceptions such as Corneliu Coposu, have in common the fact that they fully affirm their ignorance, indifference, contempt towards the Orthodox faith, towards the Church especially the Orthodox Church, which favors dictatorial behaviors. It is far too easy to accept commands and directives from foreign powers and which are a counter to the right millennial Orthodox faith of the Romanian people.

III. Dictatorship and democracy

The doctrine, in most of it, reveals the insurmountable contradiction that exists between democratic political regimes and, on the other hand, those considered to be dictatorial, or more simply, between dictatorship and democracy.

Dictatorship means the centralization and concentration of power, the denial of pluralism in all its forms, the absolute or discretionary power of the governed, the coercion and excessive limitation of individual freedoms, the rigid separation of the rulers from the governed, the non-existence or formal existence of constitutional guarantees regarding human rights, the non-existence or character fictitious, formal of some essential principles for the state organization of society, such as the principle of the supremacy of the law and the constitution. For a synthetic expression, dictatorship represents the annulment, abolition or, in the best case, the minimization of the individuality of the singular, of diversity and the affirmation of unity as an abstract and constraining generality.

In contrast, democracy is associated with the idea of the rule of law, focused on the principle that has become real and applicable of the supremacy of the law and the constitution. The centralization and concentration of power is replaced, as a way of organizing state powers, with the principle of their separation and balance. Pluralism, in all its forms, is institutionalized and guaranteed. Individual freedoms are also enshrined and guaranteed, their exercise being governed by the rule according to which: the limit of any individual freedom is the need to respect the similar freedoms of others. The legitimacy of state power implies the distinction between the being or essence of power and, on the other hand, its exercise. In a democratic regime it is not necessary to demonstrate the legitimacy of power as such, because the axiom according to which "the holder of power is the people or the nation" does not require demonstration, being a premise for the entire political and legal construction of the state-organized society. Instead, any democratic regime must find the means by which the exercise of power, or in other words, the phenomenality of power, is legitimized and legitimized. Such legitimacy is achieved when there are no irreconcilable contradictions between the essence (the power as such held by the people) and the forms of exercise (the phenomenon of power). The legitimacy of the exercise of power in the case of democratic political regimes signifies the reflection of the essence of power in its phenomenality, respectively in the way of organization and exercise.

Therefore, in the case of democracy there is always a conceptual, but also a real, distinction between the legitimacy of the essence of power that does not require demonstration, as such resulting from the simple proclamation of the principle that the power belongs to the people, and on the other hand, the phenomenal legitimacy of the organization and the exercise of power which is not a "given" but a construction, first of all constitutional, realized in the concrete forms of institutional organization and exercise of state authority. The legitimacy of the organization and exercise of power is external to the phenomenality of power, in the sense that phenomenality is not the source of its legitimacy, but it is built within a relationship whose content is the correspondence between the essence of power and the forms of manifestation.

Power, in its essence, can be considered "a thing in itself", in the Kantian sense, because full knowledge of the essence will never be possible. The reality of state power considered in the relationship between essence and phenomenon also reveals another aspect: the phenomenality of power will never be able to fully correspond to the essence of power. The object of knowledge for legal or political sciences is the phenomenon of power and not its essence. Therefore, the legitimacy of the phenomenal manifestations of power represents an ideal to which the concrete forms of organization and exercise of power come close, but without ever reaching it.

The legitimacy of the phenomenality of power consists, among other things, in realizing the principle of representation. This principle highlights very well the distinction between the being or essence of power and on the other hand the phenomenon of power. The holder of the power cannot exercise it directly, except in exceptional situations. The essence is not the manifestation of power. The exercise of power reflects the being of power without, however, encompassing it. Thus, state institutions exercise power without owning it, therefore, they need the recognition of the legitimacy of acts of power, a fact conferred mainly by applying the principle of representation.

Its power and phenomenality are undoubtedly a central place of democracy. If the phenomenal legitimacy of power is an ideal that the concrete forms of institutional realization through the principle of representation can approach, then it follows that democracy, in its essence, is also an ideal in relation to which social and political reality is constructed and manifested, but without that the democratic ideal coincides with the social and political reality. Professor Ion Deleanu's statement is relevant in this regard: "Democracy is a form of moral perfection. It measures both the organization and functioning of power in order to humanize it, as well as the way of life of citizens to shape it".

It is necessary to distinguish between ideal democracy, which is a purely speculative construction based on the possible coincidence between the essence and the phenomenality of power, but also on an ethical imperative that would mean the unity of will between the individual and society, and on the other hand, real democracy, characterized by the contradictory dichotomy between the essence and the phenomenality of power, between the individual and society. Real democracy has concrete, multiple forms of manifestation (such as the form of "parliamentary or representative democracy"), it is not an immutable fact but is in a continuous evolutionary process which, considering historical progress, has as its finality, never possible to be realized, the ideal democracy. The science of law has real democracy as its object of study, or more precisely its forms of manifestation and realization. Paradoxically, however, the legitimacy of any form of real democracy is conferred by the values and principles of ideal democracy, the latter forming the object of study mainly of metaphysics.

Unlike dictatorship, democracy involves the rehabilitation of the individual, of the particular, which is no longer absorbed and dissolved in the social abstract general or concentrated power. In democracy, the individual has ontological value and manifests itself in existential coexistence with the social general. In other words, the individual has the meaning and power of the general, the latter being legitimate, precisely because it recognizes the existential and ontological dimension of the individual. Power, even in its concrete manifestations, is the expression of the general as such, reflected for example in the notion of "public interest". In a democratic society, the legitimacy of the act of power does not consist in reflecting its own generality (of the public interest), but in respecting the individuality of diversity in all the specific forms of existential pluralism. In constitutional terms, this aspect evokes the relationship between "majority and opposition".

The problem of democracy cannot be reduced to the phenomenon of power as it seems to result from the constitutional definition of democracy that we find in art. 2 of the Constitution of the French Republic: "government of the people by the people and for the people". The essence of democracy, in our opinion, is the forms and content of the concrete relationship between society and the individual. The report expresses a one-sided contradiction, because society can contradict the individual (particular and diversity), which is typical of dictatorship, but the individual does not contradict society, a situation specific to democracy. Moreover, the dialectical relationship between the individual and society specific to democracy is an affirmative one, not including a negation as Hegel claimed. It is typical of democracy that society affirms the individual (individuality and diversity), not denying it, therefore consecrating and guaranteeing individuality and diversity. Any broader analysis of the phenomenon of democracy also involves references to the concepts of civilization and culture, to the relationships between civilization, society and the individual.

In our opinion, there is obviously a contradiction between dictatorship and democracy, but a one-sided one: dictatorship is in contradiction and excludes democracy, but democracy does not exclude forms of dictatorship. The space and object of this study do not allow us a broader analysis of this interesting problem, however we mention that in the doctrine references are made to forms of dictatorship that can characterize any democratic regime: the dictatorship of the parliament, the dictatorship of the masses or the dictatorship of the majorities. In all these situations of democratic reality, the affirmative contradictions highlighted above become negative (the majority excluded or ignores the minority). As a consequence, we end up exercising authority in discretionary forms, a fact that obviously essentially contradicts the values of ideal democracy.

John Stuart Mill, in his work "Civilization", published in 1836, considered that civilization is contrary to the state of nature or barbarism. A people is civilized when the social conditions in which it lives provide sufficient security guarantees, so that social peace is a reality. Among the consequences of the growth of civilization, the most significant, in the philosopher's opinion, is the fact that power tends to pass from individuals and small communities to the masses. The importance of the masses increases while that of individuals decreases. Along with the decrease in the role of the individual, of the person we say, the power of individual beliefs also decreases, and public opinion gains supremacy. In this ideological context, Stuart Mill emphasized that "the disadvantages of democracy consist precisely in this tyranny exercised by the masses, by majorities, by public opinion. That is why the political organization of the representative government must contain all the guarantees of the defense of the individual against the tyranny of the masses. Among other measures, Stuart Mill envisioned the representation of minority opinions in parliament.

The findings of the great philosopher are, in our opinion, fully valid for the contemporary forms of real or representative democracy. That is why the realization of the principle of representation in one of the types of electoral system must allow, as far as possible, the diminution or even the elimination of the forms of dictatorship in a real democracy by valuing individualities, of man not only as an individual but especially as a free person, of political or other minorities. In this way, the progress of a democratic society becomes a balanced one again, based on a unilateral affirmative contradiction in which the masses affirm and do not deny the person, and the majorities affirm the minorities. Thus, the famous parliamentary principle "minorities express themselves and the majority decides" should become: the legitimacy of the decision is given by the representativeness and power of expression of the minorities and above all by the respect of man as a person created in the image and likeness of God.

IV. Legality and legitimacy of state power in democracy

Legality, as a feature that must characterize the legal acts of public authorities, has as its central element the concept of "law". Andre Hauriou defined the law as a written general rule established by the public powers after deliberation and involving the direct or indirect acceptance of the governors. Ion Deleanu defines it as "the act that includes general and mandatory rules sanctioned by the coercive force of the state, when its application is not carried out out of conviction and which is susceptible to application whenever the conditions provided for in its hypothesis arise".

In a broad sense, the notion of law includes all legal acts that contain legal norms. The law in its narrow sense is the legal act of the parliament elaborated in accordance with the constitution, according to a predetermined procedure and which regulates the most general and most important social rules. A special place in the administered legislative system is given to the constitution defined as a fundamental law, located at the top of the hierarchy of the legislative system, which includes legal norms with superior legal force, which regulate fundamental and essential social relations, especially those regarding the establishment and exercise of state power.

The state of legality in the activity of public authorities is based on the concepts of the supremacy of the constitution and the supremacy of the law. The supremacy of the constitution is a quality of the fundamental law that essentially expresses its supreme legal force in the legal system. An important consequence of the supremacy of the fundamental law is the compliance of all law with the constitutional norms. The notion of legal supremacy of the law is defined as "that characteristic of it that finds its expression in the fact that the norms it establishes must not correspond to any other norms in apart from the constitutional ones, and the other legal acts issued by the state bodies are subordinated to it from the point of view of their legal effectiveness". Therefore, the supremacy of the law in the above meaning is subsequent to the principle of the supremacy of the constitution. It is important that legality, as a feature of the legal acts of the state authorities, implies compliance with the principle of the supremacy of the constitution and the supremacy of the law. Compliance with the two principles is a fundamental obligation of a constitutional nature enshrined in the provisions of art. 1 paragraph 5 of the Constitution. Failure to comply with this obligation attracts, as the case may be, the sanction of unconstitutionality or illegality of legal acts.

The legality of legal acts of public authorities implies the following requirements: the legal act must be issued in compliance with the competence provided by law; the legal act to be issued in accordance with the procedure provided by law; the legal act to comply with the higher legal norms as a legal force.

"Legitimacy" is a complex category with multiple meanings and which forms the research object for the general theory of law, philosophy of law, sociology and other disciplines. The meanings of this concept are multiple. We mention a few: the legitimacy of power; the legitimacy of the political regime; the legitimacy of a government; the legitimacy of the political system, etc. Referring to this concept, Jean Leca states: "The term legitimacy denotes the quality that gives the holder of a power the ability to order or prohibit, the ability to be obeyed without resorting to explicit physical violence or, which means the same thing , the faculty recognized as normal to successfully resort to coercion if necessary". The concept of legitimacy can also be applied in the case of legal documents issued by public authorities, being linked to the "margin of appreciation" recognized by them in the exercise of their powers.

The application and observance of the principle of legality in the activity of the state authorities is a complex problem, because the exercise of state functions also implies the discretionary power with which the state bodies are invested, or in other words, the authorities' right of discretion regarding the time of adoption and the content of the measures ordered. What is important to emphasize is the fact that discretionary power cannot be opposed to the principle of legality, as a dimension of the rule of law.

Legality represents a particular aspect of the legitimacy of legal acts of public authorities. Thus, a legitimate legal act is a legal legal act, issued within the scope of the margin of appreciation recognized by public authorities, which does not generate discrimination, privileges or unjustified restrictions of subjective rights and is appropriate to the factual situation that determines it and the purpose of the law. Legitimacy distinguishes between the discretionary power recognized by the state authorities, and on the other hand, the excess of power.

Not all legal acts that meet the conditions of legality are also legitimate. A legal act that respects the formal conditions of legality, but which generates discrimination or privileges or unjustifiably restricts the exercise of subjective rights or is not appropriate to the factual situation or the purpose pursued by the law, is an illegitimate legal act. Legitimacy, as a feature of the legal acts of the public administration authorities, must be understood and applied in relation to the principle of the supremacy of the Constitution.

V. Excess of power and exceptional situations

Antonie Iorgovan states that an essential problem of the rule of law is to answer the question: "where does the discretionary power end and where does the abuse of law begin, where does the legal behavior of the administration end, embodied by its right of appreciation, and where does the violation begin a subjective right or legitimate interest of the citizen? "

Addressing the same problem, Leon Duguit in 1900 makes an interesting distinction between "normal powers and exceptional powers" conferred on the administration by the constitution and laws, and on the other hand the situations in which the state authorities act outside the normative framework. The author divides these latter situations into three categories: 1) excess of power (when state authorities exceed the limits of legal powers); 2) misappropriation of power (when the state authority performs an act that falls within its competence pursuing a purpose other than that prescribed by law); 3) abuse of power (when the state authorities act outside their powers, but through acts that do not have a legal character).

Therefore, the application and observance of the principle of legality in the activity of the state authorities is a complex problem because the exercise of state functions also implies the discretionary power with which the state bodies are invested, or in other words the "right of appreciation" of the authorities regarding the time of adoption and the content of the measures ordered. Which is important to emphasize is the fact that discretionary power cannot be opposed to the principle of legality, as a dimension of the rule of law.

In the administrative doctrine, which mainly studies the issue of discretionary power, it was emphasized that the expediency of administrative acts cannot be opposed to their legality, and the conditions of legality can be divided into: general conditions of legality and, respectively, specific conditions of legality based on considerations of expediency. Consequently, legality is the corollary of validity conditions, and opportunity is a requirement (a dimension) of legality. However, the right of appreciation is not recognized by the state authorities in the exercise of all the powers they have. It should be noted the difference between the related competence of the state authorities that exists when the law imposes on them a certain strict decision-making behavior, and on the other hand the discretionary competence, a situation in which the state authorities can choose the means to achieve a legitimate goal or in general, when the body the state can choose between several decisions, within the limits of the law and its competence. We retain the definition proposed in the specialized literature of discretionary power: "it is the margin of freedom left to the discretion of an authority, so that in order to achieve the goal indicated by the legislator, it can resort to any means of action within the limits of its competence."

Although the issue of discretionary power is mainly studied by administrative law, the right of appreciation in the exercise of certain powers is a reality encountered in the activity of all state authorities. The Parliament, as the supreme representative body and the only legislative authority, has the widest limits to manifest its discretionary power, which is identified from the very characterization of the legislative act. Since the interwar period I.V. Gruia emphasized: "The need to legislate in a certain matter, the choice of the moment of legislation, the choice of the moment of implementation of the law, by fixing by the legislator the date of application of the law, the revision of previous legislations, which cannot limit and oblige the activity To the future Parliament, the restriction of social activities from their free and uncontrolled development and their submission to the norms and sanctions of the law, the content of the legislative act, etc., prove the sovereign and discretionary appreciation of the function of the legislative body."

These considerations are still valid today, because any parliament has the freedom to exercise its powers almost unlimitedly. The legal limit of this freedom is outlined only by the constitutional principles applicable to the legislative activity and the control mechanism of the constitutionality of the laws.

Discretionary power also exists in the activity of the courts. The judge is obliged to decide only when he is notified, within the limits of the notification. Beyond this is manifested the sovereign right of appreciation of the facts, the right to interpret the law, the right to set a minimum or maximum penalty, to grant or not mitigating circumstances, to establish the amount of compensation, etc. The exercise of these powers means nothing more than discretionary power.

Exceeding the limits of discretion means violating the principle of legality or what is called "excess of power" in legislation, doctrine and jurisprudence. Excess of power in the activity of state bodies is equivalent to the abuse of law, because it means the exercise of a legal competence without existing a reasonable motivation or without an adequate relationship between the ordered measure, the factual situation and the legitimate goal pursued.

The problem of excess of power is mainly the object of the doctrine of legislation and administrative jurisprudence. Thus, the jurisprudence of the administrative litigation courts in other states delimited the freedom of decision of the administration from the excess of power. The French Council of State uses the concept of "manifest error of judgement", to denote the situations in which the administration exceeds, through the adopted legal acts, the discretionary power. German administrative courts can annul administrative acts for excess of power or "misuse of power". In such situations, the legal acts of the administration have the appearance of legality, because they are adopted within the limits of the competence established by the law, but the excess of power consists in the fact that the administrative acts are contrary to the purpose of the law.

The Romanian administrative litigation law uses the concept of "excess of power of the administrative authorities", which it defines as: "the exercise of the right of appreciation belonging to the public administration authorities, by violating the fundamental rights and freedoms of citizens provided by the Constitution or the law" (art. .2, paragraph 1, letter m). For the first time, the Romanian legislator uses and defines the concept of excess of power and at the same time recognizes the competence of administrative litigation courts to sanction exceeding the limits of discretionary power through administrative acts.

The exceptional situations represent a particular case in which the state authorities, and especially the administrative ones, can exercise their discretionary power, there is obviously the danger of excess power.

In the doctrine, there is no unanimous opinion regarding the legal significance of exceptional situations. Thus, in the older French doctrine, the discretionary power is considered to be the freedom of decision of the administration within the framework allowed by law, and the opportunity evokes a de facto action of the public administration, in exceptional situations, action necessary (therefore timely) but contrary to the law. Jean Rivero believes that exceptional situations mean certain factual circumstances that have a double effect: the suspension of the application of the ordinary legal regime and the triggering of the application of a particular legislation whose requirements are defined by the judge. Another author identifies three characteristic elements for exceptional situations: 1) the existence of abnormal and exorbitant situations or serious and unforeseen events; 2) the impossibility or difficulty of acting in accordance with natural regulations; 3) the need to intervene quickly to protect a considerable, seriously threatened interest.

The excess of power can be manifested in these circumstances at least through three aspects: a) the assessment of a factual situation as an exceptional case, although it does not have this significance (lack of objective and reasonable motivation); b) the measures ordered by the competent state authorities, by virtue of their discretionary power, exceed what is necessary to protect the seriously threatened public interest; c) if these measures excessively, unjustifiably, limit the exercise of constitutionally recognized fundamental rights and freedoms.

The existence of crisis situations - economic, social, political or constitutional - does not justify the excess of power. In this sense, Professor Tudor Draganu states: "the idea of the rule of law requires that they (exceptional situations n.n.) find appropriate regulations in the text of the constitutions, whenever they have a rigid character. Such a constitutional regulation is necessary to limit the areas of social relations, in which the transfer of competence from the parliament to the government can take place, to emphasize its temporary nature, by establishing some terms of applicability and to specify the purposes for which it is carried out ."

Of course, the excess of power is not a phenomenon that manifests itself only in the practice of the executive bodies, it can be encountered in the activity of the parliament or the courts.

We consider that the discretionary power recognized by the state authorities is exceeded, and the measures ordered represent an excess of power, whenever the existence of the following situations is found:

1. the ordered measures do not pursue a legitimate goal;

2. the decisions of the public authorities are not appropriate to the factual situation or the legitimate goal pursued, in the sense that they exceed what is necessary to achieve this goal;

3. there is no rational justification for the measures ordered, including in situations where a different legal treatment is established for identical situations, or an identical legal treatment for different situations;

4. through the measures ordered, the state authorities limit the exercise of some fundamental rights and freedoms, without a rational justification representing, in particular, the existence of an adequate relationship between these measures, the factual situation and the legitimate goal pursued.

During the state of emergency established throughout the country, specific measures of a restrictive nature regarding fundamental human rights and freedoms are established by decrees of the President and military orders of the Government. The provisions in question are discretionary, they can at any time represent an excess of power on the part of the state authorities by illegitimately restricting these rights or freedoms or even by affecting their substance, as is the case with religious freedom. Other such measures are expected to be taken, such as compulsory vaccination of the population. Such a provision would seriously affect the freedom of conscience, the person's freedom to dispose of himself, but also the fundamental right to dignity and physical integrity, especially since so far there is nothing to guarantee that such a vaccine would not have consequences negative, unpredictable for the person's health.

All these normative legal acts, in accordance with the current constitutional provisions, cannot be censured by the courts or by the Constitutional Court, a fact that can represent a dictatorial manifestation of the power of the state in a democratic society.

That's why we support the proposal to include in the powers of the Constitutional Court also that of ruling on the constitutionality of administrative acts exempted from the legality control of administrative litigation courts, including normative acts adopted during an exceptional situation. This category of administrative acts, referred to in art. 126 paragraph 6 of the Constitution and the provisions of Law no. 544/2004 of the contentious-administrative law are particularly important for the entire social and state system, but especially for the exercise of fundamental human rights and freedoms. A constitutionality check of these normative acts is necessary, especially in exceptional situations such as the present one. because in its absence the discretionary power of the issuing administrative authority is unlimited with the consequence of the possibility of excessively restricting the exercise of fundamental rights and freedoms or of violating some important constitutional values.

The excess of power of all state authorities manifests itself, paradoxically within the limits of the law, whenever the normative acts recognize a margin of appreciation on the part of the decision-making body (Parliament, administrative authorities or courts), on the moment of the decision or regarding the measures ordered. State practice in Romania has shown that in many situations the content of the decision that can materialize in: law, Government ordinance, acts of administrative authorities at all levels, judicial acts of the prosecutor's offices or court rulings, exceed, through provisions especially of a restrictive nature what is necessary to achieve the purpose of the law or inadequate to the factual situation. Such displays of power can seriously harm fundamental human rights or the public interest in a word, the features of the rule of law. The criterion that allows the courts to censure these forms of abuse of power is, in our opinion, the principle of proportionality.

Proportionality is a fundamental principle of law explicitly enshrined in constitutional regulations, legislation and international legal instruments. It is based on the rational law values of justice and equity and expresses the existence of a balanced or adequate relationship between actions, situations, phenomena, being a criterion for limiting the measures ordered by the state authorities to what is necessary to achieve a legitimate goal, in this way being guaranteed fundamental rights and avoided the excess of power of the state authorities. Proportionality is a basic principle of European Union law, being expressly enshrined by the provisions of art. 5 of the Treaty on the European Union.

We believe that the express regulation of this principle only in the content of the provisions of art. 53 of the Constitution, with application in the field of restricting the exercise of certain rights, is insufficient to highlight the full significance and importance of the principle for the rule of law.

It is useful as in art. 1 of the Constitution to add a new paragraph that stipulates that "The exercise of state power must be proportional and non-discriminatory". This new constitutional regulation would constitute a true constitutional obligation for all state authorities to exercise their powers in such a way that the adopted measures fall within the limits of the discretionary power recognized by law. At the same time, the possibility is created for the Constitutional Court to sanction, through the constitutional control of laws and ordinances, the excess of power in the activity of the Parliament and the Government, using the principle of proportionality as a criterion.

Of course, the existence of a viable, qualitatively performing, well-structured and harmonized state institutional system, including in terms of the moral and professional quality of civil servants and magistrates, is obviously an ontological factor of substance to eliminate or at least reduce the excess of power of the state authorities in all its forms, we would especially emphasize in the situations where the measures ordered by political and legal manifestations of will take on the form of legality but sound obvious contradiction with the requirements of the principle of legitimacy

Strengthening the judicial power, the control of the courts but also the constitutional control, especially in situations where the violation of human rights or the principles of the rule of law, especially the separation and balance of powers, can be a viable solution to guarantee not only the legality of the measures ordered by the state authorities, but also their legitimacy, in order to prevent the dictatorial manifestations of those who exercise state power in a society democratic.

References

1. Archbishop Justinian Chira, Live beautifully and in joy, Nicodim Caligraful Publishing House, Putna Holy Monastery, 2014, p. 161;

2. Archbishop Justinian Chira, op.cit, p. 162;

3. See Andreescu Marius, The Church and freedom of conscience in times of trial, in the Commandment of Love April 2020, Agaton Publishing House, Făgăraş;

4. André Hauriou, Droit constitutionel et institution politiques, Ed. Montchrestien, Paris, 1972, p.137;

5. Ion Deleanu, Constitutional law and political institutions, Ed. Europa Nova, Bucharest, 1996, p.509;

6. For developments, see Marius Andreescu, Florina Mitrofan, Constitutional Law. General theory, Pitesti University Ed., pp.61-68;

7. Tudor Draganu, Constitutional law and political institutions. Elementary treatise, Ed. Lumina Lex, Bucharest, 1999, vol.II, p.362;

8.Dictionary of sociological thinking, Ed. Polirom, Bucharest, p.431;

9. Antonie Iorgovan. Foreword to: Dana Apostol Tofan, Discretionary power and excess power of public authorities, Ed. All Beck, Bucharest, 1999;

10. Leon Duguit, Manuel de Droit Constitutionnel, Paris, 1907, pp. 445-446;

11. Antonie Iorgovan, Treaty of administrative law, Ed. Nemira, Bucharest 1996, vol I, p.301;

12. Ibidem, p.292;

13. Dana Apostol Tofan, op. cit. p. 22;

14. In the doctrine, Jellinek and Fleiner supported the thesis that the discretionary power is not only specific to the administrative function, but also appears in the activity of the other functions of the state, in the form of a freedom of appreciation on the content, on the opportunity and on the extent of the legal act. (see Dana Apostol Tofan, op.cit. p. 26);

15. I.V. Gruia, Discretionary power in the functions of the State, in the weekly Pandectele, 1934, p.489;

16. Law no.554/2004, published in M. Of. no. 1154/2004;

17. Antonie Iorgovan, op. cit., vol. I, p. 294;

18. Dana Apostol Tofan, op.cit., p.81;

19. Tudor Drăganu, Constitutional law and political institutions. Elementary treatise, Ed. Lumina Lex, 1999, vol II, pp. 131-132.

25. FROM ONTOLOGICAL HAPPINESS TO THE RIGHT TO HAPPINESS

Abstract:

In our opinion, the problem of happiness can be approached ontologically and epistemologically in three ways: 1. As a state of consciousness but also existential of man in his physical, rational and spiritual individuality. It is always relative, determined or influenced by factors external to man, but especially by the various existential situations in which man finds himself; 2. Happiness as an ontological reality not only of the individual man but also of the human being, which has no boundaries of this world and of this life. It is a permanent call of man towards the acquisition of ontological happiness, it is an expression of the transcendental dimension of the human being. Such an approach to happiness involves religious meanings and meanings, especially of Orthodoxy.

3. From a legal perspective, being a fundamental human right that generates correlative obligations for the state. As a fundamental right, it can be enshrined explicitly or only implicitly in legal and political instruments. In this way, happiness is a component of the phenomenality of human existence in the social environment. The right to happiness in the legal sense has the generality and abstract nature of the legal norm, and its guarantee and realization depends on social and economic factors, on the realization of the imperatives of the rule of law and a democratic governance regime;

Happiness has a unitary ontological meaning, and none of the above ways of approaching this concept should be approached rigidly or in isolation.

In this study we propose an analysis of the concept of happiness, in an interdisciplinary way: philosophical, legal and theological.

Key words:

Happiness as an ontological state of the human being/the dignity of being happy/the legal understanding of happiness/the fundamental, constitutional right to happiness.

I. Meanings and philosophical significances of happiness

One of the most debated issues in world culture is understanding the relationship between suffering and happiness, the two terms being in principle diametrically opposed. In other words, how can suffering be removed and implicitly what are the conditions for man to be happy. Moreover, the state of happiness can characterize not only man as a person, but at the same time, it can also be a characteristic of a community, even a people.

Man's aspiration for happiness is confused with his existence and nature. Happiness, as a state of mind and existence, is opposed to suffering, death and servitude of all kinds. Religions, philosophy, but also sociological, political, and legal doctrines have elaborated different conceptions and theories about happiness over time.

All people want to be happy. No matter how nihilistic or skeptical we may be at certain moments of life, no matter how much we doubt that happiness can be achieved or that it is worth seeking it, we never stop striving - consciously or not - towards its acquisition. But even if they agree that happiness is desirable, people differ as soon as they ask what happiness consists of. Each of us seeks to avoid suffering and to achieve and perpetuate the state of happiness.

In our opinion, the issue of happiness can be approached in three ways:

1. As the existential state of man in his physical, rational and spiritual individuality, located in the exteriority and phenomenality of the world. It is always relative, ephemeral, incomplete, determined or influenced by external factors, by the various existential situations in which man finds himself and by such diverse and often contradictory states of mind;

2. From a legal perspective. Happiness as a fundamental human right, not yet enshrined in constitutions, but present in doctrinal approaches. In this way, happiness is one of the phenomenality of human existence in the social environment. The right to happiness in the legal sense has the generality and abstract nature of the legal norm and its guarantee and achievement depends on social and economic factors, on the realization of the imperatives of the rule of law, human freedom of a decent life and a truly democratic governance regime. In our opinion, man has the right to happiness in this world, but the current political and social order of the world cannot confer or guarantee it;

3. Happiness, as a perennial ontological reality of the human being, which has no boundaries of this world and this life. It is a permanent call of man towards the acquisition of perfection, of the happy life in eschatology, it is an expression of the transcendental dimension of the human being, of living in the right Orthodox faith.

Philosophical conceptions of happiness existing in history are diverse and different in the meaning and significances attributed to happiness, the ways through which man can avoid suffering and reach existential happiness, the conditions that must be met for the acquisition of happiness.

Conceptions of happiness differ by the purpose we attribute to others in achieving our own happiness. In one of his plays, Jean Paul Sartre used a shocking expression: "hell is the others"[496], and, of course, each of us can be "the other" at any time. How can we find happiness in a world where the fulfillment of our own desires depends on what our fellows want and do? Many times, the desires of two people conflict and as a result, each tries to prevent the realization of the other's desire. No one gives up without fighting for happiness. All people want to be happy. No matter how nihilistic or skeptical we may be at certain moments in life. The different conceptions of happiness are distinguished primarily by the way in which its nature is understood. Sometimes happiness is conceived as a very high idea, a distant ideal, beyond our power to attain it; true happiness would not be possible during this life.

There are existential constants different from the concepts and categories of reason, the latter explaining and guiding the process of knowing and understanding phenomenal reality. The existential constants are specific to the being, in our case the human being, but obviously they are present in the phenomenological existence, without the phenomenology of the individual and social existence of man ever exhausting the essential ontological dimension of these constants. From this perspective, the existential constants, for man's power of knowledge, were and will remain "the thing in itself, noumenon", as Kant says, to which the knowing human reason does not have access because it does not have a sensitive intuition of being, but only of the aspects and the various existential phenomenological through which it manifests itself. Existential constants are life, freedom, suffering, happiness, love, our

[496] Jean Paul Sartre, Being and Nothingness, Parallels 45, Pitesti, 2004, p. 96.

enumeration not being exhaustive.[497] Existential constants can be thought by man in their very being, but they cannot be known and conceptualized scientifically, theologically or philosophically except in their phenomenological, existential manifestation.

In the existential phenomenology related to the hypostasis of each human person, the existential constants are finite and relative, as is the case with happiness.

As we said, happiness is an existential constant, but in its existential phenomenological dimension it is conceptualized, explained and understood by philosophy, theology and even the science of law. This category, in its phenomenological expression, can also be the object of ethical or legal regulation. Thus, in the legal sciences the ontological constant of happiness is found in the phenomenological expression of: the constitutional right to happiness or the right to seek happiness.

In our study we will mainly analyze the legal concepts, the normative dimension and jurisprudence solutions regarding the right to happiness and the right to the pursuit of happiness.

The dialectic of being and existence, including regarding happiness in relation to legal normativity, generates the question: Is happiness a gift of God or a human right? The salvation and deification of man by grace is the true happiness that is complete and will never be taken from him, according to the words of our Savior the Lord Jesus Christ. Happiness is above all a priceless gift of God to man.

We propose a brief synthesis of the most important philosophical and theological conceptions regarding the existential (ontological) constant of happiness. The different conceptions of happiness are distinguished primarily by the way in which its nature is understood.

Sometimes happiness is conceived as a grand idea, a distant ideal, beyond our power to attain. True happiness would not be possible during this life. However, we all owe it to ourselves to try to reach this state, and some thoughts from the wisdom of history's greatest philosophers can help us.

---

[497]For developments, see Marius Andreescu, Existence si being. Journal of thoughts and reflections, Pro Universitaria, Bucharest, 2022.

Gautama Buddha's view of happiness places great emphasis on the fact that people should find fulfillment in the experience of living rather than in the "final destination". There is no final goal, people build their happiness along the way, believed Buddha. "Of all the forms of caution, caution in love is probably the most fatal to true happiness." Nirvāṇa is usually associated with Jainism and Buddhism and represents the ultimate state of sotheological liberation, freedom from repeated rebirth in samsara. In classical Indian religions nirvana is a state of perfect peace, freedom, the highest bliss, as well as liberation or the end of samsara (that repeated cycle of birth, life and death).[498]

Confucius' view of happiness has echoed throughout history in books and recent research on cognitive therapy, which aims to help people understand the connection between thoughts, feelings and behaviours. According to a mindset promoted by Confucius, happiness is a self-fulfilling prophecy that multiplies as we find reasons for its existence. "The greatest blessings of mankind are within us and within our reach. A wise man is content with his lot, whatever it may be, without desiring what he does not have."[499]

Solon, one of the 7 sages of antiquity, believes that no one is happy while he lives, because misfortunes can befall him at any time: we have to wait for the end of someone's life to be able to say if he was happy. In the absence of true happiness, people can console themselves with its pale traces: joy, pleasure, glory, prestige, prosperity. One who is privileged to experience such states may mistake them for happiness itself. He will then be content with surrogates of happiness, attainable in spite of our mortal condition. Or, on the contrary, he will understand that happiness is an unattainable ideal, that he is irremediably condemned to unhappiness. Small joys make our life more beautiful, but sincere and total happiness is extremely difficult to achieve.[500]

The question "What is a good life?" started most clearly from Socrates. Should a virtuous man, a moral man and deep in the holy things be a happy man? Or is it strictly about satisfying certain pleasures? Socrates says it is both.

---

498 For development networks, see Nicolae Achimescu, India. Religion and philosophy, Tehnopress, Bucharest, 2005; Henry Zimmer, Philosophies of India, Humanitas, Bucharest, 2012.

499 Confucius, Analects of Confucius, The European Idea, Bucharest, 2022, p. 67.

500 See Ioana Sarambei, Nicolae Sarambei, 99 Personalities of the Ancient World, Albatros, Bucharest, 1983, pp.101-104; Aristotle, The Athenian State, Antet Revolution, Bucharest, 2007, pp. 21-22.

That is, the ultimate good means being happy in morality or moral in happiness.

For Socrates, one of the greatest philosophers of antiquity, happiness does not come with external rewards, but with success achieved on one's own account. By lowering the level of our needs, we can learn to appreciate simple pleasures. "The secret of happiness is not found by looking for it with all your might, but by developing the ability to enjoy yourself for a little." The man who does everything to achieve happiness and relies on himself and not on others has adopted the best plan to live happily.[501]

Plato, Socrates' disciple, defines happiness in the same way as his teacher. Plato's version of happiness is a form of personal development, more precisely satisfaction derived from achievements. "Our happiness depends only on us." In the Republic, Plato asserts that those who are moral are the only ones who can be truly happy. Thus, we must understand the cardinal virtues, especially justice. Through the thought experiment of the ring of Gyges, Plato concludes that he who abuses power enslaves himself to his appetite, so he is unhappy. An essential theme for Plato in his philosophy is the theory of forms, the distinction between perceptible but unintelligible reality (science), and on the other hand imperceptible but intelligible reality (mathematics). Geometry was Plato's main motivation, and this also shows the influence of Pythagoras. Forms are perfect archetypes of which real objects are imperfect copies. In the Republic, the highest form is considered to be the form of good, the source of all other forms that could be known by reason. Glaucon, a character participating in the dialogue, classifies the three kinds of good and asks to which justice belongs: those which we accept for their own sake without regard to the consequences, those which we accept both for their own sake and their consequences, and those which we do not accept for their sake but accept for the sake of their consequences. Socrates attributes justice to the second kind of good.

The good is the highest happiness for Socrates and Plato.

He also sees a type of happiness arising from social justice through the fulfillment of social function; because this duty forms happiness. Other sources of happiness, such as leisure, wealth, and pleasure, are considered less firm

[501] Andre Comte-Sponvile, Arlette Farge, Jean Delumeau, The most beautiful story of happiness, Art, Bucharest, 2015, pp. 19-21.

forms, if not entirely false, and opposed to the form of good and happiness.[502] Plato believes that happiness is pleasure purified sensorially by intelligence, in other words, the pleasure of knowing ideas, transcendental pure forms.

For Aristotle, Plato's student, happiness is not a gift offered by other people or things, but is something created by us and it is our responsibility to protect it. "I learned to seek my happiness by limiting my desires rather than trying to satisfy them." The great Athenian philosopher claims that eudaimonia is the goal of human thought and action. Eudaimonia is usually translated as happiness. Eudaimonia involves good, truth, justice, courage, friendship, but also philosophy, arts, knowledge and creation in general. Eudaimonia is a philosophical concept superior to the state of pleasure, contentment, because it implies reaching the maximum potential and fulfillment on all levels, with the intention of continuous improvement in terms of: autonomy, personal development, self-acceptance, the purpose of life, perfectionism.[503]

Aristotle believes that, "Happiness is activity (in Greek energeia) in accordance with virtue".[504]

In the Nicomachean Ethics, Aristotle draws attention to the fact that many ends are really only intermediate goals and are desired only because they make possible the attainment of larger goals. Therefore, things like wealth, intelligence, and courage are valued only in relation to other things, while eudaimonia is the only valuable thing in isolation.

Aristotle considered virtue to be necessary for a person to be happy and argued that without virtue, contentment is the maximum that can be achieved.

Immanuel Kant was a German philosopher, one of the greatest thinkers of the Enlightenment period in Germany. Kant is considered one of the greatest philosophers in the history of Western culture who stated that "Happiness is the state of a rational being in the world, for whom, throughout his existence, everything goes according to his desire and will, and is therefore based on the

---

[502] Plato, Republica, Letterhead, Bucharest, 2010, p. 97.

[503] See Aristotle, Nichomachian Ethics, Antet Revoluţion, Bucharest, 2012, pp. 56-64.

[504] *Ibidem*, p. 114.

agreement of nature with its entire purpose, as well as with the essential determining principle of her will."[505]

Stoicism is a philosophical school founded in Athens by the philosopher Zeno of Citium around 300 BC, during the Hellenistic period of ancient history. The central teaching of Stoicism is morality derived from the laws of nature itself, or rather rational promotion, virtuous existence, or the manly attitude to the vicissitudes of life. Acceptance of this evidence offsets pain and unhappiness, reconciles good with evil, life with death. Another trait is recommending love to all other beings.

Stoics believe that happiness or fulfillment (eudaimonia) can only be achieved inside, and that which is outer is merely preferable, but essentially indifferent. This idea of happiness is common to almost all philosophies, but the Stoic way of achieving it is unique.

The ethics developed by the Stoa derive from the own principles of physics: the universe is governed by absolute laws that admit no exceptions, and the essence of human nature is reason. These principles are summed up in the famous maxim: "Live in harmony with nature!".

From this formula derives the notion of virtue, with its four cardinal aspects: wisdom, courage, justice and temperance, corresponding to the teachings of Socrates. While in Aristotelian ethics he recognized the place of passions in human nature, following that they should be repressed by reason, the Stoics demand the annihilation of passions, going as far as asceticism ("askesis"), because virtue represents the only happiness. To be virtuous is to be indifferent to pain and suffering ("apatheia") and at the same time desirous of knowledge. Hence the importance given to science, physics, logic, because they represent the foundations of morality, the roots of all virtue. A wise man is synonymous with a good man. The unhappiness and evils of the world are the results of ignorance. Hence the recommendation of the practice of philosophy, the permanent examination of one's own judgments and behavior, in order to ascertain whether they differ from the universal reason of nature.

---

[505] Immanuel Kant, Religion within the limits of pure reason, Humanitas, Bucharest, 2004, p.65.

Among the greatest Stoic philosophers are, in Ancient Rome, Seneca, Cicero, Marcus Aurelius, Epictetus.[506]

Hedonism (from the Greek hedone - "pleasure") is an ethical conception and a philosophical current, which proclaims pleasure, enjoyment as the ultimate good, and the desire to obtain it, the principle of behavior. It was founded in Antiquity, in Rome, by Aristippus of Cyrene (who emphasized sensual pleasures), and was later developed on a rationalist basis in Athens, by Epicurus, then by the humanists of the Renaissance, by the materialists and the Enlightenment of the 18th century (with anti-religious, individualistic accents). In essence, hedonism starts from the natural human inclination to seek pleasure and happiness and avoid suffering, pursuing the means by which the ratio of pleasure to suffering can be maximized.[507]

For Epicurus, one of the most important representatives of hedonism in ancient Greece, sensation, which is the criterion of knowledge, is also the guide that makes us seek pleasure and run away from pain. This happiness will therefore consist in the satisfaction of pleasures, among them those of intelligence. Epicurus's morality is a hedonism, but Epicurean hedonism is not an apology for pleasure and excess. He promotes a just regulation of pleasures, the life of the sage being temperate, contemplative and virtuous. The philosopher believed that ataraxia (imperturbability) can be achieved by cultivating the pleasures of the soul. Material pleasures were almost unimportant to Epicurus, but he advocated the exercise of wisdom as a way to achieve deep joy. An important ingredient for Epicurus in all this was friendship. He believed that imparting wisdom was far more valuable than being a lonely sage. "Self-knowledge is not a guarantee of happiness, but it is on the side of happiness and can provide the courage to fight for it."[508]

Blessed Augustine is one of the most influential thinkers, perhaps the most influential of all, especially if we take into account the fact that even Platonism influenced medieval thought through Augustine. He remains an authority more than a thousand years after his death, influencing, for example, the thought of Descartes. Augustine claims that both philosophy and theology

---

[506] For development, see Giovanni Reale, History of ancient philosophy. Cynicism, Epicureanism, Stoicism, Vol. 5, Galaxia Gutemberg, Bucharest, 2016, pp. 382-491

[507] See Giovanni Reale, *op.cit.*, pp. 305-380; Michael Flocker, The Hedonism Handbook. The art of tranquility and pleasure, Humanitas, Bucharest, 2006.

[508] Andrei Cornea (ed.), Epicurus and Ancient Epicureanism, Humanitas, Bucharest, p. 367.

pursue the achievement of one and the same goal, happiness, with the distinction of the paths: Theology-the path of faith; Philosophy-the path of reason.[509]

Baruch Spinoza, famous rationalist philosopher and pantheist from the 17th century, claims that from a well-determined purpose man in life must be happy. The desire to live happily or well is the essence of man by which the human being seeks to maintain his existence. But man is not a solitary individual, he lives in the world, in nature, and understanding this becomes primary for the intended purpose. Happiness depends on awareness of the structure of the world and the place man occupies in this universal structure. First of all it is necessary to know the nature of God, as he really is, but not according to our arbitrary imagination. For Spinoza, God is not as the Christian religion imagines him - a man. He is against anthropomorphizing God. God, says Spinoza, is identical with nature.[510]

John Look shows the social coordinates of happiness. Happiness, in the view of the English philosopher, is the natural state of man, it is a natural right that involves social conditions. He "claims that natural law legitimizes everything that a person undertakes in relation to his life. God created people free and equal, in the natural state a natural equality is imposed, there is even a law of nature that a person should not interfere with the life, health, freedom or possessions of others." The English thinker points out that this state is not necessarily a state of war. Such a state is declared only when someone violates our rights. Only then can the aggressor be punished and even killed. Conflicts in the natural state can be remedied by providing a framework, by concluding a contract with everyone else, in order to create a civilized society. We thus authorize a government that can even judge us to defend natural rights. However, this government can be dissolved at any time if it violates the laws and endangers the life, liberty or property of individuals.[511]

In the introduction to On Crimes and Punishments, Beccaria sees happiness as a basis for social organization and understanding, or, to put it another way, for constitutionalism.

---

[509] For developments see, priest, dr. Sicoe Tudor, Blessed Augustin. Theological aspects with special reference to Triadology, Andreiana, Sibiu, 2013.

[510] See Baruch Spinoza, Ethics, Bucharest, Scientific Publishing House, Bucharest, 1957.

[511] Ioan Ciochină-Barbu, "On the legal nature of the right to happiness", Acta Universitatis George Bacovia. Legal, Volume 6. Issue 2/2017, pp. 321-322.

Formulating the fundamental normative principle that must be the basis for the adoption of all laws, he says: "Let's open the history books and we will see that the laws, which nevertheless are or should be pacts concluded between free people, were generally nothing more than an instrument of the passions of a few or they appeared as a result of a fortuitous and transient necessity; by no means dictated by an impartial researcher of human nature, who would lean over the actions of a multitude of people and subordinate them, concentrating them, to the following point of view: the maximum happiness shared among as many as possible. Happy are those very few nations that did not wait for the slow evolution of human relations and vicissitudes to reach the peak of evil and only then proceed to good, but hastened the intermediate changes through good laws; and the gratitude of the people is due to that philosopher who had the courage to, from his obscure and despised cabinet, throw into the crowd the first seeds of useful truths, long remaining unfruitful."[512]

The German philosopher Immanuel Kant defines happiness as actually "continuing well-being, the joy of living, complete satisfaction with one's personal situation." In one of his well-known works on the critique of pure reason, referring to the concept of happiness, he stated: "As a finite rational being, man cannot give up his natural goal, which is happiness. But he becomes worthy of happiness only by his ceaseless striving to observe the moral law."[513]

Kant claims that "Morality is not strictly the doctrine that teaches us how to make ourselves happy, but how to become worthy of happiness... Happiness is the state of a rational being in the world, to whom, throughout his existence, everything it follows desire and will, and is therefore based on the agreement of nature with its entire purpose, as well as with the essential determining principle of its will."[514]

The great German philosopher believes that morality, the moral law, including the dignity of being happy are categories of reason and not sensory, empirical: "Happiness is the satisfaction of all our inclinations (both extensive, according to their variety, and intensive, according to degree, as well as protensives, according to duration). I call pragmatics (the rule of prudence) the

[512] Cesare Beccaria, About crimes and punishments, Humanitas, Bucharest, 2007, p. 61.
[513] Immanuel Kant, Religion within the limits of pure reason, Humanitas, Bucharest, 2004, p. 65.
[514] Immanuel Kant, Critique of practical reason, Encyclopedic Universe, Bucharest, 1999, p 102.

practical law determined by the motive of happiness; and I call that moral, if such a thing exists, which has no other motive than the dignity of being happy (moral law). The first advises what we must do, if we want to have happiness, the second orders how we must behave in order to be only worthy of happiness. The first is based on empirical principles; for other than through experience I cannot know either what are the inclinations that want to be satisfied, nor what are the natural causes that can produce their satisfaction. The second abstracts from inclinations and the natural means to satisfy them and considers only the freedom of a rational being in general, and the necessary conditions, without which there could be no harmony, according to principles, between this freedom and the distribution of happiness, and therefore it can at least be based on simple ideas of pure reason and be known a priori."[515]

The space allotted to this study does not allow us to develop further the exposition of the philosophical conceptions of happiness.

In the contemporary period, some philosophers argue that happiness is not an ideal, but a state of our soul: either as a state of joy, pleasure, exaltation, or as one of peace, reconciliation. Understood in this way, happiness is no longer intangible: it depends on each of us, we look for it within ourselves, and the path to its acquisition is also found within us. We can consider that the acquisition of happiness can be achieved through the path of knowledge, the path of love and the path of faith.

Other philosophers, however, considered that happiness does not mean being in a certain state of mind; happiness lies in what we do, in our activity. For pragmatism, including the contemporary one, the foundation of morality is utility (or the principle of greatest precision). According to this principle, people's actions are good if they bring happiness and bad if they bring unhappiness. Thus, happiness consists in pleasure or the absence of suffering, and unhappiness in pain or the absence of pleasure. From the beginning, man has only one goal: pleasure and the absence of suffering. A thing is thus desirable if it is itself a pleasure or mediates one by removing suffering. John Stuart Mill admits that such a "theory" of life can cause many dislikes because it proclaims pleasure as the ultimate goal". But he says that, "nevertheless, the utilitarians recognize the superiority of spiritual pleasures, which, by duration, certainty, intensity, are stronger than the pleasures of the body, but they add

[515] Ibidem, pp. 103-104.

that this primacy consists rather in the advantages they procure than in its nature.[516]

There are also philosophers who deny the possibility of man attaining the state of happiness. Albert Camus- the French philosopher had a different approach to happiness compared to Socrates' theory. For Camus, happiness was a rather bleak goal of life. Instead, he preferred to live meaningfully in the moment and not dwell too much on long-term goals, as reflected in his most famous work, The Myth of Sisyphus. "By pleasure we mean the absence of pain in the body and problems in the soul. A sober reasoning, the search for reasons for decisions and avoidances, the elimination of those beliefs that lead to the tumult of the soul."[517]

The Romanian philosopher Ernest Bernea, analyzing the dialectical contradiction between suffering and happiness, explains the existence of suffering through the existential freedom with which man is endowed by nature: "Why does man suffer? – asks the philosopher- Because it is double. And what is he still suffering for? Because it's free. He can be a biblical image or he can make a satanic figure. Man is double and he is free. He suffers because he walks on negation which is the manifestation of the evil deposited in his very root and he suffers because he has the freedom to choose and decide, but he may not. Man plays between good and evil, between his spiritual heroism (holiness) and the sweet softness of sin. Man cannot do everything and cannot do anyway."[518]

The same author believes that the ideal of the modern and postmodern era is the elimination of suffering, in all its forms, and the achievement of the state of ontological happiness only through comfort and the pleasures offered by science, technology, culture, transposed into everyone's life and becoming characteristics of contemporary civilization. This attempt turns out to be a failure or at best an illusion. "The man of our civilization did not want to accept suffering as a natural moral state and sought to remove it by the means available to him. However, the ideal of modern ethics could not be achieved. With all culture and civilization, with all science and technology, man's suffering could not be banished, but on the contrary, it continued to grow with

---

[516] See John Stuart Mill, Utilitarismus, All, Bucharest, 2014.

[517] Albert Camus, The Myth of Sisyphus, Polirom, Bucharest, 2020, p. 97.

[518] Ernest Bernea, He who climbs the mountain of suffering, Predania, Bucharest, 2021, p. 13.

the progress dreamed of by the Age of Enlightenment. Man was able to make his theoretical and practical knowledge grow unsuspectedly rich, he succeeded in perfecting his tools, raising his material conditions of life, having comfort and even luxury, but until the end he realized that happiness it escaped him and he suffers more than ever".[519]

The dialectical contradiction between suffering and on the other hand happiness, in its concrete expression of joy, has been misunderstood and resolved wrongly by the main ethical conceptions of history. These conceptions must not only be understood diachronically, historically, but also synchronically, because they also coexist in our times. The correct solution is that conferred by Christian morality based on supernatural revelation. "If Epicureanism, greatly updated by the bourgeois era, removes suffering without knowing happiness, if pessimism accepts suffering for its own sake, the new ethics of a deeply understood Christian accepts suffering in order to reach the enlightened spheres of joy".[520]

Petre Andrei, the well-known Romanian sociologist and philosopher, believes that happiness is not a purely subjective, internal phenomenon of an abstract human being isolated from social life, nor is it the result of social influence on the passive human soul, but is the product of personality, the processing of social material. "...The process of integrating the individual into society is carried out simultaneously, it involves the process of individualization, subjectivization of social goals. Harmonizing the soul with the social environment, as moral tendencies, establishing a balance between objective and subjective, these produce happiness. The source of happiness is the connection of the soul with itself and with the social moral environment... Happiness is a social ethical phenomenon that differs from simple biological pleasure, satisfaction or contentment. Happiness presupposes a conscious goal, an ideal, results of a value selection of a choice or employment."[521]

Elena Zamfir, believes that "Happiness is a subjective state par excellence, with a complex structure of emotional-affective, cognitive-informational, but also appreciative-valuing type. That is why our perceptions

---

[519] Ibidem, p. 9.

[520] Ibidem, p. 16.

[521] Cited by Valentin Mureşan, "Does Aristotle use the dialectical method in the Nicomachean Ethics?", Journal of Analytical Philosophy, Vol. III, 2o, July-December 2009, pp. 29-56.

of the life we live, which give us the dimension of happiness, are very different depending on individual characteristics, but also on the opportunities offered to each of us by our living environment. Happiness, as a process and not as a given (an immutable constant that can remain as our asset and that we can conserve over time), implies a continuous search; it consists of a multitude of desires, latent aspirations which, once fulfilled, are replaced by others and become just as pressing, just as important to be transformed into active demands."[522] We also agree with this opinion.

Indeed, from what has been presented so far, it follows that happiness must be viewed multidimensionally and that from whatever angle it is viewed "it is composed of a multitude of desires, latent aspirations which, once fulfilled, are replaced by others and become equally pressing, equally important to turn into active requirements".[523]

It is a certain fact that economic and social progress, facilities and social services specific to contemporary civilization, moral pragmatism, current consumerism based on the desire to "have" and not "to be", atheism, contemporary ideological and moral libertinism, they did not eliminate suffering and do not give man the existential state of happiness so much desired. This is because happiness cannot be acquired in the phenomenology of man's individual or social existence, it is not an external fact that responds to causality and material determinism but an inner dimension of man's deeper self, of his consciousness reconciled with himself, with God and with the universe, it is a state of the ones pure in heart and soul.

We will not dwell on theological conceptions of happiness. However, we conclude by affirming that the only true way to achieve the state of happiness, now and for eternity, is the fulfillment of the commands and words of our Savior Jesus Christ contained in the Holy Gospel. In the Sermon on the Mount, our Lord Jesus Christ shows what human happiness consists of and what are its conditions. It is not the only place in the Holy Gospel where the Savior refers to happiness. Therefore, happiness can be an ontological reality not only for the limited and finite existence of man, but especially for eternal life.

---

[522] Elena Zamfir in "The right to happiness, prisoner between the culture of freedom and the culture of silence. Interview with Elena Zamfir", on https://www.romaniapozitiva.ro/romania-pozitiva/dreptul-la-fericire-prizonier-intre-cultura-libertatii-si-cultura-tacerii-interviu-cu-elena-zamfir-profesor -university.

[523] Ibidem.

II. Brief considerations on fundamental human rights and their evolution

Can happiness form the object of regulation of some legal norms?

The answer to this question has certain nuances. Ontological happiness with its theological meaning and significance cannot be regulated by legal norms. It is part of the area of non-law, it is a reality specific to the human being, just like life, conscience, freedom inexpressible and indefinable by legal norms. Legal norms can only regulate the phenomenological aspects of existence, not their being; more precisely, it exclusively regulates the conduct of man as a subject of legal relations, in which his life, conscience and freedom are manifested.

Happiness can be not only an ontological reality specific to the human being, but also a phenomenological manifestation contained in the content of human social relational behavior. In this sense, happiness can be conceptualized and expressed normatively, legally.

Can a fundamental human right to happiness be conceptualized and expressed normatively, constitutionally? To answer this question, we propose a brief summary of the legal nature of fundamental human rights and their evolution.

The fundamental rights and freedoms of man and citizen are a constitutional reality with deep implications in the existence of each person, in his relations with the state. It also represents an existential reality of each person, of society as a whole and a dimension of democracy. Modern constitutionalism is based on the affirmation, recognition and guarantee of fundamental rights and freedoms, without which the notions of state, law, civil society, democratic regime, sovereign power would be inconceivable. Therefore, this institution has an important philosophical dimension that characterizes the existence of every human being, but also one of constitutional law and international law, expressing both conceptually and normatively the complex relations between man and the state.

The scientific research of fundamental rights and freedoms must be carried out on three levels: conceptual, philosophical and political. And, last but not least, legal, being, at the same time, also a problem of the international constitution.

In essence, all the authors recognize that democracy and human rights together form an indestructible unit that mutually conditions each other. Democracy marks the emancipation of the people, their becoming a subject of the government, emancipation that presupposes the power of determination of each person, thus endowing them with the rights that are inherent to them as human beings and citizens.

For the constitutional definition of this institution, several aspects must be considered:

a) Fundamental rights are subjective rights, they are the faculties of the subjects of the legal relationship to act in a certain way or to ask the other subjects for an appropriate attitude and to benefit from the protection of the state in realizing legitimate claims;

b) Fundamental rights are essential rights for citizens. It is the feature that distinguishes the fundamental rights from the usual subjective ones, being decisive for the legal status of the citizen;

The delimitation criterion between subjective and subjectively essential rights is a value one, but also a concrete historical one. From a value point of view, the rights that refer to the life, freedom and personality of each person are essential.

From a concrete historical perspective, the same subjective right can be considered a fundamental right or a simple subjective right, according to the concrete, economic, social, political conditions and according to the will of the rulers, expressed by law.

c) Due to their importance, the fundamental rights are registered in special documents, such as the declarations of rights and fundamental, constitutional laws.

The constitutional regulation of these rights is the result of the application of the value criterion, thus recognizing them as essential for citizens. Enshrined in the constitution, they are recognized as fundamental rights and guarantees are established for their protection and guarantee.

We can define the essential rights and freedoms as those subjective rights of citizens, essential for their life, freedom and dignity, indispensable for the free development of the human personality, rights established by the constitution and guaranteed by the constitution and laws.

Thus, human rights evoke the rights of the human being, endowed with reason and conscience, whose natural rights are recognized as imprescriptible and inalienable. On the level of legal reality, man becomes a citizen, integrates into a certain social and political system, regulated by moral and legal rules. Consequently, from this point of view, citizens benefit from all the rights enshrined in the constitution, while foreigners and stateless persons benefit from only some of them and, in particular, those indispensable to the human being.

In conclusion, from the point of view of universal and existential realities, human rights become the rights of the citizen on the level of the internal realities of each state.

The issue of fundamental rights and freedoms and their constitutional regulation is a consequence of the evolution of the state and its functions, and on the other hand, it is the result of the social, economic and political demands of society.

At the same time, there is a constant legal preoccupation with the consecration and, above all, the guarantee of fundamental rights, an aspect that generates a variety of legal solutions with implications also in terms of public international law.

The first documents with constitutional value that enshrine fundamental rights and freedoms with a civil and political character are: *the French Declaration of the Rights of Man and the Citizen, from 1789, the Constitution of Philadelphia, from 1787, the French Declaration of Fundamental Rights, from 1793.*

The fundamental rights and freedoms contained in these important international documents were considered, by doctrine, first-generation rights, because they directly targeted the human being in his relations with society and sought to limit the power of the state by affirming individual freedom.

From the second half of the 19th century, an increasingly broad social movement for the economic emancipation of some disadvantaged social categories is manifested in Europe. Consequently, the rulers accept economic and social concessions in favor of the working class, in the form of accepting their trade union demands.

After the First World War, under the influence of economic and social progress, but also due to the need to ensure the population a better material condition, access to culture and personality development, as well as effective control over the respect of fundamental rights and freedoms, in various constitutions are proclaimed economic and social rights, respectively: the right to work, the right to strike, freedom and trade union association, social equality, the right to social insurance, to job security, free access to justice, the guarantee of individual freedom, the right to education, etc.

In constitutional doctrine, they are called second-generation rights and freedoms.

Unlike civil and political rights, which do not, in principle, imply concrete actions on the part of the state, apart from the abstention in the face of personal freedom, social, economic and cultural rights and freedoms involve actions, measures and guarantees on the part of the state.

Social and economic rights were imposed, especially, after the adoption by the UN of the Universal Declaration of Human Rights, from 1948 and the Pacts adopted by the UN, in 1966.

Although, in some international documents, fundamental political rights and freedoms, on the one hand, and social and economic rights, on the other hand, are treated differently, modern constitutional doctrine has affirmed the indivisibility and close connection between rights, regardless of their specificity.

In the 7th decade of our century, new human rights were imposed, rights from the third generation, also known as rights of solidarity, respectively: the right to peace, to development, the right to the environment, rights specific to young people, the rights of cohabiting minorities, the right of nations or peoples to self-determination, the right of the people to exploit natural wealth, the right to a decent standard of living, the right to privacy and respect for personal life.

These new fundamental rights underline the idea of promoting human personality and valuing the complex relationships between the individual and the collective.

From an evolutionary point of view, it can be seen that the Universal Declaration of Human Rights from 1948 emphasizes, above all, individual rights, while other international documents, such as the Tehran Proclamation, from 1968, mark the evolution from the conception of human rights focused on the individual to a conception that is based on the collective.

However, the specialized literature emphasized that the only criterion for classifying citizens' rights and freedoms is their content and other criteria, such as their exercise or the possibility of realization, are not essential for their characterization.

In this sense, it can be stated that:

a) all human rights and freedoms are, at the same time, both individual and collective;

b) each right and each freedom are individual through their holder.

Using the content criterion for their classification, the following principles must be taken into account:

(i) the classification shall not be construed as a ranking of rights. All human and citizen rights have the same importance;

(ii) fundamental rights and freedoms are inalienable.

According to the criterion of content, fundamental rights and freedoms are classified, in the opinion of Professor Ioan Muraru, into:

a) Inviolability, i.e. those rights and freedoms which, by their content, ensure life, the possibility of free movement, physical and mental safety, as well as the safety of the person's domicile. In this category, we include: the right to life, the right to mental integrity, individual freedom, the right to defense, the right to free movement, the right to protect private life, the inviolability of the domicile;

b) Social, economic and cultural rights and freedoms, respectively those prerogatives which, through their content, ensure the social and material conditions of human existence: the right to education, the right to health protection, the right to work and social protection, the right to strike, the right to property, the right to inheritance, the right to a decent standard of living, the right to marriage, the right of children and young people to social protection, the right of disabled people to social protection;

c) Exclusively political rights are those rights which, by their content, can be exercised by citizens only through participation in governance: the right to vote, the right to be elected and the right to elect and be elected to the European Parliament;

d) Social and political rights and freedoms, i.e. those rights which, by their content, can be exercised by citizens, at their choice, for solving social and spiritual problems or for their participation in governance, respectively: freedom of conscience, freedom of expression, the right to information, the freedom of assembly, the right of association, the secrecy of correspondence;

e) Guarantee rights are those rights which, by their content, have the role of constitutional guarantees, respectively: the right to petition and the right of the person injured by a public authority to request compensation for the damage caused.[524]

---

[524] For development, see Marius Andreescu, Andra Puran, Constitutional law. General theory and constitutional institutions. Constitutional jurisprudence, 4th edition, C.H. Beck, Bucharest, 2020, pp. 227-234.

III. The right to happiness in legal doctrine and constitutional jurisprudence

Adopted on July 4, 1776, the Declaration of Independence of the United States of America, is the first normative act with constitutional value of a democratic state that talks about the inalienable right of man to seek his happiness. In its second paragraph, it proclaims: "*We hold the following truths to be self-evident: all men are created equal; they are endowed by the Creator with certain inalienable rights; among these rights are life, liberty and the pursuit of happiness. Governments are established among men to guarantee these rights, and their just power emanates from the consent of the governed. Whenever a form of government becomes destructive of this end, the people have a right to change or abolish it, and to establish a new government, basing it on such principles and organizing it in such form as they shall think most suitable for to give him safety and happiness*."[525]

The author of the draft Declaration is, according to historical sources, Thomas Jefferson. One of the authors of the American concept of happiness and its search is James Madison, the fourth president of the USA. He, taking some ideas about the social status of man from the work of Aristotle and John Looke, considered that "And I am sure that wherever there is restlessness there is also desire; for we unceasingly desire happiness, and it is certain that the more we feel uneasiness, the more we lack happiness, even in our own opinion, whatever may otherwise be the condition or state in which we find ourselves."[526]

In the world of our time, marked by insecurity, crises, social discrepancies, conflicts, obscurantism, intolerance, exclusivism, secularism, poverty, politicians and doctrinaires try to define the concept of happiness not only as an experience of the individual in relation to certain circumstances that determines certain feelings of pleasure, supreme joy, strong admiration, etc., but as a "right to happiness".

The UN General Assembly, by Resolution no. 66/281/12.07.2012 proclaimed March 20 as the "International Day of Happiness". "The pursuit of

---

[525] The Declaration of Independence (adopted unanimously by Congress on July 4, 1776, in Philadelphia), on https://constitutii.wordpress.com/wp-content/uploads/2013/02/declarac89bia-de-independenc89bc483.pdf.

[526] Camil Mureşan, Alexandru Vianu, President of the White House, Politics, Bucharest, 1974, p. 89.

happiness is one of the fundamental objectives of the human being", emphasizes the UN Assembly in its Resolution adopted by consensus. The document proposes to the 193 member countries to celebrate this day "in an appropriate manner, especially through educational activities" and to address public policies that increase the well-being of the peoples. The United Nations also invites international and regional organizations, as well as civil societies, including non-governmental organizations and individuals, to mark the International Day of Happiness through various public awareness activities". "The pursuit of happiness is at the heart of human endeavours. People all over the world aspire to a happy and fulfilled life, in harmony with nature. When our actions are directed towards the common good, we are all enriched. Compassion brings happiness and helps us shape the future we want," emphasized the UN Secretary General at the time, Ban Ki-moon.[527]

On March 20, 2020, the UN published the World Happiness Report.[528] According to this report, in the midst of the global health crisis caused by the coronavirus pandemic, Finland was named the happiest country in the world for the third consecutive time, followed by Denmark, in second place, and Switzerland, in third place. South Sudan and Afghanistan, two war-torn countries, occupy the penultimate and last place respectively in this ranking. The methodology used consisted in evaluating the answers taken from a sample of people from over 150 countries to a series of questions regarding the perception of the quality of personal life, on a scale from 0 to 10. Among the factors taken into account is the domestic product gross per capita, social benefits, individual freedoms or the level of corruption. Romania was ranked 47 out of 150 in this ranking, up from the report published in 2019, when it was ranked 48. The happiest countries are those "where people have a sense of belonging, trust each other and value each other," said John Helliwell, co-author of the report.

The jurisprudence of the Supreme Court of Justice of the U.S. includes solutions regarding the constitutional right to the pursuit of happiness. Jurisprudence does not recognize the right to happiness, but the right to seek happiness.

Since the idea of the pursuit of happiness is not expressly provided for in the US Constitution, one scholar argues that it is essential for the United States

---

[527] For development, see Ioan Ciochină-Barbu, *op.cit.*

[528] https://worldhappiness.report/ed/2022.

Supreme Court to recognize the ideals of "life, liberty, and the pursuit of happiness" in the Declaration of Independence as part of the American constitutional pantheon.

The pursuit of happiness, however, is enshrined in many American state constitutions and is considered by many to be a metaphor, a holdover from a bygone age. However, US state courts have applied founding principles and historical indicators to give a contemporary dimension to constitutionality review. It would seem that technological, economic and foreign policy developments and the changing course of society's ethics would make it difficult to apply the judicial interpretation of the realities of the present in the manner designed by the US Declaration of Independence. But the basic democratic principle of protecting "life, liberty, and the pursuit of happiness" is addressed primarily to Congress. Justice John Marshall, in *McCulloch v. Maryland [(17 U.S. (4 Wheat.) 316 (1819)],* stated: “the constitutional architecture must allow the national legislature a certain discretion as to the measures which will accomplish the heavy tasks assigned to it, in the manner most beneficial to the people."[529]

It has been suggested that, in the context of the 18th century, the "pursuit of happiness" should be understood to mean something more than a pursuit of happiness: "it denotes a practice or activity, a pursuit of life".

One of the first cases to address happiness and security was Beebe v. State 6 Ind. 501 - 1855. Here, the Indiana Supreme Court struck down a state law on the ground that it was contrary to the right to "liberty and the pursuit of happiness." This right, said Justice Perkins in Herman v. State 8 Ind. (Tanner) 545 - 1855 "comprises the possibility of choosing, in an individual compos mentis, what to eat and what to drink."[530]

Another example is Territory v. Ah Lim 24 P. 588 (Wash.) - 1890, in which the Washington Supreme Court rejected the defendant's argument that his right to pursue happiness was secured by smoking opium in the privacy of his home. The Court stated that “the state manifests an interest in the intellectual condition of each of its citizens, society being nothing but an aggregate of individuals. The moral or intellectual side of society rises or falls in proportion to the moral or intellectual level of its members." "Opium-

[529] https://supreme.justia.com/cases/federal/us/17/316/

[530] https://case-law.vlex.com/vid/beebe-v-state-908660614

smoking is a detestable, disgusting, and degrading practice, so that it is becoming dangerously common to the youth of the country, and its typical symptoms are imbecility, misery and crime... If the state concludes that a certain practice is dangerous for the moral, mental and physical well-being of citizens, to such an extent that it is apt to become a burden to society, it has the undoubted right to limit the commission of that act to the citizens."[531]

Similarly, the Alabama Supreme Court held in Sheppard v. Dowling 28 So. 791, 795 (Ala. 1899) state prohibitions on the sale of liquor - "The law does not permit the pursuit of happiness in this way. The feeling of ecstasy would result from drinking liquor, but the law does not approve of such a passion that involves harmful consequences for society".

An Ohio court held that a school principal violated a student's right to seek and achieve happiness, guaranteed by Article 1 paragraph 1 of the Ohio State Constitution. When they removed him from the position of student body president, members of the administration banned him from extracurricular activities and lowered his grade point average because he insisted on violating the school rules regarding hair length and style: "In non-legal terms paragraph 1 enshrines the principle that every citizen has the right to be left alone and free from any governmental interference, except as necessary for the protection of others or for the furtherance of legitimate governmental purposes. This constitutional provision places a heavy responsibility upon every governmental body when it justifies its interference with the liberty of the citizen, with the right to enjoy the freedom of his decision and to seek his happiness in his own way."[532]

In State v. Cromwell, 9 N.W.2d (N.D. 1943), the Oklahoma Supreme Court declared invalid a law requiring a photographic license because the reasons underlying it were "strange." The Court cited Henry Campbell Black, author of the Black's Law Dictionary: "The pursuit of happiness is indeed an aggregate of several rights, some of which are enumerated in constitutions, and others included in the general guarantee of 'liberty.' Human happiness can consist of many things or depend on many circumstances. It is clear that it must include personal liberty, freedom from oppression or individual discrimination, the right to follow one's individual preferences in choosing an

---

[531] http://courts.mrsc.org/washreports/001WashReport/001WashReport0156.htm

[532] See Dalia Hindawi, "The right to seek happiness", https://www.juridice.ro/439850/dreptul-la-cautarea-fericirii.html

occupation, freedom of conscience, and the right to share in family relations and family life and home. The constitutional right to pursue happiness can mean neither more nor less than the right to direct one's mental and physical forces to the attainment of an end, without any restriction or obstruction in relation to other individuals, except when necessary for to safeguard the equal rights of others. This guarantee is, therefore, one of the most indefinite, yet one of the most comprehensive that can be found in a constitution."[533]

Also, in the German Constitution, fundamental human rights are based on the principle of the dignity of the person, which is the expression of the right to happiness.

The Federal Constitutional Court of Germany has a particularly interesting argumentation and solution regarding the constitutionality of a law in relation to the principle of respect for human dignity.

In the Effes case, the applicant's request to extend the validity of his passport was rejected by the relevant authority, with no other reason than the reference to the Law on the Passport Regime. The Court began by stating that the right to leave the country is not part of the right to free movement. Despite this fact, he is not without constitutional protection. It is part of the right to free personality development. And the free development of personalities "does not only involve the development within the core of the personality that makes the human being a spiritually and morally gifted person".

Therefore, the Court deduced from Article 2 para. (1) of the German Constitution a general right of freedom, with the prescribed limits. Thus, the Court concluded that when vital areas are not protected by specific fundamental rights, the individual affected by state interference can invoke this article, if he considers it appropriate that his freedom is violated.

The condition that the Court emphasizes is also interesting, namely that a law can be considered compliant with the constitutional order only if it respects "the principles of the preeminence of law and the social welfare state". Dignity, the right to personality development, the horizontal effect of fundamental rights and the two important concepts of the active state role - Rechtstaat (which requires compliance with the principle of proportionality) and the

---

533 State v .Cromwell, 9 N.W.2d *914* (N.D. 1943), https://www.supremecourt.gov/docket/docket.aspx

social state, which obliges the state to adopt measures that guarantee the minimum level of material existence, so that people have a standard of personal safety and can lead their existence without their dignity being affected, constitute the inherent premises of the pursuit of happiness.[534]

[534] For development, see Edward J. Eberle, Human Dignity, Privacy, and Personality in German and American Constitutional Law, https://docs.rwu.edu/cgi/viewcontent.cgi?article=1067&context=law_fac_fs

IV. The fundamental right to the pursuit of happiness in Romanian constitutionalism

Currently, the fundamental right to happiness or the pursuit of happiness is not provided for in the Constitution nor in the secondary legislation in Romania, as it is not included in the international legal instruments regarding the consecration and guarantee of human rights.

Consequently, the jurisprudence of the Constitutional Court of Romania does not contain concrete references to this right.

In Romanian legal doctrine, there are several studies regarding the meanings and content of the right to happiness and even the possibility of its normative consecration.[535] Thus, in this sense in our country, some citizens' initiatives have appeared, such as for example the proposal that the "right to happiness" should appear alongside human dignity, the right to life, the right to physical and mental integrity, etc., as a distinct right in the Charter of Fundamental Rights of the European Union.[536]

In our opinion, it is not necessary to include in the Romanian Constitution a distinct right to happiness or the pursuit of happiness. All fundamental human rights and freedoms enshrined and constitutionally guaranteed, their exercise, with special reference to inviolability, the right to life, individual freedom, freedom of conscience and expression, but also the right to health protection, the protection of disabled persons, the right to a decent standard of living must aim at the dignity, good and happiness of man as a person.

The Romanian state, specifies art. 1 paragraph (3) of the Romanian Constitution, it is a social state, which signifies the involvement of the state in the social and economic field.

In the traditional conception, the essence of democracy is freedom and implicitly the limitation of state intervention in the life of society. However, economic and social freedom represent simple wishes, without a material support, without the elaboration of a global development strategy and follow-up of the elaborated program.

---

[535] We mention in this regard Tudor Panțiru, The right to seek happiness, Journal of Public Law, no. 1/2015 and Ioan Ciochină-Barbu, op cit.

[536] See The Right to happiness on http://petițieonline.com/dreptul_la_fericire.

That is why the constitutional concept of a welfare state does not contradict, but supports democracy through the lens of achieving the general interest which must be evaluated as the fundamental purpose of public services, namely: ensuring a decent standard of living for all residents, ensuring the health of the population, developing the system of instruction and education, of culture, environmental protection, etc.

Constitutional doctrine and political science have emphasized the fact that massive state intervention in the economy and social life is not preferable either, a fact that leads to the statization of society, but neither is a passive position of the state towards the issue and the realization of the general social interest.

The essence of the problem lies not in repudiating the role of the state or in amplifying this role, but in establishing the degree of state intervention, as well as the concrete forms of intervention suitable for each stage of society's development.

The social state attribute also implies positive obligations of the public authorities in relation to the constitutional powers they have to undertake appropriate actions to ensure the effective nature of human rights and freedoms, their exercise in relation to their above-mentioned purpose.

The Constitutional Court of Romania specified in this regard: "Even if, in certain situations, the public interest of society can prevail over private rights and interests, such a relationship cannot be conceived when serving the public interest has the consequence of affecting those rights that guarantees the very biological existence of the individual, as are the right to health and the right to life."[537]

As a conclusion, we propose that in a future revision of the Romanian Constitution, dignity is expressly enshrined as a fundamental human right and it is stipulated that: "The exercise of the powers of public authorities, the consecration, guarantee and exercise of fundamental rights and freedoms are aimed at the dignity, the good and the happiness of man."

In this way, an important guarantee regarding the effective nature of the exercise of the fundamental rights and freedoms of man, the orientation of the

[537] Decision no. 244 of April 20, 2021, published in the Official Gazette, no. 551 of May 27, 2021.

entire activity towards the supreme goal which is the dignity, the good and the happiness of man, and the possibility of exercising a more effective control of the Constitutional Court on the laws that have as an object of regulation the particularly complex social relations between the public interest represented by the state and on the other hand the guarantee and promotion (priority) of fundamental human rights and freedoms.

Bibliography

1. Nicolae Achimescu, India. Religion and philosophy, Tehnopress, Bucharest, 2005;

2. Marius Andreescu, Existence and being. Journal of thoughts and reflections, Pro Universitaria, Bucharest, 2022;

3. Marius Andreescu, Andra Puran, Constitutional law. General theory and constitutional institutions. Constitutional jurisprudence, 4th edition, C.H. Beck, Bucharest, 2020;

4. Aristotle, Nichomachian Ethics, Antet Revoluţion, Bucharest, 2012;

5. Aristotle, The Athenian State, Antet Revolution, Bucharest, 2007;

6. Cesare Becaria, On crimes and punishments, Humanitas, Bucharest, 2007;

7. Ernest Bernea, He who climbs the mountain of suffering, Predania, Bucharest, 2021;

8. Albert Camus, The Myth of Sisyphus, Polirom, Bucharest, 2020;

9. Ioan Ciochină-Barbu, "On the legal nature of the right to happiness", Acta Universitatis George Bacovia. Legal, Volume 6. Issue 2/2017;

10. Andre Comte-Sponvile, Arlette Farge, Jean Delumeau, The most beautiful story of happiness, Art, Bucharest, 2015;

11. Confucius, Analects of Confucius, The European Idea, Bucharest, 2022;

12. Andrei Cornea (ed.), Epicurus and Ancient Epicureanism, Humanitas, Bucharest;

13. Edward J. Eberle, Human Dignity, Privacy, and Personality in German and American Constitutional Law, https://docs.rwu.edu/cgi/viewcontent.cgi?article=1067&context=law_fac_fs

14. Michael Flocker, The Hedonism Handbook. The art of tranquility and pleasure, Humanitas, Bucharest, 2006;

15. Dalia Hindwai, "The right to seek happiness", https://www.juridice.ro/439850/dreptul-la-cautarea-fericirii.html;

16. Immanuel Kant, Religion within the limits of pure reason, Humanitas, Bucharest, 2004;

17. Immanuel Kant, Critique of practical reason, Univers Enciclopedic, Bucharest, 1999;

18. Camil Mureşan, Alexandru Vianu, President of the White House, Politics, Bucharest, 1974;

19. Valentin Mureşan, "Does Aristotle use the dialectical method in the Nicomachean Ethics?", Journal of Analytical Philosophy, Vol. III, 2o, July-December 2009;

20. Tudor Panţiru, The right to seek happiness, Journal of Public Law, no. 1/2015;

21. Plato, Republica, Letterhead, Bucharest, 2010;

22. Giovanni Reale, History of ancient philosophy. Cynicism, Epicureanism, Stoicism, Vol. 5, Galaxia Gutemberg, Bucharest, 2016;

23. Ioana Sarambei, Nicolae Sarambei, 99 Personalities of the Ancient World, Albatros, Bucharest, 1983;

24. Jean Paul Sartre, Being and Nothingness, Paralele 45, Pitesti, 2004;

25. priest, dr. Sicoe Tudor, Blessed Augustin. Theological aspects with special reference to Triadology, Andreiana, Sibiu, 2013;

26. Baruch Spinoza, Ethics, Bucharest, Scientific Publishing House, Bucharest, 1957;

27. John Stuart Mill, Utilitarismus, All, Bucharest, 2014;

28. Elena Zamfir in "The right to happiness, prisoner between the culture of freedom and the culture of silence. Interview with Elena Zamfir", on https://www.romaniapozitiva.ro/romania-pozitiva/dreptul-la-fericire-prizonier-intre-cultura-libertatii-si-cultura-tacerii-interviu-cu-elena-zamfir-profesor -university;

29. Henry Zimmer, Philosophies of India, Humanitas, Bucharest, 2012;

30. The Declaration of Independence (adopted unanimously by Congress on July 4, 1776, in Philadelphia), on https://constitutii.wordpress.com/wp-content/uploads/2013/02/declarac89bia-de-independenc89bc483.pdf;

31. https://worldhappiness.report/ed/2022;

32. https://supreme.justia.com/cases/federal/us/17/316/;

33. https://case-law.vlex.com/vid/beebe-v-state-908660614;

34.http://courts.mrsc.org/washreports/001WashReport/001WashReport0156.htm.

www.ingramcontent.com/pod-product-compliance
Lightning Source LLC
LaVergne TN
LVHW052209200926
848481LV00001B/66
9798892486835